CHARLES JAMES FOX

CHARLES JAMES FOX

A Man for the People

LOREN REID

Let him do what he will, I must still love the dog.

Edward Gibbon

UNIVERSITY OF MISSOURI PRESS

Standard Book Number 8262-0076-1

Library of Congress Card Number 69-19319

Printed in Great Britain

Published in the United States of America by the
University of Missouri Press
Columbia · Missouri

Published throughout the world except in the United States of America
by Longmans, Green and Co. Ltd,
London and Harlow

TO
GUS

Contents

Contents

Part Three

Man of the People

Part Four

Long Road Back

List of illustrations

Between pages 226–227

Foreword

The most pleasant part of writing this book has been the association with knowledgeable and gracious people who have extended their assistance.

Fox letters and documents are found in more than twenty different collections. I am particularly indebted to the trustees and staff of the British Museum for their unfailing courtesy in placing at my disposal, and in permitting me to quote from, the Fox and more recently the Holland House manuscripts. I also used the Museum's Burney collection of newspapers and those at the Colindale branch, all indispensable. I am indebted to Earl Fitzwilliam and Earl Fitzwilliam's Wentworth Estates Company, and the City Librarian, for permission to quote from the Wentworth Woodhouse Muniments at the Sheffield City Library and from the Fitzwilliam (Milton) collection in the Northamptonshire Record Office, Delapré Abbey. At the Public Record Office I read Admiralty and Treasury papers and also Foreign Office records dealing with treaty negotiations of 1783 and 1806. I have seen other materials through the courtesy of L. W. Hanson, keeper of printed books at the Bodleian Library, and R. G. Chapman, compiler of an invaluable index of major historical periodicals. J. E. Fagg, Reader, University of Durham, supplied copies of the Fox-Grey correspondence; the Probate Registry, Somerset House, provided copies of Fox's will and that of his wife. D. F. Cook, curator of Special Collections, University Library, Liverpool; J. H. Hudson, keeper of the manuscripts, University of Nottingham, and other librarians of British universities called attention to incidental Fox letters. For these courtesies I am deeply grateful.

A substantial quantity of Fox correspondence and related materials is available in the United States. The extensive collection of eighteenth-century materials on deposit at the William L. Clements Library of the University of Michigan is of the highest importance, and the courtesies extended by Howard H. Peckham, director, and William S. Ewing, curator of manuscripts, made my stay there a fruitful one. John E. Pomfret, director of the Henry E. Huntington Library and Art Gallery, and members of his staff, guided me through the extensive holdings of that institution to important Fox papers. The James M. Osborn collection of Fox letters, housed at the Beinecke Library, Yale University, is a select one; I am indebted to Dr Osborn for permission to consult these papers and to the librarian of the collection, George A. M. Wood, for putting them at my disposal. The Princeton University Library, the Miriam Lutcher Stark Library of the University of

Texas, the New York Public Library, and the Newberry Library have useful manuscript and pamphlet collections, and I am grateful to these institutions for the opportunity to see and quote from specific items.

Again, various individuals and institutions have supplied photographs of Fox portraits; more, in fact, than I have been able to include in this volume. Dr Pomfret provided a photograph of the Fox portrait attributed to Johann Zoffany in the directors' room of the Huntington library. Caroline Rollins of the Yale University Art Gallery supplied a photograph of the Fox portrait by John Opie in the Elizabethan Club at Yale. Through Gillian Thompson, editorial assistant of *History Today*, I learned of the Anton Hickel painting of Fox addressing the House of Commons, in the possession of Paul Channon, M.P. Mr Channon made it possible to secure a photograph of the painting. Viscount Galway graciously gave permission to reproduce the well-known portrait of Fox by Reynolds, formerly in the possession of the Earl of Ilchester.

Over the years various people have called attention to items and sources I might otherwise have missed. I express appreciation to Joseph O. Baylen, University of Mississippi; John Brooke, Historical Manuscripts Commission; Donald C. Bryant, University of Iowa; Alice M. Donaldson, Purdue University; Joel J. Gold, University of Kansas; Jerome B. Landfield, University of Maryland; Solomon Lutnick, Queens College; Sir John Murray, London; Joseph F. O'Rourke, Wabash College; Charles Daniel Smith, Syracuse University; J. Steven Watson, St Andrews University.

The hon. secretary of Brooks's, Major H. N. Lucas, searched the Betting Book and copied examples of Fox's wagers; he also gave information about the Fox Club, which still meets. Richard D. Girouard, hon. secretary, provided the current roster of the Pitt Club. To the editor of *The Times Literary Supplement* I am indebted for the courtesy of allowing authors to request information of *Supplement* readers; to two different inquiries I received many helpful responses. Dr Frederick Hilton of Addlestone, Surrey, Frank S. Ochs of Hassocks, Sussex, D. W. D. Yates of Chertsey, Surrey, and Colin F. Ball of the Central Library, Chertsey, graciously supplied information about St Anne's Hill.

Basically the book grows out of a professional interest in Fox's talents as a parliamentary speaker. The scope, therefore, is that of a biography, with Fox's attainments as a speaker coming to the foreground at frequent intervals. In the study of his speeches I have proceeded from the viewpoint of rhetorical theory and practice even though I have not employed much of the terminology of classical or even contemporary rhetoric. As Fox's non-speaking activities also command substantial interest, I have tried to give them proper attention. To keep a sharper focus on Fox himself I have abbreviated the political background. Here my generalizations cannot possibly do full justice to the researches of specialists. I suspect they will react as I sometimes do, when reading works primarily political in nature, to see Fox's complex personality described in one or two compressed sentences.

At the same time I must express my great debt to the labours of others. In all fields scholars profit from works like *The Correspondence of Edmund Burke* under the general editorship of Thomas W. Copeland, *The History of Parliament* under the general editorship of Sir Lewis Namier and John Brooke, and the volumes of correspondence of George III and George IV edited by Arthur Aspinall. Ian R. Christie's *The End of North's Ministry*, John W. Derry's *The Regency Crisis*, and Herbert Butterfield's *George III, Lord North and the People* not only have the merit of presenting a detailed account of movements in which Fox was heavily involved but also have the advantage of being written by scholars who have given particular thought to Fox's part in them. Studies of range and scope like Eugene C. Black's *The Association* and Archibald S. Foord's *His Majesty's Opposition* also bespeak special attention, as do the many new biographies of Fox's contemporaries and near-contemporaries. I have continually referred to J. Steven Watson's *The Reign of George III, 1760–1815* for specific background and orientation. These and other sources are listed in the bibliography.

Obviously as time goes on the Fox career can be more fully stated. Studies centred upon the latter half of the eighteenth century will continue to appear, to add to the clarity of detail and at times to affect the interpretation of a specific event. Yet many questions can never be answered. Tremendous gaps exist in the Fox correspondence, and the extant reports of his speeches are often inaccurate and incomplete.

My most heartfelt thanks go of course to those who have read chapters of the manuscript. Herbert Butterfield, Master of Peterhouse, Cambridge; Ian R. Christie, University College, London; John W. Derry, Downing College, Cambridge University; Richard B. Morris, Columbia University; Charles F. Mullett, University of Missouri; and J. Steven Watson, St Andrews University, have each read sections of the book and have supplied detailed, provocative, and stimulating queries and annotations, taking time from all manner of teaching, research, and publication commitments of their own to do so. I most readily acknowledge the wisdom of their perceptive advice, and hasten to add that they are in no way responsible for the book's shortcomings.

The long interest that A. Craig Baird of the University of Iowa has shown in this project is a debt of another sort that I gratefully acknowledge. It was he who suggested, in Iowa student days, that I should undertake a study of Fox as a parliamentary speaker. Moreover, on three separate occasions beginning in 1952 I have taught in the Overseas Division of the University of Maryland, under the general direction of Dean Ray Ehrensberger, and since my request to teach in the London area could usually be honoured along with classroom duties I was able to pursue Fox researches. The University of Missouri provided a faculty summer research fellowship in 1963 to revisit the British Museum and inspect the then newly released Holland House papers. It has since supplied grants to study at Huntington, Clements, and Newberry libraries.

The preparation of the manuscript has in itself been a major undertaking, and I indeed express my appreciation to Mrs Lyle Dorsett, Mrs Stephen I. Rosen, Mrs Henry Smits, Mrs Bill Crockett, and Mrs Larry Schulz in completing the manufacture of the final draft, facing the author's alterations with charity, patience and fortitude.

Finally I am grateful to my wife, Gus, who spent many a week reading eighteenth and early nineteenth-century newspapers in the British Museum's North Room and Colindale reading room, and who has read chapter after chapter with creative insight. When I reflect upon the persistence that has gone into this undertaking and also the affection that across the centuries Fox has been able to generate, I must admit that much of the persistence and the affection has been sustained by her interest as well as my own.

LOREN REID

University of Missouri, Columbia

Part One
Thrice In, Thrice Out

King wins, Knave loses.

Faro banker's cry

1

Genesis of a Speaker

1627-1780

> My Charles is handsome, as well as clever and good-
> natured; but I fear he won't continue long very hand-
> some, as he grows more like me.
>
> *Henry Fox*

Autumn, 1780. In Westminster, largest urban constituency of England, voters scanned the prospect of selecting two men for the new Parliament. The electorate, discouraged by the progress of the war against the American colonies, depressed because the city had been swept by riots and rioters that spring, gravely pondered its three candidates: the popular Admiral Rodney and the less popular Lord Lincoln, both choices of the court; and the intelligent, well-born, good-natured, budding statesman and professional gambler at cards and horses, Charles James Fox.

They knew him as an accomplished and gifted speaker, and that he certainly was; later Edmund Burke was to call him the world's greatest debater. They were beginning to call him the Man of the People, because he sympathized with their disappointments and voiced their aspirations. Rodney and Lincoln were less well known; Fox was the person that Westminster and London most frequently read about in the papers; he was the one they saw and heard most often. Swarthy, shaggy eyebrowed, negligently dressed in the colonial blue and buff, he nevertheless had an animated countenance, a winning smile, and, to use the old, flamboyant phrase, a way with argument seldom equalled and never surpassed.

In front of St Paul's—the church at Covent Garden, not the cathedral —officials had erected a timber structure, the hustings. In this temporary building, with mats at one end where the speakers stood and benches elsewhere for those about to speak or to engage in other official or semi-official activities, the polling place was housed. Here an elector could appear before the high bailiff or his clerks, identify himself as possessing those prescribed qualifications that magically set l.im apart from less fortunate men, and, in full view of the law and of the partisans who had bought or besought his vote, cast his ballot. Since only two of the three candidates were to be chosen, the voter could select any two of the three nominees, or he could plump down his whole favour for one name singly. The voting could easily last the best part of a month, as in this election it did, with daily totals of the progress of candidates arousing interest and priming enthusiasm through most of that September and well into October.

But first came processions, with carriages and marchers and banners: 'Freedom and Independence', 'Liberty', and a hundred thousand people, or fewer, cheering and huzzaing and shouting 'Fox!' 'Fox!' or 'No Fox!' Then would come speeches, interspersed with cheers and cat calls, dirty fists in the air, and impromptu fights when 'Fox!' found himself side-by-side with 'No Fox!' Holding to rails and lamp posts were hundreds of little boys who, like their elders, listened betimes with the utmost attention and at other times joined lustily in the yelling; and like their elders shook fists and waved hats. No matter that most of the adults had no right to vote; all, the washed and the unwashed, the suffraged and the unsuffraged, could scream for 'Freedom' and 'Independence' and Fox or Lincoln or Rodney 'for ever'.

For many days the canvass would earnestly and passionately continue. There would be ugly remarks about the parentage, the character, the virtue, the religion, the shortcomings of each candidate. Guineas would change hands; promises would be made to entice the gullible, threats to hold the wavering; faces would be bloodied and heads broken. With one candidate an admiral, the navy would need to look to its record; with another a government front man, the administration would face charges of corruption. Fox, the third, was suspected of being friendly to Catholics and known to be the son of a public official whose tenure in office had brought him hundreds of thousands of pounds; hence the Man of the People would continually need to defend old speeches and other misdeeds.

Finally all was over. Admiral Rodney and Mr Fox, said the electors; the Government's lord would have to further his career elsewhere. The crowd fell upon the hustings with hatchets, crowbars and bare hands, pulled it down and triumphantly carried off the timbers. The admiral was not on hand but Fox was thrust into a victor's chair, encircled with branches of laurel, preceded and followed with banners, and carried up and down the main streets of Westminster. Evening came and torches were lit. Eventually the battered, bruised, chair-sore victor was set down and allowed to make his final speech of gratitude. After hearing fresh rounds of congratulations, he retired to his own private victory festivities. The dark city swallowed up the mob.

That would be October 8. Two days later the high bailiff made everything legal with his official return. In subsequent years October 10 became a special date on the whig calendar. Each year rounds of dinners and speeches, in the metropolis and throughout the kingdom, through Fox's lifetime and spasmodically for a century afterward, commemorated the anniversary of his first election from Westminster. His election day thus became a time at which to recall his stand for freedom of speech and assembly, religious toleration, parliamentary reform, peace among nations—in short, political liberty. Nothing like this small, persistent tribute to the speaking of one man has ever appeared before or since.

Other Westminster elections would be held at which the yelling would be uglier—'No Fox!' 'Hunt the Fox!' 'Turncoat!' 'None of your damned speeches!' Even so, Westminster never failed to reelect him.

In this century, also deeply committed to the betterment of the human lot, Fox deserves to be known better than he is. He was a member of the House of Commons from his entrance in 1768 at the age of nineteen until his death in 1806 at the age of fifty-seven—nearly thirty-nine years. During that period he debated every major issue that arose: the American and French revolutions, the removal of civil restrictions upon Catholics and dissenters, the abolition of the slave trade. He gave his name to a libel act affording greater protection to the press, he believed in the political party as an important instrument of parliamentary government, he spelled out the vital necessity of free speech and free assembly. He believed in public speaking ('the boldness of a man's mind, which prompts him to speak, not in private, but in large and popular assemblies . . . that creates in a state the spirit of freedom'). He believed in full inquiry ('public discussion is the best security for public welfare').

One would suppose that a man who was on the right side of so many deeply rooted issues—on the side, that is, to be supported by subsequent events—would have been honoured by many years of tenure in high office during his lifetime. The fact, however, is that during those thirty-nine years Fox held office of cabinet rank less than twenty months and junior office less than thirty-eight months; the rest of the time he was in opposition, sometimes lacking a single vote of parliamentary victory, often more than 200. A few reasons why he was so seldom in office may readily be recounted. In his early speaking career he showed so little regard for freedom of speech or of the press that later when he reversed his position on these central issues he could be charged with political inconsistency. He was, moreover, a compulsive gambler, almost continually heavily in debt; hence he was vulnerable to attacks upon his financial responsibility. He kept a mistress for a dozen years, shocking the conscientious; then he married her but kept the marriage secret for seven years; then he announced the marriage, which revived and intensified the shock. On certain highly sensitive issues, such as his coalition with North after years of attacking him, and his claim that the Prince of Wales had a right to assume the powers of the sovereign during the insanity of George III, he committed impulsive blunders. It has therefore become easy and in part correct to picture Fox as never having realized his great potential because of faults of character and temperament.

Since the influence of a speaker is affected both by what he is and what he says, this book will consider the personal as well as the political aspects of his career. Here is a man who could not only manage a faro bank, operate a string of race horses, and share mistresses with a prince, but who could also read and write six languages, command on scores of occasions the full attention of the exacting House of Commons, out-argue attorneys on critical points of law or financial experts on details of a budget, correspond with professors of the classics upon subtle points of grammar and composition. Whilst he lived Englishmen divided themselves sharply into 'Fox!' and 'No Fox!' gradually mellowing, however, during his later years; when he died, practically all London and Westminster, in person, viewed the long procession that escorted him to his grave.

Deciding where to start an excursion into the ancestry of Charles Fox is like staring at the ocean, wondering where the waves begin; yet in either instance one must start within his knowledge and his view, and this narrative elects to start no further back than Fox's paternal grandfather, Stephen, who also spent a large share of his life in opposition. Stephen Fox, born in 1627, started his career about as far out in opposition as one can get, since his superior, Prince Charles, was not only out of office, but out of the country, in exile on the Continent. Stephen started by looking after the prince's hounds and horses, a position that in later years gave opponents of Charles Fox the opportunity to malign him as having descended from a stable boy; but managing horses led eventually to managing the household, and managing the household to managing the young prince's finances. When Prince Charles came to the throne in 1660 as Charles II, Fox eventually received the lucrative post of Paymaster General of all forces in England, and still later was named a Lord Commissioner of the Treasury.

Stephen chose a wife from the court family, a sister of one of the King's surgeons. She became the mother of ten, only three of whom reached maturity. Their first child, a daughter, died in infancy in 1655;

6

eventually antiquarians were able to observe that Charles Fox had two aunts that died more than 170 years apart.[1] Sir Stephen outlived not only his wife but each of the three surviving children, and at the age of seventy-seven, unwilling that 'so plentiful an Estate' should have no heirs, 'began to entertain Thoughts of Marrying'. He courted the daughter of a clergyman, who won his heart by 'reading Books of Devotion and History' to him; they were married in 1703. As he wrote, the nuptial bed was blessed with 'seasonable Tokens' of God's grace and bounty; in all, four children. One of these was Henry, born in 1705, fifty years after the first child had died.[2]

Henry went to Eton in 1715 and spent nearly nine years there and at Christ Church, Oxford. He made the grand tour of the Continent and saw the places that young men were supposed to visit. He kept in touch with politics and eventually was returned from Hindon in Wiltshire in 1735, the same year that his great rival, William Pitt, was returned for the notorious rotten borough, Old Sarum. Attaching himself to Sir Robert Walpole ('All those men have their price'), Fox continued on the Government side during Walpole's and two administrations that followed; he was given a seat at the Treasury board and eventually attained the positions of Secretary at War and Secretary of State.

In 1757, his fifty-third year, Fox accepted the office of Paymaster General of the forces, a backward step politically though it was a post with tremendous possibility for personal gain. Basically the office lay between the War Office and the Treasury; the Paymaster received funds from the latter and paid them on proper requisition to the former. Since his balances were not closely scrutinized, he could utilize them as he wished, subject to a final accounting that in practice was generally delayed for years. He could therefore lend money to the Government itself and pocket the interest; he could assess foreign countries, on loans made by the Government to them, a commission of half per cent; he could invest surpluses in government bonds. These practices netted sums regarded as legitimate spoils of office. Fox's personal fortune during his eight years in office thus increased by hundreds of thousands of pounds, and at the same time he gained an unenviable reputation as a despoiler of the public purse. If reference were made in those decades to a certain defaulter of unaccounted

---

[1] George Otto Trevelyan, *The Early History of Charles James Fox* (New York, 1881), pp. 6–7; *Notes and Queries*, 9th series ii (August 13, 1898), 125–6.

The infant daughter that died in 1655 was the first of the two aunts. The other aunt is found on the maternal side, Fox's mother's youngest sister, who died in 1826 at the age of eighty-two.

[2] *Memoirs of the Life of Sir Stephen Fox*, (London, 1717), pp. 92–3; The Earl of Ilchester, *Henry Fox, First Lord Holland* (London, 1920), i, 14–15.

millions, no listener need send to know who was meant, as Henry Fox, in the popular view, had a clear lien on the title.[1]

For many decades when enemies of Charles Fox ran short of other names they could blacken him afresh with his father's unsavoury reputation. Hence, Charles's heritage from his father was a political liability.

The narrative of Fox's maternal ancestry leads back to the same Prince Charles whom Sir Stephen had served.

Among the mistresses of Charles II was the beautiful Louise de Kéroualle. Louise, a promising fixture at the court of France, was exported by the French king to the English court, her mission being to serve as a source of inside information. Despite the competition of lovelies like Nell Gwynn, Louise soon became the ruling passion of Charles's life. She charged the King astonishing prices for her favours; she made and broke promises, then remade them at higher tariffs still; by keeping the King frantic with desire, she wrested from him one concession after another. She gained for herself the title of Duchess of Portsmouth; the King, never hesitant about acknowledging a bastard child, gave her son his own name, Charles, and created him Duke of Richmond.

On the ancestral tree of Charles Fox, therefore, are this shrewd, calculating French great-great-grandmother and her royal lover. In due course, as often happens to mistresses of royalty, she overplayed her hand, lost her high place at court, and returned to France, but by that time the house of Richmond was well established. The first duke grew up, married, and had an heir. To satisfy a gambling debt, this heir was married while still a boy, 'the young people's consent having been the last thing thought of'. The lady is not reported to have complained, but the gentleman exclaimed, 'They surely are not going to marry me to that dowdy!' Immediately after the ceremony, the groom, then known as Lord March, later the second Duke of Richmond, was hustled to the Continent and his bride went back to her mother.[2]

During the years that immediately followed the new husband gave little thought to his wife, and when he returned to England he went directly to the theatre. Looking over the spectators, he spied an amazingly charming young woman; inquiring who she was, he was told: 'You must be a stranger in London not to know the toast of the town, the beautiful Lady March.' Immediately he went to her box and intro-

---

[1] For Fox's profitable speculation with public funds, see Lucy S. Sutherland and J. Binney, 'Henry Fox as Paymaster General of the Forces', *English Historical Review*, lxx (April 1955), 229–56.

[2] The Countess of Ilchester and Lord Stavordale, *The Life and Letters of Lady Sarah Lennox* (London, 1901), i, 85–6.

duced himself as her husband. The two fell in love and forever after lived devotedly together.

One of their daughters was Caroline, who was courted by Henry Fox. Fox was not quite thirty-nine and his wife was just past twenty-one when they married. Their first son was Stephen, who had been ill from birth, suffering from a nervous ailment that the father recorded as 'Sanvitoss dance.'[1] The second son, Henry Charles, died two months after birth. For the arrival of the third child, the parents chose a house in London at Conduit Street, since Holland House was being re-modelled, and there, on January 24, 1749, Charles James was born. 'He is weakly,' wrote the father the day after the birth of his new son, 'but likely to live. His appearance improved steadily, however, for at the age of a year and four months his aunt wrote that 'pretty Charles is quite well', and his father observed, two years later : 'Charles is playing by me and surprizes me with the *éclat* of his beauty ev'ry time he looks me in the face.'[2]

The serious illness of the firstborn and the death of the second son should not be passed over too hurriedly as mere biographical detail. Had the second survived, and had both spent their early years in good health, the parents would have had ample outlet for their tenderness and indulgence without needing to heap it on Charles in excessive and unwise amounts. Even so, Charles displayed a charm and intelligence that increased the affection that his parents showed him. 'I dined at home today, *tête-à-tête* with Charles, intending to do business, but he has found me pleasanter employment, and was very sorry to go away so soon.'[3]

Before he was seven Charles was writing letters on his own. A sample :

Dear Brother : I hope you are well as I am. Papa goes to Windsor today and I fancy will see you. . . . The King of Prussia has beat the French and the Germans. I shall take it very ill if you don't write to me next Post. Fitz Gerald desires that you would send him the Cricket Ball which you Promised him a half a year ago. I am yours, Chas. Fox. Nov. 19, 1757.[4]

This letter, like hundreds to follow, was a mixture of personal matters and politics.

---

[1] Ilchester, i, 174. August 20, 1751.
[2] *Ibid.*, i, 175. To Sir C. Hanbury-Williams, November 30, 1750.
[3] Lord John Russell, ed., *Memorials and Correspondence of Charles James Fox* (London, 1853–57), i, 5. Hereafter cited as *Fox Cor.*
[4] Holland House MSS.

A fourth son, Henry Edward, had been born in 1755. This son followed a military career, fought in America during the revolution—he was at Concord and Bunker Hill—and eventually became a general.

Stories told about the indulgence of Henry Fox for his son have been too often recounted to be stated at length here. The story of the watch: Charles expressed himself as having a great desire to break his father's watch, and, receiving no parental demurral, dashed it to the floor. The story of the wall: workers at Holland House planned to dynamite a wall on the lawn, and Henry Fox had promised Charles that he could witness the explosion. As Charles, however, did not get to see the dynamiting, the father had the stones relaid, recemented, and redynamited. The dank, ever-to-be-suppressed story of the small boy's nuisance in the kitchen, the victim being a pig roasting before the fireplace; the chef nevertheless incredibly served the roast, apple in its mouth, and also two lines of poetry on a card: 'While at the fire I foam'd and hiss'd, A fox's cub upon me piss'd'—more incredibly the dinner assembly applauded the incident, the verse, the roast.[1]

Charles's early life is inseparable from spacious and imposing Holland House, a house that had belonged to the Earl of Holland, the lover of the Queen of Charles I. Here young Charles Fox had every opportunity to meet and converse with the leading social and political figures of the day. He was introduced to the guests and encouraged to take part in conversations and discussions, balls and parties; he participated in talented theatrical performances, of which more later; in general this was the type of society in which he matured so early and lived so easily. Though Henry Fox was tragically lenient, he did allow Charles to grow up with self-assurance and self-possession, gaining an intimate acquaintance with the people who ruled the social and political structure of late eighteenth-century England.

---

[1] Sources for these and similar incidents: *Kent County Herald*, September 25, 1806, quoted in Philopatris Varvicensis [Dr Samuel Parr], *Characters of C. J. Fox* (London, 1809), i, 40; B. C. Walpole, *Charles James Fox* (London, n.d.), p. 14; *Fox Cor.*, i, 7; *Crito the Euclidian; a letter addressed to the right honourable Earl Percy, M.P.*, etc. (London, [1806]).

2

Eton, Oxford, the Grand Tour
1754–1768

I hope . . . you will be able to spare one Tuesday or
Saturday . . . to hear me speak.

Young Charles, writing from Eton

You will think it very extravagant when you hear that I
have [spent] £150.

Old Charles, writing from Oxford

To educate a speaker, start with natural gifts such as Charles Fox
possessed—intelligence, quickness to learn, superb energy, a powerful
and expressive voice; let him associate freely with his elders so that he
will grow up unawed by the adult world; nourish his self-assurance;
expose him to the best schooling his generation offers. Let his educa-
tional experiences fall under two categories: formal instruction by
masters and tutors plus opportunities to speak and to debate. Those
who aspire to speak well must serve a speaker's apprenticeship, and if
they do not serve part of it in school (like Pitt, Burke, Gladstone) they
will have to serve all of it after reaching public life (like Sheridan,
Disraeli). If a speaker is to become the Man of the People, even though
reared as an aristocrat, let him develop the common touch through an
interest in those who move in humbler circles.

Various routes may indeed be followed to a parliamentary career;
Fox followed the route briefly described above.

Charles's education started, for all practical purposes, at the age of
five, with the Reverend Doctor Philip Francis, who joined the Holland
House staff as tutor and chaplain in 1754. Dr Francis had had unusual
experiences with literature, drama, and oratory. His translation of the
orations of Demosthenes, his political pamphlets, and his attendance at
parliamentary debates, had made him familiar with ancient and modern
speaking.

At Holland House, Francis not only became chaplain to Lady Caro-
line, Charles's mother, but also undertook to teach Charles to read.
Frequent guests at the house were Lady Caroline's sister, Lady Sarah
Lennox, younger of the two aunts who died 170 years apart, who was

11

four years older than Charles, and Lady Susan Fox-Strangways, Henry Fox's niece, two years older than Lady Sarah. Francis nurtured the talents for declaiming and acting of all three.

Charles planned eventually to attend Eton College, as had his father. Eton, an outstanding school, then as now beckoning to sons of influential families, had two divisions: a Lower School for lads under the ten-to-twelve age limit, and an Upper School for those older.

Henry Fox's plan had been to bypass the Lower School, supplanting it with home tutoring; in this way he could keep his favourite son longer at home. Francis had supervised certain of Charles's early studies and Lady Caroline others; but family legend has it that one day the boy asked his mother a question about Roman history and was so dissatisfied with the answer that he thenceforth resolved to have no more home schooling but to get his education from professional schoolmasters, either at the Lower School or at a preparatory school at Wandsworth. Henry Fox, worrying about the boy's coughing, thought Wandsworth might be better for his health. Charles also liked the idea of Wandsworth for his first formal education. Goodbye then to mother and home pabulum and off he went.

Customarily, biographers pass over these first school days with a shrug of the shoulder. Charles 'studied Latin grammar'; Charles 'laid the foundation of an intimate acquaintance with the classics'; Charles acquired 'an excellent French accent'. Information about Wandsworth is so meagre that Charles's Wandsworth days have been consigned to the same oblivion as the school itself. Established by a Monsieur Pampellonne, the school was for a while famous and fashionable; moreover, young Lord Stavordale, a cousin and Lady Susan's brother, was already there. Charles and the nine-year-old Stavordale immediately became rivals in their studies. When on one occasion Charles was to be sent home to recover from an illness, he refused to go until the master had given him an assignment in grammar so that he might keep ahead of his cousin.

Although there are no records of the Wandsworth school, his studies there can easily be conjectured. Since he was seeking to qualify for entrance to Eton's Upper School he would have to parallel the achievement of students in Eton's Lower School. He would need to know Latin grammar well and to have enough familiarity with Greek to be able to read one or two easy books. He would be required to translate Latin prose and to turn translations from simple Latin selections back into the original with help from a dictionary and occasional suggestion from the master. A boy thus qualified would be sent to Eton usually about the age of eleven and would be entered in the lowest part of the fourth form.[1] So having survived his home studies and more particularly his year at Wandsworth, Charles went to Eton June 22, 1758, paid his fee of five pounds and five shillings and was duly enrolled. He was then only nine and a half.

The Headmaster of Eton in 1758 was Dr Edward Barnard, an eloquent teacher and reader who so captured the enthusiasm of his pupils that Charles composed a poem calling Barnard the English Quintilian.

George Hardinge, a student of Barnard's, has written the best description of the famous headmaster. Hardinge commented on Barnard's musical voice and exquisite ear and said he could outargue anybody pitted against him. He declared that Barnard lacked only Garrick's features and figure to make him the equal of the great actor. As a classroom teacher, Barnard indirectly nurtured talents in his students that might develop their effectiveness in speaking. He encouraged them to translate and to recite in exact and gracious language. He demonstrated how the arts of delivery could enhance even the reading of their own compositions. At stated periods he would put on little demonstrations by reading aloud an entire Greek play. This brilliant teacher, quickly observing the talents of young Charles, freely predicted that he would become a distinguished parliamentarian and statesman.[2]

Education for speech making was not lost on Eton students. Eton supplied more members to the House of Commons than any other of the great public schools of the eighteenth century. One Etonian in every ten reached the House between 1750 and 1832, compared with one in fifty supplied by Westminster, its nearest competitor.[3] Eton therefore, like the other schools, was steeped in parliamentary tradition; its students well realized that a parliamentary career was easily accessible to those of suitable endowments and talents. To develop their ability as speakers, they could participate in a variety of speech activities. A month before every holiday a programme of declamations was held; there were likewise opportunities to speak before the whole school, with attention at least to the mechanical requirement of emphasis and stress. Selections were taken from Cicero and others.

1 Sir Edward Creasy, *Some Account of the Foundation of Eton College and of the Past and Present Condition of the School* (London, 1848), p. 53. Sir Henry Churchill Maxwell Lyte, *History of Eton College, 1440–1910* (London, 1911), pp. 313–14, cites a manuscript dated 1766 giving a similar description of studies at Eton's Lower School.
2 John Nichols, *Literary Anecdotes of the Eighteenth Century* (London, 1814), viii, 544–7.
3 Gerrit P. Judd, iv, *Members of Parliament, 1734–1832* (New Haven, 1955), pp. 37–8.

By the time Charles reached the sixth form he was actively participating in speechmaking programmes. On one occasion he wrote his father that he was busily perusing Cicero searching for speeches to declaim, adding: 'I hope . . . you will be able to spare one Tuesday or Saturday to come to Eton to hear me speak.'[1]

Charles's classical studies required continual translating and memorizing from Virgil, Horace, Cicero, Ovid, Homer, Aristophanes, Demosthenes, the Greek testament. Students not only translated the lines, commenting both on the grammar and rhetoric, but were also required to cite similar passages from other works. This last-named practice sharpened their appreciation of the handling of favoured themes, and filled their minds with apt phrases from better-known passages. In addition, Charles could summon Dr Francis for tutoring services.[2]

The simple fact that Charles studied classical oratory and drama does not in itself explain his later phenomenal success as a speaker. Many who studied the classics attained only mediocre skill as speakers. True enough, Fox's memorizing and reciting classical selections made him familiar with the language of great literature and supplied him with a fund of quotations that he could use to embellish his speeches. This knowledge in itself, however, might have led to a method of speaking that was imitative, formal, constrained. It could have led him to write manuscripts, polish the style, and commit them to memory. This practice is unwise for debate, because the debate may take a different turn from what the speaker imagined; but even if it does not, the speaker with a carefully plotted speech nicely tucked away in his memory is almost sure to betray his premeditated and predigested language.

Descriptions of eighteenth-century speaking suggest that many members of the House of Commons employed a style of public address that was pompous, dignified, studied, rehearsed, formalized, groomed-and-tailored. In sharp contrast, Fox developed a style that was natural, simple, unaffected, conversational. Part of this style resulted from the self-assurance that he had developed at Eton and elsewhere, part from his continual discussion of politics with young and old friends, part from his accumulation not merely of classical gems but of an ample store of contemporary fact and example, part from an analytical mind that allowed him to follow an argument closely from beginning to end, part from the habit of sharp listening to what the other speaker was actually

---

[1] The Earl of Ilchester, *Letters to Henry Fox, Lord Holland* (London, 1915), p. 191. October 18, 1763. Later Lord Holland wrote his wife that he was delaying his visit to Eton until a Saturday in order, at Charles's request, to hear him speak. He adds 'otherwise I should have gone tomorrow'. November 8, 1763. (Add. MSS. 47593, 24.)

[2] Add. MSS. 47593. Letter to Francis, presumably 1762.

saying, part from an unusual memory that would allow him to prepare a reply as he listened.

Charles enjoyed early experiences on the amateur stage that also furthered his progress as a speaker. A fashionable activity of the Holland House young set was to produce plays; the earliest record of a performance in which Fox participated was in January 1761. At that time he was twelve and had come home from Eton to take part in the production of Nicholas Rowe's historical tragedy of *Jane Shore*, an eighteenth-century drama. Charles had an important male lead, and made frequent appearances throughout the play until, toward the end, he was tragically carried off to be executed.

The third Lord Holland, a principal editor of the Fox correspondence, commented that Fox's dramatic interests gave him a knowledge of plays, 'prodigious numbers of which he had read with great delight and singular attention'. On the oratorical side Holland made two observations: that Fox's use of quotations and allusions in his speeches from passages 'not commonly known in our dramatic authors, both serious and comic, was frequent'; and that his ability to express emotion by the tones of his voice 'had no doubt been brought to perfection by his exertions on the stage'.[1] Although Fox's speaking voice was strong and powerful rather than resonant and melodious, he learned to control and modulate it.

Charles might have developed into an even sturdier citizen and scholar had he been allowed to spend more time in school. At intervals his father took him to London for amusement; one of the more important visits was to see the coronation of George III in 1761, the only coronation in Charles's lifetime. He began to form habits of extravagance that pursued him throughout the years. In the Holland House papers is a note, signed by him shortly before his thirteenth birthday: 'December 15, 1761. Receiv'd, advanced to me by my Father as part of my Fortune two hundred pounds.' The note acknowledging this formidable advance of funds is signed, in dignified copperplate script with elaborate initials, 'C. J. Fox', and must have represented an expenditure far beyond the usual, since the father elected to memorialize it by this impressive document.

In May 1763 Holland took him from school again, going first to Paris, then to Spa, providing him with five guineas a night to spend at dice and card games, and thus introducing him to a vice that plagued him

[1] *Fox Cor.*, i, 31–2.

most of the rest of his days. After four months of idleness on the Continent, he returned to Eton, attired in red-heeled shoes and Paris cut-velvet, adorned with a pigeon-wing hair style tinted with blue powder, and a newly acquired French accent. His schoolfellows could hardly endure what they saw, and Dr Barnard is said to have given him a flogging.[1]

Other interruptions were more useful. In November 1763, after Holland went to Eton to hear the speaking exercises, he took his son to London to hear the debates in Parliament on John Wilkes.[2] Charles heard debates on other occasions as well. As he sat in the strangers' gallery of the House of Commons, began to familiarize himself with forms of parliamentary procedure, and noticed the speechmaking, good, bad, and indifferent, of his older friends and acquaintances, he could easily imagine himself a participant in this political scene.

October 1764 found him at Oxford. In the manner of university students everywhere, one of his first letters home was to justify the low state of his finances. He had drawn unexpectedly upon the family banker for £150. 'I will therefore,' he wrote to his father, 'take some pains to explain it to you.' He had old Eton debts to pay: new shirts, new stockings, and a new frock to buy; and 'many other trifles' to reduce his balance to £34 11s, 'which is all I have left'. Thus £150 of student money was cut to £34, with little to show for it. Yet he had met and dined with 'Mr Burk' whom he found 'one of the most agreeable men I have known'. He carried his £34 into a gaming session, and—let him tell it—'I have been so foolish as to break all the good resolutions I had formed in regard to play, and have lost upwards of eighty Guineas.' After this debacle he met his tutor and read with him part of Aristotle's *Rhetoric*. Debts, shirts, Burke, gambling, the *Rhetoric* of Aristotle; here is Fox's college career compressed.[3]

On October 23, a few months before his sixteenth birthday, he formally matriculated at Hertford College,[4] which though small and undistinguished had gained a good reputation because of three tutors, David Durell, Benjamin Blayney, and William Newcome.[5] Charles matriculated under Dr Durell as a gentleman commoner, but Dr Newcome, who in 1767 was appointed to an Irish bishopric, wielded greater influence. It was Dr Newcome, who, learning of one of Charles's expeditions to Paris, wrote him assuring him he acted wisely

[1] Add. MSS. 47593, 34.   [2] *Fox Cor.*, i, 12.
[3] Holland House MSS. Letters to Holland, October 13, 24, 1764. *Letters to Henry Fox, Lord Holland*, pp. 202–4.
[4] *Alumni Oxonienses, 1715–1886* (London, 1888), ii, 486.
[5] Sidney Graves Hamilton, *Hertford College* (London, 1903), pp. 86–8.

in taking a vacation: 'Application like yours requires some intermission, and you are the only person with whom I have ever had connection, to whom I could say this. I suspect that you will return with much keenness for Greek, and for lines and angles.'[1] In later years when Fox was chided for hours spent in idleness instead of reading parliamentary documents, he would produce his old tutor's letter, much creased and folded, to explain that 'application . . . requires . . . intermission'.

His education at Oxford was informal even by his own standards. In February 1765 he wrote to his friend Macartney about his studies; he liked mathematics vastly, partly because it was useful, mostly because it was entertaining; he was convinced of the importance of learning French well, which he did; he thought there could not be a more agreeable place than Oxford for one who reads a great deal.[2]

From April to July Charles was in Paris—it was here that he received Newcome's letter—and then returned to Hertford, where, as his parents took note in separate letters, he worked hard and generally applied himself.[3] He spent most of one vacation with his friend Dickson, later Bishop of Down, studying and reading the early dramatic poets of England. Fox could declare that there was no play extant, written and published before the Reformation, that he had not read attentively.[4]

About this time the Duchess of Leinster reported a conversation between Charles's parents that she overheard. Lady Caroline, after expressing her fear that her husband was overindulging their children, added: 'I have been this morning with Lady Hester Pitt, and there is little William Pitt, *not eight years old*, and really the cleverest child I ever saw *and brought up so strictly and so proper in his behaviour*, that, *mark my words*, that little boy will be a thorn in Charles's side as long as he lives.'[5] In making this remark the mother was principally expressing a fear that the old rivalry between her husband and the elder Pitt would be renewed between their sons, but it was indeed a prophecy.

In the spring of 1766, a little past his seventeenth birthday, Charles left Oxford. No record exists to suggest that he did any speechmaking there. He may have been involved with Carlisle, Fitzpatrick, and Hare in writing the first two issues of *The Spendthrift*, a shortlived periodical.[6] During late spring and early summer he entertained himself

[1] Holland House MSS.; *Fox Cor.*, i, 22. May 1, 1765.   [2] Add. MSS. 47568.
[3] *Fox Cor.*, i, 23.   [4] Add. MSS. 47593. *Fox Cor.*, i, 23.
[5] Add. MSS. 47593. *Fox Cor.*, i, 25.
[6] Perhaps the issues of March 29 and August 9, 1766. The set at the Beinecke Library, Yale University, is endorsed: 'Wrote by Ld Carlisle, Charles Fox, & Mr Fitzpatrick & Hare.' A letter to Fitzpatrick from Florence, September 22, 1767, suggests that an issue edited by Carlisle was 'with all due respect to Mr Fitzpatrick, much the best that appeared' (*Fox Cor.*, i, 43).

with theatrical productions at Winterslow, Stephen Fox's home. On July 7 of that year Lady Sarah wrote of plans for the production of two plays, Dryden's *All for Love,* a representation of the story of Antony and Cleopatra in the neo-classical tradition, and a Beaumont and Fletcher comedy, *Rule a Wife and Have a Wife.* Charles had leading roles in both plays; he was Antony in the tragedy, and Michael Ferez, the Copper Captain, in the comedy.

Charles was disappointed in his rendition of the Captain, as he fell short of his own expectations.[1] In other pursuits he was more pleased with himself. In an undated letter written about this time to his good friend Fitzpatrick, he described certain financial ventures:

At Burford I touched the hounds for a couple of milles at whist. C. Blake and T. Hervey [professional gamblers] gave in 300 apiece or thereabouts. . . . I believe I shall have about 3000 gns. clear or rather more at the opening of the winter, when I have paid Cavendish, Vice, & others including even two or three hounds or tradesmen. So much for business, it has been rather a boar, but I thought you would like to know the state of the funds.[2]

The point should be made, albeit briefly, that Charles was absorbed by the private and public doings of people in public life. Nearly every letter in the slender sheaf still extant from his early years contains references to matters being talked about, ranging from current developments in the Wilkes affair, changes in the Government, and new political pamphlets, to gossip about his father's two illegitimate children. He freely entered into conversation with people around him; he was equally at home discussing the French theatre with a friend of his own age or politics with a member of the cabinet. Hence he formed the basis of a wide acquaintance with many with whom later he associated in the House of Commons.

The letters also reflect a wide variety of other talents and interests. There were, for example, summing-up impressions of his short university career. He wrote to Macartney that he understood Latin and Greek tolerably well but was 'totally ignorant in every part of useful knowledge'. That autumn he wrote to Fitzpatrick, 'For God's sake learn Italian as fast as you can, if it be only to read Ariosto.' He added

1 Add. MSS. 47580. *Fox Cor.*, i, 43. To Fitzpatrick, September 22, 1767.
2 Add. MSS. 47570.

Richard Fitzpatrick, one of Charles Fox's closest friends and associates, began a military career while Fox was at Oxford. The two roomed together in London, were leaders of the young fashionable set, participated in plays (Fitzpatrick was the better in comedy, Fox in tragedy), and later were members of the House of Commons. Fitzpatrick served with the British forces stationed in the colonies, was Fox's Secretary at War in two cabinets, and eventually attained the rank of general. More than any other achievement, however, Fitzpatrick prided himself on being Fox's friend and confidant.

that there was more good poetry in Italian than in all other languages put together. 'Make haste and read all these things,' he urged, 'that you may be fit to talk to Christians.'[1]

Nice he thought 'the dullest town in the world', according to the excerpt quoted in the sedate *Memorials and Correspondence*; what the printed volume omits is the reason: ' . . and what is a terrible thing, there are no whores.' He continued that his health was quite good, though he was still in a weakened condition from ailments he had picked up, unwittingly, from female companionship.

One of his 1768 letters from Nice to Uvedale Price may describe the eighteenth century grand tour as well as it can be encompassed in print. He did not read and travel all the time. In this letter he said:

The reason of this change [away from reading and the study of Spanish] in my way of life is a very good one; that is, a woman, or rather two women. There is a Mrs Holmes here, an Irish woman, more beautiful than words can express, and very agreeable into the bargain; this attraction draws me to Nice, which is about a mile distant from hence, every morning. Now it so happens that tho' this woman is exquisite entertainment for Charles, yet, as she is chaste as she is fair, she does not altogether do for Carlino so well. There is also at that same Nice, a silver-smith's wife, who is almost as fair as Mrs Holmes, but not near so chaste, and she attracts me thither as regularly in the evening, as the other does in the morning.

He suggested that Price ask Fitzpatrick about this estimable silver-smith's wife; Fox, Price, and Fitzpatrick had few secrets from one another. Charles continued: 'When you consider those journeys to Nice, the proper time for eating, drinking, sleeping, praying, etc., . . . you will not be surprised that I read but little.' He did, however, make verses, and promised one in Latin upon the pox, following the metre of Ovid, one of the few writers that he read during this well-filled holiday.[2]

Later that summer Price and Fox called on Voltaire at Ferney. The old philosopher gave his young visitors food, drink, advice, and a list of his own books that would open the minds of young people and free them from religious prejudice.[3] Fox spent most of August in England, but in September was back on the Continent. Meanwhile his father had quietly arranged for his son to become a member of the House of Commons. The prediction of Charles's schoolmates, who had been so impressed by his deft handling of Cicero's orations, was about to be fulfilled.

[1] Add. MSS. 47580. *Fox Cor.*, i, 42–4. September 22, 1767.
[2] Add. MSS. 47576. February 24, 1768.
[3] *Fox Cor.*, i, 46–7. See also Add. MSS. 47593.

3

The Phenomenon of the Age
1768–1770

The great speakers fill me with despair, the bad ones with terror.

Edward Gibbon

Early in 1768 Henry Fox and his brother, the Earl of Ilchester, had begun to negotiate for parliamentary seats for Charles and Stavordale. The two cousins who had competed in Latin at Wandsworth were now ready to serve their country as members of Parliament. The fathers selected a sparsely inhabited constituency, Midhurst, in Sussex, whose two proprietors over the years had accumulated title to the plots of land comprising the borough. A few days before the election the owners distributed parcels of property among their servants with instructions to vote for the two young men; after the candidates had been duly elected, deeds to the property were re-executed in favour of the original title-holders.[1] Under this system the cousins, like many others, were able to enter the House of Commons without the fuss and bother of a campaign.

The thirteenth Parliament, later famous as the unreported Parliament since so few of its debates got into print, met May 10, 1768; Charles was then nineteen, technically too young to take his seat, and as he was absent in Italy, reading, playing chess, visiting Mrs Holmes in the morning and the silversmith's wife in the evening, he did not attend this opening session. Its life, however, was short; it transacted little business and adjourned for a long holiday. When the second session opened November 8, Charles was present, to begin his 39-year career.

The motives impelling a young man to enter Parliament have been described by Sir Lewis Namier. To make a figure in the nation, he quotes Lord Chesterfield, a man must first make a figure in the House of Commons; to be out of Parliament, he quotes Admiral Rodney, is to be out of this world.[2]

Any talented, well-educated young man, of suitable political and

---

[1] Ilchester, ii, 325–6.   [2] *The Structure of Politics*, 2nd edn (London, 1957), p. 1.

family connection, could aspire to Parliament, as has already been suggested. Charles's motives can be conjectured from a letter he wrote his friend James Hare, obviously in response to an appeal from Hare for advice. As he counsels Jemmy he reveals his own ambitions. Do not enter the priesthood, he warns: 'It is the only situation where there is no hope of emerging from that damned state of obscurity and laziness.' A prime requisite of a career, therefore, is one that lifts the individual out of obscurity. Better be a Common Soldier or an Author than a Priest. For any one who has ambition, the Law 'is undoubtedly the finest profession in the world, since it not only opens the way for the most obscure to immense riches, but likewise to the greatest importance and consideration'. 'Merit makes its way' in the profession of law, he confidently urged, 'and in that profession only.'[1] To Fox the possibilities for a young man were radiant indeed.

Hare found it simpler to ask for this robust advice than he did to pursue it vigorously. Fox, with his aristocratic connections, did not need to enter law but could move directly to Parliament, where, already several notches above obscurity, he could move immediately toward the fame that he was sure lay waiting.

John Wilkes was much in the public eye when new member Charles Fox took his seat on a back bench in St Stephen's chapel, chamber of the House of Commons.

Wilkes had come forcibly to the attention of the Government in 1762 when he began, with Charles Churchill, the publication of the *North Briton*. Its famous issue, Number 45, of April 23, 1763, had sharply criticized the King's speech, calling it 'the most abandoned instance of ministerial effrontery ever attempted to be imposed on mankind'.

Responding to the frontal attack, the Government made a disastrous decision: it issued a general warrant for the arrest of authors, printers, and publishers, for printing an infamous and seditious libel. Wilkes and his growing group of followers denounced the tactic of a general warrant as a blow to the liberties of the people. The Government replaced the general warrant by a specific warrant naming Wilkes and others, but Wilkes made a spirited defence and after a weekend in the Tower was released.

In the midst of the considerable litigation that followed, the government learned of Wilkes's plan to publish a private edition of a salacious poem, *Essay on Woman*, secured a copy in a devious way, read it aloud in the Lords, and condemned it as 'a most scandalous, obscene,

[1] Naples, December 2 [1767]. (Osborn Collection, Yale.)

and impious libel'. During the debate in the Commons, Samuel Martin, ex-secretary of the Treasury, target of abuse in an earlier *North Briton*, made a bitter speech against Wilkes that led to a duel. Wilkes, wounded, left for France; in 1764 he was expelled by the Commons and later prosecuted for publishing Number 45 and the *Essay*. Although most of this action occurred while Charles Fox was a teenage school-boy at Eton, he was fully aware of all that went on. In November 1763, for example, Henry Fox had gone to Eton to hear Charles speak, and later took him to Westminster to hear the debates on the Wilkes affair. Charles had been present therefore when the Commons made its memorable resolution that Number 45 was false, scandalous, and seditious.[1] Since the father was a member of the Government that Wilkes had so forcibly attacked, the son naturally approved the sentiments uttered that day against the author.

While Charles was at Oxford and on the Continent between 1764 and 1768, Wilkes was in exile, although he returned to England in February 1768. Though a declared outlaw, he audaciously announced his candidacy to Parliament for the City of London but was soundly defeated. Even so, he managed to emphasize that the issuance of general warrants and the seizure of private papers were important questions of public liberty. He then entered himself in March as a candidate for the county of Middlesex—and here he found himself at the top of the poll by a tremendous majority.

By this time Wilkes's long fight had captured the imagination of the people, who fully and completely celebrated his victory at the polls. Boisterous groups paraded the town demanding that all good patriots put lights in their windows, heaving stones into those that were left dark. Wilkes distributed handbills urging his friends not to disturb the peace but he could not halt the celebration. At a dinner 45 gentlemen sat down at 45 minutes past 1, drank 45 gills of wine with 45 new-laid eggs in them, and ate a five-course dinner of nine dishes each; from dinner they moved to a ball to which 45 ladies had been invited, danced 45 dances, kissed each lady 45 times, and departed at 45 minutes past 3.[2] Thus Wilkes, 45, and liberty came to mean about the same thing.

When Charles took his seat, the Wilkes affair was the principal business before the House of Commons.

Standing momentarily at the entrance to St Stephen's chapel, Charles Fox, like his father and grandfather before him, could see Mr Speaker on his throne at the far end of the chamber, the parliamentary clerks seated in front of their desks a little lower down. Hanging from the

[1] *Fox Cor.*, i, 12.   [2] *St James's Chronicle*, April 23–25, 1768.

ceiling was a vast chandelier; on the ceiling at the point where the chandelier was attached was an openwork grill behind which newspaper reporters and others sometimes hid to glimpse the proceedings below. High on either side was the Strangers' Gallery: a slender balcony for relatives of members, peers, and other visitors. On the main floor, at the left, were five rows of benches, running lengthwise of the room and divided into two sections by a cross aisle, a gangway. These were occupied by members of His Majesty's loyal Government, the front bench of the section nearest Mr Speaker being the Treasury bench, reserved for the great offices of the Government. As the Duke of Grafton, the first minister, with the portfolios of Treasury and Secretary of State, had been in the Lords since 1768, on the Treasury bench, therefore, were such other officials as Sir Edward Hawke, hero of the great naval victory of Quiberon Bay, First Lord of the Admiralty; Frederick, Lord North, Chancellor of the Exchequer; and John Dunning, Solicitor General.

Separated by a narrow lane of carpet and facing the Government benches was a similar phalanx of benches occupied by His Majesty's loyal opposition, though that precise term was not to come into being until the following century. A speaker would thus stand with his colleagues at his back and side, his opponents squarely in his eye. Few if any in St Stephen's seemed concerned that there was bench space for only about three-fourths of the membership; the small, compact chamber encouraged a direct and intimate type of parliamentary debating. If more members showed up than there was seating room, they stood at the back and around the sides, the crowded condition of the chamber enhancing the urgency of the speechmaking. When St Stephen's was burned out in 1834 and that successor bombed in 1941, the Commons on each occasion decided to perpetuate the traditional seating arrangement and the traditional shortage of seats.

The atmosphere was even more challenging to spirit than to body. Listeners readily distinguished between good and mediocre speaking; since they had heard some of the best, their standards were set high. If a speaker of mediocre eloquence arose, members were likely to leave the chamber to refresh themselves at nearby Bellamy's, where the head waiter would keep them informed about who was speaking and when or whether a vote was to be taken. In the chamber itself was not only the disturbance created by members coming and going, but by various other kinds of restlessness. Best evidence of the difficulty of speaking is the simple fact that relatively few members spoke. Far less than a fourth of the membership participated in debate at all, and a list of those who spoke frequently would be limited to about twenty-five names per session.

Whatever his thoughts on the occasion of that first day, Charles Fox selected a seat at his left, presumably a back bench below the gangway. Like his forebears he was staunchly on the side of administration. He could hardly have realized that he would spend ninety per cent of his career in opposition, seated across the way.

A momentous event in the career of a parliamentarian is his maiden speech. A new member may sit for weeks quietly among the backbenchers, but sooner or later duty and conscience compel him to catch the Speaker's eye, rise to his feet, and offer his first contribution to parliamentary debate. A few new members made notorious failures. Joseph Addison was in the last decade of a brilliant career when he entered Parliament; but though he had fine command of written language, he was too timid to speak. Tradition persists, however, that once he made an attempt; gathering courage for the ordeal he gained the floor and opened with the phrase, 'Mr Speaker: I conceive . . .'; his fluency faltered and after an embarrassing pause he continued, 'I conceive'; still he could not go on, and after a final 'Sir, I conceive' sank back in his seat and uttered no more. 'The honourable gentleman has conceived three times and has brought forth nothing,' said an honourable opponent—and that retort brought to a finish the parliamentary speaking of the eminent man of letters. Half a century later Edward Gibbon could not bring himself to speak at all. Through eight sessions of Parliament he sat without opening his lips. Once he wrote that he felt chained to his seat 'by some invisible unknown invisible power'.[1]

Yet it is not possible to put a finger on any of Fox's early efforts and say with assurance, 'This was his maiden speech'. No one even made an attempt to identify his first speech until half a century or more after the event. Sir George Otto Trevelyan, who like Dr John Allen and the third Lord Holland had the first views of the early Fox papers, wrote that 'when Fox first spoke, and on what subject, is, and will ever remain, a doubtful matter', and dismissed further inquiry.[2]

[1] J. E. Norton, ed., *The Letters of Edward Gibbon* (London, 1956), ii, 64. To J. B. Holroyd, April 8, 1775.

[2] Sir George Otto Trevelyan (1838–1928), biographer, historian, member of Parliament, nephew of Thomas B. Macaulay; author (1880) *Early History of Charles James Fox* and (1912–1914) *George III and Charles Fox, the Concluding Part of the American Revolution*. For years he served as a kind of informal consultant about the Fox papers, advising the owners who should and who should not be allowed to see them.

Dr John Allen (1771–1843), Scottish physician, researcher, historian, companion, attached to the household of the third Lord Holland. Allen wrote the life of Fox for the seventh and eighth editions of the *Encyclopedia Britannica*. He also contributed notes and

Even if the problem cannot be accurately solved it can be plausibly explained. Obviously Fox did not open his career in the usual way, with a lengthy, easily identifiable maiden speech. On the contrary he was unconcerned about the necessity of making an impressive first speech; he had always been at ease in the company of his elders, he had freely discussed political matters informally with them, he had faced Eton audiences; moreover, these experiences had received encouraging praise and approval. Undoubtedly he began his career in an unpretentious manner, simply by rising and saying a few words, and then resuming his seat; such a brief utterance could hardly be called a maiden 'speech' conspicuous enough to call for the congratulations of friends and later stand out prominently in family tradition. The preferred candidate for the honour of Fox's 'first words' is an utterance of March 9, 1769:

Mr *Charles Fox*. Are we to take the construction from the sheriff of the order? He might have come up half way, and an express sent to him in return.[1]

Fox also contributed other brief interpolations to the session's debate. As the years went on, however, the March 9 utterance and others were forgotten, and a strong belief developed that his maiden speech— meaning by this term a talk of sufficient length to let the young orator show that he could sustain an argument—was delivered during the Wilkes debates of April 14 and 15, 1769. Certainly his speech on that occasion brought a mention in the manuscript memoirs of Walpole.[2] Holland, admitting that he was unable to state the exact date on which Fox first spoke, nevertheless reported this tradition: 'I have indeed

comments to the four-volume *Memorials and Correspondence of Charles James Fox* (as did the third Lord Holland, see below).

Henry Richard Vassall Fox (1773–1840), third Baron Holland, son of Stephen Fox, second Baron Holland, and nephew of Charles James, figures prominently in the latter part of this book; an activity of his later career was to collect materials for a life of Fox and to edit the Fox correspondence.

[1] Egerton MSS., 219, f. 95. Wright, John, ed. *Sir Henry Cavendish's Debates of the House of Commons* (London, 1841), i, 342, has a slightly different wording. Editor Wright, after corresponding with Allen and especially after consulting the Cavendish notes particularly on this point, nominated this brief comment as Fox's first words to the House of Commons.

Dr Allen apparently at one time thought a speech of March 2 was the maiden speech, but later concluded it was made by Stephen Fox. (See Cavendish, i, 301.) His *Memoirs of Charles James Fox* (Edinburgh, 1820), put a speech of April 15 as the maiden speech.

The statement in the *Parliamentary History* that a speech of January 9, 1770, was the 'first parliamentary essay' of Fox is in error by several months. John Almon's *History, Debates, and Proceedings of both Houses of Parliament of Great Britain*, 7 vols. (London, 1792), contains no Fox speech previous to this date.

[2] Add. MSS. 47593. Brief text of an April 15 speech appears in Cavendish, i, 361–2. When Fox was congratulated on this speech (or some other early effort), he said: 'Wait until you hear Hare.' But Hare, his classmate, had few political ambitions and as Sir Edward Creasy commented, was satisfied to be 'the Hare with many friends' (*Annual Register*, xlvi (1804), 473).

heard . . . that it was on the business of Wilkes . . . a speech of great ability and more promise.' He added that a listener was so impressed that he ripped off part of his shirt and drew a picture of the young orator.[1]

By 1769 the business of Wilkes was the continuing dispute between the Commons and the county of Middlesex as to whether Wilkes would be allowed to represent it. Repeatedly Middlesex had returned Wilkes to the House and repeatedly the House had refused to seat him. At the latest election Wilkes had polled 1143 to 296 for the government's candidate, Colonel Luttrell. The question before the House was that Henry Lawes Luttrell, Esq., not Wilkes, ought to have been declared elected by the sheriffs of Middlesex. This position Charles strongly approved; in his speech that day he acidly observed that the sheriffs have committed 'a great crime' in returning Wilkes 'in flagrant violation of our privileges'. He thus opened his career by speaking in behalf of the Commons against the people and their elected representative. Horace Walpole reported that Stephen Fox declared, in his speech on this issue, that 'Wilkes had been chosen only by the scum of the earth', and he added that Charles was not inferior to his brother in insolence.[2] Fox's father, however, expressed great pride in the talents displayed by his son: 'Few in parliament ever spoke better than Charles did on Tuesday—off-hand—with rapidity, with spirit, and such knowledge of what he was talking of as surprised everybody in so young a man.'[3]

Fox's next appearance was May 8; the brief report in *Cavendish's Debates* opens with the notation: 'Mr *Charles Fox* spoke very well.' Of this speech, also against Wilkes, his father wrote that 'it was all off-hand, all argumentative, in reply to Mr Burke and Mr Wedderburne . . . a most extraordinary thing'.[4] The *Middlesex Journal* printed a list of those who had 'distinguished themselves by their oratory': those who spoke 'for liberty' included Barré, Burke and eight others; those who spoke 'against it' included North and Fox. The division, at four o'clock in the morning, found Fox in the majority of 221, against 152;

---

1 Add MSS. 47593. *Fox Cor.*, i, 52. '[It] is still preserved in my possession at Holland House, retaining many traits of resemblance to the dark, intelligent, and animated features of Mr Fox.'
2 Add. MSS. 47593. *Fox Cor.*, i, 52. Horace Walpole, *Memoirs of the Reign of King George III* (London, 1845), iii, 359.
3 *Ibid.*, i, 52–3. April 14 was Friday, April 15 was Saturday; Holland's letter refers to a Tuesday speech. The exact date, however, is of less importance than is the description of the young parliamentarian.
4 *Ibid.*, i, 54. May 11. Burke lists Fox as a speaker in a letter of May 8 to the Earl of Charlemont (Lucy S. Sutherland, ed., The *Correspondence of Edmund Burke* (Cambridge, 1960), ii, 24; *Historical Manuscripts Commission Reports*, Charlemont MSS., i. 294. Hereafter cited as *HMCR*.

this majority, the *Journal* declared, actually voted that Luttrell's 296 was a larger number than Wilkes's 1143. It further offered an item analysis to show that the majority was corrupt, indicating members that were sons of peers or that expected peerages, office holders or hopeful office holders, possessors of contracts or of commissions in the army and navy. So it was during the various debates on John Wilkes that Fox made his first major appearances as a parliamentary debater.

Colonial problems had also come before the Commons that session. 'The grand debate on North American affairs', as the *Parliamentary History* put it, had commenced on January 26, 1769; 'the debate was very fine indeed'. As had other colonies, the province of Massachuset's Bay had presented a petition reviewing the troubles and hardships of the colony: skirmishes with the French and the Indians, hardships of living, smallness of incomes, and above all the difficulty of finding money to pay taxes, since the balance of trade was continually un- favourable. The petition had therefore prayed that 'the several Acts of Parliament made for the purpose of raising a revenue in America be repealed'. The Lords had passed resolutions dealing harshly with Massachuset's Bay: its people had threatened officers of His Majesty's revenue, its government was in a state of disorder and confusion, and above all it had passed an insulting, subversive, and unconstitutional resolution.

The opposition contended forcefully against the Lords' proposals. Fox, however, avoided the debates on the growing discontent in America. He may have, as his nephew once observed, been advised by an older member to limit his participation in debate since the question could readily have been raised on his right of speaking and especially of voting while still a minor. Later, however, Fox himself reflected that since the register of his baptism had been burned, no one would find it easy to prove his exact age and thus unseat him, although he might have been subjected to criticism or censure for doing much voting or speaking.

So much for his first speaking experiences. The session closed in May, and Parliament adjourned for the rest of the year.

The third session of the thirteenth Parliament, which met January 9, 1770, quickly became known as the horned cattle session. The address of George III from the throne was expected to discuss the growing difficulty with the American colonies, but the King instead confined his message to another kind of distemper—among the horned cattle of the kingdom.

During the debate that day Fox did not speak brilliantly, the reason being, according to a friend, Fish Craufurd, that he had just come back from Paris and had sat up all night at the Star and Garter. He did, however, get in the last word on the Government side by asserting that the language of the opposition speakers was so licentious 'it seemed as if the old decent freedom of debate was at an end'.[1] He must have spoken with impressiveness and at greater length than the extant text now indicates, since nearly half a century later Craufurd still remembered the occasion. Over the years he had thought, erroneously, that it was Fox's maiden speech.[2]

On January 25 debate was renewed on the Middlesex election by the introduction of an ingenious motion: in matters of disputed elections the House should judge according to established law and custom. To deny such a bland statement would be unwise, yet its acceptance would open the way further for debate on whether the House, in preferring Luttrell to Wilkes, had acted according to law and custom. The topic was a good one for lawyers of both the amateur and professional variety, and the parliamentary reporter observed that considerable debate ensued as to whether the various precedents cited were or were not applicable.

A strong supporter for Wilkes was Alexander Wedderburn, a Scot, who at the time of this debate had had eight years of parliamentary speaking, and for twice that many years had been a member of the bar. He was a shrewd and competent debater who had taken lessons in elocution from the renowned Thomas Sheridan, and although nominally sympathetic to the court party had joined the Wilkes crusade. This session, as he spoke out in opposition to the North administration, his enemies alleged that he took this position not because he had a great heart that throbbed for the cause of liberty but because he had a great yearning that panted for office. To cast one's lot with the opposition at this juncture, a time characterized both by public unrest and by frequent changes of and within administration, was not a bad political move. Accordingly in the debates on the legality of the Middlesex affair, Wedderburn flatly declared that no precedent could be found for a certain feature of the Wilkes business. At this point Fox, who had just reached twenty-one, completely refuted Wedderburn, producing a case decided in the courts below but the last year, and exactly

---

[1] *Parliamentary History*, xvi, 727. This source is the one most generally used in this volume for Fox's speeches. *Parliamentary Register*, pamphlets, and newspaper reports are also cited as supplementary sources.

[2] 'Charles Fox dined at the Star & Garter sat up all night & made his maiden speech in answer to Sir George Savile' (Add. MSS. 47591; *Fox Cor.*, i, 60).

similar to that of Wilkes. The court, he said, had had no precedent, but had gone on analogy. The *House roared with applause.'*[1] Thus Walpole, who did not hear the debate, and who in fact had not yet heard Fox at all, reported the incident—showing that it must have rebounded in lively fashion through the clubs. Fox's interest in many facets of current affairs, combined with an accurate and tenacious memory and an unparalleled facility for reasoning from particular to general or the other way around, made him, as Chatham had been before him, a dangerous opponent even on points of law. Wedderburn himself did not fare badly, since his continued opposition to the Government led North to conclude he would rather have the Scot on his side than on the other, so a year later he became Solicitor-General.

On January 28, the Duke of Grafton resigned his post as the head of the Government. The King had had a long struggle finding a minister to his complete liking. In rapid procession had passed Carteret, Bute, Grenville, Rockingham, and now Grafton: five governments in ten years. The king thereupon selected Frederick, Lord North, thirty-seven years old, a competent and resourceful speaker, to take charge of affairs, beginning a term of office that was to continue until almost the end of the American revolution. North, long aware of Fox's abilities, found a post for him as Lord of the Admiralty. It was a high position for so young a man. He was appointed on February 23, 'a commissioner for executing the office of High Admiral for Great Britain', and next day took his seat.

At the Admiralty Fox got to know better both Admiral Edward Hawke, scourge of the French fleets, First Lord of the Admiralty, and even better Hawke's successor the next year, the unpopular Earl of Sandwich. Fox was by nine years the youngest of the seven Lords of the Admiralty, and the only one without either naval or office-holding experience. Fox's attendance was good although not perfect, as if he were no more overawed by his election to this prestigious board than he was by his membership in the Commons. His curious, inquiring, and retentive mind was exposed to the thousand details of running the great navy of the eighteenth century. Fox learned the problems of building naval vessels and of supplying and outfitting them; of getting volunteers to enlist; of quarantine to prevent the spread of a contagious distemper; of weather and navigation and the peril of storms; of preparing an expedition or relieving a garrison.

North could well strengthen his team of speakers by anchoring Charles Fox more snugly to the Government. Fox, heartened by his

[1] *Ibid.,* i, 60.

29

new appointment, entered the debates with renewed vigour. After his February 8 speech, the *Evening Post* noted, the 'hear him' broke out into a torrent of applause.

His short speech of February 12 likewise struck fire. The House was the fullest known for several years, 451 members being present. The order for the exclusion of strangers was strictly enforced: 'even members of the Irish House of Commons were not admitted.'[1] The motion was to disqualify revenue officers from voting at elections. With some 12,000 revenue officers at liberty to support government candidates, reform seemed indicated but Fox opposed it: 'The present motion is wrong in the manner but right in the principle.' Abuses should be corrected 'but do not correct one abuse by causing many'.[2] A few days later George III was able to write: 'The seeing that the Majority constantly encreases gives Me great pleasure.'[3]

The heavy gambling to which Fox had been introduced during his latter days at Eton, and which he continued during Oxford days and his visits to the Continent, went on unabated these years as member of Parliament and Admiralty. In 1770 Walpole could write that the young men of the age lose five, ten, fifteen thousand pounds an evening. Newspapers related with awe that the son of the defaulter won £7000 at one sitting at Pall Mall, and that on another occasion by cutting the cards, beginning with £100 a cut and ending with £1000 a cut, he had won £9000 from a single opponent. Any admirer of Charles Fox must first draw a circle around him large enough to encompass substantial faults as well as massive virtues. Probably no man out-gambled him. The vast horn of plenty amassed by Holland at the paymaster's office needed to withstand repeated draughts by his son and those who took his notes. Gambling became a disorder he could not shake, an obsession that weakened him financially and politically.

Before the year 1770 was out, however, twenty-one-year-old Charles Fox had made one more speech on the wrong side of this issue: the prestige of the people versus the prestige of the House. The debate on December 6 was on Serjeant John Glynn's motion to inquire into the administration of criminal justice, with reference to the increasing tendency of judges to allow juries to consider only the fact of a cause, not the intent of the defendant. In a libel case under this practice juries could determine only whether the defendant published the suspected

[1] *Cavendish's Debates*, i, 458.   [2] Egerton MSS. 220, 75.
[3] Add. MSS. 47585. Sir John Fortescue, *The Correspondence of King George the Third* (London, 1927), ii, 132. February 28.

libel and whether the innuendoes were true, whereas judges ruled on the more important issue of whether or not the published matter were libellous. Glynn, a lawyer who had represented Wilkes, was an able speaker on legal and constitutional questions; Chatham called him 'the very spirit of the constitution itself'.[1] Increasingly, said various other speakers, people were becoming restless about the fairness of this kind of proceeding. Fox spoke heatedly, however, against the motion; those who alleged that certain complaints and grievances were made by the people, he insisted, were merely describing their own complaints and grievances. He continued:

For my part, I am not disposed to take the voice of a miserable faction for the voice of my country. Were the people really dissatisfied, I should be glad to know how I am to ascertain the reality of that dissatisfaction? I must freely confess that I know no other way but that of consulting this House. Here the people are represented, and here is their voice expressed.

How, he asked, is he to learn about the cries and the complaints of the people? From the members of the House of Commons, the legal representatives of the people, who *are* the people. Twenty years later Fox would have developed more faith in juries, and, with Erskine at his side, would present Serjeant Glynn's arguments even more eloquently than did the Serjeant. Right now he was distrustful of the people generally—on juries or off them. Opinions of members of Parliament were more representative of what was best for the public than were those of the vulgar mob, 'with their capricious shouts and hisses.'[2]

William Woodfall was in the gallery that day and reported the debate at length. Many of Fox's early speeches went unreported and unnoted, but this one found its way into print in the *London Magazine*, the *Gentleman's Magazine* and elsewhere, so that in later years when Fox securely wore the mantle of 'man of the people', his enemies could, and did, quote this and other 1770 speeches as evidence of earlier days when Fox heartily scorned the electorate. Lord Macaulay in his own classic prose noted scornfully that small men, 'when they had nothing else to say in defence of their own tyranny, bigotry, and imbecility', could raise cheers against Fox 'by some paltry taunt about the election of Colonel Luttrell, the imprisonment of the lord mayor, and other measures in which the great Whig leader had borne a part at the age of one or two and twenty'.[3] Fox himself was compelled to develop considerable ingenuity in defending some of his early speeches. Like many other statesmen, if he had had more foresight he would have needed less repentance.

[1] Sir Lewis Namier and John Brooke, *The History of Parliament* (London, 1964), ii, 506.
[2] *Parliamentary History*, xvi, 1264–6.
[3] From the essay on Lord Holland in *Historical Essays* (London, 1843), iii, 319–20.

4

In and Out of Government
1771–1774

Charles Fox is commenced patriot, and is already
attempting to pronounce the words *country*, *liberty*,
corruption, &c.

Edward Gibbon

The issues debated in parliament during 1771 to 1774 offered various
opportunities for the young speaker who became the great liberal, the
Man of the People, to join the enlightened and forward-looking. On the
domestic side was the major controversy concerning the rights of
printers to report parliamentary debates, and less hotly contested proposals to review capital punishment and the Thirty-Nine Articles of
the Established Church. On the foreign side was the persistent problem
of the management of an empire, with questions involving America
on one side of the globe and India on the other. How Charles Fox reacted to these and other issues is the theme of this chapter.

One point emerges: the infant of the House speedily became one of
its most frequent speakers. Not for him was the traditional advice that
a new member should sit respectfully and quietly on a back bench.
Along with North, who excelled everybody in number of speeches,
Burke, who was difficult to surpass in either length or quantity, and
other well-known personages like Sir George Savile, Alderman John
Sawbridge, Solicitor-General Alexander Wedderburn, and Colonel
Isaac Barré, whose name is perpetuated in Wilkes-Barre, Pennsylvania, Fox appeared often in the lists of speakers regularly forwarded
to the King. Now in his early twenties, he was seventeen years younger
than North or Sawbridge, twenty years younger than Burke, twenty-
three years younger than Barré or Savile. Reporters in the galleries
wrote paragraphs branding Fox as presumptuous, ambitious, and
violent. And outside the House he had to face the fury of volatile, articulate mobs. Fox thrived on both the missives and the missiles. Far from
suffering any damned obscurity, he was from the start fully exposed to
public appraisal.

The most prolonged and eventful debate, with Parliament and the
King on one side and the Lord Mayor and other authorities of the City
on the other, concerned the illegal publication of parliamentary debates
in eight London newspapers. This dispute came to a crisis in 1771. Fox

opened his career by taking an illiberal and reactionary point of view towards this issue, as he did toward most of the others that arose that year and the three that followed.

A newspaper that printed the proceedings of Parliament committed a notorious breach of privilege. For more than a century the publication of debates had been stoutly opposed. At the outset some members had declared that if debates were not printed, speakers would feel more free to change their minds; others noted that much public business was highly confidential; still others that speakers should not be held accountable outside the chamber for what they said inside. To print the speeches of the House, members were told, would make it appear to be the most contemptible assembly on the face of the earth.[1] To this sentiment the House had agreed without a dissenting voice.

Parliamentary news was in such demand, however, that newspapers did everything possible to print a small portion regardless of restrictions. Instead of mentioning the House of Commons or House of Lords by name, the printers at first skirted the rules by representing their excerpts as having been uttered in a fictitious Lilliputian assembly or Brobdingnagian senate. Later this fiction was dropped and speakers were identified as L—d N–rth, Mr F–x. Under this thin guise parliamentary materials were printed, but members became restless when they were misquoted or abused. Clearing the strangers' gallery on the day of an important debate was therefore for the Government a means both of protection and retaliation. Reporters knew they were allowed in the gallery only on sufferance. These restrictions, together with poor sight lines and hearing conditions that were far from ideal, contributed to the inaccuracies of parliamentary reporting.

A typical English newspaper of this half of the century had a page size approximately 14 by 18 inches; each issue comprised four 4-column pages. English printers, unlike a few of their American counterparts, did not print extra pages to accommodate special news events. Sheer mechanical limitations therefore made it possible to print only a fraction of a night's debate; the papers had to make extensive use of summary and paraphrase. A single speech might appear as much as a month late; a debate might be continued through two or three issues. 'The remainder of this excellent speech in our next issue' was a familiar sentence. Speakers had ample opportunity to supply revised texts of their speeches. Printers did not always know the names of their correspondents.[2] To speak of verbatim reports of parliamentary speeches is

[1] *Parliamentary History*, x, 806.
[2] Actually the papers freely published anonymous contributions. A speaker could therefore easily get in print a laudatory puff for himself that he or a friend had composed.

sheer nonsense. Even a speech text purporting to be a shorthand account had been exposed to possible corrections by speaker, reporter, and printer. Presumably, however, the main lines of a speaker's argument could survive intact, along with glimpses of his supporting illustrations and of his use of language.[1] The total body of texts, however, is slender indeed. If modern standards of reporting had been in force during Fox's career, his eloquence and that of his colleagues would have appeared in something like 1000 volumes instead of 27.[2]

The famous quarrel with the printers opened February 8, when Colonel George Onslow complained that *The Gazetteer and New Daily Advertiser* and the *Middlesex Journal* had misrepresented speeches and had reflected on several members. The House speedily voted to order the printers of the offending newspapers to appear before it. As the printers did not appear, they were cited for contempt.

Although the House seemed unable to seize, much less punish, the two printers, Colonel Onslow on March 12 preferred charges against three brace of printers more, from six additional newspapers. The opposition made every attempt to ridicule his complaint. In St Stephen's the method of voting was not by roll call but by division of the House into ayes and noes, the members on one side emptying into the lobby and being counted individually on their return as they filed between two tellers, the other side being similarly counted in the chamber itself. Burke and his colleagues employed the tactic of calling for one division after another so that time and again members found themselves queueing up to be counted. Eventually the House wearily marched through twenty-three divisions, before it was able to pass the necessary motions ordering Onslow's printers to attend. These labours were not completed until four o'clock in the morning.[3]

In the days that followed, the House, attempting to uphold its privileges, brought itself into open warfare with authorities of the City. When one of the printers was apprehended and taken before

[1] A. Aspinall's comprehensive article, 'The Reporting and Publishing of the House of Commons' Debates, 1771–1834' in *Essays Presented to Sir Lewis Namier* (London, 1956), describes obstacles to the publication of debates and incidents that arose as reporters attempted to carry out their assignments.

[2] An incredibly small percentage of parliamentary debate was published. For the whole of 1770 *Parliamentary History* records about 700 columns of text (less than half a volume), which at $3\frac{1}{2}$ minutes for each column would be 2450 minutes or about 40 hours of talk. For the same period *Cavendish's Debates* records about 35 hours of talk. The situation improved only slowly. The important topics of 1780 were reported in 1050 columns in the *Parliamentary History*, slightly less than a volume. During the period 1780–1800, one volume proved sufficient to contain the reports of slightly more than one year's debating; 27 volumes encompass the 39 years of Fox's parliamentary career. By 1820 the reports of a single year's debate required 3 volumes; by 1850, 6 volumes; by 1960, 17 volumes for the Commons, 9 for the Lords.

[3] *Parliamentary History*, xvii, 75–83. *Journal of the House of Commons*, xxxiii, 249–51.

John Wilkes, now an alderman, the accused man was set free and the person apprehending was charged with assault and false imprisonment. In similar fashion Alderman Richard Oliver freed another printer. Another time the Lord Mayor, Brass Crosby, and the two aldermen detained not only the printer but the messenger sent to apprehend him.

The House indignantly ordered Alderman Oliver and the Lord Mayor, both members of the House, to appear before it. Excitement was intense; crowds from the City gathered in support of its officials; attendance at the debates ran high, on some days exceeding 450. Members packed the benches, stood by the walls, jammed the area around Mr Speaker's chair. Fox made his longest recorded speech to date during the debate of March 25 for committing Oliver to the Tower. The question, he said, was whether the people or the Commons are the best judges of public welfare:

> For my own part, Sir [he continued] I shall not hesitate to pronounce positively in favour of this House. . . . I pay no regard whatever to the voice of the people: it is our duty to do what is proper, without considering what is agreeable. . . . I stand up for the constitution, not for the people. . . . I am for maintaining the independence of parliament, and will not be a rebel to my king, to my country, or my own heart, for the loudest huzza of an inconsiderate multitude.[1]

This is strange language, coming from the future Man of the People. Walpole, who had once called him the phenomenon of the age, now wrote that 'Charles Fox, as if impatient to inherit his father's unpopularity, abused the City as his father used to do.'[2] When the alderman was committed to the Tower, City officials promptly voted to pay his expenses during his confinement.

Fox did not spend all his energy abusing the multitude on the floor of the House, for he spent half an hour one day 'leaning out of a coffeehouse window in Palace Yard, shaking his fist at the people, and provoking them by all the reproachful words and menacing gestures that he could invent'. His own version was that he simply went to the windows to show that he was not afraid. George Selwyn, a parliamentary colleague who in a forty-year career never once spoke, stood behind him, as usual an onlooker, 'encouraging him and clapping him on the back, as if he was a dirty ruffian going to fight in the streets'. Fox told the House that he would rather be hissed in the company of Lord North than applauded with those who were applauded.[3]

Two days later the House debated whether to send the Lord Mayor himself to the Tower. Fifty thousand people, most of whom

---

[1] *Parliamentary History*, xvii, 149–50.
[2] *Memoirs of the Reign of King George III* (London, 1845), iv, 290.
[3] *Matthew Brickdale's Notes on the Debates in the House of Commons for the years 1770–1774*, v, 72. S. Parnell Kerr, *George Selwyn and the Wits* (London, 1909), p. 282.

could not read newspapers, milled around the streets and swamped the approaches to St Stephen's. Hostile groups insulted North, tore his hat in pieces, broke up his carriage. They threw mud and assorted articles at Charles and Stephen, ripped their clothes, upset their coach. The excitement out of doors carried into the chamber. Although speakers tried to calm violent feelings and urge that the Lord Mayor simply be placed in the custody of the sergeant-at-arms instead of being jailed in the Tower, the Lord Mayor insisted that he should be treated exactly as Alderman Oliver had been; hence an amendment to commit him to the Tower carried by a five-to-one ratio. Next day Fox complained of the treatment he had received, detailing that he had been pelted with stones and oranges, and blaming the sheriffs for their lax handling of the crowds; North answered laconically that the House had more important business and let Fox nurse his bruises without official comfort.

In every respect, however, the victory went to the City and to the printers. The end of the session meant the automatic release of the popular prisoners in the Tower; they were triumphantly escorted to their homes. They continued their publication of the proceedings of Parliament, and although as late as 1782 the German clergyman, Moritz, observed reporters taking down the debate 'rather by stealth', their position slowly but steadily improved. Even so, the galleries could still be closed, as they were during important debates on the American question, and the cry of privilege could still be raised.

The King's speech in May put an end to the session. Whatever praise goes to Fox those months is for his growing facility as a debater, but not for any qualities of vision or judgment. With his parliamentary duties temporarily at an end, he turned from debating to cricket and partridge shooting during the summer, and a visit to Paris, duly recorded by Madame du Deffand, that winter. In January the tragedy of *Jane Shore* was revived at Winterslow house, with Fox as Gloster; the press commented that it had been received with most distinguished applause by a numerous and polite audience.

After a seven-month holiday, the new session opened on January 21, 1772. One of Fox's early moves was to give notice that he intended to move an amendment to the Clandestine Marriages Act, against which his father had spoken eloquently twenty years previously, to enact changes that would offer greater legal protection to young couples who had married in irregular circumstances. Here was a kindly, liberal, and human move. His preparation for this proposed action was, however, far from thorough; Walpole asserted that when Fox moved the repeal he had not actually read the act, 'nor did till some days after'.[1] Nor was Fox informed that at this same time the King's ministers were moving in a more restrictive direction, preparing a Bill prohibiting members of the royal family from marrying unless the marriage was approved by the sovereign. Charles, who considered himself a member of the Government even though his office was a modest one, was deeply hurt that ministers had not taken him into their confidence: 'Ld North', wrote his mother, 'has always said Charles Fox was the only support he cd intirely depend on in the House of Commons,' and therefore not telling Charles what business was to come before the house 'was a most unpardonable neglect'.[2] More to the point, however, since he did not believe that one person, even a King, should pass judgment upon the marriage plans of another, even a member of the royal family, Fox determined to argue against the Bill.

In other areas, Charles was not so rebellious. Before the debate on the marriage Bill got under way, a petition was presented, signed by 250 members of the clergy of the Church of England, certain professors, and others, praying that they be relieved of subscribing to the Thirty-nine Articles of the Church, so that each might study and interpret the Scriptures for himself. Charles, not yet willing to speak for religious freedom and against religious tests, spoke briefly and voted against the petition. So again, he found himself on the side of the established order of things. Yet North's treatment of him over the marriage Bill continued to rankle, so on February 20 Fox resigned his position on the Admiralty board. Gibbon learned that Fox had turned against the administration, and in memorable prose wrote: 'Charles Fox is commenced Patriot, and is already attempting to pronounce the words *Country, Liberty, Corruption,* &c., with what success, time will discover.'[3]

Like the American colonies, Fox did not aim at political independence from the beginning; Craufurd, writing to their mutual friend, Lord Ossory, said that Charles had not really meant to leave the Government, and Fox added a postscript that the reason for his resigning was complicated but that he wanted to feel free to vote against 'this Royal Family Bill'. 'Upon the whole I am convinced I did right and I think myself very safe from going into opposition, which is the only danger', he concluded.[4] Rumours to that effect began to circulate, however, and the *Gazetteer and New Daily Advertiser* mischievously observed that Mr F-x had offered to join opposition provided it paid his debts.

[1] *The Last Journals of Horace Walpole* (London, 1910), i, 7.
[2] Ilchester, ii, 346–47.
[3] *Letters of Edward Gibbon*, i, 309. To Holroyd, February 21, 1772.
[4] Add. MSS. 47579. *Fox Cor.*, i, 73.

Since the postscript to the Ossory letter is perhaps Fox's first reference to political parties, it is worth mentioning that Fox did not think of 'opposition' as a single, monolithic party. Trevelyan observed that Fox probably never changed so many votes as he did in his first half-dozen sessions, when party limits were still undefined and party obligations far less strict than they afterwards became.[1] The detailed investigations of Namier and his students have further demonstrated the incorrectness of visualizing a two-party house, whigs on one side, tories on the other. During Fox's career the term 'tory' was used mainly as an epithet to describe someone firmly associated with administration policies, and who therefore could, loosely, be considered as reactionary or at least as conservative. The term 'whig' was more desirable; a whig was staunchly on the side of the 'constitution', especially on points where the privileges of Parliament were to be preferred to the prerogative of the Crown. An important segment of the opposition in 1773 was the Rockingham faction; although eventually Fox adhered to this group, he might have attached himself to some other connection, or sat on the opposition side simply as an independent. As will be seen on later pages, whenever a contemporary undertook to analyse voting affiliations, drawing columns on his page under which to list members, he would need several headings to describe all shades of opinion: pro, con, hopeful, doubtful, and the like.

The King was powerfully interested in the fate of his Bill, urged Lord North to exert every energy in favour of it, and determined to punish those who voted against it.[2] After one close, important vote of 200 to 164 in favour of administration forces, the King wrote to North for a list of those who had deserted to the minority. Such a list, he added, would guide his conduct in the drawing room on the morrow.

Great courage was required to defy the King's measure, but Charles led the opposing cavalry in many a charge up Administration Heights. He attacked the Bill in law, he attacked it in principle; he lashed ministers on technical points, he pointed out contradictions of the lawyers. Walpole ranked Fox's speaking above that of Burke, Wedderburn, or Townshend, declaring that Charles, above all others, 'seized the just point of argument throughout, with most amazing rapidity and clearness'.[3] The Bill passed easily by 168 to 115. 'Never', said Walpole, 'was an Act passed *against* which so much, and *for* which so little, was said.' It is still on the statute books.

---

[1] *Early History of Charles James Fox*, p. 468.
[2] 'I have a right to expect a hearty Support from everyone in my Service,' he wrote North on February 26, 'and shall remember Defaulters.' Fortescue, ii, 325.
[3] *Last Journals*, i, 70.

This defeat marked Charles's first experience in fighting the mobilized forces of George the Third. But the day came for Charles to introduce his own marriage Bill; that was a fortnight later, on April 7. Walpole was a spectator that day; he had heard many reports about Fox but had never before listened to him speak, so he went to the gallery to hear the young orator. He observed that Charles introduced his Bill with ease, grace, and clearness, and without the elegant formality of the usual young speaker. Even so, Walpole concluded that Fox did not shine particularly, though his sense and facility showed that he could shine. Walpole knew the inside story: that Fox had returned just that morning from Newmarket, where he had lost a thousand pounds the preceding day; that he had stopped at Hockerel, where he had sat up drinking all night; that when he moved his Bill, he had not even drawn it up. The Fox strategy for that day was a simple one; he planned to make the preliminary motion, let his opponents attack the Bill, and then he, powerful in refutation, would reply to these arguments.

The story of what happened is a tribute to a brilliant mind. North and Burke each argued at length against the Bill, emphasizing that the present system of regulating marriages had survived the test of twenty years of experience and had demonstrated the wisdom of forbidding the marriage of young and immature couples. Walpole described Fox running about the House talking to different persons, scarcely listening either to North or Burke; then, with amazing spirit and memory, answering them both, ridiculing North and refuting Burke.[1]

Here for the first time Fox caught the fancy of the London press, ever ready to applaud good speaking even from a political opponent. Although hardly a year had passed since Fox had viciously attacked the printers, the *Gazetteer and New Daily Advertiser* now declared that Fox's speech 'was a most masterly assemblage of arguments on behalf of the liberties of human nature, in the essential part of marriage'. So eloquent was he, the reporter concluded, that no fewer than twenty-three avowedly intended opposers of his motion absolutely voted in support of it, 'from bare conviction of its equity and necessity'. If this appraisal is accurate, it indicates that a good speech could reach members of the independent group and other less hardened partisans.

On that day Charles whipped the Government by a margin of one vote: 62–61—'a disgraceful event for a Prime Minister', said Walpole. Fox's success did not last long since he did not trouble to pursue his advantage, and, on May 19, arrived from Newmarket just in time to see his Bill thrown out without debate by a vote of 92 to 34. He took his defeat with indifference and did not continue his fight against the ministry.

[1] *Ibid.*, i, 81–2.

Negotiations to entice Fox back into administration, rumoured in the spring, were resumed toward the end of the year. One paper conjectured that since North would be elevated to the House of Lords upon the death of his aged father, the resulting shuffle of offices would make Fox Chancellor of the Exchequer; another that Lord Holland was to be the Earl of Rochester, provided he would settle his pay office accounts by 1801; another that if Holland were truly to be Earl of Rochester, the title would descend to Charles James Fox since his older brother had no issue. Out of these charges and allegations, these rumours and anxieties, these hearings and understandings, came a letter from the King appointing Fox to a seat on the Treasury board paying £1600 a year. Since Gibbon had calculated that gambling cost Fox £500 per hour, Fox's new position at the Treasury board would fortify him for three hours' good play at Almack's or White's.

Fox was elevated to the Treasury board December 28, 1772. His attendance was less regular than at the Admiralty board. At one long meeting he participated in discussions of the problem of smuggling and of the difficulties of collecting duties; he heard a letter read from wax chandlers complaining of frauds in the manufacture of candles, and seeking additional duty on imported wax and spermaceti candles. He was also introduced, by way of the problem of providing subsistence for slaves, to the question of the slave trade and the employment of Negroes by government contractors. He heard complaints from collectors of Rhode Island 'stating the great difficulties they labour under from the vexatious law suits carried on in the courts of that colony against the collectors for the execution of his [*sic*] duty'. He heard complaints from Boston and also acknowledged a remittance of more than £8000 covering duty on tea. At some meetings letters were read, at others petitioners appeared in person; thus he became familiar with the processes of discussion and administration.

From these early contacts with the executive arm of the Government, Fox, like any young statesman, absorbed a vast deal of factual information and an approach to the making of policy. Most problems have a financial underpinning, and the steady procession of letters and petitioners through the Treasury board gave young Charles Fox insight into governmental decisions and the fiscal problems accompanying them.

In 1770, his first year as the first minister, North had brought about the repeal of the Townshend duties except the one on tea, maintained to remind colonists that Parliament continued to have the right to impose taxes. The Americans had not liked this arrangement but as they lived happily on smuggled tea the result had been to relax tensions and quiet restlessness. The East India company, however, soon had found its warehouses bulging with unsaleable tea and its financial position weakening. Parliament learned about these difficulties from the King's message from the throne on November 26, 1772.

A secret committee was appointed to investigate the matter; its report was debated, the need of the company for financial help being repeatedly stressed. North proposed that the company, now possessed of 17 million pounds of tea, be allowed to export a substantial part of this supply to the colonies in America, free of usual customs and inland duties. Under this special dispensation the tea could be sold, with only the Townshend duty added, at a lesser price than smuggled tea; the colonists would be sufficiently grateful for the bargain to be willing to overlook the duty, and the company's finances would soon be put in good order.[1] There was little debate, no division; no one realized that the tea resolution was a bomb with a long, slow-burning fuse.

Although most of the rest of the session was devoted to East India affairs, the principal debate was on the conduct of Lord Clive. Clive, former governor of Bengal, who had amassed a large private fortune in India, had come under sharp criticism for his administrative practices. Fox, by now fully introduced to the India question that intermittently occupied the house in his lifetime, 'declaimed with vehemence'; to the embarrassment of the Government, he described Clive as the 'origin of all plunder, the source of all robbery'.[2] The issues that came up during this debate foreshadowed the controversy a decade later when Fox found a similar target, the abuse of Indian peoples by another governor, Warren Hastings.

During this 1771–74 period, Fox, in his mid-twenties, continued his compulsive gambling. When he was not at St Stephen's he was at Almack's, White's, the race course at Newmarket, or some other locale where the action was. His energy was inexhaustible; he went from one spot to another, ending up at the House of Commons. Walpole recorded the following account of Fox's activities in 1772, the night before the debate, already mentioned, on the Thirty-nine Articles:

[Fox] did not shine in this debate, nor could it be wondered at. He had sat up playing hazard at Almack's, from Tuesday evening 4th, till five in the afternoon of Wednesday 5th. An hour before he had recovered £12,000 that he had lost, and by dinner, which was five o'clock, he had ended losing £11,000. On the

1 *Parliamentary History*, xvii, 840–1.   2 *Last Journals*, i, 232.

Thursday he spoke in this debate; went to dinner at past eleven at night; from thence to White's, where he drank till seven the next morning; thence to Almack's, where he won £6,000; and between three and four in the afternoon he set out for Newmarket.[1]

He further observed that in three nights Charles and Stephen together had lost £32,000. He added: 'There being a report that Charles was going to be married, it was told to his father . . . who replied: "I am glad of it, for then he will go to bed at least one night."'

Walpole's description of gaming is awesome; at Almack's, he reports, £10,000 generally lay in cash on the table. The participants gambled with £50 bundles. It is difficult to appreciate the purchasing power of these sums, though it can be noted that Fox spent little more than a £50 bundle in meeting his preliminary expenses at Oxford; for ten bundles the colony of New York could hire the services of Edmund Burke as its London agent for a year; the loose cash on the table would buy a bench full of parliamentary seats. A popular game was quinze, which had most of the features of vingt-et-un or blackjack, the magic number being fifteen instead of twenty-one. Each player had a small stand nearby for his bank notes and tea, and when his funds were exhausted he would replenish the supply with loans from Jews at high premiums. Fox called his outer room where moneylenders awaited him, the Jerusalem Chamber.

Actually, Fox had been in continual debt ever since he had overspent his Oxford allowance. Over the years creditors had advanced loans, postponing the hour of reckoning because they calculated that he would some day come into the major part of a vast inheritance. Lord Holland was ill, and Stephen, himself a poor health risk, had no children. But the fact became known that Stephen's wife was expecting. A son was born on November 21—Charles himself wryly described the boy as a second Messiah born for the destruction of the Jews—and this sudden lessening of Charles's great expectations brought creditors swarming about his head. Most of them held obligations in the form of annuities and demanded that they be redeemed. Lord Holland needed to be told; and on November 26, he directed his financial adviser to settle all outstanding debts:

I do hereby order direct & require you to sell & dispose of my long annuity's, and so much of my other Stock, Estates & Effects as will be sufficient to Pay and Discharge the debts of my son The Honble Charles James Fox not exceeding the sum of one hundred thousand pounds.[2]

The paper suggests the grief and melancholy with which the old politician bent himself to this last gesture to his son. It should be said

---

[1] *Last Journals;* i, 12.   [2] Add. MSS. 35068B. Ilchester, ii, 354.

that some of Charles's debts had been co-signed by close friends, but Lord Holland assumed the entire burden.

Charles continued a member of the Treasury board. He was, however, beginning to inquire more fully into the policies of the King and his minister. These worthies might have found the long mislaid earldom for Lord Holland a cheap price to pay for words of good tory advice spoken softly to his talented son, but as they never found it convenient to elevate the father to Earl of Rochester or to anything else, the independence of the son began more and more to assert itself. Inevitably it would have, earldom or no. The break soon came.

On February 11 the *Public Advertiser*, printed by 'Memory' Woodfall, well-known parliamentary reporter, published an attack on the Speaker of the house, Sir Fletcher Norton, alleging partiality plus gross and willful falsehood. Norton, called 'Sir Bull Face Double Fee' for his love of money, was not popular, but members thought the issue involved the dignity of the House, and the motion was made that Woodfall be ordered to appear before it the coming Monday. The House agreed that a malicious and scandalous libel had been printed and ordered Woodfall to appear at its bar.

Woodfall duly presented himself, as ordered. Respectfully stating that in twenty years in the printing business he had never before incurred the displeasure of the House, he threw himself upon its mercy. A motion was offered simply that he be committed to the custody of the sergeant at arms. Fox thought this punishment too mild and moved that he be sent to Newgate prison. Although North declared the printer had behaved with decency and should not suffer long imprisonment, 'Mr Fox was exceedingly violent . . . he was peremptory in his wish that the printer should be sent to Newgate.' Horace Walpole also thought Fox violent and presumptuous as well.[1] At a later stage of the debate when North agreed with Fox that imprisonment was suitable, Newgate was dropped and Gatehouse prison substituted. Still later, when precedents were cited showing that it would be proper merely to commit the prisoner to the serjeant at arms, North sought to be released from his promise to vote for imprisonment, but Fox held him to his word. North therefore reluctantly voted with Fox in the division but urged his own friends to vote on the other side, so the division, 152 to 68, committed Woodfall to the sergeant at arms.

The King was angered at Fox's conduct. 'I am greatly incensed at the presumption of Charles Fox in obliging You to vote with him that night', he wrote to North on February 16; '. . . that Young Man has so thoroughly cast off every principle of common honour and honesty that

---

[1] *Last Journals*, i, 291. Walpole is quoted at length in *Fox Cor.*, i, 96–8.

he must become as contemptible as he is odious.'[1] It was the strongest condemnation of Fox that the King had as yet penned. Others outside the House enjoyed the mounting criticism of Fox; the *Evening Post* noted that 'the young Cub . . . has got a severe rap on the paws for his late violent abuse against printers'. The *Morning Chronicle* editorially thought the cub's conduct universally condemned by the people of the three kingdoms.

Since Fox continued to speak and vote as he pleased, it became apparent that something must be done to discipline him. He learned of his punishment through the following laconic note from North: 'His Majesty has thought proper to order a new Commission of the Treasury to be made out, in which I do not see your name.' Papers considered it prime news that he was dropped from the Treasury; some recalled again that he was the son of the public defaulter of unaccounted millions.

So he faced the critical years immediately ahead with mixed assets. His political philosophy was far from crystallized: he could denounce the multitudes but he could also attack the King's marriage Bill. He had been introduced to two issues that would sorely trouble the next decade, the American revolution and the administration of India, and to two others that would persist even longer, freedom of religion and freedom of the press. Some of his early utterances he would later need to explain; some of his positions he would need to reverse. In a sense he was his own worst enemy, but he made two others with power and influence: the King's first minister and the King himself.

Fox always had courage; he had gained administrative experience; he had developed vigorous, articulate speech. Moreover, he had abandoned the Government position as a platform for his speaking and had begun to develop one of his own. In the parliamentary sessions that lay ahead, Fox began to participate in the debates on the American question, a topic on which he was eventually to do some of his finest speaking. The incident that was to revive this issue had already occurred: the reception of the East India Company's tea in certain prominent American ports.

[1] Fortescue, iii, 69.

Part Two
The Loyal Opposition

Fox during the American war, Fox in his best days,
was the best speaker I ever heard.

Henry Grattan

5

Fox Discovers America
1774–1775

You know I have a natural partiality to what some
people call rebels.

Charles James Fox

Nothing can be more calculated to bring the Americans
to a due submission than the very handsome Majority
that at the outset have appeared in both Houses of
Parliament.

George the Third

Looking back over his stormy career, Fox could reflect that the ability
to speak well was a double-edged sword. If one spoke in behalf of the
Government, it could reward him with marks of favour. If one spoke
against the Government, it could either make an effort to win him back
or take from him such favours as it had already bestowed.

In 1774 and the years that followed nearly every major proposal of
the Government had to face his pointed, eloquent criticism. Occasionally the criticism was *pro forma* but usually it was substantive, and
either it had to be replied to, or if ignored, had to be offset by other
kinds of influence.

A silent parliamentarian can listen to the debates, or inform himself in
other ways, and then vote according to his convictions or his prejudices.
The small handful of speakers in the House, however, like North,
Burke, Fox, and Wedderburn, were invariably prepared to discuss in reasoned, articulate, fashion each issue as it came along. A
parliament considers a wide variety of proposals concurrently, foreign
affairs interspersed with domestic urgencies. The various strands that
are intertwined to make up Fox's long speaking career can be labelled
America, France, Ireland, India, parliamentary reform, slave trade,
religious and political liberty, and scores of transient matters.

Fox's resignation brought him more notoriety than he relished. It
was observed that he was tender in years but tough in politics and
already had been twice in and twice out of place.[1] George Selwyn, wit

[1] *Last Journals*, i, 309.

and bon-vivant, who as a sideline had developed a remarkable curiosity about corpses, reflected both interests by addressing him as Charles the Martyr because his political head had been severed. Selwyn prophesied, however, that Charles's head, unlike the martyred King's, could be sewed on again.[1]

Meanwhile the tea ships had met an unexpected and unwelcome reception in America. At Charleston the cargo had been seized by customs officials and left to rot in damp cellars. At Philadelphia and New York captains could not land their cargoes, and sailed back to England. At Boston on December 16 a party of 'Mohawk Indians' had boarded the vessel and dumped 340 chests of tea into the harbour. 'In two hours' time', wrote Governor Thomas Hutchinson to his superior, the Earl of Dartmouth, Secretary for the Colonies, 'it was totally destroyed.'[2] This grim word reached London early in 1774. The American problem had flared up in full force.

Not until March, however, was the issue formally laid before Parliament, when the King, supported by 109 letters and documents, with others to follow, reported the violent and outrageous proceedings at Boston, urging Parliament to take steps to put a stop to the disorder and to secure the just dependence of the colonies upon the mother country.

During the debates, North proposed to close the port of Boston altogether. As he explained the move it seemed a reasonable punishment for Boston's outrageous misbehaviour. Once America realized that Great Britain was in earnest, he declared, troubles would subside. Advice like this had previously come from Governor Hutchinson and from his successor, General Gage, who, on the basis of his first hand, on-the-spot observation had written the King a month previously that the colonies would act like Lyons if the mother country acted like Lambs, 'but if we take the resolute part they will undoubtedly prove very meek'.[3] Henry Herbert, a frequent and independent speaker who later was to oppose the Government's conduct of the war, on this day argued that the Americans 'were a strange set of people, and that it was in vain to expect any degree of reasoning from them; that instead of making their claim by argument, they always chose to decide the matter by tarring and feathering'. Charles Van, a violent anti-American, declared that Boston ought to be knocked about the ears of its citizens, and, like Carthage, destroyed. Van was the one who the following month advocated that the Government should punish Massa-

---

[1] *Last Journals;* i, 304.   [2] Peter Force, *American Archives* (Washington, 1837), i, 6, 29.
[3] Fortescue, iii, 59. The King to North, February 4, 1774.

chusetts by setting her forests on fire.[1] Old Welbore Ellis, who had opposed the repeal of the Stamp Act, now called the tea riot, 'treason', and urged that Boston be singled out as the principal ringleader and punished, in order to subdue the others.[2]

Some advice was more moderate. Rose Fuller, who had interests in the West Indies and who had spoken and voted against the Stamp Act, thought that before punitive measures were adopted, the colonists should be required to pay some £15,000 for the dumped tea. Even Benjamin Franklin was amazed by the news of the party and declared that the tea should be paid for.[3] The problem presented by the tea party was complex. Since it would be difficult to identify members of the raiding party, Parliament was tempted to punish the whole town of Boston for the misdeeds of the few; and since the political drowned out the commercial overtones, members were in a mood to be more severe than to assess a monetary fine. Germain and others repeated the argument that since the repeal of the Stamp Act simply encouraged the Americans to commit fresh outrages, strong measures should now be taken. Thus the King heard much dubious advice of the sort he wished to hear.

The Boston Port Act proved to be harsh indeed. Actually the face of Boston was turned to the sea. The city's 20,000 people, nearly all of English ancestry, lived upon its rum distilleries, fisheries, shipyards, ropewalks. To blockade its port was to threaten it with economic disaster. The Earl of Chatham declared that 'if that mad and cruel measure should be pushed . . . England has seen her best days'.[4] In subsequent debates staunch opposition speakers like William Dowdeswell objected both to the haste and the unfairness. Parliament should conduct hearings before it voted the Bill. Moreover, it was unfair on the face of it; no reason existed for singling out Boston when Philadelphia and New York had sent back the tea, and Charleston had put the tea into a damp cellar, 'and the whole has become rotten and useless'. In eighteen days the Bill passed the Commons without formal vote, nor did it meet substantial resistance in the Lords.

As a conciliatory gesture to soften the severe measures taken against the colonies, the opposition made the motion that the duty on tea be repealed. During the debate Burke delivered his famous speech on American taxation, authoritatively reviewing colonial grievances and envisioning a policy that would deal with the situation. The King's supporters could not meet the Irishman's logic and array of fact; they

---

[1] Quoted in *History of Parliament*, iii, 572.   [2] *Parliamentary History*, xvii, 1159–81.
[3] *Virginia Gazette*, May 5.
[4] William Stanhope Taylor and John Henry Pringle, eds., *Correspondence of William Pitt, Earl of Chatham* (London, 1840), iv, 337. To Shelburne, March 20.

had done what they could when that morning they had closed the gallery doors both top and bottom, so that no stranger would be admitted. Burke must have felt a twinge of despair as he noted the absence of reporters and visitors, but it was a twinge he had often felt, and one about which the minority could do nothing except print the speech in a pamphlet. Yet in the audience Charles Fox was listening attentively (he declared later that he learned more from Burke than from all his books and studies). In the debate Fox said, in part:

> Let us consider, Sir, what is the state America appears in to this country; the Americans will appear as useful subjects, if you use them with that temper and lenity which you ought to do. . . .
> A tax can only be laid for three purposes; the first for a commercial regulation, the second for a revenue, and the third for asserting your right. As to the two first, it has clearly been denied it is for either; as to the latter, it is only done with a view to irritate and declare war there, which, if you persist in, I am clearly of opinion you will effect, or force into open rebellion.

In a few brief sentences he reduced all possibilities to three, showed that no issue was involved in the first two, and prepared to battle on the third.[1] Despite the eloquent appeal of Burke, and the short but incisive analysis of his new pupil, Government forces by 182 to 49 declined to repeal the tea duty.

The House thereupon focused its attention upon another proposal of North's—a Bill to regulate the government of Massachusetts Bay. England had no right to tax America, Fox declared on April 22. 'I believe America is wrong in resisting against this country, with regard to its legislative authority . . .'—this throwback to the doctrine of a former year shows simply that Fox's conversion was gradual—'but, Sir, there has been a constant conduct practised in this country, consisting of violence and weakness. . . . [The] Bill before you is not what you want; it irritates the minds of the people, but does not correct the deficiencies of that government.[2] On May 2 he declared: 'I take this to be the question'—the words of a debater, seeking the real issue before the House:

> . . . whether America is to be governed by force, or management? I never could conceive that the Americans could be taxed without their consent. . . . There is not an American, but who must reject and resist the principle and right of our taxing them. . . . If a system of force is to be established, there is no provision for that in this Bill; it does not go far enough: if it is to induce them by fair means, it goes too far.[3]

Burke spoke only briefly, most of the time needing to shout above the noise and confusion of members anxious to get the Bill passed. It made

[1] *Parliamentary History*, xvii, 1270.   [2] *Ibid.*, xvii, 1288.
[3] *Ibid.*, xvii, 1313. The *Chronicle* noted that Fox spoke about half an hour: 'he condemned the bill throughout, and predicted the worst consequences from the present measure.'

drastic changes in the government of Massachusetts. This measure and the Boston Port Act were the first two of the four later known in American history as the Intolerable Acts; a third provided for trying in England or in another colony anyone indicted for certain types of capital offences, and a fourth legalized the quartering of troops in Boston. During all the debates the top strength of opposition forces was in the neighbourhood of three-score votes.

So Fox discovered America. She had not been entirely a stranger to him, for he had heard the debates on the repeal of the Stamp Act when he was an Eton schoolboy and he had participated in discussions of colonial problems as a lord at the Admiralty and Treasury boards. His speeches thus far had been largely rebuttal in nature, tactical rather than strategic. Yet although he still needed to extend his range of information, in these recent weeks he had heard, on the floor of St Stephen's, copious reviews of the history of British-American relations, a subject that later he took over bodily. He was, moreover, attracted to Burke's thought that if there were a solution, it lay on the side of conciliation rather than force.

Lord Holland died July 1. George Selwyn had called to see him shortly before he passed away. 'Send him in next time he comes,' said Holland, mindful of Selwyn's liking for corpses; 'if I am alive, I will be glad to see him; if I am dead, he will be glad to see me.' Walpole wrote that Holland expired easily, worn out in mind and body,[1] as he might be, considering his unfulfilled hopes and the constantly mounting debts of his older sons. Lady Holland did not long survive him. Her acute sufferings from cancer led to her death before the month was out.

The Holland estate was divided among the three sons, except that debts of Stephen and Charles totalling £200,000 were taken from their share. Charles was left a place of £600 a year, an estate of £200 and £10,000 in money.[2] Later he inherited the sinecure of Clerk of the Pells in Ireland, worth £2300 a year.

Already Fox had broken with the political ideas of his family, but the death of his parents cut any tie that might have still remained. The title of Baron Holland passed to Stephen, and when Stephen died at the year's end went in turn to his young son, Henry. If Fox had had any fear that he might be catapulted into the Lords, he could now rest easy.

The sudden dissolution of the thirteenth, the unreported Parliament, was a tactical move of George the Third. North thought the move

---

[1] *Last Journals*, i, 362. [2] Ilchester, ii, 356–7. *Fox Cor.*, i, 136.

would be unwise; 'if Parliament is now dissolved, every Member in the County of Middlesex will be a determined opposer of Government.' Although in a subsequent letter he wrote that other seats in the House would certainly be lost, the King insisted that although a premature dissolution might in a few places be disadvantageous, upon the whole the objections would not be of consequence.[1] So the thirteenth Parliament, with its John Wilkes, its horned cattle, its fight with the printers, and its punitive acts against the colonies, was dissolved in September.

The country placed its own interpretation upon the King's move. But whatever the suspicions of the nation might have been, the fourteenth Parliament that convened later gave George III a stronger following than did the thirteenth. Two weeks before the new session opened North was able to send the King a list of new members supposed to be friendly. This list, North avowed, was conservative, for every member had been left off the List of Pros 'whose sentiments are not perfectly known, & of whose conduct the least doubt can be entertain'd'.

Between St Stephen's chapel and the colonies, as Burke was to point out, were three thousand miles of ocean that could not be pumped dry; there they were, a formidable barrier to communication. Within the Colonies, however, lines of swift communication were being established. The Massachusetts assembly issued an invitation to other colonies to send delegates to an American congress. Meetings of protest sprang up all over; resolutions were framed and delegates appointed; committees of correspondence and the colonial press assured one and all that the cause of Boston was the cause of America. The Continental Congress met in Philadelphia on September 5 and drew up addresses to lay before a Parliament that would be even less sympathetic than its predecessor.

Now public opinion was beginning to question the American situation. As trade with the colonies had continued to fall off, the great mercantile cities and towns submitted petitions of protest. Gibbon, a new member, noted that Parliament spent most of its time reading papers and rejecting petitions. Fox attacked the ministry violently, but the House, by a vote of 197 to 81, supported North's delaying tactics. This division pleased the King infinitely. 'The very handsome Majority that at the outset have appeared in both Houses of Parliament', he wrote to North, would bring the Americans to a due submission.[2]

[1] Fortescue, iii, 132. [September 25]; iii, 134. September 27.
[2] Fortescue, iii, 168. January 23, 1775.

The Commons spent a stormy day on January 26, 1775, considering the situation of commercial interests. Three days earlier London merchants had sent a petition explaining that since exports to North America had come almost to a total stop, thousands of industrious artificers and manufacturers faced utter ruin. This first petition having been consigned to what was now called the committee of oblivion, they presented a second. Burke urged the necessity of hearing the petitioners, lamenting the calamities that would befall England if the present situation were allowed to develop into civil war. Fox took occasion to upbraid the ministry for its whole programme, indicating the acts of the thirteenth Parliament as being 'framed on false information, conceived in weakness and ignorance, and executed with negligence', and boldly stated that North had no system, plan, or knowledge of American affairs. Finally, Fox pledged himself to join Burke 'in pursuing the noble lord, and bringing him to answer for the mischiefs occasioned by his negligence, his inconsistency, and his incapacity'. Fox insisted his motivation was not his own dismissal from the Treasury, but that he was determined to fight 'the destructive proceedings of a bad minister'.

North replied by pointing out that Fox had once approved of his conduct; Fox declared that the noble lord could be charged with 'the most unexampled treachery and falsehood'. The Government would not tolerate such talk and the scene was clamorous as the twenty-six-year-old opposition orator was called to order; Fox sat down twice or thrice, rising after each sitting to repeat his accusations; but he was not allowed to proceed further. The house divided 250 to 89 in favour of the minister; it seemed as if every faithful member in sight had been herded into the lobby for the express purpose of giving Fox a stinging defeat.[1]

Next day North offered a resolution asking the Commons to reaffirm the principle that His Majesty should never be called upon to relinquish authority over any part of the Colonial domain. It was just such a resolution as would compel a vote of confidence from the King's following. Excitement was tense both in and out of the House; streets leading to St Stephen's Chapel were so crowded that there was hardly room for members to pass. The usual complaint having been made, galleries were cleared and the House began an important series of debates without benefit of reporters. The report of Fox's long speech that day is inadequate, but the testimony of his contemporaries shows that he was at his best. Gibbon noted that Fox, 'taking the vast compass of the question before us discovered powers for regular debate which neither his friends hoped nor his Enemies dreaded'.[2]

---

[1] *Parliamentary History*, xviii, 190–3.
[2] *Letters of Edward Gibbon*, ii, 59. To Holroyd, February 8.

Walpole wrote: 'Charles Fox entered into the whole history and argument of the dispute with great force and temper, and made the greatest figure he had done yet, in a speech of an hour and twenty minutes.'[1] The *Gazetteer* reported that even his opponents thought his speech one of the most able ever delivered within the walls of Parliament.

At the conclusion of his speech Fox moved that Lord North's resolution be amended so as to state that, in the opinion of the House, the measures taken by the ministers of the Crown tended to widen rather than heal the difference between the two peoples. It was an important moment. Should the House vote North's resolution down, the King would face a demand to form a new ministry; should the House favour North's resolution, the present ministry could continue its avowed colonial policy as before. There was little doubt of the result; Government supporters, choosing between the King and Fox, selected the former by a vote of 304 to 105.

In this speech the twenty-six-year-old Fox revealed a new dimension of parliamentary discussion. He combined historical sweep and broad review of policy with keen analysis of tactical details, and thus established a formula that he used repeatedly in his great efforts during the years that ensued. But the *Morning Post* preferred to emphasize another talent of Fox's and urged that he be sent overseas at the head of a contingent of five hundred compleat gamblers to teach the Americans gaming.

Eventually the Government decided to make a gesture of conciliation. On February 20 North proposed that the colonies should be allowed to tax themselves in raising their share of the contribution to the common defence. Any colony that would make a proper contribution would be relieved of any other duty, tax, or assessment from Parliament, except only such duties, of course, as necessary for the regulation of commerce; even these could be credited to the colony. North optimistically argued that the plan would please the English and the Americans as well; and it would facilitate the passing of legislation designed to place further restriction upon the trade of New England, Virginia, Maryland, and other provinces. He even went so far as to apprise Burke of his proposal, informing him that he intended to propose a motion relative to the American situation, and urging him to pass the word around to 'such gentlemen of your acquaintance, as may wish to be present'.[2]

Burke was on hand and so were gentlemen of his acquaintance,

---

[1] *Last Journals*, i, 428.
[2] George H. Guttridge, ed., *The Correspondence of Edmund Burke* (Cambridge, 1961), iii, 115. February 19.

including Fox. To Fox it may have seemed that firm opposition was penetrating the thick hides of the ministers. Said he:

It is the opposition which has been made in this House, although ineffectual to oppose the measures of ministers, whilst they were pleased to be violent, yet has had that effect, that they now find it their interest and their safety to be otherwise. . . . The noble lord . . . felt that even his friends and allies began to grow slack towards the vigour of his measures. . . . No one in this country, who is sincerely for peace, will trust the speciousness of his expressions, and the Americans will reject them with disdain.[1]

Fox, with more fire than judgment, here tried to substitute attacks upon the personality of a minister for logical analysis. Burke's speech was more rational; even so, the vote, 274 to 88, was for North, the King, and the continuance of punitive legislation against the colonies. 'I never doubted the zeal of the House of Commons in Support of the just Superiority of the Mother Country over its Colonies,' wrote the King to North, 'but the debate of Yesterday is a very convincing proof of it'.[2]

Chatham's reaction was entirely different; writing to Townshend, his language fairly scorched the paper:

I shall only say that it is a *puerile Mockery*, as to *America*; and will be spurn'd at *there*, and by all the true friends of America *here*. . . . Sure I am, that America will never consent . . . to be tax'd by the Parliament of England, *in such Proportion* as They judge proper; or *in any way* that does not leave America *absolute mistress* of her *Property*; to *grant* or *to withhold, freely*. If this Plan of Lord North should prevail, I am determin'd to protest against it, in all its Stages.[3]

Yet conciliation was in the air. Not North's type of conciliation, which in the long run sought to gain more than it gave, but an arrangement that would keep the colonies on friendly terms with the mother country. Burke had devised a set of resolutions as a basis for such conciliation and had planned to present them to the house, but friends were not sure his plan was politically feasible. One objection they expressed was the fear that the public would conclude that all revenue from America would be lost. To discuss this point, the opposition planned a meeting for the evening of March 7 at Grosvenor Square; Rockingham, leader of the group, thought that Barré and Dunning would attend and fourteen or fifteen others.[4] The result of this deliberation supported Burke's plan, for five days later the Duke of Richmond wrote Rockingham that although he had not seen Burke's resolutions, what he had heard of them disposed him favourably. Thus by conversation and

[1] *Parliamentary History*, xviii, 329–30.   [2] Fortescue, iii, 179. February 21.
[3] HM 22357, Townshend collection (Huntington). February 20 [1775].
[4] Earl of Albemarle, ed., *Memoirs of the Marquis of Rockingham* (London, 1852), ii, 273.

correspondence, the group planned its parliamentary coup: a carefully reasoned, carefully considered plan could have a chance in a House which was showing leanings toward the Colonies.

So the days rolled on to March 22, when Burke rose to his legs and explained this new plan of conciliation. 'It is an awful subject; or there is none so on this side of the grave.' America is a noble object; we can gain her loyalty best by prudent management of her affairs; we will lose her if we attempt to force compliance with our plans. For two hours and a half he talked, from 3.30 until 6.00, demonstrating that concession should be made and then pointing out what kind of concession was best; explaining in detail the temper of the colonies, their resources, their political condition, their inherent loyalty to the British state; and concluded by moving his resolutions for conciliation. The effort was a noble one. Rockingham wrote to Burke at once: 'I never felt a more complete satisfaction on hearing any speech, than I did on hearing yours this day'; and Richard Burke wrote that 'from a Torrent of Members rushing from the house when he sat down, I could hear the loudest, the most unanimous and the highest strains of applause'. Little reason exists to subtract anything from these partisan tributes.[1]

At least seventeen other speeches were made, eight for and nine against, but as the gallery doors were again closed that day, a scant page is all that remains of what was uttered, other than Burke's speech, which he published as a pamphlet. Fox spoke 'with the greatest ability and spirit' in support of Burke—that is all the reporter learned about the speech. Public opinion was quiescent and parliamentary opinion expressed itself 270 to 78 that it was not in the mood for conciliation.

North's proposals for conciliation crossed the Atlantic in the usual six weeks and aroused strong protest. Burke's wiser view was hardly noted, for within twenty-four hours after Burke's speech in St Stephen's Chapel, a Virginia lawyer stood in St John's Church, Richmond, and told a packed assembly that the time for conciliation had long passed; that although it was natural for man to indulge in the illusions of hope, nothing in the action of the British ministry promised relief. The war, he shouted, had already begun; their brothers were already in the field; and as for him personally, he concluded, he sought either liberty or death. Lexington and Concord were just around the corner. In a few days after Burke had spoken in Westminster and Patrick Henry in Virginia, the shot was fired that was heard around the world.

By the time Burke's speech got across the ocean, colonists were already occupied with the sombre realities of war. With deliberate

[1] *Correspondence of Edmund Burke*, iii, 139–40. Richard Burke's letter is to Richard Champion.

speed the speech had appeared in London in a pamphlet, and late in 1775 a New York printer had brought out an American edition. Although the London pamphlet went through at least three printings, there is no reason to suspect that the New York version had more than a modest sale. In the end, however, Burke exacted a grim and terrifying tribute to his eloquence from American school children. Starting about 1893 and continuing past 1932, American high schools began to require *Conciliation with the Colonies* as required reading of students in English classes. No fewer than 36 editions of the speech, complete with explanatory notes, questions, illustrations, and other study aids, appeared for the consumption of tens of thousands of American students. All the great publishing houses serving the public schools—Allyn and Bacon, American, D. Appleton, Ginn, Heath, Houghton Mifflin, Longmans, Macmillan, Scott, Foresman, and others—printed one or more editions.

The total influence of this nationwide ingestion of Burke—in city schools and in rural districts—has never been explored. Young Americans studied Burke's gift of organization, the previews and internal summaries and transitions, the evidence. They looked up the meaning of difficult words (*labyrinth, predilection, dragooning*) and marvelled at the array of epigrams ('public calamity is a mighty leveller', 'I do not know the method of drawing up an indictment against a whole people', 'a great empire and little minds go ill together'). Through prefaces and annotations they learned about the mother of parliaments herself: that the presiding officer of the Commons bore the same title as the presiding officer of the House of Representatives, that a member of the House of Commons did not have to live in the constituency he represented, that members of the executive branch of government had seats in the legislative, that the existence of pocket and rotten boroughs made possible the bartering of parliamentary seats. Young Americans memorized excerpts from their own orators, Webster, Lincoln, Ingersoll, and others, but they chewed, swallowed, and digested Burke. Perhaps at the end they devoutly wished that their revolutionary forefathers had reasoned more and tarred and feathered less, and just possibly a few pupils wearily concluded that the war for independence was hardly worth fighting if it had to be followed by such long history lessons plus so much Burke.

1775 . . . Lexington and Concord were followed by the seizure of Ticonderoga, where Ethan Allen reportedly demanded the fort in the name of the Great Jehovah and the Continental Congress, and speedily got it. The second Continental Congress met in Philadelphia, among those present being John and Samuel Adams, Thomas Jefferson, John

Jay, and, from London, after nearly two decades there, Benjamin Franklin. George Washington was unanimously approved as commander in chief, agreeing to serve without compensation other than his expenses. British troops lost and then won at Bunker Hill.

Back in London, the first session of the fourteenth Parliament received a petition from the colony of New York complaining of recent Acts of Parliament. North did not even want to review it. Fox was on his legs at once: 'The only province that was moderate, and in which England had some friends, he now treats with contempt. What will be the consequence, when the people of this moderate province are informed of this treatment?' Fox was developing a clearer insight into the issue. 'You make an Act of Parliament to raise a revenue in that country, and you not only make a capital blunder in it, but stumble at the threshold of collecting it.'[1]

North was supported by 186 to 67. Gibbon, aware of a great lassitude developing toward American affairs, wrote: 'In this season and on America, the Archangel Gabriel would not be heard.'[2] On May 26, Parliament recessed for the summer. Quite possibly this was one of the most unseasonable holidays Parliament ever took.

Without exception, the great minds that have fashioned systematic theories concerning what is and what is not effective public address have insisted that the convincing speaker must be a man of character. Typical of the Greek view is Aristotle's insistence that the personal character of the speaker is probably his most persuasive instrument—more so than his logic or his power of emotional appeal. Typical of the Roman view is Quintilian's declaration that public address is the good man speaking well. Honour, wisdom, selflessness, nobility, all illumine a man's words and endow them with persuasive impact.

Although during the American war Fox's character developed some of its finer qualities, it was also notorious for a variety of unenviable traits. Most prominent of his shortcomings was his addiction to gambling. The betting book at Brooks's still records numerous wagers that he made. February 22, 1775: Mr Fox betts General Scott fifty Guineas that Lord North is not first Lord of ye Treasury a year from this date (Mr Fox lost). Mr Fox betts Mr Fitzpatrick 50 Guineas that Lord Coleraine outlives Mr Codrington (Mr Fox won). Mr Fox betts Mr Crewe 10 Guineas Mr Chester against Berkley for Gloucestershire (Mr Fox won, though the election was close).[3] Cards and horses

---

[1] *Parliamentary History*, xviii, 648–9.

[2] *Letters of Edward Gibbon*, ii, 69. To Holroyd, May 15.

[3] These entries copied for the author by Major H. N. Lucas, hon. Secretary of Brooks's. For a dozen others, see *Early History of Charles James Fox*, pp. 452–3.

consumed most of his energies. In the summer of 1775 he was as active as ever; Storer and Selwyn kept Carlisle fully informed. Good days alternated with bad: 'Charles, to my great astonishment, . . . is elbow-deep in gold; and he wanted a guinea ten days ago.' Charles 'lost in three nights last week £3000'. Charles won £990—'and was in high cash'. But another day came and 'Charles . . . lost everything . . . at Newmarket'.[1]

Indisputably, Fox's listeners could not separate Fox the parliamentary orator from Fox of Brooks's, White's, Almack's, and Newmarket. Nor could they forget certain unwise statements or impulsive acts. At times while Fox was speaking, as will be seen, listeners would recall something about Fox's behaviour that would detract from his words. These intrusive reflections got into diaries, into letters, into public prints. Fox's career would have got under way sooner if his character had given it surer direction. Nor can the fact be overlooked that his popularity suffered from his taking a sympathetic attitude toward the colonies. Those were not the days when one could criticize the nation's war effort. Once Chatham had denounced those of his colleagues who were friendly toward Austria by bitterly declaring, 'Is there an *Austrian* among you?' With equal scorn Fox's political enemies could denounce him as an *American*, pointing to the fact that his speeches, circulated in the colonies, nourished their resistance, and that 'Charles James Fox and the English Liberals' was a favourite toast among those of democratic or republican tendency. Here is a denunciation that now reads suspiciously like a compliment. On the American issue Fox was wiser than his critics. Yet it should be said that on the American question, and on others that confronted those generations, speakers could be found on both sides of the House who defended their positions with passionate sincerity.

[1] *HMCR*, Carlisle MSS., pp. 282–94.

6

Fox in Opposition
1775-1777

To vote in small minorities is a misfortune to which I
have been . . . much accustomed.

Charles James Fox

By October 1775 the King knew he had more than an uprising on his
hands; he termed it a rebellious war. The Americans, he told the new
session of Parliament, had raised troops, collected a naval force, seized
the public revenue, and were already exercising legislative, executive,
and judicial powers, in an arbitrary manner over their fellow subjects.
The Government therefore declared it necessary to increase land and
naval forces and vote additional supplies.[1]

In each House a full-dress debate followed. Fox denounced North as
'the blundering pilot who had brought the nation into its present difficulties . . . Lord Chatham, the King of Prussia, nay, Alexander the
Great, never gained more in one campaign than the noble lord has lost
—he has lost a whole continent'.[2] He referred to the old political distinctions of whig and tory, describing the present members of administration as enemies to freedom, and therefore tories. Germain thought
him abusive, 'but able, and full of those quick turns which he inherited
from his father';[3] Fox's friend Storer observed that opposition speakers
were better than the Government's, and that Charles Fox outdid himself.[4]

North in reply told the House that he held the pity and the contempt
of the honourable gentleman in equal indifference. The debate lasted
until four in the morning: 'The most crowded and hot assembly',
wrote Germain, 'I ever remember to have been in.'[5] In the division the
ministry had 278, the opposition 108. Next day Fox renewed his
attack, declaring that he could not consent to 'the bloody consequences
of so silly a contest about so silly an object, conducted in the silliest
manner that history, or observation, had ever furnished an instance of;
and from which we were likely to derive nothing, but poverty, misery,
disgrace, defeat, and ruin'.[6]

[1] *Parliamentary History,* xxviii, 695–7.   [2] *Ibid.,* xviii, 769.
[3] *HMCR,* Stopford-Sackville MSS., i, 137.
[4] *HMCR,* Carlisle MSS., p. 298. October 27.
[5] *HMCR,* Stopford-Sackville MSS., i, 137.   [6] *Parliamentary History,* xviii, 775.

After continued parliamentary defeat members of the opposition became discouraged. Yet Fox was not one to quit. In the debate to prohibit trade with America, he attempted to prove the 'want of policy, the folly, and madness, of the present ministers'. Said he:

I have ever understood it as a first principle, that in rebellion you punish the individuals, but spare the country; in a war against the enemy, you spare individuals, and lay waste the country. This last has been invariably your conduct against America. I suggested this to you, when the Boston Port Bill passed. I advised you to find out the offending persons, and to punish them; but what did you do instead of this? You laid the whole town of Boston under terrible contribution, punishing the innocent with the guilty. You answer, that you could not come at the guilty. This very answer, shews how unfit, how unable you are, to govern America.[1]

North defended, Burke attacked, Germain defended, and the House divided: for the Government 143, against it 38. Some members of the opposition began to leave for the holidays, so that, as Walpole observed, one division commanded only 16 opposition votes.[2] In January 1776 he wrote:

What little life there was existed in the Duke of Richmond and Charles Fox. The latter bustled, tried to animate both the Duke and Marquis, conferred with Lord Shelburne, but abandoned neither his gambling nor rakish life. He was seldom in bed before five in the morning, nor out of it before two at noon.[3]

Ever unwilling to abandon the struggle, Fox rose on February 20 to move for an inquiry into the causes of the ill success of British arms in North America. Parliamentary reporters were not able to keep up with his eloquence, which one newspaper said lasted three-quarters of an hour, another upwards of an hour, and a third an hour and a half, but summarized the major part of his speech in these words: 'He painted in the strongest colours, and held to view in the most striking lights, such a scene of folly in the Cabinet, servile acquiescence in parliament, and misconduct and ignorance in office and in the field, as never before disgraced this nation, or indeed any other.'

The House, however, found comfort in observations like Welbore Ellis's, that 'a powerful fleet and army are now going out, and . . . will be sufficient to crush the rebellious Americans', by Burgoyne's defence of military operations in America, and by North's assurance that he had no objection to an inquiry at the proper season, but this was not the time; so it declined the inquiry.

[1] *Ibid.*, xviii, 1059.
[2] *Last Journals*, i, 501. December 11; refers to that day's debate.
[3] *Ibid.*, i, 512–14.

The Americans began to have troubles of their own. After their initial successes in 1775 at Ticonderoga and Crown Point, they had boldly decided to push on to Canada but the campaign was unsuccessful, and they had to abandon Canada altogether. News of English victories and American reversals brought further gloom to the Rockingham camp, as members of the opposition realized that North's administration would be entrenched more solidly than ever. In the face of the King's majorities, why continue to waste time and energy in speeches? Why attend the sessions at all? Why have a party? Writing to Ossory, Fox expressed the opinion that these victories 'will give the tools and tories here such spirits as to make them insufferable'. He continued:

I am still convinced the Americans will finally succeed whether by victories or defeats, and if they do not, I am sure . . . that it will check all future enterprise to such a degree as to give the completest triumph to toryism that it ever had. . . . Whatever happens for God's sake let us all resolve to stick by them as handsomely (or more so) in their adversity as we have done in their glory.

He declared he was not dejected by the news but had noted that some of their colleagues might become so.[1]

July 4 brought the Declaration of Independence. August 17 found Fox writing to Burke: 'The declaration of independency seems to be an event which we ought not surely to pass over in silence.' To Burke he suggested a meeting at which means and methods could be deliberated. Burke, of course, would be a key man in such a conference; he, too, was in solemn mood about American affairs. 'We are deeply in blood', he had written.[2]

Later news of the successful landing of Howe's troops on Long Island and of victories at Brooklyn further shattered the courage of the main group of Rockingham whigs to the extent that they planned a formal secession from Parliament. Fox wrote to Rockingham that such a secession was untenable; instead, he proposed a line of action: either exhort the Government to follow up the victory with offers of conciliation, or emphasize the apprehension that would result if the Crown should augment its influence by defeating the Americans. He concluded:

I hope that it will be a point of honour among us all to support the American pretensions in adversity as much as we did in their prosperity, and that we shall never desert those who have acted *unsuccessfully* upon Whig principles. . . . I am so clear that firmness in Whig principles is become more necessary than ever, that I cannot help conjuring you, over and over again, to consider the importance of this crisis. . . . I am resolved . . . to adhere still more . . . to those principles of government which we have always recommended with respect to America.[3]

[1] Add. MSS. 47579. *Fox Cor.*, i, 143. June 24.
[2] *Correspondence of Edmund Burke*, iii, 286. To Richard Shackleton, August 11.
[3] *Memoirs of the Marquis of Rockingham*, ii, 297. *Fox Cor.*, i, 146. October 13.

When the new session opened on October 31, the King's address spoke of treasonable and rebellious confederacies, the recovery of Canada, and the promise of a successful campaign in New York. The Commons had a long discussion. Cavendish, Johnstone, Wilkes, Luttrell, Townshend, Barré, all battered the ministerial stronghold. There was a weak defence by Germain, followed by Fox, in 'one of his finest and most animated orations, and with severity to the answered person'. When he sat down, no member of the Government attempted to reply. This silence impressed even Gibbon; he told Walpole 'he had never heard a more masterly speech than Fox's in his life', and that both Thurlow and Wedderburn, the Attorney General and the Solicitor General, argued among themselves as to which one should answer it, both finally declining.[1] Burke wrote that he never knew Fox to speak better than he did on that day: 'His speech was a noble performance. To my surprise none of the Ministry attempted an answer to it. . . . I waited for the Crown Lawyers expecting some of them would follow Charles Fox. But none spoke, and the debate could not lie better than he left it.'[2]

By 87 to 242, despite the fact that no one ventured a reply, the Commons continued to support North, the Crown lawyers, and their silent friends. In America the King's speech was publicly burned. Many other times would come when the debate could not lie better than Fox left it; and a few occasions would arise when ministers not only did not, but apparently could not, reply.

The opposition next proposed to revise the laws complained of by the Americans. Fox met the problem obliquely when he digressed long enough to attack again the journalistic activities of the King's ministers. 'The only proper objects of parliamentary attention were totally neglected', he stormed, 'and left to be collected from chance, vague reports, or a newspaper.' The sins of journalistic commission were even greater than those of omission; the administration was carrying on a pamphlet warfare in America no less deadly than that of Howe and Burgoyne. In America the pamphlets spoke of 'peace, conciliation, and parental tenderness'; in England nothing was heard but 'subjugation, unconditional submission, and a war of conquest'. Ministers, he continued, had sent a special pamphlet to America, 'where thousands of them were distributed gratis; while in England the title was not so much as known, till after the publication on the other side the Atlantic'.

Publications of a very different tendency are encouraged here [he went on]. America is to be subdued; taxes are to be obtained; charters are to be modified or

---

[1] *Last Journals*, i, 584.   [2] *Correspondence of Edmund Burke*, iii, 299. November 2.

annihilated at pleasure . . . while the most moderate measures and fascinating promises were held out on the other [side of the ocean], in order to insiduously trepan and deceive.[1]

No such thing, said the House, by 109 to 47, and so another effort at conciliation fell to the ground.

'From this time a great number of the minority, particularly of the Rockingham party' said the *Annual Register*, the editorial hand of Edmund Burke showing, 'began to relax in their attendance upon Parliament in either House.'[2] The King wrote to North he had heard that Fox intended to leave for Paris and therefore would not attend future sessions of the house until after the holidays; North should, therefore, bring up as much business as possible while Fox was away, 'as real business is never so well considered as when the Attention of the House is not taken up by noisy declamations'.[3]

Across the ocean General Washington could not have known that his whig friends were relaxing some of their enthusiasm for the American cause. As Fox was losing his louis at gaming, Hessian mercenaries occupying Trenton were celebrating Christmas eve. The general and his troops crossed the Delaware, took a thousand Hessians prisoner, and mortally wounded their colonel. So 1776 turned the corner and became 1777—the year of the triple gallows some called it, as they viewed the grim trio of 7's.

Meanwhile America's second line of defence, led by Rockingham, Burke, and Fox, drew its gloom over its head like a coverlet and fitfully slumbered. The projected secession from the lower House was in effect. A few, however, were beginning to feel the jab of public criticism; Sir George Savile wrote to Rockingham that at present they were 'not only patriots out of place, but patriots out of the opinion of the public'.[4] When on January 21 Parliament resumed work, Walpole was among those who noted that none of the Rockingham whigs attended the opening meeting.[5] They were not entirely idle; they gathered at Grosvenor Square, composed petitions, argued among themselves.

One day the Rockinghams heard the startling rumour that the Habeas Corpus Act was to be suspended. Walpole got wind of this proposed move of the ministers three weeks before it was brought

[1] *Parliamentary History*, xviii, 1437.
[2] Quoted *ibid.*, xviii, 1448–9. 'Lord Granby hath decamped for St. Stephen's Chappell,' wrote Blackbourne to Craufurd, 'where he is gone to add *one* to *a minority*, which, to speak the truth, at this time are rather disconcerted.' November 18. *HMCR*, Rutland MSS., iii, 7.
[3] Add. MSS. 47585. Fortescue, iii, 402. November 15.
[4] *Memoirs of the Marquis of Rockingham*, ii, 304–5, January 15, 1777.
[5] *Last Journals*, ii, 3.

before the House and communicated his news to the Duke of Richmond, Charles Fox, the Duke of Grafton, and Lord Camden.[1] They could hardly believe the report was true; the right of habeas corpus, older than Magna Carta, was firmly established in the law of the land. Nevertheless on February 6 North asked leave of the House to bring in such a Bill, and next day Germain as Secretary of State brought it in.

It was a strange Bill. The preamble seemed to apply only to treason committed in America or on the high seas but the body of the Bill seemed to apply to treason in any part of the King's dominions. Members of the opposition had grounds for imagining that even one of them could come within the scope of the Bill—Edmund Burke might be surprised reading a letter from America, suspected of treason, and lodged in the Tower without hope of trial. The contradictions and ambiguities of the Bill made it dangerous; more than one observer noted that the title was at variance with the first enacting clause. The whigs gathered at Grosvenor Square and wondered what to do. Portland argued that the secession should continue; they were helpless against the formidable majorities of the King, and to wage another hopeless fight would invite the contempt of the ministry and the court. Rockingham also thought the secession should go on, as did the Cavendishes and Burke. All, wrote Walpole, 'adhered to their stupid retreat, but Charles Fox would not'.

In the debate on the second reading, Fox declared that the proposed bill would rob America of her franchises; moreover, it would be a step toward introducing the same kind of government into England and thus to all territories belonging to the British Crown. He expressed his astonishment 'in the boldest and most animated terms, at the insolence and temerity of ministers, who could thus dare to snatch [habeas corpus] from the people, by a mandate manufactured by themselves'.

Fox's colleagues rightly predicted that Fox would find himself again a member of a helpless minority, for only 43 voted with him, 195 with the Government. The *Morning Chronicle* not surprisingly thought Fox by far the best speaker in the debate. The *General Evening Post* thought him severe and pointed, and printed samples of his ridicule. During the third reading 'Mr B— and several of the minority members left the House of Commons . . . and at the same time declared that they would not attend any more this session, as they saw that opposition to any Bill, however nefarious, was of no avail'.[2]

Yet the opposition was not entirely insignificant. The stalwart John

---

[1] *Last Journals*, ii, 5–6.
[2] *General Evening Post*, February 13–15. Storer wrote of the February 12 debate that the arguments of Fox and Dunning *against* the Bill convinced him all the more *for* it. Fox, he particularly noted, 'spoke very ill' (*HMCR*, Carlisle MSS., p. 317).

Dunning described the ambiguity of the text and proposed a clause to confine the operation of the Bill to those who have been in the Colonies and on the high seas. North, under the pressure of argument, could do nothing other than accept Dunning's clause, with a slight amendment that had been proposed; the clause as amended was agreed to without a division and it was now Fox's turn to ridicule. He congratulated the minority for correcting the Bill which North had brought in crude and undigested, imperfect and erroneous. But his moment of glory was over when he resumed his seat, for the measure passed 112 to 35, and before the month was out the Lords concurred.

The rift between Fox and the King continued to widen and deepen. The King had little appreciation of the functions of an opposition, and Fox more and more sought to mobilize and strengthen one. Intertwined with his interest in party as an agency for first discussing and then formulating measures was a growing conviction in the discussion process itself. But to the King Fox's talent for speaking was a wicked art. Moreover, Fox's personal conduct was not only unbecoming but odious and contemptible. When the question of the King's mounting debts, more than £600,000, came before Parliament, Fox not only questioned the legitimacy of certain items on the long list but the dignity of the sovereign himself. The reign of George the Second had been great and glorious, a reign of high principle; by contrast that of the present monarch was shot through and through with corruption and patronage. 'Majorities were found to support the worst measures with as much alacrity as the best.' With the Crown's control of the funds, it could call upon its followers to make good the King's debts— 'to make good the very rapine and plunder they had long since shared.'[1]

The speech was Fox's first lengthy utterance on the influence of the crown and the management of Parliament through that influence. That the image of corruption drawn by Fox and other opposition orators was overdrawn has been pretty well demonstrated. And coming from Fox, charges of corruption probably had less than usual weight. He was still branded as the son of the defaulter of unaccounted millions. His own life was associated with cards, dice, and horses. His personal finances were in an uproar. Though each of these matters can be ameliorated, collectively they do not form a stout moral base for a lecture to others about corruption. Even so, charges of corruption can be easy to make and awkward to answer.

All told, Fox was a formidable opponent. Next month an interesting debate occurred in which Richard Rigby accused Speaker Norton of

[1] *Parliamentary History*, xix, 155.

having misrepresented the state of the finances of the King's household; Fox replied to Rigby and persuaded the Commons that Norton had honestly presented the situation. Fox's motion commending the Speaker, in fact, passed 'almost unanimously'. Walpole thought this was a situation in which Fox had persuaded the House to reverse itself.[1] The King himself wished Rigby had remained silent.[2] Undoubtedly he wished even more that Fox had not spoken.

On May 22,[3] in a debate on the affairs of the East India Company, Fox reached a new peak in his sharp criticism of North's ministry.

Specifically the issue concerned Lord George Pigot, Governor of Madras, who, after a bitter controversy with local officials, had been arrested and imprisoned, and recalled by the company, which had been unduly pressured, it was argued, by the ministry. On the day of this debate Governor Johnstone, who generally opposed governmental interference in the affairs of the company, rose to Pigot's defence with a series of resolutions. North opposed them and the issue was joined.

The short debate, filled with sparkling moments, is significant in that it introduced Fox further to the complex question of the authority and responsibilities of a governor of a province of India. Pigot's difficulties foreshadowed those later embodied in the trial of Warren Hastings. The debate is further noteworthy for showing Fox's concern with a single oppressed individual. The individual, to be sure, had recently left the Government side to join the opposition, and was a brother of Admiral Hugh Pigot, one of Fox's gambling companions. These circumstances dampen any purely humanitarian aspects of Fox's position, but a speaker sometimes stands on a narrow platform on his way to a broader one, and Fox took full opportunity of the occasion to attack administration. The speech does not illustrate the low-keyed, carefully reasoned method of his great addresses but rather exemplifies his ability to weld irony and ridicule into determined censure.

Fox had incredible talent for drawing an opposite conclusion from an opponent's argument; on this day 'he justified lord Pigot principally upon the . . . representations of his enemies and persecutors', and contended that this evidence could not be controverted or explained away. Adding further praise of the virtues and military talents of Pigot, he was 'so very able, pointed, convincing, and severe', and so captivated several members that they, as the parliamentary reporter recorded the

[1] W. S. Lewis, ed., *Horace Walpole's Correspondence With William Mason* (New Haven, 1955), 28/i, 309. May 16. See *Parliamentary History*, xix, 213, 224–34.
[2] Fortescue, iii, 445. To North, May 9.
[3] *Journals of the House of Commons*, xxxvi, 519. *Parliamentary History* erroneously gives May 21.

scene then, and the *Annual Register* later, 'in a transport of approbation, forgot themselves so far, as to testify it in accents of Bravo! Hear him!—which they accompanied with a clapping of hands'—a conduct unprecedented. Many members of the Government were 'absent from this dirty business'. Fox noted that the Attorney General was ill; that the Solicitor General was probably also too ill to want to risk defending such an issue; that another noble lord (Germain) who invariably discouraged rebellion in the West chose to be absent instead of appearing to discourage it in the East. Even so, Fox feared enough were still present to defeat Governor Johnstone's resolutions.

The audience, not a mighty one because of the lateness of the session, was unusually responsive. It not only applauded Fox but during Burke's speech cried 'Go on! Go on!' Moreover, when an administration supporter made a rash claim, the House called for proof (none was produced); when later he asked that papers be read, the House became noisy. The vote was 90 to 67, so North had a narrow victory. No one knew at the time of the debate that Pigot had died in prison eleven days previously.[1]

More than likely Fox had spent the preceding night at Brooks's and would be there the following night. The summer would see him at the Newmarket races and in other attractive places as had the preceding summer. *Posts* and *Chronicles* and *Advertisers* would record these doings and more. In these regards Fox was like a hundred other aristocrats. But there were other moments when Fox could stand in St Stephen's and call the King's first minister to such hard and just account that the impact astonished even his detractors. In this talent he was surpassed by few.

The *Morning Post*, recalling Fox's speaking during the session, thought North would do well to bid high to have Fox back on the Government benches. 'His turning him out raised by much the severest enemy his Lordship has ever met with.' The *Post* strengthened its argument by paying Fox a rare tribute: 'On the day of Lord Chatham's motion in the House of Lords, a knot of members of the House of Commons, wondering at the crowd that attended, all agreed that they had heard Charles Fox as great as ever Lord Chatham had been.'[2] To compare with Chatham in matters oratorical was to compare him, in Horace Walpole's words, 'with what is beyond whatever was'.

Chatham's motion, to put an end to hostilities in America, was de-

---

[1] *Parliamentary History*, xix, 282–7. 'The most celebrated speakers of the opposition were on this day particularly distinguished; and one gentleman excited such sudden and extraordinary bursts of approbation, as were not warranted by the usual practice of that House' (*Annual Register*, xx (1777), 107).

[2] June 21, 1777. Fox had successfully sued the *Post*, a firm supporter of administration, in 1774.

feated; and so the session approached its close. 'I trust You will be troubled with no further Debates during the few days the Session will still continue,' the King had written to North.[1] In June, Parliament recessed. Late that summer Fox visited Ireland with Lord John Townshend. They took their horses over, made an excursion to Lake Killarney, and, in a country where rashness is applauded, bathed in the chilling waters of the Devil's Punch Bowl. They received countless invitations to dinners, 'where there was much conversation, and a prodigious quantity of wine'.[2] On this visit Fox made the acquaintance of Henry Grattan. More than that, he visited the Irish House and was courteously permitted to sit on the floor of the chamber. He listened so attentively to Grattan that at a dinner at which both were present he paid the Irish orator the extreme compliment of quoting passages he had heard. Fox's courtesy, tact, gentleness, and captivating manner made a deep impression on Grattan, who afterwards related the whole incident with obvious pleasure.[3] That fall London heard the report that Fox had toasted General Washington in the home of an archbishop, and was ordered out by his most reverend host.[4]

In sharp contrast to his treatment of Fox was the King's deep concern about the personal affairs of North. On September 16 John Robinson wrote the King a letter oozing apologies for perhaps being too presumptuous, but withal managing to say that North's debts were so distressing and worrisome that even in the midst of public business they preyed on the first minister's mind. The King promptly sent word of his concern and asked Robinson to suggest a sum necessary to put North's affairs in order; Robinson in two pages answered £10,000. It was then the King's turn to bite his quill, but he offered £15,000 or even £20,000 if needed. Moreover, at a future date, the King would further demonstrate his affection by giving North's family certain 'employments for life' as they became vacant.[5]

North accepted with grateful heart this sudden, unexpected, copious relief. Years later Charles Butler, in another connection, told about the Cardinal de Retz. Replying to a person who had tauntingly observed the superiority of Cardinal Mazarin over him, de Retz said: 'Give me the king but for one day, and you'll see which has the real superiority.' Fox, observed Butler, 'never had the king with him, even for an hour'.[6]

---

[1] Fortescue, iii, 448. May 29.   [2] *Fox Cor.*, i, 156–7.
[3] Henry Grattan, *Memoirs of the Life and Times of the Rt. Hon. Henry Grattan*, new ed. (London, 1849), i, 285–6.
[4] *Morning Post*, November 17.
[5] Fortescue, iii, 476–9. September 16 and 19.
[6] *Reminiscences of Charles Butler*, 4th ed. (London, 1824), i, 165.

A man matures rapidly on the parliamentary battlefield. Charles Fox could not only lead a skirmish but he also knew what it was to keep lonely vigil while others slept in their tents. Some of his colleagues, while respecting his talents, realized that at times he was likely to act rashly. While he was in Ireland he received a letter from Edmund Burke, a frank invitation to join the Rockingham group whole-heartedly, to share its councils, to have a place in its Government when and if it came into power; it was moreover a hope that Fox would not be too impulsive, here today and there tomorrow. Burke wrote:

Do not be in haste. Lay your foundations deep in public opinion. Though . . . I have never given you the least bit of advice about joining yourself in a declared connexion with our party, nor do I now—yet as I love that party very well, and am clear that you are better able to serve them than any man I know, I wish that things should be so kept, as to leave you mutually very open to one another in all changes and contingencies. . . . In order to be very great, as I am anxious you should be, . . . you will certainly want some better support than merely that of the Crown. For I much doubt, whether, with all your parts, you are the man formed for acquiring real interior favour in this Court or in any. I therefore wish you a firm ground in the Country; and I do not know so firm and sound a bottom to build on as our party.[1]

The opposition could well use Fox; as Burke wrote later, 'Dont you like Charles Fox? . . . He is one of the pleasantest men in the world, as well as the greatest Genius that perhaps this country has ever produced. If he is not extraordinary, I assure you the British dominions cannot furnish anything beyond him.'[2]

Thus one genius praised another. The British dominions could well be proud of both.

---

[1] *Correspondence of Edmund Burke*, iii, 385. October 8.
[2] *Ibid.*, iii, 390. To Garrett Nagle, October 26.

7

A Speech Without a Reply
1777-1778

'You are a corrupt and scandalous assembly,' said Sir
George Savile, 'I thought so last night, and I think so this
morning.'
'We think so, too,' said the assembly, by their
silence.

Horace Walpole

At Grosvenor Square the Marquis of Rockingham must have pondered
deeply the persistence of the North Government. Eleven years previously he had relinquished his position as First Lord of the Treasury,
first minister in the King's Cabinet; since then as the King's hand
strengthened the influence of opposition lessened. Merchants of the
great cities of England could send in petitions attesting to their loss of
trade and Government could ignore them; Burke could make a learned
and persuasive speech for conciliation, supported by Cavendish, Sawbridge, Fox, and Beaumont, and the Government could ignore them
as well; North and Germain could attack the right of habeas corpus;
the King could confess to a deficit of £600,000, get it repaid plus an
extra £100,000 a year; despite these problems, the Government continued in strength.

In front of the marquis was a letter from the Duke of Manchester,
wondering whether the party was going to do anything about the
situation; if not, the Duke would like to spend a few months in Paris.
This missive was not the first that Rockingham had received during the
past months but now they were beginning to pile up: from Richmond,
Burke, Savile, and others. All wanted to know what the marquis was
going to do about the situation and the marquis was only slightly less
perplexed than his colleagues.[1]

The least that he could do was to call a meeting, so in due course he
and his colleagues gathered at Grosvenor Square. Someone proposed
an inquiry into the state of the nation, thus to compel the Government
to show its hand—what it had done and what it planned to do. Here at
last was a plan; how to execute it called for discussion. Some argued

---

[1] *Memoirs of the Marquis of Rockingham*, ii, 315–24; *Works and Correspondence of the Right
Honourable Edmund Burke* (London, 1852), i, 351; *Correspondence of Edmund Burke*,
iii, 399.

that the approach should be cautious; that the House should simply be notified that on February 2, after the holidays, a motion would be made for a committee on the state of the nation. Others thought that February 2 should definitely be fixed as the date upon which the state of the nation would be debated; and, should this motion be agreed to, a second motion should follow, calling for papers and documents to be laid before the House. Richmond, Grafton, Fox, and several others argued in favour of the second, bolder, plan, but the group finally decided to throw the discussion into the lap of the venerable Chatham and get his analysis of the situation.[1]

The earl was in bed with the gout when Rockingham's note arrived, and his strangely worded reply seems to indicate that he was seized with fresh pains as he reviewed the alternatives. His reply, however, was soon on its way back to the marquis, who, reading that the second plan, 'the direct, right forward proceeding', was the most advisable, hastened to pass the word around to those who had been present at the morning session. Chatham's approval of the idea and his implied promise to be present on the day upon which it was launched, gave heart to the whigs. December 2 was selected as the day on which to open fire. 'Everybody concurs', wrote Rockingham.[2] One other point emerged from their discussions: they selected Richmond to lead the attack in the Lords, and as leader of the debate in the Commons they chose their newest adherent, Charles Fox.

Fox was pleased by this responsible assignment. He wrote Ossory a hopeful and optimistic note:

Though we have not yet got one vote this year, I cannot help thinking we are grown considerably stronger in public opinion, for in all the debates we have had, the Ministers have said nothing to give people hopes for the future, and little in justification of the past. I am clear the *opinion* of the majority of the House is now with us. I cannot help flattering myself that *opinions* will, in the long run, have their influence on *votes*.[3]

On December 2 Charles Fox rose to his legs and formally moved that on Monday, the 2nd of February next, the House should resolve itself into a committee of the whole House to consider the state of the nation. Lord North rose as graciously as if Charles had proposed a toast to the Speaker and declared that he cheerfully agreed to the motion, saying that the nation would be found in much better condition than many of the Opposition affected to believe. Fox then rose again, according to the strategy duly worked out at Grosvenor Square, and

1 *Chatham Correspondence*, iv, 459–60. November 27.
2 *HMCR*, Rutland MSS., iii, 10. To Granby, November 28.
3 Add. MSS. 47579. *Fox Cor.*, i, 159–60. November 29.

this time moved that certain papers and documents be laid before the House. This procedure disturbed North; he rose again, muttered something about papers not being ready, inappropriateness of the time, etc., and resumed his seat. Fox appealed to those members who prided themselves on their personal independence (even though they continually supported administration policies), saying that if they did not stand up for the dignity of the House, 'they could never after wipe away the imputation of being mere puppets to the minister, without one principle of reason, pride, or honour'.[1] A hundred and seventy-eight of the puppets lined up against eighty-nine men of independence; consequently the files of the Secretary of State for the Colonies and those of other Cabinet members would not have to be exposed to the unsympathetic survey of fact-mongers like Burke and cross-examiners like Fox. A newspaper called Fox's speech 'one of the most able, nervous, and convincing ever delivered in a British senate';[2] alert and interested, he was getting himself fully prepared for the main event.

Earlier that year a wager had been made: 'John Burgoyne wagers Charles Fox one pony [25 guineas] that he will be home from America by Christmas Day, 1777.' When that bet was made neither had taken thought of a place called Saratoga. In the months that followed Germain evolved a plan, by no means novel, for defeating the colonies by cutting New England from the rest of the seaboard. The focus of the campaign was to be Albany: Burgoyne was to move towards that point from the north, Colonel Barry St Leger at the head of a body of Hessians, Indians, and British would come from the west, and Howe would drive from the south. The hope was that General Washington would move toward off this blow, find himself engaged by the powerful forces of the British combined commands, and thus the rebellion would be crushed.

Burgoyne arrived in Canada in May and proceeded to move south in the general direction of Albany to execute his part of the plan. He was short of troops, horses, drivers, and ammunition. He seized Crown Point and Ticonderoga with little difficulty though he had to leave behind about a fifth of his effective strength to garrison these and nearby points. By the end of July he had reached Fort Edward, north of Albany, where he needed to await fresh supplies. While there he learned that Americans were gathering supplies at Bennington so he detached a raiding force to move in that direction; it ran foul of 1800 men under General John Stark, and the American victory not only cost

[1] *Parliamentary History*, xix, 513, 524. [2] *Chester Chronicle*. December 12.

73

Burgoyne 600 men but so cheered the colonists that enlistments on the American side began to increase.[1]

About that time Burgoyne learned that St Leger's forces, supposedly moving to Albany from the west, had met unexpected resistance both at Fort Stanwix and at Oriskany, and rumours that additional masses of Continentals were on the way encouraged St Leger to pull back to Canada. Moreover, Howe, instead of coming north to Albany, left New York by sea southerly to Philadelphia. Desertions of Canadians and Indians and other attrition had also reduced Burgoyne's strength.

By October even London knew the military situation was grave. General Horatio Gates had amassed a formidable force of American patriots near Saratoga, and after two bloody battles on September 19 and October 7 Burgoyne realized the full desperation of his position. There now seemed no likelihood that a relief force, which had set out from New York, would arrive in time. At a council of war Burgoyne and his officers wondered whether to capitulate; at a critical moment in the discussion a cannonball whizzed through the tent, so agreement was prompt that surrender would not be dishonourable.[2] General Gates allowed the surrender to proceed under chivalrous terms—at Burgoyne's insistence the ceremony was called a convention, not a capitulation—and so the Americans won their first great victory: the result of a calamitous mix of poor communications, confused orders, tactical blunders, uncertain chain of command, and generally poor coordination of troop movements and supplies.

At 9 o'clock on the evening of December 2, after Parliament had finished its long debate on the motion to inquire into the state of the nation, the King received a note from Sandwich, First Lord of the Admiralty, enclosing a letter which told of the surrender at Saratoga.

The report quickly spread that Burgoyne had surrendered and was on his way home. On the floor of the House of Commons Colonel Barré forced Germain to admit that the report was true, which that unhappy lord did, though he squirmed in the doing and tried to hedge by asserting that the news had been reported by deserters and was not authenticated. Fox declared that if no one else would take the responsibility of moving an inquiry into the affair, he would do it; he told the House that those who had supported the war were equally criminal with the ministers, and presented a motion that the instructions to

---

[1] Details principally from Alan Valentine, *Lord George Germain* (Oxford, 1962), chaps 14–17.

[2] *Ibid.*, p. 251.

Burgoyne should be laid before the House. This the House refused. In the Lords, Chatham's motion for copies of Burgoyne's orders and instructions was also voted down.

Saratoga might yet have some effect upon parliamentary opinion— it was still two months before February 2, which had been duly set aside for an inquiry into the state of the nation.

To feel his authority challenged hurt the King as much as the annihilation of an army corps. His advisers would not or could not help him face this central problem; they kept annoying him with rumours that France and Spain were threatening to join the Colonists, that France had already signed a treaty with them, that the stock markets were growing paler, that citizens were casting anxious glances into the eyes of their fellows wondering where everything was going to end; nobody had anything to say about February 2. But the King would not be side-tracked. He knew the seriousness of the inquiry into the state of the nation and consequently resolved to enter the lists garbed in and armed with the full influence of the Crown.

Most of the royal anger was vented upon North, who was not only conveniently near, but who could absorb more than the rank and file of the King's creatures. The King dispatched a note to North stating that even more important than the mode of conducting the American war 'is the plan on which Administration is to repell the different attacks of Opposition when Parliament meets, as to calling for Papers'. North was to be held personally responsible for instructing the Cabinet as to the best means of defence; the ministers were to agree upon a plan and follow it, for leaving matters to the spur of the moment often meant that ministers in one House would propose one thing, those in the other another. Furthermore, all this must be digested by North, and presented forthwith, in fact at the next meeting of the Cabinet.

North was taken aback at these demands and hardly knew what to do about them. 'Lord North did not understand,' he wrote, 'that it was expected of him to come prepared with any plan to the next meeting of the Cabinet for the conduct of both houses . . . upon all possible attacks, or enquiries that may be brought on after the recess.' The King's reply was calm; he did not wish North to be ready with answers for every absurd proposition that the opposition might bring up, but he did want 'the great outlines of measures' to be agreed upon before Parliament convened. The Cabinet met at Downing Street, but plans made to repel the opposition, if any, were not reported. North continued unhappy; he wrote to the King that his anxiety had deprived him of his memory and understanding, pleaded his inability to cope with the situation, and begged that some one else be chosen to take his place.

Truly the whig faction was building better than it knew; its discussions at Grosvenor Square were reverberating painfully in Downing Street. The King refused to listen to North's talk of resigning, admonished him not 'to allow such a thought to take any hold on your mind,' and emphasized again that he should submit his ideas to the Cabinet, then bring the result to him, and when the whole was thoroughly digested—he was to convey it to the principal men in the House of Commons.[1]

Grosvenor Square continued no less active than the palace. The opposition was being told to avoid the appearance of being either exulting or insulting over the Saratoga debacle; instead, it should maintain 'a manly, firm conduct, a marked decision . . . to point out how the public have been deceived and misled'. But the strategy board of the Rockingham faction was doing more than this; it was, it appears, giving Fox and Richmond help with their speeches. The party was now prepared and determined to go ahead with its scheduled inquiry into the state of the nation. As late as January 14 North thought that the Opposition would, in the debate of February 2, centre its attack upon Saratoga,[2] but the Opposition had made other plans.

All was interest and excitement the afternoon of February 2. Crowds mulled around restlessly in the lobby and environs of the House of Commons, anxious to gain admittance. Charles Fox, young, fiery, dynamic, would grind North and Germain to pulp. It would be a great show. The ladies were there too: Georgiana, the beautiful Duchess of Devonshire, charming leader of eighteenth-century society, was present; so also were Mrs Norton, the Speaker's wife, and fifty or sixty others. Members who had not graced the floor of the House since opening day were on hand; they edged their way through the crowds, grumbling because progress was difficult.

It was a restless crowd; an irritated crowd, too, because doorkeepers stood firm at their posts and refused admittance to all. Some visitors had letters from the great and near-great, some claimed relationship with members, some relied upon threat or persuasion; but despite tears, bribes, and oaths, the doors remained closed. Those seeking entrance could stand frustration just so long. Finally they broke through the doors and swarmed into the galleries, Speaker's wife, duchess, and all, and sat down to enjoy the spectacle. Members objected to this intrusion. A motion was made that the galleries should be

[1] Fortescue, iv, 14–31. January 13, 1778.   [2] *Ibid.*, iv, 17. January 14.

cleared and the gentlemen present grudgingly withdrew. It looked for a while as if the ladies might be allowed to remain, but Governor Johnstone observed in ungallant fashion that if the motive for clearing the galleries were to keep the state of the nation concealed from the enemy, there was no reason to acquaint the ladies with the arcana of state. So they left, and with them the Speaker's wife and the duchess, spending hours in the committee rooms before conveyances could be found to see them home. This enforced delay gave ample opportunity for comment; one lady declared that she should hate the name of Governor Johnstone to the latest hour of her life.[1] Reporters, likewise, were required to leave; and the report of Fox's speech that survives represents a thirty to forty minute summary of what he took two hours and forty minutes to deliver.

With infinite tact he began his speech. The diminishing of his audience he called his own personal good fortune, as he was sure he should not have lived up to expectation. His purpose was to move an inquiry into the state of the nation: 'I must, however, beg not to be considered as the mover in this momentous concern; it is the nation that calls for this inquiry, and I am only one instrument in the bringing it about.' Whigs breathed more easily; their speaker was doing well. His eyes swept over the Government benches across the way:

I would wish gentlemen would agree with me at least so far, as to divest themselves of all former opinions, of all favourite ideas, and of all prejudices which may have been contracted in the course of past debate, and take them up anew as they are the result of the present enquiry. . . . I would wish gentlemen to forget their animosities, and consider themselves neither as friends nor enemies to America, nor that country either with love or hatred, but regard it with calm and dispassionate mind, as a part, and a very considerable part, of the British empire.

Fox could hardly have made a more effective beginning. Perhaps he recalled his study of Aristotle's *Rhetoric* at Oxford, and remembered that confidence is inspired in the orator's character when he shows good sense, good moral character, and good will. Fox had already displayed all three: good sense in that he conciliated his audience rather than antagonized it; some ingredients of good character, in that, shorn of a part of his audience, he was calm and modest; good will in that he urged listeners to forget animosities of past debates and discuss the American question impartially.

The facts which he proposed to use, he declared, were taken from the papers on the table—papers put at the disposal of the House by

[1] *Morning Post, Morning Chronicle*, issues of February 3 and 4.

ministers themselves. Nothing could be fairer. First, he said, he intended to point out

that in the years 1774, 1775, 1776, and 1777 there was such an army, consisting of so many thousand men, and that such and such operations were performed; . . . secondly, state the impossibility of increasing that army; and thirdly, the enormous expence that already is incurred. . . . After having stated these facts . . . I shall . . . shew that the war has been mismanaged . . . though at the same time I will allow, that if it should turn out that there is a radical error, it is not of itself a proof of the criminality of ministers.

With a promise to be brief as possible, he reached the heart of his speech.

So far hardly a breath of political passion. Now the opposition might be more uneasy than ministers; was he going to forgive the Government side its blunders? Not quite; Fox began to discuss with energy, the principal events of 1773 and 1774—the tea party, the Boston Port Bill. Eyes of ministers, he alleged, were shut to the true state of America at that time. On he talked, the words pouring out—he was, perhaps, the most rapid speaker in the House—and in succession reviewed events of the preceding years. The attempts to change the government of Massachusetts, which led the Colonists to fear for the permanency of their legislature; the Quebec Act, which silenced the few remaining friends England had in America; the uninspired and haphazard operation of troops in and near Boston. With a little imagination one can see his eyes flashing and his heavy head indignantly shaking, and hear his voice rise, shrill and piercing. This business was serious; the fate of a nation, a people, was concerned; the situation had been bungled.

The ministers thought they could subdue the colonies by voting to send General Howe to Long Island with 55,000 reinforcements, said Fox, and the Americans whipped out the declaration of independence. The Government won minor victories in the summer campaign, he continued, and at Christmastide the Americans pummelled Hessian mercenaries at Trenton. The Government refused to revise the laws considered offensive by the Colonists; America's answer to that was shown in the failure of Burgoyne's expedition at Saratoga. Yet on this day, Fox told the House, he intended to begin with a very small part of the business. Since England had so many reasons to fear a war with France, it would be unwise to dispatch more troops to America; and he concluded with a motion that no more of the Old Corps be sent outside the country.[1]

The report in the *Parliamentary History* ends with the motion. During the speech, however, Alexander Wedderburn was busily en-

[1] *Parliamentary History*, xix, 672–83.

gaged taking notes on it. There still exist two large sheets, folded to make pages each about the size of an ordinary letterhead; along the left half of each page Wedderburn wrote a running résumé of Fox's arguments, jotting on the right half notes to use for his reply. Wedderburn's notes suggest that after making the motion, Fox continued with an appeal that did not get into the *Parliamentary History*. Here are some of Wedderburn's notations:

Premature to inquire [this is Fox speaking] whether to insist on dependence or to admit the independence of America.

There should be no disagreement now on that point.

All must wish indeed for its dependence but nominal independence may be real dependence and nominal dependence independence. . . .

They will be dependent because they want what we produce—we what they produce.

We cannot subsist without the friendship of America. Britain grew by America to greatness and without her aid will dwindle to her former insignificance.

Give up taxation, gain a party by that conception and make peace at the best rate we can. . . .

To answer this argument, Wedderburn apparently contemplated using this line of thought:

The first point to draw a line [Wedderburn might have planned to say] is the independence—necessary to settle it now for if any hope is given that this point may be obtained It is lost.

No wavering upon it can be safe for us. If a party here for it where the idea is mortifying to every man's pride, how much will that party be increased there where interest vanity ambition gratified by the idea.[1]

It is easy to read too much into these sentences, but Fox surely hit upon the illuminating idea that independence for the Colonies might turn out to be independence in name only, since the basic needs of both the mother country and the daughter would operate to the advantage of both. Independence was therefore inevitable and not necessarily a calamity. Indeed, Fox may be envisioning America, even when independent, as continuing to be a powerful friend of Britain. Wedderburn, like any good lawyer, was merely struggling to find words to put his reply in the best light.

A rebel cannonball whizzing through St Stephen's walls could not have made members more speechless than they were. The unexpected ending to Fox's speech put the ministers in a dilemma. The motion put a finger upon a thin spot in the nation's defences. For only two weeks previously the King had written to North to the effect that nothing could be more detrimental than the idea 'of sending in our present Weak State another Old Corps out of Great Britain'.[2] Not even the King had considered this move of Fox's as a possibility for February 2; the 'great

1 Wedderburn MSS., v. iii, item 4. (Clements.) 2 Fortescue, iv, 23. January 19.

outlines of measures' prepared by North and reviewed before his Cabinet made no provision for this kind of attack. The dilemma in which North and his supporters now found themselves was this: if they argued that more troops should be sent to America, they would leave themselves open to the charge of leaving the British Isles without sufficient defence, for Fox had shown, from ministers' own documents, that even now there was a deficiency of 6,000 men in the peacetime establishment. Or if they argued that the war could be carried on without sending more troops to America, they could point to nothing in support of that argument but the disastrous campaigns of 1776 and 1777. Nor could much be said to Fox's 'nominal independence' idea.

Fox's analysis was, of course, incomplete. Speakers in the House of Lords, after listening to Richmond's defence of a similar motion, found varied lines of rebuttal. In the Commons an embarrassing silence followed Fox's speech. No one rose to reply. One observer reported Wedderburn and Welbore Ellis each feverishly encouraging the other to take the floor. But Wedderburn did not give the reply that he had been industriously working on while Fox was on his legs. Perhaps North tugged at his coat tails; more likely he lost confidence in his planned speech as he noted the tremendous effectiveness of Fox's. Someone called out, 'Division!' and both sides prepared to vote.

The Speaker announced the result. Ayes 165, Noes 259. Fox had lost once more. The King sensed, however, the deep embarrassment of having no speakers ready and able to defend Government policy of the last four years. At forty minutes past ten that night he wrote, laconically: 'I trust that when next the Committee on the state of the Nation is resumed, Gentlemen will be more ready to speak. . . .'[1] He thought Germain might have put the defence in motion. The truth was again confirmed: it is easier to buy votes than eloquence.

A speech in a parliamentary debate is not an isolated event, but grows out of happenings, issues, other speeches. If its analysis, interpretation, and emphasis are cogent, it in turn requires a response. North and his colleagues had made a tactical blunder by failing to deal with the powerful impression that Fox's speech had made. The fact that no one attempted to reply struck the House and later the country with stunning force. Walter Spencer Stanhope, member for Carlisle, recorded that evening in his pocket diary: 'At the House of Commons on the inquiry by Mr Fox. He spoke for two Hours . . . & no body got up to answer him.'[2] Nothing else that happened in the House that year,

---

[1] Add. MSS. 47585. Fortescue, iv, 34.

[2] Stanhope MSS. 60635 (Sheffield). Born the same year as Fox, Stanhope entered Parliament seven years later than Fox did, and thus was in his third year as M.P. Generally he voted with the minority, and did so on this occasion.

judging by the diary, mostly a record of dining, hunting, and shooting, impressed him so profoundly as the simple fact that Fox spoke and no one replied.

Among those who heard reports of the speech was Governor Thomas Hutchinson, now a loyalist exile in London, who wrote in his diary:

He spoke more than two hours in support of the motion: nobody said one word, so that it can't be called strictly a debate. The Question was called for, and carried —259 against, to 165: a larger minority than has lately been known. Both Ld H[ardwicke?] and S[oame] Jenyns thought it impolitic to make no answer, and that the Ministry lost hands by it.[1]

The London press also noted forcefully the omission of any speeches in reply. After commenting that Lord George Germain felt the greatest weight of Fox's powerful eloquence, which, like a torrent, seemed to carry all before it, the *Public Advertiser* observed: '. . . This important resolution was not opposed by arguments but by votes.' A few days previously the *Advertiser*, a little weary of Fox's oratory, had printed a contributor's observation that Fox would prefer hell with a debate against God Almighty to the summit of celestial beatitude without any argument. The *Evening Post* lamented at the 'open degeneracy' of the present times, when a speech, replete with 'good sense, precision, and a detail of woeful information' could be passed over in silence by every member of the ministry. It went on to say that Fox 'stands high in the esteem of all the remaining good, honest Whigs in the Kingdom'. The *Gazetteer* wrote with scorn:

Ministers, chap-fallen, or struck with the impossibility of giving a rational, or even plausible reply, to one of the most able speeches ever delivered in a popular assembly, declined answering a single syllable. . . .

The very formidable minority in the lower house on Monday has greatly alarmed Administration, as they did not expect so strong a division in favour of Mr Fox's motion.

The *Morning Chronicle*, after describing the speech as 'mild and sensible . . . as full of good and real information as ever fell from that Hon. Member', noted 'what is most extraordinary', that no member from the other side of the House got up to make a reply. The weekly *Westminster Journal* recorded simply, 'Most unexpectedly the business of the day broke off here. No reply was made to Mr Fox.' The *General Advertiser and Morning Intelligencer*, praising Fox for his close and conclusive argument, declared the clearing of the House was scandalous, and the refusal to reply to his speech as an extravagantly predominant instance of ministerial influence such as perhaps had never

---

[1] *Diary and Letters of Thomas Hutchinson*, ii, 182. The editor appended a note expressing a different opinion: 'The Continuator of Hume speaks of the "contemptuous silence" with which the speech was received.'

before been witnessed. Across the channel the *Courier de l' Europe*, which had often in the past been impressed by the *orateur distingué* with his *beaucoup de véhemence*, took stern note of North's failure to reply.

One would need to search far and wide to find any other parliamentary incident of the 1770s more widely commented on than the failure of the ministry to meet Fox's argument.

Other sorts of comments appeared : the *Morning Post* spoke of Fox's usual vehemence and acrimony, repeating the observation in its columns two days later. The *St James's Chronicle* a few days later treated its readers to the revelation that Charles's family name was originally Tod, the Scottish word for fox, and that grandfather Stephen had made the change. Subsequently for some weeks the *Chronicle* and also the *Public Advertiser* frequently referred to the young orator as Charles Tod.

Still, there was more praise than criticism. The *Advertiser* and the *London Chronicle* each printed this comment :

Mr Fox's speech was masterly, forcible, and expressive, and it gave, in the course of near three hours which it lasted, the most striking proofs of judgment, sound reasoning, and astonishing memory.

Walpole wrote that Fox had tumbled Chatham from his oratorical throne, 'and if he has not all the dazzling lustre, has much more of the solid materials'. His speech was 'marvellous for method and memory', and was 'really unanswerable, for not one of the ministers knew what to say, and so said nothing, and that silence cost them many votes. In . . . the minority . . . were several Tories.'[1]

Fox himself reflected at greater length. In a letter to Richard Fitzpatrick, then in America, he wrote next day :

What the Ministers intend doing, besides keeping their places, upon which they are very decided, I can not even guess. They know as little how to make peace as war. . . . They still keep a great majority, though we begin to increase considerably. We divided last night . . . 165 to 259 which is certainly a very good division compared to the past, but a very bad one in my mind, considering the circumstances of the country.

Only rarely does one find a letter by a speaker summarizing his own speech. Fox said of his :

I made the motion in a very long speech, in which I went over the whole of the American business, and I really thought the House went a good deal with me in most of it. . . . We had several Tories with us, and . . . it was a great day for us. The Ministry, not by concert I believe, but by accident, did not say one word

1 *Walpole's Correspondence with William Mason*, 28/i, 349–50. To Mason, February 4.

which scandalised even their own friends a good deal, as I had opened the affair so very fully; for I spoke two hours and forty minutes. They now pretend to say that Ellis and Wedderburne were up (I did not see them), and while they were complimenting one another, the question was put. The fact is, that it is such a cause as no man can defend well, and therefore nobody likes to attempt it.

Fox was not unmindful of the scores of compliments that must have come to him because of his speech:

People flatter me that I continue to gain, rather than lose my credit as an orator, and I am so convinced that this is all that I ever shall gain (*unless I chuse to become the meanest of men*) *that I never think of any other object of ambition.* . . . Great reputation I think I may acquire and keep, great situation I never can acquire, nor if acquired *keep without making sacrifices that I never will make.*[1]

On this February 2, Fox made his first major contribution to parliamentary debate. Judging by the printed reports, a rough measure indeed, it was twice as long as any previous speech. Since the surviving text represents less than a fourth of this two hour and forty minute effort, the greater part of Fox's exposition and argument is lost altogether. Even so, the conciliatory approach, the broad view, the use of familiar example and illustration, the analysis of argument, the stylistic devices of question and answer, are characteristics of Fox's speaking at its best. The printed fragment that remains shows energy, vigour, directness. Richmond's argument on the same topic, developed much less effectively, provoked extensive reply from government supporters in the Lords.

As has been noted, both Walpole and Fox commented that several tories divided that day with the minority. Inspection of the minority division list of 165 members reveals a number who had not been regular members of opposition. At the head of the list, most worthy of the colourful appellation of tory, were Edward Gibbon, who had voted with Opposition the previous week (but after these two lapses he returned to the Government fold); John Montagu, son of the Earl of Sandwich; and Sir Charles Sedley, whose only known vote was cast on this occasion. Another, Lucy Knightley, was an independent of tory background. Some on the list were former Government supporters who had started voting with opposition on the American question. A thoroughgoing independent who went with Fox into the lobby that day was John Darker.[2] Twenty-nine names on the list do not appear on any of the other division lists of the fourteenth Parliament, suggesting that opposition exerted strong efforts to get out the vote. Among

[1] Add. MSS. 47580. *Fox Cor.*, i, 167–9. February 3.
[2] These statements are principally based on voting records in *History of Parliament.*

these rare attenders were John Henbury and Beilby Thompson, both of whom enjoyed notoriety for showing up in times of crisis. The *Parliamentary Register* appended to its list of those who voted with the opposition a note that 62 county members voted in this division, and 39 of them were on the minority side.[1] County members constituted the House's core of independents.

The Opposition of 1778 was far from being a permanent, cohesive group. Moreover, further inspection of the minority list shows that it was largely made up of individuals who spoke very little. So far as records show, 40 of the 165 never participated in parliamentary debate during the whole of their careers. Another 81 never spoke during 1777 and 1778; 26 spoke four times or fewer.[2] Five individuals made the most, the longest, and the most significant speeches: Burke, Townshend, Barré, Johnstone, and the most frequent speaker of all, Fox.

The majority was far too rugged to collapse before a single attack. But the debate and the general pressure of events led administration to initiate two lines of thought. One was to propose further ways of ameliorating the complaints of the Colonies. The other was to explore the possibility of getting Fox to rejoin the Government.

[1] Series 1, viii, 337–9.
[2] Specifically: January 29, 1777 to December 4, 1778, as listed in *Parliamentary History*, xxix. Additional sources would add a few names and speeches to this reckoning.

8

Fox and North: Conflict
1778-1779

If you get Charles Fox it may do for a while, but otherwise you are at your last gasp.

John Robinson

Ignorance in a minister is a crime of the first magnitude.

Charles James Fox

Even before Fox's February 2 speech, North had informed the King
that the complexities of the American problem had deprived him of
memory and understanding and had convinced him of his incapacity
for the office of first minister.

North had also advised that the time had come 'to take some step of a
pacifick kind' toward the colonies. News from the Continent carried the
threat that France would likely join forces with the Americans. The
possibility of this contingency also spurred North to urge the Commons
to appoint commissioners to negotiate with the Americans on all
matters that aggrieved them. A dull melancholy silence followed this
speech, according to the *Annual Register*; 'astonishment, dejection,
and fear, overclouded the whole assembly'. Fox agreed to the proposals, observing that they did not differ materially from Burke's,
presented three years previously.

Meanwhile, Franklin had signed a treaty providing that America
and France should become allies should France engage in war with
Britain. Here Horace Walpole's account is more revealing than the
parliamentary record. Thomas Walpole, with news from Paris that
the treaty between America and France had actually been signed,
decided to tell Fox, through the Duke of Grafton, an hour or two before
the House was to meet.[1] In the concluding moments of his speech, Fox
could therefore tell the House of his certain knowledge that a treaty
had been concluded and called upon North to give the House satisfaction on this interesting point. North, astounded, could only say
lamely that he could not answer from authority, but that it was possible,
nay too probable, that the treaty alluded to had been signed.[2]

Before many days had passed the news was generally known. Sir
Gilbert Elliot wrote that the French in London broke the news at the

[1] *Last Journals*, ii, 116–17.   [2] *Parliamentary History*, xix, 767–75.

opera and in clubs and coffee-houses with their natural impertinence. On March 17 the King sent a message to Parliament confirming the fact and stating that he had recalled his ambassador from the court of France. North by now had fully confessed that he was totally unfit to cope with the present difficulties of the nation, that 'both his mind and body grow every day more infirm and unable to struggle with the hardships of these arduous times', and insisted that the Government should be materially strengthened.[1]

William Eden, who had preceded Fox at Eton, though Fox had caught up with him at Oxford, had been delegated to learn under what circumstances Fox would be willing to lend his growing abilities to the administration. Eden, soon to be sent overseas as one of the peace commissioners, blandly set down the tone of his conversation: 'I rather speculated on changes than proposed any.' Fox, reported Eden, 'stated himself to be unconnected and at Liberty.' In a trial draft of a ministry, Fox was set down for the modest post of Treasurer of the Navy—this item eventually showed up in a note to the King.[2] Fox had been out of office four years; he had continuously and strenuously opposed administration policy, yet the Government was yearning to have him back.

Fox's terms were too high. The King's response was exquisitely definite. Rather than call upon any branch of the opposition for assistance, he would rather lose the crown 'than bear the ignominy of possessing it under their shackles'.[3] North was made to realize that he must carry on without fresh help.

Christopher D'Oyly, a Government placeman, had written during one of the debates: 'The friends of Opposition increase, and we are now in the midst of an inquiry into the state of the nation; in short, we are in a damned bad way.'[4] The House reviewed further the debacle at Saratoga, Fox placing the blame on Lord George Germain: 'The whole . . . failure . . . was owing to either the ignorance or negligence of the secretary of state . . . by which one of his Majesty's armies was totally lost, and in consequence of that, thirteen provinces were lost, to the utter ruin of this country.'[5] The debate was long and heated. Walpole describes an incident otherwise unrecorded:

Dundas . . . rose and taunted [Fox] with his moderation, and called on him to employ his usual invectives. . . . This speech, and the small minority and support of his friends, several of whom had gone away, . . . provoked Fox to the utmost rage. He burst out into a torrent of abuse, and lost all temper and conduct.[6]

[1] Fortescue, iv, 55. To the King. [March 15.]
[2] Add. MSS. 47586. *Fox Cor.*, i, 180–9. Fortescue, iv, 55–56.
[3] Fortescue, iv, 58. [? 15 March, 1778.]   [4] Quoted in *History of Parliament*, ii, 336.
[5] *Parliamentary History*, xix, 953.   [6] *Last Journals*, ii, 143–4.

When Fox heard the result of the division, 164 to 44 against him, he angrily declared he would not make another motion; he thereupon took the resolution of censure out of his pocket, 'tore it in pieces, and then went out of the House'.[1]

That, too, was the heritage of Holland House. Once a nine-year-old boy had impatiently smashed his father's watch against the tiles. Administration papers smugly interpreted Fox's leaving and deserting his own motion as showing his awareness of its impropriety. The King continued to write to North that he never, never would surrender the Government to any member of Opposition.

In the other place, Opposition was briefly divided in a stirring, highly dramatic interlude.

Chatham, though a friend of the Colonies, vigorously opposed their independence. Builder of an empire, he could not consent to its dissolution. On April 7 the Duke of Richmond moved in an exceptionally long series of resolutions that the Government withdraw its forces from American shores. For this debate Chatham, tall, gaunt, pale, wrapped in flannels, leaning heavily on crutches, supported by his son William, had left his sickbed to protest any dismemberment of the Empire. Richmond's reply was respectful, yet pointed. The old statesman suffered keen mortification as he heard the younger man, inferior in the art of speaking but that day markedly superior in evidence and judgment, earnestly develop the argument against him. Arising to reply, mentally shaken as well as physically broken, Chatham fell backwards in a fit; debate came to a halt as the stricken orator, the Great Commoner, distinguished patriot and scourge of incompetents and time-servers, was carried to the nearby Prince's Chamber.

After a few days he was taken home. He lingered a month, finally expiring on the morning of May 11. Newspapers that once found him eminently worthy of their space printed only brief notices of his death. The twenty-seven lines in the *St James's Chronicle* was not the briefest. Badly organized funeral arrangements, poor attendance of the great men of state, lack of public enthusiasm, were all embarrassing to family and friends.

The session came to an end on June 3. The opposition had reached its high point with the 165 votes it had amassed in February.

Fox felt he had deserved a holiday after his busy season, and took his ease during the weeks that followed. He wrote to Burke that he was in

[1] *Parliamentary History*, xix, 958.

June enjoying 'the most complete indolence . . . lying almost naked upon my couch all day . . . that when the weather is really warm, I want neither amusement, society, occupation, nor object'.[1] The King, busy as ever, urged North to prepare a plan that would assure better attendance at the opening of the coming session. North replied that nothing much would help but 'a change in the appearance of Public affairs' or a change in administration. Later, however, he informed the King that he had sent out a second set of letters to members, '& intends to have a meeting of the placemen etc. on Friday, in which he will request their support'.[2] Walpole also noted that morale was especially low among the country gentlemen. North hinted afresh that half a dozen places in the Cabinet, including his own, could be vacated without difficulty, but the King was not interested in this proposal, and nothing remained but for North to face the coming conflict.

Fox meanwhile was trying to organize a system of arguments to be used by opposition speakers. He wrote to Fitzpatrick that the proper stance was to act as if the independence of the Colonies were an accomplished fact, 'withdrawing our troops from North America, and making the most vigorous attacks upon France, or possibly Spain, too'. In his February 2 speech Fox had presumably advanced the notion that independence in name would not necessarily make the colonists less dependent in fact. To Fitzpatrick he reflected upon the wisdom of taking a less controversial stand: tacitly acknowledging independence without making speeches about it. In taking this view he was following a principle of Burke's, that political theory must be tempered by political experience. 'We must consider a little the state of things at home,' Fox continued, 'and think what is practicable as well as what is best.'[3] Within five years he would move to a more idealized position: independence should be acknowledged freely, openly, without bargaining or dickering.

He also urged Rockingham to convene the party for a discussion: 'Surely if ever it was necessary it is now more particularly so to be a little prepared for that strange medley of questions persons and things which must come upon the carpet next week.' Rockingham often received this kind of prodding from his associates. To Fox the need for a meeting was clear: 1778 had been an eventful year. The French were in the war. British troops had evacuated Philadephia and had moved to New York. Fox's friend and surety for his gambling debts, Carlisle, with Eden and Johnstone, had been appointed as a peace commission to Congress, and had crossed the ocean with authority to offer attractive proposals, short of actual independence.

[1] *Works and Correspondence of Burke*, i, 370. [2] Fortescue, iv, 210–11, 215.
[3] Add. MSS. 47570. *Fox Cor.*, i, 199–200. November 11.

Fox's letter continued, displaying both his generous nature and his candid straightforwardness:

Believe me, my dear Lord, tho' I certainly disapprove of some things which you have done, and of many more which you have left undone, yet there is no man in this country who wishes more heartily to agree with you in every thing, or who is more convinced that the Salvation of this country must ultimately depend upon you and your friends.[1]

Fox's speech on November 26, at the opening of Parliament, one of his finest, was reported better than most of his speeches had been up to this time. The *Morning Chronicle* commended him for his able two-hour speech. Burke, it continued, was cooler, more argumentative, and less flowery than usual.

To the statement in the address from the throne that British successes had not repaid 'the justice of our cause and the vigour of our exertions', Fox replied that the ministers had had even more success than they deserved. So when the Government argued that it deserved more success than it got, any Foxite might have predicted that Fox would reply that it got more success than it deserved. As to the plans and measures alleged to have been employed, he developed his retort by repeating words and phrases—a characteristic of style that was his life long habit:

What were those plans of parliament? for I never heard of them before. That the commissioners should be sent out in the dark as to every thing intended—was that the plan of parliament? That general Clinton should leave Philadelphia without giving the commissioners two hours warning . . . was that the plan of parliament? That they should offer terms of reconciliation . . . unlikely to be listened to . . . was that the plan of parliament?

Then, following the lines of argument suggested in the letter to Fitzpatrick, he urged the house to choose between its war with America and its war with France, demonstrating his wise understanding of the nature of the American war, and the difficulty of overcoming the sentiment that powered it:

You have now two wars before you, of which you must choose one, for both you cannot support. . . .

The war of the Americans is a war of passion; it is of such a nature as to be supported by the most powerful virtues, love of liberty and of country, and at the same time by those passions in the human heart which give courage, strength, and perseverance to man. . . .

The war of France is of another sort; the war of France is a war of interest; . . . turn your face at once against her, attack her wherever she is exposed, crush her commerce wherever you can, make her feel heavy and immediate distress

[1] Rockingham Letters, R1-1792 (Sheffield), November 18.

throughout the nation, the people will soon cry out to their government; . . . she will find the having entered into this business a bad bargain, and you will force her to desert an ally that brings so much trouble and distress.[1]

The debate was lengthy but at two in the morning the house divided for the Government 226 to 107. The King was pleased by the vote: '. . . handsome majority . . . credit to Administration . . . the Session will be much more pleasant than was expected.' Others were not nearly so relaxed about the prospect. It was then that John Robinson, the King's most valuable henchman and informant, wrote to North: 'If you get Charles Fox, it may do for a while, but otherwise you are at your last gasp.'[2] Fox had just turned thirty.

A year ago, Fox had been convinced that simply to gain credit as an orator was ambition enough. Now that he was thirty his ambition was modified. He had thoroughly experienced what he called 'a fruitless opposition'. He wanted office, the opportunity to reshape the policies that were driving the nation more and more deeply into war on land and sea. His name was on the lips of men, sometimes in connection with one Cabinet post, sometimes another.

With Chatham buried in Westminster Abbey, Rockingham was more influential than ever. So Fox wrote to the marquis on January 24, seeking to know whether Rockingham would have anything to do with a ministry not entirely of his own framing; and, furthermore, whether it would be proper for Fox to accept office in such a ministry.[3]

What Fox sought was something like a coalition, as he wrote to Burke the same day. He felt that he could write more frankly to Burke than to the marquis, and accordingly did not hesitate to state his opinion of the King:

There is no man who hates the power of the Crown more, or who has a worse opinion of the Person to whom it belongs than I. . . . I hate the power of the Crown and therefore wish not to confirm it by leaving the management of it in the hands of the most obsequious men in the country.

Continued opposition out of office he thought futile; discouragement had finally penetrated his marrow and sharpened his political perception: 'One principal cause of the astonishing strength of the present Ministry consists in their long and uninterrupted possession.' So, if members of the opposition could enter the Government only for a month, they would be stronger afterwards.

Fox knew, after the abortive attempts of that spring to bring about a

1 *Parliamentary History*, xix, 1322–30.
2 *HMCR*, Abergavenny MSS., p. 24. January 31.
3 *Fox Cor.*, i, 207; *Memoirs of the Marquis of Rockingham*, ii, 372.

partial coalition of forces, that Rockingham and his supporters would not be able to make an ideal arrangement with the North administration. If, however, 'the best possible system' could not evolve, accession of even a part of the Rockingham talents to the government would be better than the 'worst possible system' now in force.

As an endorsement to this letter, Burke wrote that before he could finish his reply to it, Fox had arrived in person. 'We had a long discourse in a Night walk on the ramparts when I think I convinced him that we were not mistaken in our Ideas.' So Fox got little encouragement from Burke to proceed with the thought of coalition.[1]

Nor did he from Richmond, who saw Fox's letter to Rockingham and undertook a reply to it. The dangers of individual members of the whig group accepting office were indeed grave. Even though changes were made and promises offered, it would be dubious wisdom to take office with the present Government. Fox should not be overly eager. Such a step would be far from his best interest. And most cordially Richmond added:

You have many of those social virtues which command the love of friends. . . . You have abilities in abundance; and your conduct of late years has done much to regain that public confidence which is so necessary to a public man. By a steady perseverance you may accomplish so essential an object.[2]

This letter may have kept Fox from plunging headlong into the arms of the ministry. On the other hand no specific invitation to join the Government was forthcoming. But from this point on Fox can more than ever be regarded as contemplating office.

One reason why the Royal Navy played a relatively minor part in the American revolution may have been that most of its engagements took place on the floor of the Commons. As First Lord of the Admiralty the Earl of Sandwich was responsible for the equipment, personnel, and tactical manoeuvres of the navy; and his mismanagement, seized upon by Fox, himself a former naval person of sorts, and vigorously presented to members of the House, proved to be one of the events that led to the fall of the North ministry and to Fox's elevation to a seat in the Cabinet.

A brief prologue to these major parliamentary engagements is helpful to the understanding of them. Between 1771 and 1778 Sandwich had received about £6 million for the navy and had little at the end to show for it. Some of this money had been appropriated to repair ships

[1] John A. Woods, ed. *The Correspondence of Edmund Burke* (Cambridge, 1963), iv, 38–41.
[2] *Fox Cor.*, i, 222–3. February 7, 1779.

that continued to rot in harbours; some to build ships that never were launched from the drafting board; some to put ships into commission mainly for political service. So when Admiral Augustus Keppel—distant cousin of Fox's—had gone to Portsmouth in March 1778, he had found that twenty ships of which Sandwich had boasted so often in the House of Commons amounted to but six ships in reality. Consequently Keppel had to spend valuable time rebuilding ships and refitting them for service. At last he had his twenty ships; he was then ordered to go out after the French, though war with France had not been declared, and he was none too sure what he should do in case he did meet a French ship.

Fortunately Keppel had learned through the papers of a captured frigate that the French fleet consisted of thirty-two ships, more than the Admiralty had supposed, so he returned to port for reinforcements. Putting out in July with thirty ships, he had soon sighted the French fleet proceeding cautiously out to sea. After four days of manoeuvring he had forced it into an engagement. The two fleets lined up, and following usual naval tactics sailed past each other on opposite tacks, firing broadsides as they went along. As the French concentrated their fire on masts and rigging, whereas the English fired on hulls, the English vessels suffered considerable loss of manoeuvrability as a result of the exchange. Keppel signalled for another line of battle but Palliser, his ship badly damaged, made no response. Nor was Keppel successful in getting prompt action from other ships in Palliser's division. Darkness came, further engagement was impossible; by morning the last of the enemy fleet was seen disappearing over the horizon. It was unfortunate for Britain that the battle was not renewed; a decisive victory would have crippled the power of France to aid the Americans.[1]

The details of the battle were not revealed to the public until an opposition newspaper, the *General Advertiser*, printed a paragraph accusing Palliser of failing to respond to his superior's signal. In retaliation Palliser blamed his superior in the columns of the tory *Morning Post*. As both men, like most admirals, held seats in the Commons, the engagement was staged again on the floor of the House. Palliser had filed charges of neglect of duty and misconduct against Keppel, and the Admiralty Board had immediately ordered a court-martial. This procedure the Opposition thought highly arbitrary. Burke and Dunning at length, Fox briefly, argued that the Board had discretionary power whether to proceed with charges, whereas North and Wedderburn declared that the Board was bound to act.

---

[1] David F. Wells, 'The Keppel–Palliser Dispute, 1778–1779,' *Georgia State College, Arts and Science Research Papers*, Number 3 (June, 1964); Captain William James, *The British Navy in Adversity* (London, 1926). The incident is discussed in Piers Mackesy, *The War for America, 1775–1783* (London, 1964), pp. 237 ff.

Fitzpatrick wrote to Ossory that it was 'the most interesting debate I ever remember to have heard. . . . The House was violently disposed to Keppel, who spoke like a man inspired, and no tool was bold enough to venture one word in favour of Palliser.'[1]

The trial was set for January 7, 1779, aboard the *Britannia*. For more than a month it progressed; it became increasingly evident that Keppel would be acquitted, and so he was. Burke declared that he could not remember any event in his time that had excited so much indignation. 'The disgust of the Major and better part of the Marine is not easily expressed.'[2]

News of the acquittal reached London on February 11 and touched off extensive illuminations and fireworks. At three o'clock in the morning Fox and other 'young men of quality', who had been drinking at Almack's, went on a tour of the streets and found a mob in front of Palliser's house, its windows broken. Then the mob marched to the Admiralty, forced the gates, broke more windows, and so terrified Sandwich that he escaped through the garden with his mistress.

As soon as the calendar was cleared in the Commons, Fox prepared to move that Palliser be dismissed from the navy, but was thwarted by the Admiral's immediate resignation. Next Fox moved that papers relative to the naval manoeuvres of 1778 be laid before the House, but the Government outvoted him by the slender majority of thirty-seven. The King sensed the seriousness of what was in the air, and prepared to do that which he did best; he directed North to improve attendance by any means he thought feasible. 'I therefore am ready to take any ostensible step to shew my disapprobation of those who do not attend', he indicated.[3]

Fox rose at four o'clock on the afternoon of March 3, in a full House, to propose a motion of censure upon the Admiralty. He recalled that the Admiralty sent Keppel with only twenty ships to fight the French; either they knew that the French at that moment had thirty or more ships at Brest, or they were ignorant of that fact; in either case they were equally culpable. As Fox proceeded, North no doubt began to wish that he himself were at sea, anywhere but on the ministerial bench in the Commons. He must have felt the attention with which his opponent was being heard; Fox could take arguments all had heard many times and cast them in such a mould that the House would listen again.

[1] Add. MSS. 47579. *Fox Cor.*, i, 204. [December 12, 1778.]
[2] *Correspondence of Edmund Burke*, iv, 34–5. To Philip Francis, December 24.
[3] Fortescue, iv, 288–9. February 23.

But Fox could use a variety of tactics. In the midst of his argument he unexpectedly paused, asked Admiral Keppel to rise, and then began to ask direct questions to substantiate what had already been said. Immediately the House was in a 'prodigious uproar'; half a dozen men jumped to their feet at once to claim the floor, protesting the unusual procedure. Was St Stephen's to be used as a courtroom? Fox's friends came to his defence; the House compromised by allowing Fox to ask the questions and Keppel to answer them, but would not allow the information to be written down. The questioning proceeded, the information thus elicited was summarized and emphasized, and Fox's concluding sentence left ministers high and dry upon the horns of a dilemma: either the administration knew the strength of the French fleet, or it did not; in either case its conduct merited censure.

North could not effectively answer the speech. He attempted to show that Sandwich was not culpable in sending Keppel out with twenty ships to meet the French fleet of thirty-two—but the House laughed in his face. Consequently after some further argument he made a bald plea for support. If you vote against Sandwich, he told the House, you will be voting against all of his Majesty's confidential servants. If any member of the Cabinet were censurable, so was every other.[1]

The division taken at one o'clock in the morning was 204 to 170 in favour of the Government—a terrifyingly close vote. Some may have recalled Sir Robert Walpole's dictum that when a minister's margin shrinks to forty he should resign. North had just barely snatched the administration's cause out of the fire. Twenty-five minutes later he wrote to the King: 'There has been a very bad attendance today, & the Opposition have conceived great hopes upon it.' Next morning at 8.15 the King's indignant answer came back:

I trust You will get an accurate List of the Absent that every means may be tried to get their attendance on future occasions. . . . If you can devise any means I can personally take to assist in getting Persons to attend better You will find me most ready to addopt it.[2]

The King's machine began to work overtime, and John Robinson began to compile data regarding absentees. Soon the list was ready to send to the King: 'Mr Robinson says it is as compleat as he can make it from all enquiries he has made & he imagines there are few if any errors in it.' The King acted promptly; so strongly must the principal defectors have been reprimanded that, almost without exception, they voted

[1] *Parliamentary History*, xx, 198. See the *Annual Register*, xiii, 72, for an observation that North might have lost the division had he not openly declared that a vote for the resolution would be interpreted as a vote of censure against him and all other ministers.
[2] Fortescue, iv, 295, 297.

thereafter on the administration side. Opposition did not have the resources to exert such powerful leverage on its waverers.

On March 13 appeared the first number of *The Englishman*, a periodical with which Fox was briefly associated. It was published irregularly until June 2, with Richard Brinsley Sheridan the principal contributor, and Fox the author of the March 14 issue. The March 31 issue compiled a list of those who voted both for and against Fox's motion on March 3. Those who voted against Fox were formally listed together with their probable reason for supporting the Government: 'nephew to a Lord of Admiralty', 'brother-in-law to the Secretary of the Treasury', 'contractor', 'brother to the Lord of the Bedchamber', and the like. Such an appellation was discoverable for two-thirds of those who voted for the Government, the compilers adding that they took no notice of 'ministerial borough-interest, Jobbs, Reversions, private Douceurs, Script, Lottery Tickets, Places in Trust, Couplings and Quarterings, Commissions for Children, Curacies for Cousins, &c'.[1] Thus *The Englishman* further battered the familiar unsavoury image of the placeman.

On March 8, in a House much more crowded than before—for Rockingham as well as the King had been rounding up the stragglers— Fox resumed his attack on the Admiralty by presenting another motion. North had checkmated his first effort by declaring that a vote against Sandwich would be a vote against the whole ministry. Very well; in order to make the issue clear, Fox would so state his motion—a general charge of neglect and misconduct on the part of all the ministers. His speech, along much the same line as the first, reviewed blunders of the past year, declaring that ministers were treacherous or ignorant and in either case undeserving of public trust.

The King's strenuous exertions to his following brought immediate result, for although Howe, Keppel, Mann, Luttrell, Grenville, Burke, and Byng spoke long and ably in defence of Fox's motion, the governmental majority was significantly larger than it was on March 3; its vote went from 204 to 246. Opposition vote, meanwhile, went from 170 to 174, a lesser improvement. The King wrote that it would be impossible for him to be more satisfied than he was, since the vote was evident of the thoroughness with which North had 'spoken out' to delinquent members. The division list of March 8 assured the King that his organization was functioning again.

For the time being administration had survived the crisis. Fox continued to present motions against the ministry in general and Sandwich in particular. A motion of censure on March 22—called by one paper

---

[1] *The Englishman*, No. 5 (March 31). See Lord John Russell ed., *Memoirs, Journal and Correspondence of Thomas Moore* (London, 1853), ii, 312.

'one of the most interesting and important debates . . . in either House
. . . the present session'—was beat down 135 to 209, but the King's
majority slowly increased as the session went on. Yet, of all the opposition, Fox was the most optimistic. When North sent Rigby to ask Fox
if he would accept the position of Treasurer of the Navy in a coalition
Cabinet, Fox remembered Richmond's letter and replied that he was
in no way disposed to become part of an administration in which
Lord North was a principal.[1]

[1] Fortescue, iv, 368.

9

Fox Goes to the People
1779-1780

The Majority of Votes, unless it is well supported by
speakers, will sink in the course of the Sessions.

Lord North

They were talking of Burke & Fox; the first has more
Bullion Says Mr Johnson, but the other coins faster.

Mrs Thrale

The continued existence of the North Government despite aggravating
domestic grievances and foreign pressures has few parallels in English history.

In Ireland dissatisfaction and despair continued to mount. The causes
were long-standing. Politically, its parliament was subordinate to the
British Parliament; the Irish executive, the Lord Lieutenant, was an
appointee of the British Crown. Economically, the country was under
harsh restriction. Export of Irish wool and food products to British
ports was forbidden. Moreover, the vast Catholic population could not
vote for representatives in Parliament, enter the House of Commons,
hold municipal office, hold rank in the army, follow the profession of
law, nor engage in various other challenging and profitable pursuits.
Countless other restrictions, even when not always enforced, added to
the general misery of Catholics, and, in fact, of others not of Anglican
faith. To escape grinding poverty and religious repression, Irishmen
by the tens of thousands had emigrated to America.

From their thousands of relatives in the colonies and from other
sources, Irishmen kept informed about the progress of the American
revolution. In many ways it stood as an inspiration to Irish patriots.
Like the Americans, they formed local groups to enforce non-impor-
tation agreements. Even more ominously, they organized groups of
volunteers primarily for defence against a foreign invader, though they
were as well a force in being in the event of domestic upheaval. By
May their numbers reached 8000; eventually they were in excess of
40,000. They secured arms and underwent training. In their ranks
were men of respectability and fortune.

Parliament paid small attention in May and June to the Irish question. In the Lords, Rockingham had called attention to parallels between Irish complaints and those of the Americans. In the Commons,

North was content to review concessions already made to Ireland without offering specific proposals to relieve her current hardships. Fox also made reference to a pamphlet that stated, among other provocative doctrines, that if a legislature exercised power over the people of another community, it usurped their natural rights.[1] This idea he modified and adapted in some of his later extraparliamentary utterances. Aside from these discussions, Parliament had risen in July without having offered any solution to the Irish disturbances.

The new threat of Spain, which had followed France into the war, added to the Government's burdens. The loss of St Vincent and Grenada to the French fleet in the West Indies also enhanced the general gloom. Fox wrote Sheridan in September about the 'cursed news from the West Indies', news so bad he could not bear it. 'If we are to lose ship after ship & Island after Island in this manner how the devil are we to recover them?' He continued: 'I can not help hoping that there is something like a chance of hanging Ld S[andwich] at last.' And if *The Englishman* were still being issued: 'How well might he explain to the world how natural consequences all these are of the neglect of ministers, & how those very parts of their conduct which we moved to censure last Sessions, have been productive of all the mischiefs we suffer.'[2]

Thus external threats combined with economic unrest added to North's mounting burden. Especially was he concerned about the ability of his Government to face the big guns of the opposition when Parliament opened November 25. Sandwich wrote to the King that North would only with difficulty be able to manage the coming session.[3] North gloomily foresaw that his majority, 'unless it is well supported by speakers, will sink in the course of the Sessions'.[4]

So dismal was the situation that George III went to the length of compiling three considerations under which a coalition ministry would be acceptable. At the head of the list was the declaration that the empire should be kept intact. Next was a statement that the war with America should be prosecuted with the utmost vigour. Finally was an insistence that there should be no wholesale undoing of steps already taken in dealing with the colonies.[5]

To discover whether members of the opposition would take positions in the Cabinet under terms like these, intermediaries were sent to interview Rockingham and Fox. Hence the thirty-year-old Fox was tempted again—the temptations by now were coming almost annually

[1] Herbert Butterfield, *George III, Lord North, and the People* (London, 1949), pp. 90–3. Chapters 3 and 4 describe the Irish crisis in detail.
[2] Osborn Collection, Box 80, no. 26. (Yale.) September 9 [1779].
[3] Fortescue, iv, 453. October 9, 1779.   [4] *Ibid.*, iv, 487. To the King, November 15.
[5] *Ibid.*, iv, 507–8. To Thurlow. [December 3.]

—by a vision of occupying high office. Here was a situation to tantalize a young man's judgment, at times over rash, at other times over cautious. At one stage of the discussions the rumour came to the King that the opposition had set Fox down as Chancellor of the Exchequer. Rockingham believed that only a total change of men and measures could have any hope of success, and even Fox, who might have supported a coalition ministry, insisted that America should be given her independence. The King, discovering that nothing could satisfy Opposition but a complete rout of the present ministry, wrote to Thurlow that he would not 'deliver up my Person, my Principles, and my Dominions into their hands', and declared that 'this formidable and desperate Opposition' must be resisted at all costs.

North's desire these days was for men who could support him on the floor of the House with eloquence and persuasion. Perhaps he looked wistfully back to better days when he was protected by the sturdy oratory of Thurlow on one hand and the legal expediencies of Wedderburn on the other. North had to meet his formidable, desperate opposition face to face—he had to deal immediately with its taunts, its piercing attack, its unrelenting argument. His supporters also had to endure the weight of evidence and ridicule that could be amassed against them. Those who honestly believed the Government had a good case would have liked to hear it eloquently stated. Even Government newspapers could and did condemn ineffectual replies to opposition speeches. North could and did earnestly complain to the King of not being supported in the Commons.

The King's speech on opening the session in November commented on the attempted invasion and on the Irish situation, but made no mention of the war with America, an omission that opposition orators quickly capitalized upon. James Grenville, who had opposed the American war from the outset, listed the failures of the Government: Dominica, St Vincent's, and Grenada captured by France, and fortunes of British subjects there crushed; diminishing trade and commerce at home and the ever-increasing danger of commercial vessels being captured at sea; distresses of Ireland; the certainty of new taxes. William Adam, however, a Scot with a mixed voting record, next announced that he was going to forsake opposition and vote with administration; but when he declared that the King already had men in his Cabinet who were 'fully adequate to the great task of saving their country', there was a loud cry of 'Name them! Name them!'[1]

During the next seven speeches Fox mulled over Adam's sentiments

[1] *Parliamentary History*, xx, 1098–107.

and finally rose to reply. At the beginning of the last session, said Fox, Adam had thought ministers wrong, but the current campaigns had convinced him that ministers were right: 'having once thought ill of them, a line of conduct, still more disgraceful, more infamous, more destructive and ruinous, had at once done away the bad impression . . . and had determined him to support them! This . . . was soaring to the very summit of political paradox, and parliamentary enigma.' Adam had declared that there were able men in administration, who enjoyed the confidence of the country. Where was one to seek these able men? At the head of the army? here he would find an officer who had entirely lost the confidence of all. In the Secretary of State's office? there he would find no person who well understood foreign courts and interests. At the Treasury or Admiralty Boards? he would have little success at either. How did it happen that on one lately-captured island were 150 pieces of ordnance and only forty men to work them? Why should the forces have in one place cannon without balls and in another balls without cannon? Where James Grenville had merely summarized, Fox struck hard, struck forcefully and ironically, struck repeatedly.

Nor did he spare the King himself. He described the bright prospects that had opened before the young monarch at the outset of his reign: immense dominions, warmest affection of the people. Now how sadly was the scene reversed: empire dismembered, councils distracted, people falling off in their fondness for his person. Fox continued by making reference to the fact that 'the present sovereign's claim to the throne . . . was founded only upon the delinquency of the Stuart family; a circumstance which should never be one moment out of his Majesty's recollection'. From this blast at the throne Fox moved to the ignorance of the throne's advisers; 'ignorance in a minister is a crime of the first magnitude'.

For nearly two hours he kept at it. North surely could not be in earnest when he declared that the American war had nothing to do with the affairs of Ireland:

What stripped Ireland of her troops? Was it not the American war?
What brought on the hostilities of France and put Ireland in fear of an invasion? Was it not the American war?
What gave Ireland the opportunity of establishing a powerful and illegal army? Certainly the American war!

Fox hoped that in dealing with Ireland the administration would not repeat the fatal plan that it followed in dealing with America, of denying 'in one session what they offer with additions the year following, yet continuing to make little bargains until they have nothing left to bargain for'.[1]

[1] *Parliamentary History*, xx, 1116–28.

Fox's speech clearly had great excitement, tremendous power. More than anything else, it foreshadowed the kind of speaking he was to do outside of Parliament. Its sharp criticism of the Government's dilatory tactics, its vivid language, its piling up of instances, its repetition of telling phrases, all characterize popular oratory. It is too emotional, however, to be called one of his leading parliamentary addresses. The number of voters that followed Fox into the division lobby totalled 134, nearly a hundred fewer than the 233 who supported the Government. John Robinson's prediction, made just before the debate opened, had been 220 or 230 against 170 or 180.[1] Hence Fox's sharp attack on King and ministers did not draw their followers to his side. Nathaniel Wraxall described Fox's resistance as factious and severe rather than constitutional and temperate.[2]

Newspaper reporters, however, outdid one another in their praise. 'His speech was, upon the whole, the most complete performance we ever heard', said the *London Chronicle*. It noted that he was on his legs an hour and fifty minutes, and liked especially that part of his speech in which he called attention to the omission of the American war from the King's address. 'But where is America ?' the *Chronicle* asked. 'Is it forgotten ? Does it exist no longer ?' The *St James's Chronicle* averred that never before had Fox shone so greatly as on this occasion. The *Morning Post*, invariably critical of Fox, took various positions on his speech, but observed that the eloquence of that long day seemed to evaporate into nothing, in comparison with his blaze of eloquence. The *Public Ledger* declared: 'Fox . . . rivitted the attention of the house to one of the best speeches ever delivered in the British, or any other senate, since oratory has been known to the world.' And as for the paradoxical Adam and his telling members that the country was better off in the West Indies now than before, Fox 'knew not how to reconcile it, unless that we were better, *because* having lost three of our islands, we had less territory left to defend'. Said the *London Courant*: '[His] speech of two hours [is] esteemed the most powerful and masterly that he ever delivered.' On this occasion reporters did not compare Fox with Burke, North, or even Chatham—the proper person with whom to compare Fox was Fox himself.

Walpole commented wittily on the event, declaring that Fox tore Adam's absurd speech with such humour and argument that the tortured patient demanded an explanation the very next day. After reading the extracts of the speech in the various newspapers, Adam wrote to Fox that since those accounts reflected upon Adam personally he was justified in 'demanding the only satisfaction that such an injury will admit of'. He wanted Fox to print a letter contradicting the newspaper

[1] Fortescue, vi, 499.   [2] Wraxall, ii, 19–21. He entered the House the following year.

reports and declaring he had a good opinion of Adam. Fox replied that the account of his speech in the newspapers was certainly unauthorized by him; he therefore refused to avoid the duel by apologizing for something printed without his sanction.

Plans for the duel proceeded at once. Walpole's letters contain almost as many references to it as they do to his own gout and rheumatism. A date was set for four days after the speech, at eight o'clock in the morning at Hyde Park. Fox slept soundly the evening before; he simply instructed his servant to awaken him at six in the morning, giving only 'business' as his reason for the early rising. The servant demurred; six o'clock was too early for business as it was totally dark; but Fox said plainly, 'If you do not call me at six, at seven, or when I wake, I will discharge you.'[1]

Accompanied by the loyal Fitzpatrick, Fox went to Hyde Park in as good a frame of mind as if he were going to Almack's. Fitzpatrick, comparing Adam's slight build to Fox's own massive frame, advised his principal to stand sideways when facing his antagonist. 'Why, I am as thick one way as another,' exclaimed the bulky orator, recklessly squaring off to receive Adam's fire, which caused a slight flesh wound in the thigh. Fox then fired, missed, and said, 'Now, Mr Adam, are you satisfied?' 'No,' said Adam, 'you must still print your letter.' Adam then fired and missed, Fox fired in the air, and the duel ended.[2]

Fox was laid up a few days because of his wound: returning later to his accustomed haunts, he was met with solemn-faced declarations from friends that the shot had undoubtedly lodged in his groin and had impared his manly vigour. Fox, equally solemn, retorted that Adam had loaded his pistol with Government powder, far too weak to penetrate a tough whig hide. The ferocity of eighteenth-century duels may be exaggerated. Shelburne next year in a duel with an army officer also received a shot in a delicate place but the wound was so slight that, coolly inspecting it, he declared that Lady Shelburne would be no worse for it.[3]

Back in Parliament Fox duelled with North on the American war:

What was the cause of our wasting forty millions of money, and sixty thousand lives? The American war. What was it that produced the French rescript, and a French war? The American War. What was it that produced the Spanish Manifesto and Spanish war? The American war.... For what were we about to incur an additional debt of twelve or fourteen millions the ensuing year? That accursed, diabolical, and cruel American war.[4]

[1] *London Courant*, November 26.
[2] *Walpole's Correspondence with William Mason*, 28/i, 481–2. Walpole to Mason, November 29.
[3] *Ibid.*, 29/ii, 14. To Mason, March 22, 1780.   [4] *Parliamentary History*, xx, 1221–2.

It was 'a strain of oratory rarely equalled,' said the report. The *Public Advertiser*, as if it had forgotten the towering press comments on Fox's speech a few days previously, now said that on this occasion he showed 'the greatest force of eloquence we ever remember to have heard him exert upon any question'. Others were less pleased. One listener called him so abusive in his performances that he should be called out to fight ten duels a day.[1]

Meanwhile the Irish people and their legislature kept up pressure on the British Parliament to the extent that in December North offered three resolutions making generous concessions in the export of wool and woollens, glass and manufactured articles of glass; and offered free trade with British colonies and plantations. For this welcome relief to Ireland, Fox, now recovered from his duelling wound, had surprisingly little to say. He is reported to have declared that 'it was the first time in his life, that he had not, on any great public question, taken one side or the other'. With rare caution he said he must first wait until the sentiment of Ireland was known; all he could add was that his silence on the resolutions was not to constitute 'active approbation'.[2] Burke also had little to say. Thereupon their Irish friends sharply criticized the Rockingham whigs for their lukewarm support, compelling Burke and Fox each to write a defence of his silence. Burke reviewed the long record of cordial friendship of the whigs for Ireland. If he had spoken on North's propositions their passage would have been delayed. Irishmen in London with whom he consulted approved his conduct. His letter also sounded an awesome sentiment. Opposition 'is now in its final and conclusive struggle'. If it is forced to quit the field, 'if I know anything of this country, another constitutional opposition *can never* be formed in it'.[3] Fox observed that an opposition position on Ireland, to succeed, could not differ too widely from the Government's position. Better give the ministry its head, he concluded, and stay in reserve to help Ireland later when she might need help. And moreover, Ireland should not forget that it was Rockingham who had opened the Irish question that spring.[4]

During the Christmas recess Englishmen began to show their disapproval of the way affairs were being managed. In mass meetings throughout the country and through petitions they expressed their steadily growing discontent.

[1] Thomas Waite to Lord George Germain, *HMCR*, Stopford-Sackville MSS., i, 264. December 13.

[2] *Parliamentary History*, xx, 1272–85.

[3] Letter to Thomas Burgh, member of the Irish House of Commons, in *Works and Correspondence of Burke*, v, 556–74. January 1, 1780.

[4] *HMCR*, Charlemont MSS., i, 369–70. January 4. Quoted in Butterfield, p. 177.

The growth of the Association movement, through which this groundswell of public opinion asserted itself, and which brought Fox into prominence as speaker to the multitudes as well as to the more select audience of St Stephen's Chapel, has been narrated in detail.[1] Later in his career Fox was to say, 'Yorkshire and Middlesex between them make all England', and it was in Yorkshire and Middlesex that the movement got under way.

The reasons have already been suggested: expense of the war, decline of trade, accumulation of taxes, disregard of the public weal. The remedies suggested were to correct gross abuses in public expenditure, to abolish sinecures and reduce pensions, and to take other steps to make government more responsible and efficient. These proposals show the extent to which the conviction that Government was corrupt had touched the people. To alleviate their miseries, the Government should first undertake fiscal reforms. Speakers debated these and related matters in an impressive meeting at York on December 30. Throughout the day and into the evening they reviewed the state of the nation. A result was a set of resolutions urging that abuses in administration be corrected.

Behind the meeting was the guiding spirit of the Reverend Christopher Wyvill, a landowner of substance in North Yorkshire, nominal rector of an Anglican parish though less active than formerly. Wyvill was persuasive not only in letter-writing and conference but also on the public platform. His moderate approach enlisted Rockingham and other men of influence in Yorkshire, and once he had attracted men of such quality, the movement gained rapid momentum. When word of the Yorkshire resolutions and petition was received, Middlesex fell in line. The movement continued to spread; petitions were signed representing Hackney, Chester, Sussex, Gloucester, Dorset, Devon, Nottingham, Kent, Northumberland, Suffolk, Cambridge, and many others. Thus a countrywide extraparliamentary movement gained momentum.

This enterprise made a deep impression upon Fox. A month after the Yorkshire meeting he went to Wiltshire, which had enjoyed a long record of supporting Opposition candidates, to give his first speech outside the House of Commons. As he said, 'though much used to Public Speaking, he had never addressed such an assembly as that then present, for he had never before spoken to an uncorrupt Assembly'. He admitted that he was not a freeholder in the county though he had property under his care. His small group of listeners knew him, of course, as member from Malmesbury in that county. He reminded

[1] Butterfield, *George III, Lord North, and the People*; Ian R. Christie, *Wilkes, Wyvill and Reform* (London, 1962); Eugene C. Black, *The Association* (Cambridge, 1963).

them that they must be active and diligent, asserting that 'it would not be in the power of the best or ablest Minister to make them great and happy, unless they had the spirit to become so'. Parliament came to the relief of Ireland because the people of Ireland were resolved to be relieved; in England also men must exert themselves if they wish to improve their condition.[1]

It was at Westminster Hall, however, on February 2, that Fox really found his talent for popular oratory. In this famous eleventh-century structure, its wide, open area free of columns or pillars, Fox faced his first large audience, a group estimated at more than 3,000 people. Eight years ago, hardly a stone's throw away, the people of London had upset his carriage and had pelted him with stones and oranges because he had denounced them and their petitions and had declared that only the House of Commons was the really true representative of public opinion. Now they listened and applauded eagerly as he pursued the opposite tack. His earnest, natural style undoubtedly was even more appealing to the popular audience in Westminster Hall than to the smaller and more select group in St Stephen's Chapel. He reminded his listeners that the Government of the country consisted of King, lords, and people; that the House of Commons was a delegate or representative of the people; and that when the house forfeits its character and responsibility, it is 'legal, constitutional, and necessary, for the people to resume that trust'. Petitions were a way of preventing further legislative mischief and now is the time to petition: 'The moment of necessity [is] the moment of relief.' Nothing but the determined resolution of the people could save them:

You must be the ministers of your own deliverance, and the road to it is open. . . . Your brethren in America and Ireland shew you how to act when bad men force you to feel. Are we not possessed with equal veneration for our lives and liberties? Does not the blood flow as freely in our veins as in theirs? Are we not as capable as they are of spurning at life when unaccompanied by freedom? Did not our fathers fight and bleed for their rights, and transmit them as the most valuable legacy they could bequeath to posterity? . . . I trust corruption has not yet extended her debilitating influence to the people, who are the vitals of the great body politic.[2]

To these questions the three thousand listeners would find it easy and exciting to say yes, difficult to reflect and ponder and say no. He advised that an association be formed to prepare a petition, as had been done at York, Middlesex, and elsewhere—all amid such 'repeated shouts of acclamation and applause' that it took time to restore order.[3]

[1] Christopher Wyvill, *Political Papers Chiefly respecting the Attempt of the County of York and Other . . . Districts . . . to Effect a Reformation of . . . Parliament* (York, 1794), i, 108–10.
[2] *History of the political life and public services, as a senator and a statesman, of the Right Honourable Charles James Fox*, etc. (London, 1783), pp. 365–75. [By Mr Laurence.]
[3] *London Evening-Post*, February 1–5, 1780. A more complete text appears in a

Fox was proposed as candidate for Westminster at the next general election and was accepted joyously. His friends began canvassing for him; the *Public Advertiser* optimistically observed that his great talents and responsibility would, for once, 'overcome the influence of overgrown power and family connections'. Thus began Fox's long career as Westminster's favourite son. On every hand, however, political opponents saw the irony of Fox, who years before had harangued against petitions, insisting that the voice of the people was to be canvassed only in Parliament, now sponsoring mass meetings and associations and the petitions that resulted. Walpole recorded how curious it was to see Charles Fox, lately so unpopular a character, become the idol of the people even though his family still owed £200,000 of the public money. At a Guildhall meeting on February 11, an old speech was quoted to the effect that Fox had once declared in the House, that he did not consider the numerous petitions presented *as the voice of the people*, which could only be collected from the majority of the members of the House. 'But now,' said the Guildhall speaker, 'Mr Fox is *out* of place, the petitions are the *voice of the people*, and he is the head of Opposition, and the chairman of the corresponding Committee for Westminster.' Truly Fox has 'changed his opinion and his conduct as much as any man living'.[1]

This was not the first time such a charge was made nor would it be the last. In debate on February 28 Fox took oblique note of it when he declared that he would always pay the greatest deference to the advice and instructions of his constituents, but should always retain an opinion of his own, and act according to the dictates of his conscience, and the best of his judgment.[2] On an earlier occasion he had said that it was the duty of members of Parliament to conform to the sentiments, and in some degree, even to the prejudice of the people. 'The wishes and wants of the people, ought in this land of liberty to be their grand rule of conduct.'[3]

So now Fox was the champion of the borough of Westminster, its candidate at the next general election and the chairman of its Association committee. Burke's contribution to the movement had been to give notice of his intention to offer a plan of economical reform. On February 11 he presented it in a distinguished speech of three hours and eighteen minutes. That day excitement was high: six hundred

pamphlet, *The Speech of the Honble. Charles James Fox delivered at Westminster on Wednesday, February 2, 1780, etc.* (London, n.d.)
[1] *General Evening Post*, February 10–12.   [2] *Public Advertiser*, February 29.
[3] *Parliamentary History*, xx, 1379.

people heard the opening prayers inside the chamber, with another four hundred still on the outside.[1] Burke stated his hope to save the public £200,000 annually and to cut off an amount of influence equal to the places of fifty members of Parliament.[2] Walpole declared that Burke was so effective he could that day have carried any point he had proposed; even North commended him, and agreed that the Bill should be brought in. Eventually the Bill was referred to the committee of the whole House, the first clause being the abolition of the Secretary of State for the Colonies, the post held by Germain.

At this stage of the debate, at one o'clock in the morning, Fox took the floor—he was, of course, the best after-midnight speaker in the House—and his lively delivery roused members on all sides. He pictured the 'monstrous influence of the Crown' that pervaded every department of the Government; told how officials had been punished for failing to vote or for voting the wrong way; argued that the abolition of the office of secretary would not only save a £4500 salary, but would strike off just so much of the influence of the Crown. The division, held at a quarter of three, was surprisingly close; a slender margin of seven votes, 208 to 201, saved Germain.

The House next took up the question of abolishing the Board of Trade, which provided eight members of Parliament with a sinecure of £1000 a year to support the Government. At two-thirty in the morning, by 207 to 199, the Board was abolished. This defeat was a bitter one for governmental forces and marked progress in the plans of the opposition for administrative reform. The opposition quickly saw that its majority would have been even larger had not most of the members of the Board voted for themselves. Yet the victory was temporary; the Government braced itself for a struggle, and bitterly but successfully fought the remaining clauses of the Bill. As the debates ran their tedious length through the rest of the session, Burke, seeing that opposition was weakening, lost heart. Burke told the House he would not 'put his weak and disordered frame and constitution to the torture, in order to fight his Bill . . . inch by inch, clause by clause, and line by line'.[3] When the Government saved the office of Treasurer of the Chamber by 211 to 158, Burke's discouragement was complete. Fox, however, rallied to the cause; he urged the opposition to keep up courage, declaring the Bill would be renewed from session to session until the Crown's influence was demolished.

Later that spring, Fox spoke in favour of annual parliaments and changes in the method of representation. Although he never contested

[1] *HMCR*, Graham MSS., p. 341. February 21.
[2] *Works and Correspondence of Edmund Burke*, i, 418–24.
[3] *Parliamentary History*, xxi, 306.

this issue with the same zeal and fervour with which he fought for other kinds of political liberty, he did lend his voice to such extent that in later years when men spoke of 'Mr Fox's principles', parliamentary reform was one of the list.

April 6, 1780. The House was if possible more crowded than it had ever been. About forty petitions had poured in from counties and towns: 'Vast parchments subscribed by thousands of names, were heaped on the table.' The opposition had kept secret its intended motions but the Government knew that something was up and rallied its forces; 'every creature was forced down that could be carried into the House'.[1] After the titles of the petitions were read, John Dunning, successful barrister and eloquent member of the opposition, took the floor and offered a motion that became famous: 'The influence of the Crown has increased, is increasing, and ought to be diminished.' It was an amazing motion. Walpole wrote that the walls of the House could not believe their own ears—they had not heard such language since they had a wainscot. Ministerial forces countered by declaring that Dunning's proposition was an abstract one, but when North, losing 'all temper and patience', said that the opposition meant to ruin the constitution, tumult followed. Members of the opposition were on their legs clamouring that North's words be taken down—the usual method of rebuking one who becomes unparliamentary; the speaker rapped for order, but no one heard him; the floor was held by everybody and by nobody. 'Am I to hear myself charged as the author of our present misfortunes?' roared North, and from across the House came many voices—'You are, you are.' The surprised North resumed his seat and held a hurried consultation with his followers. The Government invoked parliamentary strategy and counter-strategy to stave off disaster, but at midnight it could postpone the vote no longer. The House divided, and the speaker announced that Dunning's motion was carried by 233 to 215.

The influence of the Crown had increased, was increasing and ought to be diminished—thus the House had voted. Dunning next offered his second motion: that the House was competent to correct abuses in the civil list and in other public revenues. North strongly urged members to proceed no further. Burke called North a curiosity, more fit for the British Museum than the British House of Commons. The debate, however, was brief indeed, the resolution passing without a division. A third resolution urged that the House provide immediate and effectual redress of the abuses complained of in the many petitions presented

[1] *HMCR*, Rutland MSS., iii, 27. Thomas Thoroton to the Duke of Rutland, April 7.

to the House; North again implored the House not to proceed but the resolution passed without a dissenting vote. It was an incredible stampede of a house that had been solidly and stolidly the King's.

For ten years North had been a voice of the King in Parliament—at last it seemed possible that those days were about to end, that new faces would be seen on the ministers' bench. At two o'clock in the morning, North again wrote to the King that he might be allowed to retire at the end of the session. The King replied that surely North would not expect an immediate answer to this request; the resolutions were by no means personally directed against North. He added, wryly: 'I wish I did not feel at whom they are *personally levelled.*' Previously he had written to Robinson: 'It would be madness not to call a new parliament as soon as we have hobbled through the present session.'[1]

North and others wondered where the 233 had come from. If they had compared the division lists of that April 6 with the list of the minority that had followed Fox into the lobby that famous February 2, two years earlier, they would have discovered that 138 names of Fox's 165 divided with the opposition on both occasions. In fact, only one of the 165—Gibbon—voted this day with administration. North compiled for the King a list of 'persons generally with who went against'; the list included thirty-nine names, though two that he queried actually voted with the Government.[2] The rest of the 233 included the usual variety; opposition members who attended and voted irregularly; newcomers to opposition who cast their first vote against the Government; independents who usually but not invariably supported North; and here and there a prominent name like General John Burgoyne, who thought he had been ill-used after Saratoga, and the Speaker himself, Sir Fletcher Norton, who since the debate had been held in committee, had not only voted but spoken for Dunning's motion.

Fox had not participated in the early part of that incredible debate; he was chairman of a mass meeting being held next door at Westminster Hall. With other members of the committee and with a large number of Westminster inhabitants he marched to the Hall as a member of a procession behind a large banner, 'Annual Parliaments and Equal Representation'. From 3000 to 6000 people were said to be present, to whom Fox had much to say about the extravagance of the Government.

[1] *HMCR*, Abergavenny MSS., p. 29. April 10.
[2] Fortescue, iii, 419–20, dated by the editor [? 16 February, 1777], but attributed by *History of Parliament*, i, 532, to the April 6 division. Majority and minority division lists of April 6 appear in *Parliamentary Register*, series i, xvii, 474–85; *Parliamentary History*, xxi, 368–74.

A handbill signed by Fox as chairman set forth the aims of the projected Westminster Association. Its preamble listed such grievances as curtailed income and increased taxes, plus the alarming extent in the influence of the Crown. Its proposition was that a just redress of grievances could only be expected from a free and uncorrupted Parliament. Reforms should consist of: a shorter duration of Parliament, in fact, annual parliaments; the addition of 100 members to be chosen in proportion to the population of the various English counties; strict and rigid frugality in every department of the Government. It called for an end to the war with America, partly to make possible a united, vigorous, and firm effort against France and Spain. It invited all tax-paying residents of Westminster to join the association, and pledged its efforts to elect Fox at the next general election.[1]

Fox's motions were adopted by all present. 'One who held up hand and basket against Fox's motion was knocked down and trampled upon in a cruel manner', commented the *Morning Post*, which went on to declare the crowd consisted of the lowest dregs of the mob—people that disgraced the very idea of freeholders. 'When the hands were held up, such a number of dirty fists never before appeared in that place.'

Dirty fists and chosen representatives alike were on the march. Endorsing Fox as chairman, the Westminster Hall assemblage organized an association similar to that of York. On April 10 Fox reported to the Kent committee that such an association had been formed, and in his letter enclosed copies of the Dunning resolutions. He further told Kent: 'I think there is little or no doubt of our obtaining our object; but if we are lulled into security by success, it is but too probable that the representatives of the people may relapse into their former inattention to their constituents.'[2]

Yet even with this defeat North found himself still in office. Because of Mr Speaker's illness, a ten-day adjournment was agreed to. Both sides accused each other of stalling but the King was able to make better use of the time than was the Opposition. On April 24 Dunning moved that the session should not be disbanded until the influence of the Crown had been diminished and the other abuses complained of by the people had been corrected.

Fox found it necessary to defend the motives of members of the Opposition. Throughout the war he had found himself unpopular with large segments of the British public. He had been labelled as an enemy

---

[1] Handbill dated April 6, 1780, PWF 3968, Department of MSS. (Nottingham).
[2] Rockingham correspondence, R1–1890. (Sheffield.) Fox's activities as chairman of the Westminster committee are described in Christie, pp. 83–4; Black, pp. 58–61; Butterfield, pp. 269–83.

to the welfare of England. He and his colleagues were scornfully called Americans, Frenchmen, Spaniards, Dutchmen—anything but Englishmen. Arguments against Government policy made Government followers think of sedition, treason, hanging. Now the lines were being sternly drawn, with patriots on one side and men of sinister motives on the other. To recall the minds of his listeners to the victory of April 6 he read again the resolutions passed that day, but he could sense that a reaction was setting in. At the division the vote was 254 to 203 for the ministers, a substantial reversal of the vote eighteen days previously. Some of the independent members felt that the motion invaded the prerogative of the King, and although they were willing to support the abstract motion of April 6, they were not willing to implement it. Forty who voted with opposition now deserted it, 16 voting with the Government and 24 abstaining.[1] The division over, a number of the opposition began to leave; Fox, noticing their departure, declared that he never felt himself so 'hurt, mortified, and filled with indignant resentment,' and continued by saying that he had been taken in, deluded, and imposed on. It was North's turn to smile—and Fox, irritated, declared that he would make one more trial, and if that failed, quit the House altogether. North calmly advised Fox not to be rash and hasty; some day, he promised, he might again find himself in a majority. This time, instead of stamping out of the Chamber, he pulled himself together enough to modify statements and retract threats.

Although the Dunning motion had temporarily jolted the Government, the Dunning forces could not follow their advantage, and the North administration hung on. It also encountered other problems: the Dutch had not only failed to provide military assistance to Britain in her war with Spain, as required by treaty, but continued to furnish war supplies and other needed goods to France; the Russians, instead of intervening in the war on the British side, were becoming increasingly sympathetic to the Dutch and to other neutrals.

The sweetest music to a speaker's ears is the applause of his audience. The most enchanting view is a roomful of attentive and appreciative faces. The most satisfying reflection, as Fox himself would have put it, is to feel that he has the audience with him. The right to speak one's mind, to be heard out, is a precious heritage. Even when listeners seem to be disagreeing with the speaker, he knows that they may need to contend with the argument, to rise to it, to wrestle with it in their consciences.

[1] Ian R. Christie, *The End of North's Ministry, 1780–1782* (London, 1958), p. 22.

The art of speaking exists in time rather than in space. The full weight of the speaker lives only in the memories of those who hear him. But every passing day makes memory a little dimmer, a little less certain. Words may be repeated afterwards and even set down in print, but they can supply only a part of the whole. To read a speech without a lively imagination of speaker, audience, and occasion, is like reading a play without holding in the mind the way it can be staged and acted.

The vast bulk of the speeches uttered in St Stephen's Chapel died as fast as they were born. The speaker rose to his legs, spoke, sat down. When the night's debate was over, much of what was said was already forgotten; little would be noted or long remembered. Yet not everything was irrecoverable; observations would be committed to diaries, journals, letters. Printers would also seize their fragments, to appear in type the next day. Hence even a few sentences in a *Chronicle* or an *Advertiser*, or in a listener's diary, do something to identify the better speeches. Even when the testimony is conflicting, the critic of speech-making can construct a background into which to set the speaker's utterance and arrive at judgments that appraise its quality.

Englishmen realized that they were living in one of the distinguished periods of parliamentary oratory. Newspapers observed that the parliamentary speaking of the day, like everything else, was superior to what had gone before. The current speakers 'have more splendour than their fathers', and even 'the lower order of speakers' was free from 'minutiae and vulgarities'. The informed person was keenly interested not only in issues but also in the manner of speaking. Exceptionally good speaking was praised, atrociously bad speaking was condemned, mannerisms and habits were smiled at. A pamphlet, *Anticipation*, had appeared in 1778, just before the session opened, and went through six reprintings in two weeks. Its parodies of the styles of prominent speakers—the boring, the dull, the repetitive, the pompous—were eagerly read and quoted. It contained the favourite topics and the pat phrases. It commented on Temple Luttrell's excessive display of learning, for example, and on Fox's excessive rapidity of utterance. Another pamphlet, *Remarks on the Members of the House of Commons*, 1780, teamed remarks about speaking with observations about habits of voting. One member was described as 'a tedious bad speaker'; others were advised only to vote and not to speak. The *Public Ledger* in 1779 had printed these and other criticisms of parliamentary debating; and most newspapers at irregular intervals offered paragraphs or profiles about leading speakers.

Fox had entered the House of Commons at a time when newspapers were becoming increasingly concerned about the discussion of public issues. In Chatham's day, by contrast, publishers reported the customary address from the throne, but little else of a parliamentary nature; their concern was with local happenings, movements of ships, commercial events, foreign dispatches. By Fox's time they had begun to report Bills before Parliament; to mention specific motions; to summarize debates; to comment on the talents or lack of talents of individuals. Newspapers did not have the space to give one or two full pages each issue to texts of the debates, nor did they attempt to analyse argument in detail, as did British dailies in the following century when editors like McCarthy, Morley, Delane, and a host of others offered comment and appraisal. But as the eighteenth century wore on, newspapers improved steadily. Their readership was significant: one source estimated that 25,000 copies were printed daily in 1782, and that each copy had ten readers.[1]

Fox was a favourite topic. From his first years in Parliament until the last, he was praised, commended, exalted, criticized, ridiculed, deplored, condemned. Almost none of his contemporaries received as much space.

In June came the Gordon riots. The story of this city-wide outbreak has been told many times and need not be repeated in detail. Basically the disturbance started as an expression of anti-Catholic sentiment. At the last session the House had passed an Act to relieve Catholics of certain restrictions. This liberal and long-needed move nevertheless proved highly unpopular with the Protestant community. After a preliminary meeting to seek ways to repeal the act, 50,000 to 60,000 people met in St George's Fields, under the leadership of the eccentric Lord George Gordon, and marched to Parliament to present their petitions. On its way the mob showed signs of unruliness; later, not getting satisfaction from the House of Commons, it got out of hand altogether. Prisoners were set free at Newgate Prison and elsewhere, ironmongers' shops were forcibly entered and iron crowbars confiscated, wine cellars were forced open and liquor carried away in hats and pails, Catholic schools were destroyed, the stores of merchants, druggists, tea-dealers, and pawnbrokers fired and gutted. At one interval fourteen fires blazed in different parts of the city. Not until the King called out the militia was order restored; six regimental companies were encamped in Hyde Park, and all in all it took 15,000 armed men to put down the riots.

Fox and Burke both deplored the mob; Fox declared the violence shown would degrade the nation in the eyes of Europe, since the men

[1] Dennis O'Bryen to Fox, March 1782, Burke MSS., Sheffield Central Library, 1211/1056. See also A. Aspinall, *Politics and the Press, c. 1780–1850* (London, 1949), pp. 6–7.

at the head of administration would be shown to be incapable of governing the affairs of a state.[1] Eventually Gordon was acquitted of charges of treason by virtue of Thomas Erskine's inspired defence, on the principle that treason did not consist of the deed but of the intent. Others, however, were less fortunate. Walpole noted that twenty-five were executed, of whom seventeen were under eighteen, and three not quite fifteen; two were young women.[2] One effect of the riots was to strengthen the Government. Dr Johnson's observation was as wise as anyone's: 'The late Riots have done for the Ministry what the Rebellion did for the house of Hanover; established their Authority and made their Government popular.' Anything critical that is uttered now, he continued, will bring 'a Mob to rule over us'.[3]

Another effect of the riots was to subdue the activities of county associations. Since one mass meeting had got out of control and had torn up the city, so might another. The most disastrous result of all was that the King and the conservative element learned too much from the disturbance, like Mark Twain's cat, who had the bad judgment to sit on a hot stove lid and thereupon determined never to sit on another. Trouble was, she never again sat on a cold one, either. The King, having borne the brunt and felt the heat, never forgot the experience. A decade and a half later, when the people were fighting to maintain the right of free assembly, he recalled the Gordon riots and encouraged his ministers to enact harsh legislation policing and regulating public meetings.

County association activities, however, had introduced Fox to the masses. From 1780 onward to the end of his career his voice was continually heard outside the walls of Parliament. He became, in fact, a spokesman for the people.

---

[1] *St. James's Chronicle*, June 6–8. [2] *Last Journals*, ii, 327. August 9.
[3] Katharine C. Balderston, ed., *Thraliana* (Oxford, 1951), i, 450.

10

The Opposition Triumphs
1780-1782

> I saw Charles today in a new hat, frock, waistcoat, shirt,
> and stockings; he was as clean and smug as a gentleman,
> and upon perceiving my surprize, he told me it was from
> the Pharo Bank.
>
> *George Selwyn*

The fourteenth Parliament, elected in 1774, was suddenly dissolved
September 1, 1780, more than a year short of its seven-year term. The
news was 'like a thunder clap', said the *Annual Register*, 'on those who
were not in the secret'. Negotiations to strengthen the North administration by bringing in members from the opposition had fizzled out in
July; the King was convinced that acquisitions from that pool of talent
would not support his measures. Richmond and Fox had 'dipped themselves' by their strange views on short parliaments and methods of
election; Fox might be admitted to a 'lucrative, not Ministerial Office',
provided he would support the Government: 'He never having had
any principle can certainly act as his Interest may guide him.'[1] By
August plans were under way for a dissolution.

Like modern political chieftains, the Government charted its proposed course with the help of polls as well as with conjecture and
surmise. In an extraordinary document filling forty-nine pages of a
notebook, the industrious John Robinson compiled a list of members of
the Commons, checking them as *pro, hopeful, doubtful*, or *con*, adding
notes here and there about individual political leanings. The pros and
hopefuls added up to 309; the doubtfuls and cons totalled 249; thus
Robinson analysed the Parliament about to be dissolved. Projecting
the results of an election, he estimated that Government strength
would reach 343 and opposition 215, a majority of 128 in the new
Parliament as against 60 in the old. This reckoning further encouraged the ministers to recommend a dissolution and a general
election.[2]

Fox, of course, chosen in February as a candidate for populous

---

[1] Fortescue, v, 95–7. To North, July 3, 1780.
[2] Christie, *The End of North's Ministry*, pp. 34–8. Indispensable for its analysis of the
membership of the new house and for its insight into issues confronting the ministry in its
closing two years.

Westminster, had to get his campaign under way on short notice. The Government prepared to support the incumbent, Lord Lincoln, and also Admiral George Rodney, expected to win easily because of his personal popularity even though absent on duty in the West Indies. 'If Mr Fox stands we shall have much trouble and more expense', wrote North to Robinson.[1] His observation was entirely correct; as Burke wrote later; 'It is no triffle to keep out such a Man as Fox.'[2] Fox's devoted aunt Sarah thought that the Government would rather lose twenty other elections than fail to win this one.[3] Fox was active from the outset; the Reverend Dr. Warner, who kept George Selwyn informed about Fox's progress, wrote optimistically: 'Charles Fox is going on at a great rate, we hear, in Covent Garden, and many people really think he will carry his election.'[4]

The election opened with a public meeting at which Lincoln, Rodney, and Fox were nominated. Neither of the other two candidates opposed Rodney; each sought to be elected with him. Fox in a half-hour speech opened his attack against Lincoln by reminding his listeners that Lincoln's father, the Duke of Newcastle, enjoyed a lucrative office under the Government. Speakers for the other side exhumed the old charge that Fox's father was a public defaulter who had plundered the country. One voter thought it hardly necessary to charge Fox with this original sin, since he had so many more of his own to answer for. Eventually came the time for the show of hands for each candidate; the high bailiff interpreted the result in favour of Rodney and Lincoln, but Fox's friends insisted that he had a majority of the votes, so after some altercation the poll was formally opened with all three candidates listed. At the end of the first day the poll books showed Fox 296, Rodney 243, and Lincoln 160.[5] The observant Warner wrote: 'Charles Fox keeps us all alive here, with letters and paragraphs, and a thousand clever things. I saw him today upon the hustings, bowing and sweltering and scratching his black ass.'[6]

So the beginning was auspicious although Fox was by no means in

---

[1] *HMCR*, Abergavenny MSS., p. 33. August 13. The Government spent £8,000 on the election expenses of Lincoln and Rodney (*Correspondence of Edmund Burke*, iv, 282).

[2] *Correspondence of Edmund Burke*, iv, 300. To the Marchioness of Rockingham, September 27.

[3] *Life and Letters of Lady Sarah Lennox*, i, 304.

[4] John Heneage Jesse, *George Selwyn and His Contemporaries* (Boston, n.d.), iv, 376, 380. To assure his election, Fox arranged to come in for Bridgwater; as matters turned out, however, partly because he did not appear personally to campaign, he ran a poor fourth (T. Bruce Dilks, *Charles James Fox and the Borough of Bridgwater* [Bridgwater, 1937], p. 16).

[5] *Public Advertiser, Daily Advertiser.*

[6] Sheridan put the thought in other language: 'He canvasses with the greatest industry and treats his good Friends with a Speech every Day besides' (Cecil Price ed., *Letters of Richard Brinsley Sheridan* (Oxford, 1966), i, 135–6).

the clear. He faced all the problems of a candidate running for popular office. Westminster contained an estimated 12,000 voters; Malmesbury, by contrast, which he had previously represented, had only 13.[1] Listeners in his audiences asked all sorts of embarrassing questions: how could he explain his speeches in favour of relaxing the laws against Catholics? The Gordon riots had emphasized only that spring that anti-Catholic feeling was strong. With Fox, however, religious freedom was a basic tenet, so when a questioner publicly demanded that Fox declare whether he would endeavour to secure the repeal of the 'popish Bill', the questioner adding that his vote hinged on the answer, Fox flatly told him: 'I will not'.

Here was a sensitive issue which might bring defeat, and as the questions continued, Fox found it necessary to publish a reply in the columns of the newspapers. He thereupon prepared a carefully-worded statement: 'I never have supported nor ever will support any measure prejudicial to the Protestant Religion, or tending to *establish* Popery in this Kingdom', he wrote. Thus his position, more cautiously formulated, was designed to retrieve Protestant support that might be slipping. His conscience bothered him, however, and he described his political dilemma to Burke: 'If any one were to think that I had given up in the smallest degree the great cause of Toleration for the sake of a point of my own I should be the most miserable man in the world. . . . Pray judge me severely and say whether I have done wrong.' The voter's question and his own answer would appear in the papers that evening, 'and will certainly do me some mischief but I trust I am strong enough now to bear it'.[2] The Government, he continued, was publishing handbills and filling papers with abuse 'upon this Popery subject'. Hence in his first public campaign Fox learned something of the art of threading one's way through a complex issue. In the main he kept his record on religious toleration consistent.

On September 15 at the close of the polls several persons made an attempt to seize the poll books—by no means an unusual procedure. The crowds became riotous, the attempt was prevented, and three plotters apprehended and taken before a magistrate. This incident speaks in favour of Rodney and Fox, as winners do not try to destroy the evidence, but the totals at the close of the next polling day spoke even louder: Rodney 4,594, Fox 4,223, Lincoln 3,460. As the election progressed Fox continued to gain. He trudged from door to door early and late. He was indefatigable in writing to friends and in enlisting support wherever he could find it. He sought to have men of quality appear in his behalf in order to show that his support included the better

---

[1] *History of Parliament*, i, 335, 417.
[2] *Correspondence of Edmund Burke*, iv, 282–4. September 15.

sort as well as the middling sort. [1] By September 19 the loyalist exile, Samuel Curwen, could observe that the market was crowded with the mob huzzaing for Fox. [2]

September 20 papers carried the tidings that Rodney had driven the French and Spanish out of the Caribbean; this news subtracted nothing from the support of the worthy admiral. The polls closed on September 23, the total being: Rodney 5,298, Fox 4,878, Lincoln 4,157. The high bailiff declared Rodney and Fox duly elected, but the defeated and unhappy Lincoln, no doubt prompted by the Government, ordered a scrutiny, a recount of the votes, which was scheduled to begin on October 10.

The jubilant voters were not, however, to be denied their celebration. Amidst cheering and shouting they pulled down the hustings, carried off the timbers, and hustled the victorious candidates, Fox and Admiral Young, proxy for Rodney, into chairs, carrying them through the principal streets of Westminster to the great whig homes and back to Covent Garden. Next day Fitzpatrick wrote his brother: 'Charles is pretty much knocked up, he was yesterday carried triumphantly through the whole town.'[3] Fox took space in prominent papers to advertise his thanks—he should ever entertain the highest sense of the honour the electors had conferred on him, and endeavour to merit the confidence they had reposed by acting uniformly for their welfare and prosperity. The *London Evening Post* added to the universal excitement when it reported that Fox had been killed or at least dangerously wounded in a duel with Lincoln, but the *London Courant* happily spiked the rumour when it declared that not the slightest foundation existed for such a report, but that on the contrary Mr Fox was in perfect health, ready and willing to exert his distinguished talents and uncommon powers to preserve what remained of England's greatness.

Lincoln meanwhile decided to abandon the scrutiny. Instead, on that October 10, the day it was to open, the high bailiff returned Rodney and Fox as duly elected representatives of Westminster. October 10 became a date that was to be celebrated for generations as a milestone in the history of man's quest for freedom.

No need now to come in for Bridgwater or any other controlled borough. Charles Fox, the Man of the People, was Member of Parliament from Westminster; this constituency he served, with a minor interruption, to the end of his career.

---

[1] Cf. Fox to Ossory, Add. MSS. 47579, September 4, 1780; *Fox Cor.*, i, 257; *HMCR*, Rutland MSS., iii, 35. September 14.
[2] *Journal and Letters of the Late Samuel Curwen* (London, 1842), p. 277.
[3] Add. MSS. 47579. *Fox Cor.*, i, 258. September 29. Fitzpatrick added that Admiral Young thought Rodney's victory was more the result of Fox's support than of the Government's.

The new Parliament convened November 1 to hear the King's message about American politics. The war against the Colonies looked brighter, he could report; British arms had met signal success in the provinces of Georgia and Carolina. Indeed the situation was immensely better than at the time of Saratoga. But the King also noted an unprovoked attack of France and Spain upon his dominions.

Fox's reply to the King's message was lively, provocative, and entertaining, rather than brilliant. As for the American war, he with more irony than reason belittled the British successes in the southern colonies. What Fox proposed was to withdraw the troops from America, a step that undoubtedly would be followed by American independence (Fox was one of the first to express this sentiment), and turn the arms of this country solely against the House of Bourbon.

Invectives flowed freely in that debate as they did in many. Fox was less than charitable when he recalled, in Germain's presence, how that gentleman had been publicly degraded in the last war before every regiment in the army, as being incapable of serving again in any military capacity. Germain rose to denounce such personal abuse and to defend the country's military posture; Admiral Keppel followed to deplore the military situation and denounce his old foe, Palliser. Then came the division: 212 for the Government, 130 against it. Said the King: '. . . very proper.' Philip Yorke, a new member who voted that day with the Government, was nevertheless highly impressed by Fox. calling him 'astonishingly great'. He continued: 'It is impossible to hear more true wit or more pointed raillery . . . with so much fluency and elegance of language.'[1]

In the new House Fox could point to a growing circle of personal friends and followers. Moreover, the Rockingham group included three speakers that can be numbered in the front rank of talent that has been produced in the Anglo-Saxon world. Fox and Burke were now veteran parliamentarians; Sheridan, a recruit whose name was already written next to Shakespeare's as a comic dramatist, speedily joined this distinctive band of debaters.

Parliamentarians, like college students, drift home for the holidays before the recess begins; so, as usual, attendance at the late November and December sessions was slack. Fox found himself losing not only votes but also colleagues to help with the debating. The defections from his slender team were in fact so marked that he felt himself personally obliged to speak on every question and in every debate. Thus eventful 1780 had momentarily presented him and his colleagues with a majority vote but not with enough sustained support to put them in office. What on April 6 had looked like the beginning of the end, eight

[1] Add. MSS. 35379, 246 ff. Hardwicke MSS. To his uncle, Lord Hardwicke, November 7.

months later scarcely seemed, in the Churchillian phrase, the end of the beginning.

Nathaniel William Wraxall, a new member in that Parliament, faithful keeper of diaries and journals, has recorded an excellent description of Fox of 1781:

His features, in themselves dark, harsh, and saturnine, like those of Charles II, from whom he descended in the maternal line, derived a sort of majesty from the addition of two black and shaggy eyebrows, which sometimes concealed, but more frequently developed, the workings of his mind. Even these features, however, did not readily assume the expression of anger or of enmity. They frequently and naturally relaxed into a smile, the effect of which became irresistible, because it appeared to be the index of a benevolent and complacent disposition. His figure, broad, heavy, and inclined to corpulency, appeared destitute of elegance or grace, except the portion conferred on it by the emanations of intellect, which at times diffused over his whole person, when he was speaking, the most impassioned animation.

In 1781, Wraxall continued, Fox usually wore a blue frock-coat and an old and worn buff waistcoat, the colours worn by American troops. He sat on the opposition side of the House in the third row, close to a pillar and near the Speaker's chair; not until the beginning of 1783 did he move to the front bench.[1]

After the Christmas recess Parliament undertook the major business of the session. On December 20 the Government had issued a manifesto breaking diplomatic relations with Holland, and in the House on January 25 offered a list of complaints: the Dutch had not given Britain the least assistance despite treaty obligations; they had, on the other hand, facilitated 'the carriage of naval stores to France'; moreover they had suffered American privateer John Paul Jones to enjoy the hospitality of their ports. Meanwhile behind the scenes the Russian Empress was developing an alliance, the Armed Neutrality, hopefully to include the Dutch, to transport under a neutral flag enemy goods, unless specifically defined as contraband by treaty between the neutral and the blockading power.[2] The net result of such an alliance would be to lessen the effectiveness of Britain's blockade against her enemies. The Government did not reveal the whole story in the January 25 debates but was nevertheless able to beat down an amendment by a vote of 180 to 101, and so the Commons agreed to support hostile measures against a third continental enemy.

[1] Wraxall, ii, 1–3.   [2] Christie, pp. 243 ff.

Meanwhile, Robinson was compiling a new estimate of the potential strength of the Government. Whereas before the election he had predicted 343 favourable and 215 opposed, a majority of 128, on February 14 he estimated administration's top strength at 260 and opposition's almost the same.[1] This estimate was grim indeed. The most hopeful outlook now showed him that his pre-election estimates were about 100 too high. As a device to improve the Government's working majority, the general election was 'clearly a failure'.[2]

Looking forward to a fuller attendance, opposition decided that its best chance of overturning the Government was on the issue of economical reform, and obtained leave for Burke to bring in a motion on February 15.[3] On the outside some were willing to wager that Burke's Bill would be thrown out by at least 30 votes, 'so certain are the ministry of carrying everything before them, and so steady are their dependants, that they have only to count noses, and set themselves down contented'.[4] Fox did not speak in the debate, though in addition to Burke Opposition orators included Sheridan and particularly twenty-two-year-old William Pitt, whose maiden speech that day was declared by North to be the best first speech ever heard. The debate also featured copious discussion on the Government side, and the division was 233 to 190 against Burke's proposals. The Bill 'having been negatived by So great a Majority has as Lord North can easily imagine given Me much pleasure', wrote the King.[5]

What Burke and the whigs had hoped to do through the proposed Bills for economical reform was to capitalize upon the popularity of the measure, their small successes in the last Parliament, and the victory achieved when 233 persons plus tellers had voted that the influence of the Crown has increased, is increasing, and ought to be diminished. This formula had proved winning and should be exploited further. In his speech Burke therefore had the famous motion read again, urging in persuasive language that if members agreed in general that the influence of the Crown should be diminished, they should support his specific measures through which sixty members of Parliament would be separated from the Crown's tempting. On this and other proposals, however, opposition could not put together as many as 200 votes. The greatest service it did the nation in these debates was perhaps to introduce the earnest and gifted Pitt, whose eloquent address not only reminded members of his distinguished father but gave them a chance to appraise him as a potential parliamentary leader.

---

[1] *Ibid.*, p. 253. [2] *Ibid.*, pp. 161–2.
[3] Burke and his friends discussed in advance the arrangement of some of the clauses in the speech (*Correspondence of Edmund Burke*, iv, 336).
[4] *Aurora*, February 27. [5] Fortescue, v, 199. February 27.

Fox had never participated actively in the debates on economic reform other than on the clause proposing to abolish the office held by Germain as third Secretary of State. The proposals to do away with lesser offices and to regulate the payment of pensions did not arouse his enthusiasm. On May 30, however, opposition turned to a more central issue when David Hartley offered a motion to restore peace to America. The real reason, Fox declared, that the ministers continued the American war was that it kept them in power. He imitated North at an imaginary levee, persuading a follower to continue his support:

Without the American war I shall have no places, no emoluments to bestow, not a single loan to negotiate, nor shall I even be able to retain this poor situation of mine that I have thus long held most disinterestedly. . . . Make peace with America to-day, and to-morrow I shall be reduced to the level of private life. . . . If you do not vote with me . . . against a peace with America, how am I to give you any thing?

This language was not good argument nor good senatorial oratory, but it was not dull; and he had much more to say in this ironical vein. He declared further that the American war would never end while the present system continued: 'The moment that system should be changed, the good of both countries would be consulted.' The American war was as unjust in its principle and as absurd in its prosecution as it would be ruinous in its consequences. It was a speech filled with ridicule and sarcasm. It took North's argument, turned it inside out, and crammed it down his throat. Germain attempted a reply, observing that if peace could not be obtained without admitting American independence, 'he for one would forego the blessings of peace, rather than give his vote for so degrading a concession'.[1] So there were men determined to withhold independence until the bitter end. A small house participated in the division: 72 supporters voted for Hartley's motion, 106 against it.

Were Fox a man of lesser physical energy, he would have found the duties of a parliamentary session fully satisfying. In addition, however, he participated abundantly in the social life of the capital. Dinner and theatre parties he attended in abundance. He was a delightful host at small occasions or at gala functions. At one of his levees a reported thousand people were present, including the proudest names in the kingdom. Although he was an aristocrat, he kept the friendly touch. He conversed as easily with servants or tradesmen as with distinguished visitors from other countries. He was a man worth knowing; aside from his personal charm he might one day be the head of state.

Most of his off-duty hours, however, were spent in the company of

[1] *Parliamentary History*, xxii, 336–57.

his gaming associates. From St Stephen's he would go, even late after midnight, to Brooks's or some other club. About this time the old game of faro was revived, and Fox, not content merely to be a player, started a faro bank at Brooks's. As banker—operator of the game—he met the final qualification needed for the title of professional gambler. Hence we have the spectacle of the friend of America, advocate of parliamentary reform, pleader for religious toleration, leading candidate of opposition for the highest office of the land, presiding over a faro table, paying off successful winners, raking in the guineas of the losers.

The obsessive and compulsive character of Fox's gambling is shown in a statement attributed to him: that life's greatest pleasure was to win and its next greatest pleasure was to lose. Fox might have accumulated a fortune had he continued as a banker at faro or kept to games of skill like whist, but his passion for games of chance took him into situations where often he rose a heavy loser. Boswell once declared that losing at cards had a melancholy effect on him, like a Presbyterian sermon; Wilberforce gambled for a while but eventually limited his losings to £50 a sitting; Pitt was fascinated by the pastime but abandoned it when he realized it was taking too much of his time; Gibbon played shilling whist; but Fox kept on and on. Moreover, he could enjoy playing only when the stakes were high. At his own bank bets often exceeded a thousand pounds.

This season Fox's bank proved highly lucrative. Fox, Walpole declared, was the hero in Parliament, at the gaming table, at Newmarket. 'Last week he passed twenty-four hours without interruption at all three.'[1] Selwyn wrote to Carlisle that Fox's bank 'swallows up everybody's cash that comes to Brooks's'. Faro, horse racing, and debate were easily mixed, as Storer's note observed: 'He bought last week Truth, a racehorse . . . he would not own what he gave for it, so most probably it was for [a] sum of which he was rather ashamed. He comes up tomorrow for the business in the House of Commons.' 'I never see him,' Selwyn wrote to Carlisle, 'but with heaps of gold before him.'[2]

Fox had a bad day in May when his creditors, hearing of his profits—rumours put the figure at £40,000—demanded that he pay his debts. Some creditors were paid but one who was not seized Fox's property and for two days hauled away goods, clothes, books, and pictures. Fox's library went at auction; a notation he had made in a book by Gibbon was so prized that it sold for three guineas. Selwyn reported later that Charles should have kept his books at Brooks's, where they would have been forever unmolested. He computed the

[1] *Fox Cor.*, i, 264. To Sir Horace Mann, May 17.
[2] *HMCR*, Carlisle MSS., pp. 480, 511. May 7, June 30.

bank's profits at £30,000, but that fall his winnings were for a time more than £70,000.[1] In a short time, however, the man of Brooks's, as some called him, had lost it all and was again in debt.[2]

How difficult it is to appraise the staggering dimensions of Fox's finances. Fox would win or lose a thousand pounds on the turn of a single card, and after an active evening could count his wins or losses in fives or tens of thousands. Yet it was said that even with £5,000 a year a man of station and refinement could do all that might be expected of him. And only the wealthiest men in the kingdom could point to an annual income of more than £50,000. In America a century and a quarter later the New World declared in its own lusty language that a man with a million a year could get along as well as if he were rich. Although there were no million-a-year incomes in 1781, either in dollars or sterling, Fox can be said to have won and lost on what the next century would call the millionaire scale.

On June 12 Fox, shuttling between St Brooks's and St Stephen's, once more retraced the leading events in the American war to a jammed and crowded House. He held in his hand a recent copy of the *London Gazette*, in which Cornwallis had analysed the difficulties of the North Carolina campaign that had culminated in a costly victory at Guilford Court House. The logistics of continuing the war, Fox pointed out, basing his argument on Cornwallis's report, were insurmountable; difficulties included 'the obstacles of rivers, of a deep intersected country, of impassable marshes, of a disaffected people, of "timid friends, and of inveterate enemies".'

Burgoyne at Bennington, Howe at Long Island, and now Cornwallis at Guilford, Fox went on, had found Americans unconquerable. Successively Britain had fought the colonists in Massachusetts, New York, and Pennsylvania, and had then decided that the southern colonies were the vulnerable place for an attack. Now the south was being forsaken and the only colonies left in which to attempt campaigns were Virginia and New Hampshire. He therefore moved that the House resolve itself into a committee to consider the present state of the American war.

Fox's arguments were supported and attacked by several, and after long debate, the question was loudly called for. At this juncture young

---

[1] See also *Correspondence of Edmund Burke*, iv, 377.

[2] Col. Edward Smith wrote to William Eden: 'There has been a bank kept in the gambling houses here by Chas. Fox &c &c by which they had cleared above seventy thousand pounds, but Chas. is again totally set down at the last New Markett meeting and he is thirty thousand worse than vulgarly call'd nothing' (*B. F. Stevens's Facsimiles*, no. 749). November 23. *HMCR*, Auckland MSS., i, 320.

Pitt rose and the House, as it had often done for Fox, quieted at once. The war, said Pitt, as if drawing copiously from Bailey's *Dictionary*, was accursed, wicked, barbarous, cruel, unnatural, unjust, and diabolical. It was also marked with 'injustice . . . blood, slaughter, persecution, and devastation . . . moral depravity . . . mischief . . . destruction'. Two speeches later the Government benches became vociferous in their calls of 'Question! Question!' and at this moment Fox rose to make a second contribution to the debate. It was some minutes before the Speaker could restore order, but Fox proceeded, chiefly to answer arguments that had been presented that evening and to reaffirm his own steadfast opposition to the war before and since the Boston port Bill.[1]

The season was late and attendance thinner, many of the opposition having departed; so the 'fair, impartial, and unprejudiced judgment of the House' expressed itself in favour of the ministers, 172 to 99. The friendly *London Courant* said: 'Mr Fox daily rises in public estimation. His arguments against the nefarious American war were unanswered and unanswerable.' Later it tendered him one of the supreme compliments of the day, saying his abilities were not inferior to those of Chatham. The *Public Advertiser*, still calling him Charles Tod, spoke of his sound and convincing arguments.

In June came an opportunity for Fox to revive a favourite topic, the Marriage Act, when he moved for leave to bring in a Bill to amend the current statute. His speech was well received and widely printed. In it he urged the natural right of couples to be legally wed, parental consent or no, when the man was at least eighteen and the woman sixteen. He painted two contrasting word-pictures: one of a young couple that fell in love, married, and established, through affection and industry, a home; the other couple, too young to wed and unable to secure parental consent, nevertheless entering into a connection, 'in which there is more of indiscretion than of guilt', that ended in the prosecution of the man, and disgrace and a possible career of prostitution for the woman. Neither did he like the provision of the old law that made annulment possible, resulting in illegal wedlock and illegitimate children. He spoke persuasively and eloquently. The *Morning Herald* thought the speech the principal reason for the majority. The *St James's Chronicle* called it an admirable speech 'which brought over a large party to his side, and left Lord North in a minority'. The *Whitehall Evening Post* was among those that described his 'great earnestness' and 'stile equal to any thing we remember ever to have heard from this celebrated speaker'.

Fox's own love life was assorted and various. The newspapers con-

[1] *Parliamentary History*, xxii, 435–516.

tinued to report the doings of Perdita Robinson, long-ago favourite of Fox and the prince, dashing through Hyde Park in a new phaeton with four chestnut ponies and servants liveried in blue and silver. Often she was in the company of one Mrs A, sometimes named more fully as Mrs A——d, finally to be revealed as Mrs Armistead, who in her turn had also come to a parting of the ways with the prince. Mrs Robinson and Mrs Armistead will enter these chapters later. But back to Fox's Bill: it passed the Commons but was rejected in the Lords on the second reading. In July the first session of the new Parliament was recessed.

Fox's role as man of the people brought him under the continued fire of the Government press. He was vulnerable because his new interest in petitions, annual parliaments, and popular opinion generally completely reversed the sentiments he had expressed ten years earlier. He was further exposed because his fondness for gambling, though partly explainable by eighteenth-century standards, was still several notches below the kind of conduct that his admirers in their better moments had a right to expect. The shadow of his father's unpopularity, moreover, hung over him. Just as Fox could attack the Government through its past misdeeds, ministers like Germain through their personal shortcomings, and Lord Lincoln through his father, newspapers, playing the same game, could attack him. Thus the *Morning Herald*:

Mr Fox, in one of his patriotic speeches, contended, that the *voice of the people* never was wrong—this was some time after the mob in Covent Garden bawled out, 'Fox, for ever!' But in the debate of Monday last, Mr Fox laboured to prove, that the *voice of the people* was not always right, for they, *una voce*, called for his father's head on Temple Bar, as a public defaulter, when Mr Fox knew his lordship to be one of the *most virtuous*, innocent, honest, and fairest accomptants in the world ! ! ![1]

Here the paragrapher—possibly the editor himself, or a contributor who tossed the missive over the transom—reflected upon two favourite themes; *primus*, that Fox had declared that the only true voice of the people was in Parliament, not outdoors; *secundus*, that Fox was the scion of a plunderer so well known that he could be labelled 'public defaulter' with no other identification necessary.

The London press liked frequently to offer profiles of eminent personages. Then as now, news about personalities was highly readable. So occasionally readers could scan a 'Sketch of the Character of Mr CHARLES FOX' like the following:

The torrent of argument comes rolling from him with irresistible force. He does not leave his hearers to follow; he drives them before him. He is a perfect master

[1] June 15.

of the art of debate; and disguises the sentiments of his opponents with so much dexterity, that it is some time before we perceive the distortion. . . . He is *supposed* to want firmness. He is *said* to be destitute of P—le. . . . His invincible attachment to play makes it impossible for him to possess the confidence of his country; and though his abilities are admired by all, no man wishes him to be employed.[1]

In the last sentence this bitter critic touched Fox at a vulnerable point.

Early in October papers started carrying advertisements that on Wednesday the 10th, at the Shakespeare Tavern, not far from the site of the hustings where Fox had won his first electoral victory, the independent electors of Westminster would meet to celebrate that glorious day of a year ago. Familiar names appeared among the fifteen advertising themselves as stewards—Fitzpatrick, Burke, and Sheridan, to mention three—and the Hon. C. J. Fox was to be in the chair. Six shillings was the price, and reservations in by Monday.

Of vital political import to the whigs, however, as well as to the country, was the disaster that occurred shortly thereafter: the surrender of Cornwallis. How he had taken his troops to Yorktown, how American and French troops laid siege, how the English admiral arriving tardily upon the scene found the mouth of the York river bottled up by the French admiral, how a fatal combination of French and Americans, wind and storm, combined to seal the fate of the defenders, and how the defeated British marched between the long, parallel lines of victorious French and American soldiers to hand over their encased colours, is a familiar story. All this had occurred on October 17, four years to the day after the surrender of Burgoyne; dispatches bearing this news crossed the ocean in the spectacular time of five weeks, were hustled to Germain's office, and carried by him to North. There is an account of North's agitation as he received the news —like a ball in the breast, Germain recounted later—exclaiming, as he paced his flat, 'O God! it is all over'.[2]

A week after news of the surrender arrived, large crowds gathered to see the King on his way to the House of Lords to give the opening address. Many must have thought with Curwen that never did the royal crown seem to rest more heavily upon the royal head.[3] But the King's message did not betray anxiety over the situation. Like the famous horned cattle speech a decade past, it stressed the favourable appearance of affairs in the East Indies and mentioned only briefly that

[1] *Public Advertiser*, June 20; *Morning Herald*, June 21. See Loren Reid, 'Charles Fox and the London Press', *Quarterly Journal of Speech*, xlvii, 4 (December, 1961); reprinted in *Parliamentary Affairs*, xv, 3 (Summer, 1962).
[2] Wraxall, ii, 138–9.　　[3] *Journal and Letters*, p. 327.

'the events of war have been very unfortunate to my arms in Virginia, having ended in the loss of my forces in that province'. The war was to go on as if nothing of moment had happened.

The opening was thus little different from that of any other session. After the address the Commons returned to their own quarters, and, as usual, an administration follower moved that the House tender its thanks. Government speakers declared that the war must continue; though England was in debt, loyal subjects must remember that war is always expensive and a sad necessity; the real cause for the failure of English arms was the perfidy of the French; above all the members of the lower house should be unanimous in their vote of thanks to the King. Fox's reply was long and masterful. It was absurd, he declared, to ask for a unanimous vote—did the gentlemen wish to insult the opposition? He then went into an exposition of the calamities of the American war from the beginning, making especial effort to persuade the country gentlemen that they had been duped:

There was one grand domestic evil, from which all our other evils, foreign and domestic, had sprung. The influence of the crown. To the influence of the crown we must attribute the loss of the army in Virginia; to the influence of the crown we must attribute the loss of the thirteen provinces of America; for it was the influence of the crown in the two Houses of Parliament, that enabled his Majesty's ministers to persevere against the voice of reason, the voice of truth, the voice of the people.[1]

Storer, Fox's Eton schoolmate, wrote that he 'never attended to any speech half so much . . . besides [th]at, I own, he convinced me';[2] Selwyn wrote that 'Charles is for my part the only one I can bear to hear';[3] but the House faithfully determined by 218 to 129 to approve the King's speech. The opposition had not yet fully capitalized upon the disaster at Yorktown.

'Everything that can be said upon this cursed event in America has been said by this time a thousand times,' Carlisle wrote to Selwyn. Yet each party braced itself anew for the debate scheduled for December 12. 'Both sides are sending for their friends . . . ,' Selwyn wrote to Carlisle, 'and from that debate we are to judge of what is intended as to the war in America.'[4]

[1] *Parliamentary History*, xxii, 705.
[2] *HMRC*, Carlisle MSS., p. 542. To Carlisle, December 1.
[3] *Ibid.*, p. 538. 'It is as impossible not to love him,' wrote Selwyn, 'as it is to love his adversary.' But next month Selwyn wrote: 'I wish from the bottom of my heart that he had been a good man . . .; if he had, his line of conduct would have been very different' (p. 550).
[4] *Ibid.*, pp. 544, 546. December 4, 8. 'We on the side of Ministry have received our *privates*, exhorting us to attend' (p. 548. Storer to Carlisle, December 11).

The motion sought to put an end to the war. 'All further attempts,' it declared, 'to reduce the revolted colonies to obedience are contrary to the true interests of this kingdom.' Low point in the debate was touched by one Charles Turner, who opined that the Americans ought to be treated like pointers. 'Who ever heard of breaking a pointer by force? Every body knew the only way was to coax the animal, and intice him to do his duty.' Selwyn wrote that the House expected great absurdity from Turner, and was not disappointed. High point of the debate was North's spirited attack upon the motion: his principal argument focused upon the words 'all further attempts', a statement so general and loose that he hoped the House would never agree to it. Was the nation to abandon all its posts? totally withdraw its troops? Were not some posts desirable if the war against France and Spain was to be carried on? Were Charlestown, Halifax, and New York to be given up? And if any of these posts were to be kept, would they not need to be garrisoned? Were British ships now to be allowed to be insulted and beaten without striking a blow? North's speech was sufficiently effective to hold the waverers in line, and won a supporting speech from Sir Edward Deering, who reminded the House that although sometimes he voted with North and sometimes against him, the minister's speech had that day won his vote.

Fox's brief speech touched only a middle point in the debate. Selwyn said he repeated the same complaints in the same words. Fox declared that North's position would result in a war of posts, describing the difficulties of, for example, maintaining and supporting by sea a garrison of 15,000 in New York. Certainly New York did not have the commanding position of a Gibraltar, and experience had shown the difficulties of maintaining Gibraltar. Fox declared he could 'only judge of the future by a consideration of the past', and the past demonstrated the weakness in the policy of carrying on the war. The division brought encouragement to the opposition: government strength was 220, only two votes more than the last division, whereas opposition gained a flat 50 votes to reach 179.[1]

In 1781 the Admiralty repeated a blunder it had made in 1778, a blunder which had been seized upon by Fox and the whigs so effectively that the Earl of Sandwich had almost lost his political head. In 1778 Admiral Keppel had been sent out to fight a French fleet much larger; in 1781 Admiral Kempenfelt was sent out with twelve ships to intercept a French convoy bound for the West Indies, but the admiral, finding five ships more than he had expected, was forced to retreat. The

[1] *Parliamentary History*, xxii, 802–31.

oversight was especially culpable inasmuch as English ships that he might have taken with him, and thus been able to engage the French, were lying idle. In warfare, as in cards and politics, much can be said for that leader who can discover what his opponents are planning; Sandwich had a short supply of this talent. This last blunder was so glaring that he put himself beyond the help of his friends. The incident, brought to the attention of the House just before the Christmas holidays, furnished a timely issue on which to attack a principal member of the Government.

Not surprisingly, the earl found the holiday season most dismal. Also not surprisingly, Fox headed the inquiry into the ill success of the British navy. He began, on January 24, a two-hour detailed recapitulation of the operations of the navy from 1776 to the present. He had been up all night playing quinze and had the memory of a two-thousand-pound loss at the outer edge of consciousness. Some thought him languid though they did not know the reason why. The precision with which he reported the movements of fleets during those years was nonetheless impressive. He reminded the House that he had once been a subaltern commissioner at the Admiralty and he fully drew upon that experience as he developed his speech. Mainly, however, he emphasized not so much technical points as a review of broad matters of information that, having been previously debated in the chamber, came within the knowledge of those present.[1]

North was forced to assent to the inquiry, assuring the House that Sandwich would be pleased to have one, but he added that any resolution censuring Sandwich would touch the entire administration. On that note the house agreed to Fox's motion. 'Sandwich seems to be abandoned by all persons,' James Hare had written earlier, 'and many members who constantly support the Government declare that they are ready to join in a Vote for his removal.'[2]

On February 7 the committee of the whole House entered into the inquiry. After three hours had been spent by clerks in reading papers that Fox had called for, the debate opened. Fox repeated the naval misfortunes of 1781, making five specific charges, and concluding with the motion that administration had grossly mismanaged naval affairs

---

[1] *Parliamentary History*, xxii, 878–904.

Stephen Crofts sent Lord Rockingham one of Fox's speeches of about this date, calling it 'a masterly performance, but an angel would have no avail in these times'. December 20. Rockingham correspondence, R1–1971 (Sheffield).

[2] *HMCR*, Carlisle MSS., p. 561. To Carlisle, January 1. Hare added that 'it is almost impossible to conceive how bad a figure Government makes in the House of Commons in a debate. [Germain] has lost the only good part of his speaking, his arrogance and presumption, and is now all humility. Lord North is grown very heavy. [Dundas], whenever he speaks, commits some gross indiscretion that does them more harm than good; perhaps this may be his intention.'

that year. By the narrow margin of 205 to 183 the motion was defeated.

Now the battle between Government and Opposition was joined in earnest. The *Public Advertiser* predicted that the next debate would see an even larger assemblage of members than previously—perhaps even larger than the great House that years before had inquired into the conduct of Sir Robert Walpole. Lists of predictable members of the minority were circulated, one forecasting a vote of 225, another of 203. Along with the lists were speculations about the form that the motion of censure would take. Newspapers printed the voting record of all members for the general inspection. On February 20 Fox offered to the House in regular session the same motion he had offered in committee on February 7, so that the resolution would be officially recorded in the journals of the House. At the end of the debate opposition increased its total to 217 but administration its even more to 236, so the motion was defeated by 19 votes. The opposition printed further lists displaying the vote of members on the crucial issue. Behind the scenes, Dundas for some weeks had forcefully urged North to get rid of Germain; North had held back as long as possible because, among other reasons, he knew he would need Germain's information about American affairs as well as his readiness and competence to speak in the bitter debates that lay ahead. Neither, however, could North afford to lose the support of Dundas, also a ready debater, so, making the most of a hard choice, North had dropped Germain by the end of January. This manoeuvre saved him ten to twenty or more votes, thus doubtless making possible his survival of the February 7 and February 20 divisions.[1] Yet before the House adjourned, Opposition notified members that the continuance of the American war itself would next be discussed, so North needed immediately to brace himself for a further thrust.

It came on February 22. The sixty-two-year-old General Henry Conway, friend and cousin of Horace Walpole, one-time Secretary of State, survivor of various continental wars and for forty years a member of the House, rose to move that the American war be no longer pursued. Conway, not ordinarily notable as a speaker, on this day came into his own. 'The effect of his speech,' Walpole proudly reported, 'was incredible.' Later he was said to be completely master of the deliberations of the house on the subject of America.[2] The debate was not excessively long, but the vote was close—by 194 to 193 the Government survived the division. On February 27 Conway brought the motion forward again—Fox had declared that since his side was beaten by a single vote, the same question would again be urged—and on this day the opposition—despite patronage, despite influence, despite

[1] Christie, pp. 283–98.   [2] *DNB*, xii, 56.

all manner of parliamentary strategy, not only defeated a motion to adjourn by 234 to 215—a majority for opposition of nineteen votes—but went on to pass Conway's motion without a division and also a further motion to inform the King of the decision of the House.

Depressed and discouraged, North wrote to the King at two o'clock in the morning. The House had just passed the fatal motions when the first minister took pen in hand to communicate what had occurred and to urge that a new ministry, perhaps including a part of the Opposition, be formed. The King was mortified, but found himself immediately faced with the practical problem of composing an answer to the House's resolution—'it is highly delicate to find any words not liable to the greatest objections'.

London rejoiced to hear the good news of the resolution. Papers were cried about the streets: 'Good news for England, Lord North in the dumps, and peace with America.' Bells were rung, houses were illuminated; crowds gathered in public places. At Brooks's, Fox found his faro game handicapped because every quarter of an hour he needed to halt his dealing or playing to listen to advice or requests. Jimmy Hare, the friend who only a dozen years ago had been advised to avoid a career of damned obscurity, helped both the dealing and the advising: 'Hare is whispering and standing behind him, like Robinson, with a pencil and paper for mems.' There was an immense ball which Fox did not attend, though he had been invited; afterwards he was teased that twenty ladies had kept themselves disengaged in hope of having him for a partner.[1]

Eyes turned to St Stephen's to see what further action would follow. The King's reply was delicate and harmless; he would take such measures as would restore harmony to Great Britain and the Colonies. Conway moved on March 4 that the House consider as enemies those who advised the King to carry on the war; and to this motion Fox spoke persuasively. Wraxall thought the speech one of Fox's most able, and Conway's motion was carried without a division. The inquiry into the state of the navy, begun by Fox three years ago, had gathered momentum, so that now the House found it necessary to acquiesce tacitly to the statement that the ministers of the King were the proclaimed enemies of the public.

Throughout the country lists were distributed, printing in red the names of those who continued to support the Government. This kind of publicity produced a powerful effect upon the weak and the timid, observed Wraxall. On March 5 Fox made a statement that later caused him no end of embarrassment. There were persons in Europe,

[1] *HMCR*, Carlisle MSS., 586, 590. Selwyn to Carlisle, March 1, March 6.

he asserted, fully empowered to treat for peace between Great Britain and America, but who would not treat with the Government. He thereupon offered his services as negotiator, or even as messenger, to bring about a treaty, even though he would not otherwise connect himself with the present infamous ministry. North retorted that he would not employ Fox as his negotiator, so the dialogue ended with this fresh exchange of mutual animosity. Moreover, the cry was raised that Fox had claimed to have a peace in his pocket. Ministerial paragraphers even thought his claim would attract the votes of country gentlemen. But on March 8 the Government defeated a motion of censure by ten votes—226 to 216.

Even so, the end was nearing. A week later the motion to withdraw the confidence of Parliament from his Majesty's ministers was defeated 236 to 227, Fox declaring afterwards that the motion would speedily be renewed. Next day Robinson wrote to the King that the rats were very bad, and taking note of Fox's announced plan, stated frankly that they would 'increase before Wednesday, when Mr Fox has given notice they will again attack'. To aid the King in his ruminations, Robinson listed, in columns under appropriate descriptive headings, the complexion of various elements on the eve of the fall of the North ministry. It noted 'persons with before, who changed', in number, 3; 'persons who were hopeful who now came and voted against', 5; 'persons who were not to go to the length with them—but who did vote with them as before', 4; 'persons who went away', 5; 'persons who staid away', 11. And much other information of a similar sort.[1]

The King wrote to North he was indeed sorry the majority did not exceed nine: 'It looks as if the House of Commons is going lengths that could not have been expected.' He was resolved, however, not to throw himself into the hands of the opposition. North meanwhile received word that certain of the country gentlemen would no longer 'desist from opposing what appears to be clearly the sense of the House of Commons', so that when the rats strike Wednesday 'we shall infallibly be in a Minority'.[2]

This message was the last straw. North tendered his resignation on Monday and received, on Tuesday noon, a note from the King stating: 'If you resign before I have decided what I will do, You will certainly for ever forfeit my regard.' But later a messenger came to tell North that he would have the King's decision in the morning.[3] Fox meanwhile, far too busy even to go to Newmarket, was busy whipping in votes.[4]

[1] Fortescue, v, 390. [March 16.]   [2] *Ibid.*, v, 394. [March 18.]
[3] Wraxall, ii, 240.
[4] *HMCR*, Carlisle, MSS., pp. 598, 600. Selwyn to Carlisle, March 18, 20.

Wednesday morning came, then afternoon, the time for the denouement. Crowds collected around the doorways tried to judge by the expressions on the faces of newly arriving members what action would be taken within St Stephen's. The impatience of both whigs and tories was manifest everywhere; four hundred members were in their seats long before the clock struck four. Particularly they awaited North, wondering what had delayed him. Eyes turned to the great door every time it was opened, only to turn away in disappointment at seeing another ordinary member scurrying for a place to sit. The room was filled with the hum of excited voices as moments passed. Again the great door opened—the hum was subdued—there were cries of 'Order!' 'Places!'—and Lord North, First Lord of the Treasury, in a full-dress suit with a ribbon over his coat, proceeded to his place on the ministers' bench.

The House quieted and the Speaker called for the order of the day. The Earl of Surrey, in charge of whig parliamentary manoeuvres for the occasion, and North both rose. A clamour swept over the House, as Pitt, Fox, and various other members jumped to their feet, and inquired into parliamentary procedure. Above the general disturbance the commanding voice of Fox rang out as he put the motion that Surrey be heard on the motion for the day. With admirable presence of mind, North spoke out, 'I rise to speak to that motion', and the Speaker gave him the floor. North had well learned the ins and outs of parliamentary method. Calmly he surveyed the scene, the King's secret locked in his heart; he announced that he was against the motion, because—he was this moment tendering his resignation and thus announcing that the ministry was dissolved. He thanked members for their support. 'A successor of greater abilities . . . was easy to be found,' he told them; 'a successor more zealous for the interests of his country, more anxious to promote those interests, more loyal to his sovereign, and more desirous of preserving the constitution whole and entire . . . could not so easily be found.'[1]

The House adjourned. Snow was falling outside, and members huddled in the cloak room waiting for their carriages. In the midst of this confusion North's conveyance drove up to the door. North put into it one or two friends, and, turning to the crowd, composed chiefly of bitter enemies now in the moment of triumph, said with admirable good humour and pleasantry: 'I *have* my carriage. You see, gentlemen, the advantage of being in *the secret*.'[2]

In his moment of defeat, North could depart with a dignified chuckle. He had been head of Government—he had never liked to be called

[1] *Parliamentary History*, xxii, 1217–18.
[2] *Fox Cor.*, i, 295–6; Wraxall, ii, 247; *London Courant*, March 21; *Morning Post*, March 22.

'Prime Minister'—twelve years; his was the longest term since Walpole had quit forty years earlier.

History does not record how Fox and his friends got home that late afternoon nor how they spent the evening. Chances are they never got to bed at all. Chances are also that if Fox had a quiet interlude in the late-hour celebrations, he looked back over the eight years that had elapsed since he had been precipitously dismissed from the Treasury bench. He could have spent a few wry moments reflecting upon the abuse that had been heaped upon him because of his determined opposition to the war policies of the North administration. Undoubtedly he also recalled those few, scarce, moments of triumph: the great speech of 1778 that was never answered, his part in supporting the spectacular Dunning motion that the influence of the Crown ought to be diminished, the exciting contest in 1780 that put him in the House as representative for influential Westminster, and now the complete collapse of the North–Sandwich team. As he had long argued, the independence of the colonies could now be speedily affirmed. He himself might be the powerful voice in the next administration to recognize the young nation across the sea and bring peace once again to the old world and the new.

11

The First Foreign Secretary
1782

[Mr. Fox's] astonishing parliamentary exertions will
be remembered with the highest applause as long as
oratory is held in estimation—that is to say, as long as
the constitution exists.

Earl of Charlemont

Unwilling subjects are little better than enemies.

Charles James Fox

Now it was necessary to form a new Government. To manage preliminary negotiations the King had chosen his former Attorney
General, Thurlow, since 1778 Lord Chancellor. Thurlow was tall,
dignified, stately, impressive, sparkle-eyed and bushy browed: no
man ever was so wise as Thurlow looks, Fox had once said, and the
description stuck. Thurlow had enjoyed spectacular success as a
barrister before entering the Government and as a parliamentary
debater was one of North's dependable aides. His firm belief that in the
dispute with the Colonies the Crown was fully in the right also stamped
him in the King's eyes as a man of worth. He had a talent for secret
negotiation; he could keep a sturdy foot in each camp. With his
combination of gifts he was able to serve as Lord Chancellor in four
different administrations—those of North, Rockingham, Shelburne,
and Pitt.

The negotiations that ensued, starting shortly before North resigned
and continuing at full speed for several days, would stagger the imagination of anyone who believes in human reasonableness. In the name of
principle so much inflexibility was displayed on both sides that it is
easy to apportion it generously. The possibilities of forming an
administration under Gower, who had already resigned from the
ministry, and Shelburne, were explored, but neither had sufficient
strength. Rockingham was approached but he sent the King a four-
point ultimatum of terms under which he would undertake to form a
new administration. The King found little relish in any of them: he
learned that he must not veto independence for America; the contractors' Bill, excluding holders of government contracts from membership in the Commons, must be passed; revenue officials must be

disqualified from voting at elections; Burke's proposals for regulating the civil list must be approved.[1]

The King refused to confer personally with Rockingham. This studied and calculated affront the members of the opposition decided to swallow and even to proceed with their demands through Shelburne, the sole person acceptable to the King as negotiator and go-between. Shelburne, an Irishman and disciple of Chatham, had had a long record of supporting the fight of the opposition against North's management of the war with America. Like Chatham he had been opposed to the Stamp Act and other repressive measures. Like Chatham he was opposed to independence for the Colonies. In all he was a man of considerable ability and statesmanship. Yet Fox had learned at his father's knee not to trust Shelburne; the elder Fox was convinced that Shelburne had deceived him on the delicate business of the preliminaries that led to the peace of 1763 and that thwarted his ministerial ambitions. Burke had once written that in a few days Shelburne took no less than six different turns, 'which tended infinitely to raise him in the Esteem of all that had an opportunity of observing the beautiful harmony and consistency of his proceedings'.[2] Fox and Shelburne were mutually envious, distrustful, and suspicious. Moreover, Shelburne had much personally at stake in the formation of the new Government; to send messages from Rockingham to the King and vice versa through an active partisan was considerably like sending lettuce by a rabbit. Rockingham did not enjoy the King's confidence but Shelburne did, and was party not only to the main lines of the negotiation but also, especially at the palace end, to its subtle implications. These he was careful not to reveal.[3]

The outcome was that, on March 27, a government was formed with Rockingham reluctantly put at the head as First Lord of the Treasury. Shelburne himself was one Secretary of State, Fox the other; Thurlow continued as Lord Chancellor. No place was made for Burke in the Cabinet, a grave disappointment to him; he had to content himself with the non-Cabinet spot of Paymaster of the Forces. No major appointment was found for young William Pitt, and he did not seek small glories. Lafayette wrote to General Washington that the principles of the new administration would not be any better than those of the old: 'Can those people think that by covering the trap with new leaves they may better take in the people of America?'[4]

[1] Fortescue, v, 392 [March 18, 1782]; v, 452–3. April 12.
[2] *Correspondence of Edmund Burke*, ii, 509.
[3] See Add. MSS. 47582; *Fox Cor.*, i, 289–94, for details of the negotiations as recorded by Fitzpatrick.
[4] Louis Gottschalk, ed., *Letters of Lafayette to Washington* (New York, 1944), p. 248. March 31 [1782].

Fox commented to Shelburne that the new ministry consisted of two parts—one part belonging to the King, the other to the public.[1] Of the eleven members of the Cabinet, five were in the Fox bloc: Rockingham, Richmond, Cavendish, Keppel, and Fox himself. Shelburne with four others constituted the other bloc; and General Conway, 'that *innocent man*', as Shelburne once observed to Fox, 'never perceived that he had the casting vote of the Cabinet'.[2] Fox's letters describe the discord: much teasing and wrangling, doubts, creation of difficulties, little personal projects.[3] Later he liked to recollect that in 1782 he was in the Cabinet with three lawyers, Thurlow, Camden, and Dunning, and no business was done, but that in 1783 he was in the Cabinet and there was no lawyer, and business got done.[4]

In the creation of the new Government little opportunity had been afforded for meeting of minds, much less for exploration of differences. The King emphasized the divisiveness of the Cabinet when he notified both Rockingham and Shelburne that he would give their separate advice attention, but would give greater attention to recommendations on which they concurred.[5]

Fox received a new kind of publicity in the London press. 'Now Chatham is no more, Fox is the man to whom the people should look to as their *avenging angel*', said the *London Courant*. The *Morning Herald* reported a rumour that Fox had now pledged never to play at any game on any pretext. The *General Advertiser* editorialized that the Government needed to be 'the most powerful that ever was established in this country' in order to cope with the great and weighty matters before it. Its owner-editor, William Parker, stated his position in glowing terms: '[Fox] is by far the man of the greatest abilities this country has ever been blessed with' and offered Fox's name as the paper's candidate for Prime Minister. The Association at York met and decided to trust the new ministers, at least for the present.[6]

It was necessary for Fox, having accepted a post in the Government, to stand for re-election; this requirement gave the electorate the chance to decide whether the holding of an 'office of profit' conflicted with the office-holder's desirability to his constituents. On April 3, at half-past ten in the morning, a procession of 150 coaches, preceded by a 'Band of Musick', paraded from Palace Yard to the hustings in Covent

[1] Add. MSS. 47582; *Fox Cor.*, i, 292.   [2] *Fox Cor.*, i, 454.
[3] *Ibid.*, i, 314–16. To Fitzpatrick, April 12, 15.
[4] James Greig, ed. *The Farington Diary*, 2nd ed. (London, n.d.), i, 175.
[5] Lansdowne MSS., quoted in Fitzmaurice, *Life of William, Earl of Shelburne*, 2nd edn. (London, 1912), ii, 92; Fortescue, v, 447.
[6] *Fox Cor.*, i, 311.

Garden. Banners carried such legends as 'The Man of the People' and 'Freedom and Independence'. According to one report a hundred thousand people participated in the festivities.

At the hustings were the customary speeches. Fox promised to pursue 'that open, that liberal, that patriotick line of Conduct' to which he was impelled by 'the virtuous Ambition of rescuing his Native Country from Threatened Destruction.' Popular oratory now came easy to him. He had made many speeches to loyal and enthusiastic supporters since that Westminster Hall appearance more than two years earlier. 'Loud and long-continued Shouts of Applause' greeted his more choice sentiments. At one stage of his talk he trusted that something might be done for the welfare of the people. Here a voice from the mob shouted 'Amen!' and such uproar and laughing followed that Fox could not proceed for some time. Fists waved in the air, eager voices yelled 'FOX FOR EVER,' and he replied that he was warmed in their cause 'FOR EVER AND EVER.'

In short order the head bailiff declared Fox elected, the men with the banners fell in line again, Fox was put in a gilt armchair and carried to his office in Cleveland Row, people lining the streets and peering from windows; everywhere were yells and cheers. An onlooker wrote: 'Fox was chosen with unanimity and general acclamation. He was called in his procession the man of the people. The concourse of people was astonishing. He is become a man of application to business, and has given up his clubs.'[1] Officially Fox's title was 'one of his majesty's principal secretaries of state'; assigned to deal with other countries, he thus became the first Foreign Secretary. The office of Secretary of State for America, Germain's old job, was abandoned; problems of the colonies, together with domestic responsibilities, fell to Shelburne.

Carl Philipp Moritz, visitor to England from Germany, visited the Strangers' Gallery and later wrote his impressions of Fox:

It is impossible for me to describe, with what fire, and persuasive eloquence he spoke, and how the Speaker in the chair incessantly nodded approbation from beneath his solemn wig; and innumerable voices incessantly called out, *hear him*! *hear him*! and when there was the least sign that he intended to leave off speaking, they no less vociferously exclaimed, *go on*; and so he continued to speak in this manner for nearly two hours.[2]

On a Tuesday in June, a hanging day, given the choice between observing a public hanging and a Westminster election to choose a successor to Rodney, elevated to the peerage, Moritz opted to view the

[1] *HMCR*, Emly MSS., pp. 164–5. Lord Lucan to William Cecil Pery (Speaker of the Irish House of Commons), April 3.
[2] *Travels of Carl Philipp Moritz in England* (London, 1924), pp. 56–7.

latter. In front of St Paul's church, he saw a temporary wooden build-ing, erected to serve as the hustings. At one end were mats on which the speakers stood, the rest of the space being filled with benches. The multitude of people that gathered was, he observed, mainly of the lowest order; but the speakers, in the manner of campaigners every-where, bowed low and called them gentlemen. Little boys clambered up and hung to rails and lamp posts, listened with the utmost attention, joined lustily in the cheers and waved their hats. In the distance Moritz could hear the tolling of the hangman's bell.

Mr Secretary Fox was not a candidate that day but he arrived on the scene at the beginning of the election and, Moritz recorded, was received with a universal shout of joy. When the election was nearly over, Moritz continued,

the people took it into their heads to hear him speak, and every one called out *Fox! Fox!* I know not why; but I seemed to catch some of the spirit of the place and time; and so I also bawled, *Fox! Fox!* and he was obliged to come forward and speak: for no other reason that I could find, but that the people wished to hear him speak.

So Moritz spent his tourist day, and must have concluded when he retired to his room that for sheer uncultivated excitement that blended the tradition of the past with the awareness of history currently in the making, the hustings was superior to the gallows. His vivid impressions of Fox's power and persuasiveness as a speaker, in and out of the House, are indispensable.

Much work needed to be done and Fox entered upon it diligently. Some of his supporters, however, were vexed, annoyed, disappointed. Among them were those who paid their back dues at Brooks's and elsewhere so that they could be seen in the company of the clubman who now was Foreign Secretary. Fox, however, found it possible to suspend his gambling. It is much easier to break a habit by a change of environment and activity than by a raw, bleeding effort of will, so he turned from faro at Brooks's to the excitement of politics. He found an occasional similarity; the game of assigning hundreds of office seekers to dozens of available places involved a shrewd calculation of the odds. At times even the banker himself felt insecure. The King held most of the capital and the influence of Shelburne loomed excessively large. Fox spent countless hours on appointments, winnowing the supplicants and making recommendations to Rockingham.[1]

[1] Rockingham letters, R1–2061 (Sheffield); Add. MSS. 47568.

The legislative hopes of the Rockingham ministry as it assumed office centred on ways of limiting the influence of the Crown. As Fox later said: 'Provided we can stay in long enough to have given a good stout blow to the influence of the Crown, I do not think it much signifies how soon we go out after.'[1] The shortlived ministry successfully passed an Act preventing revenue officers from voting and another excluding those who held contracts from the Government from sitting in Parliament, but as matters turned out its major problems were concerned with Ireland, Holland, and America.

The pleasant sounds of the swearing-in ceremonies had hardly died out when the Irish problem arose. Irish sentiment, largely under the leadership of two of Fox's good Irish friends, the Earl of Charlemont and Henry Grattan, increasingly insisted upon a larger share for the Irish in managing Irish affairs. The Irish volunteers, now more than 40,000 men in arms, gave added point to Irish discontent. The Lord Lieutenant, Carlisle, had sent his secretary, William Eden, to explain these developments of the Irish problem to the London Government, but Eden, when he found that the ministry was planning to send over a new Lord Lieutenant, refused to have any communication with him but instead hurried to Westminster to appeal directly to Parliament over the heads of ministers.

The session of April 8 was, therefore, an extraordinary one. Eden, introduced as the bearer of intelligence from Ireland, gained the floor and explained the Irish demands for legislative independence. Basically, the Irish legislature was made subordinate to the British Parliament by two ancient acts: Poynings' law of the fifteenth century, providing that no Parliament could be held in Ireland unless the King gave his approval, and the Declaratory Act enacted in the reign of George I, affirming the right of Great Britain to legislate for Ireland. Eden also reminded the Commons that the Irish Parliament had planned a session for the following week, on April 16, at which strong representations for Irish legislative independence would certainly be made. He closed his speech by precipitately moving that the Declaratory Act of George I be repealed.

Fox, who could be vehement, impassioned, impulsive, extravagant, and hasty, was this day, in his first speech as Mr Secretary Fox, calm and statesmanlike. It would have been more decent and respectful, he observed, for Eden to have consulted the Government before bringing such an important topic to Parliament. The ministry was inclined cordially and sincerely to do Ireland ample justice and in a few hours would bring forward its own proposals. He did not like to vote the motion down, but hoped instead that Eden would withdraw it. When

[1] *Fox Cor.*, i, 316. April 28.

Eden demurred, General Conway, ever the voice of integrity and independence, threatened to move a vote of censure which aroused such a cry of hear! hear! that Eden withdrew his motion.[1]

The Irish legislature met on April 16, with lines of volunteers drawn up outside its doors, to hear Grattan move the famous declaration: 'No power on earth but the King, lords and commons of Ireland is competent to bind Ireland.' The Rockingham administration moved swiftly, and in May Fox presented to the House specific proposals to meet the Irish demands. He declared that although he did not approve the way in which their demands had come to Westminster, he nevertheless thought they should be given full consideration. 'He had rather see Ireland totally separated from the crown of England than kept in obedience only by force. Unwilling subjects were little better than enemies.'[2] Commons and Lords alike approved the Government's proposals that day, and a grateful Irish Parliament soon thereafter voted £100,000 for the British navy—and a £50,000 estate to Grattan. And Fox himself felt a surge of party strength: whig principles had been given an onward thrust that renewed his own enthusiasm. He had written to Charlemont: 'Why should not the Whigs (I mean in principle not in name) unite in every part of the empire to establish their principles so firmly that no future faction shall be able to destroy them?'[3] Yet he was not the kind of person who could evolve the party organization necessary to bring this dream to practical fulfilment.

The problem of ending the war with Holland was more difficult. Holland had joined the Armed Neutrality organized by Catherine II of Russia. Her aid of the Americans by shipping needed goods despite the British blockade, and especially her shipping of naval stores to France, had brought on a declaration of hostilities. At a Cabinet meeting the day after the ministry came into office, the King was advised to direct Fox to enter into a treaty of peace with the Dutch, acting through the Russian minister in London.[4] Fox had thought that Russia and Prussia might be united in an alliance as a counter to France and Spain, so the interest of the court of St Petersburg was sought for this reason as well as to help bring to an end the conflict with the Dutch. These proposals encountered objection and delay. During the negotiations with the Americans in Paris the next few weeks Holland was in the background,

[1] *Parliamentary History*, xxii, 1241–64.   [2] *Ibid.*, xxiii, 23.
[3] *HMCR*, Charlemont MSS., i, 57. April 4.
[4] *Fox Cor.*, i, 331; Fortescue, v, 427. The basic issues are interpreted by Isabel de Madariaga in *Britain, Russia, and the Armed Neutrality of 1780* (New Haven, 1962).

urging France not to sign a treaty without her, and offering Vergennes a reason to say loftily, when hard-pressed, that he could not act without consulting his allies. During the fighting Holland had lost Trincomalee, her fine harbour in the Bay of Bengal, and Negapatnam, a minor port on the mainland of India, and sought to have these restored, along with a more favourable definition of the rights of neutral shipping. She asked much but offered little; she could exert little influence at the peace discussions and was fortunate to retrieve Trincomalee. Nearly two years passed before her disagreements with Great Britain were settled by treaty.

Peace negotiations with the Americans and with France and Spain were involved and prolonged. Here the two-headed division of the post of Secretary of State, with Shelburne at the head of colonial business and Fox at the head of foreign affairs, provided sturdy opportunity for confusion, since the Americans stood between the two offices : as they had fought themselves clear of the mother country they were not colonies, but neither had they had their independence formally conceded.

At its meeting on April 23 the new Cabinet turned its attention to the treaty discussions with France, Spain, and the Americans, deciding that independence for America should be dependent upon Great Britain's being restored to the situation she was placed in by the treaty of 1763.[1] Although the achievement of this aim would require the closest sort of discussion among the powers involved, the Cabinet nevertheless chose to be represented by two people : Richard Oswald, the nominee of Shelburne, and a second individual to be chosen by Fox. Fox's representative turned out to be young Thomas Grenville, second son of the framer of the Stamp Act. Since Oswald was to receive his instructions through Shelburne and Grenville his through Fox, Great Britain was in effect represented in a complex, overlapping negotiation by two separate missions.

Fox's mistrust of Shelburne erupted at the outset; on April 28 Fox wrote Fitzpatrick that Shelburne was jealous of Fox's encroaching on his department and wanted to encroach upon Fox's. 'He affects the Minister more and more every day, and is, I believe, perfectly confident that the King intends to make him so.'[2] Yet regardless of private feelings, and especially regardless of the awkward administrative arrangement, the persons concerned tried at first to get the negotiations off to a proper start. Much correspondence followed but failed to produce the close-working arrangement that might have been hoped for.

[1] *Fox Cor.*, i, 345; Fortescue, v, 488 (date given as April 25).
[2] Add. MSS. 47580. *Fox Cor.*, i, 316.

Most of May was frittered away because the instructions under which the two British envoys operated were too loose in one respect and too circumscribed in another. They were too loose, to cite Fox's instructions to Grenville, in that Grenville was 'to use his judgment as to whether the views he stated were official or personal'. For diplomatic negotiations to be successful, it is important that envoys have full accreditation. The instructions were too circumscribed, in that the Cabinet did not want to accede to American independence unless in other respects the situation would be restored to the status defined by the 1763 treaty.[1] The Americans, however, demanded independence outright, and Vergennes did not want to restore matters to the 1763 status: 'For his part he could not read the last peace without shuddering.'[2] Oswald on his part returned to London for fresh instructions, but his visit was not fruitful. Back in Paris he was further convinced, and so wrote Shelburne, that the grant of independence should be unconditional.[3] The American and continental diplomats quickly discovered that both Grenville and Oswald operated on a short leash and were kept in close check by the Rockingham Cabinet.

By May 21 Grenville received full powers through Fox, but independence was still tied to the treaty of 1763.[4] Shelburne, meanwhile, disturbed because the negotiations were bogging down, directed Oswald to keep him fully informed about all phases of the negotiation and to emphasize that the Cabinet was fully united on 'the great Subject of Peace and War'.[5] By May 23 the Cabinet finally agreed to direct Fox to instruct Grenville 'to propose the Independency of America, in the first Instance, instead of making it a Condition of the General Treaty'.[6] When eventually revised full powers were supplied allowing Grenville to treat not only with France but with 'any other of the Enemies of Gt Britain', Spain objected because she was not mentioned by name, and Grenville reported Franklin's complaint that a reference to 'princes' and 'states' in another part of the document did not seem clearly to embrace America.[7]

Circumvented by insufficient authority and also by Oswald's presence, Grenville wrote to Fox that although at first Franklin appeared to wish to deal confidentially with him, Franklin became reticent and evasive after Oswald appeared on the scene. Vergennes

[1] FO 27/2, 42–6. Fox to Grenville, April 30.
[2] FO 27/2, 61. Grenville to Fox, May 10.   [3] FO 95/511. May 18.
[4] FO 95/511. The Cabinet on May 18 submitted this proposal hoping that Vergennes would decline it, which would produce 'salutary effects' in both Europe and America (Fox to the king, Fortescue, vi, 32).
[5] Shelburne MSS., lxx, 2. May 21. (Clements.) FO 27/2, 87.
[6] FO 95/511. This decision was communicated to Grenville May 26 (FO 27/2, 109).
[7] FO 27/2, 117–28, Grenville to Fox, May 30, June 4, June 25; Fox to Grenville, June 10; FO 27/2, 161–2, Franklin to Oswald, June 27.

also quickly sensed that Grenville's channel of communication was troubled. Nor were the Spaniards taken in by the business; Grenville's contribution, they observed, consisted largely of polite courtesies, cordial protests, and long discourses.[1] Franklin kept his fellow commissioner, John Adams, now at The Hague, informed about the tortuous manoeuvres, on which Adams perceptively commented that the British ministers were too divided among themselves, too formidably opposed by the King, and too little assured of the confidence of the nation, to have the courage to make concessions.[2]

In May came news of a great naval victory over the French admiral de Grasse, in which Rodney captured the French flagship and its admiral, broke the back of the French fleet, and ended French control of the West Indies. Unfortunately Rodney had come under censure because previously, when he had captured the little island of St Eustatius with its bulging warehouses of contraband and other supplies, a convenient and needed supply depot for the colonies, he had treated British merchants so sternly, considering them traitors rather than loyal subjects of the Crown, that commercial interests back in London successfully urged the Rockingham ministry to recall Rodney and substitute Pigot. The day after Pigot sailed to take over his new command, word arrived about the Rodney victory. The ministry was assailed for its recall of a victorious admiral, though the news stiffened Britain's backbone for the treaty negotiations.

One incident of the negotiation has been exaggerated beyond its importance. Franklin had long nourished the thought that Canada should be ceded to the United States. He prepared a paper on this subject that he handed Oswald; when next in London Oswald showed it to Shelburne. Franklin had not discussed this proposal with Grenville, who learned about it later only through a slip of Oswald's. Grenville wrote to Fox in detail about it on June 4. Fox showed the letter to Rockingham, Richmond, and Cavendish, who were 'full of indignation at its contents'. Fox took this incident as further evidence of Shelburne's duplicity and intrigue. Apparently Shelburne did not present the Canadian proposal to the Cabinet, and the idea had no place in future negotiations.

By June 10 Fox was writing Grenville to stay on a while longer in Paris, though he now saw the mischief done was irremediable.[3] He spoke of further full powers being enclosed. His gloom was fully

[1] *Archivo histórico Nacional*, 4079, 2. Florida Blanca to the Count de Aranda, May 20. (Clements.)

[2] Francis Wharton, *The Revolutionary Diplomatic Correspondence of the United States* (Washington, 1889), v, 491.

[3] FO 27/2, Grenville to Fox, June 4; Fox to Grenville, June 10.

matched by Grenville's, who replied that his opportunity for service was completely annihilated.[1]

So June followed May; Grenville was still unable to get an adequate directive from Fox's office and saw himself displaced by Oswald in such negotiations as were held.

Meanwhile back in London the Cabinet continued to hold itswrangling, teasing meetings. The last week in June, on the 28th, Fox called on Grafton and complained in detail of the awkward situation in the Cabinet. Anything he proposed, Fox declared, met decided opinions to the contrary. Rockingham, meanwhile, had fallen gravely ill, so that the future of the Government looked delicate indeed.

The Cabinet accordingly held a long discussion on June 30. Fox urged again his view that the American colonies should be granted their independence in advance of a treaty of peace. This move would put the peace negotiations squarely within his department. The opposing view was that independence should be granted but as a part of the treaty, a basis for further discussion.[2] Quite possibly it was also a part of Fox's notion that the independence of the colonies should be enacted by Parliament; this view he had long held and had formally expressed on the floor of the House. Shelburne reported to the King that the Cabinet sat late 'but came to no final Resolution'. Grafton, however, recorded that the majority outvoted Fox, and Walpole later set down his version of the outcome; four had voted with Fox for immediately declaring America independent, the usual group had voted in opposition to this, with Conway's casting vote making a majority. Fox thereupon announced that he would resign from the Cabinet though he would defer this step considering the desperate illness of Rockingham.[3]

Next day Rockingham died. On July 2, during a debate on the Colonial Place Bill, Fox, concealing his own personal disappointment and dissatisfaction, undertook to present a solid front to the Commons and to assure them that the Cabinet was unified on the issue of acknowledging American independence. This position was technically correct: the Cabinet had favoured independence though it had sharply disagreed on when and how. At any rate, he hedged, he would not stay in the Cabinet one minute if he should discover there any intention of bringing America to obedience.[4] The brief report in the *Parliamentary*

[1] Holland House Photostats, ii, item 36. June 16. (Clements.)

[2] William R. Anson, ed., *Autobiography and Political Correspondence of Augustus Henry, Third Duke of Grafton* (London, 1898), p. 323.

[3] *Idem.*; North to Eden, September 30, *B. F. Stevens's Facsimiles*, x, 1054; Fortescue, vi, 69; *Fox Cor.*, i, 435.

[4] *Parliamentary History*, xxiii, 138.

History is augmented in a pamphlet, in which Fox's speech is given in more detail:

It is the interest of no parent state to restrain the mature independence of their colonies. When colonies have power to be free, independence is their natural, as well as political, charter. . . .
   A confiding state is . . . more desirable than a distrustful colony. . . .
   If we would preserve our constitution, we must disdain the idea of governing America . . . [America] is now in possession of her rights, and no coertion will ever oblige her to resign them.[1]

Nothing could be more sensible and realistic. Within a few days, however, Fox had to tell the Commons that the Cabinet was not in agreement on the principle of American independence. In private circles the Duke of Leeds could report a conversation in which Fox declared that he sought unconditional independence but the Cabinet voted against him; Fox 'thought himself so far pledg'd on that subject as to render his continuance in office totally improper'.[2]

The remainder of the Rockingham group, having climbed the greasy pole to the top, sought to nominate the new prime minister. For this position Fox proposed the Duke of Portland. Fox's claim that the Cabinet could select the head of state was a constitutional theory far ahead of its time.[3] But this situation was not suitable for the hewing of new constitutional timbers. Portland was little known and undistinguished. The hatred of the King for Fox and all his works, and the bitter contempt of Fox for the King, were equally notorious. Moreover the King, who had favoured Shelburne as North's successor in March, wanted him now as the head of administration.[4] Fox, Richmond, and other close associates knew they were not welcome in the King's chamber, so out of sheer lack of an appropriate channel asked Shelburne to carry to the sovereign the request that Portland be named. Shelburne, 'with equal mummery', as Walpole, no friend, reported, accepted the commission, and 'returning with modest confusion and friendly grief' reported to his uneasy colleagues that to his own extreme surprise and affliction His Majesty had been pleased to appoint none other than the messenger himself.[5]
   Fox now seemed less than certain about his own next move. July 4

---

[1] *The speech of the right honourable Charles James Fox on American independence: spoken in the House of Commons on Tuesday, July 2, 1782* (London, n.d.).
[2] *Political Memoranda of Francis, Fifth Duke of Leeds*, p. 73. [July 8.]
[3] On this issue see Richard Pares, *King George III and the Politicians* (Oxford, 1953), pp. 121 ff.
[4] Fortescue, vi, 71. Draft of a letter to Shelburne, July 1.
[5] *Last Journals*, ii, 449.

was long, eventful, tense. He wrote to Fitzpatrick that 'this cursed anxiety and suspense' made him miserable.[1] He also wrote to Lee:

Ld. Shelburne will I believe be 1st Lord of the Treasury. . . . *I did last night intend to resign today*, but the D. of Richmond has been bringing me messages which I did not wish to receive & which have a little embarrassed me. I wish too to see Ld. Fitzwilliam before I determine. To act with that amiable & respectable set of Men whom it is the *King's ambition to destroy*, is as much the comfort as it is the honour & pride of my life, and what nothing shall ever make me sacrifice. The D. of Richmond I am sorry to say it is imposed upon by *the second Villain in this Kingdom* in a manner that is as ridiculous as it is mischievous.[2]

No doubt can exist that Fox is here nominating the King and Shelburne respectively as the first and second villains of the piece. Later that day he confronted Shelburne in the King's drawing room: 'Are you to go to the Treasury?' Shelburne replied, 'Yes'; whereupon Fox declared, angrily, 'Then I must resign. But I wish to accommodate, and to hold the Seal for as many days as may be thought necessary to a new arrangement.' Fox then went in to confer with the King but left the seal. The King according to one report asked him to reconsider, but Fox declined and within five minutes came out with no seal.[3] Even as late as July 6, however, North thought it possible that Fox might be persuaded to resume his office.[4] The King sought no such outcome. He wrote to John Robinson about Fox: 'Every honest man and those in the least interested in the support of this constitution must wish to do the utmost to keep him [*sic*] out of power.'[5]

Fox's sudden action caused a tidal wave of consternation. His lovely Aunt Sarah described it simply as an act of violent passion.[6] In a letter to his brother, Fitzpatrick more rationally analysed public sentiment by saying that 'all persons who have any understanding and no office, are of opinion that Charles has done right, all persons who have little understanding are frightened, and all persons who have offices, with some very few brilliant exceptions, think he had been hasty.'[7]

Gibbon wrote that all were confused and amazed by Fox's resignation. Noting that the move had split the party, he commented that 'three months of prosperity has dissolved a Phalanx which had stood ten years adversity'.[8] Walpole thought that Fox might have borne

---

1 Add. MSS. 47580.
2 Lee Papers, [July 4]. To [John Lee], solicitor general in the Rockingham administration. (Clements.)
3 *HMCR*, Sutherland MSS., p. 210; Auckland, i, 2. Loughborough to Eden, July 4.
4 *HMCR*, Abergavenny MSS., p. 53; *HMCR*, Sutherland MSS., p. 210.
5 *HMCR*, Abergavenny MSS., p. 54. August 7.
6 *Life and Letters of Lady Sarah Lennox* (London, 1901), ii, 18. To Lady Susan O'Brien, July 6.
7 Add. MSS. 47579. July 5.
8 *Letters of Gibbon*, ii, 300–1. To Francis Hugonin, July 6; Lord Sheffield, July 6.

with Shelburne a few months until peace with America was concluded, Ireland settled, continental alliances cemented, Holland reconciled. When he asked Fox whether or not France would be pleased to hear about the schism between him and Shelburne, Fox candidly replied: 'Oh, it will do a great deal of mischief.'[1] Yet Fox continued high in Walpole's regard: 'I have no hesitation in saying that I think Mr Fox the fittest man in England for Prime Minister; I say it aloud and everywhere.'[2]

Fox himself, after reflection, thought the situation not entirely black. He wrote Portland that he hoped the party would stick together: 'and that we shall always keep up a standard which all Whigs may repair to when they are so inclined.'[3] To Fox's disappointment, however, some of his colleagues refused to give up their offices. Richmond thought he should keep his post as Master General of the Ordnance until he had completed certain reforms. Keppel decided to stay on at the Admiralty but only until peace should be signed. Cavendish as Chancellor, however, and Burke as Paymaster, among others, resigned. 'The secession of such a weight of talents and integrity from the service of government,' recorded the *Annual Register*, 'could not be regarded with indifference.'

The Rockingham party met at Fitzwilliam's July 8 to survey the damage. A short report still exists: Fox gave his reasons for retiring and Richmond his for remaining, but the latter was 'so pressed and stung in this nest of hornets' that at length he burst into tears. Burke spoke two hours, 'and it is said he made the best speech he ever was heard to utter'.[4]

William Knox, no supporter either of Fox or the Americans, wrote Germain, Viscount Sackville, that Fox's imprudence in advocating independence 'pending the Treaty and without any equivalent' gave Fox's friends who wanted to keep their places and perhaps win promotions an excuse for not following him out of office.[5] Germain replied that he was puzzled to account for Fox's conduct. Moreover, he predicted that if Pitt should accept office, 'Mr Fox will have little chance of being again a minister; and you will see him act as a desperate opposer of the new Administration.'[6] As the pages of history slowly turned, Germain was proved to have predicted well, in the general if not in the particular; for the rest of Pitt's life Fox was minister only for the brief period to be related in the next chapter, the rest of the time

[1] *Walpole's Correspondence with William Mason*, 29/ii, 263. To the Reverend William Mason, July 8.
[2] Cunningham, viii, 245–6. To the Countess of Upper Ossory, July 7. Wrote Lord Ossory: 'I look upon . . . Fox . . . to be one of the most extraordinary men that ever existed.'
[3] Add. MSS. 47561. July 6. *Fox Cor.*, iv, 274–5.   [4] *HMCR*, Carlisle MSS., pp. 632–3.
[5] *HMCR*, Stopford-Sackville MSS., i, 78–9. July 6.   [6] *HMCR*, Knox MSS., p. 185.

being a powerful opposer of administration, though not always a desperate one.

Fox found it necessary to explain to the House the reasons for his resignation. The helpful Moritz was in the gallery to record what went on; he was wise in seeking his seat early, since the gallery was filled at 11, though the debates did not begin until 3 and Fox did not arrive until 4. Fox spoke at first with great vehemence, recorded Moritz, but gradually became more and more moderate and at length vindicated the step he had taken:

> . . . and shewed it to be [Moritz reported] in every point of view, just, wise, and honourable,—he added, with great force and pathos, 'and now I stand here once more, as "poor as ever I was".' It was impossible to hear such a speech and such declarations unmoved.[1]

Three different times that day Fox rose to defend his action in resigning. He had joined the Government, he insisted, because it stood for certain principles. When those principles were departed from, when the Government no longer pursued the line chalked out for it by the House and by the people of England, he felt it imperative to resign.[2]

That there certainly was grave disagreement in the Cabinet on the question of American independence clearly appeared in Shelburne's speech to the Lords on July 10. Although he declared that the American business had never been stated in the Cabinet as a reason for the 'late resignations' (of Fox and Cavendish), he took something away from the completeness of that statement when he spelled out his own position: the independence of America 'would be a dreadful blow to the greatness of this country; and that when it should be established, the sun of England might be said to have set'. Independence would be a misfortune, a dreadful disaster. He had made every effort, in private and in public, to avoid it. Now the fatal necessity of granting independence appeared in full view; he might be obliged to give way on this point, but nothing short of necessity would bring him to this melancholy event, this greatest of misfortunes. 'The sun of England would set with the loss of America; but it was his resolution to improve the twilight, and to prepare for the rising of England's sun again.'[3] So although Grenville could show the American commissioners in Paris Fox's letter that independence was unconditional, Shelburne's speech told them that independence would be a disaster and a misfortune.

---

[1] *Travels*, p. 218. [2] *Parliamentary History*, xxiii, 159–79. [3] *Ibid.*, xxiii, 193–4.

Fox continued to try to refute the charge that he had resigned because of personal resentment to Shelburne. At a public meeting held on July 17 at Westminster Hall, he came forward, partly to deplore Shelburne's sincerity as a genuine exponent of parliamentary reform, but chiefly to defend himself against the allegation that he had resigned because Shelburne had been appointed to the first seat at the Treasury. He declared he could quote Richmond, Keppel, Conway, Cavendish, and several other members of his Majesty's cabinet that he had planned to resign even before Rockingham died.

Fox went on to intertwine two arguments: one, a defence of his own resignation, and the other, a direct attack upon the head of the new government. In closing he offered a plea for the independence of the Colonies, a measure not only 'absolutely necessary for the political salvation of this country, but in itself considered in the abstract, a just, wise, and equitable measure'. Americans are Englishmen—they have English habits and English feelings—and should be treated with generosity. Shelburne, he reminded his listeners, had gone on record as saying that if American independence were granted, 'the splendour of this country would be gone, its sun would be set, and his government would take place in the *twilight* of the empire'. Fox then concluded with a cordial tribute to Sir Cecil Wray, whom he was supporting as a candidate from Westminster, calling him 'an upright, able, independent senator, and an honest man'—commendation and solid support that would be recalled, in a different context, two years later when Wray bitterly opposed Fox for a Westminster seat.[1]

A more patient and tenacious person could have kept the administration afloat longer; Fox had striven for office so many years that he might have been expected to appreciate the importance of patience and tenacity although neither he nor Rockingham had ever gained any real support from the King. Fox was widely accused of having left the administration when he might most effectively have served it. 'Cease then vainly to court popularity,' said the *Gazetteer*, scornfully; 'your art and cunning will no longer prevail; your oratory will now lose all its charms . . . hide then your guilty head in humble retirement.'

Fox's reasons for resigning obviously are complex. The personal reason emerges foremost, despite his own explanations and protests. True enough he announced his intention to resign before Rockingham died, but he did not actually resign until after Shelburne had been appointed first minister, and not even then until after deliberation and consultation. Like many individuals of unusual good-nature and

[1] *The speech of the Right Honourable Charles James Fox at . . . Westminster Hall, July 17, 1782*, etc. (London, [1782]).

patience, Fox reacted violently once certain limits were exceeded, and Shelburne was a person with whom Fox could not work in harness. Fox refused to continue in Shelburne's cabinet in 1782, and after a year's reflection refused to rejoin it when given an opportunity.

The issue of American independence stands on a higher level. Fox was one of the first to advocate independence for the Colonies. As early as 1778 he had espoused the idea that the relationship between the mother country and the Americans would continue, even despite a formal separation, because of mutual ties and interests. His 1782 speeches continued in this strain. He strongly urged independence— immediately, in advance of the treaty, without antecedent concessions and bargaining. Hence it is a measure of the strength of his conviction in favour of immediate American independence (and admittedly also of his dislike of Shelburne) that he was willing to abandon a career in office, which he found challenging and absorbing, even despite the frustrations, to resume the burden of opposition.

Ironically enough, many of Fox's associates continued to believe that he had resigned for personal reasons, nor did the Americans especially feel that they had lost a champion. The American delegation was undisturbed by the fall of the Rockingham ministry and the elevation of Shelburne to the chief post. British treaty-making machinery was confused, divided, cumbersome, and would simply need to be endured longer. The Americans realized that Shelburne did not stand on entirely solid ground; and, along with other members of the diplomatic corps in Paris, they wondered about his integrity. Despite Shelburne's wobbling on the point of independence, the Americans decided that he was sincere enough. On other matters, such as drawing boundary lines, he was more generous than Fox. John Adams even thought he was a better friend to America than either Fox or Burke.[1]

Grenville heard from Shelburne on July 5 that the death of Rockingham and the resignation of Fox would make no difference in the measures to be pursued. But there was, of course, a difference: the eloquent voice that argued for unconditional American independence was no longer in the Cabinet. Not many days passed before the rumour was afloat that independence, instead of being conceded, would now have to be negotiated.[2] Shelburne finally found it necessary to write to

[1] So Adams wrote in the *Boston Patriot*, January 25, 1812. Quoted in L. H. Butterfield, ed., *Diary and Autobiography of John Adams* (Cambridge, 1961), iii, 135. See also Steven Watson's discussion of Shelburne in *The Reign of George the Third* (Oxford, 1960), pp. 249 ff.

[2] FO 27/2, 185–6. Oswald to Shelburne, July 12. Franklin wrote Oswald July 12 that he had heard that 'some opposition given by his Lordship to Mr Fox's decided *Plan of unequivocally acknowledging American independency* was one cause of that gentleman's resignation' (FO 27/2). See also Sheridan to Grenville, July 4, in *The Letters of Richard Brinsley Sheridan* (Oxford, 1966), i, 153.

Oswald, reassuring him upon 'the most unequivocal acknowledgement of American Independancy' but the rumour persisted longer than it should have.[1]

During summer and fall peace negotiations continued. Adams was a forceful addition to the American team. He entered the discussion in October, fresh from a successful parley with the Dutch. As an important point in the treaty, the Americans insisted on a statement affirming their unlimited right to fish; this right they considered a part of the doctrine of the freedom of the seas. Long before, Congress had discussed the importance of the fishing trade and had supplied its representatives with argument and precedent.[2] Adams insisted he would never put his hand to any treaty without satisfaction about the fishery, Laurens agreed, and John Jay declared that otherwise no peace would be possible, only 'an insidious Truce'.[3] The Americans gained their point, urging among other reasons that fish caught by their countrymen meant more dollars to spend in Great Britain.

Another sensitive issue centred on the loyalists whose property had been confiscated by the states. Congress resented paying indemnity to those who had opposed the revolution, arguing that such payment was not only unfair to American citizens who had suffered war's ravages but also impracticable, since much of the property had already gone through a variety of hands. Shelburne, however, was under pressure from loyalist emigrés and their friends to bargain for adequate restitution. The question also arose about debts owed by Americans to British creditors. The Americans did not want to concede either issue, but finally evolved the formula that creditors could sue for their debts through the courts, and that Congress would recommend to the states that the loyalists be recompensed. Shelburne welcomed this solution, which left the door ajar for further discussion even though it actually offered little. The Americans were impatient to have the definitive treaty signed. They wanted to be rid of their 'troublesome guests'

[1] Shelburne MSS., lxxi, 61–9 (Clements.) July 27. As late as September 10 Oswald reported to London that commissioner John Jay frequently referred to the Grenville offer 'to acknowledge their independence in the first instance'. Jay 'could not conceive the reason why that which we were willing to give them in May, should be refused in August' (FO 27/2, 274). Actually these discussions continued in the Cabinet throughout the autumn; as late as November 19 the King was still boggling at the idea of 'independence', in one communication crossing it out and substituting 'seperation'. Independence was a concession to be bargained for: it should be offered as part of a general arrangement that included, possibly, payment of debts to British merchants, restitution for damages claimed by loyalists, boundary lines, fishing rights, and the like. See Godfrey Davies and Marion Tinling, 'The Independence of America: Six Unpublished Items on the Treaty in 1782–83.' *Huntington Library Quarterly*, xii, 2 (1948–49), 213–20; Fortescue, vi, 157. November 19.

[2] *Journal of the Continental Congress, 1774–1789* (Washington, 1922), xxiii, 477–8.
[3] *Diary and Autobiography of John Adams*, iii, 81. November 29.

in order to retrieve their homes, release their prisoners, and even to keep their slaves, whom the British insisted upon freeing when possible.

The document signed by the British and American representatives was not to go into full force until terms of peace had been agreed upon by Great Britain and France. These discussions consumed almost another two months. The long treaty with France was mostly a matter of islands and fish. Both were vital. Islands, of course, meant harbours for naval bases; fish was a staple of commerce. Moreover, a fishing fleet was a nursery of seamen in time of peace that could provide experienced recruits in time of war.

A beginning was also made on the long-standing problem of the British logwood cutters in British Honduras, who were now to be allowed by Spain to cut and carry away logwood in a district the boundaries of which were to be set later. Logwood was so valuable a commodity, at one time selling upwards of £100 a ton, that pirates even ceased their piracy to become logwood cutters and shippers. It was useful because from it could be extracted a chemical used in dyeing wool, cotton, and other fibres. As Spain had previously harassed the logwood cutters, the provision in the treaty was important, but it was so vaguely worded that later it proved to be a troublesome point that Fox had to renegotiate.

What had Fox accomplished in his hundred days as Britain's first Foreign Secretary? So far as the preliminaries of peace were concerned, he could show only negligible results. He had little control of the negotiations, he did not or could not move rapidly or surely, and his resignation removed him from the scene while the discussions were at a tender stage. He argued that independence should be offered to the Americans unconditionally, without reference to past treaties or present bargaining points, and this point of view necessarily prevailed. He was never able, however, to shake the belief of many that he resigned because of a personal dislike of Shelburne rather than because of a principle, even a principle luminous enough to split the Cabinet for months, provoke hours of parliamentary debate, and puzzle the negotiators in Paris. So far as Russia, Prussia, and Holland were concerned, although he did not develop a consistent foreign policy he nonetheless recovered Russian friendship and improved British relations with Prussia. His attempt to drive a wedge between Holland and France was less successful because of counter pressure from the French court.[1] His attitude towards Ireland and the legislation which the Cabinet sponsored pleased Ireland mightily, though her troubles quickly

[1] de Madariaga, esp. Chapter 16, 'Fox's Foreign Policy', pp. 387–412.

mounted as time went on. Actually a hundred days is only a brief interval, especially in the field of foreign affairs.

Not to be overlooked is the fact that for a little while Fox achieved a complete reversal of his personal habits. He abandoned gambling, certainly not a simple accomplishment for one so enamoured of it and addicted to it, and poured his abundant energies into the duties of his office. His secretary hated to leave before his chief employer: 'Whilst light remained Fox never seemed tired.'[1] His traits of fairness and candour, his range of information and wide personal acquaintance, his gift for clear exposition and cogent argument as shown in his state papers, undoubtedly increased his stature as a statesman in the chancelleries of Europe. Closer home, he still could not like Shelburne and the King still did not like him.

Fox made the transition from Westminster back to Brooks's as effortlessly as he had a few months previously made the transition from Brooks's to Westminster. Moreover, about this time the word got around that Fox was in love with Mrs Robinson, the attractive and intelligent young woman who had achieved prominence as Perdita in *The Winter's Tale*. The Prince of Wales had taken an ardent liking to her, and promises were exchanged by which she became his mistress and was to receive a bond for £21,000 when he became 21. Apparently there were other obligations as well, for only the last year the King had learned that she threatened to publish his son's letters unless she were paid £5,000 for them, and had to appeal to North to secure them. This action separated Perdita from her royal lover. Now Charles discovered her. Of this romance George Selwyn and others saltily observed that nobody was so fit for the Man of the People as was the Woman of the People. Fox, the son of a duke's daughter who in her own right was a peer of the realm, and who himself was at ease in the stately homes, found his romantic attractions and later his permanent connection entirely outside the great families.

Here it must be recorded that some time between summer and fall, Fox and Perdita came to a parting of the ways, and Fox began to be seen even more in the company of Mrs Elizabeth Bridget Armistead, previously mentioned, a woman of unknown origins who had shared equal billings with Perdita in the columns of the London press. Known to London readers as Mrs R—n and Mrs A—d, they lived a gay life in the company of lords or gentlemen also identified with hyphens. By the end of the year Fox was fully sharing with Mrs Armistead his political hopes and dreams, writing that if his good friends Portland,

[1] Dorothy Margaret Stuart, *Dearest Bess* (London, 1955), p. 138.

Devonshire, and Fitzwilliam set out on a different course, 'I can never have any comfort in Politicks again.' In the letter was this note: 'God help my dearest Liz whose kindness to me makes up for all.'[1]

Paragraph writers were delighted with the theme of the Man of the People and his new consort, also called the Woman of the People. During the months ahead when Fox was struggling for his political existence, attempting to shrug off the attacks of the press on his coalition with North, London readers, as an obligato on the main theme, were treated to the subtle harmonics of Mrs A——d's companionship with the Foreign Secretary, party leader, and first parliamentary orator of the kingdom, the Right Honourable Charles James Fox.

[1] Add. MSS. 47570 [December 28, 1782].

12

Road to Coalition
1782-1783

[Fox and North] cannot be supposed to have either my
favour or confidence; . . . I shall most certainly refuse
any honours they may ask for.

George the Third

In July 1782 Fox was in his thirty-fourth year. 'I am a young man,' he
had told the Commons the opening day of the last session, 'but I cannot be called a young member of the House.' During his thirteen years
in Parliament, he had sat two years at the Admiralty board, thirteen
months at the Treasury, and three months in the Foreign Office—a
total of forty months. The rest of the time he had been in opposition.

Once again he resumed his customary seat on the third row of
opposition benches. Looking at the Government talent across the
carpet, he could observe a few changes. Thomas Townshend now sat
as Secretary of State for home affairs, the post just vacated by Shelburne,
now elevated to First Lord of the Treasury. The principal change,
however, was the presence of Pitt as Chancellor of the Exchequer. Pitt
had refused to accept a minor post in the Rockingham administration.
When Rockingham died, Pitt had expressed his concern to Fox that
the Government would break up. Fox said, 'it would; and the whole
system be revived'; adding; 'They look to *you*; *without* you they cannot succeed; *with* you I know not whether they will or no.' 'If', replied
Pitt, 'they reckon upon *me*, they may find themselves mistaken.'
Afterwards Fox, recounting the dialogue, added; 'I believe *they do*
reckon on Pitt, and I believe they will *not* be mistaken.'[1] Fox was
right. Shelburne had been able to enlist Pitt.

Most of the power of the new administration was in the Lords.
Shelburne, along with Camden, Thurlow, and Grafton, continued
there, and Fox could reflect ruefully that his colleagues Keppel, now a
viscount, Richmond, and Dunning, now Lord Ashburton, had joined
them. Also in the upper house was Grantham, Fox's successor as
Foreign Secretary. But all was not lost. Near Fox sat Cavendish and
Burke, who with him had forsaken posts in the Government to join
opposition.

[1] *Fox Cor.*, i, 446–7.

The two sides eyed each other warily. Wedderburn, for two years now in the Lords as Loughborough, friendlier to Fox than during the earlier years of the American revolution, thought the first move to strengthen opposition should be to reconcile North and Fox. 'The first, you know, is irreconcilable to no man; the second will feel his ancient resentment totally absorbed in his more recent hostility.'[1] The King wrote that the mask was now cast off; the issue was whether 'I am to be dictated to by Mr Fox, who avows that He must have the sole direction of this Country; Lord Shelburne certainly must and shall have my fullest support.'[2]

On the floor of the House of Commons it was Pitt versus Fox, just as a generation before it had been the elder Pitt versus the elder Fox. The sons, different from each other in temperament, seemed destined for political opposition. Now a new era had begun. In the years that followed, whenever Pitt rose to speak on a major issue, Fox was there to make immediate reply. Fox was therefore Pitt's chief obstacle; Fox, who could not be bought, won over, or frightened, could invariably be counted upon for a two-hour or three-hour sharp, penetrating, biting analysis of Pitt's measures. Sometimes Fox's opposition was better grounded than at other times, but it was always there. Pitt, later called 'the pilot that weathered the storm', was often right on lesser issues, sometimes wrong on mighty principles. In the passage of time Fox's blunders, it was noted, became inconsequential. His better ideas weathered the centuries.

Fox's persistent dislikes and obsessive hatreds are often recounted. Certainly this otherwise friendly, cordial person, entirely capable of forgiving affronts and even of suffering fools, found it well-nigh impossible in his lifetime to give his confidence to a few people—principally three. During the next few months he contended with all three at once: Pitt, across from him on the Treasury bench; Shelburne, in the other House as first minister; behind the scenes, the King himself.

Parliament rose in July, immediately after the formation of the new ministry. The King's speech at the opening of the winter session puzzled opposition orators with its statement that the treaty had been settled—a statement that implied that the independence tendered the Colonies could later be retracted. Thus again the old question was raised: were the Americans offered independence unconditionally or not?

Fox spoke heatedly on this issue. He recalled that the King had given him orders to write Grenville in Paris, unconditionally offering inde-

[1] Auckland, i, 9. To Eden, July 14, 1782.   [2] Fortescue, vi, 85. To Jenkinson, July 13.

pendence to America. Yet soon afterwards Shelburne had declared that the orders to Grenville had constituted a conditional offer of independence that could be recalled in certain circumstances.[1] The significance of this equivocation was not lost on those who had misgivings about Shelburne anyway. Opposition speakers pressed him to explain whether the concession of independence to America did, or did not, hinge upon the concluding of a treaty with France. In the other house, Fitzwilliam told the Lords 'it was impossible to walk the streets without being told of the inconsistency of ministers . . . it was the subject of all the newspapers, and the topic of general conversation'. To get a clearcut statement, Fitzwilliam wrote the question down and read it aloud: Is the independence of America contingent or not? Shelburne, however, refused to answer. He was bound to keep the King's secrets and would not divulge them.[2] The refusal was suspicious, the excuse ominous. It now became clear that only Fox's presence in the last Cabinet had kept alive the proposal to offer the colonies immediate, irrevocable, independence. Once he had left, the Cabinet took a temporizing, equivocal position.

The preliminary articles of peace were finally presented on January 27. Shelburne was of course eager to have Parliament approve them although he fully realized he might not be able to command the necessary vote. He therefore began to feel out the opposing camp to determine whether an arrangement could be made to strengthen his Government. His following was estimated at 140, North's at 120, Fox's at 90.[3] So there were three distinct groups of such a size that an alliance of two groups was necessary to command a majority. Pitt, understanding this arithmetic, asked Fox to state the terms on which he would support the Government. The reply was that there were no such terms while Lord Shelburne remained, and so the brief interview ended. W. W. Grenville, Thomas's younger brother, who reported the conversation to Lord Temple, concluded that Pitt must be 'very desperate' and Fox 'very confident' for such a question to be 'so put and so answered'.[4]

Since a Fox–Shelburne alliance was impossible on the face of it, the alternatives were either Shelburne–North or Fox–North. North therefore held the pivotal position. It was to his interest not to drift away from the centre of power. As banker Thomas Coutts put it,

[1] *Parliamentary History*, xxiii, 231–44.   [2] *Ibid.*, xxiii, 305–6.
[3] *Letters of Gibbon*, ii, 311. To Sheffield, October 14. In July the figures had been about the same: Shelburne 130, North 120, Fox 80 (*HMCR*, Carlisle MSS., Selwyn to Carlisle, pp. 633–4).
[4] *Court and Cabinets*, i, 149. February 11, 1783. *Fox Cor.*, ii, 33. Another version of the dialogue states that when Pitt told Fox that Shelburne would continue at the head of any new arrangement, Fox declared: 'It is impossible for me to belong to any administration of which Lord Shelburne is the head.' Pitt replied, 'Then we need discuss the matter no further; I did not come here to betray Lord Shelburne' (Stanhope, i, 93).

North's friends would desert him 'if they find he is no longer to be dispenser of loaves and fishes'.[1] William Adam, Fox's duelling opponent, adroitly approached North to sound out the possibility of a junction with Shelburne. The terms of this union were not, however, agreeable to North.[2] Moreover, Pitt and Richmond inflexibly opposed a Shelburne–North alliance; to them, North's management of the war and his subservience to the Crown stamped him to them as a person not to be associated with.[3] North decided that the only way to prevent the dissolution of his party was to approach Fox. Meanwhile Fox, despite reservations about coalescing with North, had decided that such a union would be feasible even though it could not be permanent.[4]

At their first meeting on February 14, Fox and North were able to evolve a working agreement. In other meetings their intermediaries pounded out the details. The two agreed to oppose the address; they agreed to lay aside their former animosity; they concluded they would not press economical reform; they declared each man could follow his own bent on parliamentary reform. Fox argued that the King should not be suffered to be his own minister. North agreed, saying that 'the appearance of power is all that a King of this country can have'. He further argued that government by departments was 'a very bad system'; one man or a cabinet should govern the whole. 'Government by departments was not brought in by me,' he continued. 'I found it so, and had not vigour and resolution to put an end to it.'[5]

Each had friends who opposed the juncture. John Robinson had written to North: 'If you and Mr Fox should overthrow the present administration and form one, your heart will tell you that it could not be permanent or pleasant.'[6] Fox's hunting friend of many years, Coke of Norfolk, had called it 'a most revolting compact'. Only Fox's assurance that North had agreed to act on his opinion, not the other way round, redeemed the prospect in Coke's mind.[7] Grafton told Fox that he did not like the arrangement, 'yet in the present state of the country, I do not see what better can now be substituted'.[8]

The final discussions between the two and their go-betweens were not concluded until four or five o'clock on the morning of February 17.[9] The debate on the preliminaries was scheduled to open that afternoon. So Parliament formally turned its attention to the acceptance or rejection of the proposals for peace. Were they 'such as merited applause, or deserved disapprobation?'

[1] Ernest Hartley Coleridge, *The Life of Thomas Coutts, Banker* (London, 1920), i, 161. February 22.
[2] *Fox Cor.*, ii, 29–36.   [3] Wraxall, ii, 415.   [4] Grafton, p. 355.
[5] *Fox Cor.*, ii, 37–8.   [6] *HMCR*, Abergavenny MSS., p. 57. February 1.
[7] A. M. W. Stirling, *Coke of Norfolk and His Friends* (London, n.d.), i, 212.
[8] Grafton, p. 374.   [9] Wraxall, ii, 422.

The debate in the Lords was earnest and thorough. The advantages of peace were generally admitted: the nation was tired of war, men of landed property were burdened by the increasing tax load, men of commerce were eager to revive old channels of trade and open new ones, and in general all desired the tranquillity of Europe, Britain, and America.

To opposition debaters, however, the terms were onerous. The new boundary line between the States and Canada was not only too generous in its disposal of territory, but seemed to have been drawn by men who had no knowledge of North American geography. The territory ceded the new states contained powerful forts, constructed by the British at great expense. To yield them would leave Canada defenceless against the Indians, and moreover, the fur trade would be 'totally and absolutely lost'. The fisheries were, moreover, irretrievably gone. Furthermore, to give up Penobscot, 'a nursery of masts', was unwise and unfortunate. And to expect that the new Congress would be able to persuade the several states to repeal the wartime laws that had banished loyalists and confiscated their property was entirely too incredible and naïve. The situation would be especially hard on those loyalists who had actually borne arms on the British side.

Shelburne ably defended the treaty. Opening with the conventional disarming statements that he would rely on facts, not emotion, and attempting to reassure the Lords of his own personal integrity in the matter, he discussed one by one the objections that had been raised. He stated that the wisdom or lack of wisdom in drawing the boundaries depended entirely upon the gain or loss of trade, and that the exports to Canada were of the order of only £140,000 and the imports were no more than £50,000. Even if the entire fur trade of £50,000 were sunk into the sea, he asked, is this a sufficient reason for continuing the war?

As for ceding advantageous fishing rights to the Americans, Shelburne declared that Britain had ample fishing resources left, including superior facilities for curing and drying. The rivalry, he persisted, would be stimulating. As for the loss of masts in Penobscot: 'I will oppose a fact to [the] bare assertion. I have in my pocket a certificate from one of the ablest surveyors . . . that there is not a tree there capable of being made into a mast.' Loss of the phenomenally tall and straight timber of the colonies—a kind almost unknown in Britain— would have been serious. Masts in an eighteenth-century conflict were vital, like oil in the middle of the twentieth.

Finally, he urged, the advantages of a peace were overwhelming. Britain was hardly in a position to continue the war or demand more at the peace table. 'We are 197 millions in debt . . . our credit is beginning to totter . . . our navy is in poor shape . . . naval stores exhausted, cordage rotten . . . magazines in a low condition.' To this last observation the new Viscount Keppel, standing on sure ground, offered a firm but brief denial, but the Lords decided, by a majority of thirteen, that they were contended with the peace. Shelburne's career here reached its summit.

In the Commons the debate on that February 17 took a different turn.

The presence of Fox and North side by side on the front opposition bench confirmed the rumours that the two had made an arrangement. Fox, whose late hours at Brooks had accustomed him to going without sleep, was fresh and alert. North, however, unable to keep awake during the opening speeches, left his seat and went to the gallery to sit beside Wraxall. There he fitfully dozed, first asking Wraxall to awaken him whenever Government speakers uttered uncomplimentary remarks. After an hour and a half of such interrupted repose, he began to arouse himself and resumed his place next to Fox.[1] Soon afterwards gaining the floor, he made a pointed attack on the provisions of the treaty. Though he sympathized with ministers in the difficult task of framing an acceptable treaty, he found little in the proposed articles with France, Spain, or America that pleased him. He did not like the liberal granting of fishing rights off Newfoundland or the cession of St Lucia. Nor did he like to see Spain in the possession of Minorca and the Floridas. Most of all North was concerned with the fate of the loyalists: those who had not fought on the British side were promised a sort of protection, but those who had fought for the British were apparently promised only a twelve-month amnesty during which they could endeavour to recover their confiscated properties. The mother country should show more gratitude and offer more protection.

As the debate progressed, however, and members saw the expected alliance between North and Fox in action, Government speakers capitalized further upon the incongruity of this situation. Here was the former first minister unsympathetic to the problems of drafting a peace; and here especially was a man who had clamoured repeatedly for peace not only now backing rapidly away from it, but in so doing embracing the support of the minister he had so persistently and bitterly attacked. Among those who ridiculed the coalition was Dundas; claiming that Fox had once boasted that he had a peace in his pocket, he asked that Fox's peace should now be produced, in order that members could compare the Fox peace with the Shelburne peace.

During the evening Daniel Pulteney wrote: 'Fox and Lord North have been laughed at for their alliance by nearly every speaker. It is

[1] Wraxall, ii, 423–4.

now a quarter past one, and neither Fox or Pitt have yet risen.'[1] Pulteney, an independent, voted with Fox on this occasion though later he became a supporter of Pitt and a sharp critic of Fox.

When Fox did rise he found it imperative to answer the many personal accusations that had been hurled. The circumstances under which, said Fox, he had urged peace, were different from those that existed today; furthermore, he could never have yearned for such a peace as was now being tendered:

You call for peace, . . . you urge the necessity of peace, you insist on peace; then peace you shall have, but such a peace, that you shall sicken at its very name. You call for peace, and I will give you a peace that shall make you repent the longest day you live, that ever you breathed a wish for peace. I will give you a peace which shall make you and all men wish that the war had been continued . . .

As he went on he had better to offer than such rhythmical cabbage (Pitt later effectively parodied it) when he denied the charge that he had ever said, 'I have a peace in my pocket':

The learned lord [Dundas] called upon him to produce the peace which he had projected. This was a very loud and sounding word; but the learned lord not being a cabinet minister, was at liberty to hazard bold things, which, if he was a cabinet minister, he was pretty sure he would not do. Will any one of the King's ministers, said Mr. Fox, give me the same challenge? Will they call upon me to produce the peace? I dare them to do it. I challenge them to do it. They know what it is; they have it in the office.

Few were more effective than Fox in answering unfounded charges. Neither Dundas nor Mr Secretary Townshend cared to take the floor for a rejoinder.

Next, in a passage that has become famous, he explained why he had joined hands with one 'whose principles I have been in the habit of opposing for the last seven years of my life'. He declared:

It is neither wise nor noble to keep up animosities for ever. . . . It is not my nature to bear malice, or to live in ill will. My friendships are perpetual, my enmities are not so. . . .

When a man ceases to be what he was, when the opinions which made him obnoxious are changed, he then is no more my enemy, but my friend. The American war was the cause of the enmity between the noble lord and myself. The American war, and the American question, is at an end.

Fox did not enter into the details of the treaties, however, although he did declare that the terms were obnoxious in the extreme, laying his finger on points 'which above others were ruinous and fatal to our commerce'.[2] Pitt, who followed, also commented on 'the unnatural alliance', which was 'undoubtedly to be reckoned among the wonders of the age'. Such political apostasy not only astonished a young man

[1] *HMCR*, Rutland MSS., iii, 68. To the Duchess of Rutland [February 17, 1783].
[2] *Parliamentary History*, xxiii, 485–9.

like him, he added, but also confounded the most veteran observers of the human heart.

At seven-thirty in the morning the House divided: 208 for the ministry, 224 against it. Sixty additional members were reported to have paired. Accordingly, in one of the large houses of the century, the ministry was defeated by 16 votes. The reversal was a pretty broad hint to Shelburne, as the situation was described later, that he was not altogether so popular as he had imagined.[1]

Much of the press vividly expressed its disapproval of the coalition. The *Morning Post* called it a gross and unpardonable insult to either or both men. The *Post* emphasized Fox's inconsistency. It recalled that once he had said, 'the moment he should make any terms with [North], he would rest satisfied to be called *the most infamous of mankind*', or that he 'so much detested Lord North, he could not even bear to sit in the same room with him!' Seldom has a politician furnished his opponents with so much volatile fuel. A pamphlet, *Fox against Fox*, lining up pairs of these opposite sentiments delivered before and after the juncture, had a wide sale. Another reviewed his political inconsistencies from his earliest speeches onward; Fox's 'political conduct contains incontestable proofs of tergiversation, duplicity, and inconsistency'.[2] The always loyal Fitzpatrick stated the situation more realistically: 'The apparent juncture with Lord North is universally cried out against, though . . . all moderate and reasonable men approve of it as the only means of establishing any government in this country.'[3]

On February 21 Cavendish offered five resolutions, the last one censuring the peace treaty for more generous terms than the adversaries of the nation had earned. Near the close of a long debate, Fox rose to his feet and made a long speech—the *Whitehall Evening-Post* clocked him at nearly three hours—in which he 'entered minutely into his political principles'. Going through the treaty in detail, he cited the many concessions made to England's foes and the few made to England herself. Treaties should be made either on the basis of *uti possidetis* [possessions now held], he explained, as when one combatant in a superior position can lay claim to all the territory of the other that it had conquered; or on the basis of general restitution, as when the combatants have an equal desire for peace and seek to restore to each other all lost possessions. This treaty, however, combined both the dishonour of *uti possidetis* and the disadvantage of restitution. 'France retains what she has taken from us, and receives a general restitution of all we have taken from her.' But more than to denounce the treaty, Fox

[1] *Parliamentary History*, xxiii, 521. Debate of February 21.
[2] *A state of facts: or a sketch of the character and political conduct of . . . Fox* (London, 1783).
[3] Add. MSS. 47579. To Ossory, February 22. *Fox Cor.*, ii, 18–19.

rose to defend the coalition: 'Only from the coalition of parties . . . [can] the spirit of constitutional power . . . be restored to its former vigour.' In conclusion he trusted that the consequence of the coalition will be the salvation of the country.

The principal defender of the peace in the Commons had to be young Chancellor Pitt. That night, however, he was so unwell that, during Fox's speech, he had to retire to Solomon's Porch, just behind the Speaker's chair, to relieve his tortured stomach. He held the door open, however, so that he would miss none of Fox's argument.[1] Pitt's speech, also three hours long, is briefly reported, but enough remains to demonstrate its logic and its eloquence. Reviewing the items of the treaty, he held them up as a better bargain than Fox had alleged. More particularly he accurately declared that the opposition was not so eager to defeat the peace as to remove Shelburne:

It is not this treaty, it is the earl of Shelburne alone whom the movers of this question are desirous to wound. . . . This is the aim of the unnatural coalition to which I have alluded. If, however, . . . this ill-omened marriage is not already solemnized, I know a just and lawful impediment, and, in the name of the public safety, I here forbid the banns.

He reminded the House forcefully of North's ill-starred administration of the war and concluded with lofty lines from Horace.[2] New Foreign Secretary Grantham wrote: 'I hear nothing ever equalled the speech which he made upon the state of the navy, army, and finance, all concurring to contradict . . . the resolution. He is a most extraordinary phenomenon, . . . and his character untainted.'[3]

It was the first of the great Pitt–Fox debates. If Pitt's eloquence came even in part from the visit to Solomon's Porch, then every legislative assembly should install one.

The resolutions were carried by 17 votes: 207 to 190. The news greatly distressed the King: 'I am sorry it has been my lot to Reign in the most profligate Age and when the most unatural coalition seems to have taken place, which can but add confusion and distraction among a too much divided Nation.'[4]

The defeat of the peace brought on Shelburne's resignation, followed by an interregnum of six weeks filled with all manner of proposals and counter proposals. A Fox–North coalition could command the votes but was unpopular. As Fitzpatrick wrote: 'unless a *real good Government* is the consequence of this junction, nothing can justify it to the publick.' Pitt was approached on the subject of forming a new

[1] Robert Isaac Wilberforce and Samuel Wilberforce, *The Life of William Wilberforce* (London, 1838), i, 26.
[2] *Parliamentary History*, xxiii, 498–555.
[3] Malmesbury, ii, 35. To Sir James Harris, February 22.   [4] Fortescue, vi, 245.

Government and apparently at one stage of the negotiations agreed to do so, Dundas assuring him that he would have a majority in Parliament. He had, however, asked for time to reflect, and later in the day wrote that he had decided he could not count either on North's support or North's remaining neutral.[1]

The name of the Duke of Portland was then put forward, word going to the King through North that Fox and his friends could not form a part of any administration unless Portland was at the head. Fox wrote the Prince to that effect, adding: 'This negociation is therefore entirely at an end, and not only the country is now without a Ministry, but there does not appear at present any prospect of making one.'[2] The King had many reasons for not wanting Fox in the Government, one being the friendship between Fox and the Prince. The Prince had warmly espoused the cause of the coalition and was declared to have exclaimed aloud in the drawing room 'that his father had not yet agreed to the plan of the Coalition, but, by God, he should be made to agree to it'.[3] The King glumly thought about abdication. In his collected papers under date of March 28 is a trial draft in which he stated that he was determined to 'quit this Island', retire to 'the Original Patrimony of my Ancestors', and turn the kingdom over to the Prince.[4]

After a final, unsuccessful plea with North to take the ministry, the King consented that Portland should be the nominal head of the new Government, with the rest of the Cabinet as follows: Secretaries of State—North (home department), Fox (foreign department); President of the Council—Stormont; Lord Privy Seal—Carlisle; Chancellor of the Exchequer—Cavendish; First Lord of the Admiralty—Keppel. The King much wanted to keep the rugged and indestructible Thurlow as Lord Chancellor, but had to give way on this point and put the great seal into the custody of a three-man commission. To pry Thurlow out of office was not a small achievement. He had been Lord Chancellor nearly five years, and once he got back in would serve many more. Fitzpatrick became Secretary at War; Burke, Paymaster of the Forces; Sheridan, a Secretary to the Treasury; and Mansfield, Speaker of the Lords.[5]

'Both Lord North and Charles Fox suffer in the estimation of the impartial,' said the *Whitehall Evening-Post*. By turns it was ironic and critical; North, for his charity and meekness in reconciling himself to his greatest political enemy, should be made Archbishop of Canterbury.

---

[1] Melville MSS., February 27 [1783]. To Dundas. (Clements.) Earl Stanhope, *Life of the Right Honourable William Pitt*, 3rd edn (London, 1867), i, 107.
[2] A. Aspinall, ed., *The Correspondence of George, Prince of Wales, 1770–1812* (New York, 1963), i, 103. [March 4, 1783.]
[3] *Last Journals*, ii, 496–7. [4] Fortescue, vi, 316–17.
[5] Arrangements for Fitzpatrick and others are reviewed in letters from Eden to Fox, April 3 and Fox to Portland, April 4 (Welbeck Abbey MSS. PWF 3970/1). (Nottingham.)

The coalition was democratic insolence, it was superior deceit and barefaced imposition, it possessed not a single virtue; public honour had gone to the dogs and public safety was following it; treason was rampant and loyalty was at her feet; liberty had shot herself through the head. The *Morning Chronicle* fairly sputtered: apostasy, effrontery, profligate indecency; democracy bid fair to ruin England; mistakes of ignorance and the designs of bad men are equally fatal. The *Herald* denounced the coalition as universally execrated. 'Not fiction herself can produce a parallel in infamy . . . the one is as vilely reprobated by his Majesty as the other is by the Majesty of the People.' The *Morning Post* observed that members of the House now got up and left when Fox rose to his legs, as they had generally done with Burke; no fewer than twelve members, it reported, walked out on Fox during a recent parliamentary rhapsody. French newspapers spoke of *cette monstreuse coalition, cette éxecrable union, cet objet de l'horreur*. To climax all, the *Post* served this delicacy: a woman caught in bed with another man declared, when upbraided by her husband, that since the coalition there is nothing left to blush at.

In entering into a coalition with North, Fox earnestly felt that he had devised an arrangement that would give him a relatively free hand in developing his policies. Moreover, the American question, over which he and North had had their most violent disagreements, was now, in the main, behind them. Again, he was not, as he said, inclined to continue personal animosity toward North. On the other hand, he did not want to move in Shelburne's direction either personally or politically. Nor did he want to continue in opposition; he had enjoyed many aspects of the minister's life during the months he had held office. He was fairly warned that the coalition was politically dangerous—he had the counsel of friends like Coke and others—and his own experience of having his youthful speeches continually quoted against him had made him painfully aware of the persistence of human memory. Nor was there any popular clamour for him to assume office. Notwithstanding, he made the decision to coalesce—and the paragraphers, the pamphlet writers, cartoonists, speakers on the hustings, the platform, and in Parliament, and the general public as well, bitterly assailed him for more than a decade.

Although Shelburne had resigned on the 26th of February, not until the 8th of April was the coalition ministry finally admitted to office.

Again it was necessary for Fox to go before the electors of Westminster. Up to the day of the election an effort was made to scare up an opponent, but without success. The usual parade got under way. The primitive sounds of marrow bones striking meat cleavers alternated with the more civilized music of a band. Men carried standards of blue silk and gold lace and the usual banners proclaiming 'Liberty' and 'Independence'. But there were notable differences. Instead of being received as 'The Man of the People', the *Morning Post* reported, 'there were calls of *Hunt the Fox!—Holloo, turncoat!—None of your damned speeches!—You shan't make fun of us any more!—Knock him down!*' The *Morning Chronicle* moreover proposed that the following alterations were to be made in the next edition of Johnson's *Dictionary* at the request of the *two friends*:

Traitor.—An honest man; one who serves his country.
Scoundrel.—A gentleman, every inch of him.
Consistency.—Turning round to all the points in the compass.

The *Public Advertiser* put its sentiments into doggerel:

> The Broad-Bottomed Administration: or, Mr. F's Genuine Thanks
> to His Westminster Electors.
>
> Quoth N— to F—, 'You've got your Ends,
> In spite of all your foes!'
> 'I have,' says F—, 'See how my friends
> I do lead by the Nose.'
> 'I see't,' says N— again; 'such Blocks
> Prove Country's Good a Farce is;
> So we broad-bottomed'—'Right,' Says F—,
> 'We bid them kiss our —.'

Lord John Townshend witnessed the installation of the new ministers. In later years he would say that he had predicted the coalition would not endure, for he was at court when Fox kissed hands and observed 'George III turn back his ears and eyes just like the horse at Astley's, when the tailor he had determined to throw was getting on him'.[1] The King wrote Lord Temple that the new ministry could not enjoy his confidence; he planned at the outset not to support its requests for peerages or other honours, and he hoped that the Grenvilles, the Pitts, and other men of abilities and character would relieve him from this situation. 'My sorrow may prove fatal to my health if I remain long in this thraldom.'[2]

---

[1] *Fox Cor.*, ii, 28.   [2] Fortescue, vi, 330. April 1; *Court and Cabinets*, i, 219.

13

Mr Secretary Fox
1783

Great Britain and the United States must still be inseparable, either as Friends or Foes. This is an awful and important Truth.

David Hartley

King and press spoke as one: the coalition was unpopular. But unpopular or not, it was in the saddle. For the second time in thirteen months, Fox found himself at the post of Foreign Secretary, and resumed his duties with earnestness and zeal.

On the floor of the Commons the new Government had to perform certain housekeeping duties; among other matters, to repeal the prohibitory Acts against the Americans and to make better arrangements to manage trade and commerce between them and the mother country. From Fox to the King flowed a steady stream of notes, just as in earlier days the stream had flowed from North. Fox's communications were gracious and explicit, models of correctness; the King's replies brief and pointed. Fox concluded one of his longer epistles: 'Whenever Your Majesty will be graciously pleased to condescend even to hint your inclinations upon any subject, that it will be the study of Your Majesty's Ministers to show how truly sensible they are of Your Majesty's goodness.'[1]

This passage carries particular significance. Considering his many strong utterances against the throne, Fox indeed humbled himself to write it. The King's dislike was broad bottomed, however, so on the letter he wrote only the grim endorsement: 'No answer.' Perhaps Fox can be accused of obsequiousness, but at least one person was confident that Fox was sincere in attempting to create a working relationship with the King: the Duke of Queensberry later told George that Fox had every disposition to comply with his wishes. 'I can assert as an undoubted fact that there was scarcely any proof of his personal devotion, or any sacrifice that he would not have made, to acquire your favour.' The King retorted that Fox never said as much to him. 'No, sir,' replied the Duke, 'assuredly he did not, because your Majesty never gave him any encouragement. . . .'[2]

[1] Fortescue, vi, 357. April 16, 1783. *Fox Cor.*, ii, 123–4.
[2] Wraxall reports the conversation, iii, 119–20.

The King was more kindly disposed to a petition from Portland begging the customary leave to lay himself at his Majesty's feet and to 'offer his most devout and fervent prayers for Your Majesty's uninterrupted enjoyment of every Blessing which The Divine Providence can bestow. . . .' To this overture the King responded in a short but amicable sentence: 'The D. of Portland's very feeling expressions for my welfare and that of my Family are not thrown away upon Me.'[1]

Even with Fox promising to be sensible of his Majesty's goodness and the Duke's offer of devout and fervent prayers, the line of communication between King and ministers was slender and uncertain. Who can say what changes would have been wrought in the shaping of the whig party had the King replied even with measured grace both to Fox and Portland? A decade later the latter two drifted apart: Portland, with obvious reluctance, split with Fox, joined the Government, and, as Home Secretary, policed the mass meetings that Fox addressed and reported Fox's language to the King as faithfully as Pitt ever did.

A full House assembled on May 7 to hear Pitt speak on parliamentary reform. So crowded was the chamber that members were obliged to stand in the passages; the doors of the gallery were locked at eleven o'clock, and after that no strangers were admitted. Fox supported, North opposed, the motion. In a striking passage contrasting Pitt and Fox, Walpole foresaw that Pitt's character was more likely to set him at the head of Government than was that of any other man, though his native abilities were inferior to Fox's. He continued:

Had not Pitt so early aspired to be his rival, Fox would have cherished Pitt as his friend and disciple. Fox was charmed with [him] . . . and loved him. Pitt [once said], 'Mr Fox had never been answered.' When he forced Fox to answer *him*, it was with such facility of superiority, that Pitt had better have remembered that neither Thurlow, nor Dundas, nor both together, could defeat Fox.[2]

For an hour and a half, this May day, Fox 'commanded throughout the most general attention,' as the *Gazetteer* observed. Others spoke in turn; then Burke sought the floor. It was not much after midnight, but many members, fearing a long-winded speech, rose and left the House. Half a dozen newspapers commented on the slight, the *Gazetteer* recording this sympathetic note about a speaker sometimes, unfairly, called the 'dinner bell':

The House of Commons gave a marked proof of their unwillingness to hear a gentleman who is one of the first orators in the world—but who is addicted to long-winded harangues. When Mr Fox concluded his brilliant speech, during

---

[1] Fortescue, vi, 377–8. May 7, 8.   [2] *Fox Cor.*, ii, 81.

which every member was arrested in his seat, Mr Burke rose, but could not command the attention of the House.—There was a general retreat to dinner.

North's opposition to reform was apparent in the division. The house voted Pitt down by 293 to 149, a majority of 144 votes.

In June the House passed a Bill providing that receipts be stamped. The two Westminster members disagreed on the Bill, Sir Cecil Wray opposing and Fox supporting. Their differences would be echoed in detail at the next general election.

A factor that prevented George III from abdicating those bleak days of the spring of 1783 was the persistent, bitter thought that the Prince would be elevated to the throne. Had George Augustus Frederick been a beloved son the King could have stepped down with relief. But the Prince's life, in sharp contrast with the King's quiet and sombre demeanor, caused the parents continued anguish. The Prince's habits were extravagant, he could swear in three languages, he was not always truthful, he gambled excessively, he could drink any quantity of liquor without passing out under the table. Both his political and female companions were of the wrong sort. In addition to the other grievances of the King against Fox was the major one that Fox and his son were confederates in all of this wickedness. Thurlow told the King that he would have no peace until he clapped both of them into the Tower.[1]

Now the Prince, approaching twenty-one, needed a regular income to support his personal establishment. This issue was the sort that could break any ministry. Fox was in an especially sensitive position as he was now compelled to request funds to enable the Prince to carry on his highly disapproved social and political escapades.

At first the lavish sum of £100,000 was proposed, an amount that had no doubt been mentioned in the hearing of the Prince in the days of the Shelburne ministry. Apparently the King agreed to this sum at the outset and instructed Portland to ask Parliament for it. Meanwhile the notion suddenly seemed repugnant to the King. A violent reaction set in; he even invited Temple to take over the Government and sent a servant in livery to stop the Duke of Richmond from going to France; Richmond would be useful if there were to be a change.

Meanwhile notes and letters fluttered back and forth. Portland and the Cabinet reflected upon a compromise: if the King could allow his son £50,000 from the civil list, Parliament would be asked to provide the remaining £50,000. With humility the Duke wrote this suggestion into a letter to the King, but as quickly added the proviso that if the

[1] *Last Journals*, ii, 497.

King, looking ahead to a future day when he would need to provide for all the younger princes and princesses 'with which Providence has blessed Your Majesty', found he could not afford even the £50,000, the Duke would certainly call upon Parliament for that additional sum as well. Another long and involved paragraph, revealing to his Majesty that the Prince had accumulated £29,000 in debts, was accompanied by the gentle suggestion that these be offset by 'the great liberality of Your Majesty'.

The effect on the King was immediate: 'It is impossible for me to find words expressive enough of my utter indignation and astonishment.' The sum of £100,000 was unbelievably extravagant, and whatever lesser sum that was appropriate should certainly come principally from Parliament. The Duke quickly offered to follow any plan the King wished, but the reply to that letter brought little cheer. The King declared his feelings were not altered and that the financial weight of the Prince's establishment was one that he was not able to bear. To pay the debts, moreover, would be a shameful squandering of public money and would encourage additional extravagance in the Prince.[1]

Like other ministers, Fox was dismayed at the turn events were taking. He wrote to Northington, Lord Lieutenant of Ireland: 'There is great reason to think that our administration will not outlive tomorrow, or that at least it will be at an end in a very few days', adding that a week ago every one had believed the matter had been 'perfectly agreed upon'.[2] As he wrote this he did not know that a solution was in sight: a crashing *deus ex machina* in the person of the King himself. Portland was summoned to the King, *'who, in an agony of tears, kissed the Duke, confessed he had gone too far, and begged the Duke to rescue him'*. The words and the italics are Walpole's.[3] Eventually the King's new attitude was conveyed to Fox as the likeliest person to manage the Prince. In a careful letter Fox counselled the Prince to accept a lesser sum than £100,000, even though it did not meet his expectations, and, 'whatever you may feel, . . . conduct yourself so as to put the world on your side'.[4] In order to keep harmony within the royal family and between the King and his ministers, the Prince accepted the King's newest proposal. So Fox could soon get off another note to Northington: 'There is reason to think that the storm is for the present dissipated. . . . The Prince has behaved in the handsomest manner.'[5]

On June 25 a revised arrangement was reported to the House. The

[1] Fortescue, vi, 401, 403. June 16.
[2] Add. MSS. 38716, 69; 47567. *Fox Cor.*, ii, 114. June 17.
[3] *Last Journals*, ii, 525. June 16.
[4] *Correspondence of George, Prince of Wales*, i, 127. June 20 [1783.]
[5] Add. MSS. 38716, 71. June 19. See also Add. MSS. 47567.

crisis was passed but no wounds really healed. The King more than ever determined not to show his ministers any favour. There would be civility enough, as Fizpatrick wrote, but 'no peerages, no marks of *real* support'.[1] The King told Lord Hertford that every morning he wished himself eighty, or ninety, or dead.[2]

Concomitantly with the business of the Prince, Fox worked spring and summer on negotiations with America, France, and Spain. He selected, as plenipotentiary to the Americans, David Hartley, long-time friend of Benjamin Franklin. Hartley had steadily opposed the American war and was a loyal member of the Rockingham group.

The negotiations are worth recounting briefly since they reveal something of Fox's capacities as a minister. His generous nature is shown in the correspondence with 'trusty and welbeloved' David Hartley, transmitting in conventional language authority to deal with 'our good friends the United States', and advising him to negotiate 'fairly and ingenuously'. Franklin was pleased with these 'handsome words'—'our good friends the United States' struck him as indeed neighbourly since he could recall other language used in times past.[3] To Robert R. Livingston, former member of Congress, then Secretary of Foreign Affairs, Adams confided that Hartley's disposition was good and his judgment liberal and fair.[4]

But Franklin and his colleagues were not to be wooed simply by handsome words. They knew the temper and the spirit of England and Englishmen. Through London and continental newspapers they kept abreast of parliamentary debates and legislation enacted. Informants back in the Colonies supplied other details. To Livingston, Adams reported the consensus of a lively discussion among him, Franklin, and Jay, in which they agreed that the Fox–North coalition was a rope of sand, that Fox's 'pushing the vote . . . disapproving the peace' meant that 'no confidence can be placed in him by us', that only men like Shelburne, Townshend, and Pitt 'had just notions of their country and ours'. 'Whether these men', concluded Adams, 'if now called to power, would pursue their former ideas I know not. The Bible teaches us not to put our trust in princes, and *a fortiori* in ministers of state.'[5] The Americans therefore learned to deal realistically with the British Government as they found it. They could only hope that this time it would last long enough not only to negotiate a treaty but to ratify it. Hartley quickly

[1] Add. MSS. 47579. To Ossory.   [2] *Last Journals*, ii, 529.
[3] FO 4/2, 3–7, 55–60. Fox to Hartley, April 10; Hartley to Fox, May 20.
[4] Wharton, vi, 447. May 24.
[5] *Ibid.*, vi, 512. July 3. But Jay once angrily declared: 'It is evident thro'out that Ld. Shelburne had no settled ideas or principle about anything' (unsigned note, FO 4/3, pt. 1, 5).

saw, and reported to his chief, that they were 'well apprized' on all vital subjects.

The Americans, who took advantage of their vast distance in time and space from Congress to trim its instructions to fit the occasion, had learned in dealing with Thomas Grenville that streams of authority did not flow easily in the pipes of the Foreign Office. Accordingly, they questioned Hartley as to whether he had full power to act, and were impatient of delay as he had to shuttle every inquiry back across the Channel before he could provide an answer.[1] Fox, however, cannot be held accountable for flaws in the system under which he operated. The British Cabinet was no more unified to wage peace than it had been to wage war.

The greatest conflict between Hartley and the Americans was British insistence that American ships be subject to British regulatory Acts. For example, it was proposed that American ships could carry only American goods to Great Britain or the West Indies.[2] Fox was adamant that Hartley was not to bargain away this point, and when Hartley tried to nibble at it, Fox repeated the point. He stressed the importance of trade and commerce between the two countries in his first instructions to Hartley, stating that produce of the thirteen states should be admitted to Britain without duties ('those imposed during the war excepted') and in return produce *and* manufactures of Great Britain should be admitted into the United States in like manner. Fox then admitted that this was not completely a reciprocal arrangement, since it excluded manufactured products of the new country, but he went on to write, with the free spirit in which one man can dispose of another's privileges, that the introduction of American manufactured products into Great Britain would be of no service to either and might fraudulently allow importers to substitute European goods for American. Moreover, he reminded Hartley that, following present restrictions 'wholly in our power' to impose, American ships could carry only American produce and no other merchandise to the West Indies.[3]

Hartley's closely reasoned prose stated the American position with eloquence. The American commissioners, he said, see their own country thus:

. . . as new states the world is before them, open and free, that a plentifull commercial supply to themselves, unconnected with any political system of commerce,

[1] FO 4/2, 63–5. Hartley to Fox, May 22. For an analysis of congressional instructions to its envoys, see Richard B. Morris's learned work, *The Peacemakers* (New York, 1965), Chap. 1; also Chap. 18.
[2] Cabinet minute, April 8. Fortescue, vi, 349. Holland House photostats, ii, 38. (Clements.)
[3] FO 4/2. Fox to Hartley, April 10. Fox reemphasized the point in his letter of May 15. Copies of these and other letters and documents in Hartley's handwriting may be seen in the Hartley Papers (Clements), vols i–iv.

is their only concern; that the rising trade of America will become the great object of all European states, and that the wisest European nation will be that which shall first unite in the most unlimited reciprocity with them.[1]

No 'American bottoms limited to American goods', but complete and unlimited reciprocity.

The American argument put a halt to Fox's original line of reasoning. Fox, however, had not for nothing debated a dozen years in St Stephen's. He had his back to the wall since British navigation Acts and orders in council continued to seek to regulate the movement of American ships and cargoes. He therefore shifted his ground and took a different approach: he requested Hartley to advise the Americans candidly that a new proposal at this time with all its difficulties would embarrass an English administration. Let the preliminaries be signed, he urged, regardless of this conflict of interest; later, after the treaty, American wishes and American opinions could come through English subjects and English merchants, 'and not through . . . negociators who are considered as triumphant with respect to this country. . . . You, sir, know enough of this country to know in how very different a manner the whole of this matter will be considered.' In a subsequent note he added that he had seen Laurens, 'who is clear we can agree'.[2]

Strong as was Fox on general principle, he was at times dilatory in keeping up his end of the correspondence. On July 2, for example, an order in council was proclaimed, regulating trade between the British West Indies and the American states; Hartley had his first news of this document from the American commissioners and not through his own diplomatic channels. He was deeply embarrassed and said as much. Fox, never hesitant to admit his own faults, replied: 'I am very ready to acknowledge my own omissions, and certainly do regret that I did not write at the time of the Proclamation. However it is not now too late to set that matter right.'[3] In August, after another vexing lull, Hartley had to write of 'the long silence of your dispatches'. He rightly felt himself handicapped because he had so little mail from London. He wrote the Duke of Portland: 'I stood out a blockade of seven weeks without the chear of a single letter or the prospect of relief, with that Proclamation to boot.'[4] The Americans sensed the difficulty: 'British

---

[1] FO 4/2, 55–60. Hartley to Fox, May 20.   [2] *Idem.* Fox to Hartley, June 10, 14.
[3] FO 4/2, Hartley to Fox, July 17; Fox to Hartley, July 29.
[4] Hartley Papers, iii, 74. August 22. (Clements.) The Americans, too, had experienced their long silences; Franklin went from January to June with no word about the reception in Congress of the preliminary articles. See Jared Sparks, ed., *The Works of Benjamin Franklin* (Boston, 1840), ix, 525. Adams took note of Hartley's seven-week blockade: 'Hartley had been 7 weeks without a letter from his principals, and then received only an apology for not having written, a promise to write soon, and authority to assure the American minister that all would go well' (Wharton, vi, 643).

politics . . . are mysterious and unintelligible. . . . The things which happen appear as unexpected to [Hartley] as to us.'[1]

Fox continued to urge that new matter be kept out of the preliminary articles. Hence they were ratified on August 13, and a definitive treaty formally signed on September 3. Even Franklin, some of the annoyances forgotten, wrote later of the 'Spirit of Conciliation . . . Frankness, Sincerity and Candour' that pervaded the negotiations.[2] In his turn Fox was pleased by the behaviour of the Americans, especially when, at the end of the decade, he had occasion to contrast them with the French.

Negotiations with France, Spain, and Holland were in charge of the Duke of Manchester, long-time friend of the American cause and member of the Rockingham whigs, who took over from Alleyne Fitzherbert, Shelburne's man in Paris. The principal problem, and one that required a good deal of correspondence between Fox and Manchester, related to logwood cutters in Honduras. The British Cabinet was eager to set down, in the treaty, a specific region in which logwood cutters would operate without continued interference from Spain, and sought territory nearly equivalent to the whole of modern British Honduras. The Count de Aranda, in behalf of the Spanish court, for some time held firm to a counter offer of territory amounting to about one-fourth of what the British wanted. Manchester's early dispatches indicated that the Count would not yield,[3] but at later conferences he, with prodding from the French, extended the territory considerably though not to the point the English originally wished.[4] The counter proposal was discussed in a Cabinet meeting July 18, the conclusion being that Manchester should try to get the article deferred if possible, but otherwise to sign it. What Fox called 'the cursed Clause in the 6th Spanish article' caused him deep anguish before it was settled. Nevertheless he wrote to Manchester congratulating him on his progress with the French treaty though he could not help including his regret that the 6th Spanish article had not been settled more advantageously.[5] Fox was more successful in dealing with the Dutch, rejecting their demands for a neutral code, and, as already stated, restoring Trincomalee and regaining Negapatnam.[6]

[1] Wharton, vi, 553. Adams to Livingston, July 16.
[2] FO 4/2, 214. September 5.
[3] Manchester to Fox, May 23. Holland House Photostats, vol. iii, item 127. (Clements.)
[4] *Archivo Histórico Nacional*, 4203, 2. Aranda's memorial on logwood, July 9, delivered to Manchester, July 11. (Clements.)
[5] Holland House Photostats, ii, 65, 100. (Clements.) *Fox Cor.*, ii, 132, 134–6.
[6] L. G. Wickham Legge, *British Diplomatic Instructions 1689–1789* (London, 1934), pp. xxix ff.

On July 16 the third session of the fifteenth Parliament was prorogued. Next day Fox wrote Northington with excessive optimism that the King was neutral toward the coalition, or at least he now had no other administration in mind. 'If this is so we shall last the summer, and when Parliament meets, I own I am sanguine.' He admitted that in the next session, however, he would bring on a question of a very delicate nature, the India Bill. If the people think the King 'has made up his mind to bear us', all will be well.[1]

Word quickly spread that the King was giving the new administration only limited support. Having no peerages to bestow, Mr Secretary Fox busied himself with managing such patronage as he could. But the pickings had become slimmer over the years. No leader of a coalition can ever hope to find enough pasture for the beasts he has to feed.[2] Perhaps administration would still have to rely chiefly upon rhetoric. At least the *Gazetteer* advised M.P.s to spend the recess preparing speeches: the *mercantile* folk, it ironically stated, should study military affairs, the *military gentlemen* should review exports and imports, the *landed* interest should compose harangues against the East India Company. Thus with everybody studying the other man's specialty, it caustically predicted that oratory would reach new summits when Parliament reconvened.

Mr Secretary Fox, however, kept to his work; his command of French and Italian facilitated his continental correspondence; he had meetings at his office and home of all who could keep him informed; he busied himself with matters ranging from Turkey to Russia and westward; he complained that so many mails had been delayed 'that we are in total want of information from the Continent'. He reminded one of his envoys that it was necessary not only to 'execute your commission with zeal, but to pay particular attention to the manner in which your request is received, and the effect it produces'.[3] At his house in Grafton street he received and entertained foreign ministers from various European courts 'with distinguished *éclat*. They, who were never weary of his conversation, respected his talents [and] admired the immense variety of his information on all diplomatic points.'[4] 'Witness our friend Fox,' wrote Charlemont to Burke, 'whose passion for gaming instantly gave way to the political duties of the minister.'[5]

Perhaps a few could agree with the *Gazetteer's* appraisal, that the Rockingham, the Devonshire, and the Bedford interests united, formed a mass of parliamentary influence difficult to equal or resist, particularly when managed by a leader as uncommonly able as Fox.

---

[1] Add. MSS. 47567. *Fox Cor.*, ii, 115–21.   [2] Lord Chesterfield, quoted in Pares, 88–9.
[3] Add. MSS. 47563.   [4] Wraxall, iii, 120.
[5] *HMCR*, Earl of Charlemont MSS., ii, 369 (undated).

The definitive treaties with France, Spain, and the United States were discussed at the opening session of Parliament on November 11. Pitt put his finger squarely on the twofold point; the definitive treaties were little more than a copy of the preliminary articles, so why was it that the ministers asked the House to approve now what these same individuals so violently disapproved at the last session? Moreover, since the two sets of agreements were so similar, why had the final treaty been so long delayed?

For true it was, that after all the letters and dispatches, the commissions worded and reworded, the inquiries and the answers, the continual shuttling between London and Paris, the discussions and the dialogues, these two sets of documents agreed in every major particular: practically the same territory, the same forts, the same fish. The two agreements with the United States showed the greatest resemblance. London and Philadelphia had agreed independently, almost at the outset, to settle on the basis of the preliminary articles unless something better came along, and nothing did. In his reply to Pitt, even Fox himself did not think it worth while to comment on the American treaty or even on the Spanish treaty, which contained a more specific definition of the logwood-cutting boundaries, but limited himself to describing four differences, none very spectacular, between the preliminary and the definitive agreements with France. These changes, he averred, were worth the time required to achieve them. With his commanding majority Fox could afford the luxury of a brief reply, especially since Pitt had announced that he was going to support the treaties anyway. The opening debate was the shortest known for at least ten years; it lasted two hours and was over by six o'clock.

Fox spoke with infinite energy, reported the friendly *Morning Chronicle*, stating surprisingly that even Pitt nodded his approbation and that the cry of 'Hear! hear!' was almost universal. Next day it went further to say that Fox's reply to Pitt 'was allowed by all who heard it, to be one of the ablest, and at the same time one of the most fair and honest ever delivered from the mouth of a Minister at the opening of a session of Parliament'. Even not-so-friendly Germain, now Sackville, wrote: 'The present Ministry have opened the session with all the appearance of support which they could wish for.'[1]

Thus the issue on which Fox and North had tumbled Shelburne from his high post was settled much as Shelburne would have settled it. Fox's record had almost as many flickerings and flutterings as Shelburne's. Shelburne's backing and filling came on the issue of giving the Americans their unconditional independence. Once he reached a stand on this issue he was reasonably steadfast. Fox was consistent on this issue and

[1] *HMCR*, Stopford-Sackville MSS., i, 145. To General Irwin, November 13.

resigned Cabinet office rather than dicker with Shelburne on it, but out of office he could not give the Americans their treaty until he had first disposed of his own personal rival. Once Shelburne was thrown out, Fox was forthright in the treaty negotiations and eventually succeeded in allaying American doubts. Shelburne never again, however, attained office. Too many besides Fox did not trust him. In the closing years of their lives he and Fox evolved a kind of understanding out of their mutual opposition to Pitt, but Shelburne died before either of them could capitalize upon it.

Meanwhile the conflict between the volunteers and the Irish legislature deepened, Fox writing Northington to stand firmly for the Government against the volunteers. The Irish problem thus persisted. Just ahead, however, was an even more demanding issue, the India question. The King's message at the opening of the session had said that the situation of the East India Company would call for the utmost wisdom. Fox, who had formed one stout bottom to his career with the coalition, was now about to elaborate it into a double bottom with his notorious India Bill.

14

The India Bill
1783

The Bishops waver and the Thanes fly from us.
Richard Fitzpatrick

Now Fox was to proceed by unwise and uncharacteristic steps from the teetery base of the coalition to the precarious India problem.

Everybody had talked about doing something for the natives, the princes, the East India Company, but nobody had done anything systematic. Yet in one form or another India had been before Parliament as long as Fox had been a member of the House. He could look back to debates on tea duties, adjusted to help the Company unload its surplus, that led to the affair in Boston Harbour. He had heard reports of secret and select committees. The India question was a complex of officials that got too rich, a Company that was too poor, natives and princes who were exploited, commercial and political responsibilities that were tangled. Certainly Fox had observed that any aspect of India touched sentiments and sensitivities, strongly vested loyalties and interests.

The Shelburne ministry had called the attention of the House to the financial affairs of the East India Company but had not held office long enough to propose legislation. Between ministries the company had petitioned for relief, but its petition had been laid on the table. As the Prince's financial affairs and the preliminary and definitive articles of peace had compelled the prior attention of Parliament, India had been further postponed. Now the long-promised legislation regulating the affairs of the Company was to be introduced into the House of Commons.

Building on his already extensive background, Fox had studied diligently during the interim, attempting to master topics 'of infinite importance not only to the credit of our Administration, but to the well-being of the country'.[1] Astonishingly enough, considering his usual approach to the study of an issue, he did not consult London officials of the East India Company. Had he done so, he would undoubtedly have evolved a plan more acceptable to them; failing that, he would at least have been made fully aware of their objections. He had, however, written to friends like Ossory, urging them to read the official docu-

[1] Add. MSS. 47567. *Fox Cor.*, ii, 163–71. To Northington, November 1, 1783.

ments so they could take part in the debates. Finally the scheduled date of November 18 arrived. As early as noon the crowds had begun to collect. The floor of the House was filled, and so were the galleries. At 3.30 Fox rose to introduce his motion.

Wraxall, who spent fourteen years in Parliament, thought this was one of the exciting events of that period. 'I scarcely ever remember . . . a day on which public expectation was wound up to a higher pitch than when Fox opened his bill,' he wrote.[1]

Starting with careful exposition and objectivity of tone, as he invariably did in his better speeches, Fox said his proposed Bills were being introduced not by choice but by necessity. As he spoke of the complexities and inefficiencies of the present system, however, he warmed to his topic. The East India Company's government in India, he declared, 'was critical beyond description; nay, it was a government of anarchy and confusion'. The governor-generals robbed the people committed to their care, and, if there were danger of being called to account for their plunder, they robbed the people again. They had borrowed half a million pounds, begged for remissions of customs to the extent of seven hundred thousand, and were still eight million in debt. Ever sensitive to unfairness, Fox described the treatment of Prince Cheyte Sing and the princesses of Oude, and the Rohilla and Mahratta wars, as breaches of public faith growing out of the maladministration of affairs in India. 'His eloquence in this part of his speech', noted a parliamentary reporter who was reacting to Fox's magic, 'was truly great and masterly.'

Next he outlined his plan of presenting two Bills: one to establish a board of seven commissioners to have control of the government of India; this board to be named at the outset by Parliament, and after four years by the Crown. He further proposed a group of eight assistants, later nine, subject to the control of the board of seven, to have immediate charge of commercial concerns. A second Bill would provide regulations to halt corruption. The governor-general was to be prevented both from declaring war upon native princes and from making alliances with them. Monopolies like that on opium were to be abolished. Company servants were forbidden to receive presents from princes.

Fox confessed that he was proposing strong measures. He knew that the task was extremely arduous and difficult, that it offered considerable risk, but declared that when he took an office of responsibility, he had made up his mind to the situation and the danger of it. 'This was not a season for a secretary of state to be idle: the minister that loved his ease, or rather, who was not determined to exert himself, had no

[1] Wraxall, iii, 155.

business with green boxes and green bags.'[1] Despite a severe cold and considerable hoarseness he spoke nearly three hours.

North was not in the House that day because of illness, but like a good debater he had reviewed mentally the arguments that would be advanced against the Bill. He realized that although Fox had spent most of his career fighting the influence of the Crown, his opponents could this day turn the tables and argue that the Bill itself would add to the Crown's influence. He also saw that objectors would claim that the Bill would give its sponsors too much power. So he had written to Fox that morning: '*Influence of the Crown, and influence of party against Crown and people* are two of the many topics which will be urged against your plan.'[2] Pitt, who rose immediately after the brief seconding speech, went straight to the first argument that North anticipated, by alleging that the seven persons making up the board, having been appointed by the minister, would allow the minister himself virtually to be the governor of India. And as for the influence of the Crown, 'had it ever been in its zenith equal to what it would be, when it should find itself strengthened by the whole patronage of the East, which the right hon. secretary was going to throw into the hands of the Crown?'[3] Fox's position was vulnerable because of the method of appointing commissioners and because directors and proprietors of the Company, not having been consulted, could charge that the Company's charter was being violated. Fitzpatrick wrote to his brother with true insight: 'The die is cast and Administration is to stand or fall upon the issue of the question.'[4]

On the occasion of the first reading of the Bill, much discussion ensued over Fox's motion to read it a second time one week later. Fox, although accused of haste as well as greed, carried his motion without a division. Fitzpatrick wrote Ossory that Charles shone as much if not more than usual in a very warm debate. He also observed: 'Pitt spoke violently and far from well, and Jenkinson came out with as foolish a speech as I ever heard'; but Fox hoped to carry the second reading by 100 or 150 votes.[5] On the other side, Pulteney wrote the Duke of Rutland that he thought Fox's Bill 'the most barefaced, violent act since the Act of Settlement, and will really give him if carried a power of five or six years' continuance, independent of the Crown, over all the Eastern Empire'.[6]

On November 27 came the long-awaited debate on the second reading of the first Bill. It would be 'the great contest', Fox had written,

---

[1] *Parliamentary History*, xxiii, 1187–1208.
[2] *Fox Cor.*, ii, 218.   [3] *Parliamentary History*, xxiii, 1210.
[4] Add. MSS. 47579. November 18. *Fox Cor.*, ii, 212.
[5] Add. MSS. 47579. November 21. *Ibid.*, ii, 215.
[6] *HMCR*, Rutland MSS., iii, 71. November 23.

'the most important question . . . ever likely to come on'. Members were, in Wraxall's words, looking forward to the clash. 'Every other topic of conversation . . . was suspended.' The debate opened with extra ammunition for the opposition in the form of a strong representation by the City of London against the Bill, and also one by the proprietors and directors of the East India Company, alleging that their finances were in better condition than Fox had represented.

Fox's performance that day was amazing. Since the issue of finances had come up, he announced that he would review the company's report, article by article, requesting members to set down his points as he enumerated them, as they would not be able to remember the figures from memory. One by one he took up the items: one for £4,200,000, then a group totalling £422,011, next one of £609,954, and thus for many columns. He rested his case, however, on sentimental grounds. If he should fall in this enterprise, 'he should fall in a great and glorious cause, struggling not only for the Company, but for the British and India people; for many, many millions of souls'.[1]

Pitt was still to be heard. Fox's eloquence, Pitt declared when he got the floor, would lend grace to deformity. His impassioned appeal in behalf of the natives of India would help gentlemen forget oppression at home. Pitt then led the House back through the maze of figures presented by the East India Company and analysed by Fox, though he admitted that he was unable to answer all of Fox's arguments since that gentleman spoke with a 'volubility that rendered comprehension difficult, and detection almost impossible'. Concluding, he hoped that the debate be adjourned until the next day, but Erskine, Mansfield, and others came to Fox's support, and at four-thirty in the morning the House rejected Pitt's motion 229 to 120, thus giving Fox a majority of 109, just within the majority of 100 to 150 he had anticipated.

Fox's speech was not without its admirers. One paper called his near-three-hour performance 'a force of reasoning and argument, and in a style of eloquence the most powerful and commanding', another wrote of his 'brilliant and elaborate reasoning', and still another rose to the heights: 'One of the completest performances ever heard in Parliament, both for accuracy, in the part of it dependent on arithmetical statement, as well as for the finest energy of thought and expression.' But Fox himself quickly sensed that the Bill was becoming unpopular. As he wrote:

They are endeavouring to make a great cry against us, and will, I am afraid, succeed in making us very unpopular in the city. However, I know I am right, and must bear the consequences, though I dislike unpopularity as much as any man.

[1] *Parliamentary History*, xxiii, 1261–78.

. . . Whether I succeed or no, I shall always be glad that I attempted, because I know I have done no more than I was bound to do, in risking my power and that of my friends when the happiness of so many millions is at stake.[1]

So the Bill went on, speech after speech, debate after debate. Most of the debate of December 1 was monopolized by Burke, Pitt, and Fox. Burke had been a prime mover throughout; 'he was responsible for both its inspiration and much of its form', and in debate he carried the burden of explaining it.[2] After a detailed exposition of the Bill, he eloquently defended his colleague, declaring that Fox was hazarding his ease and security for the benefit of a people he had never seen. He declared:

I am happy that I have lived to see this day . . . when . . . I am able to take my share, by one humble vote, in destroying a tyranny that exists to the disgrace of this nation, and the destruction of so large a part of the human species.

The night was filled with long and distinguished speeches. Pitt took the floor for two hours to oppose the Bill forcibly. Eventually it would operate to increase the influence of the Crown; in the meantime it increased the influence of Fox and North. Pitt even claimed that 'should they be driven from their places, they would carry this influence with them into private life'.

Fox also was more than usually eloquent. The period of his life when he struggled most for the real, substantial cause of liberty, was this very moment. He continued:

Freedom . . . consists in the safe and sacred possession of a man's property, governed by laws defined and certain; with many personal privileges, natural, civil, and religious, which he cannot surrender without ruin to himself; and of which to be deprived by any other power, is despotism.

No longer would a handful of men be able to execute the most base and abominable despotism over millions of their fellow creatures. The end of all government, he went on, perhaps recalling Aristotle, is the happiness of the governed; government should not spring from the calamities of its subjects, should not aggrandize itself out of the miseries of mankind. These sentiments sound too lofty from Fox in 1783, either in the immediate context of the India Bill itself or in the larger context of Fox's body of utterances up to this point. Not until later would Fox be able to seize such lofty themes and be heard with belief and assent. Right now he was not able to offset the hard-core political charge that his commissioners would be in power long after he himself had returned to private life, even though he insisted that a new administration could replace his appointees.

[1] *Fox Cor.*, ii, 219.
[2] See the evidence of Burke's authorship in Lucy S. Sutherland, *The East India Company in Eighteenth Century Politics* (London, 1952), pp. 397–401.

Eighteenth-century parliamentary debaters delighted in *argumen-tum ad hominem*. Both sides of the House hurled personal assaults and affronts, accompanied or unaccompanied by logical argument. Count-less times Fox needed to listen to recitals of his shortcomings as an individual and his inconsistencies as a politician. Nor was he reluctant to abuse his opponents. Members felt this type of argument was unfair, unparliamentary, and illogical, and said as much, but it continued. In this debate Fox needed to defend both his own character and that of the coalition, 'infinitely more having been said concerning me, than con-cerning the question, which is the proper subject of agitation'.

Turning to Pitt at this juncture, Fox recalled that Pitt had termed him 'the most dangerous man in the kingdom'. Pitt immediately called out across the House, 'dangerous only from this measure'. Fox instantly retorted that Pitt therefore was now expressing approval of Fox's other actions up to this point. 'Compare this [statement] with his opposition during the last and the present session. . . . I shall not press the advantage he gives me, farther than leaving to himself to reconcile his practice and his doctrine in the best manner he can.' This mere debating tactic illustrates Fox's alertness and readiness. Pitt opened up only a trivial chink but Fox drove through it with his coach and four.

Fox was highly conscious of the fact that he stood as the leader of a party that was effecting profound changes in the interior workings of government. He had a few caustic words for the independent, the man-above-a-party:

There are a set of men, who, from the mere vanity of having consequence as decisive voters, object to all stable government; these men hate to see an adminis-tration so fixed, as not to be moveable by their vote. They assume their dignity on the mere negative merit of not accepting places; and in the pride of this self-denial, and the vanity of fancied independence, they object to every system that has a solid basis, because their consequence is unfelt.

Earlier Thomas Pitt, older cousin of William, had expressed his detestation of 'systematic and factious opposition', and of members of a coalition that had seized the reins of government by force, planning to conclude their careers 'by giving the death-blow to their country'. Looking directly at Thomas, Fox retorted that he and his colleagues 'are not to be brow-beaten by studied gesture, nor frightened by tremulous tones, solemn phrases, or hard epithets'. He had not seized the government, but had entered office in consequence of a vote of the House. 'The votes of parliament have always decided upon the duration of ministry, and always will, I trust: it is the nature of our constitution; and those who dislike it, had better attempt to alter it.' Pitt had assisted in the change of 1782, calling it glorious, whereas the change in 1783 was disgraceful. 'Why? For a very obvious, though a very bad reason. The right hon. gentleman assisted in effecting the first, and strenuously laboured to prevent the second. The first battle he fought with us; the second against us, and we vanquished him.'

Fox is here not merely vanquishing an opponent, the head, in fact, of the house of Pitt: he is hammering out his theory of party government and of the responsibility of ministers to the Commons. But he was not yet completely through with Pitt. He continued:

He says he is no party man, and he abhors a systematic opposition.

I have always acknowledged myself to be a party man; I have always acted with a party in whose principles I have confidence; and if I had such an opinion of any ministry as the gentleman professes to have of us, I would pursue their overthrow by a systematic opposition.

I have done so more than once; and I think that, in succeeding, I saved my country.

Those who would like to tear another page from Fox's manual of parliamentary debating can see a principle in operation here: state the opponent's argument, answer the argument, repeat the answer in two or three different ways. So he went on:

Once the right hon. gentleman, as I have said, was with me; and then our conduct was fair, manly, constitutional, and honourable. The next time he was against me, and our conduct was violent and unconstitutional, it was treasonable.

And yet the means were in both instances the same, the means were the votes of this House.

During the debate others had attacked the theory of systematic opposition. 'A systematic opposition to a dangerous government is, in my opinion, a noble employment for the brightest faculties.' 'Opposition is natural in such a political system as ours.' But, he went on, opposition should not flow from disappointment or whim or the people will be against the opposers. Opposition should flow from public principle, from love of country rather than from hatred to administration, from a conviction that the public welfare is to be served.

Fox stated the theory better than he practiced it. Even so, the concept of a formed, systematic opposition was slowly emerging despite the King's passionate belief that opposition in its very nature was factious and mischievous. Fox closed with a defence of his own character and motives:

I risk my all upon the excellence of this Bill; I risk upon it whatever is most dear to me, whatever men most value, the character of integrity, of talents, of honour, of present reputation and future fame; these, and whatever else is precious to me, I stake upon the constitutional safety, the enlarged policy, the equity, and the wisdom of this measure.[1]

---

[1] *Parliamentary History*, xxiii, 1306–1434. See also *Substance of the Speech of the Right Honourable Charles James Fox, on Monday, December 1, 1783*, etc. (London, 1783).

He had talked for an hour and a half. The House divided: 217 votes for the Bill, 103 against it.

Fox's speech was impressive. The *Morning Chronicle*, as might be expected, declared it 'exceeded even his two admirable speeches on the same subject in former debates'. It noted that he ably replied to Powys and Dundas, 'obtaining the cry Hear! Hear! more than once, at the expence of each of those gentlemen'. The *Gazetteer* thought his speech, 'in point of argument, point, novelty, and grandeur of sentiment, was one of the most astonishing pieces of eloquence we ever heard even from him, and no other can be compared to him'. The reporter for the *Morning Herald* was locked out with hundreds of others, 'fortunate only in not having been squeezed to death by the crowd that was in vain pressing forward for admission'. Next day, however, the *Herald* managed to collect four columns on the debate. If its parliamentary reporter missed Fox's speech, its crime reporter nevertheless managed to get an item to the effect that on Sunday night Fox was attacked by five footpads, dressed in sailor's jackets, armed with cutlasses, who beat him and robbed him of his watch, four guineas, and a pair of shoe buckles. The *Public Advertiser*, in an open note to Fox, declared: 'Your alliance with Lord North can never be reconciled with any Principle of Truth, Honour, or Honesty', and charged that his Asiatic Bill would fill his own pockets. When on December 3 Fox presented the names of the seven commissioners, now to be called directors, and their nine assistants, press and people saw that they were Foxites and Northites and promptly labelled them People of the Man.[1] At the third reading of the Bill on December 8, Fox's support held; on division the vote favoured him 208 to 102.

Although at the outset the King did not indicate disapproval of the Bill, others speedily acquainted him with powerful objections to it. Temple and Thurlow jointly warned that the Bill would take away half his power; it should be defeated in the Lords and could be if he would make his views known.[2] Atkinson, one of the East India Company's proprietors, and Jenkinson and Robinson, devised a way out of the difficulty: interposition by the King himself. 'Every thing stands prepared for the blow if a certain person has courage to strike it', wrote Atkinson to Robinson. Jenkinson wrote Robinson: 'I have talked with Lord Thurlow on all this, and have settled with him what should be done. . . . You may be assured that the King sees the bill in all the horrors that you and I do.'[3] Meanwhile lists of peers were being compiled, to be carefully scanned in order to forecast the possible outcome

---

[1] See Wraxall, iii, 159–60; *Morning Chronicle*, December 9.
[2] A. Aspinall, ed., *The Later Correspondence of George III* (Cambridge, 1962), i, xxv.
[3] *HMCR*, Abergavenny MSS., p. 61. December 3, 5.

of the Bills in the Lords. In the Robinson correspondence also appear the names of lords that were to be spoken to.

On December 9, Fox, 'attended by an immense body of members', accompanied the Bill to the House of Lords, which after brief debate agreed to read it a second time the following week. Here the Bill ran into serious opposition, most speakers observing that the new plan carried such immense patronage that the influence of the Crown would be irreparably weakened. 'The King will, in fact', said Thurlow, 'take the diadem from his own head, and place it on the head of Mr Fox.' Meanwhile the King had agreed to allow the statement to be made—when it shall be necessary—that whoever votes in the House of Lords for the India Bill is not *his* friend.[1] This word spread so rapidly that although Fox at Brooks's spoke with great confidence of having a majority of 30,[2] that same day he wrote Portland:

I have heard of so many defections tonight that the thing appears to me more doubtful than I ever thought it before. I really think you should call a Cabinet tomorrow and some way of acting should be adopted in concert. If you call it at three, I will endeavour to see Ld. Mansfield first. Onslow, Essex, and Brudenell will all be against us or at best absent. I think you should see every doubtful Peer you can in the morning.[3]

As the situation became more clear, the name of Temple, 'that terror of administrations,' as Windham described him in a letter analysing the source and circulation of the rumours, emerged as the one who carried the word that the King disapproved of the Bill as unconstitutional and that he should consider as his enemies all who voted for it.

Outside of Parliament, sentiment continued to mount against the Bill and its authors. Fox had always been an easy mark for cartoonists. Now they had a field day. James Sayers drew the most famous cartoon of the decade when he pictured Fox as Carlo Khan, corpulent, black-bearded, dressed in the garb of an Indian potentate, riding an elephant with a face like North's, lead by a lackey, Burke. Friends of the East India Company declared that the Company's charter was being violated. Fox was suspected of selfish motives despite his pleas for the oppressed millions of India. All these factors added to the growing unpopularity of the Bill, but the uncloaked interposition of the King put it beyond rescue.

During the December 15 debate the fact of the rumour formally emerged. From a London paper, dated Saturday, Richmond read a statement that his Majesty had intimated his displeasure with the

---

[1] *HMCR,* Abergavenny MSS., p. 62. December 3, 5.
[2] *The Windham Papers* (Boston, 1913), i, 54. At Brooks's, wrote Windham, 'one supposes that no disguise is used' and that men therefore speak their real thoughts.
[3] MSS. English letters, c. 144, 66. December 13. From the Morison collection (Bodleian).

India Bill and that his ministers had thereupon resigned. The article further stated that Temple was alleged to be the bearer of the news of the King's displeasure. Temple thereupon took the floor, admitted having had a conference with the King, admitted further that he had advised his sovereign in a manner unfriendly to the Bill—but what the King had said was 'lodged in the breast of His Majesty', and Temple would not reveal it. Fitzwilliam called this statement a positive evasion and repeated again his own version of ministerial responsibility. The issue was drawn hard and fast by Temple's request that Fitzwilliam's words be taken down so he could be censured; following the usual procedure the galleries were cleared, but differences were adjusted and the motion, on adjournment, was passed by a majority of eight.[1]

Now arose the question: did a minister have the right to hold office when the King had disavowed him, especially if the minister had the confidence of the House? Which took precedence: the prerogative of the King or the privilege of Parliament? On December 17 the motion was to declare that the reporting of the King's opinion on a pending Bill was a breach of privilege. Pitt, standing forward as the spokesman of opposition, declared that Fox and other ministers should retire if they could no longer answer for their own measures. This step Fox flatly refused to take. In a long speech he recalled the thoroughness with which the question had been debated, only to be thrown out by secret influence. Even had the King decided to veto the Bill, Fox declared, he should have consulted 'the safety of his ministers'. Fox solemnly avowed:

I did not come in by the fiat of Majesty, though by this fiat I am not unwilling to go out. . . . We only beg when the revolution, which it is supposed may be effected in the royal breast, is authentically announced, we may be allowed to judge for ourselves. I will apprise gentlemen, however, that the situation of ministers is at present extremely delicate. They stand pledged to the public and a very honourable majority of this House, not to relinquish the affairs of state while in so much anarchy and distraction . . .

If, however, a change must take place, and a new ministry is to be formed and supported, not by the confidence of this House or the public, but the sole authority of the crown, I, for one, shall not envy that honourable gentleman his situation. From that moment I put in my claim for a monopoly of Whig-principles. The glorious cause of freedom, of independence, and of the constitution, is no longer his, but mine. In this I have lived; in this I will die. It has borne me up under every aspersion to which my character has been subjected. . . . I accepted of office at the obvious inclination of this House: I shall not hold it a moment after the least hint from them to resume a private station.

In short, the minister should be sustained in office by a majority of the House rather than solely by the confidence of the sovereign:

[1] *Parliamentary History*, xxiv, 154–60.

189

Is [Pitt] weak and violent enough to imagine, that his Majesty's mere nomination will singly weight against the constitutional influence of all these considerations ? . . . It is undoubtedly the prerogative of the sovereign to choose his own servants; but the constitution provides that these servants should not be obnoxious to his subjects.[1]

He had been at Brooks's until three o'clock the night before, confident that the coming day would bring victory to the India Bill. After that the rest would be easy. The Commons, in scarce half a House, divided for him 153 to 80. But the Lords, remembering Temple's warning, divided against him 95 to 76, a majority of 19 votes. The Prince, who had voted with the minority on December 15, was among those absent. The India Bill was defeated. The figure of 19 was to burn in the losers' minds.

Fox wrote his dearest Liz a short note :

I am too much hurried to write to you an account of our misfortune. We are beat in the H. of Lds. by such treachery on the part of the King, and such meanness on the part of his *friends* in the H. of Lds. as one could not expect either from him or them.

The King's victory, however, would be shortlived : 'We are so strong that nobody can undertake, without madness; and if they do, I think we shall destroy them almost as soon as they are formed.'[2] To an unknown recipient he wrote in similar vein about the 'indecent and notorious' unconstitutional interference that had beat his Government in the Lords. 'Unless vigorous measures are taken immediately, Parlt. will be dissolved & every species of confusion may be expected.'[3]

Next day came the end. As the ministers had not yet resigned, the King took the initiative. At midnight a special messenger called upon Fox, informed him that the King had no further occasion for his services, and asked him to give up the seals of his office. North, in bed when the messenger arrived, told him that if he entered he would have to see Lady North also. When the messenger insisted upon having the seals of office, North gave him the key to the closet where they were kept, and went back to sleep.

'Only think, Sir,' said Dr Johnson, 'it was a struggle between George the Third's sceptre and Mr Fox's tongue.' More than that, it was another stage in the process of determining the proper sphere of the influence of the Crown on the legislative process and on procedures by which new governments are to be selected. Eventually this sphere was to be sharply contracted. For a while longer, however, the sceptre was able to halt the onward thrust of history.

[1] *Parliamentary History*, xxiv, 196–225.
[2] Add. MSS. 47570. (Undated.) *Fox Cor.*, ii, 221.
[3] Fox MSS., December 16. (Clements.)

The Commons was quickly informed who would be the new minister. Fox and North had hardly taken their seats on the Opposition bench December 19 when young Pepper Arden rose to announce that William Pitt had accepted the office of First Lord of the Treasury and Chancellor of the Exchequer. Pitt was not quite twenty-five, and, as his enemies were quick to point out, had been carried to office by the votes of nineteen peers. Against him was a hostile majority of the Commons.

In his cabinet were Gower, President of the Council; Temple, especially in bad odour, Secretary of State for the home department; Carmarthen, Secretary of State for the foreign department; Rutland, Lord Privy Seal; Howe, First Lord of the Admiralty; Thurlow, Lord Chancellor. All were peers. None could aid him in the Commons in the bitter debates that loomed ahead. Nor could any of them, except Thurlow, supply much speech power in the Lords.

Pitt, youngest ever to hold the post of Prime Minister, had not made his decision hastily. At the breakup of the Shelburne ministry the year before, he had seriously considered an invitation to this office but declined when he realized that his support would be too uncertain. Now he had apparently agreed, even before the King had scuttled Fox's India Bill, to accept the first place. His decision was based not on hunch but on the calculations of John Robinson, probably made during the second week in December.

Robinson's elaborate analysis had predicted, in the event the King dismissed the coalition and Pitt assumed office, that the new minister could anticipate 149 pro plus 104 hopeful, or 253, as opposed to 231 against plus 74 doubtful, a total of 305. This opposition was formidable, but Robinson went on to forecast that if Parliament were dissolved, a new general election would bring in 253 pro plus 116 hopeful, as opposed to 123 against plus 66 doubtful; in other words, 369 for Pitt's Government as against only 189 in opposition.[1] The strategy was clearly to hang on now even with a majority of votes on the other side, and, at the propitious moment, dissolve Parliament, take the issue to the nation and come back into power with commanding support.

At the outset Pitt faced weighty problems in selecting and holding his Cabinet. The name of Shelburne was conspicuously absent. Pitt, who months previously had proudly declared that he would not betray Shelburne, now just as firmly decided he could not endure Shelburne as a colleague, and abandoned him to political oblivion. This decision he maintained despite the fact that some he would have liked to have in his Cabinet refused. Moreover, Temple resigned, a personal blow to the new Prime Minister. Temple had been pondering the consequences

[1] W. T. Laprade, *Parliamentary Papers of John Robinson* (London, 1922), pp. 66–105.

of his interference with the legislative process and feared he would be impeached.[1]

Nevertheless, as Wilberforce recorded in his journal, Pitt was nobly firm and called a meeting of his friends at Downing Street. Among those present was his brother-in-law, Lord Mahon, a strongvoiced, vigourous personality, described as emphasizing points with extended arm and clenched fist like Christie, the auctioneer, banging his hammer. Pitt ever dreaded 'the falling force of his noble kinsman's arm'. At the meeting Pitt asked the uppermost question: what could be done if the Opposition stopped the supplies—refused appropriations? Mahon's certain trumpet rang out: 'They will not stop them; it is the very thing which they will not venture to do.'[2] His forceful statement seemed to resolve the matter.

Pitt sent out precautionary feelers, however, towards the opposition. Temple wrote to the King: 'Mr Fox, the D. of Portland & L. John Cavendish have determined that they cannot consider this as a proper moment for a negotiation in general.' Failing to trap the leaders, Pitt started looking for rats. Palmerston noted in his journal that peerages were offered to principal persons in the Commons to induce them to desert their friends, but only three or four of the shabbiest accepted.[3] Sir Gilbert Elliot heard that Spencer went directly to Fox with a proposal to abandon North and join Pitt: 'This honourable proposal was received with the respect it deserved. . . . Fox's only answer was, "Why don't they advise us to pick pockets at once?"' Other approaches, he added, met the same kind of indifference.[4]

One who profited by the change was John Frederick Sackville, who found himself appointed ambassador to France. 'We have been in a terrible bustle . . .' he wrote. 'I firmly believe now things will take another turn and people will return to their senses.' His observation about Fox was more pointed than prophetic:

I hate confusion more than any man and much less do I like a despotic minister. C. Fox has attempted that despotism by the late East India Bill and I sincerely hope he never rise again as long as he remains in those principles. I think the dispute is now who shall be k—g and I trust the nation will now see what C. F. is aiming at under false appearances.[5]

Of such opinions were ambassadors created that Christmas season.

The brief debate on December 24 was the calm before the storm. Both sides agreed to adjourn until January 12. As yet Pitt had not had to face an actual vote.

[1] See the convincing analysis by Aspinall in *Later Correspondence of George III*, i, xxvii.
[2] Wilberforce, i, 48–9. December 23.
[3] *Portrait of a Whig Peer*, p. 147. December 31.
[4] Malmesbury, ii, 59. To Harris, January 1, 1784.
[5] Lacaita-Shelburne MSS. To Hanbury, December 25. (Clements.)

15

The Westminster Election
1784–1785

I glory in being one of those who were called 'Fox's Martyrs'.

Thomas Coke of Norfolk

The events of the opening day of Parliament, January 12, 1784, were a preview of what lay ahead. Pitt wanted to plunge immediately into the India business and introduce a Bill of his own to correct the defects of Fox's effort. Fox, however, sought to go into a committee of the whole House on the state of the nation. The danger of a dissolution of Parliament, he declared, hung over their heads; this step, he argued, would be inimical to the true interests of the country.

The debate was long and heated. Pitt, Fox, and North were sharply criticized: Pitt, because he had come into office by the back stairway as the minister of the Crown rather than of the House; Fox, because of the odium of the coalition and the India Bill; North, for these and for the further reason that he was still tagged as the man responsible for the loss of America. At two-thirty in the morning, by 232 to 193, the House voted to go into committee on the state of the nation. The margin of thirty-nine votes against him was hardly more hopeful from Pitt's point of view than the fifty-two that Robinson predicted. But many were absent. Neither side revealed its full strength.

Late in the morning though it was, Fox next offered a resolution that no pay officer could pay out any sum of money after Parliament was dissolved, if the dissolution occurred before funds were appropriated. Such action made it essential that Parliament be allowed to continue in session until money for the necessary functions of government was provided. This and other resolutions were passed without a division.

The Earl of Surrey, once a friend of Shelburne's but now, in the words of Robinson, a violent Fox man,[1] moved resolutions deploring the use of the King's name to influence parliamentary deliberations, and further deploring that a minister had been installed without the confidence of the House. At seven in the morning Fox and his followers beat down a motion to adjourn by 196 to 142, and then passed Surrey's resolutions.

[1] *History of Parliament*, ii, 645.

Next day Pitt called a Cabinet meeting to review the impasse. His new Secretary of State, Carmarthen, thought the young minister seemed discouraged enough to give up the contest. For Parliament had awesome and difficult work to do before it could be dissolved. First, it had to vote the necessary appropriations; Fox had made this fact clear during the preceding day's debates. Second, it had to renew the annual Mutiny Bill, the Bill that made a standing army legal, scheduled to expire on March 25. How could these steps be taken in defiance of the Opposition's majority? The question of dissolution was further discussed at later cabinet meetings. The King, being consulted, declared it was his fixed and unalterable determination not to be bound hand and foot and put into Fox's hands, and that rather than submit he would leave the kingdom for ever.[1]

Fox did not have the shrewd political prognostications of a Robinson to guide him. He did not, however, wish an immediate dissolution of Parliament. He could amass strong arguments. Parliament had been in session only four years. Moreover, urgent business had to be done: not only the passing of supplies and the renewal of the Mutiny Bill, but also the still persistent decision about India. He upheld also the constitutional principle that ministers should be responsible to a majority of the House; ministers who could not command a majority should resign. His hope was to defeat and discredit the young Chancellor before he could take his case to the country.[2]

The India Bill loomed as the first test of strength. On January 14 Pitt introduced and explained his own version, differing from Fox's Bill in that the King, not Parliament, was to appoint the new board of control; and instead of Fox's proposed administrative unit of nine members, the East India Company itself was to continue to manage these matters. Pitt's Bill therefore met the approval of the Company, which had in recent weeks managed to exert a good deal of influence against Fox by warning other companies that since Fox had threatened the East India Charter, he might attack some other charter next. Pitt presented his plan—in a speech reputedly two and a half hours long, though only a meagre report survives—and Fox replied. Both speeches were speculative, in that each speaker, looking to the future, argued that his own plan would be more practical and less corruptible.

A description is still extant of this debate between the twenty-five-year-old Pitt and the thirty-five-year-old Fox. Pitt 'already appears in

[1] Oscar Browning, ed. *The Political Memoranda of Francis, Fifth Duke of Leeds* (Westminster, 1884), pp. 94 ff.
[2] The constitutional issues are further discussed in Pares, 125 ff.; *Later Correspondence of George III*, i, xxii, ff.; *History of Parliament*, i, 87 ff.

Debate a Scholar a Philosopher a Statesman and a Patriot—and will I think in Time be, more than any Man living, *an Orator'*. Fox showed the greatest 'Fertility and Ingenuity', he 'attributes certain Motives to his Adversaries, and explains Actions with the most wonderful Ingenuity into these Motives . . . he constantly surprizes you with the strangest Association of Ideas . . . he is so various copious and quick that it is impossible to chain him down.'[1] Here is Fox's speaking being described when the issue was in the realm of speculation—whether the governing board proposed by Pitt would behave less efficiently than that proposed by Fox, or whether the system would be less liable to corruption if managed in India than it would be if managed in London— as opposed to situations in which Fox could use another style, of forceful exposition with cogent facts leading the way.

On January 16 the House again went into committee and advanced the Bill to second reading, but opposition was then able to take up the motion that the Pitt ministry did not have the confidence of the House and should be removed. The rankest whigs, said Fox, would not deny the Crown the right to choose its own ministers. He asked: 'Is it not also the privilege of this House, and of Parliament, to decide upon the conduct of administration, on the peculiarity of their introduction into office, and on those circumstances which either entitle them to the confidence or the reprobation of the House ?'[2] The vote for removal was 205; against, 184. The majority had shrunk to twenty-one. Pitt, however, still refused to resign.

Public opinion against the opposition crystallized ominously. In January an ambitious pamphlet appeared, priced handsomely at 3s 6d, *The Beauties of Fox, North, and Burke*, in which the inconsistent utterances of these three statesmen were revealed in striking fashion. The exhaustive and comprehensive index to the whole was printed in full in the papers. Its skilful irony shines through to the present day. Below are a few entries under the heading, 'Charges Against North by Fox or Burke' :

	Page
charged with treachery or falsehood	3
charged with negligence	ib.
leads the House of Commons blindfold	4
suspected of being bribed	7

[1] MSS. 23K53, Royal Irish Academy (Dublin). To Dr L. Parsons. [January 15, 1784.] In similar vein Sir Thomas Durrant wrote the Earl of Buckinghamshire: 'The friends of the present Ministers are fond of contrasting the virtues of Mr Pitt's private character with the excesses of Mr Fox.' (*HMCR*, Lothian MSS., February 25, 1784, p. 428.)
[2] *Parliamentary History*, xxiv, 364.

pronounced deserving an axe	. . . . .	20

[and so on to]

Mr Fox thinks it would have been better Lord North had never

been born	.	33

[and thus to]

freezes Mr Burke's blood, and harrows up his soul	. .	60

[etc.]

No rejoinder was possible. The pamphlet came straight from life. Fox's repeated declarations that situations were different, that what applied yesterday was no longer applicable, that he ever stood ready to forgive men's mistakes, could get no serious hearing except among his most devoted admirers. He was impaled upon the vigour of his own expression and the colour of his own words. For him it would have been better if certain speeches had never been reported; if, like Burke, he had put into pamphlets only those sentiments that he wanted preserved. The *Beauties* was followed by a companion, *The Deformities of Fox and Burke*; later the two were combined into one single, politically delectable, volume.

Meanwhile Pitt could demonstrate that the sovereign stood solidly behind him. He secured a peerage for cousin Thomas—the first peerage for a long while. Pitt would not accept the Clerkship of the Pells of Exchequer which became vacant, but instead gave it to Barré, who in turn relinquished a pension granted during the Rockingham administration. This exchange took Barré off the public rolls. For this manoeuvre Pitt would gain 'immortal credit' according to the simultaneous announcement in the *Morning Chronicle* and the *Morning Herald*. But on January 23, Pitt's India Bill was thrown out during the second reading 222 to 214, a majority of only eight. When the House heard the aye vote of 214 announced, Pitt and his friends raised a shout, thinking that number was sufficient to pass the Bill, but their triumph was shortlived when the noes proved to be 222.

Late in January sentiment grew for a union of parties. Addresses came from Middlesex, Southwark, Leicester, Ipswich. Country members meeting at St Alban's tavern appointed a committee to sound out Portland, Fox, Pitt. The negotiations struck hard rock at the outset: Pitt would not give up the ministry, Portland and Fox would not move into a cabinet swarming with Pitt's friends.[1] Portland set forth his views about the possibility of 'forming an extended and united Administration on a wide and solid basis'—a delicate substitute for the unpopular term, 'coalition'—in a letter that promptly reached the King. The King thought this 'curious Epistle' brazenly meant that

[1] *History of the Westminster Election*, etc. (London, 1784), pp. 23 ff.

everything was to be put in Portland's hands, and thus in Fox's hands, and wrote that it forever closed negotiations between him and that party, until 'time should bring it to more moderate Ideas, indeed such as will ever be found in those who really love their Country and do not centre their affections with the narrow limits of a party'.[1]

Even in the new United States of America Fox lost ground. The *Pennsylvania Gazette* reflected that if the willingness to coalesce were the essence of patriotism, the first patriot in the kingdom was Fox: he had coalesced with Shelburne against North, he had coalesced with North against Shelburne, and now showed willingness to coalesce with Pitt, leaving North to shift for himself.[2]

The debates were as lively as the paragraphs and the pamphlets. On February 2 a motion of censure against ministers was carried 223 to 204, majority nineteen. Pitt proudly refused to resign: 'I refuse to march out of my post with a halter round my neck, to change my armour, and meanly beg to be readmitted in the ranks of the enemy.'[3] Next day a similar motion was carried 211 to 187, majority twenty-four. The subject was renewed February 20 and featured another confrontation between Fox and Pitt; Pitt stood his ground boldly, and the vote on the motion showed that the majority had dropped to twenty. 'Pitt rises every day in character and estimation, as to abilities,' wrote Cornwallis, 'and he positively declared . . . in one of the best speeches that ever was made, that he would not resign.'[4] The English, invariably responsive to a show of pluck and ever a little partial to the under dog, admired not only Pitt's boldness but also his obvious talents.

Pitt's advisers had assured him before the holiday recess that the opposition would not dare to refuse to vote funds to carry on the Government. Now Fox and his colleagues had to determine whether to make such a drastic move. A group at Fox's home thought that a good tactical procedure would be to postpone navy supply. It also debated the renewal of the Mutiny Bill. Fox warned his colleagues earnestly that they would need to decide how far they would go in the contest. 'The question of ultimately refusing supplies, and passing the Mutiny Bill for a short time, were those which we must seriously consider.' Others also spoke, and Sir Gilbert Elliot, who reported the meeting, wrote that he was sorry to observe a boggle about the extreme, but decisive, measure of refusing supplies.[5]

[1] *Later Correspondence of George III*, i, 36. February 16. Townshend Collection (Huntington).
[2] July 7.　　[3] *Coke of Norfolk*, i, 218.
[4] *Correspondence of Charles, First Marquis Cornwallis*, 2nd edn. (London, 1859), i, 168. To Lieutenant-Colonel Ross, February 23. For letters from the Duke of Portland on this topic, see *Fox Cor.*, ii, 234–41.
[5] *Diaries and Correspondence of James Harris, first Earl of Malmesbury* (London, 1844), ii, 60–1. To Harris, February 26.

On February 18 Fox took an obviously cautious step when he moved that the discussion of supplies be postponed. The vote was 208 to 196, the small majority of twelve further encouraging Pitt to try to break the deadlock. On February 27 opposition's majority was reduced to seven. 'A number of our friends were shut out at the division,' wrote Elliot; '. . . we found seven or eight of them in Mrs Bennet's room, looking like the foolish virgins somewhere in the Bible.'[1] Even though on March 1 the majority had inched up to twelve, Pitt's government was clearly riding out the storm. By March 5 the majority was down to nine, and by March 8, one. *One*, the printer put it, in italics.

The story was told that one evening when Fox's majorities were decreasing, Sheridan said, 'Mr Speaker, this is not to be wondered at, when a member is employed to corrupt everybody in order to obtain votes.' Instantly there was an outcry: 'Who is it? Name him! name him!' 'Sir,' said the imperturbable Sheridan, 'I shall not name the person. It is an unpleasant and invidious thing to do . . . but don't suppose, Sir, that I abstain because there is any difficulty in naming him; I could do that, Sir, as soon as you could say Jack Robinson.'[2]

Sentiment mounted. The Duchess of Devonshire recorded an exciting night at the opera when the Duchess of Rutland shouted 'Damn Fox' and heard in reply a shriek of 'Damn Pitt' from Lady Maria Waldegrave. Georgiana added that she herself also had several good political fights there.[3] On the streets men yelled 'Fox! Fox for ever!' or, in reply, 'No Fox! No Fox!' On March 24, the king announced the end of the session. That night the great seal, a massive silver emblem, was stolen from the Lord Chancellor's house, an event that caused even more uproar than the dissolution of Parliament. Each side accused the other of pilfering it. Some wondered whether any business whatever could be transacted, and even whether the office of Lord Chancellor ceased now to exist. Others recalled the day when James II had hurled the great seal into the Thames, thus bringing the functioning of the Government to a temporary halt. With more mischievousness than accuracy, the *Herald* reported that Fox and the Duchess of Devonshire were seen on the streets at two a.m. carrying crowbars and a lantern. Another seal was speedily manufactured so the dissolution could be made legal.

A tumultuous prelude to the election of the two members for Westminster set the stage for the election itself. Fox and Wray had drifted

---

[1] *Diaries and Correspondence of James Harris, first Earl of Malmesbury*, ii, 62. To Harris, February 28.
[2] Horace Twiss, *Life of Lord Chancellor Eldon* (London, 1846), i, 114.
[3] Earl of Bessborough, *Georgiana* (London, 1955), pp. 78–9.

sharply apart at the time of the coalition. In a series of public meetings in Westminster, each man tried to mobilize Westminster sentiment. The Wray group passed resolutions thanking the King for dismissing the coalition and expressing confidence in the present administration. The Fox group passed resolutions declaring that Fox's conduct deserved the perfect esteem of his constituents.[1]

The climax was a general meeting called for Westminster Hall on February 14. Each faction attempted to seize the chair and hence possession of the platform. The hall itself was 'most prodigiously crowded'. In the general tussle the chair was demolished and the hustings itself broken down. Fox slipped and fell and 'some wretch, for man we can not call him, threw a leather bag, filled with assa foetida' in his face. This substance is the prince of stenches. Fox attempted to speak but was drowned out. Moreover, he was jostled out of the hall itself. But he took in his stride the asafoetida, the noise, and the jostling, any of which would have lessened the zeal of an ordinary man for public deliberation, and collected a fragment of an audience outside.

Thus even before Parliament was dissolved and the general election begun, the two Westminster members had divided sentiment in the borough on parliamentary reform and also on the coalition.[2] Pitt had also had an evening of extraparliamentary political excitement. During a procession returning from a dinner where he had been acclaimed as the saviour of the nation, he was attacked by a body of men armed with bludgeons, and escaped injury only by seeking refuge at White's. Fox himself was accused of participating in the assault but he had his own alibi: he declared he was in bed at the time with his mistress, Mrs Armistead, who was prepared to substantiate the fact on oath. The origins of this candid declaration have always been somewhat clouded and are best left so.

In this charged atmosphere the general election itself got under way. On April 1 the poll at Westminster opened to elect new candidates. The hustings was again erected in Covent Garden under the portico of St Paul's church. The voting was to to go forty days, unless concluded sooner by mutual agreement. To replace Fox, the Government backed the popular Admiral Hood, whose election was never in doubt, and Wray. So at the outset the real contest was between Wray and Fox.

[1] Part of this chapter has appeared in Loren Reid, "The Westminster Election and Scrutiny", *Quarterly Journal of Speech*, lii (February, 1966).

[2] *History of the Westminster Election*, pp. 60–4. *HMCR*, Abergavenny MSS., p. 66. Jenkinson to Robinson, February 14.

Black, pp. 112 ff., discusses the issue of parliamentary reform in the early stages of the 1784 election.

All kinds of propaganda were thrown into the campaign. Banners appeared everywhere. On a large banner for Wray and Hood was written 'No Bribery—No Receipt Tax', the last being a reference to the stamp tax on receipts, opposed by Wray, supported by Fox. On Fox's banners were written 'Fox and the Constitution', 'No Tax on Maid Servants', and 'May Chelsea Hospital stand for ever'. The reference to maid servants was to a suggestion by Wray, at the time the receipt tax was being debated, of substituting instead a tax on maid servants. This proposal was shouted down when it was presented and gave Wray no peace during the campaign. The reference to Chelsea Hospital was to Wray's speech opposing it, even advising that it be torn down. As Chelsea was maintained largely for war veterans, Wray's adverse sentiments were continually revived by Fox and his friends in order to stimulate the veteran vote. Speakers could denounce Wray as a Judas, a betrayer of men who had lost arms and legs in their country's service; speakers could also praise splendid old Chelsea, an asylum for those brave fellows who had grown grey and had been disabled while fighting for their country. Each side could accuse the other of stealing the great seal (this sentiment is well suited to hissing). Hundreds of times during the next forty days Westminster electors were awash with references in speeches, broadsides, cartoons, and newspapers to the receipt tax, to maid servants, to the welfare of Chelsea veterans. The only issue more prominent was Fox's effort to take over the patronage of India and the possibilities of corruption that went with it.

Admiral Hood spoke first, to launch the campaign, and held forth a few minutes. Fox could get in only a few words above the general clamour (*Morning Chronicle*)—version 1. He was heard with the most flattering attention (*Morning Herald*)—version 2. Wray, a poor speaker, was even less successful in making himself heard. Westminster electors did not need much reminding to recall that Fox had sponsored Wray at the 1782 by-election and thus had given him a political start; now Wray was opposing his one-time benefactor. At the opening session were the two lovely duchesses of Devonshire and Rutland, fresh from their political bouts at the opera. Wray was not a strong candidate; in fact the rumour started that ministers planned to disgrace Fox by having him defeated by a mediocre opponent. Rhymsters readily cast Wray in the role of goose: 'the electors of Westminster never will choose/to run down a Fox and set up a Goose.' The polls started at two and closed at three, with these results: Fox 302, Hood 264, Wray 238. On the second day a gang of Hood's sailors intimidated electors who wanted to vote for Fox but a gang of Irish chairmen drove them off, and the poll stood: Fox 1,243, Hood 1,234, Wray 1,104.

Then came a swing. Hood went to first place, Wray to second, and Fox dropped to third. The goose was doing better than the fox. Violence increased on both sides. So much fraud was evident that the poll had been under way only a few days before each side talked of a scrutiny of the votes; alleged bribes, generally attributed to the Government, sought to beat Fox at all costs. The rumours, the parodies, the paragraphs, the cartoons, the bulletins, the advertisements, the lampoons, on both sides, became so extensive that later they required a 538-page volume to contain them.[1]

Hundreds of stories were circulated. A Government female supporter approached 'an honest tradesman' and threatened him with the loss of the Queen's custom if he dared vote against Wray. His honest and independent answer was, 'I assure you, Madam, I have every respect for their Majesties, but still more the constitution of my country. You'll excuse me, Madam, but I vote for Mr Fox.' Fox's friends advertised that his supporters should gather at Lowe's Hotel, from whence they would be conducted in great safety to the hustings. Hood and Wray urged their electors to proceed to any of three named places, there to be conducted without delay to the polling place. Voters were urged to cast their ballots: 'Come forth, then, like BRITONS and give your suffrages in defence of your own FREEDOM!' Courage was indeed required, for a stray head on either side was in danger of being broken. Fox supporters declared that the number of false votes for Wray was incredible. Wray supporters asserted that those for Fox were far in excess. Fox supporters screamed that Wray forces marched a company of troops to the hustings. Wray admirers bellowed that Fox had corralled fifty weavers from Spitalfields and quantities of his coalition friends from other places and fraudulently voted them all. Each side accused the other of graverobbing—voting the names of electors who had long since died.

The voting was open; there was no secret ballot; every man's vote was known and noted. A man who had sold his vote had to deliver. Especially prized was an elector's plumper—the single vote cast for one candidate by the voter who chose to show his full and complete enthusiasm in that manner instead of casting two votes, one for each of two candidates. On April 27 Fox's supporters bragged that most of the 5,827 votes cast for him were plumpers; that loyalty proved, they insisted, he was truly the man of the people.

Fox solicited a tradesman for his vote. Said the man, refusing: 'I admire your abilities but damn your principles.' Said Fox: 'My friend, I applaud you for your sincerity, but damn your manners.' Another

---

[1] *History of the Westminster Election.* See also *The wit of the day, or the humours of Westminster,* etc. (London, 1784).

offered him not a vote but a halter. Said Fox: 'I should be sorry to deprive you of it, for it must be a family piece.' Said the *Gazetteer*: 'Suppose . . . Mr Fox should not come into Parliament at all, where will be the check, the control, that all ministers require?'

Fox left his own record of the campaign. April 3: 'Plenty of bad news from all quarters, but I think I feel that misfortunes, when they come thick, have the effect rather of rousing my spirits than sinking them.' April 5: 'I have still hopes but their beating me two days following, looks ugly.' April 7: 'Worse and worse. Hood 4,458, Wray 4,117. Fox 3,827.' April 8: 'I must not give up yet though I wish it. Bad news from York, and . . . Bedfordshire. I have serious thoughts, if I am beat here, of not coming in to Parliament at all. . . . Adieu, my dearest dearest Liz.'

On April 9 a ray of hope: 'We had six majority . . . a chance, but a small one.'[1] At this juncture some one in the whig high command had a happy thought: intensify the canvassing and call upon some of the party's charming ladies to help.

Georgiana, Duchess of Devonshire, a truly beautiful eighteenth-century lovely and devoted whig, was one of Fox's most loyal admirers. She and her sister, Viscountess Duncannon, and others, drove their carriages into all parts of the city, and some alleged, to villages outside the city's voting limits, zealously and indefatigably soliciting votes for Fox. The legend that she gave a butcher a kiss for his vote is too persistent not to acknowledge and applaud. She insisted, however, in a letter to her mother, that she had behaved entirely properly; not she but her sister and another lady had been kissed, 'so it's very hard I who was not shd have the reputation of it'.[2] It is very hard also to contemplate that the butcher might have voted for Fox anyway.

Wray partisans enlisted beautiful tory ladies to canvass on their side. But their thirty-four-year-old Countess of Salisbury was not equal to the twenty-six-year-old duchess. Nobody outcanvassed Georgiana: 'she was in the most blackguard houses in Long Acre by eight o'clock this morning,' wrote Cornwallis on April 9.[3] Temple wrote Rutland that during the election the Duchess 'had heard more plain English of the grossest sort than ever fell to the share of any lady of her rank'.[4]

The papers noted, moreover, that after the ladies began taking part in the canvass, Fox's lead began to increase. Whereas for days he had trailed in the tally, now he quickly mounted to second place. A part of

---

[1] Add. MSS. 47570. *Fox Cor.*, ii, 267–8. [2] *Georgiana*, p. 79.
[3] Cornwallis, i, 166. To Lieutenant-Colonel Ross.
[4] *HMCR*, Rutland MSS., iii, 88. April 12.

the shift in sentiment from Wray to Fox (Hood, represented as the naval hero, the gallant captor of the *Ville de Paris*, was steadily in the lead) grew out of the knowledge that Fox, the under dog, was being attacked by the full influence of the court party.

The campaign went on. When on April 14 Fox polled an even 45 votes, many interpreted this as a happy omen. 'Wilkes and 45' had been an effective slogan; now it was 'Fox and 45.' Other publicity was less pleasant:

> Queries to Honest, Loyal, and Independent
> Electors of Westminster
>
> Who is the notorious and infamous *liar* that formed a coalition with Lord North?
> Who *robbed* the India Company of their charter, trade, and revenue?
> Who hired a gang of ruffians to *murder* the king's minister?
> Who *stole the Great Seal* from the Lord Chancellor?[1]

And other similar interrogatories described a man for whom no free Briton would give his suffrage.

April 17, it was Hood 6,054, Wray 5,465; Fox 5,305. Were there that many eligible voters in all Westminster? The *Herald* said not: 'There can be no doubt but there must be no small number of bad votes on both sides—but Sir Cecil has most . . . in the proportion of seven to four.' Thomas Townshend, formerly Shelburne's Home Secretary and now Baron Sydney, described Fox's soliciting the votes of 'Roman Catholic hairdressers, cooks, &c.' and also making appearances on the hustings with their arch-foe, Lord George Gordon.[2] April 19, 500 independent electors of Westminster dined in honour of Fox, drank toasts to one another, to the cause of liberty throughout the world, and to the Duchess. April 20, the *Chronicle* wondered why the hustings officials of Westminster did not have the tax books on hand so the qualifications of each doubtful voter could be checked before he was allowed to cast his vote. The high bailiff took the hint and brought the books—whereupon each side claimed that from then on it would have a clear advantage. 'I have gained 32 today so that we are all in spirits again', Fox wrote to his dearest dearest Liz. April 27, Fox passed Wray in the polls; 600 to 800 electors dined with him, and when Colonel Fitzpatrick proposed a toast to their candidate, it was drunk with 21 cheers, the number of votes he was ahead.

Pitt, worried about the reversal of events, wrote to the King that as Fox had apparently gained a majority the contest would not be carried on much further, adding the ominous hint of trouble to come: 'Mr Pitt

---

[1] *History of the Westminster Election*, p. 214.
[2] *HMCR*, Rutland MSS., iii, 89. To the Duke of Rutland, April 17.

still trusts the ground will be regained by a scrutiny.'[1] April 29, betting odds rose 500 guineas to 50 that Fox would be elected.

May 10 a group of constables sent for from Wapping shouted 'No Fox! No Fox!' In the scuffle that followed a constable was killed. After an unsuccessful effort was made to close the polls a few days early, the election was continued the full forty days though by mutual agreement polling was stopped an hour early to accommodate the funeral for the slain man. On May 17 the final vote was: Hood 6,694; Fox 6,233; Wray 5,998.[2] Fox's victory was compleat, said the kindly disposed *Gazetteer*, despite the fact thatWestminster had in its bosom 'all the influence of the Court, the influence of £900,000 in civil list money distributed annually; the influence of all the private fortunes dependent on, or attached to, the Court'. In Derby Fox's victory was drunk with 235 cheers, his plurality over Wray. The victorious candidate was immediately chaired, and a triumphal procession formed headed by heralds on horseback; a squadron of gentlemen on horseback in the blue and buff uniform; the laurel-decked chair with the right honourable Charles James Fox seated thereon; stately conveyances of the Duchesses of Devonshire and Portland; about 30 other private carriages at the end. Toward the head of the procession were twenty-four marrow-bones and cleavers—that is to say, twenty-four butchers each beating on that masterful persuader, the meat cleaver, with a substantial beef bone— their summoning, primitive, pulsing percussion threading in and through and around the blare of the trumpets.[3] In the procession was the Prince, wearing Fox's colours of buff and blue. Next day at Carlton House he gave a breakfast that started at noon and lasted until six o'clock. That evening, at a dinner given by Mrs Crewe, he offered the celebrated toast, 'Buff and Blue and Mrs Crewe', to which she graciously and memorably replied, 'Buff and Blue and all of you'.

Writing to Mrs John Wentworth in America, the widowed Lady Rockingham, in a remarkable letter, described events:

I must mention the particular wicked absurdity that was imposed upon the poor freeholders in the ministerial manner of canvassing. They were ask'd whether they were for Pitt and the King, or Fox and the D—vl: I know this will make you laugh, and you will not believe it, but I can assure you that these vile methods of giving the idea that *Mr Fox aim'd* at being *King* have been shamefully possible, and practiced with too good success; but these sort of infatuations are too preposterous to last long.[4]

Fox's jubilation, however, was dampened by the action of Thomas

[1] *Later Correspondence of George III*, i, 57.
[2] *Journal of the House of Commons*, xl, 588.
[3] *History of the Westminster Election*, pp. 371–2; Curwen, pp. 404–5.
[4] Governor Wentworth's Correspondence, Wentworth Woodhouse Muniments (Sheffield). September 20.

Corbett, high bailiff of Westminster, who, prompted by the Government, received the protest of the defeated Wray and agreed to a scrutiny of the votes. The high bailiff needed to return the writs for summoning the new Parliament on or before May 18. Since the election was not completed until May 17, Corbett obviously had no time to conduct a scrutiny and still meet his May 18 deadline. At this point he had three choices: he could return Hood and Fox, leaders of the poll; he could return all three, leaving to the commons the final decision of which two to seat, a procedure for which precedent existed; or he could break with precedent (and, opposition was to argue, with the law) and order a scrutiny, delaying his return until a later date. He chose to follow the last course, so that the new Parliament meeting on May 18 contained no representatives for Westminster. Fox, meanwhile, was returned for Kirkwall, in Tain Burghs, Scotland.[1] Some protested the legality of this step, arguing that according to Scottish law he was ineligible to represent this borough since he had no property and paid no tax there, but he was nevertheless a member from Scotland when the sixteenth Parliament opened. This interlude was the only break in his long representation of Westminster.

The Westminster election had lasted forty days. But the scrutiny that followed lasted forty weeks. During this period Fox made one of his most celebrated speeches, the Westminster Scrutiny speech of June 8, 1784.

The overriding business of the commons on May 24 had been, after the election of a new Speaker, to discuss the ramifications of the Westminster election. During the debate that day and later the House heard legal and political arguments for and against the action of the high bailiff. Speakers drew analogies from such precedents as were available and cited statutes as far back as Richard II, Henry IV, Henry VI, and William III. Lawyers like Shelburne's attorney-general Sir Lloyd Kenyon, the coalition's attorney-general John Lee, and Pitt's attorney-general Pepper Arden took varying positions. Pitt himself drew from early experiences as a student at Lincoln's Inn and as a lawyer on the Western circuit. Members with no pretension to legal acumen commented on differing aspects of the thorny issue.

Arguments supporting the bailiff's action were that the polls were so jammed that he could not verify the legality of each vote as it was cast, that 4,000 more votes were cast than there were qualified electors, that under the circumstances he could not in conscience and judgment identify two legally-selected candidates. Arguments condemning the

[1] *History of Parliament,* i, 511; ii, 460.

bailiff were that he was specifically directed to make a return to his superior, the sheriff, on or before May 18, that the assembling of Parliament on that date was of such pre-eminent national importance that bailiffs and sheriffs should not delay the performance of this duty, that in previous cases of doubt the returning officers had certified all candidates, leaving the final choice to the house itself. The most-quoted statute, the 10th and 11th William III, prescribed the duties of sheriffs of counties in making their return to the King, but was silent with respect to returns made to the sheriffs by such lesser officers under their jurisdiction as bailiffs. This omission was seized upon by both sides of the dispute.

If the poll and the scrutiny could both have been concluded before May 18, one whole category of objections to the bailiff would have been removed. Fox was, in fact, accused of spinning out the election until the end of May 17 so that the bailiff would not have time to hold a scrutiny. Moreover, much discussion ensued about the legal status of the bailiff after May 18. Fox's side argued that the bailiff was legally dead and that a scrutiny could not be conducted by a dead hand. Pitt's side retorted that if a dead hand could not conduct a scrutiny after May 18, by the same reasoning it could not make a return of candidates after May 18.

Some arguments therefore came under the heading of expediency, some under legality. From the outset there were generous areas of doubt and probability, so that those who approved of the bailiff's action and also those who disapproved could find much to support their stands.

Fox hoped, early in the deliberation, to be able to refer his claim to a committee of the House, chosen by lot under the Grenville Act, empowered to examine witnesses under oath. He argued that if not the letter at least the spirit of the Act favoured his case, but the House speedily decided under Pitt's urging that the Grenville Act did not apply and that Fox would have to find other relief. Moreover, the House decided to hear arguments from attorneys representing Wray and Fox and to examine witnesses.

Fox himself claimed that he was being politically persecuted by the administration. Nor is it possible to acquit Pitt of the charge. As has been seen, when Fox began to gain a winning position in the polls, Pitt wrote to the King about the political expediency of a scrutiny. Early in the parliamentary discussions Pitt was not sure whether to allow the bailiff to proceed with the scrutiny or to allow him to return all three candidates and let the house choose. 'In either case', he wrote to the Duke of Rutland, 'I have no doubt of Fox being thrown out, though in either there may be great delay, inconvenience, and expense, and the choice of the alternative is delicate.'[1] In the preliminary debates Fox's own support slowly dwindled, at one time touching a low of 77 against the Government's 212. On the other side of the chamber, several members 'would have been ready to vote any censure or even expulsion against him'.[2]

The motion before the House that June 8 was that the high bailiff of Westminster should be ordered to make his return forthwith, naming the two successful candidates. Fox knew that many of his listeners were hostile and that some of his friends were not so enthusiastic as he would like. He was in that rare situation where with little to lose and much to gain he could speak as he pleased.

At the outset he observed that those who might especially have been expected to offer arguments against the motion had as yet remained silent. It would have been fair, he continued, to grant him the favour of being allowed to be the last speaker. But, he declared: 'I have no reason to expect indulgence, nor do I know that I shall meet with bare justice in this House.' The feeling of being politically persecuted was uppermost in his thought. His strong words brought such murmurs of disapproval that he reminded the murmurers that there was a regular way of censuring any member who used improper language in debate, namely, to have the words taken down by a clerk:

If any gentleman is offended by any thing that fell from me, and has sense enough to point out, and spirit to correct that offence, he will adopt that parliamentary and gentleman-like mode of conduct; and that he may have an opportunity of doing so, I again repeat, 'that I have no reason to expect indulgence, nor do I know that I shall meet with bare justice in this House'.

Fox's declaration squelched the murmurers. The medicine was bitter but they had to take it.

Fox lingered over this theme of political injustice somewhat, before proceeding to the logical part of his talk. The Grenville Act, he reminded members, was passed because of the conviction that a select committee, not the whole House itself, should judge disputed elections. The house had already barred him from the relief afforded by this Act. Accordingly he could say again, 'and say with truth, "that I expect no indulgence, nor do I know that I shall meet with bare justice in this House".' One after another he referred to three members whose previous speeches showed their prejudice against him and their preference for his opponents. When one of these three started to comment, Fox said in stern language: 'Is there any interruption, Sir? I hope not.'

[1] Stanhope, i, 213–14. May 24.
[2] *HMCR*, Rutland MSS., iii, 100. Pulteney to Rutland [June 3].

His personal indignation firmly established, Fox methodically stated the leading points of his discussion: whether the high bailiff of Westminster had sufficient evidence to warrant his granting a scrutiny, and, moreover, whether any returning officer can by law grant a scrutiny. Under these two headings he sought to organize the principal arguments offered during several days' debate. Fox attempted to demonstrate that the bailiff did not act impartially in throwing out bad votes, but instead received information from incompetent men like the witness Affleck, whose testimony the House itself had rejected. Moreover, Fox alleged, the bailiff acted in concert with Fox's adversaries, 'secretly, collusively':

To have received such information with the least attention, was in itself criminal enough; but studiously, cautiously, and deliberately to have concealed it from me, was base and wicked in the extreme. . . . [To have granted a scrutiny] upon this sort of evidence, and under these circumstances, was, to say no worse of it, an act that cannot be justified upon any obvious principle of law, reason, common sense, or common equity.

He insisted that the poll itself was properly conducted:

The parish books were constantly at the hustings, and each voter's name, profession, and description, collated with the books. . . . When the names of voters could not always be found in the parish books . . . a gentleman in the interest of each side frequently went to the very street in which the voter said he lived; that the vote was suspended until that inquiry was made.

Although it was true that the polls had been crowded on certain days, Fox asserted those were the very days when Wray had gained a great majority: 'I began to gain upon my adversary, not when thousands polled of a day, but when only a few hundreds, and less than a hundred polled on each day.'

Fox assured the House that he did not come as a newcomer to the problem of scrutinies. He recalled the Westminster election of 1780, when the defeated Lord Lincoln demanded a scrutiny, which the bailiff granted, and which Lincoln afterward abandoned:

I remember to have investigated the matter then. I consulted the greatest dead and living authorities, the best books, and the most learned men in my circle; and the result was, that the granting a scrutiny before the return was legal; but no book, no lawyer, no man, before that time, ever, to my knowledge, maintained that a scrutiny could be continued, much less begun, after the day on which the writ was returnable.

The literature on disputed elections was not extensive in 1780, but few if any excelled Fox in the art of collecting speech materials through inquiry and discussion. In fact his interest in scrutinies no doubt dated back even earlier, as Henry Fox had played an active role in the notorious Oxfordshire election and scrutiny of 1754.

To develop the second leading point, that the bailiff had no legal right to grant a scrutiny, Fox turned to what proved the longest and most serious part of his speech. I am not a professional man, he said in effect, but I can follow principles of common sense that tell me four different ways exist by which, in a case of doubt, I can ascertain the law. 'First of all, I should look into the statute book . . . if . . . I find an act of parliament upon the point in dispute . . . all is clear and certain.' If no act applies, I would then inquire into what has been done in similar cases. If precedent is clear, then everything is plain and easy; but if neither statute nor precedent can be found, I would then turn to legal analogies, and after that source, if necessary, to the experience of mankind. He thus set up a logical framework within which to mobilize the complexities of the situation.

If some of these various modes of defining the law should favour him, he continued, he might still be right, but not with that certainty that he would like. But to return to the words of the text:

The case, however, is so entirely otherwise, that I do venture to prove to the satisfaction of every man capable of being satisfied . . . that all and each concur in supporting me. . . . The high bailiff of Westminster, in granting this scrutiny, has violated the law of the land, by the combined force and testimony of these four tests: by the statutes—by the common law—by the analogies of law—by policy and expediency.

Fox might have been more persuasive had he not claimed so much, but the eighteenth century was not so subtle in these matters as is the twentieth. To support his first point, he turned principally to the statute of William III so often referred to. Fox recalled that this statute specifically mentioned *sheriffs* but not *bailiffs*. Kenyon, for example, had argued that the statute could not be made to apply to the election duties of a bailiff. This type of reasoning Fox termed a low, vile, dirty quibble, an outrage upon common sense: it was idiotic to suppose that the Act 'provided against the partialities, corruption, and roguery of sheriffs, and . . . left the nation at the mere mercy of mayors and bailiffs, without restraint, redress, or punishment'. Never in his career had Fox hesitated to match arguments with men of the law. He had cut his teeth on Wedderburn and Thurlow and he was not now to be overawed by any of Pitt's legal talent.

In detail Fox reviewed the available arguments under the headings of precedent and legal analogy. As the Westminster case of 1749 dealt with an election to fill a vacancy, not with a general election, it was not a suitable precedent. The Oxfordshire case of 1754 was settled in the House itself, since the sheriff returned all four candidates. In the chamber was Charles Jenkinson, an active participant in that settlement; Fox challenged him to give the correct details but Jenkinson kept his seat. He was no match for Fox and he knew it. Legal analogies also were offered to establish the point that a sheriff or other officer cannot operate under a writ after the day named for its return.

Although the heart of the speech consisted of examples and reasons, the net result of these logical arguments and those of other speakers was inconclusive. The election had truly been disorderly, with faults attaching to both sides. The law was incomplete and imperfect. Precedents were not entirely applicable. The greatest impact of the speech, therefore, was made by Fox's strong feeling of indignation at the opening plus his closing assertion that the scrutiny was unexampled persecution. He further reminded members that a scrutiny was an expensive operation, costing perhaps £18,000, and that his purse was no match for the Treasury's. And although he said that Pitt alone was not the author of the persecution, he closed by warning Pitt not to let the nation see him employ the power of office to overwhelm an individual.

Though he may exert all the influence of his situation to harass and persecute, he shall find that we are incapable of unbecoming submissions. There is a principle of resistance in mankind which will not brook such injuries; and a good cause and a good heart will animate men to struggle in proportion to the size of their wrongs.[1]

Pitt's reply exists only in brief summary. To Fox's argument about harassment, Pitt was content to say that Fox was being treated generously in even being allowed to speak in his own defence. '[Could] a gentleman who had the liberty of speaking three hours at a stretch on his own cause . . . be called a persecuted man?' He insisted that the House could not order the bailiff to return two members, nor could it punish him for doing what the circumstances of the election justified. Nothing in the extant text suggests that he tried to offset the bulk of Fox's logical arguments, nor did he offer any justification of the measures being taken to keep Fox from taking his seat for Westminster.

The division was 195 to 117 against the motion to direct the bailiff to return two members, 178 to 90 against adjournment. A further motion to direct the bailiff to proceed with the scrutiny was then put and carried without a vote. Fox was defeated but his speech had increased his support in the House. 'Many of our best friends were a little too conscientious', Pulteney wrote to the Duke of Rutland. Pulteney had frequently written disparaging notes about Fox's brand of eloquence, but now he conceded that Fox had made 'an astonishing speech', and that Pitt's dependable majority had pulled him through a business 'which would have been troublesome enough to a weak ministry'.[2] The *Gloucester Journal* also observed many of Pitt's friends voting with Fox.

[1] *Parliamentary History*, xxiv, 883–928.   [2] *HMCR*, Rutland MSS., iii, 106. [June 11.]

Wraxall, on the other hand, thought Fox's speech too long and too imprudent, but concluded that it comprised 'all that eloquence sustained by a just cause could combine to persuade . . . his judges'.[1] Holland thought it one of his uncle's three finest efforts.[2] It was reported, he said, by one of Fox's devoted partisans, and afterwards corrected by several friends.[3] These corrections would rob the text of verbatim accuracy, but undoubtedly helped to improve its temper, evidence, and structure.

The divisions having come at 4.30 a.m., London newspapers were tardy in reporting the debates. In general the reaction was on partisan lines, papers like the *Whitehall Evening-Post* and the *Gazetteer* commending the speech, the *Morning Post* criticizing it. The impact of Fox's eloquence, however, can not be measured entirely by the results of the divisions. Fox's speech put before the House and thus before the people a line of thought that persisted in its influence.

John Scott, the future Lord Eldon, arch tory, for many years Lord Chancellor, always liked to recall that he had defended Fox.[4] But Fox never lived to hear the most elaborate praise of all. Wraxall, in his indispensable journal of the debates during his years in Parliament, wrote that he considered the scrutiny 'one of the strongest acts of Ministerial oppression and persecution' that he had witnessed in his time.[5] Even more glittering and bespangled was the acclamation of one of Fox's political disciples, Lord Henry Brougham, Scottish-born scholar, amateur physicist, contributor to the *Edinburgh Review*, powerful parliamentary speaker and barrister, and for four years Lord Chancellor. Brougham advised another distinguished whig, Macaulay, to study the scrutiny speech and learn it by heart in order to acquire the art of parliamentary oratory.[6] Brougham's essay on Fox, well balanced in its distribution of praise and criticism, put the Westminster speech at or near the top of all of Fox's parliamentary addresses.[7]

Fox's genius clearly lay in linking local Westminster issues with a moving appeal for political justice. Pitt, most of his supporters, and many newspapers, did not grasp the import of the Westminster scrutiny set in motion that day. They did not realize that public opinion would turn against them. They were confident that once their mighty

---

[1] Wraxall, iii, 417.
[2] *The Greville Diary* (London, 1927), i, 41. The two others: War with France, Bonaparte's overtures.
[3] *Fox Cor.*, ii, 266–7.   [4] *Life of Eldon*, i, 121.   [5] Wraxall, iv, 95.
[6] William Fraser Rae, *Wilkes, Sheridan, Fox: the Opposition Under George the Third* (London, 1847), p. 459.
[7] Brougham, i, 229.

engines of influence started to turn, Fox would be rejected as member from prestigious Westminster.

Pitt's narrow-gauge plans did not materialize, however, and forty weeks later the opposite result was plain for all to see. The scrutineeers set slowly to work, proceeding with such deliberate leisure that in eight months they inspected only a fourth of the votes. No such evidences of fraud were revealed as had been prognosticated: the totals had been altered by a mere twenty-five votes, whereas the election had ended with Fox 235 ahead of Wray. From time to time the progress of the scrutiny was reported to the Commons, Pitt making stout resistance at every opportunity. 'Damn the fellow,' declared a good whig, 'he speaks so well, I wish his throat was cut.'[1]

As the scrutiny was exhuming so few bad votes, Fox's friends sought to have it terminated by a motion ordering the high bailiff to return Hood and Fox as members for Westminster. The debate on February 9, 1785, was defeated by the slender margin of 39 votes; thus had parliamentary opinion shifted away from Pitt. On February 21 the Government's majority shrank to 9. By March 3 the tide had completely turned: Pitt was defeated by 38, and next day Hood and Fox were returned. The scrutiny officials had dealt with a level hand: from Hood's total they had subtracted 106 fraudulent votes, from Fox's 107, and from Wray's 103.[2] Hence Fox's conduct was justified both in theory and in fact.

When Sir Cecil Wray heard the news, he fainted and had to be taken to the pump to be revived. By eleven that night, however, nearly every house in Westminster was illuminated, as the jubilant *Morning Herald* viewed the scene. The *Gazetteer* declared with unwarranted optimism that the defeat of the first minister showed that the country was beginning to totter. More significantly, the groundswell of public opinion against the scrutiny was compelling. The county of York instructed its members to stop the scrutiny; other counties might have followed suit.[3] Westminster could well rejoice; it was once again represented in Parliament by its favourite son.

The Westminster affair thus set the stage for two of Fox's great triumphs. His campaign utterances were typical of his eventful career as speaker-outside-of-Parliament. Whereas Pitt's voice was seldom heard outside the Commons, Fox spoke to thousands. When a man speaks from the hustings he stands, to use Burke's phrase, upon a conspicuous stage. The triumph of Fox's Westminster campaign is,

---

[1] *HMCR*, Rutland MSS., iii, 168. The statement was uttered by Lord Derby, staunch friend of Fox's.

[2] *Journal of the House of Commons*, xl, 588.

[3] Hamilton-Greville MSS. Greville to Hamilton, March 10. (Huntington.)

therefore, not to be overlooked. But the triumph of the scrutiny, set in motion by the June 8 speech, was even more spectacular. During the long seventeen-year period of Pitt's ministry, even though Fox spoke on such lofty issues as freedom of speech, peace, the state of the nation, and religious toleration, he was continually bested in debate by the administration's majority. Hence his parliamentary victories were few and far between. On the issue of the Westminster scrutiny, however, he was able to reverse the Government's substantial majority, upset its best legal minds, and beat the minister himself on an issue involving his personal prestige. The magnitude of the odds against Fox underscores the significance of his brilliant espousal of the rights of disputants in contested elections.

16

Mr Pitt and Mr Fox
1785–1787

> Damn his good speeches, let me hear of his making a bad one.
>
> *Charles James Fox*

So far in the contest between Pitt and Fox, Pitt had achieved a luminous victory on the coalition issue but Fox had emerged as the champion of Westminster. Now Pitt was to suffer reverses on two other issues debated in the early months of 1785.

A month after the scrutiny had been abandoned, Pitt faced one of the crowded Houses of his career to date to unfold a plan of parliamentary reform. Among other changes he proposed to disfranchise thirty-six rotten boroughs, each returning two members, and to assign these seats to the largest counties and to the cities of London and Westminster. The changes were to be made gradually, with recompense to those interested in the boroughs being disfranchised. North and Burke spoke against the proposal; Wilberforce and Dundas supported Pitt. Fox, overlooking his shabby treatment at Pitt's hand, earnestly entreated both sides of the House to support Pitt's motion. The division was 248 to 174 against it. More than a decade went by before it was again seriously taken up in the House.

The complex Irish question also came up for debate. A year previously the Irish Chancellor of the Exchequer had visited Pitt, bringing with him ten resolutions to reduce tariffs and in other ways to liberalize commercial intercourse between Great Britain and Ireland. This notion appealed to Pitt, but he later introduced a highly provocative issue: that in return Ireland should make a substantial contribution to imperial defence. In January 1785 the British Cabinet had approved the revised plan, and its proposals were passed by the Irish Parliament after heated debate, emerging as a series of eleven resolutions.[1] The Irish in their turn made an important alteration. Pitt wanted the surplus of the Irish hereditary revenue above the sum of £656,000 to be contributed to the common defence; the Irish Parliament modified this proposal by stating that the surplus should be allocated 'in such manner

---

[1] See the invaluable analysis of the Anglo-Irish proposals in Vincent T. Harlow, *The Founding of the Second British Empire, 1763–1793* (London, 1952), i, 558 ff.

as the Parliament of this kingdom shall direct', a reservation that would allow Ireland to spend the surplus on Irish ships.

Pitt was angry and embarrassed by this hitch in his plans. Regardless, he sought to present the advantage of mutually beneficial trade agreements and to minimize for the time being the embarrassing condition that the Irish Parliament had attached to its contribution to defence.

The commercial aspects of Pitt's proposals did him honour. His vision was to see Ireland admitted as a partner in the commercial enterprises of the two kingdoms. He was not dismayed that in some respects Ireland might rival, and perhaps beat England. This eventuality, however, should not be painful. Competition might trouble some manufacturers but the end result would make Ireland a rich customer instead of a poor one. Pitt's statesmanship faltered on his insistence that Ireland contribute to imperial defence, and it was on this point that the Irish, like the Americans in the preceding decade, offered a strong counter. He had to confess that this particular Irish resolution was 'not so clear' as he would wish.

Much of Fox's rebuttal that day was a holding operation. Already he could see that the proposals were generating grave doubts among British commercial interests. Angered by Pitt's rancorous treatment of the scrutiny issue, Fox was in no mood to give ground. If the opposition could prevent Pitt from moving too rapidly, it could mobilize sentiment against the proposals. Fox therefore quibbled that they had been taken to the Irish Parliament before they had been brought to St Stephen's. This manoeuvre would make it appear mischievous to reject them or even freely to debate them.

Meanwhile the merchants of Liverpool presented a petition urging that the privilege of supplying British markets with the produce of British colonies be preserved inviolate to the kingdom of Britain. The whole of Lancashire joined the protest and sent to the House a petition signed by 80,000 names—a document so bulky that it could not be held in the hands but had to be lain on the floor. Among other arguments offered in petition and in debate was the one that smuggling would increase. The propinquity of Irish shores would make possible wholesale dumping of goods into England. Because of Irish cheap labour, Ireland would be able to undersell Britain, and 40,000 men would be thrown out of work in Lancashire alone. Pitt's tax on cotton goods had been ruinous enough; the new proposals would annihilate the industry.

For two months the House heard lawyers and examined witnesses. A Government supporter admitted counting sixty-four petitions against the proposals. Petitions came from Bristol, Birmingham, Glasgow, Stafford, and elsewhere, hoping for delay until the implications of the crisis could be studied. Manufacturers of nails and ironware, cotton goods, tanned leather products, glass, sailcloth, and other merchandise pleaded their distress. A prime mover and shaker among manufacturers was the famous potter, Josiah Wedgwood. Few things are so unpopular as a good idea ahead of its time. Stirred partly by fact, partly by fear, British interests were not ready to extend commercial opportunity to the Irish. On the other coast, Irish manufacturers sought to continue the shelter of protective duties.

Pitt found it necessary to make notable concessions to the manufacturers and to his own parliamentary opposition. As an age that has developed the common market and other regional trade agreements well knows, general principles must be supplemented by specific tariffs, quotas, scales, schedules. Pitt came back to the House on May 12 with a drastically revised version of his first proposals: the original eleven plus sixteen supplements. He began his explanation of the new set at 9.15 and did not sit down until midnight. After a brief comment by North, Fox took the floor and held it until 4 a.m. He lampooned the proposals both as to quantity and particularly as to extensiveness of revision. He listed specific ill effects that would have resulted if Pitt's original propositions had been hastily passed: thus, he declared, the House was clearly shown the benefit of deliberation. Because opposition speakers had sounded the alarm, he claimed, manufacturing communities all over the kingdom had been made aware of their danger and had been given time to prepare their case.[1]

Pitt had, in fact, made many alterations. The new proposals required bonds, cockets, certificates of origin, and other documents from Irish vessels. Special provisos accommodated brandy, rum, beer, flour, biscuits, arms, gunpowder, and other manufactured articles. The Irish Parliament was notified that, to keep navigation laws consistent in the two countries, it must in the future agree to enact whatever legislation under this heading that the British Parliament enacted. This, the notorious fourth resolution, raised grave constitutional issues. Fox promptly pointed out that it demanded a surrender from Ireland of her legislative independence. Irish vessels were to keep within the Cape of Good Hope and the Straits of Magellan; this restriction, reviewed later in the Irish Parliament, spawned a good deal of seasoned ridicule.

Unlike his colleagues, Burke approved of Pitt's modified plan.[2] But Fox's part in the controversy has been freely regarded as factious and mischievous. True enough, he took full advantage of Pitt's difficulties and changes of position. 'Fox declared he would fight the whole of it

---

[1] *The Speech of the right honourable C. J. Fox . . . on May 12, 1785* (London, 1785), pp. 9–10, 20. *Parliamentary History*, xxv, 591–625.
[2] On this point see Carl B. Cone, *Burke and the Nature of Politics* (Lexington, 1964), ii, 174–8.

inch by inch,' wrote Burke afterwards; 'he would debate every resolution, every amendment, and divide the House on each; that it was a measure that went completely to the commerce, manufacture, revenue, and maritime strength of the century.'[1] Representing a solid block of English and Irish opinion, Fox hit Pitt hip and thigh on both commercial and constitutional implications.

During the final debate on May 30 Fox made his famous statement:

I wish to appear what I really feel, both an English and an Irish patriot. . . . I considered the whole plan as a lure to divert the Irish from constitutional points by throwing the trade of England at their feet. . . . If this conduct, Sir, constitutes an Irish patriot, then am I one; and if to struggle to save the trade of England from annihilation, gives any claim to the appellation of an English patriot, I possess that claim. . . .

I will not barter English commerce for Irish slavery; that is not the price I would pay, nor is this the thing I would purchase.[2]

As the issues became more complex, various members protested their confusion. Even Wraxall noted that many members could not understand the proposal and confessed as much.[3] The resolutions—now consolidated into twenty—passed the Commons in a thin House and also the Lords, with additional changes, after long debate. Six lords speedily entered a minority protest; all of them, Sydney observed to Rutland, were *âmes damnées* of Fox's.[4] Back in the Commons, Pitt presented the revised resolutions in the form of a Bill and pushed it through the first reading. In July Fox wrote to Ossory: 'Was there ever a history of folly like this Irish business? When you are in Ireland you will see the ridicule of this plan to conciliate your countrymen still more strongly.'[5]

The Irish Parliament found itself in the eye of the hurricane. Protests against the resolutions were heard on all sides. The Government, able to mobilize a majority of only nineteen for its request to bring in a Bill, saw that it would inevitably lose in the later stages. The British Parliament recessed without taking further action. In the two kingdoms, bonfires, illuminations, parades celebrated the defeat of the measure.

That autumn Walpole noted that Fox and his colleagues were received at Manchester with many compliments both on their opposition to the Irish propositions and to Pitt's new taxes. Fox himself wrote that the reception and parade were as fine as a Westminster chairing. A dinner, he continued, was attended by 150 of the principal people;

---

[1] Grattan, iii, 252. To Sir John Tydd, May 13, 1785. Pulteney wrote Rutland that Fox utilized every conceivable parliamentary trick to delay the vote (*HMCR*, Rutland MSS., iii, 206 [May 13, 1785]).
[2] *Parliamentary History*, xxv, 777–8.   [3] Wraxall, iv, 133–4.
[4] *HMCR*, Rutland MSS., iii, 230. July 20.
[5] Add. MSS. 47579. *Fox Cor.*, ii, 270. July 11, 1785.

one of them made a speech in which he confessed how prejudiced he had been in favour of Pitt and against Fox, but he declared that when he got acquainted with both men he found he had been mistaken in each. Later Fox wrote: 'I never saw more apparent unanimity than seemed to be in our favour; and all this in the town of Manchester, which used to be reckoned the worst place for us in the whole country.'[1]

Pitt's plan deserved better success than it received. Fox and his colleagues did not understand the economics of it and capitalized upon the opposition of commercial interests. It is interesting to speculate what might have happened had Fox joined with Pitt to attempt to urge upon the country a venture in this common-market type of endeavour. Had an economic union emerged, the political difficulties might have been adjusted. The realities, however, line up on the other side. Fox was not cordial to Pitt; Fox was no disciple of Adam Smith; British and Irish commercial interests cannot be accused of being stupid about their short-term interests, although hindsight can sagely advise them about the wisdom of the longer view; constitutional complexities and Irish sensitivities growing out of them were grave.

Although Mr Pitt lost the dialogue to Mr Fox on the Scrutiny and the Irish issues, and both together were defeated on parliamentary reform, Pitt had unusual success in the new Parliament with other domestic measures, particularly those designed to improve the nation's finances. He sagely reduced duties on tea and liquor in order to counteract the amazing growth of smuggling, correctly reasoning that lighter duties would make smuggling unprofitable. His proposals that government loans should be awarded, not through channels of patronage, but to the lowest bidder, and his legislation providing new taxes and imposts were readily passed, though some of his new taxes, like the additional tax on male servants and the new one on female servants, invited ridicule by opposition speakers. His tax on retail merchants understandably proved unpopular with shopkeepers, and in the years immediately ahead provided Fox with a persuasive argument. Yet in the main the Government drew strength from Pitt's measures.

The parliamentary session opening in January 1786 was given over mainly to debates on the India situation. The preceding year Warren Hastings had returned to England, having served as governor-general for more than ten years, an India fortune in his pocket; and, proud and confident, expectant of reward, he was eager or at least not unwilling to face his accusers. Of many charges, two were paramount: corruption

[1] Add. MSS. 47579. *Fox Cor.*, ii, 270–1. September 10.

among officials and employees of the East India Company, and particularly inhumane treatment of Indian princes and subjects.

Foremost among his accusers was Philip Francis, son and namesake of Fox's boyhood tutor. Francis had been one of the first members of the supreme Bengal Council of four, provided for by the Regulating Act passed during North's ministry. It was this Regulating Act, with its ingenious provision for disposing of the East India Company's surplus tea, that had led to the Boston tea party of 1773. As a member of the council, Francis had found himself in continual conflict with Hastings. When, in 1780, Hastings called Francis 'void of truth and honour', Francis challenged him to a duel and was severely wounded. Brilliant, energetic, articulate, vindictive, Francis proved an implacable enemy.

Burke also had long been interested in the conduct of Hastings. Since 1781 when Burke had been head of a select committee, he had urged that Hastings should be recalled and punished. The India Bill had presumably helped solve immediate problems, but Hastings' alleged crimes and inhumanities still remained, in Burke's eyes, unpunished.

Fox's interest in Hastings was no less keen and no less competent, though shorter-lived, than Burke's. In the debates on the ill-fated India Bill offered during his own administration, Fox had demonstrated a detailed knowledge of the financial and political operations of the East India Company. In nearly every session since he had first concerned himself with the broad sweep of political and commercial problems in India, Fox had participated extensively in debate on these topics, often sharply criticizing Hastings' policy and action. And as months wore on and evidence accumulated, Fox, like Burke, more and more had begun to talk about oppression and plunder, and underlying principles of humanity, justice and freedom.

Sheridan was another who was interested in bringing Hastings to account. Although since his entrance into Parliament in 1780, he had taken no great part in debate, he had proved his fearlessness and independence, he had demonstrated that on the floor of the House he could not be bullied by Pitt or by anybody else, he had developed a reputation for parliamentary repartee; his alert mind, however, was equal to more than superficialities. He was capable of a solid and sustained preparation that the House as yet had not suspected.

So the situation in India again came up for debate in the 1786 session. In February Burke moved that correspondence since 1782 relating to presents received by Hastings be laid before the House. Major John Scott, who on other occasions had defended Hastings on the floor of the Commons, now boasted that Hastings welcomed inquiry. After ridiculing Burke ('Year after year he had pledged himself to God, this House, and to his Country, to prove Mr Hastings a most notorious delinquent') and gratuitously instructing Fox ('The Rohillas were not a nation, as the right hon. gentleman Mr Fox styles them'), he boldly expressed Hastings' wishes for an inquiry, and the die was cast. Quite possibly if Hastings, through Scott, had not pressed for an inquiry, seven years of choice oratory would have been strangled at birth. But Hastings was eager for a peerage and Pitt had said he could not recommend him for such an honour until the sting of the resolutions moved against him had been replaced by a vote of thanks.

Further calls for papers and further debates gradually developed the case to impeach Hastings. In four mighty installments Burke presented twenty formidable charges. The accusation: high crimes and misdemeanors. In May a full House saw Hastings at its bar, carrying an immensely weighty document that needed to be read entire. His reading was far from eloquent—later he was to write, 'I am in a singular degree deficient in the powers of utterance'—and clerks continued the reading of the never-ending document. After all, twenty separate charges needed to be refuted: answer to the first charge, with twenty subheadings . . . answer to the third charge—parts I through V . . . preface to the fourth charge . . . charge the fourth . . . and so to the end. Members stole away one by one, wondering who was the more tedious, Hastings or Scott.[1]

Of all the charges, the most serious were those that involved the Rohilla war; Cheyte Sing, the rajah of Benares; and the two begums or princesses of Oude. Burke opened with the Rohilla charge. But after two days of debate Pitt and 119 others voted against the charge, only 67 for it.

Although the Rohilla charge was lost, others remained. Fox followed with the charge relative to Hastings' conduct toward Benares, pointing out that Benares was an independent nation, and its rajah, Cheyte Sing, an independent prince, and therefore not bound to support the British Government at Bengal. It was therefore unjust in the highest degree to levy a fine of £500,000 as punishment for delaying the payment of £50,000; the very use of the word 'fine' was a miserable cavil and a gross perversion. Surprisingly enough, Pitt, although objecting to Fox's argument, and contending that Benares was a vassal, not an independent state, declared that Hastings could have been properly assessed a fine—though nothing so large as £500,000. This proceeding was 'arbitrary, tyrannical . . . grinding . . . overbearing . . . disproportionate . . . shamefully exhorbitant'. He therefore announced his intention to support the charge, and it carried by 119 to 79. The *Morning Herald* sought to give Fox the credit for Pitt's change of

---

[1] Stanhope, i, 299; *Journal of the House of Commons*, xli, 668–733. See Cone, ii, 101–2, for details of Scott's incompetence.

mind ('it may be said that the arguments of Mr Fox carried with them such conviction as to disable the Minister from personally giving the vote his negative'). Quite likely, however, Pitt had decided before or even during the day's session that he could not protect Hastings much longer.[1] Despite Burke's impatience little more of the Hastings business could be carried on that session, and in July Parliament recessed for the rest of the year.

Fox's unusual affair with Mrs Elizabeth Bridget Armistead, already referred to in these chapters, now had begun to develop into a steadier attachment.

Little was known about any Mr Armistead or about her own past. Much was known about her present. She was friendly, gay, attractive. With no intellectual pretensions of her own, she was nevertheless able to listen, to absorb, to appreciate. At one time or another she had enjoyed the company of an assortment of distinguished gentlemen and lords. Because of the prominence of her associates, she had seen her conquests and exploits dragged through the columns of the papers. Invariably her experience with each new admirer had followed the same pattern: favours, costly gifts and presents, and then he would take his leave and another enter.

She had no reason ever to expect any sort of permanent loyalty or devotion. Then there came into her orbit the distinguished and fascinating member of Parliament, leader of the opposition, twice Foreign Secretary, scion of aristocracy, Mr Fox. Unquestionably she thought of their first associations, whenever and wherever they were, as something entirely transient. And indeed she should, as Mr Fox himself had had his own previous string of companions. But he himself was steadily maturing as a person.

Their relationship had its ups and downs; at one time she angrily burned all his love letters. Starting with a present of £1,000 a year, as the paragraphers reported, the arrangement with its superficiality and uncertainty grew into something appealing and durable. With her Fox began to share not only social pleasures but political aspirations. As his politics was layered with disappointment and disillusionment, he increasingly found in her affection the depths of understanding that

---

[1] *Stanhope*, i, 303, citing a letter from Hastings to Elijah Impey of April 19, 1818, thirty-two years afterwards.

Wilberforce wrote: 'I well remember . . . Pitt listening most attentively to some facts which were coming out in the first or second case. He beckoned me over, and went with me behind the chair, and said, "Does not this look very ill to you?" "Very bad indeed." He then returned to his place and made his speech, giving up Hastings' case' (Wilberforce, v, 340–1).

he needed. As far back as coalition days, when his ministry had been shipwrecked by the King's action on the India Bill, he had turned to her in his despondency. A surviving note reflects his satisfaction in sharing his thoughts with her and also his own deep personal conviction, since he had no reason to be other than wholly candid:

Indeed my dearest Liz it is no hypocrisy in me to say that the consciousness of having always acted upon principle in public matters and my determination always to do so is the great comfort of my life. I know I never did act more upon principle than at this moment when they are abusing me so. If I had considered nothing but keeping my power, it was the safest way to leave things as they are or to propose some trifling alteration. ... I write very gravely because the amazing abuse which is heaped upon me makes me feel so. I have the weakness of disliking abuse, but that weakness shall never prevent me from doing what I think right.[1]

During the early days of the Westminster polling, when he had despaired that he could ever surmount the implacable forces against him, he regularly sent her the results of each day's voting. Later he could share with her his electoral celebration. When he realized that, despite his victory, he was to be deprived of his Westminster seat and could see no way of overturning Pitt's rancour, he comforted himself with her society, as his Aunt Sarah wrote Lady Susan, '& all he seems to lament is the want of £2,000 for to buy the house at St Anne's Hill which he longs for'.[2]

Again, shortly after he had triumphed in the scrutiny and could again stand in the House as the member for Westminster, he wrote her:

I feel every day how much more I love you than even *I* knew. You are *all* to me. You can always make me happy in circumstances apparently unpleasant and miserable in the most prosperous. Indeed my dearest angel the whole happiness of my life depends upon you. Pray pray do not abuse your power. Adieu.[3]

By 1786, Fox, then past thirty-seven, had established himself with her at St Anne's, a small acreage with a delightful cottage. More on her insistence than his, they had decided not to get married. They were, however, entirely contented, and did not care what the world would say or think. The new domicile helped Fox to break the connection with the habits and routines of gambling. To his wide interests he added one in agriculture, and his letters began to contain references to field and garden. Like any farmer he worried about hay, oats, weeds, insects. He liked tennis, hunting, swimming, whist, chess, and other pleasures of countryside society. Often he and Mrs Armistead would read to one another.

[1] Add. MSS. 47570. December 30 [1783]. *Fox Cor.*, ii, 219–20.
[2] *Life and Letters of Lady Sarah Lennox*, i. 369. To Lady Susan O'Brien, September 8, 1784.
[3] Add. MSS. 47570. May 7 [1785].

The long summer and autumn recess accordingly found Fox enjoying an entirely different kind of life. Politics was less important, although in Paris young Thomas Jefferson heard a wild rumour about an attempt to assassinate George III. 'No man upon earth has my prayers for his continuance in life more sincerely than him,' Jefferson wrote to his good friend, Mrs John Adams. 'Twenty long years has he been labouring to drive us to our good, and he labours and will labour still for it if he can be spared. We shall have need of him for twenty more.' Let the Prince of Wales come to the throne, he continued his irony, with Fox in the ministry, and the United States would certainly be undone.[1]

So 1786 ended: George Washington not yet president, Louis XVI still with a head on his shoulders, George the Third not assassinated but well into his second quarter-century, the Irish restless, Hastings cleared on one charge, condemned on another, eighteen still to go. Mr Pitt in office, Mr Fox in opposition, had completed two years of dialogue with nineteen yet ahead.

Mr Fox and Mr Pitt interspersed their discussion of the Hastings affair with debates on the desirability of a trade arrangement with France. Pitt had presented to Parliament a draft of a treaty of navigation and commerce with France. As a market for British goods, he argued, France was even better than the colonies for it was eight times as populous, as Adam Smith had observed, and closer at hand. Pitt, still seeking to move towards free trade, proposed reductions in vinegar, brandy, cotton and woollens, hardware and cutlery, and numerous other items. Silk was excluded as a gesture to the weavers of Spitalfields.

Fox's opening speech protested Pitt's haste in bringing the treaty forward, and reminded the house of the political implications of a commercial agreement with a former enemy. Although Fox's correspondence contains few references to his own speech-making, a letter to Mrs Armistead comments on this debate:

It was thought by others as well as by myself better that I should speak & not let the thing go off quite silently which if I had not spoken it would have done. I spoke pretty strongly against French connections and France, and Pitt made as bad a speech in answer as could be wished. There was no more debate and no division so that I was time enough [*sic*] to go to dinner at Derby's where every body seemed to think I had done right.[2]

His language against France was even stronger in his speech of

---

[1] Julian P. Boyd, ed., *The Papers of Thomas Jefferson* (Princeton, 1954), x, 202. August 9.
[2] Add. MSS. 47570, January 26. *Fox Cor.*, ii, 276.

February 12. 'France', he said, 'was the natural political enemy of Great Britain'; not because of Creasy and Agincourt, but because of France's overweening pride and boundless ambition to hold sway over all Europe. As she was the natural foe, undoubtedly she wished by entering into a commercial treaty to tie the hands of Great Britain, and thus prevent her from entering into alliances with other powers. Although Fox took care to say that France's attitude toward Great Britain could change, even to the point where she might desire to 'act amicably with respect to this Kingdom', such an event was scarcely probable.[1]

Pitt defended his proposals skilfully. To be sure the treaty would be advantageous to France, but even more so to England. 'She procured a market of eight millions of people, we a market of twenty-four millions.' France stood to gain perhaps £100,000; England must necessarily gain a million. Important benefits would flow from a treaty between France, primarily agricultural, and Britain, primarily industrial. The debate, extending over many days, was one in which several participated; not only the principals, Fox and Pitt, but also Sheridan and Burke; and a new member, Charles Grey, a strong admirer of Fox, and later a confessed disciple, made his maiden speech against the treaty. Pitt himself declared at the close of the long debate that he had never before heard a subject handled on both sides of the House with greater ability.

Yet Pitt was no doubt reflecting more upon his own contribution to the debate than to that of his opponents. Obviously, he had much the better of the argument. And as the treaty was generally popular with commercial interests, Fox's position met further criticism. A Manchester manufacturer, though recalling that Fox's Lancashire friends were grateful because he had opposed the Irish propositions that 'had a tendency injurious to our trade,' declared that Fox should have supported the French treaty, 'replete with advantages to us and to the nation at large'.[2] Pitt's proposals did not meet serious resistance in either House. The treaty demonstrated a resourceful interest in extending British trade and was an important stimulus to British industry for the few years before peace was interrupted by the long war with France. As for the long war between Mr Pitt and Mr Fox, these lesser skirmishes over trade, duties, taxes, budgets, and other executive details of managing a growing empire were only a conditioner for the bitterly fought, highly emotional battles that lay just ahead.

---

[1] *Parliamentary History*, xxvi, 397–8.
[2] *A letter from a Manchester manufacturer to the right honourable Charles James Fox, on his political opposition to the commercial treaty with France* (Manchester, 1787), p. 9.

17

Fox, The Prince, and Mrs Fitzherbert
1784–1788

> There is reason to suppose that you are going to take
> the very desperate step of marrying her.
>
> *Charles James Fox*

The affair of the Prince of Wales with Mrs Maria Fitzherbert was one of the strange episodes of eighteenth-century politics. It came forcibly to the attention of Parliament in 1787, and loomed ominously in the background of the regency issue the following year. As a warm personal friend and political associate of the Prince, Fox received the full sting of the backlash of its repercussions.

The attractive and high-principled Mrs Fitzherbert had been twice widowed when the Prince first met her. Although she was naturally intrigued by the attention he paid her, she did not take him seriously. As a devout Catholic, she fully realized that a permanent connection between them was out of the question, but her demurrals and hesitancies made him more ardent than ever. By the autumn of 1784 he was contriving every means to spend hours daily in her society. He vowed that he would not and could not live without her, giving way to tears when it seemed that he could not legally marry her because of the formidable difficulties presented by two British laws. One was the Act of Settlement of 1689, providing that anyone who wedded a Catholic would forfeit all rights to the throne. The Prince might have made this sacrifice, but a second law complicated the problem: the Royal Marriage Act of 1772, forbidding any member of the royal household under twenty-five years of age to marry without the King's consent. As for Mrs Fitzherbert, it was marriage or nothing. Since marriage to the Prince was impossible, she refused to see him or to answer his letters, a refusal that brought a fresh barrage of tears from him.

Fox had advised the Prince to accept the gracious widow as his mistress, a proposal she would not only not hear of, but that led her to develop a cordial dislike for Mr Fox in the bargain. Above all, Fox did not want to imperil the Prince's right to the throne, since the eventual prospect of a friendly king was politically gratifying to an opposition that for so long had fought the present ruler. The Prince, finding marriage necessary in fact although impossible in theory, decided upon a strategem. One day in November Mrs Fitzherbert was informed that the Prince had stabbed himself and that only her immediate presence at Carlton House would save him. Refusing to jeopardize her honour by going alone, she finally consented to go with the Duchess of Devonshire. They found the Prince pale and bleeding. Almost losing her mind when she saw the plight of her lover, Mrs Fitzherbert hysterically promised to marry him, and a deposition was drawn up, sealed, and signed on the spot. The Prince recovered almost immediately. Next day, realizing that she had been the victim of play-acting, she wrote a scathing letter and left for the Continent.

In December 1785 she returned as suddenly as she had left. When again the Prince was seen continually in her company, Fox wrote him a long, carefully worded letter, pointing out that 'there was reason to suppose, that you were going to take the very desperate step (pardon the expression) of marrying her at this moment'. Next day the Prince answered: 'Make yourself easy, my dear friend; believe me the world will now soon be convinced that there not only is, but never was, any grounds for these reports, which of late have been so malevolently circulated.'[1] On December 15, however, unknown to Fox, a secret marriage between the Prince and Mrs Fitzherbert was solemnized by a clergyman of the Church of England. Illegal though it was, not having the sovereign's permission, the ceremony satisfied the religious principles of the bride.

In the months that followed, however, she and the Prince were seen together so continually that Londoners began to gossip about their marital status. No one particularly objected to his having a Catholic mistress but gradually ugly rumours began to circulate that he had actually married her. These rumours, entwined with the perennial comments about the Prince's financial extravagance, caused repercussions in the highest social and political circles.

The matter was brought to the attention of the Commons on April 20, 1787, in a peculiarly oblique fashion. That day Alderman Newnham announced his intention to offer a motion a fortnight hence inquiring into the embarrassing situation of the Prince of Wales. Newnham's laconic statement aroused curiosity. Would his proposed motion limit itself to the Prince's finances, inviting a discussion of ways of increasing his allowance so that he could make repairs to his house, keep up his personal retinue, and liquidate his debts? Or was the motion an entering wedge for the discussion of more delicate topics?[2] A persistent Devonshire tory, John Rolle, commented that it had extremely grave

[1] *Fox Cor.*, ii, 278–85.   [2] *Parliamentary History*, xxvi, 1009–10.

1 Charles James Fox from a portrait by Karl Anton Hickel

2 Charles James Fox
from a portrait by
Sir Joshua Reynolds

R.t Hon.ble C.J. F

3 Charles James Fox
Attributed to
Johann Zoffany

4 Charles James Fox
from a portrait by
John Opie, 1802

5 Pitt and Fox in the
House of Commons

6 Charles James Fox speaking in the House of Commons from a painting by Karl Anton Hickel

7 Charles James Fox
by Joseph Nollekens

implications, and in reality involved 'our Constitution in church and state'. By now the cat was out of the bag. The question which alone involved church and state was the marital status of the Prince and Mrs Fitzherbert.

Fox sought to clear the air the following Monday. He felt that he was in a position to deny the marriage; he had asked the Prince about the persistent rumours and had been met with such comments as 'pooh', 'nonsense', 'ridiculous'.[1] Fox therefore, flatly asserted that no marriage of any kind had taken place, and that he spoke from direct authority—from that of the Prince himself.[2]

Next day after Fox's declaration, a friend sought him out at Brooks's, and said: 'Mr Fox, I hear that you have denied in the House the Prince's marriage to Mrs Fitzherbert. You have been misinformed; I was at the marriage.'[3] Fox therefore began to realize that he had been duped. Yet, because of loyalty, because of expediency, and because of the cloudiness of the incident, he did not retract. But his statement had grievously aggravated the situation. Obviously his declaration offended Mrs Fitzherbert, although for the time being the Prince felt relieved. At midnight that day he wrote that he 'felt comfortable' about the affair.[4] He did not feel so comfortable the next morning when he faced Mrs Fitzherbert, but declared that Fox had acted without authority. He sent for Charles Grey, confessed the marriage, said Fox had gone too far, and asked Grey to smooth it over. Grey refused, and the Prince declared: 'Well, if nobody else will, Sheridan must.'[5]

Thus Sheridan found himself involved in a tricky constitutional issue. He must somehow say that a marriage had taken place, in order to salvage the good name of a lady and in order to restore domestic tranquillity to the Prince. Equally obviously he must declare that no marriage had taken place in order to save Britain the internal strife that might follow should the succession to the throne be invalidated. In one speech he must both affirm and deny.

When the House convened that May 4 with more than four hundred members present (short-memoried parliamentary reporters, generally astonished by any crowd of more than four hundred, declared they never remembered the House so filled), Alderman Newnham briefly announced that he would not present his motion inquiring into the

[1] Louis J. Jennings, ed., *The Croker Papers* (New York, 1884), i, 292.
[2] *Parliamentary History*, xxvi, 1070.
[3] W. H. Wilkins, *Mrs Fitzherbert and George IV* (London, 1914), p. 138.
[4] *Fox Cor.*, ii, 288.
[5] Wilkins, pp. 140–2. See also Lord Holland, *Memoirs of the Whig Party During My Time*, i, 205; Charles Langdale, *Memoirs of Mrs Fitzherbert* (London, 1856), p. 29.

debts of his royal highness. Over the week-end an agreement had been reached concerning ways of financing the Prince's obligations.

Some contemporary accounts indicate that this announcement caused general relief, but an examination of the parliamentary record shows a dangerous undercurrent of perplexity. The persistent Rolle threatened to denounce the terms of the agreement if he should later learn that they were humiliating to the country. After a retort by Fox, Pitt showed signs of wanting to terminate debate but Sheridan could not let the house adjourn without making his speech. The situation was even more ticklish than before since Sheridan now had to bring the dilemma of the Prince's marriage before the house so that he might resolve it.

Sheridan's first words were highly conciliatory: he joined with Pitt in expressing the hope that the conversation would not be prolonged. He went on to assure his listeners that he was sure that 'upon that day there existed but one sentiment in the House—that of a heart felt satisfaction at the auspicious conclusion to which the business was understood to be brought'.[1] So far as he was concerned, let the King and his ministers have the credit, but let every one remember that throughout the Prince had acted with good judgment and good sense.

Sheridan then moved directly to the first of the two tasks before him: to create goodwill for the Prince, who, let it be remembered, had offered to answer questions of any sort about his conduct. 'That no such inquiry had been adopted, was a point which did credit to the decorum, the feelings, and the dignity of Parliament.' If it had been decorous, sensible, and dignified to refuse to question the Prince two weeks ago, it was certainly decorous, sensible, and dignified to refuse to do so now.

As for the complementary problem of restoring the good name of Mrs Fitzherbert, Sheridan's handling of this fragile situation was highly tactful. The exact language he used intrigued the fancy of the various individuals who reported the speech. One can imagine the hurried note-taking that went on and later the mental effort of each reporter to reconstruct Sheridan's rhetorical strategy. The reporter for the *London Chronicle* set down these words: 'It was only from the prejudiced and uninformed that the conduct and character of the person he alluded to could fail to meet with the truest and sincerest respect.'[2] The speech was not long, but when Sheridan had finished members were willing to let the matter rest.

[1] *Parliamentary History*, xxvi, 1079–80.
[2] For a discussion of other versions, see Loren Reid, 'Sheridan's Speech on Mrs Fitzherbert', *Quarterly Journal of Speech*, xxxiii (February 1947), 15–22. See also *Public Advertiser*, *Gazetteer*, *Whitehall Evening-Post*, and other London newspapers for May 5; *Bath Chronicle*, May 10.

Nobody was fooled, however, by the day's business. Pulteney wrote to the Duke of Rutland: 'Sheridan . . . said to-day in the House her situation was truly respectable, at which every one smiled.'[1] Edmund Malone wrote ironically: 'The best of all was Sheridan's very gravely saying in the House, when the whole business was over, that he was sure it was impossible this lady could suffer in the smallest degree in the mind of any one of sentiment, delicacy, and honour!'[2] Members smiled at Sheridan's words but they kept their seats. And to keep one's seat at that particular moment indicated that one had been persuaded (entirely without reason?) to ignore the statutes regulating royal marriages with their implications for church and constitution. Keeping one's seat also indicated a primary concern for the Prince rather than for Mrs Fitzherbert's sensitivities.

The incident had several outcomes, all interesting.

For a time Mrs Fitzherbert's position in society was enhanced. Tories and whigs, Catholics and Protestants surrounded her. Some thought the predicament invested her with a new glamour; others sympathized because they felt she was being persecuted. Indeed she deserved sympathy, for although she was given a passing respectability by Sheridan, subsequent pressures of politics inevitably drove the Prince to make a formal marriage with another. Later Mrs Fitzherbert consoled herself by writing her memoirs. As for the Prince, his financial situation was greatly improved. Of even greater importance to him was the fact that Sheridan's speech forestalled an exposure of his illegal marriage.

Fox did not speak to the Prince for more than a year. In the autumn he again visited Coke at Holkham for the partridge shooting; the Prince wrote proposing a visit also, but Coke replied that 'Holkham is open to *strangers* on Tuesdays'. Fox departed to be with Mrs Armistead, who was ill, but the Prince came anyway, arriving one evening and assembling with the company for dinner at eight. As soon as dessert was served, the Prince proposed a toast: 'The health of the best man in England—Mr Fox!' At nine o'clock the next morning he returned to London. Obviously he had come to make peace with Fox.

Fox was able to forgive even if not to forget, but his embarrassment was deep and was revived in the regency debates more than a year later.

The trial of Warren Hastings opened February 13, 1788. Managers of the trial were chosen from the opposition. Burke, because of his wide knowledge and long interest, became chairman; Fox, Fitzpatrick,

[1] *HMCR*, Rutland MSS., iii, 387. May 4.
[2] *HMCR*, Charlemont MSS., ii, 53. To Charlemont, June 9.

Burgoyne, Windham, Sheridan, and Grey were others in charge of the impeachment.

The scene was Westminster Hall. In the procession were the Commons, with Burke, Fox and other managers in wigs and swords, then certain officials, then the Lords. Hastings, on his knees, faced his accusers as he listened to the charges. England's social as well as political leaders were there to see.

After two days of preliminaries, Burke, impressive in a dark brown suit, speaking in a voice that filled the hall, opened for the prosecution. In all, his speech required four days. Fanny Burney, the novelist, who had never visited a session in the House of Commons, attended the trial on several occasions, found 'the whole of this public speaking . . . quite new', and was eager to relate her impressions.[1]

Several days later an involved and bitter discussion arose on matters of precedence. Should the evidence for the prosecution on charge one be followed by the evidence for the defendant on charge one, before proceeding to charge two and subsequent charges? Or should the prosecution present its entire case on all charges, the defendant then replying to all at once? Fox, who had been up the whole of the preceding night and had won £1,000 at the New Club, contended against four lawyers with vehemence and conviction in favour of the first way of proceeding. He foresaw that the trial would be lengthy and argued that the Lords should hear the full discussion of both sides on one charge before proceeding to the next. This was not the first time in his career that he had debated legal points with lawyers. 'Charles Fox . . . fairly laid the lawyers on the opposite side on their backs', wrote one observer.[2]

Fox's own thoughts about his speech were recorded by his friend Storer. Fox ruminated that he should have avoided speaking that day, 'as he had drunk so much wine the night before, that, as he said, he had not a clear idea in his mind'; but as he went on, 'the mists were quickly dispelled, and on all hands it is agreed that he acquitted himself beyond everybody's expectation'.[3]

Two days later, however, the Lords decided against Fox. Fanny Burney learned about this unfavourable decision and reported it in her *Diary*, which contains more dialogue than many a novel:

I could not pretend to be sorry, and only inquired if Mr Fox was to speak.

'I know not,' cried he [Windham], hastily, 'what is to be done, who will speak, or what will be resolved. Fox is in a rage! Oh, a rage! . . . To-day will be nothing, he is all rage! On Tuesday he was great indeed. You should have heard him then.

---

[1] Charlotte Barrett, ed., *Diary and Letters of Madame D'Arblay* (London, 1876), ii, 527.
[2] *HMCR*, Charlemont MSS., ii, 72–3. Malone to Charlemont, March 12.
[3] Auckland, i, 470. To Eden, February 22.

She awaited Fox's speech with anticipation, later recording that 'his violence had that sort of monotony that seemed to result from its being factitious'. Before the speech 'he looked all good humour and negligent ease'; then came a speech of 'uninterrupted passion and vehemence'; and 'the very instant he had finished,' he 'wore the same careless and disengaged air'. So, she concluded:

A display of talents in which the inward man took so little share could have no powers of persuasion to those who saw them in that light; and therefore, however their brilliancy might be admired, they were useless to their cause, for they left the mind of the hearer in the same state that they found it.[1]

Fanny Burney as a critic of public address spoke more wisely than she realized. Others noted, among them the *World*, that 'the vehemence of his utterance frequently impeded his speech, and rendered his voice occasionally inarticulate'. Fox ever had difficulty with his onrushing, cascading flow of words, and equally with his impulse to become more emotional than his facts would support. And the Hastings trial was one of the lesser interludes of his career. So far as Hastings was concerned, Fox never had Burke's persistence or malice (this choice of words is here freely tendered).

The speeches went on endlessly. Members of the great families changed their living habits. 'Everybody is up by nine o'clock,' Storer wrote; 'the ladies have finished their toilette by that time, and are at the door of Westminster Hall, pressing and squeezing to get good places within.' Newspapers ran a daily column: 'The Impeachment'. After the speeches of the trio of managers, proceedings became less exciting. Fanny Burney and hundreds of others ceased their attendance. 'If sermons were half as long and half as dull as the speeches made every day in Westminster Hall,' wrote the *St James's Chronicle*, 'their eloquence would be very moving—it would move everybody out of church.' Thirty-five days were required to get through the second charge and it became plain that years would likely be required for the trial. By November the Duchess of Devonshire could report that Sheridan was 'heartily tired of the Hastings trial, and fearful of Burke's impetuosity says he wishes Hastings would run away and Burke after him'. Fox's opinion, not reported, would probably have been similar.

In June rumours spread that Fox was to marry an heiress, Miss Pulteney, but that romance fizzled out and in the summer Fox left for Switzerland with Mrs Armistead. Edward Gibbon met them in Lausanne and reported two days of delightful conversation. They talked steadily from ten in the morning until ten at night: a little about

[1] Barrett, ii, 520–9.

politics, much about books, including Gibbon's; much about gardening, 'which he understands far better than I do'. 'The people gaze on him as a prodigy but he shews little inclination to converse with them.'[1]

Rumours of an illness of the King, generally reported as attacks of biliousness, pursued the couple, but the attacks were not believed to be serious, and certainly nothing to keep Fox from enjoying a long and pleasant holiday. He even planned not to read newspapers, except, perhaps, the racetrack news. He might or might not be on hand when Parliament opened. From Switzerland he went to Italy once more to see the famous works of art that he had always enjoyed. In Italy a disturbing rumour reached him that his young nephew was dead. Apart from his personal grief, Fox realized only too well that should the rumour prove to be true he would be elevated to the House of Lords as the third Lord Holland, 'all his parliamentary hopes destroyed'.[2]

---

[1] Gibbon, iii, 132. October 4.
[2] From the diary of the Duchess of Devonshire, quoted in Walter Sichel, *Sheridan* (London, 1909), ii, 406. Hereafter cited as *Georgiana's Diary*. Georgiana kept a journal throughout the King's illness. As she enjoyed the confidence of the Prince of Wales and of prominent members of opposition, she kept well informed about the march of events from their point of view, and wrote with unusual perception about their actions and motivations.

18

The King's Illness
1788–1789

That Charles Fox should pretend to principle is a phenomenon that will astonish every one who ever heard of
him. His political conduct contains incontestable proofs
of duplicity and inconsistency.

Anonymous pamphlet writer

As early as the spring of 1788 the health of the King had worried his
physicians. Their usual regimen did not result in any improvement, so
they persuaded him to visit Cheltenham, in Gloucestershire, to drink
the mildly laxative waters of the springs there. This treatment he
entered into with such enthusiasm that he drank bumpers-full of his
prescription. As days went on he was seen doing all sorts of strange but
harmless things: he ran a race with a horse, he led a small crowd in
three cheers for Gloucestershire new bridge, he disobeyed orders to
rest and instead went hunting for five hours, his physician later writing
Pitt that his Majesty was 'in an Agitation of Spirits bordering on
delerium'. The agitation and the delirium continued: he launched an
embarrassing flirtation with an old flame, he carried on a conversation
with an oak tree imagined to be the King of Prussia, he ate unwisely
and exercised erratically, he displayed his backside to his attendants to
prove that he did not have the gout.[1]

Back at Windsor in August, he still continued unwell. By the end of
October, the Duchess of Devonshire recorded, the opposition had
heard the first accounts of the seriousness of the King's illness, and on
or about November 7, Fish Craufurd wrote her: 'The truth is, I
believe, that the King is quite disordered in his mind.' The humour, he
continued, had fallen upon the King's brain, and the prince had sent for
Fox, a fact supposedly a deep secret but freely circulated at Brooks's.[2]
Newspapers began to print items about 'slight derangements . . .
[that] have not excited much alarm'. *The Times* of November 10 still
only hinted at the King's sickness, but reported that the opposition
was worried about the absence of Fox and had sent two messengers
after him, knowing only that he was somewhere in Italy, perhaps in

---

[1] *Georgiana's Diary*, ii, 402. See also for other details of the King's illness, Charles Chenevix-
Trench, *The Royal Malady* (London, 1964).
[2] *Georgiana's Diary*, ii, 402–3.

Rome, perhaps somewhere on the road between Venice and Rome. Next day it called the King's malady a dropsy in the brain.

Soon it was obvious to all: the King was seriously ill. For years historians and biographers have considered his recurrent illnesses as insanity, in particular as a manic-depressive psychosis. Not until 1966 was it diagnosed as acute intermittent porphyria, a complex disease, hereditary in origin, characterized by abdominal and thoracic pain, paralysis of limbs, delusions and hallucinations. Eighteenth-century physicians, however, had to treat the King's symptoms within the compass of their own theory and practice. Naturally they disagreed among themselves about the method of treatment, and also in the advice they could give ministers and other members of Parliament about the duration of the disease or its outcome.[1]

The palace medical staff was augmented by consulting physicians, two of them playing an especially prominent part in the treatment of the malady. One of these was the immensely wealthy Dr Richard Warren, who took a pessimistic view of the King's condition. Later Dr Francis Willis was added to the staff and gradually took charge of the King; he was more optimistic about the King's recovery.

Some of the remedies were heroic indeed. The physicians reasoned, as they reviewed the history of the case, that the ailment of the King originally started as a humour in his legs. His rash consumption of Cheltenham's purgative waters drove it from the legs to the bowels. The medicines the physicians felt they had to use then to save his life had obviously driven the humour into the brain. Following an approved method of drawing it out of the brain, they applied blisters to the King's shaved head. This procedure caused him such exquisite torment and so aggravated his symptoms that the physicians decided they should bring the humour down again into the legs, which nature had originally pointed out as the basic source of the disorder. Blisters tried for this purpose brought a violent reaction; warm baths and warm coverings brought some relief. All in all there were purges and emetics to rouse the patient, woollen boots and straitjackets to restrain him, sedatives and milk baths to quiet him. Among other symptoms he had fever, he was excessively talkative, he had violent spells when he would almost tear his pages apart, he had irrational periods as when he nearly burned the Queen with a candle while trying to identify her.[2] Each day the

[1] See the articles by Ida Macalpine, Richard Hunter, C. Rimington, John Brooke, and Abe Goldberg in *Porphyria—A Royal Malady*, British Medical Association, 1968.
[2] Chenevix-Trench, pp. 69–73; *Georgiana's Diary*, ii, 405, 409; Duke of Buckingham and Chandos, *Memoirs of the Court and Cabinets of George the Third* (London, 1855), ii, 6–7. To the Marquis of Buckingham, November 20, 1788.

physicians issued a bulletin that public as well as politicians faithfully read; the language, however, was cast in such vague terms as 'unquiet', 'disturbed', 'restless', 'four hours' sleep last night', and the oft-repeated, depressing, 'no change from yesterday'.

Dr Willis brought a notable change of atmosphere into the sick room. He was relaxed in his treatment, quieting and soothing in his manner. Whereas Dr Warren fed his Opposition friends pessimistic information about the King's condition that led them to be bolder than they should be, Dr Willis was more hopeful in his conversation with the Queen and Pitt and encouraged them to move cautiously. In November and December, however, the Warren view had much to sustain it.

Opposition was not idle these days. Warren freely expressed his belief that the longer the King's illness persisted the less likely the eventual cure. 'Nothing', wrote W. W. Grenville, member of Pitt's Board of Trade, 'can exceed Warren's indiscretion on this subject.'[1] The Opposition was taking inconceivable pains, he continued, to spread the idea that the King was incurable, and that the Prince of Wales should become regent, put an end to Pitt's Government, and install Fox and his colleagues in power. Wheels began to spin and wheels within wheels. The Prince was a prime mover, as was the Duke of Portland, presumably to be the nominal head of the proposed new whig Government.

First it was necessary to see that the Prince came into the regency without undesirable and unpalatable restrictions. Here the Lord Chancellor, Thurlow, could wield a useful influence; so, handily overlooking the savage blow he had dealt its India Bill, the Opposition opened negotiations with him. If he would do his utmost to see that the regency came to the Prince without restrictions, Thurlow could be President of the Council in the new administration. Thurlow agreed to part of the bargain, but having served as Chancellor under North, Rockingham, Shelburne, and now Pitt, he insisted upon continuing as Chancellor with Portland and Fox. Like the vicar of Bray he clung to office regardless of who was in power. The Opposition was embarrassed, as Loughborough had been practically assured that seat, but the crafty Thurlow could set his own price and insisted upon the chancellorship.

Nor did Thurlow elect to keep Pitt informed about his discussions with the other camp. Windsor Castle proved to be an excellent place for intriguing, as the Queen and Pitt and their group transacted their business in one part of the castle and the Prince and his advisers in the other; thus Thurlow could go easily from one to the other. His

[1] *Court and Cabinets*, ii, 9. To the Marquis of Buckingham, November 20.

manoeuvrings, however, came to light. On one occasion, in the company of a group of Pitt's ministers at Windsor, he suddenly missed his hat. Before he could leave to look for it, a page brought it to him, saying aloud: 'My lord, I found it in the closet of His Royal Highness the Prince of Wales.' Thurlow's obvious embarrassment confirmed the dark suspicions of the others.[1]

All this plotting made it necessary to have Fox on the scene of action, but no one knew where he was. Parliament met November 20, but was immediately recessed until December 4. Fox's not being on hand for the opening session though he was aware of the scheduled date, added to the general speculation; *The Times* served up the whimsical notion that he had been taken prisoner by Barbary pirates. Elliot heard later that Fox read no newspaper, foreign or English, except once to look at Newmarket results, and then found that his races had been lost.[2] Eventually, however, Fox, in Bologna, learned that an express had arrived for him at Lausanne; his first thought was that it confirmed the death of his nephew, but when the message came it brought the news that the King was dying and that he should start home at once. This startling reversal the duchess recorded in her diary: 'What a revolution in a man's Ideas!'[3] So relieved was he that the news did not involve his nephew 'he fell down on a couch and cried violently for some time'.[4]

Not as much is known about Fox's wild, urgent trip from Bologna to London as one would like. Along the way he must have thought up half a dozen cabinets, planned scores of speeches, projected numberless interviews. He always had maintained that a post-chaise was a fine place to arrange and order one's thoughts, and this magnificent ride of rides gave him abundant opportunity for all sorts of mental gymnastics. What he could not do, lacking information, was to lay out bold plans of action. He seldom trusted his own judgment unless he could first confer with others. At Lyons he heard the rumour again that the King was dead. But from Lyons to Calais he travelled in a vehicle not so comfortable nor so well sprung as his own English carriage, which, together with the bad condition of the roads, affected his health. He arrived in London on November 24. His appearance was shocking: 'his body . . . emaciated, his countenance sallow and sickly, his eyes swollen, while his stockings hung upon his legs.'[5] He was much too ill to attend the meeting of the Privy Council on December 3, at which Warren insisted no one could tell whether or not the King could be cured, though other physicians saw a probability in favour of recovery.

---

[1] Stanhope, i, 396–7.   [2] Elliot, i, 237–8. To Lady Elliot, November 25.
[3] *Georgiana's Diary*, ii, 406.   [4] Elliot, i, 237. To Lady Elliot, November 25.
[5] Wraxall, v, 203.

The Commons held only a brief session on December 4. Fox dragging himself to his seat rather than walking to it, was able to make but brief remarks. 'Fox looked ill, and spoke worse than I ever have heard him,' wrote Grenville. 'His object was to beat about, and feel the pulse of the House with respect to further examination.'[1] Next day Fox was so desperately ill he thought he was dying, but another twenty-four hours found him better and he was able to be present when the House met again.

Fox had political concerns as well as bodily ailments. He did not like the agreement that had been arrived at with Thurlow, writing Sheridan, however, that he had swallowed the pill, bitter as it was, and had written Loughborough that he must consent to Thurlow's continuing as Lord Chancellor. 'What', he queried Sheridan, 'is to be done next? . . . I do not remember ever feeling so uneasy about any political thing I ever did in my life.'[2] Fox's unease is further shown in that he seldom asked Sheridan for advice. At a meeting at Carlton House, Loughborough, the Prince, Fox, and others in opposition, debated their best course of action. Loughborough advised that 'the Prince of Wales possessed an inherent and indisputable right to take on himself the Regency under the present circumstances'. The time when he should exercise his right, however, Loughborough admitted, should be decided by the two houses of Parliament.[3] Pitt and his advisers were worried; the King continued disordered and unquiet as the daily bulletins repetitiously put it. The Pitt ministry appeared to be in its last days, just short of its fifth anniversary.

At the session of December 8, both Commons and Lords agreed to appoint a committee of twenty-one, Fox and Sheridan included, to examine the physicians. But this step only delayed the major decision—the question of determining the proper lines of executive power when the executive is incapacitated, one of the touchiest problems in constitutional law. Ample precedent is available when the head of government dies or is assassinated, but the situation is delicate when the executive is desperately stricken. Regencies had been provided in the past but not when a prince of full age was at hand. This prince, however, would overturn the present ministry and bring in a new administration; names of its members were already being widely circulated. *The Times* published what it felt was an authentic list: on it were Portland, Chief Minister; Loughborough, Lord Chancellor; Fox and Stormont,

---

[1] *Court and Cabinets*, ii, 31, 34. To the Marquis of Buckingham, December 3, December 6.
[2] Fox Papers, Beinecke Library (Yale). Quoted in Thomas Moore, *Memoirs of The Life of the Right Honourable Richard Brinsley Sheridan*, 3rd edn (London, 1825), ii, 31.
[3] Wraxall, v, 209. A draft in the handwriting of Loughborough entitled 'Materials for a Pamphlet' lists the arguments supporting the right of the Prince, the objections to them, and answers to the objections (*Fox Cor.*, ii, 291–9).

Secretaries of State; Sheridan, Paymaster of the Navy and President of the Board of Control; Burke at the modest post of Paymaster of the Forces. Other names were also mentioned. Nineteen new peers would be created, it predicted, to give the Government a majority in the House of Lords. As every commission would need to be resigned, the new Secretaries of State would start with a windfall of £20,000 sterling in fees. Such rumours and speculations were on the streets as the Commons began on December 10 what was to be a vitally important debate.

The debate opened calmly enough. The report of seven examining physicians was presented, though their opinions offered small guidance. The King was too ill to attend to public business; at present no clear signs of improvement were evident; eventual recovery was entirely likely but it was extremely difficult to conjecture when it might take place. Any one could draw the obvious conclusion : the King might get well but no one could tell when.

So that members might be guided by the wisdom of their ancestors, Pitt moved that a committee be named to search precedents. To this step Fox objected strongly. Everyone knew, he asserted, that no precedent whatever existed, for now there was, readily available, an heir apparent of full age and capacity to exercise the royal power. Not a single moment should be lost, therefore, in turning to this person. The Prince of Wales had, moreover, as clear, as express a right to assume the reins of government, during the continuance of the King's illness, as if the King had died. Naturally he could not take possession of this right and exercise it until the two Houses of Parliament pronounced that he could. For that reason, the Prince patiently awaited the decision of Parliament rather than urge a claim that a majority of people admitted. Why make him wait further, therefore, while precedents were uselessly reviewed?

Pitt, listening to these words, is said to have smiled triumphantly, slapped his thigh, and declared that he would unwhig Fox for the rest of his life. To assert such a right as inherently belonging to the Prince, Pitt declared, independent of the decision of the two Houses of Parliament, was little less than treason to the constitution of the country. Speaking of strict right, the Prince had no more *right* to assume the government than any other subject in the country. The *claim*, of course, was entitled to the most serious consideration.[1] The House agreed to the appointment of a committee on precedents; Sheridan and Burke were on it, but not Fox.

[1] *Parliamentary History*, xxvii, 706–16.

In both Houses were members who followed the debates and pursued the rumours with more than usual concern, scenting every tainted breeze, as Burke might have phrased it, in order to be able to come in on the side of the winner. This group became known as the 'armed neutrality', after the alliance formed by Holland and other northern countries to harass English shipping during the American revolution. So Georgiana could write on December 7: 'The arm'd neutrality are with us.'[1] But on the whole Fox's speech, though his sturdy declarations about right were applauded during the debate by his followers, was later disapproved even by them. The Prince became increasingly disturbed by Fox's position. *The Times* called the debate unusually violent, but it sensed that Pitt must soon go out of office. Grenville wrote to his brother that Fox had shown complete lack of judgment in bringing his party into a scrape by advocating such a high tory doctrine.[2]

Next day the Lords heard their report from the physicians and made their move to search for precedents. Lord Camden declared that the claim of the Prince's was strange indeed—new, extraordinary, unknown to any reputable lawyer or book of law. Loughborough denounced the contrary doctrine, that the Prince had no more right to assume the regency, than any other individual subject whatever, as bold, arrogant, and presumptuous. The two Houses, having no executive head were not, he declared, even competent to make a turnpike Act, and yet Government speakers were claiming that they could appoint a regent or perhaps even several regents. In a delicately balanced speech, Thurlow urged study of the precedents and caution in arriving at a decision, although he concluded with a slight nod in Pitt's direction: 'While the crown remained firmly fixed on his Majesty's head, the appointment of a proper Regent must prove a consummation beyond expression difficult.'[3] *The Times* continued to editorialize that a change of administration was nearer than most people imagined.

Fox did not appear particularly repentant during the December 12 debate. He took occasion to explain his speech of December 10, repeating that the Prince had a right, but the adjudication of that right belonged to the two Houses. Pitt on his part denied that the Prince had any right whatever, and upon that point he and Fox were still at issue. Since Fox was well unwhigged and caught on the tory side, Pitt had the superior position in the debate and did not relinquish his advantage. 'A glorious fellow, by God, Young!' exclaimed an admirer. 'His speech

[1] *Georgiana's Diary*, ii, 412. John W. Derry's monograph, *The Regency Crisis and the Whigs, 1788–89* (Cambridge, 1963), gives an authoritative analysis of the motives and manoeuvrings of this group, pp. 93 *et seq.*
[2] *Court and Cabinets*, ii, 54. To the Marquis of Buckingham, December 11.
[3] *Parliamentary History*, xxvii, 674.

is that of an angel.'[1] Sheridan moved into the debate with the threat that the Prince should not be provoked into asserting his right, a statement that pleased his opponents and brought him abuse from his friends.[2] Members of the armed neutrality, observed *The Times*, stood ready to join either party. Prominent in that group, which numbered more than fifty people, was the Duke of Northumberland, who 'was giving sumptuous entertainments every day'. On December 15, Thurlow, another wavering person, not connected with the armed neutrality, saw that he could not straddle the fence forever; leaving the woolsack to address the lords, he said, with a flood of tears: 'When I forget my Sovereign, may my God forget me.' John Wilkes, who happened then to be seated on the steps of the throne, 'eyeing him askance with his inhuman squint and demoniac grin', declared: 'God forget you! He'll see you damned first.'[3]

Fox's own popularity took a staggering blow. The *St James's Chronicle* noted: 'The firm friend of the constitution . . . appears now desirous by one stroke to level this most glorious fabric to the dust.' Fox's doctrine, it continued in a later issue, has given such general alarm that ladies and gentlemen alike talk of nothing but the nature of the British constitution. The *World*, termed the 'Court Gazette' by opposition papers, noted that there seemed to be a destiny that shifted Charles Fox to the unpopular side of every point; Fox's friends were again apologizing for his shocking doctrine. Fox's own view, transmitted to Liz:

We shall have some hard fights in the H. of C. this week and next, in some of which I fear we shall be beat, but whether we are or not I think it certain that in about a fortnight we shall come in; . . . the Prince must be Regent and of consequence the Ministry must be changed.

He thought the chance of the King's recovery was very small, but did not think there was any probability that he would die.[4]

The Times revived an old argument: people who might have forgotten the monstrous coalition and the dangerous India Bill would have their memory freshened by these recent events and could put the

---

[1] *Court and Cabinets*, ii, 56. To the Marquis of Buckingham, December 12.
[2] *Georgiana's Diary*, ii, 416; *Court and Cabinets*, ii, 56. To the Marquis of Buckingham, December 13.
[3] John, Lord Campbell, *Lives of the Lord Chancellors* (London, 1846), v, 589–90; *Parliamentary History*, xxvii, 680. 'There can scarcely be a doubt, that Lord Thurlow's sudden fit of loyalty resulted from the unexpected improvement in the King's health' (*Life of Wilberforce*, i, 386). The Pitt forces could not entirely trust Thurlow. Said Richmond: 'That man will ruin us all yet' (Leeds, p. 140).
[4] Add. MSS. 47570. *Fox Cor.*, ii, 299–300. December 15 [1788]. Another view was that the Prince would negotiate, leave Pitt in the Treasury post and force Fox into a subordinate position (*HMCR*, Fortescue MSS., i, 365).

character of Fox and other 'patriots' in proper perspective. The Opposition, however, continued to 'mislead and inflame' the minds of the people by pasting up handbills and printing paragraphs that were 'grossly false and violent'.[1]

The debate in the Commons on December 16 was held before a crowded assembly.[2] Pitt offered three resolutions to the House, then in committee of the whole. The first formally stated the fact of the King's illness and the second asserted the right and duty of the two Houses to provide for the exercise of the sovereign authority. The third was technical: the Houses should determine a method of giving the royal assent to the Regency Bill they expected to pass. The method proposed was an awkward arrangement authorizing the Lord Chancellor to affix the great seal to the Bill, a procedure the Opposition promptly dubbed a phantom. Pitt's speech in support of his resolutions was eloquent and forceful.

Among those who spoke that day was Lord North, now infirm and blind, who was led down to the House. Wearing a green bandage over his eyes, leaning on a stick for support, he made an able speech against Pitt's resolutions. It was left to Fox, however, to provide substantial reply to Pitt. During his speech Pitt had discussed at length various precedents, drawn from the reigns of Edward III, Richard II, and especially during the infancy of Henry VI, when Parliament had provided for a regency, and had limited and defined the powers of the regent. Fox denied the applicability of these precedents: 'Was the practice of the present [enlightened] times . . . to be grounded on precedents drawn from so dark and barbarous a period of our history as the reign of Henry VI?' The Speaker of the House was then in prison; the House of Commons was prostrate at the feet of the House of Lords; moreover, the decision which resulted led immediately to the wars between York and Lancaster. In none of the precedents, he went on, was there available a Prince of Wales of full age and full capacity. As in the scrutiny debates, Fox could fully exploit the strength and the weakness in the method of reasoning by analogy.

Following Pitt through the details of his legal reasoning, he urged that 'the legal metaphysics which distinguished between the Crown and its functions, were to him unintelligible'. He reiterated his conviction that Pitt's precedents did not apply to the present instance, and he repeated that the proposed resolutions were unnecessary. But he did not lay his mind fairly alongside Pitt's; the central issue was that even

---

[1] *Parliamentary History*, xxvii, 682.

[2] The date of December 1 given to this debate in the *Parliamentary History* is obviously an error.

The *St. James's Chronicle* counted 523 members on the floor of the House and in the galleries.

though the precedents were not exactly parallel, on past occasions a vacancy had arisen and Parliament had been the effective agent in determining how to fill it. He turned to a personal attack upon Pitt, accusing him of trying to agitate the matter 'for the little purpose of personal triumph'. He declared that Pitt had been so long in the possession of power that he could not endure to part with it; he had experienced the full favour of the Crown, and enjoyed the advantage of its prerogatives. Now he was determined to cripple his successors.[1]

Fox was on his legs three hours. Wraxall, present in the chamber, observed that throughout a debate of at least nine hours Pitt and Fox and only they contended for superiority. 'These two extraordinary individuals seemed by common consent to take the debate exclusively into their own hands.'[2] Pitt's reply was highly effective; he observed that Fox digressed from the question of right, then before the House, to enter upon the question of expediency, 'and that not so much for the purpose even of discussing that expediency as to take an opportunity of introducing an attack of a personal nature on him'.

When Pitt sat down, the debate quickly concluded. The division that followed was the only one taken on the momentous issue: 268 voted with Pitt, and 204 with Fox, a total of 472, with a majority of 64; and the newspapers reported that another 48 members paired off before the division. Grenville thought Fox made 'one of the best speeches I ever heard from him', and as for Pitt's reply, 'I never heard a finer burst of eloquence'. He was less optimistic than some about the division: 'all of the neutrals, and many of the wavering people, and some of the most timid of our friends' voted with Fox on the ground of the inexpediency of agitating theoretical issues.[3] Sheffield wrote, a few hours after the division: 'Nothing could be marked more strongly in the debate than the superiority of Fox over Pitt.'[4] So each man had his stalwart admirers.

Fox's persistent illness also caught the attention of all. His malady was variously reported as the flux, a kind of cancer, the stone and gravel, an obstruction on the neck of the bladder. Elliot wrote to his wife that the other side inquired after Fox's illness with a most bloodthirsty eagerness.[5] Ministerial newspapers were finally able to unveil the true nature of the disorder: the coat of Mr Fox's stomach had been totally destroyed by his having had to eat his own words without being able to digest them. This gem reached the King's bedside. Fox's malady was actually a dysentery, an illness that had afflicted him inter-

---

[1] *Parliamentary History*, xxvii, 756–71. [2] Wraxall, v, 225–30.
[3] *Court and Cabinets*, ii, 63. To the Marquis of Buckingham, December 17.
[4] Auckland, ii, 257. To Eden, December 17. [5] Elliot, i, 248–9. December 20.

mittently since coalition days, and was now aggravated by tension and fatigue. In his later years he declared feelingly that a flux was the worst ailment that could afflict humankind. 'I know by experience', he once wrote, 'that there is nothing worse for bowel complaints than fatigue, and that fatigue from long speaking is just as bad in these cases as in any other.'[1]

The King was considered as only slightly irrational when he was overheard talking very rapidly and in the third person—'The King did so—The King thinks so—' etc., explaining that he was borrowing from Burke's eloquence, 'saying too much on little things', but when he was heard to declare that Pitt was a rascal and Fox was his friend, he was adjudged to be mad indeed.[2]

On December 19 the three resolutions that had been agreed upon in the committee of the whole House, now came before the Commons for a formal vote. The first resolution was agreed to; the second also carried, Fox speaking only briefly, saying that the House had already decided against him and to that decision he bowed. At a later session the third resolution was called up, proposing to give the two Houses the power to provide a royal assent to the Bills they passed. By 251 to 178 the House expressed its approval of Pitt's plan; his majority had slightly increased. The Lords debated the resolutions two days. In the only division taken, on an amendment, they confirmed the ministerial plan 99 to 66. Observers noted that 66 was a huge number for a minority. Noted and listed were the rat peers and the members of the armed neutrality.[3]

Meanwhile the Speaker fell ill and died, despite the fact that Dr Warren had attended, bled, and blistered him, and W. W. Grenville, whose comments on the debates have been freely cited in these pages, was elected Speaker. At Brooks's the faro table was allegedly hung with black, mourning the loss of the dead Speaker and the elevation to that post of a member of the Government (the victory represented the *Friends of the Constitution* against the *Man of the People,* as others put it). Pitt formally notified the Prince of the restrictions proposed to be placed on him as regent. The care of the King was to be the responsibility of the Queen. Pensions, offices, honours (with stated exceptions) could not be awarded. No peerages, other than to members of the royal family, were to be created. These restrictions the Prince reluctantly agreed to accept. Placing the King under the care of the Queen, for

---

[1] Add. MSS. 47594. To Lauderdale (undated).
[2] F. McKno Bladon, ed., *The Diaries of Robert Fulke Greville* (London, 1930), pp. 86, 128.
[3] *Court and Cabinets,* ii, 79.

example, gave her the disposition of the royal household with its £200,000 in patronage. Not to be able to confer peerages kept these rewards and favours out of the regent's hands.

The January debates can be briefly disposed of. Fox, far from well, was back in the Commons but so emaciated he could hardly be recognized. A lean Fox is as difficult to imagine as a fat Pitt. Pitt wrapped up the restrictions upon the regent in five resolutions, which he steamrollered through with a majority of about sixty. John Rolle caused a bad moment at the close of one debate when he stated that he had supported the regent because of Fox's assurance last year that the Prince was not married. He now demanded that Fox reassure him. Fox was not usually caught speechless but at this moment he had nothing to offer. Others came to his rescue by abusing Rolle for his indecent behaviour.[1] Pitt, who was receiving weekly reassurances from Dr Willis that the King was steadily recovering,[2] decided not to embarrass the Opposition more than it already was and Rolle's inquiry remained unanswered. The Lords concurred in the five resolutions, and the Queen and the Prince formally accepted the conditions set forth. The next step would be to follow the resolutions with a Regency Bill.

Public excitement was intense. The green rooms of the theatres, reported the *World*, had become debating societies: at Covent Garden, Pitt was the greatest minister of all; at Drury Lane, Fox reigned; everywhere actors talked about rights and regencies. When Burke had a bad day in the House, using violent language that led the Speaker to call him in order, someone wrote with chalk, in large letters: 'Very irritable in the evening, no sleep all night, and very unquiet this morning.'[3] Even the weather was portentous. So bitterly cold was the winter that the Thames froze and men walked across it.

The *World* reported fifty-four addresses of thanks to Pitt, only a few against him. It estimated that those who signed the address circulated at the London Tavern were worth an aggregate £50 million sterling. Many of these addresses were the aftermath of considerable local agitation between Foxites and Pittites. So the debate went on interminably, in St Stephen's, in local halls and taverns, in an avalanche of pamphlets. 'We have been waiting so long for the creation of a Regent,' wrote Storer, 'that I begin to imagine it will never happen. The creation of one has already taken up ten times the period, which the creation of the world did.'[4]

---

[1] 'Rolle shot his bolt . . . with respect to a certain lady. . . . He was trimmed handsomely by Ld. N[orth]' (*Correspondence of George, Prince of Wales*, i, 450; ?Robinson to Sir John Macpherson [? January 20, 1789]).
[2] PRO 30/8, 228/1, Chatham MSS. Letters of December 18 and subsequently.
[3] Auckland, ii, 292. *Star*, February 6.   [4] *Ibid.*, ii, 268. To Eden, January 16.

A long Regency Bill was presented to the Commons on February 5. Provisos had multiplied like Falstaff's men in buckram. Most of the thirty-three clauses were debated. Many of them had been scooped out of other Regency Bills, Pitt blandly explaining that it would be better to have them in than to leave them out. The status of the Established Church was reconfirmed, as was the statement that marriage to a papist would cause the Regent to forfeit the throne. Fox was in Bath throughout the debates. *The Times* declared that he went there and stayed there so he would not have to face Rolle. It also printed a bulletin of Fox's illness: 'In bed at half-past four, very restless, and unquiet—dreamed of the majesty of the people, of the King's recovery, of Mr Pitt, and the Devil.' For a while he was too ill even to drink the famous waters. 'His death', wrote new Speaker Grenville to his brother, 'would throw them into complete confusion.'[1] In a few days, however, he was reported better, and on the way to recovery. He took part in the debate of March 10, having been absent about seven weeks.

Fox, looking forward to the day when the Prince would actually assume the regency, had not been idle at Bath. He wrote Portland a long letter, mentioning fifty names for Cabinet and lesser posts: names to fill not only the great offices but also lesser situations like the Lords of the Treasury and Admiralty, the India board, the parks. It was a troublesome business, with so many names at hand and so few places to bestow. His slate was much like that published in *The Times* two months previously; Lord Rawdon, however, was proposed for a Cabinet position, to satisfy the armed neutrality.[2] Fox meditated calling a huge public gathering at Westminster to offset the effect of the addresses pouring in from Pitt's supporters, but decided to abandon it. So out of touch was he with the King's condition that he wrote Fitzpatrick on February 17: 'Let me know by the return of the post on what day the Regency is like to commence.'[3] Pitt, however, continued to receive reports from Dr Willis commenting that the King was mending rapidly, and suggesting that these sanguine thoughts be not divulged.[4] An encouraging bulletin, moreover, had appeared.

'What a revolution in a man's ideas', to repeat Georgiana's phrase, Fox experienced when he returned to London. A very good drama can be written around one reversal of the plot; in ninety days Fox had had two. For his planning was never executed. The Regency Bill had passed the Commons on February 12 and the Lords were about to pass it, when they learned that the King was improving. As his condition continued steadily better, the Lords saw that the best part of wisdom

---

[1] *Court and Cabinets*, ii, 103. To the Marquis of Buckingham, February 2.
[2] *Fox Cor.*, iv, 282–5. February 16.   [3] *Ibid.*, ii, 302.
[4] PRO 30/8, 228/1, Chatham MSS., Letter of February 10 and bulletin of February 14.

was to postpone action on the Bill. The *World* stated on February 20 that the King was considered perfectly and completely recovered, discussing public business and family matters with composure and recollection. The *Public Advertiser* continued to ride the opposition as having yearned for the demise of the King and the rise of the Prince to power. It described the jam of coaches in the street, so dense that the mail was three hours late, when the King went out for airing. It named the rats that had deserted the King during his illness.

The King's recovery crushed the hopes of the Opposition. On April 23 the nation held a solemn service of thanksgiving at St Paul's. A long procession of stately coaches wound through the streets on the way to the great cathedral. The newspapers, in fact, gathered up two columns of names of important private individuals. The throngs that lined the route readily identified the coaches of Pitt, of Fox in a carriage with Burgoyne and Fitzpatrick, of Sheridan, of the Lord Chancellor, even of Mrs Fitzherbert. Fox was hissed from St Clement's all the way to the cathedral, declared the *Public Advertiser*; this indeed is a majestic and impressive hiss. The *Morning Post*, however, heard few hisses but instead loud and fervent plaudits, with 'Fox and no shop tax', 'Fox and the repeal of the test acts' frequently echoed. Suffice it to say that onlookers revealed their partisanship. The cries of 'Fox for ever' and 'God bless Fox' were answered with 'Pitt for ever', which in turn inspired 'Damn Pitt—Fox for ever'.[1]

The day, however, belonged to the King. The occasion was, in fact, a kind of coronation, honouring, instead of a new king, an old king recovered. City and provincial newspapers pridefully described the excitement. The Houses of Parliament were superbly illuminated; the Ordnance Office was ablaze with glory; the pillars of the Admiralty were wrapped around with lamps. Drury Lane had never seemed so elegant; the Bank of England had never been decked out so luxuriously. The fine houses, whig, tory, and rat, alike proclaimed their loyalty: Carlton, Burlington, Northumberland, Cavendish. Inside the cathedral, however, the solemn gratitude of the nation expressed itself. Both the King and Pitt, each in his own way, had won a long, uphill battle. The soundness of Pitt's legislative strategy was proved in 1810; the King became incurably ill and the Prince became Regent under restrictions similar to those that Pitt had drafted that bleak winter of 1789.

What were the long-term effects of the regency fiasco upon Fox's career? Fox had never shown any capacity for high-level party strategy,

[1] Elliot, i, 281–3.

either in office-seeking or office-holding, and the regency debates eloquently confirmed the fact. Were one to erect an Arch of Disaster in his honour, the edifice would be tall and imposing, with such corner-stones as Resignation, Coalition, and now Regency. Whereas in the coalition debates he had gone down with banners flying, in the regency debates, as in those on the issue of his hasty resignation from the Rockingham Cabinet, he could only defend and explain, he could not seize the initiative. But it is as easy to underestimate Fox's management of the constitutional subtleties involved as it is to overestimate them. Some of his December and January speeches won grudging praise even from his adversaries, as has already been noted; and when in February he had to withdraw from the debates altogether, Wilberforce, a reasonably neutral observer so far as Fox was concerned, wrote: 'You cannot imagine how insipid and vapid our debates are without Fox. They serve us up the same tasteless mess day after day.'[1] Even Dundas said, on the floor of the House, that he missed Fox a thousand times, to which Burke retorted that *he* missed Fox ten thousand times. But undeniably, however, the party was left more divided, more frustrated than before. What must have been Burke's feeling, for example, to have been excluded from a Cabinet post even in a shadow government?[2] And the party as a whole was in a weakened condition to face the political upheaval to be presented by the French Revolution.

After the King's recovery, press and public relaxed and viewed with amusement the predicament of the losers. One of the first to scurry for better cover was the Prince himself; his behaviour and that of his brother needed careful explaining to their parents. An extremely long letter written by the Prince to explain himself was sent to the Queen; she, however, was not interested in effecting a reconciliation between the two sons and either herself or the King. She calmly wrote the Prince that the King did not care to converse about topics that might agitate him, and withheld her own affection for nearly two years.[3]

The late armed neutrality, the rat peers and rat commoners, were given the full treatment by the Government press, as were the leaders of the opposition. Bogus announcements offered for sale to the highest bidder the entire property of Fox, Burke, Sheridan and Co., now bankrupt, including divers full dress suits, never worn, calculated for secretaries of state, paymasters, treasurers of the navy, gentlemen belonging to boards of admiralty or treasury; and along with these were offered new blue frocks, lined with buff, plus a large stock of

[1] *HMCR*, Kenyon MSS., p. 527. To Lord Kenyon, February 12.
[2] See Derry, chaps. 4 and 5, for a perceptive analysis of Fox's and Burke's tactical and strategic errors.
[3] *Fox Cor.*, ii, 308–55.

inflammatory papers and handbills. Decorations set up in houses and buildings to celebrate the recovery of the King included a few also to note the despair of his opponents; in one window appeared a fox, surrounded by torches, the sign underneath reading 'The Death of the Fox'.

An elaborate pageant was written, to run serially for some days: 'The Funeral of Mrs Regency'. The chief mourners, naturally, were Fox and Sheridan. In the long procession were six peers with their coats turned, walking two by two: Northumberland, Hawke, Lothian, Queensbury, Malmesbury, Rawdon. In line were twenty paragraph writers, carrying silver pens and bottles of gall, with flags displaying the titles of their employers: *Morning Herald, Morning Post, Gazetteer, General Advertiser*. No one exceeded eighteenth-century Englishmen in contempt for time-servers, sail-trimmers, fence-straddlers, foot-kissers, ship-jumpers—in short, for rats. Burke walked also, in sackcloth and ashes, carrying a straitjacket. Surely he was as mad as the King himself.

In the public prints appeared orations, last wills and testaments, farewell sermons, lives, characters, testimonials, soliloquies, contrasts of The Great Statesman and The Unprincipled Dissolute. But those who expected Fox to bow out, permanently crushed, were soon disappointed. His health restored, he was heard speaking against Pitt's shop tax even before the King's recovery was celebrated at St Paul's. After that came the great issues with which his name is permanently identified: peace, the fight against the slave trade, the struggle for religious and political freedom. The memory of the coalition, to be sure, persisted; that of the regency soon faded.

Part Three
Man of the People

I give you this toast: The Sovereignty of the Majesty of the People.

Charles James Fox

19

Genesis of a New Whig
1789–1791

On religious subjects I must be permitted to think and
act as I please.

Charles James Fox

Fox shrugged off the criticisms against his alliance with North, his
ambitious India Bill, and his regency tactics as if he had lost only minor
skirmishes. Though opponents in later years did not let Fox forget the
coalition, they let the regency issue subside altogether. Of those last,
bitter, hard-fought, discouraging ninety days, he himself may have
remembered most poignantly his colossal and persistent bellyache.

Even before the King had been honoured at the solemn thanksgiving
service at St Paul's, Fox had attacked the shop tax, as already stated,
because it fell upon storekeeper rather than consumer. No one spoke
in its favour and it was quickly repealed. Now the time had come for
Fox to have his own celebration. So, on April 4, at the 'Crown and
Anchor', he had presided over a group of 1,500, described as the largest
that had even assembled at a tavern. With forgivable pride he buried
the late tax with a final jab at Pitt, its author. He thanked his listeners
for supporting him both in and out of office. He concluded in the manner
of politicians in all seasons and places that next to the approval of his
own conscience, he considered the approval of his constituents as
his greatest happiness.[1]

The shop tax was not a vast issue but it was something; and Fox,
who had been bedevilled by friends and opponents alike on the regency
issue felt comfort in the cheers of the people. Just ahead, however,
were three sturdier topics: religious toleration, the slave trade, the
outbreak of the French Revolution. The first and last of these issues
led Fox to stake out beliefs and principles that drew him away first
from Burke and later from other of his more conservative political
companions.

For more than a century the principle had been established in England
that only those who professed to adhere to the state-supported Anglican Church were eligible to hold public office. The reason was stated

[1] *Stuart's Star*, April 4, 1789.

251

by Burke as well as by anybody: the Established Church was the guardian of the morals of the national community because those in high position would be more likely not to abuse their power if they were always mindful that God sat in judgment on their acts. Since religious and political issues had proved to be closely intertwined both in the ousting of the Catholic Stuarts and in the installation of the Protestant Hanoverians, those who held public office should also support the state Church. The Test Act required those who held civil or military positions to prove their loyalty to the state Church by receiving the sacrament of the Lord's Supper in the Church of England. The Corporation Act extended the requirement to those who held office in municipal and other quasipublic corporations. Obviously this principle operated not only to the disadvantage of Catholics, who also suffered other pains and penalties, but to Protestant dissenters and nonconformists as well, mainly Presbyterians, Independents, and Baptists, none of whom could conscientiously take the sacrament of communion according to the rites of the Anglican Church. Both these Acts damaged the cause of religious liberty and kept from civil and military office (though not from Parliament) a large segment of Protestants, even though annual indemnity Acts had eased the burden of occasionally-conforming dissenters.

The dissenting ministers of London were especially active in seeking relief for their group. At first they were not friendly to Fox nor he to them. In 1772, for example, he had briefly defended the thirty-nine Articles of the Anglican prayer book, voting with Burke and North against the dissenters. That Bill for the relief of the dissenters had passed the Commons but had been defeated in the Lords. The following year he had debated the question again, briefly. He declared that individuals were compelled to attest to the truth of a string of propositions of which they were as ignorant as they were of the man in the moon. Again the House passed the Bill and again the Lords defeated it. Later the alliance with North, a stout enemy of the Bill, had resulted in Fox's loss of dissenter support in the 1784 elections. The London ministers did think, however, they had a friend in Pitt.

Back in 1787 the dissenters had attempted to secure the repeal of the parts of the Test and Corporation Acts that affected them; they had approached Pitt and had also decided to supply Fox with materials supporting their point of view.[1] On March 28 of that year Henry Beaufoy had introduced, at the request of the dissenters, a motion to repeal the appropriate parts of the Acts. Beaufoy, who has been met before in these pages, had then been in Parliament four years. He was

---

[1] See Ursula Henriques, *Religious Toleration in England, 1787–1833* (London, 1961), for a statement of the basic arguments for and against the Acts, and for an account of the activities of the London dissenters.

about a year younger than Fox. Born a Quaker, he later had joined the Anglican Church although throughout his life he was sympathetic to dissenters.

In an impressive speech that Wraxall praised for its language and judgment ('I have indeed seen few more luminous displays of intellect in Parliament'), and for its characteristic oratorical cadence (unlike Fox's natural, conversational style, Beaufoy had acquired, possibly from Thomas Sheridan, an elocution teacher, some kind of semi-eloquent drone), Beaufoy opened the subject fully for consideration. He gave the history of the Test and Corporation Acts and cited instances showing how they discriminated against the 'many hundred thousands' of the King's faithful subjects. North argued to the contrary that discomforts of dissenters were not so great as pictured. The constitution was ever in danger, he concluded, when the Church was deprived of its rights.

To the surprise of many, Pitt also opposed the motion. An established Church is a necessity. No means can be devised to bring moderate dissenters within the fold and keep out the more violent, so the bulwark must be held against all. Limitations imposed upon dissenters were no mark of infamy. Some men, for example, did not have the right to vote; are they considered to be marked with infamy? Thus he used one disability to excuse another.

These are the typical and flaccid arguments against religious toleration, against the separation of Church and state, as expressed in that decade. It was later said of Fox, contrasting him with Pitt, that Pitt was more often right than Fox—but that on great issues, worth more than all the others, Fox would likely be right and Pitt wrong. Here is one of those issues. Fox's speech that March 28 was no eloquent declaration of faith; in fact he seemed to be stumbling for suitable words and suitable arguments. For example, he thought dissenters were on the whole a decent set of people who did not depart from principles consistent with the constitution of the land. More fundamental were his observations, though expressed with only slight force, that religion should not be a test in politics and that he, and presumably the House, should never lose sight of principles of toleration.[1]

The motion was lost by 78 votes, 176 to 98. That was in 1787. The King expressed his amazement that 98 persons could be found in the House to support 'so ill-advised a proposition'.[2] The regency issue came and went, the King resumed his duties, and on May 8, 1789, the question of repealing the two Acts again came up.

Just before one of Fox's major speeches on the Test and Corporation

[1] *Parliamentary History*, xxvi, 780–831.
[2] *English Historical Documents*, xi, 671. To Pitt, March 29. (Chatham Papers.)

Acts, a delegation of dissenting ministers visited him to ask him to speak on the issue between them and the Established Church. At the moment he was about to go horseback riding but he listened to their arguments and asked four or five searching questions; then, promising to comply with their request, he picked up his whip and departed. Members of the delegation went directly to the Commons and heard the preliminary speeches on the question. Before long they saw Fox enter the chamber, carrying his whip, as if he had just dismounted outside the door. Soon he rose to his legs and addressed the House, making the speech as promised. One member of the group, Dr Abraham Rees, declared later that Fox's mastery of the subject was so profound and so convincing that it seemed as if the question at issue had been the main subject of a lifetime of study.[1] This substantial tribute came from a man who was a gifted, popular, and eloquent preacher, and editor of a general encyclopedia.

The incident is worth citing because it throws light upon Fox's methods of preparing a speech. Dr Rees, to be sure, was overly impressed by what he saw. For a dozen years or so Fox had participated in debates that touched the issue of religious freedom. The topic, therefore, was not new to him. Clearly what Fox did, during that horseback ride of an hour or so (and one can not refrain from visualizing what a lot of Fox there was, now recovered from his ailment and thicker than when he fought his duel—and what a lot of horse would be required to carry him) was to review the available arguments. His mental process, therefore, was one largely of sorting and arranging. The exact language he could leave to the moment of speaking. It is impossible to imagine him, like the young Churchill, trying a sentence aloud several different ways, in a kind of rehearsal, before selecting a proper wording for a secretary to write down. No—Fox's words came with the moment of delivery. The willingness to leave this detail of preparation to chance explains the awkwardness of language with which his contemporaries charged him: that he would plunge into a sentence trusting to God Almighty to get him out of it.

What Fox lost in precision and eloquence he gained in directness. His listeners could sense that he in fact was wording his ideas as he went along; he was coining his phrases, not recalling them; his tones were therefore convincingly natural, not memorized, artful, or cadenced. Observers commented on this spontaneity as if it were rare in the eighteenth-century parliament (which it was, save for the briefer rejoinders), and although they felt that the memorized style was not to be condemned since it was widely used, they were nevertheless forcefully struck by Fox's informal type of delivery. Where

[1] *Living Age*, ii (September 28, 1844), 484. From *Gallery of Portraits*.

twentieth-century students of public speaking theory refer to the 'prepared' speech, Fox's associates used the word 'premeditated'; Fox no more premeditated his speeches, a contemporary might observe, than he premeditated the hour of his own death. What is missing from Fox's preparation is the pen-and-paper stage. Unlike Burke and Sheridan, he never used any kind of note or outline. To twentieth-century political speakers this silent-thinking method of constructing a speech must appear entirely believable, but to Dr Rees, who likely followed the older method of writing out and memorizing, Fox's performance was astonishing.

The galleries that May 8 were crowded. In a thoughtful speech, Beaufoy again offered his motion to repeal the Acts and North again opposed it. In this debate, Fox's support was firmly grounded in principle. He declared unequivocally that religion should always be distinct from civil government. 'No human government had a right to inquire into private opinions, to presume that it knew them, or to act on that presumption.' Men should be judged by their actions, since the action is the ultimate and only effective spokesman, and not by their thoughts. Even if a man speculated that he did not like the constitution, he still should not be debarred from office unless he put his opinion into practice.

Almost as if Fox foresaw a police state with its system of thought control, he visualized what would happen if government prejudged men because of their opinions. Such a doctrine 'would sow the seeds of jealousy and distrust, it would give scope to private malice, it would sharpen the minds of men against one another'. This doctrine would lead one man to inform against another 'and thus to prove that he ought to incur disabilities, and be fettered with restrictions'. The result? It would bring about 'every species of party zeal, every system of political intolerance, every extravagance of religious hate'.

And what of the many men not belonging to the Established Church, 'to whose services their country had a claim'? Should any such man be examined upon his private opinions before he came into office? 'Was it not sufficient that he did his duty as a good citizen? Might he not say, without incurring any disability, "I am not a friend to the Church of England, but I am a friend to the constitution, and on religious subjects must be permitted to think and act as I please".' Quite likely the irreligious man or the man of no principle at all would not find his road to power barred by the test act; 'the test excluded only the man of tender conscience. . . . Was a tender conscience inconsistent with the character of an honest man? or did a high sense of religion show that he was unfit to be trusted?' These were hard, practical questions.

Fox argued further that the length of time the Acts had been in force was not necessarily in their favour. Ancestors were not invariably wiser than descendants. Moreover, it was morally indecent for one to go to the communion table, not to make peace with heaven and repent of sin, but only because he had received an appointment as First Lord of the Treasury. Fox did not want England to be the last nation to adopt a new, liberal principle : 'Should a people, who boasted of their freedom . . . reject those liberal principles of toleration which other nations had adopted?' These are the ideas that Fox might have mobilized on horseback.

Pitt opposed Fox's point of view, arguing simply that since the opinions of dissenters might lead them to commit a civil inconvenience, the Government ought to be able to prevent it rather than wait until beliefs were carried into action and the inconvenience had arisen. If dissenters were given civil rights, they might use their new power to overturn the Established Church. The debate was ended soon after Pitt sat down, and the House again rejected Beaufoy's motion, 122 to 102.[1]

Dissenters rejoiced that even though the total vote was small, the majority was down from 78 two years before to 20. Two days preceding the debate they had met in strength at London Tavern and proposed toasts not only to the King and Beaufoy, but also to Fox as a zealous and unequivocal advocate of repeal, a toast that met with more acclamation than any drunk that evening.[2] Many papers, too, liked Fox's speech : it was able and judicious, it was truly honourable and dignified, it deserved universal acclamation for uncommon vigour of argument and eloquence of persuasion. Last year, said the *Gazetteer*, Fox undid the lawyers in Westminster Hall; in this speech he evinced a knowledge of divinity equal to that of the mitred fathers. The *St James's Chronicle* expressed an opinion of another sort : although the dissenters were pleased by the speech of the Man of the People (the *late* man, that is), they must wonder indeed that he knew anything at all about religion.

The *Morning Star* and other papers recalled that Fox had won several thousand pounds the preceding week at Newmarket. That summer the *Public Advertiser* said he won not less than £50,000 at the Newmarket races.

---

[1] *Parliamentary History*, xxviii, 1–41. See also *Facts submitted to the consideration of the friends to civil and religious liberty . . . containing the substance of Mr. Fox's speech on the repeal of the test laws* (London, [1789]).
[2] *Gazetteer*, May 9.

The echoes of the Test Act speeches had hardly died away before the House turned to another liberal and humanitarian proposal, to abolish the slave trade.

The name of William Wilberforce is invariably connected with the long fight to regulate and later to abolish the trade. No member of the House supported Wilberforce so steadfastly as did Fox. Even though Wilberforce was a warm personal friend of Pitt and a reasonably consistent supporter of Pitt's policies, whenever the issue of the slave trade came up, Fox was at Wilberforce's elbow.

As early as 1785, Wilberforce had determined to inquire into the growing charges against the cruelty and inhumanity of the slave traders. As the word of his proposed intentions had become known, commercial interests had begun to protest and to produce evidence not only of the commercial necessity but even of the humanity of the trade in slaves. Wilberforce being absent because of illness, Pitt, in 1788, had offered the resolution that at the next session of Parliament the circumstances of the slave trade should be considered. Fox then had declared that the slave trade ought not to be regulated but destroyed. To consider the subject on any principles other than those of humanity and justice was idle and absurd. Later Fox was to learn that not only humanitarian but also commercial and military aspects of the slave trade would need to be argued at length, but he took his enlightened, humanitarian, view at a time when many statesmen in Great Britain, on the Continent, and in the new United States were opposed to abolition for commercial or even for military reasons. Sir James Johnstone, a friend to abolition, reported that in Grenada the slaves were so full of the subject that the common exclamations among them were, 'Mr Wilberforce for Negro! Mr Fox for Negro! God Almighty for Negro!'[1] Fox is seldom bracketed with either God Almighty or the saintly Wilberforce.

The outcome of that 1788 debate had been to pass a mildly regulatory Bill. It had become law early that summer, about the time the King had shown the first symptoms of his disorder. In May 1789, a week after the motion to repeal the Test and Corporation Acts had been voted down, Wilberforce took the floor of the House to condemn the slave trade and to offer a series of resolutions against it. His long speech was filled both with statistics and word pictures to emphasize not only the inhumanity of the trade but also the shortsighted view that its defenders took of the national interest. In a brief speech, Pitt, approving Wilberforce's resolutions, took special note of the argument that if England abandoned the trade, other nations would take it up. Fox also spoke to this point, declaring that other nations would catch a spark

[1] *Parliamentary History*, xxvii, 495–506.

from England's fire, and 'run a race with us in promoting the ends of humanity'.[1] This position was more idealistic than realistic, but Fox amply made it clear at the outset that he was opposed to the trade on humanitarian principles. To put a frame around this sentiment, contrast it with the cool, reserved speculation of the *World*: although it would be an act of humanity to abolish the slave trade, if only England abolished it, she would simply be handing the trade over to the French.[2]

July 1789. Hardly had the King resumed his daily routine at Buckingham (life now was just one bow and curtsey after another, complained the young bloods of the palace) when news of events preceding the French Revolution thundered across the channel. The sudden decision of Louis XVI to summon the Estates-General, which had not met since 1614; the storming of the Bastille; the overnight abolition of tithes, feudal dues, and titles of nobility; the Declaration of the Rights of Man with its rosy assurance that men are born and remain free and equal—these actions made thinking Englishmen examine anew their concepts of liberty and equality, and in accordance with their examination they applauded or condemned the stirring drama being enacted across the channel.

Important news from Paris crossed in three days or less and was variously received by Englishmen. Some were hopeful, some were fearful, some were joyous. Among the hopeful was Pitt, who thought that the overthrow of the old regime would probably be followed by orderly constitutional government, and that while Frenchmen were devoting their energies to working out this exercise in self-government, Englishmen could enjoy peace and light taxes. Among the fearful was Burke, who predicted that the mob would become so violent that in the end France would be worse off than before, and that the revolutionary spirit would spread to other countries and ultimately endanger established institutions of all kinds. Among the joyous was Fox, who wrote to Fitzpatrick on July 30: 'How much the greatest event it is that ever happened in the World! & how much the best!' thus expressing his opinion of the Paris revolt and the taking of the Bastille. Fox even thought he could be a friend to France if the revolution succeeded.[3]

Parliament, still in session, officially took no notice of what was going on across the channel. In August it recessed.

On November 4, the anniversary of the Glorious Revolution of 1688, Dr Richard Price, the eminent Unitarian preacher, held forth

[1] *Parliamentary History*, xxviii, 41–94. [2] March 21.
[3] Add. MSS. 47580. *Fox Cor.*, iv, 361.

before the Revolution Society on events in France. In a famous passage he said:

> I have lived to see the rights of man better understood than ever; and nations panting for liberty which seemed to have lost the idea of it. I have lived to see thirty millions of people, indignant and resolute, spurring at slavery, and demanding liberty with an irresistible voice. Their King led in triumph, and an arbitrary monarch surrendering himself to their subjects.

The society then sent its congratulations to the national assembly of France, an expression of sympathy that was the first of a long series exchanged between radicals on both sides of the channel. Three weeks later Fox received the thanks of a meeting of Protestant dissenters who voted to transmit their gratitude to him for having supported the motion to repeal those parts of the Test and Corporation Acts that affected them.[1]

The new session of Parliament opened on January 21, 1790, and soon took up the Government's proposal that the armed forces of the country should be increased. In a later debate Burke made a long speech deploring events in France. As a political light, France was 'to be considered as expunged out of the system of Europe'; the French were 'architects of ruin'; they had 'completely pulled down to the ground their monarchy, their church, their nobility, their law, their revenue, their army, their navy, their commerce, their arts, and their manufactures'. He declared that he had not wished to speak so strongly in opposition to what had occurred in France but that he would have felt unhappy if he had not expressed himself.

Fox felt deeply pained to have to disagree with his friend of many years. Such was the esteem, he said, in which he held Burke's friendship,

> . . . that if he were to put all the political information which he had learnt from books, all which he had gained from science, and all which any knowledge of the world and its affairs had taught him, into one scale, and the improvement which he had derived from his right hon. friend's instruction and conversation were placed in the other, he should be at a loss to decide to which to give the preference.

This tribute was not an empty one. Fox in his lifetime had continually sought the advice of any who might be helpful. But although he uttered these words in all sincerity, he had in fact ceased to become Burke's pupil. The two had come to a parting of the ways. After paying Burke a tribute, Fox resumed his argument. The two revolutions in England and France were more similar than Burke had admitted. Much more despotism existed in France that still needed to be destroyed.

[1] Holland House MSS. Meeting of November 26.

Burke replied that the separation of a limb from his body could scarcely cause him more pain than to differ with Fox, but he nevertheless reiterated his views. Sheridan entered the debate at this point, stating that he disagreed decidedly with his right honourable friend in almost every word he had uttered respecting the French Revolution. Burke's judgment was biased, said Sheridan; Burke was an advocate of despotism. Burke, more exasperated than ever, declared that 'henceforth he and Sheridan were separated in politics'.[1] The split in the party was alarming and Fox undertook to act as conciliator. He and Sheridan called on Burke, and there were other conferences, but the wound was healed only temporarily.[2]

French revolution or no French revolution, Fox decided to support the movement to bring up once again the question of repealing the Test and Corporation Acts. Now the atmosphere was highly charged. The violence of the changes in France made proposed changes at home suspect. Within the party itself were new tensions and anxieties. But the dissenters had appealed to Fox in February and so he had deliberated whether to support them once more. He sought opinions not only from dissenters but from Roman Catholics, and expecially from his good friend Charles Butler, who was well schooled in the law and a distinguished member of the profession, though he could not be called to the bar nor hold office because of his religious beliefs. Fox asked Butler what he thought was the strongest argument that Catholics could mobilize against the laws in force against them. Butler declared that it was that Catholics maintained no tenets contrary to the moral or political creed of the country. 'It is both unjust and detrimental to the state,' he reasoned, 'to deprive any portion of its subjects of their civil rights on account of their religious principles, if these are not inconsistent with moral or civil duty.'

Fox, however, wanted to put the argument on a more basic level. 'No, sir!' he is reported to have declared, with great animation, 'that is not the best ground; the best ground, and the only ground to be defended in all points is, that *action* not *principle* is the object of law and legislation; with a person's principles no government has any right to interfere.'[3] He tried out some of his ideas at a dissenters' dinner at London Tavern on February 13, at which pro-French sentiments ('glasses were filled and the Revolution of France drunk with nine huzzas, all

[1] *Parliamentary History*, xxviii, 351–71.
[2] Countess of Minto, *Life and Letters of Sir Gilbert Elliot* (London 1874), i, 351.
[3] Add. MSS. 47578. Charles Butler to Lord Holland, April 12, 1808; *Reminiscences of Charles Butler*, 4th edn (London, 1824), ii, 71–2.

standing') were freely mixed with pro-repeal convictions. His declaration that he had been an enemy from his earliest years to the Test and Corporation Acts, and 'would never cease to oppose them in every station of life, though he was a member of the Church of England', brought the dissenters to their feet for another filling of the glasses and nine more huzzas.[1]

Fox decided not only to support repeal but to make the motion himself. The news spread rapidly that he would open the question on March 2. By 10 a.m. the gallery was full, though he did not begin to speak until 4.30. 'Those who were fortunate as to gain admittance . . . did not think they paid too dear for it, though they were shut up in the gallery for near seven hours . . . and were greatly incommoded by excessive heat.'[2] Fox's speech was long and eloquent. The French Revolution reaffirmed, he insisted, recalling the massacres at Paris, that persecution led to horrid and detestable crimes; it proceeded on the absurd principle that one man could judge the religious opinion of another better than the man himself could. Toleration proceeded on the contrary principle. But let Fox put the thought in his own words:

Persecution always said, 'I know the consequences of your opinion better than you know them yourselves.' But the language of toleration was always amicable, liberal, and just: it confessed its doubts, and acknowledged its ignorance. . . . Persecution had always reasoned from cause to effect, from opinion to action, [that such an opinion would invariably lead to but one action], which proved generally erroneous; while toleration led us invariably to form just conclusions, by judging from actions and not from opinions.

Hence, he went on, every political and religious test was extremely absurd. In his opinion the only test ought to be a man's actions. No harm could come to the state until a man's opinions were put in action; if then the actions were detrimental, the doers could be punished. Innovations were considered dangerous in view of the situation in France, but this move for repeal could not be considered an innovation as it had been introduced years ago, long before the French had revolted. Actually, he repeated, this outbreak could well serve to remind and caution the Church of England that persecution generally terminated in the punishment of its abettors.

In reply, Pitt argued again that the Acts should not be repealed. They had stood the test of time, having been adopted 'by the wisdom of our ancestors to serve as a bulwark to the Church, whose constitution was so intimately connected with that of the state, that the safety of the one was always liable to be affected by any danger which might threaten the other'. Burke, his feeling against the French still strong, thought it necessary to support the Established Church especially at a

[1] *Public Advertiser*, February 16, 18.   [2] *General Evening-Post*, March 2–4.

time like the present. He argued that the motion would be a beginning that would continue 'till the whole of the Church establishment was levelled to its foundations'.

Fox rose to reply both to Pitt and Burke and especially to the latter, whose speech 'had filled him with grief and shame'. He spoke of Burke's 'strange dereliction from his former principles', and tried to account for it by suggesting that Burke's feeling 'had been shocked and irritated by a mistaken idea of the transactions in France'.[1] Fox's motion was defeated 294 to 105, so his further defence of religious toleration fell on sterile ground and the ties of his friendship with Burke were further stretched. Fox's efforts that day had also been weakened by the distribution to members of extracts from a letter of Dr Joseph Priestley, Unitarian minister and famed scientist, calling upon clergymen to avert revolution by religious reform, and describing his own efforts as grains of gunpowder for which his opponents were providing the match. Priestley's arguments were thus used against him in a way he undoubtedly had not foreseen.

George the Third added this last speech to the long list of Fox's faults. When the King received the news that the Government had won the division, he replied that he hoped Parliament would not be troubled again with this most improper business.[2] On Fox's behalf let it be said that he not only always voted for religious toleration but nearly always troubled Parliament with a speech on the business.

These words of 1790 were long remembered. When Lord John Russell renewed the fight for the repeal of the Test and Corporation Acts in 1828, he reminded the Commons of Fox's argument and eloquence ('no man was more splendid in the one or forcible in the other'). The miscarriage in 1790, Russell said, affected him so much, that he would resign the case as hopeless but for the conviction that if he could not wield the same arguments as Mr Fox, he had not the same enemies to encounter. Lord John, later one of Fox's biographers, was a logical rather than an emotional speaker, and invariably addressed the House in a thoughtful, serious, almost distant manner, but this speech had its eloquent moments. There were cries of 'hear, hear' at the mention of Fox's long-ago struggle and there was also stout debate, but within two months the Acts were repealed.

Fox's finances improved. Seagull won at Ascot by a whip's length, netting 6000 guineas. That year Fox had thirty horses in training.

[1] *Parliamentary History*, xxviii, 387–452; *The speech of the Right Hon. C. J. Fox, in the house of commons, on Tuesday, March 2d, 1790, upon his motion for the repeal of the corporation and test acts* (London, 1790).
[2] *Later Correspondence of George III*, i, 464. To Pitt, March 3.

Later he sold Seagull and Chanticleer for 4,400 guineas. Men recalled that in April 1772 Fox had won £16,000, the greater part by betting against the celebrated Pincher, who lost by half a neck.

In Westminster Hall the trial of Warren Hastings went slowly forward. An eyewitness on April 29 was Gouverneur Morris, one-time member of the committee that had drafted the American constitution, later to be minister to France, himself a lawyer and debater. He wrote in his diary:

> The Speakers this Day are Mr Burke and Mr Fox. The former has Quickness and Genius but he is vague, loose, desultory and confused. His Speech contained Matter to make a fine one and to marr the best. Mr Fox . . . is obliged to abstract himself so much in pursuit of the Matter that he is extremely deficient in Manner. . . . His Mind appears like a clouded Sun, and this I believe results from the Life he leads.

After another session he noted: 'Mr Fox summs up the Evidence with great Ability.'[1] So came to light observations on what were undoubtedly run-of-the-mill speeches by two distinguished speakers.

And here let a difference be noted between great speakers like Fox, Burke, Sheridan, and Pitt, and the near-great. The great speakers, like the near-great, deliver an abundance of average, mediocre speeches. But the great attain heights of inspiration that the near-great can never approach. It is with speaking as with writing: the same mind that produces *Coriolanus* also creates *Hamlet*. On the day that Morris heard him, Fox's mighty engine, to use an eighteenth-century metaphor, was grinding but slowly.

The general election was held in June. Despite the outcry raised against him the previous year, the lampoons and the sarcasms and the streets filled with spectators that had hissed him during the long ride to the cathedral, Fox did not expect a contest at Westminster. 'The election was to have been carried off cheap and snug,' the *Public Advertiser* reported; the clerks did not even have pens to take down the votes. Unexpectedly, however, Horne Tooke announced his candidacy, and attacked both Hood and Fox to 'repeated bursts of applause'. Any opinion of Fox's speech that day must be formed by whichever reporter one reads: according to the *Public Advertiser*, Fox 'ran over, as well as could be collected, all the cant phraseology of independence, public virtue &c. to no purpose'; according to the *London Chronicle*, Fox

[1] Beatrix C. Davenport, ed., *A Diary of the French Revolution by Gouverneur Morris* (Boston, 1939), i, 493, 537.

reminded the electors of his fight for the repeal of the shop tax, and challenged one and all to show a single instance when (since first representing Westminster) he had not supported the rights of the people in general and the interest of Westminster in particular. The election dragged on until July 2. Fox stood at the head of the poll with 3,516 and Hood was second with 3,217; Tooke ran a poor third with 1,697. On the last day, 'Mr Fox thanked the electors, Mr Horne Tooke made a short harangue, Mr Fox was chaired, and the day ended without mischief.'[1]

Fox scored a notable victory in outpolling the popular Admiral Hood, though Hood was after all a political cipher who seldom attended Parliament and seldom spoke when he did. A silent senator, with little talent or potential, is a poor representative for an energetic and populous borough. Yet the Government did what it could to support Fox's opponents. As Fox wrote to Fitzwilliam: 'There is no doubt of the Treasury's having made every possible exertion.' Fox sought to learn how much Fitzwilliam could be set down for in the event of a shortage of funds, and enclosed a list of subscribers. The principals: Portland £1,500, Devonshire £2,500, Bedford £2,000, Spencer £1,000, Fox himself £500, Sheridan £200, etc., totaling £12,000.[2] Later Horne Tooke protested the election of Fox and Hood through a petition to Parliament, but since an act of 1789 made petitioners responsible for the costs whenever their complaints were frivolous and vexatious, Fox felt Tooke's petition was one such, and sued him.

At St Anne's Hill in August. Fox rested from the cares of politics and enjoyed the companionship of Mrs Armistead. Anthony Morris Storer described Fox 'surrounded by the arts, lolling in the shade. Mrs Armistead was with him; a harper was playing soft music; books of botany lying about; . . . like Solomon, he is to seek wisdom in the search of herbs and flowers.'[3]

Burke, meanwhile, was working on his famous *Reflections on the Revolution in France*. It forwarded many of the ideas he had advanced on the floor of St Stephen's. The revolution of 1789–90 was in no way to be compared with the revolution of 1688; change was to be encouraged when it was in harmony with the traditions of a people but a people that tore its past up by the roots could expect only war and tyranny. Men who destroyed 'the whole original fabric of their society . . . would become little better than the flies of a summer'. Soon in France there would be no cherished ideals such as religious freedom,

---

[1] *Public Advertiser*, July 3, *London Chronicle*, July 1–3.

[2] Fitzwilliam MSS. F115. (Sheffield.)

[3] Bishop of Bath and Wells, *Journal and Correspondence of William, Lord Auckland* (London, 1861–2), ii, 369–70. To Auckland, August 6.

property rights, or personal culture. Two days after publication 7,000 copies were sold.[1] There were formal answers a-plenty to the pamphlet, including Mackintosh's *Vindiciae Gallicae* and Paine's *Rights of Man.*

Pitt's request in March 1791 for additional funds with which to take action against Russia, is regarded as his first major blunder. The preceding year England had made a successful stand against the Spanish in the Nootka Sound affair. English fishermen in the Pacific had settled at Nootka Sound, on the west coast of what came to be named Vancouver Island, but the Spanish, trying to establish title to the whole western American coast from Cape Horn to Alaska, had seized English ships. Parliament had voted a credit of £1 million and prepared for war; Spain backed away; the British right to Nootka and to other Pacific fisheries was conceded. Now Pitt, successful in that manoeuvre, proposed a power play against Russia. An ultimatum sent to Catherine of Russia demanded that she make peace with Turkey and restore conquered property, but Catherine would not return the city of Oczakov, a valuable base on the Black Sea. Accordingly Pitt requested additional funds to keep up steady naval pressure on Russia.

Fox opposed the move from the outset. On March 29 he spoke at length, declaring it impolitic of Britain to go to war for a single town, Oczakov, which Catherine could demolish in a few days rather than surrender. He thought the plan of increasing naval armament in order to impress continental powers was ruinous. The division taken that day, however, gave the Government a majority of 93.

The debate was continued on April 12 with a series of resolutions by Grey, the first being that it was to the interest of the nation to preserve peace. Fox wrote to Mrs Armistead that the Government 'made a terrible figure indeed in debate'. He noted that Pitt did not speak so that it was not necessary for him to either, but Sheridan made the best speech he ever made in his life.[2] The House voted the resolution down 253 to 173, so the Government's majority had shrunk from 93 to 80. Fox thereupon, in the closing moments of the debate, commented that Pitt's sullen and obstinate silence when he was about to plunge the country into war could not be endured. The division must certainly convince him that his war was unpopular and that he should be held accountable for the deceptive language he had put into the King's speeches from the throne. Pitt replied briefly that Fox's rude words would not prevent him from stating calmly that the language of the King's speeches was accurate at the time it was uttered. The opposition

[1] *General Evening-Post,* November 6–9.   [2] Add. MSS. 47570. [April 1791.]

served notice that the debate would be resumed April 15; Grey's remaining resolutions went down without a vote.

When debate was renewed Fox reiterated that sufficient cause for war did not exist and took further opportunity to attack Pitt's system. 'Nothing could justify an armament which could not justify a war; for, the nation that was once discovered to have armed in bravado, would find little regard paid to her armaments again.' Eventually, declared Fox, and his language steadily became stronger, the minister, after his bullying and blustering, would withdraw his arrogant demands, 'and we should have nothing in return for an expense of perhaps half a million, but the shame of having interfered where we had no right to interfere, and the disgrace of having completely failed'.

Fox should have taken his seat at that point while he was still ahead. For then he turned to internal conditions in France to contrast its present state with its former condition. He paid France an elegant compliment, stating that her new constitution was 'the most stupendous and glorious edifice of liberty, which had been erected on the foundation of human integrity in any time or country'. As he spoke these words Burke became highly agitated. Later he rose, 'in much visible emotion, but the cry of "Question!" being general, he unwillingly gave way to the division, which immediately took place'.[1] Grey's motion was defeated 254 to 162, but Fox later regretted that Burke had not been allowed to speak.

Grenville's report to Fitzwilliam described the scene:

Charles ended a very eloquent speech which contained much dissertation upon foreign politicks by alluding to the change of situation which France had undergone. . . . When he spoke of the revolution in that country he added that he knew his opinion did not coincide with a very large proportion of the House, but that he could not help considering that revolution as a most stupendous work, however it might appear to those who took a more superficial view of it: Burke at this time walking up the House attracted much attention; he rose to speak when Charles concluded, but gave way to the impatient cry for the question with so much readiness that I took for granted he felt no great anxiety to enter into any debate.

Later Grenville wrote that the Government was capitalizing fully upon the difference of opinion between Burke and Fox. He and Fox called on Burke, and although 'Charles [was] as conciliatory as possible' and 'Burke talked cheerfully enough', Grenville concluded that the situation was fraught with enough mischief 'to answer all the purposes our adversaries wish'. Portland had also had a conversation with Burke and realized that Burke's feelings about the situation were grim and solemn indeed. In fact, Portland wrote to Fitzwilliam, a political schism and division might follow that could end in the dissolution of the party.[2]

[1] *Parliamentary History*, xxix, 244–9.
[2] Fitzwilliam MSS. F11 5. April 19, 22. (Sheffield.)

So Fox's words about France were grievous to Burke. But the part of the speech that dealt with Russian armament was tremendously effective. One onlooker declared that he had never heard anything equal to Fox's eloquence on both occasions.[1] Fox was invariably powerful when he spoke for peace. Pitt himself saw that he should back away from his warlike stance. His envoy to Berlin, Joseph Ewart, then in London, described an interview in which Pitt explained that his attempts to justify the situation in the House of Commons were fruitless. Tears came to Pitt's eyes, Ewart recorded, as Pitt told about 'the greatest mortification he had ever experienced,' observing that he would manage affairs so that he would not appear to have given up his point but would nevertheless prevent any bad consequences stemming from his taking a new direction.[2] Later Pitt wrote Ewart that to have persisted would have risked both the Government itself and with it 'the whole of our system both at home and abroad'.[3]

The next week Fox turned from war and armament to deliver another stirring appeal for the abolition of the slave trade. When the debate opened on April 18 Wilberforce and Francis were the principal speakers, Fox contributing only briefly. Next day, however, he and Pitt both spoke at length. Although Fox had read widely from the hearings before the select committee, he based the opening part of his speech on the strong assertion that the question before the House was one of personal freedom. No man would suspect him of being an enemy to political freedom, he asserted, but even political freedom, when compared to personal freedom, sank to nothing; it was really no blessing at all. To the argument that if England did not trade in slaves some other country would, he offered the analogy of a highwayman who reasoned that if he did not rob the traveller another highwayman half a mile further along the road certainly would. Although by this level of argument and example he made the slave trade difficult to defend, in the main he based his appeal on the even stronger basis that it was opposed to every decent and humane consideration. He assured the House that his warmest efforts would always be exerted in promoting the cause of abolition.[4] Yet the vote went against him by a majority of 75, and the *Evening Mail*, reflecting upon the debates, wondered why the extraordinary abilities of Pitt, Fox, Burke, and

[1] Add. MSS. 47568. S. Rolleston, April 26.
[2] John Holland Rose, *The Life of William Pitt* (New York, 1924), i, 617–18. Rose notes that the Cabinet was also divided against the move: Richmond and Grenville, and Stafford later, were opposed to the use of coercion against Russia.
[3] Stanhope, ii, 117. May 24.   [4] *Parliamentary History*, xxix, 344–56.

Wilberforce, were not able to carry a humane question like the abolition of slavery when no possible objection could arise except the private interests of a few wealthy individuals.

After the debate, Fox wrote to Mrs Armistead, partly to excuse himself for not writing sooner, partly to comment on his speech and on his
way of living:

I have led a sad life sitting up late always either at the H. of C. or gaming and
losing my money every night that I have played, getting up late of course, and
finding people in my room so that I have had no morning time to myself and have
gone out as soon as I could tho' generally very late, to get rid of them, so that I
have scarce ever had a moment to write. You have heard how poor a figure we
made in numbers on the slave trade, but I spoke I believe very well and indeed it
is the thing that has given me the most pleasure since I saw Liz, for I do think it is
a cause in which one ought to be an enthusiast and in which one cannot help being
pleased with oneself for having done right.[1]

Twentieth-century generations that have heard countless hours of
debate on such bitterly controverted topics as woman suffrage, the
graduated income tax, the proper scope and purview of international
government, the extension of civil rights, the gradual abolition of
duties and tariffs, and have observed that what is hotly argued one day
becomes freely accepted the next, can readily see that political leaders
of the late eighteenth and early nineteenth centuries found in the abolition of the slave trade a fully debatable, entirely arguable issue. On the
questions of the slave trade and of religious freedom as well, people of
the twentieth century would find themselves more comfortable alongside Fox than on the Government benches opposite him. It was some-
time in 1790 that Mirabeau, himself a moving and eloquent speaker,
attempted to disparage Fox in Pitt's presence. Pitt replied simply:
'You have never seen the wizard within the magic circle.'

On May 6 the House of Commons was considering a Bill for the regulation of the government of Quebec, and the motion before the house was
whether the clauses of the Bill should be considered paragraph by paragraph. Burke gained the floor and immediately began to talk about the
subject closest to his heart—the French constitution. For many days
thoughts on this topic had been simmering inside him. As he warmed to
the occasion he was sharply called to order for failing to speak to the
question: whether the Bill should be considered by paragraph. Fox
took the floor and in a strain of delicate irony stated that his friend

---

[1] Add. MSS. 47570. *Fox Cor.*, ii, 362. April 1791. The editor of Fox's letters included
only the latter, statesmanlike, half of the letter, though of all the Fox correspondence this
holograph best illustrates the speckled and checkered mixture of events that constituted
so much of his life.

Burke was not out of order, as this was a day of privilege when anyone might abuse any government he pleased, whether or not it had reference to the question before the House. Half a dozen country gentlemen successively implied that this was no time for trifling. Confusion followed: Fox declared that if Burke would simply state whether or not his discussion of government was for or against reading the Bill paragraph by paragraph, he would take him at his word and would leave for the duration of his speech. Once, he said, Burke had taught that it was impossible to draw a bill of indictment against a whole people, but now he urged the contrary of his former teaching. Moreover, he concluded, neither Burke's books nor his speeches could make him change his position.

Fox himself said later that he had spoken more than he intended. Burke rose and charged he had been greatly abused. He reaffirmed his belief that as these were dangerous times, all attempts to subvert the constitution should be watched with jealousy and circumspection. As for himself he would risk all; his last words would be: 'Fly from the French constitution.' Fox readily understood that Burke would, in fact, risk all, including his lifelong friendships, and whispered to Burke, 'there was no loss of friends'. 'Yes, there was a loss of friends,' replied Burke, 'he knew the price of his conduct—he had done his duty at the price of his friend—their friendship was at an end.' At the end of his speech he walked across the floor to the Treasury bench and sat next to Pitt. It was the most dramatic moment in St Stephen's since North's resignation.

What followed then was an amazing speech by Fox in which he attempted to set things straight. He had often taken the floor of the House to correct an impression that he had unintentionally given, but perhaps never with greater concern than on that May 6. At first 'his mind was so much agitated, and his heart so much affected by what had fallen from Mr Burke that it was some minutes before he could proceed. Tears trickled down his cheeks, and he strove in vain to give utterance to feelings that dignified and exalted his nature.' Members of Parliament, for years having listened to Fox in situations where he never seemed to be at a loss for a word or an argument, were touched: 'The sensibility of every member of the House appeared uncommonly excited.'

Fox recalled their friendship of upwards of five-and-twenty years, dating from his boyhood. He could remember previous differences of opinion but never before one that had threatened their personal friendship. Yet friendship should not stand in the way of public duty. If Burke wanted to blast the French Revolution he must do so, but he must allow others that thought differently to speak differently. Burke replied that he liked the beginning and end of Fox's speech better than the middle part, reiterated his own views of the French situation, and resumed his new seat.[1] The debate was continued on the days that followed, but the quarter-century friendship between Fox and Burke had come to a shattering close.

Newspaper after newspaper attempted to give an accurate account of the rupture between Fox and Burke. Some thought Pitt had provoked the quarrel. Others merely regretted the tragic disagreement between two eminent men. Especially at first, Fox seemed to stand in higher stature for his behaviour during the dispute. Said the *Morning Post*:

Nothing could be more manly and firm than his declaration of the principles which he had espoused:—nothing more interesting and dignified than the subdued tenderness with which he expressed the sentiments of . . . his preceptor and friend.

The *Morning Chronicle* suggested that Pitt and his friends had hoped Fox would say something in the heat of debate that they could use against him, but praised Fox for his manly, statesmanlike, English speech. The *Public Advertiser* correctly saw that the two men were now forever 'at an irreconcileable distance . . . it is impossible they should ever again coalesce', and felt that Burke was largely at fault. The *World* said, under the heading, 'Burke versus Fox': 'The quarrels of vulgar politicians go to no account . . . but characters of the first eminence . . . who have trod the steps of opposition together, as *leaders* and bosom friends, must excite an anxious curiosity.'

Two or three days later the paragraphers were at work. The *Morning Chronicle* thought Fox gracious and kindly: 'Placable in emotions, he was not to be moved in principles.' The *Public Advertiser* noted: '. . . though Burke's party had separated from him . . . mankind at large . . . would approve.' As for Fox, it wondered whether his tears were the size of peas or hailstones, or as large and thick as walnuts. The *Whitehall Evening Post* characterized Fox as a whig inclining somewhat to republicanism, Burke a whig inclining more to aristocracy, hierarchy, and monarchy. Burke, moreover, whatever the subject being discussed, was likely to introduce the French Revolution just as Lord George Gordon on all occasions was wont to harp on popery.[2] Gibbon had mixed feelings about the quarrel: Burke, he concluded, was the 'most eloquent and rational madman' that he knew; and as for Fox, he struggled with his conscience: 'I love Fox's feelings, but I detest the political principles of the man and of the party.'[3]

[1] *Parliamentary History*, xxix, 364–401.   [2] Issues of May 9 to May 16.
[3] *Letters of Gibbon*, iii, 229.

Quaintly enough Burke was deeply proud of his part in the altercation. That following September he told Sir Joshua Reynolds and Edmond Malone that 'the second most brilliant day of his life' was when he was attacked by his own party in the House of Commons on the matter of the French Revolution. His 'most brilliant day' also centred upon a difficult moment: when he appeared before the bar of the House of Lords with the censure of the House of Commons in his hand, referring to the conduct of the managers during the impeachment of Warren Hastings.[1]

What Burke did not realize was that his career as a speaker had passed its zenith long before. His moments of brilliant oratory came less and less frequently and finally faded away altogether. The language used on the floor of the House by his close friends showed that they had ceased to respect his judgment. Less friendly members, both by walking out and in other ways, showed an unwillingness to listen to him. Burke easily found, however, a more durable way to express his philosophical sentiments: to write pamphlets instead of make speeches. In the *Reflections* he was able to develop his views to the fullest. Later, in the *Appeal from the Old to the New Whigs* he could explain in detail both why he should have been allowed to speak and also what he wanted to say. Hence, even as his reputation as a speaker declined his reputation as a political writer attained new heights.

Fox gradually became the leader of a new opposition: the new whigs. With the old opposition he had broken with Shelburne over American independence, he had incurred the King's wrath over the Bill to provide India with a more responsible government, he had differed with Pitt on the method of replacing George III with a regent. One needs to brush aside layers of political opportunisms and personal differences to see, as Fox at the time insisted, that his actions had a bedrock of principle. He moved to the new opposition on a series of more compelling issues: by fighting the injustice of the slave trade, by attempting to loosen the grip of established religion on political affairs, by defending the right of the French to seek liberty in their own way. Probably no spokesman ever defended such high principles so frequently or so eloquently, with so few followers in Parliament and so many out of it.

---

[1] Sir James Prior, *Life of Edmond Malone* (London, 1860), pp. 181–2.

20

Defender of Political Liberty
1791–1793

> Sir, whenever . . . Englishmen are so subdued; when
> they shall consent to believe . . . rejoice . . . grieve, just
> as it shall suit . . . the ends of ministers, then I pronounce
> the constitution of this country to be extinct.
>
> *Charles James Fox*

During his long career, Fox saw his name attached only to three measures. His India Bill has already been discussed. Fox's Embargo, promulgated the last year of his life, was thus called by Americans who resented it. In 1791 he initiated what is known as Fox's Libel Bill, most important by far of the three. Biographers have made little or no mention of it, though it looms large in the history of English law.

Before Fox's Bill, one who censured public men or the country's institutions ran the risk of facing a charge of seditious libel. The prosecutor needed to establish two principal points: one, that the material had been printed or uttered, and the other, that it was libellous. As the law had developed, the first, easier question, became the province of the jury, and the second, subtler question, was determined by the judge himself. This procedure put the question of fact into the hands of the jury and the question of law into the hands of the judge. As fact and law were often intertwined, and as some judges had been felt to be too harsh or abstract in their definitions of libel, Fox contended that since the jury was required to arrive at a general verdict of guilty or not guilty it should also have the right to consider not only whether the matter at issue had been published but also whether it was libellous. Wedderburn and Erskine were others who felt that a jury of twelve men would give a more reasonable interpretation of what was libellous than would a judge.

The Bill, bearing the title, 'An Act to remove doubts respecting the functions of juries in cases of libel', simply stated that since doubts had arisen whether the jury had the right to review both the fact of publication and the question of libel, it should be declared that the jury should consider the whole matter at issue. Among other provisions was one that the judge at his discretion could offer the jury his opinion, as he would in other criminal cases. Fox's Bill thus proposed to bring libel law into harmony with the growing feeling of the people that public affairs should be fully and freely discussed.

Fox's speeches in May 1791 in support of his Libel Bill, therefore take their place alongside his many utterances in behalf of free speech. At the outset he candidly stated that he believed in the liberty of the press, though he freely acknowledged that he did not believe one man should be able to libel the actions of another with impunity. The difficulty was that no man 'could really freely discuss the actions of government, in the way in which . . . it was the right of every man to discuss them, without a greater risk to his person and property than prudent men would choose to hazard'.

The issue of seditious libel was even for Fox a topic involved and complex. This was no speech to be prepared while riding on horseback, plucking arguments from personal knowledge. For this cause he needed to engage in lengthy, reflective research. Although he was an avid reader in six languages of history, drama, oratory, poetry, news items, and parliamentary documents, he studied legal questions only in preparation for specific debates. As he told the House, to understand this complicated business he had looked into several books on the subject, beginning with the most modern writers, and continuing 'as deeply . . . as it was possible for him to do'. Among other lines of thought, he, like any debater, sought to discover 'if there was any argument on the other side of the question' and learned that wherever he turned he found notable differences even among eminent lawyers. Fox concluded that when law and fact were united, as they often were in libel cases, the jury should have not only the right but the power to decide. A collateral analogy was furnished by murder cases. Murder was a crime consisting of law and fact, and in murder trials juries regularly judged both law and fact. In trials for high treason, moreover, how unendurable it would be to Englishmen if juries could determine only the fact of publication of a treasonable statement and not other circumstances. He touched on the knotty question as to whether a libel were more of a libel because it was true, again concluding that the jury should determine whether the fact of the libel's being true justified the libel or aggravated it. Erskine warmly supported the Bill and Pitt also gave it his approval, so it passed the commons with little debate and with no divisions.[1]

Both friends and foes of Fox in the newspaper world praised him highly. The *World* declared he was 'entitled to the best thanks of his

[1] *Parliamentary History*, xxix, 551–602.

country, and of the literary world, for his noble exertions to rescue the press from oppression, and to restore it to its genuine freedom'. Fox, who had provided the press with so much copy in the space of his more than twenty years in Parliament, who in his younger days had led the fight against printers for trespassing upon the dignity of the House, who constantly complained that newspaper reports of his speeches were irresponsible, who fought his only duel because his opponent chose to be offended by a newspaper version of a speech, now was lauded as the eminent defender of the freedom of the press. *The Times* and *Evening Mail* declared:

Mr Fox's successful speech on Friday and the assent of the minister to the truth and the justice of the argument against the present doctrine of libels will have this good effect—that every jury before whom the merits of a prosecution come to be tried, will determine on the law and the fact, and investigate the nature of the complaint before they give their verdict. When such men unite in opinions the Constitution must be firm indeed.[1]

About this time Fox was corresponding frequently with his nephew, the third Lord Holland, who was becoming increasingly interested in politics. He wrote: 'I am very happy to have succeeded in it because I think the thing essentially right, & because I have reason to think that it will do me a good deal of credit, which I am sure will give you as much pleasure as myself.' Other than this brief reference, Fox's extant correspondence is silent about his part in the Libel Bill. Though he understated his motives ('it will do me a good deal of credit'), his initiative in introducing the Bill actually suggests his concern about the freedom of the press. He himself had been the victim of nearly every imaginable sort of character assassination at the hands of London printers, involving both his personal as well as his political morals, but he did not hesitate to seize this opportunity to remedy what had become bad judicial practice.

Although the Bill passed the House, it made little further progress that session. Largely at the instigation of Thurlow the Lords decided to defer its consideration. Next year the Bill again ran into determined opposition, but it received such powerful support, principally from the venerable and able Camden, that it passed and became the law of the land. Again the *Evening Mail* and *The Times* praised this notable landmark in the history of the freedom of the press: 'Thus the great constitutional point is at last decided by the Lords and Commons—that

---

[1] During this period the *World*, *The Times*, *Oracle*, and *Herald* were on the list of newspapers receiving regular subsidies from the Government. The *Morning Chronicle* was the principal Opposition paper (A. Aspinall, *Politics and the Press, c. 1780–1850* (London, 1949), pp. 68 ff.).

JURIES ARE JUDGES OF BOTH THE LAW AND THE FACT.' *The Times* called the Libel Bill 'a monument to the name of Fox'.

Oddly enough, for the next few years after the Bill was passed, more convictions were secured for seditious libel than ever before. In essence the decision of what was libellous came down to what the twelve men of the jury thought was libellous, and during the early years of the troubled war with France juries were capable of being persuaded that certain writings were seditious. Gradually, however, as the public conscience became more sympathetic to criticism of the Government, trials for seditious libel became rarer and after the Reform Bill of 1832 ceased almost altogether.[1] Editors could express political opinions much more candidly when they could operate less exposed to charges of libel.

An aftermath of the Russian affair was Burke's charge that Fox had sent his friend, Robert Adair, to St Petersburg, to counteract the efforts of the Government's own envoy. Burke felt so vehemently about the matter that he composed articles of impeachment that appeared in the newspapers and years later were published as a pamphlet.[2] Pitt did not accuse Fox of this kind of manoeuvring, though on the floor of the House he insisted that better terms could have been secured from Russia had it not been for circumstances hostile to the interests of England. In later years Adair denied the charge, declaring that it was not only untrue but improbable ('It is always better to search for what is true in what is probable.')[3] The Empress of Russia herself was hardening her attitude toward Pitt. She had had in her collection for some five years an excellent bust of him, but now she began to show obvious public interest in securing one of Fox;[4] when she acquired one, she put it in a gallery between Demosthenes and Cicero, as her tribute to a man who had saved two nations from ruinous war.[5] As the session ended the Opposition was inquiring vigorously into the reason for continuing to spend money on armaments if no war with Russia was intended.

[1] For discussion of the issues involved and the history of the Act, see Sir James Fitzjames Stephen, *A History of the Criminal Law of England* (London, 1883), ii, 348–74; Sir William Holdsworth, *A History of English Law* (Boston, 1938), x, 688–94.
[2] *A letter from the Rt. Honourable Edmund Burke . . . containing 54 articles of impeachment against the Rt. Hon. C. J. Fox* (Philadelphia, 1797).
[3] A statement of his denial is in *Fox Cor.*, ii, 383–7.
[4] *The Diary, or Woodfall's Register*, August 11, 1791.
[5] Busts of Fox by Nollekens were very popular. At least thirty-two were made at sixty guineas each, and were ordered by the Dukes of Devonshire and Portland, several by the Empress of Russia (Philopatris Varvicensis [Dr Samuel Parr], *Characters of the late Charles James Fox* (London, 1809), ii, 68). One of Sayers's cartoons shows the Empress personally adjusting into a niche a bust of Fox, a rope around his neck to support him as he was winched into position between Demosthenes and Cicero, each with a scornful look on his face.

The King's speech opening the session in January 1792 sounded an optimistic note, reporting that preliminary articles of peace were being concluded between Russia and Turkey and that although war still raged in India, 'friendly assurances from foreign powers' and 'the general state of affairs in Europe' augured continued tranquillity. Present naval and military expenditures might even be reduced in order to cut taxes.

Since the national prosperity had produced substantial revenue during the last four years, Pitt proposed to repeal the recent tax on malt and the taxes on female servants, carts and wagons, houses having fewer than seven windows, and the last half-penny per pound on candles. These were the fringes of governmental income of that day. He then declared that 'unquestionably there never was a time in the history of this country when from the situation of Europe we might more reasonably expect fifteen years of peace than we may at the present moment'.[1] Fox was left with little ground to stand on but managed to insist in his reply that the House itself should have the privilege of determining which taxes should be repealed, rather than the minister, in his arbitrary manner that bordered on the unconstitutional. Pitt's proposals were agreed to, however, without a division. *The Times* noted that his lead, last session 2 to 1, was now almost 3 to 1.

On Leap Year day, February 29, the Commons debated Samuel Whitbread's resolutions criticizing the Government's policy towards Russia. Whitbread, a new member of Parliament, had at the outset of his career attached himself to Fox, and especially distinguished himself in the debate on Russian armament. The significance of the fortress of Oczakov and of other Russian claims was mentioned many times in the discussion and Fox particularly was called upon to speak. The debate, however, was adjourned to March 1, members still impatiently awaiting Fox's speech. 'Some members then very irregularly called upon Mr Fox' says the report; the *Morning Herald*, more explicit, noted that the House called loudly and repeatedly for Fox. On that occasion he delivered what has been ranked as one of his great speeches. The attack on Pitt was forceful indeed:

Half a million of money is spent, the people alarmed and interrupted in their proper pursuits by the apprehension of a war, and for what? For the restoration of Oczakov? No; Oczakov is not restored. To save the Turks from being too much humbled? No; they are now in a worse situation than they would have been had we never armed at all. . . . We are now tied down by treaties, and fettered by stipulations! we have even guaranteed to Russia what we before said it would be unsafe for the Turks to yield, and dangerous to the peace of Europe for Russia to possess.

[1] *Parliamentary History*, xxix, 826. February 17, 1792.

He went on to reiterate that Pitt gained for all his rashness only an excuse to sacrifice wantonly the public money and the public quiet.[1]

The *London Recorder* observed that the attention of the 360 members in the House was 'perfect and constant' throughout a nearly three-hour speech; 'during that time not one person left his seat'. Pitt, it reported, was 'overcome . . . by the incontrovertible arguments of Mr Fox. . . . His *ore rotundo* utterance was gone, his right arm forgot its favourite sway; and his looks of complacency and confidence strayed no more even to the Ministerial benches'. Thomas Coutts, banker and Fox's financial adviser, to be mentioned later in these pages, confessed that 'it is generally admitted that the argument on the Russia business was in favour of opposition'.[2] The *World* gamely breasted the tide of praise: 'Mr Pitt's speech . . . was one continued chain of incontrovertible argument. Mr Fox's speech was brilliant, but it was evidently an effort against conviction and truth.'

In the early part of his speech, Fox had foretold that Pitt's tactic would be to wait until the close of the debate, make a speech which Fox would not have opportunity to contradict, and then throw himself on his majority, 'and that makes you dumb for ever'. The prediction was not entirely true, in that Pitt made a speech of moderate length, to which Fox offered a brief reply; but Pitt's majority had the final word as Fox and everyone else knew it would, and declined to pass Whitbread's critical resolutions. The only division taken favoured the Government 244 to 116. 'Not one convert was made,' ruminated Coutts, 'notwithstanding the wonderful oratory displayed on both sides of the question.' He marvelled that Pitt had been minister for seven years, and was likely to continue for seven years more, even though 'no man . . . ever had so many personal friends as his opponent, Mr Fox'.

These decades produced a quality of parliamentary debating seldom excelled. No speaker was always the best; twoscore different people each had his moment in the limelight. One moment impressed Bishop Tomline, the tutor, friend, and biographer of Pitt. One evening while Pitt was dining with Tomline, Burke called, predicted that the debate that night would turn on a phase of the French Revolution, and reviewed arguments that he planned to use. Taking a small piece of paper out of his pocket, Burke 'read over these heads, and descanted a

[1] *Ibid.*, xxix, 990–4.
[2] *Life of Coutts*, ii, 8. Coutts was a steadfast admirer of Fox. In 1787 he had written a generous letter, offering to refinance Fox's annuities or debts ('such a sum as I can spare would extricate you from hands that are less liberal than *I Hope* mine are') (Holland House MSS.).

short time upon each as he proceeded', in a manner that Tomline found impressive. Tomline therefore followed Pitt and Burke to the House and took a seat in the gallery in order to hear Burke actually deliver what he had rehearsed. The debate, however, took an entirely different turn from what Burke had forecast. 'At last Burke rose,' recalled Tomline, 'and made a most admirable speech, but wholly in reply to what had been said that night.' With no opportunity to use any material he had rehearsed for Pitt, Burke spoke on the spur of the moment. The speech that evening was not distinguished, but the incident shows the readiness and competence with which an intelligent, informed, and articulate member could enter into debate.[1]

Fox, strong advocate of party government, sat down in March to write a long letter in which he set forth his own beliefs. His correspondent was Fitzwilliam, who, like himself, 'hated the two extremes equally', but differed 'with respect to the quarter from which the danger is most pressing'. Fox said:

There are three points in which I know that I have not the general support of our Party. The first of these relates to religious liberty. . . . I am sure you have no objection to putting an end to all penal laws and disqualifications on Catholics and Dissenters in this country, . . . but there are some of our friends especially of those belonging to the other wing of the Coalition where sentiments on this regard are very different.

A second was the slave trade; but on this point Fox felt 'so seriously and so warmly' that he preferred the abolition of it to the achievement of any party or political gain. On this subject he would not seek concession from his friends because 'I am determined to make none myself'. A third was parliamentary reform, and since Fox was never believed to be an ardent parliamentary reformer, it is interesting to read his own words as he refines his position:

The truth is I am more bound by former declarations and consistency, than by any strong opinion I entertain in its favour. I am far from being sanguine that any new scheme would produce better parliaments than the present mode of election has furnished.

So whereas he was uncompromising in his views about the abolition of slavery, on parliamentary reform his opinions were not adamant. As he took up the question of party, his beliefs became more positive:

I am firmly convinced that the existence and union of our party is useful to the country, and as such that it is our duty to maintain it by every exertion and effort. We must console ourselves with knowing that what we do is right without expecting either power or emolument, or popularity or thanks or even fair construction with respect to our intentions.

[1] Lord Rosebery, *Tomline's Life of Pitt* (London, 1903), p. 181.

The time may come, he continued, when the country would reap advantage 'from the existence of a party of men who are passionately attached to the principles of liberty'. As he concluded : 'The times are bad, very bad for us, but perhaps we are of that sort which in bad times is most useful, and we may be in our proper place.'[1]

It was a great year for those two parliamentary giants, Fox and Pitt, and not a bad year for Sheridan and Wilberforce. On April 2 the last-named, despite his defeats of years before, again offered his motion for the abolition of the slave trade. Once more he described the cruelty of the system by which slaves were collected for barter (sometimes African villages were burned and fleeing Negroes seized as they attempted to escape); by which they were shipped on the unbelievably inhuman middle passage from Africa to the West Indies (hundreds perished en route, and Wilberforce offered the statistics); by which slave ship captains could commit unspeakable instances of brutality.[2] For three hours and a quarter Wilberforce spoke : 'He was uncommonly eloquent and animated, and during so long a speech rivetted the attention of the House, which was extremely crowded with members.'

The quality of attention that long, three-hour speeches could command is, by today's standards, beyond imagination. Speakers who venture longer than an hour today usually trespass unforgivably upon the listener's patience. Most keep comfortably within the harbour of a fifteen to thirty-minute voyage. London is repeatedly described as stinking (later Shelley described hell as a city much like London); St Stephen's chapel as hot, airless, crowded, uncomfortable; yet again and again galleries were packed to hear the debates, and although members then, as now, could freely walk out in the midst of a speech, at times parliamentary reporters noted that 'not a member left his seat'. Each member had his own friends among London printers, but when a really fine speech was made, other papers would praise it even though they usually had disapproved of him or his politics. Athens, Rome, and Paris have each produced great speakers, but no list can surpass Chatham, Burke, Fox, Sheridan, Pitt, O'Connell, Disraeli, Gladstone, Bright, Lloyd George, and Churchill on one side of the ocean, and Henry, Clay, Calhoun, Webster, Lincoln, Wilson, and Roosevelt on the other. And a third of these names are associated with the explosive, revolutionary years of the latter eighteenth century.

[1] Fitzwilliam MSS. (Milton), 44/9, 1–4. March 16. (Northamptonshire Record Office.) Quoted in Herbert Butterfield, 'Charles James Fox and the Whig Opposition', *Cambridge Historical Journal*, ix, 3 (1949), pp. 297–8.
[2] *Parliamentary History*, xxix, 1069–71.

Those supporting the slave trade could argue either that the brutalities were not so excessive as alleged, or no worse than were found in other situations—the treatment of prisoners in Old Bailey, for instance. They could calculate the extent of the trade commercially—300,000 tons of shipping, involving important interests in Bristol, Liverpool, and throughout the kingdom. The triangle of trade was well established and profitable: fabricated articles and textiles from industrial England were traded on the Gold Coast for slaves; the slaves were shipped to the West Indies and sold; the ships were then loaded with sugar and rum and taken back to England. In addition exchanges between the West Indies and the States involved molasses, timber, pig iron, tobacco. Those favouring the slave trade could moreover summon experts on naval defence to testify to the value of the slave fleet, with its 30,000 trained seamen, as a naval reserve in being; the trade was 'the very nursery of seamen'. They could enlist the arguments of misguided humanitarians, who argued that since charity begins at home, members should turn their attention first to inmates of prisons or mental hospitals—suffering Englishmen, here, at hand—rather than to black people a thousand miles away. They could command the silky talk of opportunists who admitted, or professed to admit, the evils of the trade but who contended that abolition should be gradual, not sudden, and who suggested that if England withdrew from the trade, the Dutch, the Portuguese, the Spanish, the Yankees, would quickly pick it up. Public opinion, however, favoured abolition; petitions to Parliament prayed for an end to the slave traffic.

Fox spoke in favour of Wilberforce's motion, though on that April 2 Pitt made one of the truly impressive speeches of his ministry. In that early morning speech, achieving one of the fine moments of his career, he spoke as a man inspired.[1] By 193 to 125, the House agreed that the word 'gradually' should be introduced into the motion; and by 230 to 85, majority 145, the House carried the main motion as amended, that the abolition of the slave trade should be gradually accomplished.

Later the Commons set 1796 as the year of abolition; the Lords, however, thought the principle of abolition was of a piece with principles flowing from the French Revolution ('insubordination, anarchy, confusion, murder, havock, devastation, and ruin' as Lord Abingdon phrased it in 1794), and, moreover, was an assault upon the rights of private property. Fox trusted that the Lords would not delay the question, nor shun it, nor shrink from it, nor shift and neglect it,[2] but the

---

[1] *Life of Wilberforce*, i, 347. Dr Parr also thought this speech was Pitt's masterpiece, though ordinarily he had no high opinion of Pitt as a speaker: 'he suspected Pitt of a settled design of subverting the idiom of the language, as well as overturning the constitution' (Charles Whibley, *William Pitt* (Edinburgh and London, 1906), p. 309).
[2] *Parliamentary History*, xxx, 1448.

Lords replied, in due course, the Commons have no right to dictate to us; let them mind their own business and we will take care of ours, 'and in the rejection of this Bill, this will not be the first time . . . that this country and this constitution have been saved by this House, from the rash and intemperate measures of the other'.[1] For the time being the anti-slave-trade movement was not to have the benefit even of deliberate speed. Yet the slavers these years received due warning that the business was offensive and unholy so that when Fox and Wilberforce brought it under fire a decade and a half later the outcome was different.

On May 11, Fox resumed his long struggle for religious freedom by taking up the cause of Unitarianism. Specifically, he proposed the repeal of certain statutes which defined as blasphemy and profaneness beliefs such as those professed by the Unitarians. The cause was not a popular one: the year before on July 14 rioters at Birmingham had sacked the home of the eminent Dr Joseph Priestley and had destroyed his books and laboratory equipment. Priestley and other Unitarians had taken an active part in politics through the establishment of societies and the publication of pamphlets and Fox decided the time had come to support the group.

Fox's speech that day was characterized by a mood of calm reasonableness. All would agree, he said, that toleration was abstractedly just; the difficulties arose in the application of its principles. Toleration was not merely a thing convenient and useful to a state, but a thing in itself essentially right. In a state having an established religion, men could be bound only by that part of the establishment that was consistent with the pure principles of toleration. These principles were founded on the fundamental, unalienable rights of man: 'To call on man to give up his religious rights, was to call on him to do that which was impossible. . . . No state could compel it; no state ought to require it.' Yet in the last century four persons professing Unitarian doctrines had been burnt; others had suffered persecution. Though Unitarians were not now actively persecuted by the legislature, they were in a manner under the lash of divines of the Established Church.

How unjust, inhuman, and cruel, Fox concluded, it is to say to a man:

Read the scriptures, study them, make them the guide and rule of your action and opinion; but take care you interpret them as the professors of the church of England do, or else you shall be deprived of all the enjoyment which belongs to a man in a social state. Read attentively, and understand clearly the whole of the scriptures; but take care, in understanding them, you understand exactly as we do, or

[1] Lord Abingdon, March 2, 1794. *Parliamentary History*, xxxi, 469–70.

else you shall lose all the benefits of a member of society, every thing that is dear and valuable to you.

Burke followed him, opposing the motion. Government has a general superintending control over all the actions and over all the publicly propagated doctrines of men without which it could not provide adequately for the wants of society. To be sure, Burke argued, this power should be used with discretion. But the question to be decided was not a theological one but one of legislative prudence. The evidence for urging the repeal of these statutes was not sufficient, and nothing had been said about prudence and policy. North and Adam supported Fox; North declared that 'no time could be improper to do justice, or proper to continue injustice'; Adam urged that the petitioners were respectable and the time not improper. Pitt opposed the motion. 'The statutes in question had stood long, and were thought necessary by our ancestors.' To repeal them would make the public feel that the House had taken a first step 'towards a gradual abolition of all the establishments and fundamental principles of the constitution'.

Fox offered a brief rejoinder, concluding that the more the subject of toleration was discussed, 'the more its justice would be perceived and acknowledged'. The House divided against him, 142 to 63.[1] He had done his Unitarian friends little good, since the penal laws against them were not repealed until 1813, and he had given his conservative friends another reason to shake their heads at what they considered an unwise and unnecessary espousal of a radical notion.

One can with little difficulty envisage Pitt's position as Prime Minister during those long years when Fox and Pitt stood diametrically opposed to one another on nearly every issue. The remark of the Duchess of Leinster, made a quarter of a century previously, that strictly brought up, clever, properly behaved, eight-year-old William Pitt would be 'a thorn in Charles's side as long as he lives' worked the other way as well. Fox was one of the first to approve and commend Pitt's maiden speech in 1781, and initially thought of their working together during the years of the American revolution and those that were to follow, but the echoes of that maiden speech had hadly died away before the two had found themselves in disagreement.

Fox's shortcomings have been narrated at length, but Pitt was not altogether blameless. More than one contemporary noted a trait variously described as haughtiness, severity, aloofness, formality, reserve. In his youth he had missed the hard knocks that come from school and playground. Unlike his father, he had not even had military

[1] *Parliamentary History*, xxix, 1372–1403.

training. His ways of relaxation also drifted towards the solitary: drinking, horseback riding. Entering public life, he stepped almost immediately, with little struggle, to the highest position, where he became accustomed to more than the usual amount of deference. Sheridan, once discussing Pitt's character, regretted that it had often been his fate to oppose him. Aside from disagreeing with his measures, Sheridan admitted: 'I may have considered that there was somewhat too much of loftiness in his mind which could not bend to advice, or scarcely bear cooperation.' These qualities were slow to mellow. Generally it could be said of Pitt, as of his father, that he could not bear the lightest touch of command.

Attempts at coalescing those early years had found each man unwilling to accept the other as first minister and also unwilling to work together under a third man as nominal chief. Neither had a markedly superior array of talents over the other, and neither enjoyed at crucial moments overwhelming popular support. Now in the critical days after the fall of the Bastille, Pitt knew that almost anything he proposed on the floor of the Commons in the way of budget, armament, or treaty, would meet Fox's opposition: pointed, eloquent, lengthy, fortified with resources of argument, statistic, example, precedent, or reason (the logical basis of discourse) and of scorn, ridicule, belittlement, and appeals to patriotism and humanity (the emotional basis). Fox showed little charity: any given proposal of Pitt's could be attacked because it was untimely, insufficient, ill-begotten, unconstitutional, ill-advised. Fox's experience in office had been short but intensive; he had learned the inner workings of Admiralty, Treasury, and Foreign Office; he had spent many months travelling about the Continent, visiting its historic cities and discussing all manner of topics with its leading citizens. With ten years more parliamentary experience than Pitt, he had debated every topic not once but many times. Little could be said on Admiralty, budget, courts martial, the constitution, the establishment, America, France, Germany, the Low Countries, Russia, Turkey, that he had not heard many times before. Or if a new topic came up he would learn of it about as quickly as anybody. He had a wide range of serviceable example. As for formal reasoning, he very well knew his syllogisms, his enthymemes, his sorites, his ratiocinatory states, his *onus probendi*, his *argumentum ad hominem*, his dilemmas and table-turnings. Pitt would have cheerfully created a new Earl of Rochester—the title old Holland yearned for and never received—to have had Fox out of the Commons and in the Lords.

Yet on certain types of legislation Pitt and Fox could work together. Apprising Fox of his intentions, Pitt would receive in advance assurances of hearty support, or a qualified promise that while endorsing the basic principle, Fox would debate the lesser details.

During 1792 various societies had been organized to sponsor reform movements. The London Corresponding Society, consisting mainly of working men, was organized by shoemaker Thomas Hardy at the beginning of the year to advocate parliamentary reform. Eventually it attracted 6,000 members. A similar organization was the Society for Constitutional Information. In April, Grey founded the Friends of the People, also to agitate for reform. This society was more influential than the others as its charter group included members of Parliament and other men of substance. Fox was not a member of the society but Erskine, Whitbread, Sheridan, and Sawbridge were, and it resolved to arrange for notice in the Commons of a motion for reform. This motion Grey offered on April 30. Fox supported him, saying that parliamentary reform was not popular in the House, but that the public regarded the matter in a different light. The greatest beauty of the constitution was that it admitted of perpetual improvement. Its permanency, however, must depend upon what the people thought of it. Before they could have any great reverence for it they should be convinced that the voice of their representatives was in unison with their own. He drew a line between the type of reform sought in Paine's *Rights of Man* and the type of improvement that time and circumstance might render necessary in the constitution as it stood. In this debate Fox heard Burke and other old friends speak against him. Fox's speech was popular outside the walls of Parliament, the London Corresponding Society ordering 500 copies for distribution.[1] The King, however, could find no merit in the speeches of Fox and his cohorts: 'If men are to be found willing to overturn the Constitution . . . it is most providential they so early cast off the mask.'[2]

Anxieties fostered by the revolution laid hands of fear on any movement that could possibly be construed as change. Such movements were radical, were Jacobin, were revolutionary, were republican. When the Government planned to issue a proclamation against sedition, aimed at societies like Grey's and pamphlets like Paine's, even the whigs found they were in deep disagreement. The Duke of Portland, having been consulted on the advisability of the proposed proclamation,

[1] T. J. Howell, comp., *A Complete Calendar of State Trials . . . Continued From the Year 1783 to the Present Time* (London, 1817), xxiv, 774.
[2] *Later Correspondence of George III*, i, 591. May 1.

called a meeting at Burlington House. Arriving there, the Duke of Bedford inquired if Fox were expected, and on being told that he was not, picked up his hat and drily observed, 'Then I am sure I have no business here', and left the room.[1]

The debates in Parliament revealed further the deepening split in the Opposition. In the Commons Fox and Grey spoke against the proclamation, but Windham, Grenville, the young Lord North and others supported it. In the Lords the Opposition was also divided: the Prince himself spoke for it as did Portland. When Lauderdale attacked Richmond in the debate and the duke replied in kind, Lauderdale challenged Richmond to a duel and was himself challenged by General Arnold; the first quarrel was peaceably settled, but Fox himself was Lauderdale's second in the other, which ended without injury to either party. These and similar incidents became increasingly painful to those who hated to see the party break up. James Harris, first Earl of Malmesbury, who had represented the nation on various missions to the courts of The Hague, Catherine the Second of Russia, and Frederick the Great, arrived in England on June 2, and immediately found himself in consultation with the Prince, Portland, and others. At an evening meeting at Burlington House, June 9, he has recorded how Burke complained of Fox, whose conduct had disqualified him for office: 'he was tainted with French politics and principles; that he . . . deserted his old friends, and had preferred a new set in the party.' Fox was the sort of person to be seen either in the company of great harm or great good, Burke continued, yet differences must somehow be resolved: 'A union of all the abilities, all the weight, and all the wealth of this country was necessary —the times required it.' After Burke had left, Loughborough expressed his agreement with what Burke had said, but declared that it should not be repeated; still, 'the times called for a junction'. It would be disagreeable for many of those present to separate from Fox, but to remain would be to assent to Fox's sentiments on the French Revolution, parliamentary reform, the repeal of the Test Act, the repeal of the Act against Unitarians, the abolition of the slave trade, and similar radical views.[2]

Next day Malmesbury conversed further with Portland and the notion of a coalition gained momentum. During a two-hour conversation on June 13. Fox told Portland that he favoured coalition if a neutral man such as the Duke of Leeds could be put at the head and if it could be arranged that power and patronage would be equally shared. On June 14, at a conversation between Loughborough and Pitt, Pitt spoke 'with great openness and sincerity', said that although he did not have the King's command to form a coalition, he was sure it would

---

[1] *Fox Cor.*, iii, 18. Holland, *Memoirs of the Whig Party*, i, 16.
[2] Elliot, ii, 44. William Elliot to Sir Gilbert, June 19.

please the King and the Queen as well. Pitt did not seem to feel that their parliamentary altercations had produced language that would later prove embarrassing. It might not be easy to give Fox the foreign office immediately, but 'in a few months he certainly might have it'.

Later discussion revealed that the controversial issues, not so much between Pitt and Fox as between Fox and the Portland–Malmesbury axis, were: parliamentary reform, abolition of the slave trade, repeal of the Test Act, and 'the system to be observed relative to French politics'. Despite seemingly insuperable disagreements the idea of a coalition continued to be nourished. Fox at the outset distrusted Pitt's sincerity; later Fox thought a coalition possible if he could come into the Government on equal terms; at one time he said he 'loved coalitions'. As the conversations went on, the name of Portland sifted towards the top. Fox was reported as saying that a coalition was 'so damned right, to be sure, that I cannot help thinking it must be'. Burke was pessimistic to the last; his phrase was, 'Mr Fox's coach stops the way'; there was no doing with Fox or without him. By July 30 Fox seemed set in his own mind that Pitt's giving up the chief post was a prerequisite to further negotiation, 'and was so opinionative and fixed about it, that it was impossible even to reason with him on the subject'.[1]

Leeds thought it worth while to interview the King, but concluded that the King's dislike for Fox 'remains in full force'. The only possible compromise, the King insisted, was to yield anything complimentary to the opposition 'but no Power'. But when Leeds later talked to Pitt he received no encouragement whatever. The circumstances did not call for any alteration in the Government, Pitt declared, nor did the people wish it. No new arrangement, either by a change or a coalition, had ever been contemplated. Moreover, a union with Fox was even more difficult than it had been before, because of Fox's conduct towards the close of the last session.[2]

The negotiations had no chance to succeed. The force was irresistible, the target immovable. The coalition, as some liked to term it, of the King and Pitt, could not be displaced. The mutual dislike between the King and Fox was as strong as ever. Nor did Fox and Pitt have any genuine wish to work together. Hence the mixture continued as before.[3]

---

[1] *Diaries and Correspondence of James Harris, First Earl of Malmesbury* (London, 1844), ii, 453–72.

Fox wished it known that no offer would divide them—'or that we can come in *under* Pitt though we could and should be willing to act with him in administration' (Fitzwilliam MSS. (Milton), 44/8/2. July 22. Northamptonshire Record Office).

[2] Leeds, pp. 187–95. August 14, 22.

[3] For other details of the negotiations see Butterfield, 'Charles James Fox and the Whig Opposition', *loc cit.*

Events across the channel figured in the discussions. In July the Duke of Brunswick issued his manifesto, threatening Paris with destruction if the King and Queen were mistreated, and suggesting other forms of retaliation. In August the Tuileries was attacked, the Swiss mercenaries defending it being slain either on the spot or later, as were also many retainers and servants; and the King and his family were imprisoned. In September came the notorious massacres, prisons being emptied and captives slain. The number of revolutionary victims has been exaggerated but even the careful estimates of 223 priests and other political victims plus from 800 to 1,100 common criminals is appalling.[1] The violence alarmed even eighteenth-century Englishmen, accustomed to daily multiple hangings; Fox declared there was not 'a shadow of excuse for this horrid massacre'.

Fox was at St Anne's Hill with Mrs Armistead during these events, shooting, playing tennis, viewing the Richmond boat races and the Newmarket horse races. He declared the Brunswick manifesto was revolting to the feelings of mankind. At first the news of the imprisonment of the King disturbed him, but later he reconciled himself to it; however, as he wrote his nephew: 'It is impossible not to look with disgust at the bloody means which have been taken, even supposing the end to be good, and I cannot help fearing that we are not yet near the end of these trials and executions.' To the National Assembly he had these reactions:

There is a want of dignity and propriety in everything they do. . . . And yet, with all their faults and all their nonsense, I do interest myself for their success to the greatest degree. It is a great crisis for the real cause of liberty, whatever we may think of the particular people who are to fight the present battle. I wish they were like our old friends the Americans, and I should scarcely be afraid for them.

He also heard the news that Brunswick's army had been stopped by the French, aided by a savage epidemic of dysentery reportedly caused by eating unripe grapes. This sudden turn of affairs left him exultant: 'No! no public event not excepting Saratoga and York Town, ever happened that gave me so much delight. . . . The defeats of great armies of invaders always gave me the greatest satisfaction in reading history, from Xerxes's time downwards.'[2]

After the defeat of Brunswick came the successful invasion of Belgium by General Dumouriez. The newly summoned National Convention, its representatives elected practically by universal suffrage, abolished the institution of royalty, and as French troops gained new victories, spoke with new boastfulness. It issued an order opening navigation on the Scheldt and also its famous decree of November 19

[1] Georges Lefebvre, *The French Revolution from its Origins to 1793* (London, 1962), p. 243.
[2] Add. MSS. 47571. *Fox Cor.*, ii, 369–72. September 3; October 12.

offering assistance to oppressed peoples. The activity of French agents in Holland, England, and elsewhere put a fine edge to the concern of those governments. Throughout England meetings were held to celebrate the success of French arms, although the opening of the Scheldt officially involved Britain's treaty obligations. Debating societies and corresponding societies became more active than ever, and riots broke out in Scotland. Thomas Paine was brought to trial, though he himself was in Paris, but not even Thomas Erskine's eloquence could prevent the hand-picked jury and the judge from pronouncing a sentence of outlawry against him.

That autumn Carlisle attempted to appraise Fox's activities. He saw much to shudder at:

Fox's unfortunate encomium of the French Revolution. The dispute with Burke. His dashing so deeply into the slave trade. The little management he has had about the Church. His conversation and speeches concerning the association (though I acquit him of any real love of reform of parliament).

There they are—listed as he put them, like separate felonies to be regretted and deplored. Asked to speculate upon whether Fox would join Pitt's Government, Carlisle was certain that Fox would not. Pitt needed strength in the Lords, in parliamentary speaking, in the law posts, Carlisle thought, but would neither break up his administration to found another, nor accept an equal station with Fox under a third person.[1] Fitzwilliam also had doubts: '. . . however we might to look to Charles, as a great, leading, necessary spring in the machine, still there were some requisites wanting in him, to be the representing Head of the party.'[2]

At the same time there were those who wanted Fox to go even further than he did. Tierney, active in the work of the Society of the Friends of the People, wrote Grey to urge Fox to 'come forth in his true natural Colours and speak boldly what I am certain he thinks' on the issue of parliamentary reform. 'Either Fox must ruin the cabal at Burlington House,' he concluded, 'or that Cabal will ruin him.'[3]

Fox's principles emerge more clearly when his views on political liberty are contrasted with Pitt's. In the autumn of 1792, worried about the restlessness in the country, Pitt wrote Dundas outlining the kind of legislative action that should be initiated when Parliament next convened:

[1] Fitzwilliam MSS. (Milton), 44/6/1. To Fitzwilliam, October 19. (Northamptonshire Record Office.)
[2] *Ibid.*, 44/5/3. October 31.
[3] Grey MSS., Durham University. November 15. Quoted in Black, pp. 291–2.

I am much inclined to think [he wrote] that when Parliament meets the Penalty on publishing Seditious Libels . . . should be augmented. I do not see that it would be too much to make it even Felony, in any Person who should persist in Acts of Publication, after Notice served upon him from some officer of Government in a form to be prescribed. This would at least check the Publication of anything mischievous enough to be of much Note.

Pitt also reflected that, without interfering with the liberty of the press, it might be possible 'to make it highly penal' to print material on political subjects. Pitt offered these notions as loose ideas on the subject, but at the same time he was persuaded of the 'Absolute Necessity' of taking effectual measures. In other letters he discussed the feasibility of suspending habeas corpus, especially in order to deal with refugee Frenchmen in England and other foreigners.[1] So while Fox was trying to enlarge the right of British subjects to express their opinions, Pitt was contemplating additional restraints, restrictions, punishments.

On December 1 when Pitt called up part of the militia, Fox wrote Portland that if members of the Government mentioned danger of rebellion or insurrection, 'surely the first measure all honest men ought to take is to impeach them for so wicked and detestable a falsehood. . . . I cannot trust myself to write any more, for I confess I am too much heated.'[2] Regardless of the September massacres, regardless of the stream of propaganda poured into the country, regardless of mounting sales of the *Rights of Man*, regardless of the grim predictions of Edmund Burke, to Fox party was worth speaking for, and free speech and assembly were worth fighting for. He was decidedly in that frame of mind when the session opened December 13. He had written Adair: 'It is good not to despair but I do assure you I am forced to use considerable exertion with myself to avoid it.'[3]

We are to hear more and more about the Whig Club of England. Founded about this time, it became extremely successful as a forum in which whig views could be sympathetically presented to other whigs. As Aristotle would have put it, it offered a fine opportunity to praise Athens in the presence of Athenians. Its popularity led Pitt's followers to organize their own club.[4] In the years ahead the Whig Club became more and more a Fox Club of England, and eventually changed its name to Fox Club. He was its brightest light and his was the voice it heard most frequently. On December 4, he had spoken to it; his sentiments were gathered into a twopenny pamphlet that went through at least three editions. He said:

[1] Pitt Papers, November 8, 27. (Clements.)   [2] *Fox Cor.*, iv, 291–2.
[3] Add. MSS. 47567. November 29.   [4] Black, pp. 217–18.

I am attached to the House of Brunswick—because I hope, because I believe, that *they will never forget the principles which placed their family upon the throne of Great Britain.*

For the same reason I am attached to *the Constitution, according to the principles asserted at the Revolution. . . .*

It follows, therefore, that I am, and I declare myself to be an advocate for *the rights of the people.*[1]

The speech echoed and re-echoed through newspaper columns even more than many of Fox's parliamentary utterances. Paragraphers observed that Fox's toast had been to the House of Brunswick but not to the King himself (a gesture approaching sedition?), and these brought forth a torrent of protesting letters and counter-letters in the *Sun, Oracle, Morning Chronicle,* and others. Yet the talk of some kind of coalition persisted. 'The duke [Portland] . . . was tossed like a tennis ball from side to side,' wrote Stanhope; 'almost quite determined to join the ministry whenever he met Lord Malmesbury; almost quite determined not whenever he met Mr Fox.'[2] Newspapers reported Fox's statement to Portland: 'Having suffered so much unmerited obloquy by one coalition, I am firmly resolved—*never to consent to another. . . .* I am too old, too indolent, and now too unambitious, to fight under the banners of Government.' If his absence were desired, he would retire to a foreign country; otherwise he would continue to discharge his duty, approving measures, not men, according to the dictates of his conscience. Hearing this declaration, those who favoured coalition were 'astonished and dejected'; Burke, the papers went on to report, shed tears of sorrow. Another arrangement with Portland as premier and Pitt as Chancellor of the Exchequer was proposed, but Portland said he could not accept without Fox, and Pitt never sent a final answer.[3]

The King's speech on December 13 reminded Lords and Commons that seditious practices had been openly renewed and had actively increased; that tumults and disorders had required calling out the militia to support the civil magistrate; that this subversion of order and government had been pursued in concert with persons in foreign countries. Lords and Commons should therefore proceed to adopt measures that would force obedience to the laws and repress 'every attempt to disturb the peace and tranquillity of these kingdoms'. Pitt's views, as he had expressed them in his correspondence with Dundas, were thus about to be enacted into law.

[1] *The speech of the Right Hon. Charles James Fox containing the declaration of his principles*, etc. 3rd edn (London, 1793), pp. 6, 9.
[2] Stanhope, ii, 183. [3] *Lloyd's Evening Post*, December 5–7; *Oracle*, December 7.

Without much debate, and without a division, the Lords agreed to legislate measures for enforcing obedience to the laws and for repressing attempts to disturb peace and tranquillity. The Commons in its debate proceeded in the same direction, but here Pitt's plan ran into determined opposition from Fox. Fox's speech was at once an answer to the King, a defence of himself, and a plea for reasoned thinking. On many occasions Fox could be acrimonious and critical, but this speech, like that on the Westminster Scrutiny, illustrated an unequalled ability to keep his admittedly strong and deep feelings restrained by parliamentary decorum. He said:

I am not so little acquainted with the nature of man as not to know, that in public speaking, in order to engage the attention of the hearers, besides the efficacy of fair and candid reasoning, a man ought always to be in temper and unison with his audience. He ought to show that, however they may differ upon points, they are pursuing in reality the same object, namely, the love of truth.

He thus showed something of the conciliatory mode often lacking in eighteenth-century parliamentary speeches dealing with warmly contended issues.

Two points in the speech first drew his fire: one, that there was an insurrection in the kingdom, and, two, that a dangerous spirit existed when it could be seen that many people despaired upon hearing the rumour that General Dumouriez had surrendered. As to the alleged insurrection which presumably had existed for fourteen days, he demanded, 'Where is it?' and if Government is keeping it a secret: 'This is really carrying the doctrine of confidence to a length indeed.' Some tumults had been reported, to be sure, but these arose because sailors wanted their wages increased, not because they wanted to overthrow the constitution. As to the Government's growing tendency to be alarmed by the mood with which people reacted to news, he eloquently asked:

But what, Sir, are the doctrines that they desire to set up by this insinuation of gloom and dejection? That Englishmen are not to dare to have any genuine feelings of their own; that they must not rejoice but by rule; that they must not think but by order. . . . Sir, whenever the time shall come that the character and spirits of Englishmen are so subdued; when they shall consent to believe that every thing which happens around is indifferent both to their understandings and their hearts; and when they shall be brought to rejoice and grieve, just as it shall suit the taste, the caprice, or the ends of ministers, then I pronounce the constitution of this country to be extinct.

'Our constitution was not made', he went on to declare, 'in a day. It is the result of gradual and progressive wisdom. . . . Never has the protecting genius of England been either asleep or satisfied.'

Pitt wanted to move in the direction of surveillance of aliens, censorship, and repression. Here is Fox's plan:

We are come to the moment when the question is whether we shall give to the King, that is, to the executive government, complete power over our thoughts. . . . This I call a crisis . . . imminent and tremendous. . . .

What would I propose to do in times of agitation like the present? I will answer openly.

If there is a tendency in the dissenters to discontent, because they conceive themselves to be unjustly suspected and cruelly calumniated, what would I do?—I would instantly repeal the test and corporation acts, and take from them, by such a step, all cause of complaint.

If there were any persons tinctured with a republican spirit, because they thought that the representative government was more perfect in a republic, I would endeavour to amend the representation of the Commons, and to shew that the House . . . should have no other interest than to prove itself the representative of all. . . .

If there were other complaints of grievances, I would redress them where they were really proved; but above all, I would constantly, cheerfully, patiently listen. . . .

What, instead of this, is done? Suppress the complaint—check the circulation of knowledge—command that no man shall read; or, that as no man under £100 a year can kill a partridge, so no man under £20 or £30 a year shall dare to read or to think! . . .

Sir, I have done my duty, I have, with the certainty of opposing myself to the furor of the day, delivered my opinion at more length than I intended, and perhaps I have intruded too long on the indulgence of the House. [A general cry of 'Hear him!' bespoke the perfect attention of the House.] I have endeavoured to persuade you . . . to avoid involving the people in the calamity of a war, without at least ascertaining the internal state of the kingdom . . .[1]

Only 50 divided with him; 290 opposed.

Fox of course knew that he would have little support. The meetings at Burlington House, faithfully reported by Malmesbury, describe how the whigs were divided. The day before, December 12, opposition lords had met at Burlington House and had decided that the address from the throne would be allowed to pass without a division. After their meeting had broken up, and most of those present had left, Fox came, with a copy of the address, and upon learning that the Lords had decided not to push the matter to a vote next day, Fox 'with an oath,' declared 'that there was no address at this moment Pitt could frame, he would not propose an amendment to, and divide the House upon'. This, noted Malmesbury, 'was putting an end to all discussion'.

Malmesbury thought that Fox's fifty votes that December 13 included twenty-one reformers, four of Lord Lansdowne's members (Lansdowne himself felt strongly opposed to the address), and the rest people 'personally attached to Fox, and who, from this feeling, and

[1] *Parliamentary History*, xxx, 12–34. December 13.

against their sentiments, voted with him'.[1] Fox's own sentiments were expressed to Liz:

. . . the King is at the moment quite master of the country, and every effort one makes for the people of the country only renders one unpopular among them and if possible still more odious at Court, but it does not signify as long as one is satisfied that one is doing right, and I am quite sure I am completely.

Later he observed that Burke had done him great mischief, but Fox confided in Liz that he was 'not apt to hate', and that he tried to remember Burke's 'many, many good qualities'. He continued:

I told you the cry was very great against me, and so I fear it continues and will because I am for treating openly with France which Pitt is doing clandestinely. But the cry be it as loud as it will does not make me feel a tenth part of the uneasiness that I suffer and have suffered from the apprehension of separating from the D. of P. and Ld. Fitz, which I still hope will not happen, indeed I think it will not.[2]

An undated draft of a letter to Grenville further suggests Fox's reaction to the breakup of the party:

To tell you the truth every time any of you of the new party which I call the *allarmists* get together I always fear some mischievous consequences. . . .
   If this is true I am sure my life has been a very ridiculous one, and all yours not much better, but I do not want to go on with the dispute if you all think the keeping up of the party a useful & good thing. I will not quarrell with you about the inconsistency of the opinion in which I concur with those opinions in which I differ.[3]

That autumn Lady Malmesbury had written to Lady Elliot, that someone had written on a wall, 'D—n Pitt; d—n the Duke of Richmond! *no king*!' Sentiments like these alarmed her, and she frankly confessed: 'As for Fox and Grey, I wish they would utter treason at once, and be beheaded or hanged.' Sir Gilbert Elliot wrote to his wife, 'You can hardly conceive the degree of reprobation in which Fox and his party are held.'[4] The *General Evening Post* struck a reasonable pose when it declared that no sane man could believe that Fox would deliberately work against the real interests of his country. Nevertheless, it went on, many moderate men of the soundest character felt that Fox had abandoned the path of discretion in defending the French nation so eloquently and ardently; for his own reputation and for the interest and honour of Britain he should not deceive or delude himself. Sheffield deplored that Fox had 'said everything we wished him least to say, and everything his bitterest enemy could wish'.[5]

[1] *Diaries and Correspondence*, ii, 475–6.
[2] Add. MSS. 47570. [December 15, 18, 1792.] Coutts wrote, December 22: 'There has been a great deal of abuse poured forth on Mr Fox . . . but I cannot see on cool examination what it is he has done; and I believe he will be found as strenuous a supporter of the Constitution, King, Lords and Commons as any among them' (*Life of Coutts*, ii, 22).
[3] Osborn Collection, 80/26. (Yale.)   [4] Elliot, ii, 71, 85.
[5] Auckland, ii, 482. To Auckland, January 3, 1793.

Subsequently, Fox moved to recognize the French republic and to send a minister to Paris. Pitt was absent but the debate was lively. Fox was too hoarse to make a long speech but he made a forceful one. That evening and Sunday Fox's conduct was reviewed by his colleagues and the stern necessity of separating from him amicably if possible, but decidedly, was grimly discussed. Portland himself was silent: 'He seemed in a trance, and nothing could be so painful as those two hours, for our conversation lasted as long as that, reckoning intervals of ten and fifteen minutes' silence.'[1] There were other meetings, but by Christmas Portland had agreed to accept the leadership of the party— he rationalized that this move in the long run might be best for Fox, since it would hold a segment of the group together; and he was further persuaded that public opinion favoured his point of view. So Fox quickly found himself with only a remnant of support, his friends abandoning him, his eloquence ineffectual, his good name abused.

The full depths of Fox's despair are difficult to sound. His nature made him a man of party. Take party away, or even a segment, and his loss was sharp and personal. 'I cannot help loving the D. of P.,' he wrote to Liz, 'and if with him the D. of D. and Ld. F. are to go I never can have any comfort in politics again.'[2] He enjoyed the discussion of ideas, the give and take among men of united purpose as they debated how best to implement their strategies. And, more effectually than almost anyone else, he could present the fruition of this group dialogue in the urgent and tense atmosphere of St Stephen's.

Those from whom he had separated also had their moments of despair. Fox's talents combined with his qualities of heart and temperament were a serious loss. When early in 1793 the Prince of Wales wrote to Portland expressing a hope that the whigs would not only reunite but also give warmer support to administration policies, Portland firmly replied that he could not give his confidence to the administration, that the differences between him and Fox were not irreconcilable, and that Fox, moreover, was a man of complete loyalty, zeal, and integrity.[3]

Among other measures to curb the nation's restlessness was an Alien Bill, placing restrictions on foreigners in England. Introduced into the Lords, it swiftly went through all stages of legislation with little discussion and without a division.

Dundas, in Pitt's absence, had explained the Bill in the Commons on

---

[1] Malmesbury, ii, 477–8.   [2] Add. MSS. 47601. December 18.
[3] *Later Correspondence of George III*, i, 649–52. The Prince sent both letters to the King, January 24.

December 28. Fox spoke briefly, hoping that he could continue to act in harmony with those whom he esteemed and loved, but with respect to the Alien Bill he hoped he had sense enough to discern his duty and fortitude to perform it.

Burke, strongly on Pitt's side, insisted that ministers knew better than others the full danger that confronted the country, and the present ministry was worthy of trust. The present Bill would keep out of England murdering atheists who would pull down Church and State. The danger of murder and assassination was very real. Already an Englishman had ordered three thousand daggers from a firm in Birmingham, of which seventy had been delivered. It was not known how many of these were for export and how many for home consumption. At this point he drew a dagger which he had kept concealed under his coat, and threw it vehemently on the floor. 'This,' said he, pointing to the dagger, 'is what you are to gain by an alliance with France: wherever their principles are introduced, their practice must follow. You must guard against their principles; you must proscribe their persons.' He then picked up the dagger and held it up to public view, continued the parliamentary reporter; it was a weapon, he declared, that never could have been intended for fair and open war, but solely for murderous purposes.[1] So without a division the Bill passed the second reading and three days later went swiftly through the committee stage. Lord Eldon apparently got Burke's dagger ultimately, as one with a five-inch handle and foot-long blade was found among his papers.[2]

Fox made his principal contribution during the final reading on January 4. Primarily his speech is notable because he insisted that opinion and argument could not be overcome by force:

Opinions were never yet driven out of a country by pikes, and swords, and guns. Against them the militia was no defence. How, then, were they to be met if they existed? By contempt, if they were absurd; by argument, if specious; by prosecutions, if they were seditious; although that certainly was not a mode which he would recommend, but it was a mode which ministers had before resorted to, and which they still had in their power.

He regretted, in view of the increasing strength of the armies and fleets of France, that England 'had no public means of communication by which any differences that had arisen, or might arise, could be explained . . . the circumstance alone of having no public communication would in itself be a great cause of peril'. This statement can be read against a twentieth-century practice of providing not only diplomatic channels for communication but also a hot line as an ultimate means of

[1] *Parliamentary History*, xxx, 180–9.
[2] Horace Twiss, *The Public and Private Life of Lord Chancellor Eldon* (London, 1844), i, 151–2.

preventing an irreversible misunderstanding. Fox went on to hope that his utterances would not make it necessary to remind his listeners that he loved the constitution; that document, however, was not perfect, 'and if it were, it would not long continue so, unless the practice of it was carefully watched, and if that spirit of vigilance on the part of the people, which was its best security, were lulled to sleep'.

To this line of thought Pitt set himself in total disagreement. Serious and conscientious opinions ought always to be treated with deference, he asserted, but certainly not the 'wild and violent notions, assuming the name of opinions, but tending to overturn every established government' that were coming out of France. After Pitt's speech the Bill passed without a division and became law.[1] Later Pitt wrote to the King that not more than ten or twelve persons would have voted with Fox.[2]

Under date of January 26, 1793, Fox addressed a letter to his Westminster constituents in which he reviewed the position he had taken during the session. Ten days before, by a vote of 361 to 360, the National Convention had voted death to Louis XVI; five days before, on January 21, it had executed him. Two days before, on January 24, Fox had observed his forty-fourth birthday. Never before had he shown much interest in the public reception of his parliamentary utterances; he had never revised a speech for the newspapers, professing not to care whether he was quoted accurately, inaccurately, or at all; he must have felt that even if his name were reviled truth would in the end prevail. That he now reversed the practice of a lifetime to make a specific appeal to his constituents showed how keenly he felt public criticism of his position. That this appeal should be made in writing—for him a difficult mode of self-expression—is one more unusual fact about this unusual letter.

Many observations could be made about the pamphlet, which in large part reviewed his December speeches. He charged the Government with exaggerating the restlessness of the country as an argument for imposing severe restrictions of speech and assembly. 'To these systems of crooked policy and pious fraud I have always entertained a kind of instinctive and invincible repugnance.' Moreover, he urged that if the Government felt the nation aggrieved by actions of the National Convention, rather than rattle the sabre it should ask redress or demand explanation or disavowal. To this end, Fox reminded his constituents

---

[1] *Parliamentary History*, xxx, 194–238. Fox's speech also appears in *The speech of the right hon. Charles James Fox . . . on the Alien Bill* (London, 1793).
[2] *Later Correspondence of George III*, i, 640. January 5.

that he had recommended sending an authorized minister to France. As for the objection speedily raised that the sending of a minister would pay some compliment or imply some approbation of the French Government, he reminded objectors of the ample precedent for the proposal to send a minister to a nation whose policies were disapproved (we have sent a minister to the piratical republic of Algiers, others to emperors of Morocco who had waded to their thrones through the blood of their murdered relatives). He was a man of peace and he thought his position would best preserve peace in a tense world situation.[1]

The pamphlet was widely read. Sixteen printings quickly sold out. The printer happily informed newspapers that ten thousand copies were swallowed up in a few days, and that his press could not begin to cope with the demand. Pamphlets of Fox's speeches were more numerous than were those of any contemporary, but the *Letter* enjoyed an even greater circulation than any of his speeches. A copy of the fourteenth printing found its way into the library of George Washington.

On February 1 the National Convention, successor to the Legislative Assembly, successor to the National Assembly and the Estates-General, having abolished the monarchy and executed Louis Capet, declared war on Great Britain, Holland, and Spain. On one side of the channel, the Reign of Terror lay just ahead; on the other, repressive measures against revolutionary agitation, trials for high treason, and increasing preparation for war, with Fox a lonely, eloquent figure, defending political rights and pleading for peace. How far he was from the solid, respectable, conservative thought of that year is reflected in a judgment of its most eminent and distinguished historian. Edward Gibbon had dipped his pen in his inkwell that New Year's Day and had written: '[Fox's] inmost soul was deeply tinged with Democracy. Such wild opinions cannot easily be reconciled with his excellent understanding, but tis true tis pity, and pity tis, tis true.'[2]

---

[1] *A letter from the Right Honourable Charles James Fox, to the worthy and independent electors of the city and liberty of Westminster* (London, 1793). For a brief note on its reception, see Parr, i, 62.
[2] *Letters of Gibbon,* iii, 308. To Sheffield.

21

War with France
1793-1794

> The love of liberty is not necessarily connected with a
> thirst for blood.
>
> *Charles James Fox*

Pitt's hoped-for fifteen years of peace turned out to be only the single year of 1792. Rising in the Commons on February 1, 1793, and noting that the execution of the King and other violent actions in Paris called to mind the horrible scenes of the massacre of St Bartholomew, Pitt declared that the armed forces must be increased. Fox, gathering that 'war was not absolutely determined on', retorted that no case had been made for such aggressive preparation. He shared the general horror of the execution of Louis XVI; neither propriety nor wisdom, however, warranted one nation's passing judgment upon the internal actions of another. 'The people are the sovereigns in all countries . . . they might amend, alter, and abolish the form of government under which they live at pleasure.'[1]

Though the ultimate result was a declaration of war, first by the French Government and then by the English, on February 18 Fox offered five resolutions in opposition to the administration's move. He wanted the House to declare that war should not be begun to suppress or punish the French form of government. Nor did complaints now being lodged against the French Government provide a sufficient basis for war; they should be negotiated. A full House stayed for the division although only 44 voted with Fox and 270 against him. Years later the story was told that Pitt and Dundas appeared in the House obviously the worse for the liquor they had consumed; their dialogue was set to verse:

> I cannot see the Speaker, Hal, can you?
> What! Cannot see the Speaker, I see two.[2]

Contemplating Fox's slender group of forty-four, Storer wrote to Auckland: 'Mr Fox is almost deserted. He may come into Administration now without being embarrassed to make room for his followers.

---

[1] *Two speeches of the Right Honourable C. J. Fox*, etc. (London,1793); *Parliamentary History*, xxx, 301–14.
[2] Rose, *The Life of William Pitt*, i, 279.

The door has not to be opened very wide to let in his whole suite. . . . Opposition is splintered into a thousand pieces.'[1] In Naples a British emissary, who later gained attention as the husband of Nelson's Lady Hamilton, had heard of Fox's part in the debates and neatly capsuled the position of the English orator: 'Poor Fox seems nearly to stand alone.'[2] What Fox had done those opening months of 1793 was to take a strong stand, as he had done before and would do again, for peace. War should be declared only as a last resort, after grievances had been fully stated and negotiations had failed. As he had been branded an American for attempting, a dozen years ago, to end that war, now he was to be called a Frenchman because of his wish to bring hostilities to a conclusion. Although those who cry 'peace' when the nation is at war are seldom popular at the time, Fox's speeches meant later that his name became associated not only with civil, religious, and political liberty but also with the always complex, ever elusive issue of peace.

The Traitorous Correspondence Bill, a proposal to prevent commerce with, and aid and assistance to the enemy, brought Fox to his feet many times to protest it as an attack upon fundamental liberties of Englishmen. He had 'never seen a bill so unfounded in policy . . . so contrived . . . to violate every principle of justice, humanity, and the constitution. . . . The bill was much better calculated for entrapping individuals, than for guarding them against the perils of high treason.'[3] Partly because these notions gained some headway and partly because Government attendance slipped, the Bill passed by a single vote, 154 to 153. The Lords speedily approved it, however, 62 to 7.

Fox's motion in June to re-establish peace with France received only 47 supporters, 187 dissenting. A few days later Parliament was prorogued for the rest of the year. Fox wrote to Holland that he found only small comfort in seeing that 'while the French are doing all in their power to make the name of liberty odious to the world, the despots are conducting themselves so as to show that tyranny is worse'. He went on:

I believe the love of political liberty is *not* an errour, but if it is one, I am sure I never shall be converted from it, and I hope you never will. If it be an illusion it is one that has brought forth more of the best qualities and exertions of the human mind than all other causes put together.[4]

---

[1] Auckland, ii, 497–9. February 19.
[2] *Sir William Hamilton Autograph Letters to Charles Greville.* March 12, 1793. (Huntington.)
[3] *Parliamentary History*, xxx, 634.   [4] Add. MSS. 47571. *Fox Cor.*, iii, 40. June 14.

To Fox, liberty was still paramount, even despite French excesses.

The notorious trials in Scotland late that summer of Thomas Muir for sedition and of the Reverend Thomas Fysche Palmer, Unitarian minister, for seditious practices, aroused Fox profoundly. The court decided Muir was much too dangerous to be allowed to remain in the country; his writings were inflammatory, 'very near to treason'. He was therefore sentenced to be transported overseas for fourteen years, a period that would give him time to repent so that later he would have an opportunity 'to live under the constitution which he seemed to despise so much'. Palmer was transported for seven years.[1] Fox wrote: 'The very name of Liberty is scarce popular.' Those who defended liberty were labelled enemies of the public. As he put it:

We live in times of violence and of extremes, and all those who are for creating or even for retaining checks upon power are considered as enemies to order. However, one must do one's duty, and one must endeavour to do it without passion. . . . Good God! that a man should be sent to Botany Bay for advising another to read Paine's book![2]

Both Houses of Parliament reviewed the severe sentences of the Scottish courts the following year. Palmer's petition for relief was flatly opposed by Pitt, over objections by Fox and Sheridan. The London Corresponding Society cordially proposed a toast to Citizens Muir and Palmer: 'May their sentence be speedily reversed, and *Botany-bay* peopled with a colony of *real* criminals.'[3]

In France, the Reign of Terror. Fox wrote his nephew, 'the horrours there grow every day worse'. Parliament opened on January 21, 1794, after its long recess. The King's speech commented on the favourable progress of the war and requested from the Commons such further provision as the exigencies of the time required. Fox argued that in the eyes of the Government the conflict had now become a war against the French system; again he insisted that the internal concerns of one nation, repugnant though they might be in this instance, were not properly the affair of another; and he moved an amendment that the Government should take the earliest means of concluding peace, on such terms as may be reasonable and prudent.[4] The vote was 277 to 59 against his amendment.

[1] *State Trials*, xxiii, 117–382.
[2] Add. MSS. 47571. *Fox Cor.*, iii, 51, 61–2. To Holland, September 17, December, after Christmas.
[3] *State Trials*, xxiv, 446.   [4] *Parliamentary History*, xxx, 1251–77.

By now the separation of the whig party into two factions was complete. Fox wrote Holland that Portland, Fitzwilliam, and Thomas Grenville had all come to him before Parliament opened, and, although they had assured him of their personal esteem, they felt they should support the administration: 'in short to declare formally the separation, or rather the dissolution, of the Whig party.'

You can easily imagine [Fox wrote to Holland] how much I felt the separation from persons with whom I had so long been in the habit of agreeing . . . there remains nothing but to get together the remains of our party, and begin, like Sisyphus, to roll up the stone again, which long before it reaches the summit, may probably roll down again.

Despite Pitt's great majorities, Fox was sure the House felt restless about the war: 'Every thing we say against it is heard with great attention.' In a later letter he reiterated that 'arguments against the war and our alliances are heard favourably . . . though they do not get us a vote; but sentiments of liberty and complaints of oppression are very little attended to, however well founded. In short liberty is not popular.' And at the end: 'Though weak, we are right, and that must be our comfort.'[1] Fox, who loved popularity as much as any living mortal, these days had less of it. And if he could have read the Government's mail, he would have learned further that the King still considered Fox malevolent and his speeches ungrounded and mischievous.[2]

From these pages the reader may have gathered the impression that Fox spent the bulk of his time in St Stephen's, debating one complex issue after another, and therefore had little social life. That impression is easy to create, partly because materials on Fox's political life are more plentiful than are those on his social activities, partly because the purpose of these chapters focuses on Fox's career as a speaker.

Entirely aside, however, from his political gifts, Fox was an extremely social and sociable individual. The aristocratic circles that he frequented had the means and the leisure to entertain frequently and extravagantly. Fox was almost as much at home at Devonshire House, Carlton House, Bedford House, Burlington House, as at St Anne's Hill. Like other members of Parliament, he frequently attended dinners and receptions held by the Prime Minister, the Speaker, and other greater and lesser officials of government. Countless small dinner parties gathered together those of congenial temperament. As Fox was a good listener as well as a good talker, as he had the graces of kindliness, thoughtfulness, and even temper, as he was widely-read and well-informed, he was a popular guest.

[1] Add. MSS. 47571. *Fox Cor.*, iii, 64–71. March 9, 18, 1794.
[2] *Later Correspondence of George III*, ii, 183. To Pitt, March 6.

During that April, 1794, Fox was one of a small group invited to dinner at the home of a political friend, Sir Francis Burdett, later to become famous, even notorious, for his radical ideas. Present also was the Reverend W. B. Stevens, chaplain to the Burdett family, who was so delighted by the range of the evening's conversation that he set it down in his diary as well as he could recall it. Fox was easily persuaded to talk at length, and the Stevens diary records fragments of the conversation:

Fox. Writing was a very agreable Employment to those in the habit of it to others nothing so irksome.
Wycombe. Nothing makes Time appear so short.
Fox. I think the reverse my Lord (with a smile) I know nothing that can make Time appear so long!
Adam. How feelingly he speaks!

The topic turned to religious freedom:

Wycombe. The speech of Mr Fox from which he had deriv'd the greatest pleasure was that on the Test Act.
Adam. Mr Fox is indeed an equally able advocate for Religious and Civil Liberty.

The guest of honour had much to say about current politics:

Fox. He was more and more convinced every day that the resources of this country were beyond calculation. The war he thought wd last as long as it could & as we were very able it would last a long time. The Emperors resources would be first exhausted but he would lay any wager that the war would last 2 years by which time perhaps the nation would be heartily sick of it. Another year's campaign he thought would bring around many of his old allies. Lord Fitzwilliam he said had been the Ringleader of the Alarmists. . . . The Speeches he was told were worse detail'd in the papers this year than ever. No man's speech he said would bear printing as it fell from his Lips.[1]

This last sentence, of course, echoed one of Fox's famous beliefs about speechmaking. With an orator in their midst, those present could not resist the temptation to ask him about the usefulness of oratory; his defence of the art appears two chapters hence.

The Burdett dinner was an occasion that brought Fox out to the fullest. Fox was also a member of Dr Johnson's club, where he was not nearly so talkative. Especially during these trying days with 'Windham and Burke, and . . . the whole nation, being on one side, and Fox and his little phalanx on the other', members of the club kept as clear of politics as possible.[2]

Actually, Fox's social life these days was undergoing marked

[1] HM 26405, W. B. Stevens Diary. April 18. (Huntington.) I am indebted to J. Steven Watson for calling my attention to this source.
[2] George Birkbeck Hill, ed., *Johnsonian Miscellanies* (Oxford, 1897), ii, 25, citing *HMCR*, 13th Rep., App. viii, 239.

change. Gradually drifting away from some of his old haunts, he had pitched his personal life as well as his political notions on a higher plane. Holland put the middle of 1793 as the time when, for example, Fox stopped going to Newmarket.[1]

On May 16 the Government laid before the House the first report of its committee of secrecy respecting seditious practices. The papers accompanying the report consisted of letters from and between the Society for Constitutional Information and the London Corresponding Society, already mentioned, with strongly worded statements about reform, universal suffrage, and annual parliaments. Members addressed one another as 'citizen' and carried on correspondence with a score or more branch societies throughout the kingdom. They deplored the exiling of individuals for utterances supposed to be seditious; they passed resolutions of praise for those who had been convicted and for the attorneys who had defended them. Their proceedings were at times printed and distributed, on one occasion at least to the number of 200,000 copies.

Pitt argued that to control this flow of publications the right of habeas corpus should be suspended. The resolutions of these societies, he declared, threatened the sovereign, insulted the Lords, accused the Commons. Even Burke said that although the administration's proposed measure was severe, it was salutary: 'It was withholding, for a short time, the liberty of the country to preserve it for ever.' Fox's speech, though brief, was forceful. Sometimes lacking common, ordinary, good sense, on this occasion he abounded in it. Much of what the secret committee reported, he declared, had been widely published in the newspapers. In a pompous, public, formal, manner, the committee presumed to inform the house in detail about matters that had already passed before it, day after day. What was worse, from these stale facts the committee had arrived at unwarranted inferences. The committee saw seditious opposition to the power of government rather than simply a desire to seek redress of grievances. Certainly the constitution 'had too many admirers, too many defenders' to listen to any group of men that sought to overturn it. The mischief that would follow the suspension of habeas corpus would be infinitely greater than the mischief that the bill proposed to remedy. This measure was being brought forward as the result of a fancied terror, a groundless alarm, a supposed expediency, and it was being brought forward with such haste, with such precipitation, that many members would be deprived of the privilege of debating it.

[1] *Memoirs of the Whig Party*, i, 65–6.

Fox's anguished cry went unheeded. In a series of eleven divisions, all taken before 3.30 in the morning, the administration put the Bill through various legislative stages. The vote of the opposition, 39 at first, gradually dwindled to 13; the Government's 201 votes shrank to 108. So weak was opposition that nearly half of Pitt's troops could go home.[1] Twenty-four hours later the Commons passed the Bill. On May 22 the Lords passed it even more expeditiously. The 'allarmists', as Fox called them, were in full control. Thus easily was the ancient right of habeas corpus suspended.

The *Oracle* thought it well to remind its readers of the dubious character of the man who fought the suspension. It was this Mr Fox who had laid the basis 'of all defalcation of principle and moral tergiversation' when he had entered into a coalition with Lord North. The coalition was then a full decade in the past, and North had been in his grave nearly two years.

Fox turned immediately from the debates on suspending habeas corpus to the final stages of the Hastings trial. Nearly seven years had elapsed since Hastings, before a huge throng in Westminster Hall, had heard the weighty and wordy charges against him. Attendance had dwindled after the opening series of orations by Burke, Sheridan, and Fox; the trial had dragged slowly on, interrupted by long recesses, Burke now and then reporting to the House on its progress. Interest revived, however, as the trial drew near the close. Fox, on May 20, began summing up the Benares charge. Before a large audience he spoke three hours, then, pleading weakness and indisposition, requested to be heard another day. On May 21 he spoke nearly four hours. Burke had the last word, or nearly the last word, in a 'warm, eloquent, and beautiful appeal to the High Court'.[2] Hastings was acquitted, however, and the long trial was over. Shortly the word was spread that Burke, at sixty-four an old man, would retire from public life and vacate his seat for Malton.

The session closed July 11. On the same day Portland was appointed third Secretary of State and Fitzwilliam became Lord President. Other appointments were announced along with fresh elevations to the peerage. Thomas Grenville. Fox's plenipotentiary in Paris during American treaty discussions and one of his long-time adherents, now became a supporter of the Government. Burke was to be created Lord Beaconsfield, but about that time his only son, Richard, died. Burke thereupon declined the peerage but accepted a pension to help meet his debts.

[1] *Parliamentary History*, xxxi, 523–5.   [2] *Morning Chronicle*, June 17.

Fox's feelings as he heard of continued favours bestowed on his former colleagues can easily be imagined. He was especially saddened to learn of Fitzwilliam's entering the Government. In July Fox wrote that he was anxious to see him. 'I know I shall hear nothing pleasant, but my affection for you is such, indeed it is, that I can not bear to hear what you are about from general report only.' He continued:

. . . nothing ever can make me forget a friendship as old as my life and the man in the world to whom I feel myself in every view the most obliged, and I should like to know from the best authority, tho' I know beforehand that I shall not approve, the reasons which have led you all to the present measure.[1]

Fitzwilliam's defection hurt him deeply: 'Since I was a child Fitzwilliam has been, in all situations, my warmest and most affectionate friend, and the person in the world of whom decidedly I have the best opinion.'

I think they have all behaved very ill to me, and for most of them, who certainly owe much more to me, than I do them, I feel nothing but contempt, and do not trouble myself about them; but Fitzwilliam is an exception indeed.

Still, 'I do not think we shall be much weaker as an opposition,' yet he confesses he is quite sick of politics and keeps on only because it is his duty. In another letter written three days later, referring to himself, Fox quoted Cowper: 'How various his employments whom the world/ Calls idle.' He wrote at length about the party system, the best, if not the only way, 'for supporting the cause of liberty in this country'. The party system alone, he averred, prevented Britain from falling into 'what Hume calls . . . the Euthanasia of absolute monarchy'; it is therefore, 'my duty, and that of those who think like me, to use the utmost endeavours to preserve together what little remains of this system, or to revive it if it is supposed to be quite extinct'.

The letter showed courage and persistence, coming as it did at the bottom of his political fortunes. For Holland he reviewed the basis of such a revival of his party: Coke, the Duke of Bedford, Guilford, and Derby, 'and some others, with myself'; undoubtedly a weak start, 'but then how glorious it would be from such small beginnings to grow into a real strong party, such as we once were'. All this at the age of forty-five, after ten years of opposing seemingly impregnable power.

Those who belong to a party are less likely to be influenced by improper motives than are the independents, he declared, since one who is member of a party has fewer occasions for new decisions and therefore fewer occasions exist upon which he can be corrupted. Fox's enthusiasm waxed as he proceeded:

[1] Fitzwilliam MSS., F115. July, 1794. (Sheffield.)

In short, it appears to me that a party spirit is the only substitute that has been found, or can be found, for public virtue and comprehensive understanding. . . .

Whatever teaches man to depend upon one another, and to feel the necessity of conciliating the good opinion of those with whom they live, is surely of the highest advantage to the morals and happiness of mankind; and what does this so much as party ? . . . Ought we to abandon a system from which so much good has been derived, because some men have acted inconsistently, or because, from the circumstances of the moment, we are not likely to act with much effect ?[1]

Thus Fox was strong for the notion of party even when his own was at its weakest point.

Nor did those on the other side of the ocean react with distinguished and judicial calm to events in France. In the United States as in the mother country, news was managed, freedom of inquiry discouraged. In 1794 Washington wished to prevent discussion of the newly signed Jay treaty—the sequel to problems left unsettled in 1783—but despite this specific request the *Aurora* published the text, and terms of the agreement were soon known everywhere. When in 1797 John Adams succeeded to the presidency, his administration was so belaboured by the French that the Federal Government enacted repressive measures: the Alien Act, the Alien Enemies Act, the Sedition Act. So President Adams and a large segment of the American people 'no longer tolerated the wearing of the French revolutionary cockade, which had before been so popular, and any American editor who should have printed an opinion or a piece of news taken openly and clearly from a French source would have suffered'.[2] Those who championed almost any freedom were, at this time, suspect and alone.

So although Fox's close friends had gone over to the Government, he continued in opposition. When the observation was made that the entire Opposition could fill a single hackney coach, a former member for Middlesex retorted: 'This is a calumny. We should have filled *two*.'[3] Fox's persistence and optimism command admiration. Even at the close of 1794 he wrote to his nephew that the parliamentary situation might improve. Although at the moment of writing he could not name any new accessions to his party in the House of Commons, 'in the House of Lords we have hopes of Thurlow and the Duke of Leeds, and some talk of the Duke of Richmond. . . . The circumstances of the times must bring these, and many more soon.'[4]

[1] Add. MSS. 47571. *Fox Cor.*, iii, 79. August 18, 21, October 5.
[2] Bernard Faÿ, *Notes on the American Press at the End of the Eighteenth Century* (New York, 1927), pp. 17, 24.
[3] John C. Campbell, *Lives of the Lord Chancellors* (London, 1846), v, 614.
[4] Add. MSS. 47571. *Fox Cor.*, iii, 98. December 25, 1794.

But the circumstances of the times were against him. The war had gone badly. In the early part of 1793 the allied armies, later to become Pitt's first coalition, had driven the French out of the Netherlands and had put such steady pressure on French frontiers elsewhere that the British Cabinet thought the war must soon be concluded. The French conscripted every available man, however, and forced the enemy back from its borders. An English force under Admiral Hood established at Toulon was shattered; the English hastily retired with as many refugees as possible but others were left behind to suffer the vengeance of the French armies. By 1795 French troops had swarmed over the Low Countries. In Haiti, half a million slaves under Toussaint L'Ouverture, made famous in the United States by the brilliant eulogy of Wendell Phillips, had expelled 40,000 settlers. On the whole it was a poor season for oratory about freedom of discussion; and criticisms of the Government and appeals for peace commanded even less support than did these themes during the American Revolution.

22

For Freedom of Speech
1794-1795

When the power of speaking is taken away, what is left
but . . . implicit submission?

Charles James Fox

During the parliamentary session that opened on December 30, 1794,
and its successor, Fox continued to speak frequently for the freedom
and the dignity of the individual.

His party was still split; some of his closest friends still sat across the
chamber. Hence in his greatest speeches during these years he would
be followed into the lobby, not by a hundred or more as in the better
days, but by numbers in the forties or fifties. Even so, he continued on
the line he marked out for himself. His nineteenth-century reputation,
not too surprisingly, was enhanced not only because of his ideas but
also because of his persistence against enormous odds.

The forcible overturning of the French monarchy, the succession of
despotic governments with their mass drownings and guillotinings,
the impassioned French oratory, the violation of long-established
property rights, the sour odour of republicanism, alarmed the British
Government. In France men indeed seemed to be acting like flies in the
summertime, cutting themselves off from the past, making little provision for the future. In England the anxiety was ever present that
mass meetings if allowed would get out of hand with frightening
consequences. Memories of the Gordon riots of 1780 had been
freshened by the Paris riots of 1789. Simple, elemental prudence seemed
to dictate that meetings should be placed under stout governmental
surveillance. Seditious writings should also be made subject to severe
legislation, in order to intimidate and shackle authors. Fox vigorously
opposed all manoeuvres of this sort.

The King's address opening the session on December 30 mentioned
disappointments in the war with France but called for firmness and
perseverance. Military reverses encouraged a slight increase of peace
sentiment in the Commons. Fox urged the House not to delay to an
extremity that left no room for choice; the country 'was already sorely
beaten; it had received wounds both deep and wide, but the obstinacy

of ministers was not yet conquered'. Insufficient forces had been sent to the West Indies; the force at Toulon 'was too small for defence, and too great to retreat with honour'; the projected invasion of France 'served only to weaken our strength in quarters where it ought to have been more powerful, without even an attempt to carry it into execution'.[1] In January even though Sheridan made an eloquent plea for the repeal of the habeas corpus suspension Act, suspension was renewed by substantial votes in both Houses.

Troubles also broke out in Ireland over the issue of Catholic emancipation. Fitzwilliam, who had broken with Fox to join the Pitt Government, had been sent to Ireland as Lord Lieutenant with instructions not to agitate the Catholic question. Upon arriving, however, he took steps that embarrassed the Government: he dismissed two officers and he lent his encouragement to the bringing in of a Bill to improve the Catholic lot. Unanimously the Cabinet, including his old friend Portland, voted to recall him. Fox wrote Holland that at first he did not believe that the Government had disavowed Fitzwilliam, but rumours nevertheless proved true: 'He is to come home immediately, and states himself publicly to have been betrayed and deserted not only by Pitt, but by the Duke of Portland.'[2] As for Catholic relief, Fox thought it little short of madness to dispute over the few concessions that were proposed.[3]

In March a ten-year-old boy, Harry, out riding in Hyde Park, saw the famous Mr Fox for the first time. 'I never saw a man so fat in all my life.'[4] The boy grew up to become the third Viscount Palmerston, twice Prime Minister of Britain. On March 24 the portly Mr Fox offered a motion that the House consider, in committee, the state of the nation. The House was not truly, nor even virtually, the representative of the people, for it did not take upon itself 'the guardianship of their rights, nor show the smallest alacrity in the superintendance of their interests'.

Fox thus combined his wish to inquire into the state of the nation with his growing conviction that the House of Commons must be reformed. The speech was, however, a state-of-the-nation speech and not a reform speech. He bolstered his request for an inquiry by listing

[1] *Parliamentary History*, xxxi, 1046–61.
[2] From Halifax came a letter commending Fox's stand on Lord Fitzwilliam: 'I have been very angry with Fox . . . ,' said this correspondent from the New World, 'and had taken down a little portrait you gave me of him because I conceived him a Democrat—but his fair opinions of Lord Fitzwilliam . . . restored him to my . . . respect . . . and his little picture is replaced in my dressing room (Ch. Wentworth to Wentworth Fitzwilliam, July 18, 1796. Fitzwilliam MSS. (Milton) 50. Northamptonshire Record Office).
[3] Add. MSS. 47572. *Fox Cor.*, iii, 99–101. March 6.
[4] Brian Connell, *Portrait of a Whig Peer* (London, 1957), p. 322.

questions to which he sought answers. How many British troops had been lost in the war? and how many other troops in the pay of Britain? How have the revenues been spent? and by what resources would the war continue to be supported? What is the state of Britain's trade and commerce? How well has the Admiralty protected British merchant ships?

For nearly four hours he probed the various phases of the war. He passed in review events in Prussia, Austria, Italy, Spain. He discussed Switzerland, Genoa, France herself. He condemned the ministry for not clearly stating its war aims. He reviewed the evacuation of Toulon and the loss of Holland. He had much to say about the injustices done to the Catholic population of Ireland, declaring that at the moment she was not only in a state of irritation but in a state of danger.

Fox also touched on the great intangible, the importance of morality in foreign policy:

> The common proverb, of honesty being the best policy, is as applicable to nations as to individuals. . . . If, therefore, we have been deficient in justice towards other states, we have been deficient in wisdom. . . . Justice is fairly to be ranked among the number of our resources; and it is the duty of the House to inquire whether or not our conduct since the commencement of the war has been such as to entitle us to the good opinion of the wise and observing part of mankind.

Fox realized that members would argue that the principal reason for an inquiry was the removal of the present ministers. He did not deny having this ultimate purpose in mind but he nevertheless insisted that the inquiry should come first. If it should turn out that ministers had acted wisely, the House could continue to give its confidence; if the contrary, then they should be called to account.

> This inquiry [he continued] . . . will discover to the nation the true causes of all our late failures and calamities. . . . If the House should agree to go into the inquiry, they will prove that they are really affected by the interests of their constituents. If they should resolve to go on without knowing who are our allies, or whether we have any, there will be too much reason for saying that our constitution is gone.[1]

Pitt's reply, one of his least effective, especially as regarded the state of Britain's allies, ended in his moving that the House adjourn, 219 supporting him and 63 Fox's position; a majority for the Government of 156.

Unquestionably this effort was one of the outstanding speeches of Fox's career; it falls if not in his first five then in his second. Even the *Sun* praised it: 'Mr Fox certainly made a very brilliant speech on

---

[1] *Parliamentary History*, xxxi, 1345–1413. The speech was widely circulated in pamphlet form: *Speech of the Right Hon. Charles James Fox, in the House of Commons, on Tuesday, March 24, 1795*, etc. 2nd edn (London, 1795).

Tuesday evening'—although modified by a disclaimer: 'Yet it contained nothing new, except about Ireland . . . a topic which is clearly not ripe for public discussion.' Said the *Morning Post*: 'If Ministers are not afraid of exposure . . . why refuse to enquire into the State of the Nation ? . . . it is what the People require', and if not granted, 'after the unanswerable and invincible arguments of Mr Fox,' the opinion of Parliament will be lowered in the eyes of the people. It observed that during Fox's eloquent and comprehensive speech, confusion, apprehension, and dismay were alternately reflected in Pitt's countenance, and that in his reply, his usual arrogance and assurance forsook him and he was incapable of answering a single argument. Canning, it reported, tugged at Pitt's sleeve as a gentle hint to get him to stop speaking: 'Administration was sufficiently exposed without his assistance.'

Fox therefore gave his friends among the newspapers an opportunity to renew their support. The *Morning Chronicle* criticized Pitt's arguments:

The Minister . . . has a *swivel* argument, relative to the war. When we are successful, it is glorious to go on; when we are not so, it is disgraceful to stop. He now has another swivel argument, as to Ireland; when Mr Fox talked of that country, last session, his enquiries were improper, because all was *well*; on Tuesday night they were equally so, because all was *wrong*.

In a subsequent issue, after having canvassed the opinions of various listeners, it set forth its own conclusion about Fox's speech: 'For extent of knowledge, accuracy of information, clearness of arrangement, force of argument, perspicuity of illustrations, and energy of delivery, it seemed almost to exceed every former effort of his own transcendent eloquence.' Each new topic he opened up, it reported, reached a higher level of impressiveness, and thus for three hours and three-quarters 'attention hung unwearied on his lips'. When Pitt rose to answer him the contrast was so striking that 'before he had spoken half an hour both the House and the Gallery were three parts empty'.

Holland wrote nearly two months later from Florence: 'Your speech on the state of the nation has made a great sensation here and is admired as much as it ought to be.'[1] In his reply Fox made one of his rare observations on his own speaking:

I believe I did speak very well . . . and yet I am very much surprised it should have been so; for my mind had been for some time in a state of great uneasiness, and I never felt less inclined to speak in my life; however, all my friends flattered me about it, and even as it is taken down in the newspapers you seem satisfied with it: how it so happened is one of those paradoxes about the human mind which I am sure I cannot explain.[2]

[1] Add. MSS. 47572. May 12. [2] *Ibid.*, 47572. *Fox Cor.*, iii, 107–8. May 17.

Even so he felt sure that scarcely twenty members could be found in the House who did not favour peace.

Another letter had a sad note; Fox felt himself losing interest in public affairs. The Bills of this year, he wrote, 'appear to me to be a finishing stroke to everything like a spirit of liberty.' He pondered the wisdom of seceding altogether. He was recalling, of course, the futile days during the American war when a segment of the Rockingham whigs did stop attending Parliament. Although he decided not actually to secede, the wish persisted:

I am perfectly happy in the country. I have quite resources enough to employ my mind; and the great resource of all, literature, I am fonder of every day; and then the Lady of the Hill is one continual source of happiness to me. I believe few men, indeed, ever were so happy in that respect as I.[1]

The question of Fitzwilliam's recall came before Parliament in May. After long debate, the Lords voted 100 to 25 not to inquire into the recall; the Commons nevertheless went ahead with its discussion. Fox warmly supported his old friend and former comrade in politics, stressing Fitzwilliam's popularity with the people he had been sent to govern. Then followed some useful observations about law and about religious toleration:

It was essential to the welfare of a country that the common people should have a veneration for its laws. This was by no means the case in Ireland; and why? Because the law was there regarded as an instrument of oppression . . . made upon a principle of pitiful monopoly, and not for the general protection, welfare, and happiness of the people. . . .

[This principle] was also applicable to religion. . . . All men should be estimated in society, by their morals, and not by the mode of religious worship. To root out prejudices altogether was not a thing to be accomplished at once; but it was a thing to be attempted, and every step towards it would be an advantage to the country.

Pitt's reply ignored Fox's speech but went to another issue: that resignations were not invariably followed by inquiries, and that no good could result from the agitation of this particular, delicate, subject. He thought, in fact, that the motion should not be entertained at all, and moved the order of the day, which was carried 188 to 42.[2]

In a letter to his nephew the following month Fox commented that Pitt 'does not know what the feelings of honour are. He has no natural instinct upon the subject, and it is a part of his education which seems to have been omitted.'[3] Two days later he commented on another old enemy, Shelburne, now Lansdowne; still distrusting Lansdowne's

---

[1] Add. MSS. 47572. *Fox Cor.*, iii, 105–6. April 12.
[2] *Parliamentary History*, xxxi, 1537–58.   [3] Add. MSS. 47572. June 14.

sincerity, Fox affirmed: 'I never can have a good opinion of him, and still less a great one.' He had, however, dined with him once, and might even do so oftener next year. Lansdowne's conduct the last three years 'has had an openness and consistency' that at least entitled him to outward marks of respect; moreover, the two had agreed that if one were approached by the court, he would communicate and consult with the other.[1] Thus an understanding, cool and civil though it was, arose between them. The old wounds of the mid-eighties and earlier seemed in the process of being healed in the mid-nineties.

That autumn Fox and Mrs Armistead were married. Why they had delayed more than ten years before going through a formal ceremony is a mystery that still puzzles biographers. John Drinkwater suggested that the existence and demise of a possible Mr Armistead might be the solution.[2] Letters in the Fox correspondence suggest entirely plausible reasons why they had delayed their marriage and why they should no longer do so. In a letter of September 25, 1795, Fox argued the pros and cons. 'By following our plan', he insisted, 'we are doing for the best. In case of anything happening to me, I am sure your having been my legal wife will make your situation less uncomfortable.' She had feared that if he married her his affection for her might diminish, but he declared he 'would never, never repent of being married to her and wishing himself free'. He reassured her that the secret could be kept but even if it got out there would be no great harm ('indeed after the first talk it would be pleasanter that it should be known than not'), and the worse that could happen would be a few additional paragraphs in the newspapers.[3] He was able to overcome her scruples, for on

[1] *Ibid.*, 47572. *Fox Cor.*, iii, 112–13. June 16.

[2] *Charles James Fox*, p. 279. This volume has perhaps the most detailed account available of circumstances attending the wedding ceremony. Little is known of descendants of Charles Fox. Drinkwater cites the Reverend Edward V. R. Powys, Fox's great-grandnephew, who recalled two old ladies who were daughters of Charles and Elizabeth Fox, but the direct line has not survived (p. 287). Samuel Rogers in his *Table Talk* (New York, 1856) mentions a natural son of Fox, a dumb boy, 'the very image of his father', who died at the age of fifteen. 'To him Fox almost entirely confined his attention, conversing with him by the fingers: and their eyes glistened as they looked at each other. Talleyrand remarked to me, "how strange it was, to dine in company with the first orator in Europe, and only see him *talk with his fingers!*"' (pp. 80–1).

[3] Add. MSS. 47570. This correspondence contains no reference to a Mr Armistead. Years later Mrs Armistead, announcing her marriage to Fox, stated that Fox himself did not want to announce it previously because of some situation; that situation no longer existing, she continued, Fox was willing to make the announcement (see below, p. 382).

Presumably at the request of Lord John Russell, then working on *Life and Times of Charles James Fox*, a Mr Beadham journeyed fourteen miles to get local information about the Fox marriage. He asked for a copy of the *Life and Times* in return for his efforts if the author thought they were worth it (Add. MSS. 47601). See also *Notes and Queries*, 4th ser., x (October 26, 1872), 330.

September 28, in the parish of Wyton in Huntingdonshire, they were married by the rector, J. Pery, friend of the groom's. The marriage, however, was not announced until they made a trip abroad together in 1802.[1]

Domestic disturbances plagued the kingdom, treason trials or no. The Corresponding Society's public meeting in June was attended by many thousands. Annual parliaments and universal suffrage were demanded, the high cost of living was deplored, peace was sought. In France the Constitution of 1795 was proclaimed in August, its executive power vested in a directory of five. When Parisians rose in revolt, one of the new directors exclaimed: 'I have the very man we want, a little Corsican officer whom I knew at Toulon.' General Bonaparte was thus put in charge of troops, fired a whiff of grapeshot that was heard round the world, quieted the rioters, and put the Directory in business.

Fox continued to feel earnestly that rights of Englishmen were being severely curtailed. In the summer when General Doyle was sent to France with 4,000 British troops, plus emigrants, Fox reacted so bitterly that the editors of his published letters omitted this one:

Violent as the wish may sound, I would much rather hear they were all cut to pieces than that they gained any considerable success for in the latter case the war may be prolonged to the utter destruction of both countries and to the total extinction of all principles of Liberty and Humanity in Europe.

This desperate expedition, he continued, 'has not the smallest chance of success'—and fortunately Fox's view did not get into the newspapers or he would have found his position even more difficult to justify on patriotic grounds than it was.[2]

On October 26, three days before Parliament opened, the London Corresponding Society sponsored a mass meeting in a field near Copenhagen House to discuss the nation's critical and calamitous state and to urge universal suffrage and annual parliaments. The pamphlet that recorded the events of the day claimed that not fewer than 100,000 persons were present; the *Annual Register* observed more cautiously that the number of members, auditors, and spectators was extremely great.[3]

[1] On July 28, 1802, Fox wrote Lord Holland: 'Mrs A. and I have been married for some years, so long ago as 1795. Even in England there has been some inconvenience resulting from this not being known, and abroad I think there might be more, so that I do not wish it to be any longer a secret' (Add. MSS. 47601).
[2] Add. MSS. 47572. September 2.
[3] *Account of the proceedings of a meeting of the London Corresponding Society, held in a field near Copenhagen-House, Oct. 26, 1795,* etc. (London [1795]); *Annual Register* for 1795, *Chronicle,* p. 37.

Outwardly the meeting was orderly but inwardly a spirit of unrest was growing. Three days later as the King went to Parliament to deliver his opening speech, he heard cries of 'Bread!' 'No War!' 'No Famine!' 'No Pitt!' 'Down with Tyrants!' 'No King!' A missile struck the window of his carriage, breaking the glass. Entering the House of Lords he quietly said to the Chancellor, 'My Lord, I have been shot at,' and proceeded to read his speech 'perfectly composed', a member from Warwick observed, 'without any person uninformed being able to judge that all had not passed as usual'.[1] The royal message noted satisfaction at the successes of Austrian arms in Germany and Italy, held out a hope that although the Government would seek peace if just and suitable terms could be negotiated with hope of reasonable permanence, the better design for the present was to prosecute the war with the utmost vigour. The address also took note of the restlessness of the people, increased by the high price of grain and the poor harvest, and urged that Parliament adopt regulations to alleviate distress and also to encourage the spirit of order and submission to law.

Fox spoke severely against the address. Whatever hope of peace the Government offered, it snatched away. No time ever seemed suitable to negotiate. As long ago as December 1792, he recalled, he had made a motion that he hoped would lead to a beneficial peace. In every session since that period he had renewed in one way or another the same motion. Yet the answer was ever the same: the time was not ripe. As years went on, however, instead of being offered more favourable conditions to negotiate, we instead 'entangled ourselves deeper, and rendered the practicability of peace upon safe and honourable terms more hopeless'. The Government would not treat with Robespierre because he was a tyrant, but neither would it discuss terms with his successor. Would you, said the Government, negotiate with a country that changes its constitution so often? Yes, declared Fox, I would: 'If they changed their constitution every week, nay, every day, if they had seven constitutions a week, I would treat with them.' As he developed his line of argument: 'If a rational treaty is made, and it is the interest of the parties to keep it, that is the only true and wise dependence which you can have for the continuance of peace.' Treaties the French had made with Sweden and with Prussia, he instanced, had been regularly maintained.

So Fox reiterated the topic so close to his heart, the search for peace. He admitted that the terms of a peace ever depend upon the relative situation of the contending parties. Nor would he accept terms

---

[1] Hamilton-Greville correspondence (Huntington). Charles Greville to his uncle, Sir William Hamilton. [November 2, 1795]. Charles, Lord Colchester, ed., *The Diary and Correspondence of Charles Abbot, Lord Colchester* (London, 1861), i, 2–3.

inconsistent with the honour and the interests of Britain. 'But he would not admit of that eternal evasion that the time was improper. One year we were too high to treat, another year we were too low; and thus the continuance of the war was prolonged.' As he said:

> When we were masters . . . and France was beset on every side, with insurrections raging in her bowels, that was the favourable time to treat. But no, we were then too high. What! treat when she almost lay expiring at our feet? We suffered that moment to pass. Last year, again, we had great success in the West Indies . . . France was obviously desirous of peace. No, then again we were too high, and we were asked in a lofty strain in the month of June last, What, shall we treat with her when she lies in her last agony? Nothing, they said, could save her. . . . The event has proved that the prediction was not well founded; and here we are, after three years war, reduced to a state in which we are said to be too low to treat, with nothing left us but the hopes that some day or another a favourable opportunity will arise for negociation.

Fox insisted again that a war against opinions was not just nor pardonable. He concluded by moving a long amendment to the address, that the Government propose a pacific negotiation. If, however, suitable terms could not be negotiated, then he on his part would support a vigorous prosecution of the war.

Pitt did not meet Fox's reasoning, lofty and generalized though it was, head on, but instead repeated his assurance that 'to sue for peace . . . must inevitably bring disgrace on the country'. He pointed to improvement in the present state of the country and promised to do whatever he could to reduce the high price of grain and to make the situation of the poor more comfortable. The vote supported him 240 to 59.[1] In his diary Charles Abbot recorded that the Opposition had hoped for a vote on its side of 100, but that some who had come to town to vote for Fox went away without voting after hearing his pacifistic amendment. Abbot also added that the Government could have had an additional thirty votes from supporters who at the time were in the House of Lords and who therefore missed the division.[2] Pitt also noted these absences in his usual report to the King, setting the figure at twenty, however, instead of thirty; he added that Sheridan spoke with great violence and that Fox's amendment gave great dissatisfaction. The King could not have been more pleased: 'The general complexion of both Houses is such as all friends to the Constitution must rejoice at. . . . The times may be difficult, but with energy cannot fail of success.'[3]

Yet the situation was gloomy. A few days later Pitt commented, 'My head would be off in six months were I to resign,' and introduced into

[1] *Parliamentary History*, xxxii, 163–88.   [2] Colchester, i, 4.
[3] *Later Correspondence of George III*, ii, 415, 416. October 29, 30.

the Lords in November a Bill defining and extending the law of treason, providing penalties for those who by writing or speaking stirred up the people to hatred of the sovereign or the constitution. This Treason Bill was followed by introducing into the Commons on November 10 a Seditious Meetings Bill, empowering magistrates to disperse, by force if necessary, meetings believed seditious, and requiring a licence for houses, rooms, or fields where admission was charged to hear speeches or lectures. Fox's opposition was forcefully stated:

Say at once, that a free constitution is no longer suitable to us; say at once, in a manly manner, that upon an ample review of the state of the world, a free constitution is not fit for you; conduct yourselves at once as the senators of Denmark did; lay down your freedom, and acknowledge and accept of despotism. But do not mock the understandings and the feelings of mankind, by telling the world that you are free—by telling me that, if out of the House, for the purpose of expressing my sense of the public administration of this country, of the calamities which this war has occasioned, I state a grievance by petition, or make any declaration of my sentiments, which I always had a right to do; but which if I now do, in a manner that may appear to a magistrate to be seditious, I am to be subjected to penalties which hitherto were unknown to the laws of England.

To allow a magistrate the right to approve or disapprove of a public opinion was a proposal Fox regarded with genuine horror:

Behold, then, the state of a free-born Englishman! Before he can discuss any topic which involves his liberty, he must send to a magistrate who is to attend the discussion. That magistrate cannot prevent such meeting: but he can prevent the speaking, because he can allege, that what is said tends to disturb the peace and tranquillity of this realm.

He went on to say that freedom of speech is a vent for political humours; if grievances could not be discussed, the aggrieved had no alternative but to use violent means of adjusting their complaints.[1] The usual forty—in this instance 42—stood with Fox in the division, 214 supporting the Government's proposal. Pitt wrote to the King the same evening that Fox and others opposed the motion with great violence.[2]

The partisan *Morning Post* heralded a forthcoming meeting in Westminster Hall in capital letters, on page one:

THE REAL FRIENDS
OF THE CONSTITUTION
Are earnestly requested to attend in
WESTMINSTER HALL
On Monday next, November 16, to take
into their consideration
A Petition to Parliament AGAINST the OUTRAGE with which
THE BILL OF RIGHTS IS THREATENED[3]

---

[1] *Parliamentary History*, xxxii, 276–83.   [2] *Later Correspondence of George III*, ii, 418.
[3] November 14.

At first the hustings was erected in Westminster Hall as advertised, but the Chancellor and Chief Justice of the Common Pleas objected to a meeting being held where courts were sitting, so the hustings was moved outside to Palace Yard. Fox, Sheridan, Grey, Bedford, Lauderdale and others were present. As seen through the eyes of one observer: 'It was not a large mob—very far short I should think of the numbers which they expected and I apprehend that Government had great strength there. It went off quietly and they determined to petition.'[1] As seen through the eyes of the ministerial *True Briton*, Fox, 'the Hero of the Day', used the same misrepresentations and perversions that he and his associates had used elsewhere. Fox undertook to defend his political conduct, 'carefully omitting all reference to his coalition with Lord North' and his 'unqualified admiration' of the principles of the French Revolution. After the meeting, Bedford, Fox, and Sheridan took a coach to the gaming house in St James's Street. Thus the *True Briton* reported the scene in its November 17 issue. Three days later it said with mock charity that they did not alight at the gaming house, but only halted and then went on to Mrs Armistead's in South Street.

Letters to Holland written just before and just after this meeting give Fox's own reaction to it. He had approached it in a spirit of distress and discouragement; he had been beat down in the House and felt impelled to take the argument to the people. He saw no choice between 'absolute surrender of the liberties of the people' and 'a vigorous exertion, attended, I admit, with considerable hazard, at a time like the present.' Looking forward to the meeting at Westminster Hall next day, he expressed his fear that the Government might send persons who, 'under pretence of opposing our measures', will endeavour to incite a riot. 'This is a great crisis.'

The day after the meeting, however, he wrote Holland that it had succeeded beyond all his hopes, 'incredibly numerous, yet very peaceable'. He continued:

It is clear that here we have the popularity, and I suspect we shall have it universally among the lower classes. I need not tell you how I dislike this state of things, but I can not submit quite passively to Mr Hume's Euthanasia which is coming on very fast.[2]

On all of these assemblings the Government kept a wary eye. The constabulary was under the direction of Fox's good and great friend and former companion in politics, Portland, Home Secretary since July of the preceding year, who in November fully described the activities of Fox, Sheridan, and other former associates. The speakers, Portland

[1] Fitzwilliam MSS. (Milton), 49. November 18. W. Baldwin to Fitzwilliam. (Northamptonshire Record Office).
[2] Add. MSS. 47572. *Fox Cor.*, iii, 126. November 17.

reported, urged the people to hold their tempers; on the whole there was 'no sort of sourness or even seriousness, but . . . an appearance of good humour prevailed generally'. As for Fox, the sentiments expressed for him 'indicated much more of compassion for his situation than any determination or intention to place him in one more conspicuous or advantageous'. The Duke thought the crowd was not very large, nor even very attentive, and when an hour passed after the meeting without disturbance, he dismissed his military forces and kept at hand only his constables. This report the King approved, only repeating his former sentiment: 'It is highly necessary that this business should be correctly watched'.[1]

In the debates in the House that followed, Fox's voice was earnestly lifted in powerful support of freedom of speech and of the press. In a free society speech should be completely free; and by being completely free, he meant, in his words, 'freedom in the first instance'; a man could be punished if he abused that freedom yet still he had perfect freedom 'in the first instance'. Never had he heard of any danger arising to a free state from freedom of the press or freedom of speech; so far from it, he was perfectly clear that an independent state could not exist without both. Newspapers today operating in a free society would not fail to approve to the utmost Fox's declared opinions on this subject, just as they endorse the pungent, succinct 'I disapprove of what you say, but I will defend to the death your right to say it,' attributed to Voltaire. Those who proclaim that sentiment should also recall the eighteen-year-old English lad who had visited Voltaire in 1767, who received a list of Voltaire's works that might free the mind from religious prejudices and perhaps other prejudices as well, and who, on November 25, 1795, uttered words like these:

It is not the written law of the constitution of England, it is not the law that is to be found in books, that has constituted the true principle of freedom in any country, at any time. No! it is the energy, the boldness of a man's mind, which prompts him to speak, not in private, but in large and popular assemblies, that constitutes, that creates in a state, the spirit of freedom. . . . If you suffer the liberty of speech to be wrested from you, you will then have lost the freedom, the energy, the boldness of the British character.

Fox's warning was plain enough. If this Bill passed the people could retain for a while the institution of juries and the forms of a free constitution, 'but the substance is gone, the foundation is undermined;—your fall is certain and your destruction inevitable'. To this enduring sentiment and sublime language the House disagreed, 267 to 70.[2]

[1] *Later Correspondence of George III*, ii, 419–20, 425–6.
[2] *Parliamentary History*, xxxii, 409–22.

Fox fought the Alien and Sedition Bills in the House and out of it. He went to Epsom to take part in a debate at a meeting of Surrey free-holders gathered to petition against the Bills. He appeared before another Palace Yard meeting; a sixteen-page pamphlet summarizes what went on. Fox, in the chair, spoke against the two Bills: 'A daring attempt has been made upon your liberties—an attempt to subvert the Constitution of England.' Everyone regrets the insults and indignities to his Majesty, but certainly the law as it stands is sufficient to punish those who are guilty. The Bill for preventing seditious meetings and assemblies could give a magistrate power to dissolve a meeting like this one. Even if a magistrate suspects that a meeting is to be held for the discussion of a political subject, 'and you pay money for your admission, he may attend, and he is to have power to disperse you, under the penalty of rioting in a disorderly house'.

After other speeches, the crowd accompanied Fox to his home in South Street. From his window he addressed them briefly and then asked them to disperse quietly. In ten minutes the street was cleared, 'and all that numerous body of people retired with a tranquillity and good order that was hardly equalled, and never exceeded'.[1] Against this report may be abutted the *True Briton's* comment: it declared that he eulogized the most worthless characters, a proof that he had lost all sense of discrimination between virtue and vice.

The Bills passed notwithstanding, and the Rockingham club in Yorkshire, like many groups throughout the country, made formal inquiry as to whether their meetings would be 'subject to the visit of a magistrate'. Fitzwilliam, however, thought the new Bills did not apply to the club, and so its meetings could proceed.[2] Alongside this small, affrighted inquiry and its measured, cautious response may be placed a solemn and awesome couplet, quoted by Fox:

> Between two seas, on one small neck of land,
> Wearied, confounded, and amazed we stand.

And a narrow isthmus it was. Looking back over the preceding years, the durable opposition could recall dividing 50 against 290 on December 13, 1792, on the address of thanks; 44 against 270 on February 18, 1793, on Fox's resolutions against the war with France; 41 against 282 on May 7 that year on Grey's motion for parliamentary reform. Beginning a new session on January 21, 1794, opposition did slightly better with its 59 against 277 on the address of thanks, but on the notorious Scottish libel trials, Adam's motion on March 10 brought

---

[1] *Account of the proceedings of a meeting of the inhabitants of Westminster in Palace Yard, November 26, 1795*, etc. (London, 1795).
[2] Fitzwilliam Papers, F-41 (Sheffield).

out only 32 against 171, and Fox's May 30 motion on ending the war with France called up 55 against 208. The first and best division that same month on the repeal of habeas corpus was opposition 39, Government 201. Sheridan's motion on January 5, 1795, to repeal the Habeas Corpus Suspension Act gained 41 supporters against 185; the same month the Bill for continuing the Act was carried 239 against 53. And as 1795 ended the Opposition made much its best showing when it divided 70 to 267 against the Seditious Meetings Bill. Little wonder that Fox or others who viewed the record could feel wearied, confounded, and amazed. On these issues, all close to his heart, odds ranged from 4 to 1 to 7 to 1 against him.

In a real sense, Fox was closer to the mind and spirit of the people than Pitt or any member of Pitt's administration. More than any of them, he had faced the people in the public discussion of controversial issues. At Covent Garden, at Palace Yard, in Westminster Hall, and in numerous other public places, he had confronted both the praise and the abuse of scores, hundreds, thousands. He had been applauded and he had been jostled; he had heard his statements cheered and he had also heard them drowned in jeers and cries. Yet although he had frequently witnessed public discussion accompanied by noise and other kinds of disorder, he was certain in his own mind that when the speechmaking was over the crowd would quietly adjourn. He himself had often successfully brought gatherings to a conclusion simply by requesting the crowd to disperse orderly. The approval of magistrates for a public gathering and the presence of constables to maintain order was to him not only unnecessary but unwise, a frightened judgment of the temper of the times, an affront to the dignity and the liberty of the British people. And as for his utterances about freedom of speech, no one in the entire Greek-Roman-Anglo-Saxon tradition has ever defended more warmly, more earnestly the vital significance of speaking in public.

23

Great Whig
1796-1797

To propose negotiation is not to sue for peace.
Charles James Fox

Pitt's parliamentary forces swept everything before them in the early months of 1796. Principally the topic was peace, but the Government was in no mood for peace. Grey's motion was beaten down 189 to 50 in February, and Fox's four-hour speech in May gathered in only 42 votes to the administration's 216. Pitt wrote to the King that the arguments were the same old arguments; certainly the vote was the same old vote. When the Lords also beat back pacific sentiments, the King noted: 'This decided support in both Houses at the close of a Parliament not only will have its due weight in the country, but must much influence a similar conduct in the approaching new Parliament.'[1]

On this note Parliament was dissolved, and the country proceeded to a new general election. At a meeting of the Crown and Anchor on May 3, Fox, presiding, announced that he would again stand for Westminster, running independently of any other candidate. The election began May 27, with Fox, Horne Tooke, and Sir Alan Gardner as the candidates, the latter receiving the support of the Government. During the election speeches on May 31, Fox thanked the electors for their support: 'The people approve of those principles which it has been my anxious endeavour to maintain.' Tooke made a short talk and Gardner attempted to speak, 'but the roaring voice of that lion, the populace, prevented a single word from being distinguished'. By June 1, Gardner headed the poll, and in his speech he commented that if he possessed the eloquence of Fox and the faculty of using as many words as Tooke he would express his thanks in better terms.[2] Reporters caught Fox at an eloquent moment addressing Westminster electors:

[The Ministers] have been the cause of squandering more of the public money, and of spilling more of the blood of human creatures than any other Government or Power that ever was in this or any other country in Europe whatever. With the words of Religion and Humanity in their mouths, they have destroyed more of God's creatures, and spilt more human blood, than any Prince, Emperor, or Despotic Tyrant in the annals of History. They have spilt as much blood as the

[1] *Later Correspondence of George III*, ii, 473. (Chatham Papers.)
[2] *Gazetteer*, June 1, June 3, 1796.

greatest Conquerors, and lost as much as those conquerers have obtained. . . .
They have sent men out of their country, contrary to law, to Botany Bay; after
trials conducted in such a manner, that every lover of justice shudders when he
reads them.[1]

In his election speeches he made the point that it was the constitution of
1688 he loved, and that he detested the innovations that had been made
in it, 'particularly the innovations in 1796'.[2]

The polls ended on June 13, Fox and Gardner being easily in the
lead, Tooke a poor third. Fox was seated in a triumphal chair, and was
escorted by 2,000 admirers to the Duke of Devonshire's in Piccadilly,
and congratulated with 'those marks of love and esteem due to his
patriotic exertions'.[3] At Devonshire House a disturbance was created,
the chair being broken and windows smashed, but Fox entreated the
people, 'for his sake and their own honour', to disperse. 'There was an
immediate cry of "home, home,"'—and the group disbanded without
further violence.[4]

The House of Commons of the eighteenth Parliament opened its
deliberations September 27 by choosing Henry Addington as speaker.
Addington, a man of low-level talents, is forever associated with
Canning's doggerel: 'Pitt is to Addington, as London is to Padding-
ton.' The King announced the Government's intention to send a
representative to Paris to treat for peace. Pitt was finally going to do
what Fox had urged all along. The address also commented on the
fortunes of war on the Continent, with praise for Austria and scorn for
Spain, and hoped that the new harvest had improved the food supply.
Fox, who a week previously had written his dissenter friend, William
Smith, that 'we ought to make a stand against acknowledging the
justice of the war' and that 'there is not the smallest chance of Peace',[5]
could not avoid reminding the House that often he had advised negotiation and always without success, and now a hundred millions of additional money and thousands of lives had been expended in the cruel
contest. He then repeated one of his maxims: 'To propose negotiation
is not to sue for peace.'[6]

---

[1] *Ibid.*, June 13. A slightly different version of Fox's speech appears in the pamphlet *The
Speeches of John Horne Tooke, during the Westminster election, 1796: with . . . the speech of the
right hon. C. J. Fox, on Saturday, June 11*, etc. (London, 1796).
[2] *Jordan's complete collection of all the addresses and speeches of the Hon. C. J. Fox, Sir A.
Gardner, and J. H. Tooke, Esq. at the late interesting contest for Westminster*, etc. 3rd edn
(London, 1796), p. 11.
[3] *The Gazetteer*, June 13. Colchester, i, 59–60.
[4] *Jordan's complete collection*, etc., pp. 53–4.
[5] Osborn Collection, September 28. (Yale.)
[6] *Parliamentary History*, xxxii, 1194–201.

Invasion is a word of terrifying import to the twentieth century. For ten years during the war with France a threat of invasion of the coast of England was posed; for these years part of the general conversation of Englishmen was where and when invaders would strike. In October, Pitt called the problem to the attention of the Commons, in committee, and quite properly without revealing specific plans proposed to augment the numbers of seamen and soldiers, and provide short periods of emergency training. Dundas, who supported him, happened to praise the preceding Parliament as ranking with 'the most venerated parliaments this country had ever known'. This sentiment aroused the ever-listening Fox, who, immediately following, offered this impromptu yet eloquent denunciation:

> . . . the last parliament . . . had done more mischief to the country than any that ever sat since parliaments were recognized in England. . . .
>
> Show me a parliament, in consequence of whose proceedings the people have been drained so much, and from which they have had so little benefit!
>
> Show me a parliament since the year 1688, the era of our Revolution, that has diminished the best and dearest rights of the people, so shamelessly, so wickedly, as the last parliament have done!
>
> Show me a parliament since that period that has so uniformly sacrificed the liberty of the subject to increase the influence of government, as the last parliament have done! . . .
>
> Sir, I consider the last parliament to have been a curse to this country. . . .
>
> This is the only war that has ever been conducted on the part of this country, in which there never has been one inquiry on the part of parliament. You see to what a state that has led you already. Should this parliament be like the last (God in his mercy avert it!) this country will soon be in a condition, in which it will be of little importance, whether they have a parliament or not.[1]

One must imagine these words being uttered, not hesitantly or dispiritedly, but forcefully, vigorously, bitingly. No one rose to deny any part of this sentiment; only one speaker followed, who spoke briefly on a side point, and Pitt's proposal was agreed to without a vote.

As the year ended, Pitt was forced to tell the House that negotiations of peace entered into with France had been broken off by the refusal of that Government to negotiate, and by its ordering the English plenipotentiary to leave within forty-eight hours. Fox principally argued that the Government had not properly demonstrated its sincerity in the negotiations, largely through not giving its representative proper instructions; but only 37 voted with him, as opposed to 212 for the Government.[2] French Laurence writing Fitzwilliam said that Fox's speech was three and a half hours long, 'going through every personal topick with great violence': 'He said, the country could now only be saved by a change of men and measures, and after peace reforms . . . to

---

[1] *Parliamentary History*, xxxii, 1216–18.   [2] *Ibid.*, xxxii, 1466–93.

bring back the spirit of the constitution and make the voice of the people of England prevail over the voice of the minister.'[1]

1797. No lack of news. Three of Stonehenge's giant stones, dislodged by the stresses of winter, crashed to the ground. John Adams became the second President of the new United States; the winner of second place in the election, Thomas Jefferson, became the Vice-President. One Sir Godfrey Webster secured an uncontested divorce from his wife, Lady Elizabeth, charging an adulterous relationship with Lord Holland over two years' time and in various places such as Florence, Padua, Vienna, etc. etc., and the birth of a child; Sir Godfrey was awarded his divorce and later £6,000 damages; Holland immediately married Lady Webster. Victory over the Spanish fleet resulted in an elevation to an earldom for Admiral Sir John Jervis and a knighthood for his commodore, Nelson.

Parliament returned from the Christmas holidays just in time to face a financial crisis: a run on the Bank of England. In the last days of February the demands for cash increased so steadily that the directors appealed to the Government for advice. An order in council was issued, prohibiting them from tendering any cash in payment until the sense of Parliament could be taken and proper measures adopted. Pitt moved that a committee be appointed, not to inquire minutely into specie holdings, but into the general state of the Bank's funds and obligations. In a long speech Fox objected to the procedure on every conceivable ground, principally that the inquiry was not to be full and complete. 'We have for a long time had a confiding House of Commons,' he declared. 'I want now an inquiring House of Commons.'[2] The Government's strength that day was measured at 244 to 86, and from then on Pitt had his way. An alleged cause of the emergencies, which Pitt consistently denied, was that the Government had shipped too much cash to the Continent, principally to Vienna, in the form of subsidies. Pitt, thus warned, began to curtail his financial support to his allies, the public rallied to the measures taken to issue bank notes in lieu of cash, and financial disaster was averted.

Late in March, Fox moved that the Government consider the disturbed state of Ireland, 'to adopt such healing and lenient measures . . . best calculated to restore tranquility'. He noted the unhappiness occasioned

---

[1] Fitzwilliam MSS. (Milton), 50. December 31, 1796. (Northamptonshire Record Office.)
[2] *Parliamentary History*, xxxii, 1526–49.

by the recall of Fitzwilliam, but particularly commented on Catholic grievances. Although Catholics could vote for members of Parliament they could not themselves hold office; thus 'civil liberty can have no security without political power. To ask for civil liberty without political power, would be . . . to ask for the possession of a right for the enjoyment of which they can have no security.' Fox recalled parallels between Ireland in 1797 and America in 1774; unless the discontent of the Irish is allayed no way was left to keep them obedient except the use of force. 'My wish is', he said, 'that the whole people of Ireland should have the same system, the same operation of government. . . . I would have the whole Irish government regulated by Irish notions and Irish prejudices.' Moreover, he declared, the more Ireland is governed by the Irish the more will she be bound to English interests.

Pitt's rejoinder embraced two points: first, that since the Irish legislature was independent, Great Britain's attempt to deal with Ireland's internal affairs would be an unjustifiable interference with that nation's legislative and executive government. This belief, he declared, was the real ground on which he opposed Fox's motion. Assuming, further, only for the sake of argument, that regulation could be accomplished without interfering with Irish legislative processes, Pitt asserted that Fox had not even hinted at any possible moves and had left the Government entirely in the dark as to what remedies he prescribed.[1] The debate was not long and the Government was not shaken by it; the motion was beat down 220 to 84, and in his dispatch to the King Pitt found it sufficient merely to mention the speakers pro and con and the vote.[2] The King was grateful for the 220, but commented that 'every well-wisher to the Empire must feel hurt' that the minority was so large.[3] In Dublin, however, the speech was applauded.

In America, dispatches from London noted that 'reports of a change of ministers continued to occupy the conversation of every political circle. . . . Pitt's retirement from office is universally admitted to be . . . indispensable . . . friends have abandoned hopes . . . every man forms such [a ministry] as he wishes, but no man includes Mr Pitt in his arrangement.'[4]

Fox contributed to this thought in an outdoor speech in Palace Yard in April. With an umbrella over his head to protect him from the weather, he discussed a wide range of topics: the Treason and Sedition Bills, the burdens on the people from the war, the prosecutions of the

---

[1] *Parliamentary History*, xxxiii, 139–71.   [2] *Later Correspondence of George III*, ii, 555.
[3] J. Holland Rose, *Pitt and Napoleon* (London, 1912), p. 241.
[4] *Aurora General Advertiser* (Philadelphia), May 12. Dispatch of March 15, 1797.

societies. 'Leave no means unturned', he concluded, 'to get the ministers out.'[1]

Pitt, however, survived this blast to face still new crises. One was a serious mutiny in the Channel fleet and another in the North Sea fleet. Sailors complained bitterly about low pay; poor food, generally consisting of weevily biscuits and ancient salted pork; excessively severe punishments; tardy pay; unfair distribution of prize money; irregular and infrequent liberty. Sailors of the Channel fleet at Spithead addressed a petition to Fox to come to their aid, but apparently the petition was intercepted by the Admiralty and never reached its destination.[2] The Spithead mutiny was resolved and the sailors returned to their duty, but the later rebellion of the North Sea fleet was savagely handled and nearly two-score men hanged before the disturbance was quieted.

Opposition capitalized upon the fact that the Government had delayed and temporized. Whitbread moved, Fox seconding, that Pitt should be censured. In the debate that followed, during part of which Pitt at Mr Speaker's request absented himself from the chamber, the motion was modified, among other changes substituting 'his majesty's ministers' for Pitt. In a relatively brief speech Fox spelled out the extent of the delay but especially took occasion to restate his firm belief in the necessity for full inquiry and debate:

Public discussion is the best security for public welfare, and for the safety of every good government. That energy which is to be had from secrecy stands upon the authority of but a few, and they have never been the wisest nor the best, but those who, from age to age, have endeavoured to enslave mankind.[3]

This motion, like others supported by the opposition, was defeated, the vote being 237 to 63.

Increasingly Fox began to be discouraged by the uneven numbers. 'It is sad work to be urging people against the grain', he had written.[4] Pitt's reports to the King on parliamentary debates occasionally fanned his Majesty's bitter dislike. With reference to a budget speech of April 26 the King replied to Pitt: 'I think Mr Fox's attempt to aggravate the difficulties must . . . convince every impartial man that from personal pique at me and my Administration he is become an open enemy of his country.'[5]

---

[1] *The Times*, April 4.
[2] The situation is detailed in James Dugan, *The Great Mutiny* (New York, 1965), chs. 6 ff. A younger, more energetic Fox would have taken up the sailors' cause and, drawing fully upon his experience as a former member of the Admiralty board, given full exposure to administration delays and shortcomings.
[3] *Parliamentary History*, xxxiii, 509.   [4] Add. MSS. 47569. January 15.
[5] *Later Correspondence of George III*, ii, 566. April 27.

In May Fox spoke energetically for the repeal of the Treason and Sedition Bills, which had been on the statute books for more than two years. He mentioned examples of the caprice and vexatiousness with which sheriffs and magistrates had prevented public meetings, but was particularly effective, however, when he pleaded for the fundamental principle of free speech:

Do you think that you gain a proselyte where you silence a declaimer? No; you have only by preventing the declaration of grievances in a constitutional way, forced men to more pernicious modes of coming at relief. In proportion as opinions are open, they are innocent and harmless. Opinions become dangerous to a state only when persecution makes it necessary for the people to communicate their ideas under the bond of secrecy.

Ireland, he continued, was an example of a country driven to hostility because other means of expressing grievance had been forbidden.

To those who promised to repeal the Bills when peace and tranquillity was restored, he had only scorn:

You tell the people, that when every thing goes well, when they are happy and comfortable, then they may meet freely, to recognize their happiness, and pass eulogiums on their government; but that in a moment of war and calamity, of distrust and misconduct, it is not permitted them to meet together, because then, instead of eulogizing, they might think proper to condemn ministers.

What a mockery is this! What an insult to say that this is preserving to the people the right of petition! To tell them that they shall have a right to applaud, a right to rejoice, a right to meet when they are happy, but not a right to condemn, not a right to deplore their fortunes, not a right to suggest a remedy! ... If you mean that freedom is not as conducive to order and strength as it is to happiness, say so. . . .

Liberty is order. Liberty is strength. . . . Liberty not only is power and order, but . . . it is power and order predominant and invincible . . . the heart of man has no impulse, and can have none that dares to stand in competition with it.

Pitt did not speak in the debate; and those who followed Fox offered principally the arguments that the Acts had served to quiet the country, that the situation called for continued firmness and order, that constitutional and proper meetings were still allowed, that it was unjust to call the present ministers hostile to liberty because they were obliged to enact some temporary restrictions. The vote on the motion followed the familiar pattern: 52 for it, 260 against it.[1]

The advisability of seceding from Parliament began to be talked of among members of the Opposition. From Fox, wearying of the constant and fruitless struggle, the proposal met little objection. A motion for the reform of Parliament was projected, and the opposition made every attempt to rally its forces for the debate set for May 26.

[1] *Parliamentary History*, xxxiii, 613–39.

Fox's long speech that day was one of the eloquent efforts of his career: reasoned, analytical, judicial. He opened by answering those who claimed that the motion was motivated by party politics, undertaking to define party in its best sense—not party as 'an unprincipled combination of men for the pursuit of office and its emoluments, the eagerness after which leads them to act upon feelings of personal enmity, ill-will, and opposition to his majesty's ministers'—but rather in the sense that 'men of honour, who entertain similar principles, conceive that those principles may be more beneficially and successfully pursued by the force of mutual support, harmony, and confidential connection'. This sort of party, Fox declared,

... is an advantage to the country; an advantage to the cause of truth and the constitution; an advantage to freedom and humanity; an advantage to whatever honourable object they may be engaged in, that men pursue it with the united force of party feeling; that is to say, pursue it with the confidence, zeal, and spirit, which the communion of just confidence is likely to inspire.

Further: those who think party is a good thing for ordinary occasions must admit that it is peculiarly so in emergencies like the present.

To convince his hearers that on this occasion he was, in this sense of party, more concerned with measures than with personalities, he conceded that some mixture of personality was inescapable when one attempted to suggest change or fix responsibility. Certainly his position was not conceived out of hostility to Pitt, since Pitt himself had again and again spoken on this subject, and at least on three occasions when Pitt had done so, in 1782, 1783, and 1785, Fox reminded his listeners that he had given his support.

Fox in 1797 was a vastly more mature individual than even in the towering days of the American Revolution. In 1797, entering his second quarter-century of active, intense, parliamentary speaking, he could in any debate draw copiously upon his experience in comparing and contrasting one set of conditions with an earlier set. In this speech when he argued in favour of parliamentary reform, he could describe in detail the failure of the Government to extend reform to Ireland; and how, since reformers could get no relief through the Government, they turned more and more to societies. Thus the comparatively small number of societies in Ireland in 1791 became stronger and stronger by the accession of thousands who at first thought they had little in common with the charter members, so that from small beginnings their numbers had increased to 100,000 men in Ulster alone.

Is it improbable that the original few were not more than ten or twenty thousand in number? What, then, do I learn from this? That the impolitic and unjust refusal of government, to attend to the applications of the moderate, made 80 or

90,000 proselytes from moderation to violence. This is the lesson which the book of Ireland exhibits! Can you refuse your assent to the moral? Will any man argue, that if reform had been conceded to the 80 or 90,000 moderate petitioners, you would have this day to deplore the union of 100,000 men, bent on objects so extensive, so alarming, so calamitous? I wish to warn you by this example.

'What England is now, Ireland was in 1791.' Let us then try to effect a reform 'without touching the main pillars of the constitution, without changing its forms, or disturbing the harmony of its parts'.

Fox declared that so basic was the failure of the House to represent the people, not even a general election could remedy the matter. In the general election of 1780, he insisted, even though sentiment against the prosecution of the American war was considerable, only three or four members were added by the election to the side of those who protested the war. Actually, as has already been seen, Government majorities were much less in early 1781, after the election, than they were in the middle of 1780, before the election. But as Pitt, arguing for parliamentary reform in 1782, had reasoned that the election of 1780 did not reflect the true sentiment of the country, Fox contended that the same line of reasoning was still valid:

You see [Fox is quoting Pitt as of 1782] that so defective, so inadequate, is the present practice, at least of the elective franchise, that no impression of national calamity, no conviction of ministerial error, no abhorrence of disastrous war, is sufficient to stand against that corrupt influence which has mixed itself with election, and which drowns and stifles the popular voice.

The texts of Pitt's earlier speeches on parliamentary reform, particularly that of his 1782 speech, are too incomplete to check Fox's recollection of them, though the impression is speedily gained that here Fox is enlarging upon a shred of memory. He went on to say:

I aver, that as in the American war the public opinion had changed, though no change was produced by the general election of 1780, so now, for the last two years, the present war has been universally unpopular in England, though it has not made its voice to be heard in the choice of representatives.

Even though opposing candidates in the last election campaigned on the war issue—one side boasting of opposing it, and the other apologizing for supporting it, the outcome of the election did not reflect the sentiment of the people against continuing the conflict.

Fox went on to develop a host of other arguments: the fallacy of the notion of virtual representation; the hypocrisy of a member who paid £5,000 for a seat making a vehement speech against bribery; the importance of reducing the property qualification for voting; the difference between the plan suggested and, to him highly undesirable, universal suffrage. He argued that extending the right of election to householders was the best and most advisable plan. 'It is the most perfect recurrence . . . to the first known and recorded principles of our constitution.' 'Household suffrage' became, of course, the great issue in the debates on reform in the nineteenth century. Fox was not ready to advocate universal suffrage, which might extend the vote to three million men, and would include a large number of men like soldiers, servants, and other persons 'whose low condition necessarily curbed the independence of their minds'. The plan before the House might bring the electorate to a figure in the neighbourhood of 600,000, which he thought desirable, and would provide for the largest number of 'independent' electors.

Compared with the discussions of 1866 and 1867, this debate was on a generalized level. Fox, Grey, and their colleagues insisted that details could be worked out at the proper time. They had no settled convictions about redistribution of seats or extension of the franchise that could not be modified by later discussion.

In the conclusion of his speech, Fox announced his intention, not to secede totally from the House, but to give more of his time to other pursuits. Regardless of what opposition could demonstrate about the failures and incapacities of government, the House continued to give the ministers full support; accordingly Fox declared that he would spend less time in parliamentary discussion.

Whenever it shall appear [he assured members] that my efforts may contribute in any degree to restore us to the situation from which the confidence of this House, in a desperate system and an incapable administration, has so suddenly reduced us, I shall be found ready to discharge my duty.[1]

The effectiveness of the speech is found in the division: 256 opposed Fox, but 91 voted with him, a larger number than usual. George Rose, Secretary to the Treasury, close friend of Pitt, wrote that to his utter astonishment the minority had attracted 'about a dozen of our friends'. Opposition papers proudly counted twenty-one county members in the division. Lord Morpeth, Government supporter, called Fox's speech 'the finest and most impressive I ever heard him make'.[2] Pitt's letter to the King was brief and factual but the King's reply revealed a royal wince: he thought the minority would have been less, but Fox's 'art' succeeded in keeping his party together.[3]

Next day the papers were filled with reports of Fox's powerful effort. Some of them wondered exactly what Fox had actually said about retiring; several papers, quoted this passage:

[1] *Ibid.*, xxxiii, 699–734. See also the pamphlet: *The substance of the speech of the Right Honourable Charles James Fox, on Mr Grey's motion, in the House of Commons, Friday, May 26, 1797, etc.* (London, 1797).
[2] The Rose and Morpeth comments are quoted in *Later Correspondence of George III*, ii, 582.
[3] *Pitt and Napoleon*, p. 241. May 27.

I hear it said, 'You do nothing but mischief when you are here; and yet we should be sorry to see you away.' I do not know how we shall be able to satisfy the gentlemen who feel towards us in this way. If we can neither do our duty without mischief, nor please them with doing nothing, I know but of one way by which we can give them content, and that is, by putting an end to our existence.[1]

The *True Briton*, which in the past had sharply criticized him, described his speech as having 'unparalleled force and brilliance', and the *Oracle* thought it 'one of the most brilliant and animated speeches ever delivered by this distinguished orator'. The *Oracle* freely discussed the possibility of Pitt's retirement. Attempting to view the political situation more impartially than usual, it observed that no one could deny that Fox's abilities were transcendentally great, his views comprehensive, and his politics open and manly, but it did not judge him indispensable. On balance it hoped he would reconsider his decision to retire and in some way unite his powers with the country.

The *St James's Chronicle* put its sentiments in these words: 'Mr Fox's speech . . . is universally allowed to have been one of the most masterly pieces of reasoning, and one of the most profound political disquisitions that has been heard within [St Stephen's] walls for the last twenty years.' The opposition *Morning Post* thought he had never spoken with more effect, his language being singularly plain and pointed.

The preceding day *The Times* had blamed him for inciting revolt in Ireland and insurrection in the navy; it recalled that his motion on the repeal of the Sedition Bill was not supported by any prominent member of his party; it went on to formulate this dilemma: 'If he keeps on he will lead a revolution that "cannot fail to bring on an overthrow of the Constitution"—if he alters his conduct "he pays a tacit homage to an Administration which he constantly reviles".'[2] Next day, however, after the speech, it paid him the tribute of having uttered 'one of the most brilliant and argumentative speeches perhaps ever delivered in Parliament'. It further observed that the Commons was 'awfully attentive', that he had never spoken with greater ability in his life, and that his speech was characterized by sound reasoning and mature reflection. More to the point, it admitted that if the times were not so adverse, it would willingly give assistance to a temperate reform.

The *Morning Chronicle*, with the *Oracle* and the *St James's Chronicle* particularly in mind, chuckled that the Treasury's own hired writers had mutinied, quoting with relish their praises of Fox's effort. Outside Parliament the speech was eagerly discussed; Debrett's pamphlet containing the text went through at least a dozen printings.

Fox was criticized then and later because he advocated reform at a

---

[1] May 29–31. 1797. *Parliamentary History*, xxxiii, 731.   [2] Issues of May 26 to 30.

time of national stress. When England was fully occupied with enemies foreign and domestic, many were convinced that the reform movement was not only inopportune but even unpatriotic. One can easily imagine that if a Bill had been introduced and debated, public and parliamentary tempers would have been well heated. Assuming that the Bill passed the Commons, it was almost certain to have been defeated in the Lords. Hindsight quickly brings to mind the disturbances of 1831 and 1832, and, for that matter, the monster meetings of 1866. It proved easier to defeat Napoleon than to bring about a change in the structure of Parliament. What the efforts of Fox and other early reformers did was to open the question and ventilate it. In the 1820s and 1830s Fox's words, cited with approval, gave moral support to that generation. In the twentieth century it does not seem so out of place to criticize the party in power, even when it has its hands full.

So Fox departed with a promise to return should England need him. That need did not appear for some interval. In fact, the unexpected appearance of a Burke pamphlet, containing fifty-four articles of impeachment against Fox, written four years earlier, must have led some to feel that England would never have further use for the speech-making talent of the Republican Hercules.[1] Meanwhile, leaving Fox at St Anne's Hill with his wedded wife, still known to friends and the public alike as Mrs Armistead, this narrative can be halted to inspect and appraise certain aspects of this talent.

---

[1] *A letter from the Rt. Honourable Edmund Burke to the Duke of Portland . . . containing 54 articles of impeachment against the Rt. Hon. C. J. Fox* (Philadelphia, 1797).

The advertisement by the editor states that the pamphlet was originally printed without the approbation of Mr Burke. As soon as it appeared it was suppressed on complaint to the Lord Chancellor. The injunction was so suddenly carried into execution that 'not more than between 70 and 80 copies got abroad'. Whether or not this information was correct, the editor claimed the pamphlet was scarce in England. See also Cone, ii, 418, fn.

24

Speaker for the People

I will now describe an orator for you.

Cicero

If [Pitt and Fox] had not been orators, I have known
many wiser, abler, and much better men than either.

The Bishop of Lichfield and Coventry

In the year of Fox's forty-fifth birthday, Sir Francis Burdett entertained
at a modest social event mentioned two chapters back. In a congenial
dinner group of like-minded folk, talk ranged widely from the cruelties
of the French Revolution to the origin of man's belief in God, and finally
lit on speechmaking, one diner arguing that eloquence was of no avail
in either House of Parliament. Oratory never influenced a single vote,
he contended, and was useful only to reach the minds of the people;
parliamentary orators should therefore above all else hope that on
important occasions galleries would be well filled. At this juncture
eyes must have turned to Fox, who countered with the rejoinder that
although oratory would not bring over a single vote on the spot, the
eloquence that carries conviction to a man's bosom will influence him
in his cooler moments. 'It does influence even ministers,' he concluded.[1]

Long before, Burke had sturdily defended the art of public address.
It is indeed worth while, he told Sir Joshua Reynolds, for a man to take
pains to speak well in Parliament. Though a Bill ably opposed may
nevertheless pass into law, he continued, it underwent modification
through debate. Again, a minister not supported by good speakers
would soon be forced out of office. Moreover, a man who speaks well
will be politically rewarded himself.[2]

Fox was, however, on this and other occasions, an even more
fervent apologist for oratory. As a parliamentary speaker he stood on a
higher rung than did Burke, whose fame rested more on the written
version of his speeches than on the reception of them in the Commons.
If pressed, Fox could have argued that evening that eloquence could
change votes on the spot. As early as 1772 he had observed that his
own speech on the Royal Marriage Act persuaded listeners to change
sides; his 1778 speech on the Old Corps brought new faces into his

---

[1] HM 26405 (Huntington).
[2] Sir James Prior, *Memoir of the Life and Character of the Right Honourable Edmund Burke*,
2nd edn (London, 1826), i, 320–2.

lobby; Pitt's speeches during the constitutional crisis of 1784 undoubtedly garnered votes. Instances were not plentiful but they existed. As to the way in which eloquence influences ministers, he could have recalled that debates on the American war softened measures as they passed through the House. In 1777 he had declared that 'opinions will, in the long run, have their influence on votes'.

Charles Butler, distinguished Catholic lawyer, is another who stressed the utility of effective parliamentary debate: 'It is idle to say that a single vote is seldom gained by a speech in the House of Commons.' He recalled an 1817 debate in which Sir Robert Peel spoke against Catholic emancipation. Peel's speech did not then, perhaps, gain votes, but since no reply was made to it, the House adjourned with an impression that his strong argument against Catholic emancipation had not been answered. 'Compared with it,' observed Butler, 'a division of ten more votes in favour of the minister would have been trifling.'[1] In later years Sir Robert found reasons to change his own position. Fox often felt that his better speeches had an effect and an influence even upon those who at the moment voted against him. He realized that a speaker can give an idea such forcible utterance that its impact lingers. Victor Hugo also observed: 'The persistence of an all-absorbing idea is terrible.'

The ancients identified three influences that can alter human action: wealth, generalship, rhetoric. Fox had little wealth, and that speedily slipped through his fingers; he commanded no army; but he was a master of rhetoric. Not rhetoric in the ordinary sense of the ornate, decorative use of language, but rhetoric in its solid, Greek sense: the faculty of discovering in controversial issues the principal persuasive arguments. Fox was not a person to be put aside, overlooked, ignored. He was such a person that the Government must not only offset his and his friends' votes with its votes and those of its friends, but it must also provide a forceful counter to his arguments, his evidence, his facts, his interpretations and appraisals. Otherwise it would be seriously embarrassed, as North and Pitt were at times seriously embarrassed, and the fact of its embarrassment would be known in every coffee house in London.

A talent for conversing and discussing often accompanies skill in public speaking. When Fox chose he could be a delightful participant. Georgiana once wrote 'that the great merit of C. Fox is his amazing quickness in seazing any subject, he seems to have the particular talent of knowing more about what he is saying and with less pains than

[1] *Reminiscences of Charles Butler*, 4th edn (London, 1842), i, 200.

anyone else. His conversation is like a brilliant player at billiards, the strokes follow one another piff puff.'[1] 'He is above the petty vanity of playing the great man at table, and running away with all the conversation', wrote the Reverend Mr Stevens. 'Fox's manner of speech was very quick with a broken sharpness of tone. He seems to have an air of melancholy about him. He smiles delightfully. . . . He has almost constantly the forefinger of his left hand on his eye, an odd habit!'[2] Sir Philip Francis noted that in conversation he seldom opened up a subject but he liked to argue or discuss views launched by others.[3] Wilberforce recalled: 'Fox was often truly wonderful. He would begin at full tear, and roll on for hours together without tiring either himself or us. . . . Fox in general society was quiet and unassuming. . . . Fox was truly amiable in private life.'[4]

Wraxall spoke of his irresistible smile. Others also noted his charm, his good-natured disposition, his disarming candour. Fox once said in Rogers's presence—and this comment will meet a sympathetic response from those who speak in public—'Often in speaking, when a thing occurs to me and it is not time to bring it out, I know I shall lose it when I want it, and never fail to do it.' The Irish orator Curran thought Fox had no relish for broad humour; he thought that when he sported too playfully in the presence of this slumbering lion, Fox seemed to laugh inwardly. 'It was not easy to say what Fox would call a *mot*,' Curran went on, 'but when said, I thought I saw a smile rippling over the fine Atlantic of his countenance.'[5]

Much of what Fox had to say about Ireland, the India Bill, the Libel Bill, the Test and Corporation Acts, and other major issues came from informal discussions. Chief among his informants, as he once said in the Commons, was Burke; but Burke was only one of a host. Fitzpatrick throughout his life, Erskine, Lauderdale, Grey, and Whitbread in later years, General Henry Fox, members of the diplomatic corps, farmers, sailors, dissenting ministers, Catholic priests, scholars, poets, all poured information into his hopper. 'There's not a man I can't get something from if he talks,' he once said. Of the brilliant Sir Philip Francis, Fox once said in Burke's presence: 'I have sucked many brains in my time, and seldom found more to reward me.'[6] Fox could give as well as take. Holland heard Sheridan more than once praise Fox's generosity in providing speakers on his side with the best arguments and liveliest illustrations that occurred to him.

[1] *Georgiana*, p. 32. [1777].   [2] HM 26405 (Huntington).
[3] Beata Francis and Eliza Keary, eds., *The Francis Letters* (London n.d.), ii, 450.
[4] Wilberforce, v, 260.
[5] W. H. Curran, *Life of the Rt. Hon. J. P. Curran* (Redfield, N.Y., 1858), p. 525.
[6] Tom Taylor, ed., *Autobiography and Memoirs of Benjamin Robert Haydon* (London, 1924), p. 558; Francis, ii, 376.

Heads of state can put to effective use in their speeches the personal information they acquire from interviews with heads of other states, with officials at lower echelons, with executives of industry and trade unions, with knowledgeable professional people. 'So and so told me', quoted in a public utterance, implies authoritative, timely, data. True as the statement is in modern days, it is especially true of the eighteenth century. Until semaphore relays were built about 1797, news could travel no faster than a human body could be moved through space. The captain of a ship docking in the Pool of London could bring with him the newest word from his last port of call. Government officials and members of Parliament at times got word of battles won or lost, treaties signed or edicts proclaimed, through rumours borne by or dispatches carried by ships' personnel. Ships brought foreign newspapers, also invaluable sources. A personal letter from New York, Vienna, St Petersburg, could carry vital, exclusive information. Adverse winds that delayed ships also delayed news. Although for the large part of his career Fox had to operate without benefit of the pipelines of news that flowed to those in office, he was more active than most of his contemporaries in keeping his information up to date. Through receptive members like Fox the daily experience of men in the market place and in the public streets can eventually find its way into the legislative chamber.

Even so, Fox lived and died having seen only a modest way into the process of informal discussion. Review the impasse that Fox and Pitt quickly erected between themselves when the question arose of Fox's joining the Shelburne Government. Fox, in effect, said, 'I will not serve under Lord Shelburne'; Pitt replied, 'I did not come here to betray Lord Shelburne'; and so the conference began and ended—no exploring, no search for a common ground, no leaving the door ajar. The prophet Amos once warned that two could not even walk together except they have agreed. Pitt and Fox could have agreed on one point: neither had any liking for Shelburne. Many hoped fervently at various times during Pitt's Government when the nation was threatened by an aroused foe on the Continent, that Fox's gifts could be put at the service of the administration, but Fox would not take the first step, or hardly more than the first step, toward such discussions. Pitt, by his superior management of Parliament and with the energetic support of the Monarch, seemed always to have enough votes to do the Government's business. Fox, meanwhile, could only remind Englishmen forcefully that it was not necessary to curtail their liberties even though they were fighting an unrelenting enemy. Pitt was overly fearful of noisy assembly and disturbing utterance at home, Fox was overly irresponsible toward danger from abroad. At this distance it is easy to see that these two positions are reconcilable. The sharp corners of these brittle arguments could have been rounded to the greater service of humanity on both sides of the channel.

Public address was to Fox the bold expression of ideas—ideas gathered mainly from persons and returned to persons. Public address was also to Fox the bold use of language. And it is rather amazing that although he spoke or wrote various languages and deeply appreciated the artistic and sensitive use of words by others, he did not himself use words artistically or sensitively. Porson, who probably drank more than any grammarian that ever lived, who at banquets was observed to consume as much as any one present and then before leaving gulp down whatever remained in the glasses, was no doubt cold, stone sober when he made the famous observation: 'Mr Pitt conceives his sentences before he utters them. Mr Fox throws himself into the middle of his, and leaves it to God Almighty to get him out again.' Grattan stated it otherwise: 'His sentences came rolling like a wave of the Atlantic three thousand miles long.' Pitt phrased ideas more easily. Fox was heard to say once that although he himself was never lacking for words: 'Mr Pitt is never without the very best words possible.'[1]

What Fox did succeed in achieving through the arts of language was clarity. He would state an argument in such a way that his meaning was invariably lucid. Butler said: 'There was never a moment in which Mr Fox was either intentionally or unintentionally obscure.' Sir Francis Boring told Farington: 'Mr Fox went *forward & backward*, not satisfied with his first expression, He would put it another way.'[2]

Although much of Fox's repetition was rough-hewn, contrived on the moment, he used this procedure so much that at times he achieved a measure of artistry with it, as when he said in repetitive fashion, 'Show me a parliament . . . that has so diminished the best and dearest rights of the people . . . show me a parliament . . . that has so uniformly sacrificed the liberty of the subject,' and, 'They are not fighting, they are pausing . . . that man is not dead—he is only pausing . . . their country thinks there should be a pause.'

During a debate in January 1778 North complained that 'he was unfortunate in having censure so frequently cast upon him'. The word *unfortunate* caught Fox's ready ear, and in his reply he played upon the word for above an hour, as the *Public Advertiser* noted. The speech is a

[1] Add. MSS. 47590, Rogers MSS., p. 40. London newspapers also complained about his grammar and refinements of rhetoric ('solecisms of language . . . violations of grammatical accuracy . . . unpardonable' (*Morning Post*): 'careless of his language' (*Courier*); Rogers, p. 34; Colchester, i, 23.
[2] Butler, i, 191. *The Farington Diary*, iii, 260.

jewel of its particular sort, and although it does not appear in the published collections, the *General Advertiser and Morning Intelligencer* gave a lengthy excerpt of which the following is a sample:

The noble Lord was indeed an *unfortunate* man in the veriest sense of the word. Never hero in the annals of history, or the records of romance experienced so unbroken and so lengthened a chain of *misfortunes* as he has done. . . . It was his *misfortune* to have plunged the nation into its present unnatural contest, and his *misfortune* to have transacted it all along to the *misfortune* of his country, and dismemberment of the empire. Had he been indeed *fortunate* enough to have discovered, that imposing the Tea Tax, would produce universal discontent in the minds of the colonists, . . . he would have saved millions . . . When he discovered that he could not preserve the peace of the province of Massachusetts Bay, . . . had he been *fortunate* enough to have discovered that the gentle application of amenable measures would have been more effective than the breaking of their charter, . . . he would then have been *fortunate* in the *fortune* of the nation. . . .

As a rhetorical device it is almost an instance of having too much harness for the horse, but viewed as an attention-compelling design, it produced an emotive force above and beyond the mere words themselves. Long after having left the chamber, members would be able to recall and would want to share with their friends parts of what Fox had said, as did reporters in various London newspapers.

Fox had acquired Latin and Greek at Eton, French and Italian while travelling on the Continent, Spanish by clawing rules and words out of a grammar and dictionary. Once when Irish editor, politician, and historian Justin McCarthy inaccurately wrote a statement that Fox used French poorly, an earnest American admirer of Fox, Charles Sumner, eloquently defended Fox's ability to speak excellent French, supplying chapter and verse.[1] To read literature in the original tongue was for Fox a lifelong avocation. His own style was described as Demosthenean; and rugged Demosthenean prose indeed was an effective counterirritant to the neatly measured and balanced rhythms of eighteenth-century rhetoric. Fox well recognized that oral language is something else again from written language. No man's speech, he told Burdett and his guests, would bear printing as it fell from his lips. A good speech bore its special hallmark; it lost by being set down in words and confined within the narrow columns of newspaper and pamphlet; the written version could not fully represent the spoken effort. Fox's oft-repeated and best-known observation: 'Does it read well? Then it was not a good speech.'

On rare occasion Fox offered comments upon the style of others. He had great affection for Lauderdale and constantly sought his advice, but when he learned that Lauderdale was planning to draft a document, he wrote Holland: 'If he does it, it should be done in time for you or

[1] *Reminiscences* (London, 1899), i, 249–50.

somebody else to put it into English.'[1] On one occasion when Fox declared Burke too wordy, Holland left the room, returned with a Burke pamphlet, and asked Fox to support his remark. Fox turned a few pages and rewrote a passage. 'Those present thought he had made his point.'[2]

Fox's language is not invariably quotable. Chatham, Burke, Disraeli, Gladstone, and Churchill in England, and Webster, Lincoln, Roosevelt, and Kennedy in America, have each left behind more that has entered living speech. Much of Fox's diction has been muddied by eighteenth-century, third-person reporting ('Mr Fox said that where there was the opposition of assertions from different gentlemen it was extremely difficult to act'). But Canning liked to quote Fox's aphorism, 'A Restoration is the worst of Revolutions'.[3] Other Fox sayings well deserve to be put into circulation: 'Unwilling subjects are little better than enemies', 'To propose negotiation is not to sue for peace', 'Liberty is the essence of the British constitution', 'I know of no way of governing mankind but by conciliating them', 'No man can be certain of his footing on ground that is unexplored', 'Ignorance in a minister is a crime of the first magnitude'. At times, to be sure, Fox never quite captured the diamond sparkle: 'The wishes and designs of men enter into composition of their opinions' ('We are such stuff as dreams are made of'). Or: 'I will fight the whole of it inch by inch; I will debate every resolution, every argument, and divide the house on each' ('I am in earnest. I will not equivocate; I will not excuse; I will not retreat a single inch; and I will be heard'). Or: 'I can only judge of the future by a consideration of the past' ('I have but one lamp by which my feet are guided, and that is the lamp of experience. I know of no way of judging of the future but by the past').

Hence only infrequently did Fox give his admirers a convenient handle to hold him by. His great utterances, too long to be portable, could not be easily managed, and eventually were set to one side. Exceptions can be noted, but usually the brief speeches and those of modest length are the ones that are read and re-read and that are compiled in anthologies. After the magic of a three-hour speech has worn off, even though it has passed into law, custom, or the land's history, there is not much you can do with the speech text itself except line a shelf with it.

Any technical observation of Fox's speaking genius must pay tribute

---

[1] Add. MSS. 47573. January 7, 1798.
[2] *Circumstantial details of the long illness of the right honourable Charles James Fox, p. 24.*
[3] *Letters of George IV*, iii, 161.

to his mastery of argument. 'He took the argument as it was meant, and answered it if he could', wrote Sir Philip Francis. It was common knowledge, recorded Henry Rogers, that Fox stated his opponent's arguments so convincingly that his friends trembled that he would be unable to answer them. Samuel Rogers, whose friendship with Fox extended over fifteen years, wrote: 'Never in my life did I hear any-thing equal to Fox's speeches in reply.' A contemporary pamphleteer thought it only fair to say that Fox fairly met and routed his opponent where he was strongest.[1] Scribbled on the inside front cover of a Bodleian manuscript is a medley of comments written by an unknown hand: 'Fox follows the grain of the argument. [He is] as careless of words as he is of dress. Can't quote from a greater authority than him-self ... does not affect wit ... a great man ... explosions of elo-quence.'[2] Butler declared that the moment of Fox's grandeur was when, after he had stated the argument of his adversary with greater power than his adversary had done, 'he seized it with the strength of a giant, and tore and trampled on it to destruction'.[3]

Statements like these occur so frequently that it hardly seems neces-sary to qualify them. Set them down as a matter of common knowledge and belief. Fox liked to state an argument before replying to it. He knew the method of accepting an opponent's facts but using them to support the opposite conclusions: 'You say you deserved better suc-cess than you had ... why, you have had more success than you deserved.' Or: 'Put the question the other way. Suppose Ireland were to legislate for England.' When the opponent spoke, Fox had an eye for the jugular, so that if the corpus of his arguments revealed a weak-ness, Fox could put his finger on it. He could attack the premises, the reasoning, the facts underlying the reasoning, the inferences; if a flaw appeared he could detect it. Often, to be sure, he concluded a well-reasoned argument with unnecessary sarcasm: 'I defy imbecility itself to string together a more motley pack of excuses than the right honour-able gentleman has laid before the House this night.'

Occasions arose when Fox so completely answered the arguments before the House and so overwhelmingly demoralized his opponents that no one could make any sort of reply. The most striking instance was his 1778 speech on the motion that no more of the Old Corps should be sent out of the kingdom. Lesser occasions arose in 1776, when he attacked North's management of American affairs (it was then that Burke said he kept waiting for the Crown lawyers to reply,

---

[1] Francis, ii, 455; *Essays* (London, 1855), iii, 99; *Recollections of Samuel Rogers* (London, 1859), p. 78; *A short view of the political state of Great Britain and Ireland at the opening of the new parliament* (London, 1807), pp. 43–4.
[2] MSS Add. C 254 (Bodleian).   [3] Butler, i, 159.

but none did, 'and the debate could not lie better than [Fox] left it'),
and in 1805 when he criticized Pulteney's abuse of eloquence, and
when he supported the right of the House to censure Melville. The
natural fate of an Opposition speaker is to appear late in the debate, after
ministers have offered their proposals. One reason why Fox's name at
times appears as the last speaker of the evening may be that, after he sat
down, ministerial speakers found themselves with nothing remarkable
to say.

Times occurred when Fox's reply contained more of the form of
rebuttal than of substance; Burke's phrase, 'the smartness of debate',
applies here. Another friend called one of Fox's efforts a mere 'debating
speech'. North and Pitt could in fairness then complain that nothing
whatever satisfied Fox. Fox's reputation was not built on speeches of
this sort. Actually, his speeches may be put in three large categories.
One is the 'debating speech', in which he raised merely tactical objections: the procedure or protocol was wrong, the House was being
rushed to a decision, the proposal was unseasonable. Such a speech
served primarily as a holding or delaying action. Another is the impulsive, vehement, 'Good God!' speech, mainly built out of such emotional
appeals as ridicule, scorn, indignation. The third category, the 'over-
view' speech, contains his greatest efforts. These were better reasoned,
more reasonable; the motion before the House was placed in historical
perspective; assertions were supported by specific instances—
precedents, resolutions, statutes; objections were convincingly dealt
with; the emotional appeals were on a high plane—justice, fairness,
humanity; the theme was lofty—peace, religious freedom, political
liberty.

Nor did there seem to be a boundary to his talent for debate. No
genius in his own finances, he could shake and rattle a budget, as he
did some of North's, until the maker was glad to have him resume his
seat. No constitutional historian, he could pile precedent upon precedent, as he did in the Westminster Scrutiny speech, so that eventually
the Crown's talent had to let him take his place in peace. No lawyer, in
his twenties he could cite precedents that Wedderburn and Thurlow
had overlooked; in his thirties, in the Hastings trial, argue the law
lords to a standstill; in his forties, sponsor the Libel Bill. Francis was
correct in his studied judgment that if Fox had entered the bar, he
would have become, 'in a shorter time, and with much less application
than any other man, the most powerful litigant that ever appeared
there'.[1] And Francis had heard Erskine, Mackintosh, and other brilliant barristers of those contentious years.

---

[1] Add. MSS. 40758. Francis, iii, 43–4.

Fox sensed that good debating deeply involved the listener as well as the speaker. The arrangement of seats in St Stephen's chamber, with its five rows of Government adherents seated face to face with five rows of vigilant opposition, facilitated directness: the speaker has his potential objectors prominently in his eye. Fox kept them there. If one so much as shook his head, Fox was capable, if he wished, to take note of it in his next sentence. If one offered question or interjection Fox could react to it without losing his stride. In this way he gave his ideas immediate, distinctive emphasis by linking them to the people in front of him. He could tell whether or not his listeners were lively and attentive. 'There seems to be a sort of deadness in the House of Commons,' he once wrote; 'worse than even in the worse times of the House of Lords.' He wanted to be clear to the listener and also to be understood and believed by the listener. In his public appearances he often commented on the practice of public speaking, as when he declared a speaker 'ought always to be in temper and unison with his audience'. Wraxall observed that if Fox saw latecomers enter the chamber, he would review arguments they had missed.[1]

London reporters liked the word 'rivitt'; Fox 'rivitted' the attention of the listener, they would say. He did not give the longest speech known to his generation—a four-hour effort was his maximum in the House—but he often spoke upwards of two and three hours. On many such occasions the papers would speak of the close attention with which he was heard. At times they would record, unbelievable as it seems and improbable as it is, that the whole House would listen for hours and not a single person leave his seat. Yet the Duke of Somerset once declared that he had listened to Fox for four hours and had been sorry when he left off.[2]

Once called 'greater than Lord Chatham ever was', he lacked entirely Chatham's mastery of the arts of delivery. Chatham, who could roar so loud in one chamber that he could almost be heard in the other, who within the chamber could whisper so as to be heard to the farthest bench, whose gesture reminded listeners of Garrick, whose flashing eye and forbidding manner could threaten and command, had developed these characteristics far beyond the talent of most speakers. Yet although Fox had a shrill, penetrating voice, he used it well, at times pitching his tones low with good effect. He had a rapid rate which in itself had a compelling quality that swept the listener along with the speaker. His gestures were limited to simple pokings with the index

---

[1] Wraxall, iii, 225.

[2] Sir William Fraser, *Disraeli and His Day*, 2nd edn (London, 1891), p. 315.

finger. His enunciation was not always distinct—reporters sometimes found him incomprehensible, probably from a combination of rapid rate, indistinct utterance, and insufficient loudness. He used the old-fashioned pronunciation of 'London', calling it 'Lonnon' to the end of his days. One observer said that he had a habit of saying, 'But, sir,' repeatedly.[1]

Great speakers come in all sizes. Fox was well on the massive side. Coke claimed it was no measy matter to provide a horse sturdy enough to carry Fox. At Holkham an argument once arose as to whether Fox was heavier than Coke's fat chef. Both were weighed, 'but history is silent upon the result'.[2] Fox was solid and bulky. His head, neck, and chest were large. His face, despite its coarse features, was so expressive that listeners could sense the workings of his mind. His shaggy eyebrows helped to punctuate his thoughts. Fox was therefore an impressive speaker to watch in action.

Fox had a bright mind and a retentive memory. Charles Abbot, later Speaker, wrote in 1795: 'The debaters themselves very rarely take any notes at all during the speeches which they intend to answer. Pitt and Fox, never.' When Abbot became Speaker, a member started to read a long speech; the Speaker rebuked the practice, lest it become a precedent, and the House entirely assented.[3] The preparation of a speech was a continuing mental act. Fox's listeners could sense a creative process going on at the moment he uttered his words. They could fully appreciate his alertness and spontaneity. No long glances at a manuscript suggested that something prepared at home was being warmed over. 'The debaters . . . rarely take any notes . . . Pitt and Fox, never.'

So much for the speaker in the man; now to the man in the speaker. He had strong and persistent dislikes but his friendships covered a wide field. He was honest, candid, frank, guileless, unassuming, unpretentious. He had unlimited personal courage—he could have honourably avoided the duel with Adam, but he went through with it and made a lifelong friend out of his opponent. He would accept loans and gifts freely and unabashedly ('How will Fox take it?' 'Why quarterly, of course!') but he would not take a peerage from either Pitt or Grenville. He was tempered by defeat. He knew what it was to outargue the other side, only to have it outvote him; to watch, fast, and sweat in the House of Commons, night after night,[4] wondering what move to make, which way the division would go. He could forgive much: he coalesced

[1] *Idem.*   [2] *Coke of Norfolk*, i, 328–9.   [3] Colchester, i, 24; ii, 60.
[4] Burke's description in his speech to the electors of Bristol in 1780.

with North, he excused Burke's refusal to see him when Burke was mortally ill; he continued his association with the Prince even after the Prince had lied to him.

He was loyal to his political friends. He did not like to make a move without consulting Fitzpatrick, Spencer, Fitzwilliam, Carlisle. His support helped each of them to high post. As he was, however, in office so brief a time, he was not always able to reward many of those whose claim was purely personal. Once he regretted that of this latter group he had been able to help only William Dickson, his Eton and Hertford classmate, whom he assisted to a bishopric. Some considered him thoughtless. 'You have heard me say,' wrote Selwyn, 'that I thought he had no malice or rancour; I think so still, and am sure of it. But I think he has no feeling, neither, for anyone but himself.'[1] Lady Sarah Napier would have agreed. Fox might have secured for her husband the command of a company in the guards, an extremely welcome appointment, but instead he secured it for a stranger. She wrote: 'I had a great mind to be in a *rage*, but I have overcome my anger upon the reflection that Charles has good quallities enough to attone for a thousand faults.'[2]

Fox had no Boswell but many boswells. Wraxall, Creevey, Carlisle, Selwyn, Grattan, Farington, Malmesbury, and a score of others recorded in their correspondence and in their journals such trifles of Fox's everyday living and speaking that came to their ears. Fox's opinions on the odds and ends of life bespeak his own character and personality. For example:

On poetry: Poetry is 'the great refreshment of the human mind'. 'Not a sum of arithmetic could be cast up at first without the aid of poetry . . . men first found out they had minds by making and tasting poetry.' If he had a boy he would make him write verses, 'the only way of knowing the meaning of words'.[3]

On writing: 'As to altering and correcting I know by experience that one often alters twenty times without mending, but yet sometimes one may light on an improvement.'[4] 'I write with difficulty—perhaps the greater ease with which a man speaks, the harder it is for him to write. I believe so.'

On English: '. . . the most difficult of all languages—a union of many.'

1 *HMCR*, Carlisle MSS., p. 591. March 12 [1782].
2 *Life and Letters of Lady Sarah Lennox*, ii, 40–1. November 10, 1783.
3 Except as otherwise noted, these comments are from Add. MSS. 47590, Rogers MSS.
4 Add. MSS. 47573. To Holland.

On Chatham: 'Lord Chatham, I think, delivered finer things than Demosthenes—; but he had a greater theatre and men are made by the circumstances. "America, they tell me, has resisted. I rejoice to hear it." This passage I think excels any in Demosthenes.'

On miscellaneous pleasures: When an acquaintance said it was delightful 'to lie down on the grass in some wild spot the whole day long with a book,' Fox asked: 'But why with a book?'[1]

On disagreeable correspondents: When once he received a missive from a pompous somebody whose name has charitably been forgotten, he is reported, perhaps apocryphally, to have replied: 'Sir—your letter is before me, and in a few minutes it will be behind me.' The pungency of this note, said the writer who exhumed it, 'found favour in the lobby of the House—its impromptu was whispered through every opera box— its attic salt was *gouté* in the highest garret.'[2]

Gladstone's political opponents liked to say of him that he was Oxford outside but Liverpool inside. Fox never displayed any sort of front or façade. He was the same stuff all the way through. Aristocratic Oxford and Eton were there, showing in his fondness for travel, his passion for fashionable recreation, his delight and even expertness in poetry, history, drama, oratory. But London was there, too, showing in his enthusiastic participation in the life of its hustings, theatres, markets, shops. Hence, wherever he went he was as much at ease in the company of domestics and tradesmen as he was in conversation with lords and their ladies.

But now back to the main stream of Fox's career. Gloriously in his immediate past was his commanding, impressive, masterly, ill-timed plea for parliamentary reform. Invitingly in his immediate present was a recess from parliamentary speaking. The *True Briton* announced on May 31, 1797: 'Mrs Armistead rejoices in the secession of Mr Fox from the House of Commons. She likes him better at St Anne's Hill than in St Stephens.' His party was tiny, but he was chief of it, and the prose was not too lavish that described him as 'the inmate of baronial halls, the guest of palaces, the companion of princes, the *preux chevalier* of dames, the associate of sages and scholars, himself a classic and wit of the first order, one of the *haute-volée* in all points'.[3] This was the view from one direction of that bulky bit of English architecture known as Charles James Fox.

[1] Add. MSS. 32566, Mitford.   [2] *The Times*, August 12, 1854.   [3] *Idem.*

Part Four

Long Road Back

I always say, and always think that of all the Countries
in Europe, England will be the last to be free.

Charles James Fox

25

Secession; St Anne's Hill
1797-1799

His standard is in the hearts of men.
Georgiana, Duchess of Devonshire

No politician today in his right mind would formally announce that he was seceding from office. If he did, voters would relieve him of his duties in full at an early opportunity. Fox had announced his secession in 1797 with mixed and mingled feelings. Largely they were compounded of his disappointment and frustration, but it must be remembered that he was no longer as energetic and vigorous as he was when two decades formerly he had disputed the wisdom of secession by his Rockingham colleagues. He had little doubt, of course, of his hold on his Westminster constituents.

Elsewhere, even in that day the move was attacked. Fox asked Holland to defend it by stating that the secessionists, after losing out on parliamentary reform, had decided that they might stay away, 'considering the preceding events of the Session and the behaviour of Parliament upon them'.[1]

At St Anne's, with its garden, lawns, and thirty acres of land, retired Mr Fox had ample opportunity for leisurely reading, strolls, and modest ventures in horticulture. After breakfast at eight or nine, he read some Italian author with his wife, and spent the rest of the morning in further reading and writing; dinner was at two or three; walking and conversation occupied the day until tea-time; much reading aloud, principally of history, until ten; a light supper of fruit or pastry ended the day, and by ten-thirty the family was abed.[2]

Burke died that summer, two years short of man's threescore and ten. His death caused hardly a ripple. Occurring on a Saturday, it was so generally known on Sunday that it barely qualified as news for the few Monday papers that chose to print a brief statement. Only an occasional word of praise appeared, like this in *The Times*: 'Mr Burke will live as long as strength of imagination and beauty of language

[1] Add. MSS. 47572. *Fox Cor.*, iii, 136–7. August 7, 1797.
[2] John Bernard Trotter, *Memoirs of the Latter Years of the Right Honourable Charles James Fox* (London, 1811), p. 16.

shall be respected by the world.' Neither Burke's ideas nor his personality caught the fancy of Londoners, however, and in their minds the world moved on as if he had never lived.

Fox, of course, was deeply touched, and wept bitterly when he heard the news. When Burke lay dying Fox had gone to see him, but Burke stubbornly refused an interview on the ground of principle.[1] Later Fox related the incident to Coke, who lamented Burke's obstinacy, but Fox was philosophical: 'Oh, never mind, Tom; I always find every Irishman has got a piece of potato in his head.'[2] Burke's will, dated 1794, had a statement asking forgiveness if his friendship with others had been broken off by political differences. This declaration, also, Fox needed to view with philosophical detachment. His friendship with Burke, going back to Hertford College days, had been strengthened by the long struggles over America and India, but fell apart over the violent issues that arose in France.

Fox came briefly out of retirement on October 10 to speak at the Shakespeare to a large group of electors and other friends, gathered to commemorate the anniversary. He was in good form that evening as he spoke on a variety of topics. Naturally those present expected him to comment on his retirement, but he merely said that people would believe, if he attended, his presence would lend support to the notion that there actually was an effective Parliament. He repeated a favourite maxim: 'Being easily discouraged by majorities . . . is not one of my faults.' He grieved at the steady erosion of freedom of speech, citing examples of meetings broken up by magistrates, newspaper men imperilled, a faculty member rejected from a deanship for opposing the repressive Bills. He offered to leave the Commons in order to give way to some other representative, but cries of No! no! no! 'resounded instantly from every part of the room'. In government, he concluded, a complete change was needed, but, he added, a change consistent with the fundamental principles of the constitution with its monarchy, Lords, and Commons. Thus he differed entirely from the French radicals.[3]

Fox appeared at other Whig Club meetings but on the whole his life these years was literary, or quasi-literary, as much as it was political.

In December 1796 Fox had received from the distinguished scholar, Gilbert Wakefield, an edition of Lucretius. Wakefield, a scholar with a side interest in politics, dedicated his book to Fox, a politician with a

---

[1] *Circumstantial details of the long illness*, etc., p. 31.   [2] *Coke of Norfolk*, i, 384.
[3] *The speeches at length of the right honourable C. J. Fox, T. Erskine, &c. &c. &c. at a meeting held at the Shakespeare Tavern*, etc. (London, 1797). Excerpts are from this pamphlet.

side interest in literature. This gift was the beginning of a correspondence about literary matters, with select political digressions, that lasted
nearly five years. Fox read the book and asked the author questions
about the meaning of passages not completely clear. Wakefield replied
in detail—scholars love to instruct statesmen—and the correspondence
was on.[1] Fox in his turn was proud to think of himself as a scholar:
'We Etonians hold ourselves (I do not know whether or not others
agree with us) of some authority, in matters of this sort.'

The Lucretius did not sell very well, and Fox suggested that his
name on the dedication page was partly the reason; Wakefield gallantly
responded that such could not be the cause at all. Wakefield then turned
from literature to politics and wrote a pamphlet in which he called
attention to the poverty of the people, deplored the existence of a titled
aristocracy and an established Church, called Pitt a demon of destruction with a prostitute majority in the lower house of borough-mongers,
loan jobbers, military officers, pensioners, and official sycophants. As
the laws clearly prohibited this sort of prose, Wakefield found himself
brought to trial, and, despite or because of a long speech in his own
defence, was sentenced to Dorchester jail for two years.

The correspondence continued, Wakefield in jail and Fox at St
Anne's. Friends took up a collection of £5,000 to ease the misfortune
of the scholar turned politician and provided him with materials for
writing.[2] Fox was profoundly distressed by the severe punishment
inflicted upon his friend. He wrote another correspondent that the
liberty of the press was virtually annihilated: 'The only thing left us,'
he declared, 'is the trial by jury, and if ever that shall be found materially
inconvenient to our rulers, I am convinced they will find as little
difficulty as they will feel scruple in getting rid of that also.'[3]

Eventually Wakefield served his sentence, which, wrote Fox, 'I shall
ever consider to have been as disgraceful to the Government of the
Country, as it has been honourable to you,' and after more words on
books recommended and books read, the correspondence came to an
end.

Parliament opened on November 2, 1797. The absence of Fox was
lamented. With Fox and his friends away, one division went 139 to 8

[1] *Correspondence of the Late Gilbert Wakefield, B.A. with the Late Right Honourable Charles
James Fox, in the Years 1796–1801*, etc. (London, 1813).
[2] *State Trials*, xxvii, 679–760.
[3] Christopher Wyvill, *Political Papers Chiefly Respecting the Attempt of the County of York
and other . . . districts . . . to effect a reformation of the Parliament of Great Britain* (York,
1794–1802), vi, 28–9. To Wyvill, March, 1, 1799. Fox wrote O'Bryen about Wakefield's
punishment: 'The more I think of the verdict . . . the more I consider it a death blow to the
liberty of the press' (Add. MSS. 47566. July 29).

for the Government. For the first time in his long career Pitt could speak almost without opposition and without inquiry. For example, on November 24 he proposed to augment the Government's income partly by a new loan of £12 million and partly by increasing the assessed taxes on windows, servants, horses, carriages, and such articles. As he explained in his speech, however, he recommended a graduated rate, based on the taxpayer's wealth. The more opulent classes might pay three and a half or four times the former assessment, whereas those of lesser means might pay half or three times the previous rate. This tremendous increase, immediately affecting 800,000 people, was agreed to in committee ten days later with only fifteen dissenting. Pitt's mastery was complete: the graduated income tax was launched with hardly a voice raised against it.

As Fox had formerly been attacked for opposing Pitt's measures, now he was attacked for not appearing in Parliament. Yet his secession from Parliament did not mean that he had completely seceded from politics. He used the Whig Club as a platform from which occasionally to make a public utterance. *The Times* took a particular interest in the meetings of the Club, described it as being composed of 'broken-down gamblers and needy adventurers, who bellow for reform, but pant for the moment of revolution', and regretted that such men as Fox and the Duke of Norfolk associated with it. It scolded Fox for declaring 'that he will accept no share in the Government, until the *public mind* is made up to a complete and radical reform'. On this version of his speech, it wondered whether he would determine 'public mind' from the toasts of the Whig Club or the resolutions of Corresponding Societies; and if he meant by 'complete and radical reform' the repeal of the Test Act (thus opening church benefices to dissenters), the Act against Treason and Treasonable Practices (thus exposing the King's person to insult and injury), the Act against Unlawful Assembly (thus reviving Mr Thelwall's lectures, and the meetings at Copenhagen House). These dangerous doctrines, said *The Times*, require an explanation, so the country would know what to expect from an administration in which Fox had a share.[1] The excerpts are worth citing, if only to show that on the points cited history proved Fox resoundingly right and *The Times* capitally wrong.

Pitt's proposed new taxes brought Fox and the other seceders back to the Commons for the second reading on December 14. A burst of applause and cries of 'Clear the lobby' greeted Fox as he entered the chamber. 'Every one in the gallery rose as with one impulse, and the effect seemed to communicate itself to the House.'[2] Acidulous remarks greeted the appearance of the vacationers, which Sheridan took note of,

[1] December 7, 23. [2] *Parliamentary History*, xxxiii, 1100.

adding that the war was being continued to keep nine worthless ministers in their places. Fox in his turn commented on a sly retort that his absence had given him a chance to study history and therefore reform his opinions. To this statement he retaliated in his best debating style:

I have been told this night that . . . I in my retirement have had leisure to reconsider my former opinions; and that I, like others, may have had much to learn. Those who think they have arrived at that degree of knowledge beyond which they have nothing to learn, are in a state which, when they affect it, show they have learnt but little.

Fox obviously was still a formidable opponent. He continued:

But I should hold myself much indebted to the right honourable gentleman who made this observation, if he would tell me, in what book of ancient or modern history—in what school of philosophy—in what system of any admired politician . . . I am to find, that perseverance in a system which has led you to the brink of ruin is the way to extricate you from your difficulty. That, indeed, is one of the lessons which I have yet to learn.[1]

He then entered into a detailed analysis of the presumed efficacy of the new income taxes and declared that he would have no part of a new administration until there had been thorough reform and 'a direct return to the genuine principles of the British Constitution'. Pitt replied at length, and the division recalled the old, familiar, presecession quantities of 175 to 50.

Fox's vacation from Parliament turned out to be one of the most interrupted holidays ever planned. On January 4 he was back again in the Commons for the final debate on the Tax Bill, to hear his absences condemned once more and his motives assailed. Most of his three and a half hour speech was in self-defence: 'I am not very dexterous at any thing, but I ought to be so at explanation, he said, '. . . because [it is] impossible for a man who has been so often misrepresented as I have been not to have acquired some art in making his defence.' He declared that the wisdom of ministers was not equal to the wisdom of the people in deciding political matters. Many that day spoke against Pitt's bills but none so masterfully. Although Fox did not believe the day for universal suffrage had come, and woman suffrage seemed so novel that he hardly felt it necessary to say he opposed it, he again urged a substantial broadening of the base of representation. He said:

You can do nothing by saying in this House, 'this or that is the opinion of the people,' but you should have that opinion from themselves freely expressed, by a

[1] *Parliamentary History*, xxxiii, 1111.

true, substantial, as well as virtual representation of the people. . . . These are the only means to show the real strength of this country.[1]

The House adjourned at five o'clock in the morning, the opposition recording votes of 75 and 71 against the Government's 202 and 196 respectively. Opposition in the Lords was equally trivial, and Pitt's new Tax Bill speedily became the law of the land.

The annual observing of Fox's birthday was by now as well established as that of the King's or Queen's. On January 24, 1798, a reputed 2,000 persons attended a public dinner at the Crown and Anchor, with Fox present and the Duke of Norfolk in the chair to give the toast of the evening:

We are met in a moment of most serious difficulty to celebrate the birth of a man dear to the friends of freedom. I shall only recall to your memory that not twenty years ago the illustrious George Washington had not more than two thousand men to rally round him when his country was attacked. America is now free. This day full two thousand men are assembled in this place. I leave you to make the application. I propose to you the health of Charles James Fox![2]

These sentiments were uttered at a time when Ireland was dangerously on the edge of rebellion. Later when a toast was offered to the Duke, he rose and said: 'Give me leave, before I sit down, to call on you to drink our Sovereign's health:—The Majesty of the People!' These were also dangerous words. As a result, the Duke was dismissed from two offices he held.

Pitt wrote to Wellesley in detail about the parliamentary and extra-parliamentary debates of the immediately preceding weeks. He confessed that those weeks had produced more fatigue and anxiety than had attended any other parliamentary campaign, yet he felt fit and equal to fighting the battle as long as necessary. He thought he had saved the assessed taxes by showing that at all risks he was determined to persevere, 'and by that means alone I believe it was carried'. Members of the Opposition, he went on, only added to the odium and disgrace of their secession by their conduct and language in these debates. On the extraparliamentary side, Pitt continued, was Fox's birthday celebration:

The two most distinguished Traits were a speech from the Duke of Norfolk, which I think even the Crown Lawyers will hardly prove to be much short of Treason,

---

[1] *Parliamentary History*, xxxiii, 1221–61. See also *Speech of the Right Honourable Charles James Fox, in the house of commons, on Friday the 4th of January, 1798, on the assessed-tax bill,* etc. (London, 1798).

[2] *Early Life of Samuel Rogers*, pp. 378–9; Stanhope, iii, 91. *Annual Register*, 1798, *Chronicle*, pp. 5–6.

and a Public Profession from Horne Tooke of Reconciliation and Coalition with Fox with which I think you will be delighted.[1]

So much criticism followed the birthday celebration that Fox at the Whig Club defended the toast of 'the sovereignty of the majesty of the people', and said that if it were imprudent, he was as guilty as the Duke of Norfolk. Later Fox wrote that the Duke's dismissal from his offices, because of the toast, provided a means of distinguishing between whig principles and those advocated by the administration.[2]

In March he wrote to Dennis O'Bryen that he had 'quitted London with little exception *for good and all* as the phrase is. I know there must be many who blame me; but I am convinced that in these times I can do no good, and therefore think I have a right to consult my ease.'[3]

Still another interruption to the secession had been the annual slave trade debate. Wilberforce's usual motion had been slated to come up in April, and after much urging Fox agreed to be present. He wrote Fitzpatrick that he was going against judgment and against inclination, since he had learned that it was useless to attend the early sessions on the slave trade Bill. Moreover, he added: 'I do not think it fair when a Man has considered a subject, and after listening to others, formed his opinion, to heaze him into acting contrary to it by mere importunity.'[4] Nevertheless, he and other seceders were in their places on April 3 when Wilberforce moved that leave be given to bring in a Bill to abolish the slave trade, at a time to be fixed.

Over the years the arguments against the trade were gradually wearing down. The old contention was repeated that England should not act unless others did: on this day it was argued that vigorous steps should be taken by the colonial legislatures of St Vincent, Grenada, Antigua, and others. Another weary argument was that males exceeded females in the proportion of five to three; consequently importations of slaves should continue in order to equalize the numbers of each sex. A novel argument also appeared in the form of a story describing a war between two African kingdoms, a vast number of prisoners being taken on both sides. One king had all male prisoners brought before him, and in accordance with his usual practice, had their throats cut in his presence; the other, having learned that French traders were operating on the Senegal river, sent his captives there to be sold into slavery.

---

[1] *Letters from William Pitt to Lord Wellesley*, 1796–1804. January 26, 1798. (Clements).
[2] Add. MSS. 47564. *Fox Cor.*, iii, 276. To the Earl of Lauderdale, February 4.
[3] Holland House MSS., March 19.   [4] Add. MSS. 47581. April 1.

Slavery therefore was an institution that preserved men's throats from being cut.[1]

Pitt's speech was brief but the House had the rare opportunity of hearing Fox praise him. Pitt, Fox declared, speaks always with great force, but what he advanced this night was of immense weight. But Fox went on to inquire why the House, which had supported Pitt on points infinitely less clear, could refuse to support him tonight, unless it was hostile to liberty in general. Why, he demanded, 'is Pitt's eloquence deficient in effect in this cause? How am I to account for it, unless there is a deliberate system in this House to discourage the principles of liberty?'[2] Fox must have thought the cause was lost regardless of what he said, as he did not achieve the topmost height of conciliation in his speech. In a slender House the motion failed, 87 to 83. The close vote did not arouse much excitement. It was late in the parliamentary year; foreign affairs were in the foreground of public attention; yet many of those who divided that day in favour of the trade and those who profited from it must have felt that the question would continue to be agitated and that abolition was certain even if slow.

The incident of Norfolk's toast was not yet closed. At the meeting of the Whig Club at Freemason's Tavern on May 1, when the Duke offered 'The man who is, and dares be honest in the worst of times— Mr Fox', Fox, in the chair, remarked: 'I'll give you a toast . . . the Sovereignty of the People of Great Britain'.[3] Fox's continued defiance angered Pitt. He wrote to Grenville that although he hesitated to prosecute Fox because it was likely Fox would be triumphantly acquitted, he might very well order him to attend the House and be reprimanded by the Speaker. If after a reprimand, Pitt wrote, 'he offers a fresh insult at the next Whig Club, [he might be sent] to the Tower for the remainder of the session; which . . . would be enough to assert the authority of the House.'[4] Pitt's final decision was to recommend to the King that Fox's name should be stricken from the list of privy councillors;[5] the King on May 9 personally drew an ink line through Fox's name. No longer, then, could Fox be addressed as 'right honourable'.

Lascelles's comment is appropriate: 'It was Pitt at his pettiest.'[6]

Fox's repeated absences from the House afforded more opportunity for voluble George Tierney to speak. Tierney had refused to join the

[1] *Parliamentary History*, xxxiii, 1385–92.   [2] *Ibid.*, xxxiii, 1403–10.   [3] *The Times*, May 3.
[4] *HMCR*, Fortescue MSS., iv, 187. May 5. He wrote Dundas in similar vein also on May 5. See the bound volume, *Autograph Correspondence with Lord Melville* (Clements), printed in Stanhope, iii, 127–8. On May 7 he wrote to Wilberforce (Wilberforce, ii, 422).
[5] Pitt to the King, May 8. Fortescue transcripts (Clements).   [6] *Charles James Fox*, p. 285.

seceders but in their absence speedily became one of the frequent speakers in the eighteenth Parliament. In May, during the debate on a Bill to increase navy personnel, Tierney spoke up with such asperity—the word is one from his own vocabulary—that Pitt declared that he was obstructing the defences of the country. When Tierney retorted that this language was not parliamentary, Pitt stiffly refused to retract or explain; whereupon, next day, Tierney challenged Pitt to a duel. It was Fox and Adam, a great man needlessly exposed to danger from a lesser one, all over again. The two met at Putney Heath, took stations twelve paces apart, and blazed away without effect. With fresh pistols they fired again, Tierney at his target, Pitt into the air; the seconds then put a stop to the business, declaring that everything had been conducted with perfect honour to both parties. Pitt wrote to Wellesley later that week to report on his duel, concluding: 'I believe we parted better satisfied with each other, than on any other occasion in our Lives.'[1]

Next week Pitt was seriously ill. This fact, by no means related to the duel, is a reminder that Pitt, like his father, was a sick man most of his life. As a youngster he had been in such poor health that he was tutored at home, instead of, like his father, being sent to Eton. Physicians had prescribed port wine as a medicine and over the years Pitt had drunk more and more of it: two bottles at a sitting, as many as seven with a competent companion like Dundas; a respectable achievement even when men drank brandy like tea. The story is told that one on occasion he appeared at the House having had so much wine that his speaking was evidently affected. A clerk told the Speaker that seeing Pitt's distressing condition gave him a violent headache. Pitt, hearing the story later, observed: 'I think that is an excellent arrangement—that I should have the wine and the Clerk the headache!'[2]

Pitt endured poor health until the end of his life, though he was not subjected to the sort of criticism and abuse because of his drinking that was levelled at Fox for his gambling.

The Irish problem broke out again in 1798. As a matter of personal observation, members of the Government knew little about the Irish. Sheridan and Burke had been born in Dublin and Fox had visited Ireland, but most of those who had to formulate policy on the Irish question had never been there. It was not the habit of prime ministers to go take a personal look. The Irish were mainly Catholic, which ran them

[1] Stanhope, iii, 130–1; Sidmouth to Pellew, *Life of Lord Sidmouth*, i, 205; *Letters from William Pitt to Lord Wellesley, 1796–1804*, May 31. (Clements).
[2] *Life of Lord Sidmouth*, i, 153. Quoted in Stanhope, iii, 136–7.

foul of the Test Act and the privileges extended those of the Anglican communion as opposed to those of Catholic faith. Trade restrictions were irksome despite concessions that had been made. The Government's headquarters in Dublin, the Castle, was a symbol of oppression. The differences between the English and the Irish were too complex to be resolved, either with a subordinate Parliament at Dublin or a united Parliament in London.

In 1798 an aspect of the complicated problem was the eagerness of the leadership of the United Irishmen to have France help Irish plans for revolt. One of their group, Arthur O'Connor, undertook to go to Paris to negotiate this dangerous mission. With him was a Roman Catholic priest, the Reverend James O'Coigley, and three others. All were captured in England, and were taken to Maidstone for trial. Meanwhile in Ireland the Government's troops began a systematic search for arms and seized not fewer than 70,000 pikes and 48,000 guns. Risings followed in Leinster, Ulster, and Wexford; Protestant prisoners were massacred and rebels were executed.

Out of this background began the trial, in May, of O'Connor, O'Coigley, and their confederates. O'Connor summoned as character witnesses the principal leaders of the opposition—Fox, Sheridan, Erskine, Norfolk, and others—and was subsequently acquitted, though he was immediately arrested on another charge, held in custody a few months, then allowed to retire to France. The Reverend Mr O'Coigley was found guilty, and later hanged and beheaded.[1]

Fox was shocked by what he considered a grave miscarriage of justice. The selection of Maidstone as a place for the trial, he declared, was especially unfortunate. He had become especially concerned about O'Connor, noting his altered appearance because of 'his long imprisonment having shaken his health and shattered his nerves'. He added, with great human sympathy: 'What an engine of oppression this power of Imprisonment is!'[2]

In June Fox once more attended the House to take part in the debates on resolutions that Irish Catholics should be treated with greater liberality, and that those who disapproved of measures of concession and conciliation towards Ireland were not effectual channels of administration. At the outset of the debate it was moved that the standing order against permitting strangers in the gallery be enforced; as a result there was little record of the debate, which included a 'long and able' speech by Fox followed by his motion that the system of coercion in Ireland and the scourges and other tortures employed to extort confession were disgraceful to the British name and should be ended. All

[1] *State Trials*, xxvii, 142.
[2] Add. MSS. 47581. *Fox Cor.*, iii, 277. March 9, 1798.

motions were lost, however, by a ratio of three to one.[1] Thus was treated the eloquent protest against flogging, picketing, half-hanging and other styles of torturing. Further protest was entered on the lords' journals: 'When an Irishman is tortured, an Englishman is tortured; for the same men, who, in violation of the laws of their country, and of every dictate of humanity, dare to put Irishmen to torture, will not hesitate, when they think it expedient, to put Englishmen to torture also.'[2] Buried in ageing volumes of the *Parliamentary History*, these protests represent a bold but futile step on the narrow, ill-marked trail, lined with gallows and gibbet, flogging post and dungeon, and, more ominously, with sealing-wax on parchment; a trail believed to lead eventually to human freedom. As the nineteenth century unfolded, this trail widened and at times brightened, but as the twentieth century knows, the summit has not yet been reached.

In 1799 Fox did not appear in the House of Commons. Debates on repealing the suspension of habeas corpus, on the proposed union with Ireland, on the abolition of the slave trade, on suppressing Sunday newspapers, on the budget, continued without him. Keeping abreast of what went on, however, Fox wrote to Holland that Pitt's new Tax Bill seemed dreadfully oppressive. On political parties, a subject that had fallen low in popular opinion, he felt on the defensive:

When a Man has taken an opinion, he takes everything to be a confirmation of it, but I can not help feeling every day more and more, that in this country at least an Aristocratick Party is absolutely necessary to the preservation of Liberty, and especially to give any consequence to the inferior classes, but this I fear is all over.[3]

He was shocked by the proposed union of the Irish and British Parliaments, calling it 'the most monstrous proposition that was ever made',[4] but urged Holland to attend the debates, though he himself did not. He could have argued, as he wrote to Holland in detail, on the theme that Parliament was not competent to effect a union with Ireland; his reason being that Parliament was appointed to uphold the constitution, and a union would be a way of destroying it; Parliament could not even legislate Great Britain into an absolute monarchy or a republic, though it might believe the change would be for the better. For alterations so radical as these—union, monarchy, or republic—the unequivocal consent of the people should be secured, though Fox does not spell out how this should be done; perhaps by special convention, perhaps by a

---

[1] *Parliamentary History*, xxxiii, 1513–17.
[2] *Ibid.*, xxxiii, 1517–19. Oxford and Mortimer.
[3] Add. MSS. 47573. *Fox Cor.*, iii, 149. January 5, 1799.
[4] Add. MSS. 47573. *Fox Cor.*, iii, 150. January 19.

Parliament elected for that purpose. What is clear is that he considered union 'not only a Revolution, but a Revolution of a more complete kind than any other'; in a sense each of the united Parliaments would become, to use his word, 'annihilated'.[1] To another correspondent he called the proposed Union 'the most equivocal instance of Despotism that we have seen, and that is saying a good deal'.[2]

Fox appeared at other Whig Club meetings, but on the whole his life these years was literary rather than political. The solemn editors of the *Memorials and Correspondence* omit reference to the deluge of poetry in English, Latin, and Greek on the subject of the death of two of Fitzpatrick's dogs. There were versions marked first, second, and third:

> Of Faddle's death I know the cause;
> 'Twas that, disdaining Nature's laws
> And deaf to voice of sober Reason
> He courted Flora out of season.

This entire literary venture now seems out of season, but the correspondence also contains interesting fragments of literary and rhetorical criticism. From time to time Fox elaborated his theory of poetry, his general idea being that poetical language should deal in simple words conveying simple ideas rather than in involved words conveying complex or abstract ideas. He was sure that poetry should appeal to the senses rather than to the understanding.[3]

The criticism of speakers and speech making he especially felt to be his province. His high regard for Demosthenes has been noted before; he advised Holland to read Cicero's letters to Athens, and if he were not able to do it in Latin, to try it in French.[4]

These literary and semi-literary pursuits, combined with battledore and shuttlecock, whist, hunting, and a variety of social activity contrasted strikingly with those of the old days at Brooks's and Newmarket. He would have been happy to pursue his current interests longer, but his retirement was sharply interrupted by a communication from the First Consul of France to the King of Britain that brought an opportunity for Fox to speak once again on a subject that invariably touched his heart: peace.

[1] Add. MSS. 47573. *Fox Cor.*, iii, 153–64. February 18, 19, 23.
[2] Osborn Collection, 85/15. To William Smith, February 2. (Yale.)
[3] Add. MSS. 47581, 47583. *Fox Cor.*, iii, 156. To Fitzpatrick, January 13; to Holland, February 18, 19.
[4] Add. MSS. 47581. December 1799.

26

Quest for Peace
1799–1800

They are not fighting—Do not disturb them—they
are merely pausing!—this man is not expiring with
agony—that man is not dead—he is only pausing!

Charles James Fox

While Fox was enjoying his leisure at St Anne's, Bonaparte was planning political manoeuvres that effectively disrupted it.

Now the First Consul of the newly established republic, Bonaparte was a person of extraordinary talent who had an exalted belief in his own capacities. 'Never speak unless you know you are the ablest man in the room,' he once said, a maxim that still allowed him to discourse freely on a multitude of topics. He could stir men with well chosen words, or he could use forceful positive action as the situation required : a whiff of grapeshot to overawe a mob, a movement of an army corps to humiliate a kingdom. He was a man of tremendous energy. And he was resilient; he could absorb defeat at one spot and direct victory at another.

In 1798 the Directory had assigned him to train an army for the invasion. The difficulties of this venture, however, have made more than one general take a second look, so Bonaparte had decided instead to carry the war to Egypt. Although Pitt had sent a squadron under Nelson to the Mediterranean, Bonaparte eluded the British fleet and landed his army at Alexandria. His first skirmishes had been successful, but in August Nelson located the French fleet and sank all but four French ships. Bonaparte's troops, marooned, launched a campaign into Syria but had to retreat back into Egypt.

By the spring of 1799 the Second Coalition had been formed, including Austria, Russia, Turkey, and Naples. During the summer the allies had been able to drive the French out of Italy and advance into Switzerland. Military setbacks plus the state of affairs at home had threatened the existence of the Directory, so Bonaparte hurried to Paris, overthrew the Directory, and in November set up a republican form of government headed by three consuls. Meanwhile the Russians had met reverses, and, discouraged, pulled out of the coalition.

Bonaparte now thought the time opportune to seek an armistice. On

Christmas Day 1799, he wrote to George III, expressing a wish for peace. The King reacted promptly and vigorously. He wrote to Foreign Secretary Grenville that it was impossible to 'treat with a new Impious Self created Aristocracy', and that the only consideration was how to reject the proposal with 'Dignity and Seriousness'.[1] Over the signature of Grenville, Pitt's Government responded with aloofness; his Majesty thought it could negotiate only with a stable government, and since there was no evidence that Bonaparte spoke for such a state, his Majesty's forces must pursue the present just and defensive war.

Fox had reacted strongly against the refusal of Pitt to negotiate; the Government's position was an insult to the intelligence of the English people. How absurd it was, he thought, in time of war, to require Bonaparte to restore the French monarchy, or at least to demonstrate that he could behave peaceably, before negotiations could be opened.[2] Fox did not want to forsake his leisure at St Anne's and plunge into a heated political debate, but he realized that he could not in good conscience decline an opportunity that might help bring the war to an end. His associates also strongly urged him to participate in the debate. Seldom had a man a more bitter struggle within himself to reconcile preference with duty. He had not been in the House for more than a year; he was convinced that his return would have no effect upon the outcome; he was now a man of limited energies, and his zest for life entirely centred upon the delights of St Anne's.

The insistence of his friends finally led him to return to the parliamentary scene but on the whole he felt that he had been overpersuaded, 'and when one does a thing against not only one's inclination, but one's judgment too', he could not be expected to do his best. He decided to visit Lord Holland on his way to Westminster, but left the country with such reluctance that he promised to stay at Holland House only two nights. While there he learned that because of Pitt's illness the debate had been postponed, and the news of this further absence from home so vexed him that tears stole down his cheeks.[3]

Having decided to appear, he demonstrated the customary reflexes of a party leader; he hoped that attendance would be good so that his return would appear less absurd.[4] Moreover, he thought a preliminary meeting at the house of some notable person like the Duke of Bedford would be desirable if the debate were to be successful, going on to say that by 'success' he could not hope to carry the question—the old party was too routed and dispersed for that—but to gain advantage in point

---

[1] Fortescue transcripts, January 1, 1800. (Clements.)
[2] Add. MSS. 47574. *Fox Cor.*, iii, 175–6. To Holland, January 1800.
[3] Add. MSS. 47574. *Fox Cor.*, iii, 176. Wyvill, vi, 55. *Memoirs of the Whig Party*, i, 157–8.
[4] Add. MSS. 47574. *Fox Cor.*, iii, 177. To Holland, January 21.

of numbers. Positive he was that the refusal of Bonaparte's offer was a fault in judgment without parallel in history.[1]

The great debate took place Monday, February 3. The benches of the House of Commons were crowded. Most enthusiastic report was an eyewitness account that described impatient politicians hovering about the entrance to the parliamentary chambers almost as early as the day broke; later the bustle became prodigious as various individuals presented their claims to admission. The gallery was insufficient to contain half the candidates for seats. One unsuccessful contender had an arm fractured, and endured a long delay while others attempted to disengage him from the crowd. Most papers, however, were able to get full reports of the speeches. *Lloyd's Evening Post* could say that Fox made his appearance about half past four o'clock, but was not received by the *outside passengers* with any of that *acclamation* which announced his return on one or two former occasions; other papers did not gainsay this observation. In the House Sheridan and Erskine sat on either side of Fox (what a trio! a supremely eminent comic dramatist, a debater, and a court-room pleader). Next to Erskine sat Tierney. Wilberforce was there, although as matters turned out both he and Sheridan, along with others, were prevented by the length of the principal speeches and the lateness of the hour from speaking. Grey was in the gallery, ill, his arm in a sling, but he heard the debate and participated in the division.

Fox told Holland as they walked down to the House of Commons that he never spoke without nervousness, and that he felt an unusual degree of it that day. 'I shall be sorry, however,' he added, 'if it were to spoil my speech today, for I should not wonder if it were to be the last I shall ever make in Parliament.'[2] Listening to other speeches, however, often has a steadying effect. Dundas spoke first, moving thanks to the King and approving the vigorous prosecution of the war. Whitbread, Canning, and Erskine followed, so that two speakers approved the motion and two disapproved.

Pitt found it necessary in replying to his learned friend Erskine's arguments, to go back to the beginning of the war in 1792, and establish France as the aggressor nation: 'You cannot look at the map of Europe, and lay your hand upon that country against which France has not either declared an open and aggressive war, or violated some positive treaty, or broken some recognized principle of the law of nations.'[3] He noted, among others, aggressive wars against the

[1] Add. MSS. 47574. To Holland, January 24.
[2] *Memoirs of the Whig Party*, i, 157–8.
[3] Text of speeches quoted comes from *Parliamentary History*, xxxiv, 1301–97.

German empire, against Austria, against the King of Sardinia. He described Bonaparte himself, drawing inferences from his character and conduct. He looked at 'the dreadful catalogue of all the breaches of treaty', confessing himself unable to name a single treaty that Bonaparte had not broken. Nor was there reason to expect that the new Government would endure; other French Governments had lasted, on the average, two years each. 'What, then, is the inference I draw from all that I have now stated? Is it, that we will in no case treat with Bonaparte? I say no such thing. But I say . . . that we ought to wait for experience . . . before we are convinced that such a treaty is admissible.' He declared he was not trying to impose monarchy upon France, against the will of the nation—'I never thought it, I never hoped it, I never wished it.' In proper circumstances the restoration of the monarchy by the people themselves might be entirely practicable. Finally, he described the resources of England as increasing and its spirit as indomitable, whereas France was becoming weaker and more exhausted.[1]

Fox, whose speech was awaited with the greatest expectation, began with words his hearers recognized as familiar; he described Pitt as using the old arguments that he had employed many times before.

Gracious God! Were we not told, five years ago, that France was not only on the brink, but that she was actually in the gulf of bankruptcy? Were we not told, as an unanswerable argument against treating, that she could not hold out another campaign—that nothing but peace could save her—that she wanted only time to recruit her exhausted finances—that . . . we had nothing to do but persevere for a short time, in order to save ourselves for ever from the consequences of her ambition and her Jacobinism?

He rebuked the Government for using harsh language in reply to the French offer to negotiate : 'It is not by reproaches and by invective that we can hope for a reconciliation.' And to go into the early history of the war 'with such severity of minute investigation . . . ought not to influence the present feelings of the House'.

Fox was never one to be overawed by an opponent's analysis; an outstanding feature of his debating was his ability to discover a still more fruitful field of argument. Thus he declared that the lengthy part of Pitt's speech which recounted the controversies leading to war—a train of thought into which Pitt had been led by Erskine—had little bearing on the present offer of the French. Pitt in a later part of his argument had detailed acts of aggression of the French against the English; Fox did not particularly attempt to deny these, but either interpreted them differently or offset them by citing acts of aggression

[1] Fox thought that Pitt's speech 'had more of the faults of his oratory and less of its excellencies,' than usual in his speaking (Wyvill, vi, 62).

of England's allies against the French. Thus each speaker, with an anchor in the facts of the case as he understood them, debated the broader field of application and interpretation. Fox offered one argument that his listeners had heard him make before: in a circumstance in which one nation offends another, the offended nation should offer every chance for investigation before taking drastic action. Fox alleged that Pitt was less ready to negotiate and more ready to retaliate. So, rather than dismiss the French ambassador because his explanation of an act of the French Government was unsatisfactory, Fox averred:

Did you tell him you were not content with this explanation? And when you dismissed him afterwards, on the [execution of Louis XVI] did you say that this explanation was unsatisfactory? No; you did no such thing: and I contend, that unless you demanded farther explanations, and they were refused, you have no right to urge the decree of the 19th of November [proclaiming the promise of French aid to all nations seeking to be free] as an act of aggression.

This degree of the 19th of November, Fox had also declared, this indiscriminate provocation thrown out at random, never should have been seriously considered in the first instance. This example illustrates again his forceful reappraisal of a statement advanced by his opponent. It also emphasizes his insistence that a government should not fail to practice the arts of peace—fair statement, discussion, negotiation—before lining up its heavy cannon.

Pitt had outlined various contingencies that faced the Government and how each contingency could properly be met. Fox followed Pitt's reasoning through this portion of his argument but countered that peace would be a better means of meeting a contingency than would war, and that Pitt could get better terms from Bonaparte now than later. It was therefore Fox's position that the nation, under Pitt's plan, would suffer another year or two of human misery in pursuit of gains doubtful at the most.

In the debate in the Lords on this subject the previous week, Grenville had declared that rather than negotiate with Bonaparte, Great Britain should await events. The Earl of Carnarvon, supporting Grenville's argument, had said that Grenville was recommending a pause in order better to understand France's new constitution. In the Commons, Dundas had spoken of a pause: 'Sir, . . . I hope Ministers will pause and weigh well the consequences to which it would lead.'[1] Pitt apparently did not use the word *pause*, but he expressed the same idea when he argued that Britain must delay negotiating, and, in the future, 'be regulated by the course of events'. Fox, gathering together the lines of his argument for a towering conclusion, touched the summit of eloquence in his long career. His interest in negotiating rather than in

[1] *Parliamentary Register*, x, 272. *Parliamentary History*, xxxiv, 1249.

fighting and his abhorrence of war were rolled into an ironic but vivid picture:

We must keep Bonaparte for some time longer at war, as a state of probation. Gracious God, Sir, is war a state of probation? Is peace a rash system? Is it dangerous for nations to live in amity with each other? Is your vigilance, your policy, your common powers of observation, to be extinguished by putting an end to the horrors of war? Cannot this state of probation be as well undergone without adding to the catalogue of human sufferings? 'But we must pause!' What! must the bowels of Great Britain be torn out—her best blood be spilt—her treasure wasted—that you may make an experiment? Put yourselves—oh! that you would put yourselves—in the field of battle, and learn to judge of the sort of horrors that you excite. In former wars a man might at least, have some feeling, some interest, that served to balance in his mind the impressions which a scene of carnage and of death must inflict. If a man had been present at the battle of Blenheim, for instance, and had inquired the motive of the battle, there was not a soldier engaged who could not have satisfied his curiosity . . . they were fighting to repress the uncontrolled ambition of the grand monarque. But, if a man were present now at a field of slaughter, and were to inquire for what they were fighting—'Fighting!' would be the answer; 'they are not fighting, they are pausing.' 'Why is that man expiring? Why is that other writhing with agony? What means this implacable fury?' The answer must be, 'You are quite wrong, Sir, you deceive yourself—They are not fighting—Do not disturb them—they are merely pausing!—this man is not expiring with agony—that man is not dead—he is only pausing!

Another minute, and Fox's speech was finished. But in this final moment he made a further telling point. Suppose the ministers this night had proposed to accept Bonaparte's overtures for peace instead of rejecting them. Fox declared that he would ask for no gentleman's vote who under those circumstances would have voted against the ministers. But, in all honour, in all consistency, in all conscience, Fox felt he could demand the vote of every gentleman who would have voted with the ministers had *they* proposed the opposite of the motion now before the House.

Fox resumed his seat. No one rose to reply. Dundas and Pitt had already spoken; some who might have taken the floor had, by Pitt's generous action, been long ago translated to the Lords. Sheridan and Tierney must have felt that the debate could not lie better than Fox left it. Moreover, the hour was late. The division eloquently declared, however, 265 to 64, that the war should go on. At 4 a.m. Pitt wrote to the King: 'The general Impression in the House upon the whole Question appeared to be highly favorable and satisfactory.'[1] The King could hardly have been better pleased. He would have been still better pleased had he known that Fox would not appear in the chamber again that session.

[1] Fortescue transcripts, February 4. (Clements.)

Noting that Fox 'never was listened to with a more earnest and fixed attention,' the *Oracle* quoted:

> Still, they gaz'd, and still the wonder grew,
> That one man's head should carry all he knew. (*sic*)

Even so, it judged that he had done even better in other debates.[1] The *Sun*, for example, was among those that observed that 'towards the latter part of his speech, in one instance, Mr Fox hesitated considerably, having apparently lost the chain of his reasoning'. The silence must have indeed been dramatic when the plunging cascade of Fox's never-failing eloquence suddenly stopped as he groped for his next thought. Listeners were accustomed to his hesitant openings—like Patrick Henry of Virginia, Fox often uttered his first sentences haltingly—but they were startled to hear him fumble after having gained a fair hold on the argument. The *True Briton* commented on his confusion with partisan satisfaction. It had no praise even for this speech, contenting itself with scolding Fox for non-attending, leaving thousands without any representation. But these criticisms are trivial in view of the substantial merits of the speech. Holland thought Fox's exposure of Carnarvon's policy of pausing was perhaps 'one of the finest specimens of his oratory for argument, for feeling, for pleasantry, and for animation, that has been preserved'.[2] In her *Journal*, Lady Holland later recorded that Fox was at his finest when he answered those who had declared 'that we should *pause*'.[3]

In view of these comments, and the fact that the 'pausing' argument strikes a reader vividly, it is surprising that London newspapers overlooked it altogether. Since Fox had spoken at a late hour—he finished at 3.30 a.m.—some papers condensed his speech, others deferred it to the next issue. One paper after another failed to include this excerpt. Said the *London Packet*:

It was said by some, that we could afford to pause and examine matters for twelve months; but if we were to pause, would it not be better to pause in peace.[4]

Said the *Morning Chronicle*:

. . . and all this that we may pause, and for what? merely, that we may better ascertain the character of an individual or the probable stability of his power.[5]

With all their shortcomings, London printers could report more accurately than this, and missed a good opportunity to record Fox's remarkable peroration. The passage, however, appeared in an edition

[1] February 5. Other papers praised Fox's speech more generously: cf. the *Star* ('commanding . . . impressive . . . masterly').
[2] *Memoirs of the Whig Party*, i, 157.   [3] ii, 47–8. February 14.
[4] February 3–5. This text also appeared in *Gentleman's Magazine*, lxx (June, 1800), 540.
[5] February 4.

of the speech published by Debrett,[1] the *Parliamentary Register* and the *Parliamentary History.*

According to Holland, Fox had heard the debate in the Lords and thus had ample opportunity to phrase a memorable retort to the policy of 'pausing.' As was his lifetime practice, he delivered the long speech with its stirring conclusion entirely without notes. Disraeli or Gladstone could duplicate this feat, though invariably they fortified themselves with six to a dozen pages. Churchill would have written and rewritten and would have worked from a finished and polished manuscript.

Next evening, Fox attended the Whig Club meeting at the Crown and Anchor and, before an estimated 300 people, discussed his speech and reviewed the arguments he had used. On the whole he had decided that his effort and those of others 'who spoke the sense of the country' had gained not more than three votes. 'The active power of the Constitution was gone, as it must be gone when the representative body does not respond to the public opinion.' He reminded his friends, as he had the Commons, that if Pitt had proposed the opposite course of action and had agreed to negotiate, the same persons would have voted with Pitt 'for opening the road to peace'. He therefore declared he was going to continue his plan of non-attending, though he did not want to recommend secession to others who were more optimistic.[2]

The *Evening Mail* editorialized: 'Many persons are vexed and indignant at seeing Bonaparte defended by a British Opposition. Think what it would be if he were to be flattered and sustained by a British Ministry!' A fortnight later, learning that Fox was reading Tacitus, it wondered that Fox should study the character of mankind rather than his own, and should so profoundly investigate the duties of others while he neglected his own. *The Times* paid the art of speaking a tribute by suggesting that if Fox's reasoning did not succeed in persuading the House, the war must surely be just and necessary. Certainly if 'the most able, the most experienced, and the most eloquent adversary' could fail to convince, the cause he opposed must be wise.

Early in 1800 Fox revived an idea that had long lingered with him: to become a historian. He chose not to write about his own turbulent

[1] *The speech of the honourable Charles James Fox in the House of Commons on Monday, the 3d of February, 1800, on a motion for an address to the throne, approving of the refusal of ministers to treat with the French republic. A new edition.* (London, n.d.)

[2] *Star, London Packet, Oracle, Sun, True Briton, Whitehall Evening Post,* others, dated February 5 and later.

times—nothing ever led him to want to write memoirs or to keep a sustained journal—but instead he looked back to the days of the Stuart kings: *History of the Early Part of the Reign of James the Second.*

Fox had often before turned to Lauderdale when in need of information. Now he needed advice of another sort:

I am seriously thinking of becoming an Historian and have indeed begun. . . .

I find one of my greatest difficulties to be, how to discover the authorities upon which the Historians advance their facts, for they very often do not refer to them.

Thus, like many others since him, he deplored the absence of footnotes and other references. Could Lauderdale supply the information requested?

For instance [Fox went on], the first point I would inquire about is the generally received opinion that it was Charles the II's intention to change his measures, if death had not prevented him. I should like very much to know upon what authority either written or traditional this opinion is founded. I have a vague notion that the Duchess of Portsmouth told my grandfather the Duke of Richmond so . . . but I should imagine there must be something more than such slight authority for an opinion that has so generally prevailed. Can you inquire?[1]

He suffered other pangs of the writer, also: 'It is dreadful how slowly I proceed', and still later: 'I have at last finished my Introduction which after all is more like a speech than it should be.' Another note in the correspondence reveals the problem of the historian as he struggles with his conscience: 'His [Laing's] book I think is a treasure. I hope he will not mind my stealing from him a little or indeed more than a little.' By the middle of May he had several perplexities:

Can you tell me what books to resort to, to find who were in the different great employments in different years? Who was Attorney General in the early part of James's reign? This particular officer I suppose I shall find by the state trials, but not others.

By June he had run into references that he needed to run down: where, for example, could he see a journal kept by the Duke of Monmouth? Other authors had quoted from it, 'but one should judge better if one were to see it all'.[2]

The word got out that Fox was working on a history. Various reports were that it was to be a history of England, beginning with the Glorious Revolution. Some time was to elapse, however, before it could be finished.

There was more work on the *History* during the summer but in September he observed that 'the speaking season puts a great stop to history writing',[3] and in October he expressed a sentiment that every

[1] Add. MSS. 47564. [Undated; early in 1800.] *Fox Cor.*, iii, 289–90.
[2] Add. MSS. 47564.
[3] Add. MSS. 47581. To Fitzpatrick, September 10.

author will, with feeling, challenge: 'I am the slowest writer that ever took pen in hand.'[1]

By this time the yearly celebration on October 10, the anniversary of the first election to Westminster, was a feature of whig politics. 'After an absence of two years,' said a friendly pamphlet, 'it is not easy to conceive the applause with which he was received.'[2] Three to five columns of his speech found their way into various papers and pamphlets. He declared:

> If I speak at all; I must speak out those principles which have distinguished England for so many centuries. I must say, that in every country . . . the *only legitimate Sovereign is the People*, and that only in proportion as Governments are the genuine representatives of that Sovereign, they are legitimate, and calculated to promote the happiness of the people . . .
>
> Upon those principles the French, and not the English, were the proper persons to determine, whether the Bourbons ought to reign in France. . . . We have thus *spilt our blood, squandered our treasure, and contracted a load of national debt we are unable to bear, not in support of our independence, not in support of our commerce, not in support of our colonial possessions, not even to add to our military fame, but alone to* DEPRESS FREEDOM *and promote the* CAUSE OF DESPOTISM.

So he reiterated the principles on which he fought Pitt's conduct of the war. A people should have the right to determine its own form of government. The avowed purpose of the war was wrong, since it attempted to deny to the French this basic right of being allowed to solve their own problems in their own way. As the war was not for possessions but a challenge to the very independence of France, it would unite her from top to bottom. Fox cannot justly be accused of lack of patriotism. Fully aware of French crimes and French atrocities, he was nevertheless certain that the principles he advocated would in the longer term be best for Englishmen. Never did he urge violent reform of the Government, but only modifications, consistent with the constitution, that would give greater voice to the people.

For his views he was castigated by being called *Frenchman, Jacobin, republican,* even *democrat*; just as twenty years previously he had been denounced as an *American*. On this anniversary occasion, however, special songs were written and sung to offset part of this bitter criticism. One rouser ended:

> Here's the MAN OF THE PEOPLE, so honest in fame,
> That no foul-mouthed apostates can tarnish his name.

Though 'I'm a Democrat called,' ran another, 'I will stand or I'll fall under LIBERTY'S TREE'; so,

> Come fill me a bumper from LIBERTY'S SPRING—
> Here's the Friend to Reform, CONSTITUTION, and KING!!!!

[1] Holland House MSS., October 17.

[2] *The celebrated speech of the honourable C. J. Fox,* etc., 4th edn (London, n.d.).

As for his secession, he stated simply that if his constituents could find a person who by attendance in Parliament could do better, who could 'rectify abuses and restore the constitution to what it has been, I shall cheerfully make way for him.' His continued retirement rested upon the approval of his supporters: 'I am too old to embrace any new systems; the principles I have invariably followed, I must still persevere in. [I cannot] adopt a lower tone than that which I uniformly held during and since the American war.' As no one was seriously considered to oppose him, the secession went on. It had never been, however, a complete withdrawal from public life: his January birthday speech, his October Westminster anniversary speech, his Whig Club talks, his appearance at St Stephen's on occasions such as the debate with Pitt on Bonaparte's overtures, and his not infrequent speeches to mass meetings, kept him in the public eye.

27

Pitt Resigns; Secession Continues
1801–1802

*When men . . . heard Fox they heard much that was
ordinary, and some things that were unrivalled.*

Henry Grattan

The Irish problem, which had so long occupied both Pitt and Fox,
finally brought to an end Pitt's long tenure of office.

Under the leadership of Henry Grattan, Ireland had demanded and
received parliamentary independence in 1782. This independent Parliament was by no means a complete solution. None of its 300 members
could be Catholic, nor, for that matter, could the large Presbyterian
group in Ulster be represented. Most members came from rotten
boroughs controlled by Anglo-Irish families.

The Protestant majority in the Irish Parliament, not wishing to lose
its power and patronage, had in 1799 voted down a proposal for Union;
whereupon the Government proceeded to manufacture a majority by a
liberal bestowal of peerages, offices, and pensions. Catholics had been
induced to support the Union by being persuaded that Catholic emancipation would follow. In 1800 the Act of Union had passed both the
Irish and the British Parliaments, and on January 1, 1801, the United
Parliament had met in London with a hundred Irish members added to
the Commons and 32 Irish peers and bishops to the Lords.

Once parliamentary union had been secured, the implied promise of
Catholic emancipation had to be redeemed. Here Pitt ran head-on
into the views of the King, who felt that his coronation oath would
never permit him to sanction such a move. The King was eager for him
to stay on as minister; he even wrote to Pitt offering to abstain from
talking on the subject if Pitt, in turn, 'will stave off the only question
whereon I fear from his letter we can never agree'.[1] This compromise
Pitt was unwilling to make. Discussions and negotiations followed:
gradually the rumours of Pitt's resignation, 'widely circulated and
eagerly believed' as Opposition papers had it, became more positive.

Early in January the Whig Club had met at the Crown and Anchor to
celebrate Fox's fifty-second birthday, Fox being received with the

[1] Fortescue transcripts, February 1, 1801. (Clements.)

the usual thunders of applause. In the days that followed massive tributes were heard, such as this in the *Morning Post*: 'He stood against the Court—he stood against the Country—he stood against both united—he was the isthmus, lashed by the waves of democracy on the one side, and the billows of despotism on the other, unmoved by either, and superior to both.' Young William Wordsworth sent Fox a copy of *Lyrical Ballads*, asking him to accept it principally to read 'The Brothers' and 'Michael'. 'I am convinced,' said Wordsworth, 'that if since your first entrance into public life there has been a single true Poet living in England, he must have loved you.' Wordsworth further praised him for realizing 'that the most sacred of all property is the property of the poor'. The time may come, Wordsworth concluded, 'when the country may perceive what it has lost by neglecting your advice'.[1] Fox also speculated with O'Bryen whether the name of Bonaparte or Fox would ultimately achieve the greater fame, observing that although he was not indifferent to personal glory he recognized Bonaparte's might surpass his.[2]

But now the persistent rumours of Pitt's resignation brought a new turn to these pleasantries. After years of semi-retirement, Fox realized that the time had come for a strategic, or at least a tactical, decision. He wrote to Fitzwilliam that he had no feelings of personal ambition; he could not be induced to take a post at the head of public affairs. Although he was sure that nothing at all would do any good: 'If there is a possibility of any good being done I must admit the present state of things affords the most favourable opportunity.'[3] Although Fox especially in these later years intuitively arrived at the proper stand on broad issues, on purely political manoeuvres he as intuitively called for help. Now with a decided personal inclination to remain at St Anne's, he needed to consider whether duty outweighed love of leisure. If the rumours were indeed true that Pitt was out, he would have to make a sudden decision whether to attend Parliament, and if so, what to say and do; he therefore wrote to Fitzpatrick: 'I shall want your advice very much . . . come as soon as you can.'[4]

As to the basic realities of the situation he was clear enough. He wrote to Grey deploring the 'clandestine and unconstitutional bargains for support'. He added a quaint sentiment: 'I wish some strong expression of popular joy could take place upon Pitt's going out. . . . It would do more good than anything, and certainly not tend to strengthen

---

[1] Add. MSS. 35344, ff. 142–3. *Correspondence of T. Poole*, 1765–1837, ii.
[2] Add. MSS. 47566. January 23.
[3] Fitzwilliam MSS. (Milton) 58/3, 5–7. February 1. (Northamptonshire Record Office.)
[4] Add. MSS. 47581. *Fox Cor.*, iii, 319–21. February 3.

but weaken his successors. . . . Pitt was a bad Minister; he is out—I am glad.'[1]

The King's choice for his new minister was Addington; this choice seemed to Fox totally incomprehensible, 'a strange juggle'. Time was required for Addington to complete his Government, the King being consulted each step of the way. Then, in the middle of February, the King fell ill. Addington, however, who had an interview with him, reported the King wandering on a few matters but calm on others. The political situation was confusing, with Addington prime minister *de jure* and Pitt prime minister *de facto*. With the memory of 1789 still in mind, Pitt, apparently with Addington's consent, advised the Prince to accept the regency, if the King did not improve, under restrictions similar to those proposed at the time of the last royal illness. Fox raised no objection—his memory also stretched back to 1789—and Parliament was silent on the matter. The King recovered for a time, however, so Addington completed his Cabinet and was installed in office.[2]

After seventeen years on the Treasury bench, Pitt was now out of power. Men recalled the Christmas season of 1783 when the young man of twenty-four had agreed to head the Government despite the fact that the combined forces of Fox and North controlled a majority of the votes. Save Walpole, no one had ever sat in the first seat so long.

Fox had learned in February that Grey planned to debate the state of the nation in March. He wrote Lauderdale that he would return to speak on Grey's motion, simply to put the House to a test, but added: 'When we are beat on the State of the Nation, I mean to attend no more; unless the Catholic question is brought on, and in that case upon that only.'[3] Grey made his motion on March 25; his speech, like those of Dundas and Pitt that came later, dealt with the conduct of the war and the capabilities of members of the present Government. On these points Fox, making his first appearance in the Parliament of the United Kingdom of Great Britain and Ireland—the Imperial Parliament—had much to say. Fox thought Dundas's speech a series of insulting puerilities; and he summarized part of Pitt's claims as follows:

Have you restored monarchy?—Its very hopes are entombed forever.
Have you destroyed Jacobinism, as you call it?—Your resistance has made it stronger than ever.
Have you reduced the power of France?—France is aggrandized beyond the wildest dreams of former ambition.

[1] Add. MSS. 47565. *Fox Cor.*, iii, 324. Grey MSS. (Durham.) To Grey (dated 1800; postmarked 1801).
[2] Fox specifically wrote Addington that Opposition would not object to a regency on the basis of 1789 (Colchester, i, 250).
[3] Add. MSS. 47564. *Fox Cor.*, iii, 328. February 19.

Have you driven her within her ancient frontiers?—She has enlarged herself
to the Rhine and to the Alps, and added five millions to her population in the centre
of Europe. . . .

Could all this be chance? No, Sir; it is the true succession of effect to cause. It
is the legitimate issue of your own system. You began in foolishness, and you end
in mischief. Tell me one single object of the war that you have obtained? Tell me
one evil that you have not brought upon your country? Yet this House will not
inquire.[1]

The old wizard still had some of the old magic. Addington spoke only
briefly; yet in the division Government had 291, Opposition 105.

Some of Fox's friends greatly wanted to see his speech in print.
Adair secured the transcript of the shorthand reporter, and asked Fox
to look it over and correct it, but Fox could not bring himself to do this.
The speech was poorly adapted for the reading audience, he contended,
as so much of it was in reply to Pitt and Dundas: 'The very identical
things, which make a speech good to hear make it bad to read and vice
versa; and consequently an opening speech which is never quite so
pleasant to hear, is the only sort of speech that ought (if any ought) to
be published.'[2]

Fox's continued unwillingness to attend Parliament was wistfully
revealed in a demurrer to Holland's renewed request that he be on
hand: 'Never did a letter arrive in a worse time my dear young one
than yours this morning; a sweet westerly wind, a beautiful sun, all the
thorns and elms just budding and the nightingales just beginning to
sing.' Only 'Tooke's business (which I could not desert without
shabbiness) and the May Whig Club' would bring him to town this
year.[3]

'Tooke's business' had grown out of his return in February as
member for Old Sarum. The issue arose whether Horne Tooke, who
had once taken holy orders, could now renounce them; and if he could
not, was it legal for him, as a priest, to occupy a seat in the House of
Commons? Fox argued that his former Westminster opponent was
entitled to a seat. Although Erskine and Sheridan sided with Fox, the
eccentric Horne Tooke was a difficult person to defend, and a Bill
carried to prevent persons in holy orders from sitting in the Commons
was carried by a large majority. He was grateful, however, for Fox's
support. 'Mr Fox,' said Tooke, 'has taken a severe revenge. I have
passed my life in attacking him, and he has now, for the second time,
defended me nobly against the arm of power.'[4]

The negotiations for peace that Pitt had spurned in the great debate of
February 1800 were now going forward under the auspices of the

---

[1] *Parliamentary History*, xxxv, 1148–9.   [2] Add. MSS. 47566. April 5.
[3] Add. MSS. 47574. *Fox Cor.*, iii, 189–90. April 19.   [4] *Memoirs of the Whig Party*, i, 180.

Addington administration. The preliminary articles signed October 2, 1801, involved substantial concession on the part of Great Britain. Her own conquests, excepting Trinidad and Ceylon, were returned to France, Spain, and Holland; concessions to balance these were minor enough so that Addington's supporters were not happy about the negotiations. Nevertheless, London celebrated with illuminations, rockets, pistol firings. The Government named Cornwallis to interview Bonaparte in Paris and then proceed as plenipotentiary to Amiens to negotiate the definitive treaty with the French.

Meanwhile on the October 10 anniversary 400 persons gathered at the Shakespeare to help Fox celebrate. They heard him say that twenty-one years had passed since they first did him the honour to elect him as the representative of Westminster. He rejoiced that peace was once more in prospect, and declared that he would not inquire critically into the terms—an island in the West Indies or a province in the Mediterranean could not be set against the evils of war for a month, much less for a year. During the celebration he gave his usual toast of 'The cause of Liberty all over the Globe', quite possibly the most controversial words he uttered that evening.

Fox's speech with its plea for peace with the French fuelled sharp retorts from his opponents. Charles Yorke wrote to his brother, the Earl of Hardwicke, that Fox was certainly mad on the subject of peace. 'None but a perfect madman, or a consummate villain, could have made such an oration on such an occasion. However, like many other of his speeches it will serve as a *warning* to all honest men.'[1] His fervour brought dismay to his friends. Thinking ahead to his participation in debates on the preliminary articles of peace, Fox feared he might utter other indiscretions:

The truth is, I am gone something farther in hate to the English Government than perhaps you and the rest of my friends are, and certainly farther than can with prudence be avowed. The triumph of the French Government over the English does in fact afford me a degree of pleasure which it is very difficult to disguise.

He went on to say, however, that he clearly felt the only chance of England's being saved arose from peace being concluded this year— the evil would be ten times worse if peace were concluded later.[2]

As expected, Fox appeared in Parliament to repeat his strong approval of the peace. He said:

I urged then, and still urge, that the question of the stability or instability of the government ought not to be treated as of great consequence. . . . But, Sir, we were

---

[1] Add. MSS. 35701. Hardwicke Papers. October 13, 1801. 'Mr Fox's speech . . . is a specimen of what may be expected from Jacobin factions in this country' (*HMCR*, Fortescue MSS., vii, 62. Mulgrave to Grenville, October 18).
[2] Add. MSS. 47565. Grey MSS. (Durham.) *Fox Cor.*, iii, 347–50. October 22.

told by his majesty's ministers to pause. We did pause from January 1800 to
October 1801, and we have added 73 millions of debt since the impertinent answer
. . . returned to the overtures of the chief consul.[1]

Next day, however, the preliminaries were approved without a division. In the spring the definitive treaty itself was signed at Amiens and
was approved by both Houses.

In the fall of 1801 Fox summed up his personal feelings in a letter. He
reviewed part of his credo:

The three points I most feel are those you mention [parliamentary reform, abolition of all religious tests as to civil matters, and abolition of the slave trade] and
Catholic emancipation in Ireland, but I think . . . that for the present they are
unattainable and while they are so I personally will have nothing to do with any
administration.

On other points there was not so much reason for despair: the Sedition
Bills, the proposal for a modest military establishment, a change of
system for Ireland. Then he asked himself the question: 'Well but
you may say, what do I intend to do with myself?'

To this I must answer truly that I do not know. If I represented a quiet borough,
I would certainly not refuse, tho' I should not seek to come in again. As it is, I will
certainly not give myself or my friends any trouble.[2]

Meanwhile, as 1801 ended, he once again turned from speaking to the
writing of history. He was only in the first half of the reign of James II,
and was spending his time correcting and adding to what he had already
written, rather than in forging ahead with new chapters. He experienced, also, other pangs of the beginning researcher: taking notes
and then misplacing them, reading without recording, later realizing
that he should have taken ample notes, wondering what 'esteem for
veracity' certain of his sources possessed, realizing that despite his
study at Paris he still needed to locate much source material.

Francis Russell, fifth Duke of Bedford, long-time admirer of Fox, died
on March 2, 1802. Fox's grief at the loss of a fine friend was followed
closely by the realization that he should pay tribute to the deceased;
this circumstance meant preparing a speech, leaving St Anne's, and
going to London to deliver it. He dreaded making this kind of speech—
throughout his career Fox almost never participated in a purely ceremonial occasion—and wrote Holland that if he undertook it, he would

[1] *Parliamentary History*, xxxvi, 80.
[2] Add. MSS. 47569. To William Smith, November 15. Osborn Collection, 85/15. (Yale).

very probably 'burst out crying and be quite unable to proceed'. This, he added, 'is one of the few occasions where I had rather write than speak'.[1]

The speech, neither remarkably long nor brilliant, was noteworthy in part because of his intense personal feeling. He touched on the usual topics of the character of the Duke, the friendships he had formed with others, the activities he followed to make his a useful life. When toward the close he said, 'I hope the House will forgive me for having said so much', a cry of hear! hear! arose from every part of the House.[2]

After the speech came the necessity of revising it for publication; to accomplish this task Fox endured exquisite torment. He asked Lauderdale to send him the paper that had the best report to use as the basis for revision: 'I will look it over,' he added, 'and send you a corrected, maybe improved, copy.'[3] Two days later he was still worrying; 'I shall have no scruple', he wrote, 'in introducing new topicks if any occur that I think I can manage tolerably,' though he did not want to make so many changes that the result would seem like a new composition. He realized, of course, that if he made too many changes readers might be tempted to compare the refurbished version with the early printed report. This grim fact, however, seldom serves to keep speakers honest when they gaze at the shorthand transcript of their remarks and mentally contrast what actually came out with what they hoped they had said. Meanwhile Ridgway had printed a pamphlet version that Fox found intolerably bad though the account was a full one.[4] Still later he commented that the 'vile publication' of Ridgway's would be ten times more read than his own version in the *Monthly Magazine*.[5]

In the British Museum is a proof of the speech corrected in Fox's own handwriting; the final version with his revisions resembles closely that appearing in the *Parliamentary History*. Many changes are slight—a comma in here, a comma out there, 'derive' for 'receive', 'bodily pain' for 'torture'.[6] 'Perhaps there is a little vanity in all this,' he wrote, 'but . . . the credit of the subject is a little involved in that of the speech.'[7] Any lover of eloquence may today express proper regret

---

[1] Holland House MSS. [March 4, 1802.]   [2] *The Times*, March 17.

[3] Add. MSS. 47564. *Fox Cor.*, iii, 364. March 17.

[4] Add. MSS. 47564. *Fox Cor.*, iii, 366. To Lauderdale, March 25.

[5] Add. MSS. 47564. *Fox Cor.*, iii, 367. April 6. When Fox submitted his copy to the *Monthly Magazine*, where it appeared in the April 1802, edition, he observed 'that he had never before attempted to make a copy of any speech which he had delivered in public' (*Parliamentary History*, xxxvi, 365).

The vile publication of Ridgway's: *A sketch of the character of the late most noble Francis Duke of Bedford, by the Hon. Charles James Fox*, etc. (London, 1802). It has few resemblances to Fox's version (Add. MSS. 47564).

[6] Add. MSS. 47564.

[7] Add. MSS. 47564. *Fox Cor.*, iii, 367. To Lauderdale, April 6.

that he devoted so much energy to the preservation of a minor speech, when, for example, his speech of March 22, 1775, the day when Burke made his celebrated effort on 'that awful subject', conciliation with the colonies, went unreported and unpublished.

Burke's death had been painful enough but the death of the Duke signalled the passing of the first of Fox's truly close friends. O'Bryen, who had noticed Fox's declining interest in politics since the summer of 1798, thought the Duke's death contributed materially to Fox's desire to retire altogether to private life.[1] Fox, however, was not inactive the rest of the session. When friends of Pitt offered a motion praising their chief, Fox retorted that nothing in Pitt's administration 'became him like the leaving it', and declared that praise had been forfeited by Pitt's own actions. Next week came the debates approving the treaty signed at Amiens.

Pitt and his friends were, of course, restless about their position as members of Opposition. Pitt himself was active in attempting to keep together the fragments of his party. He took a special interest in young George Canning and tried to enlist his support by correspondence.[2] The attention shown by the great minister gradually had its effect upon the young parliamentarian. When word of plans to commemorate Pitt's birthday reached Canning, he seized the idea eagerly and promoted it vigorously. The outcome was the celebrated birthday party of May 28, with more than 800 present and another 200 turned away. Frankly an effort to outshine the Fox parties, the Pitt celebration was a huge success. A feature was Canning's poem, read to the crowd assembled, calling Pitt 'the pilot that weathered the storm'. For several years the annual Pitt and Fox birthday parties intensified the rivalry between the two groups.[3]

During this session the whig secession came to an end. Yet Fox's political conscience never let him secede totally. He broke the silence with notable utterances both within the House chamber and outside it. As a tactic, however, either to influence the Government or to arouse the people, secession was a failure. No parliamentary opposition ever again tried it.

The Westminster election opened on July 7. The candidates were the two incumbents, Fox and Admiral Gardner, plus Mr Graham, an auctioneer living in Chancery Lane.

[1] Add. MSS. 47566. [1802.]
[2] Canning Papers (Clements). On October 26, 1801, for example, Pitt attempted to enlist Canning's support in the debates on the peace terms.
[3] Archibald S. Foord, *His Majesty's Opposition, 1714–1830* (Oxford, 1964), pp. 425–7.

It was a burlesque of an election, rowdy and disorderly. When Fox was nominated, 'the whole place rung with applause, ten thousand hands were raised in favour of Mr Fox'. The nomination of Lord Gardner was received 'with very partial approbation. . . . Many exclaimed, "O Admiral! you have been but three times in the house since you was last elected."'

Fox offered to yield to anyone the electors might prefer who was 'possessed of more youth, activity, energy, and better abilities', but promised that whenever he thought his presence in Parliament would be helpful, 'I will be as diligent, if not equal in other respects to, a more young and active man.' The reporter wrote: 'It is not possible to describe the effect produced by this speech. The plaudits, clapping of hands, shouts and exclamations, did not cease for several minutes.'

Lord Gardner had a difficult time getting a hearing. Some one yelled: 'Noble Admiral, order those noisy fellows a dozen.' Over the clamour the noble admiral tried to be heard as he pledged himself to do his duty at sea, trusting to be forgiven if he did not always do it ashore. Truly Westminster was offered that day a quaint brace of incumbents indeed, insofar as regular attendance at the House was a criterion.

The third candidate, however, gave a speech so grotesque and laughable that 'even the gravity of Mr Fox could not withstand such an irresistible provocative to mirth'. Some called, 'Read us a few pages from one of your catalogues'; others, 'Well, said, auctioneer, knock 'em down.' Fox got his boos on subsequent days: 'Charley, my boy, we, the majesty of the people, desire to know immediately whether the poll is closed or not'; 'Go home, Charley, and repent, or you'll die an old sinner'; and continually, 'No coalition'. For this last cry the majestic memory of the people reached back nearly twenty years; it was as if the mature Churchill were rebuked for mistakes made as a Liberal early in the century.

After a week of this splendid outdoor sport, polls were formally closed on July 15, whereupon the mob descended upon the hustings with hatchets and crowbars and pulled it down. Gradually the excitement dissolved and the people dispersed, a few with broken heads but most without.[1]

Ridiculous and hilarious though it was, this Westminster election of 1802 was not inexpensive. The sum of £800 paid in, £200 from each from the Dukes of Northumberland, Devonshire, Bedford, and Fitzwilliam, underwrote a major part of the costs. Newspaper ads. totalled £57 2s.; the Shakespeare's bill amounted to £132 2s 6d. The High Bailiff's fee amounted to nearly £1,000, to be apportioned among the three candidates. It included such items as twenty-four

[1] Details from *The Times*, July 8–16, 1802.

clerks for nine days at £1 1*s* each and 3*s* 6*d* for their dinner, totalling £264 12*s*.[1]

Thus ended what proved to be Fox's last contested election campaign.

[1] Fitzwilliam Papers, F115 (Sheffield).

28

Road to War
1802–1803

A speech more craftily formed to inspire despondency
and dismay was perhaps never delivered.

The Times

The truth is . . . it was my best.

Charles James Fox

The Peace of Amiens aroused in many Englishmen the desire to see
Paris again. Thousands made the trip across the Channel that summer,
Fox among them. His immediate excuse was to locate materials for his
history, so he invited his private secretary, John Bernard Trotter, a
nephew of his good friend the Bishop of Down, to go along to read and
copy. Trotter not only served in this capacity but also took notes for a
life of Fox; although at first he intended to write a full biography, like
many others who have undertaken Brobdingnag he settled for Lilliput.
His *Memoirs of the Latter Years of . . . Charles James Fox*[1] proved to be
a curious account of Fox's doings as they intrigued Trotter, his close
associations with Fox and with the great and near-great they met on
the continental trip, with a delightfully blended image of Fox and
Trotter, Trotter and Fox stirred in throughout. Other letter writers
and journal-keepers on the Continent that summer also recorded Fox's
visit but Trotter provides the most intimate narrative. The party,
including Mr and Mrs Fox—for the 'Mrs A' of all these years was now
revealed as his long-wedded wife[2]—and Trotter, left St Anne's Hill,
by coach, on July 29, 1802.

As Fox's carriage went from city to city on the way to Paris, the
travellers noted many changes produced by the war. The revolutionary
fury had spent itself upon a convent in Cassell, demolishing the convent and destroying its garden; in Lisle there was not a single gentle-

---

[1] Quotations in this chapter not otherwise identified are from this volume.
[2] On August 1 she wrote Harriet, signing herself—for the first time in her life ?—'E. Fox.'
'This is has [*sic*] long been my name but till now Mr F. had reasons for not wishing it to be
known but has them no longer.' On August 12, she wrote Caroline the same news, saying
that 'a Secret which never need have been one is now divulged' (Holland House MSS.).

Lady Bessborough, Georgiana's younger sister, reflected a prevailing opinion when she
wrote: 'The odd thing is that people who were shocked at his having a mistress are still more
so at that mistress having been his wife for so long' (*Georgiana*, p. 250).

man's carriage whereas formerly there had been 300; Antwerp and Ghent, their commerce declined, presented a view of fallen grandeur. As the coach travelled to Utrecht, Amsterdam, The Hague, and Brussels, and thence back into France, its occupants listened to Trotter read Fielding's novels, principally *Joseph Andrews* and *Tom Jones*, and discussed passages from the *Aeneid*. At most cities municipal officers welcomed the small party; wherever Fox spent the night became the scene of a dinner or other social gathering, with Fox discussing literature, politics, paintings, or his newest hobby, agriculture. Fields of battle that they passed, scenes of slaughter, fortifications and sieges, however, did not interest him.

Fox was an excellent travelling companion. Aside from the charm of his conversation, he was 'easy, affable, and cheerful'; the 'little obstacles, disappointments, or unpleasantnesses' never ruffled him; he paid the bills in the coinage of the country with expertness; he consulted Mrs Fox's comfort and convenience in everything. Moreover, he was invariably the first 'to extenuate or find an apology for deficiencies in others'.

So a month went by. Then, toward the end of August, they entered Paris, staying at the Hotel de Richelieu, one of the fashionable hostelries, now a common hotel, though still with its superb furniture, rich silk hangings, noble mirrors. Trotter, impressed, almost expected to meet a French marshal at every turn. Other English vistors to the city made their presence known—the Hollands, General Fitzpatrick, Lord Robert Spencer, Hare, and Adair.

At the theatre Fox was quickly recognized: 'every eye was fixed on him, and every tongue resounded Fox! Fox!' The centre of this attraction was so embarrassed that he could hardly be brought to acknowledge the applause. The First Consul was there and was received with applause, 'but much inferior to that bestowed on Mr Fox'. The Holland House papers still contain the original invitation, addressed to Monsieur, not Citoyen, Fox, to dine with the First Consul at the Palais des Tuileries, along with invitations to various civic celebrations in his special honour and an invitation to become a member of the Institut National des Sciences and des Arts in the distinguished category of science morale et politique. Mrs Fox had memorable occasions of her own, as when she dined in the Talleyrand home and was shown the utmost courtesy by her hostess.

At visits to the Louvre, Fox admired the attractions that invariably draw visitors; but a history needed to be written, so eventually he began his studies at the French Archives, working every day from eleven to three. The keeper, eager to be of service, provided a special room, with pens, ink, paper, and other accommodations; and thus for two months Fox read letters of Barillon and various materials on Louis XIV.

Evenings were available for socializing; there were Kosciusko, Talleyrand, the Abbé Sieyes; there was Lafayette; there were princes, counts, marquises, earls, dukes, members of the corps diplomatique, and countless others. And there was Napoleon, who, flustered and flurried, very rapidly said: 'Ah! Mr Fox! I have long admired in you the orator and friend of his country, who, in constantly raising his voice for peace, consulted that country's best interests—those of Europe—and of the human race.' Lady Holland reported the interview: Napoleon's speech, 'evidently got by heart', referred to Fox as one of the greatest men of one of the greatest countries, whose voice had always been exerted on the side of humanity, justice and peace.[1] And much more to the same effect. Fox, who could have spoken fluently in French or Italian, usually found it difficult to respond to compliments in any language, and so said little or nothing; after desultory conversation about Fox's tour, the interview ended.

A delightful interlude during the Paris stay was the acquaintance that the Foxes formed with the charming, vivacious, and intelligent Madame Récamier, the twenty-five-year-old reigning beauty of the city, and hostess of one of its envied salons. Government officials, philosophers, men of letters and arts, all found themselves at ease at her social affairs at her home in Clichy.

On one occasion Lucien Bonaparte, brother of the emperor, was one of those present when a carriage rolled up and Mr Fox, with Lord and Lady Holland were announced. Something like the following conversation ensued:

Mr Fox. We have come to take you by surprise, and I think you will also have other guests this morning. . . .

Lucien (to Mr Fox). Have you done Paris already?

Fox. Not as much as I should like. I have had things to do. I have friends, time flies, and there are so many interesting things, so that, really, for fear of not seeing all of them, sometimes I find myself saying I will look at nothing at all. Since I must leave so soon the things I should admire, why go to see them?

Mme Récamier only smiled, but with a look that expressed many words.

Fox. You think me ridiculous to speak so? But it is partly true. In England we have a proverb that says, 'It is better never to meet, than to meet merely to part.'

Thus went one of the possibly half-dozen Fox conversations that have been recorded, out of a lifetime of social, literary, and political talk.

Other guests came, and the conversation turned to a variety of topics, literary and political. Fox was enchanted by Madame Récamier:

[1] *Journal of Elizabeth, Lady Holland*, ii, 150.

'What a charming creature!' he said. 'She is really the work of the Deity on a holiday! How sweet she is! What a smile! What a glance! And the sound of her voice! . . . And how happy her expression, so calm and pure, it portrays the self-content of a sweet soul.'[1] She in turn was so captivated by Fox that she persuaded him to take a drive with her so that she could show off the distinguished Englishman to Parisian onlookers.

Fox several times was in the company of Napoleon. While visiting the Louvre, they with a group of others passed a globe of extraordinary size. One of Bonaparte's followers pointed to the British Isles and remarked that England filled but a small space in the world. 'Yes,' replied Fox indignantly, 'that island of the Englishmen *is* a small one.' But, he added, approaching the globe and stretching his arms around it, 'but, while the Englishmen live, they fill the whole world, and clasp it in the circle of their power.'[2]

On another occasion Napoleon discussed the feasibility of building a tunnel under the English Channel, thus joining the two countries. He had reviewed the engineering plans and was intrigued by the possibilities of the project. Fox was enthusiastic, exclaiming: 'Oh! this is one of the great things that we will be able to do together.'[3]

October 6 was the last day in the Archives:

> I shall not easily forget [Trotter noted], Mr Fox walking up stairs, taking off his hat, and sitting down in our room, oppressed with heat and the fatigue arising from it; and then applying with the same ardour and industry every day, copying, reading aloud the passages leading to any discovery, keeping his friends busily employed, and always cheerful and active.

Indeed it had been a lively and gregarious way of writing history, in marked contrast to the lonely researches of professionals. At three in the afternoon work would be summarily ended and visits to museums and galleries begun, with entertainment in the evening, and, betimes, weekend visits to an elegant country home.

From July 29 to November 17, Fox kept a journal—two small volumes bound between light mottled green cardboard covers, the blank pages interleaved with purple sheets of blotting paper. Quite possibly it was the only journal he kept in his lifetime. Brief and unimpressive, the entries are mainly lists of sights and entertainments. At

---

1 Duchesse d'Abrantés, *Histoire des Salons de Paris*, vi, 336–8. Quoted in Henry Dwight Sedgwick, *Madame Récamier* (Indianapolis, 1940), p. 84.
2 Edward S. Creasy, *Memoirs of Eminent Etonians* (London, 1850), p. 383.
3 Albert Sartiaux, *Le tunnel sous-marin entre la France et l'Angleterre* (Lille, 1907), pp. 16–17; A. Thome de Gamond, *Étude pour l'avant-projet d'un tunnel sous-marin entre l'Angleterre et la France* (Paris, 1857), pp. 3–6. Georges Viernot, *Le tunnel sous la manche* (Paris, 1908), p. 13.

Lisle he recorded an excellent dinner served to fifty to sixty persons; from the table the group went to the 'Comedie' and afterwards viewed illuminations—'one of the most beautiful spectacles I ever saw'. At Amsterdam on a hot August he tried two places before he could find lodging. The canals were full of bad smells. Late in August he began his work; many entries read simply 'Worked as usual', though at times he recorded that he rose so late it was not worth working that day.

All sorts of brief comments are found. On inns: they ranged from dirty and noisy to tolerable and nice. On food: often good, but there was one vile dinner. On the theatre: *Amphitryon* was delightful; the new actress in *Andromaque* was ugly and ungraceful. On art: he liked a crucifixion by Van Dyck, but Rubens's 'The Death of Lazarus' was one of the finest things he ever saw, and Titian's 'St Peter' was the first picture in the world. At Leyden the library was not worth seeing but the fish market was gay. He went hunting and shot nineteen rabbits, he played whist on one occasion and lost his money, he saw a balloon ascension, he broke his spectacles and thus had to halt his research, he attended a natural science museum and debated whether the birds were as well stuffed as back home, he often found it difficult to get horses when he wanted them. He heard terrible talk of war being renewed, 'but I can not believe in it'.

The Channel crossing back to Dover from Calais took a little longer (four and a half hours) than a steamboat crossing (what passengers lost on sail they gained on customs). The carriage broke down three miles out of Dover—'a sad scrape indeed'—so they completed their journey by post coach and stage. Finally, on November 17, by Clapham and Kingston, they reached 'dear dear home where we arrived about six, very very glad to be here and happy *so* happy that my Liz bore all the fatigues of the journey so well'. The leg from Dover to St Anne's had taken twenty-four hours.[1]

Meanwhile, the peace that had been concluded at Amiens earlier that year was proving to be uneasy. As months wore on it became increasingly obvious that it was more advantageous to France than to England. Moreover, Napoleon used peace as he had war to further his own desires. He built naval vessels; he sent an army to Haiti; he declared himself President of the Cisalpine Republic; he kept troops in Holland; he strengthened his stance in Switzerland and Germany. English merchants, principally in Liverpool, grew restless as they faced the difficulties of exporting to French-controlled markets.

[1] Holland House MSS.

Fox, however, left the Continent more convinced than ever that Britain's policy should be peace; that commercial problems should be worked out by other than warlike means; that the extension of the French system did not of itself constitute a reason for breaking the treaty. With undue optimism he wrote Lauderdale on November 18 that war would not break out again: 'I can tell you my reasons for this opinion in two sentences. 1st, I am sure that Bonaparte will do everything that he can to avoid it. 2d that, low as my opinion is of our Ministry, I can not believe them quite so foolish as to force him to it.' He added that he planned to attend the opening session of Parliament, to oppose the ministry if it were warlike, to support it if were pacific.[1] He also wrote Georgiana that he was strongly in favour of peace, and that she could relay this message to all who wished to know his views. The folly of the last two wars makes another war doubly detestable: 'Mad Kings and foolish Ministers must govern the world in our times.'[2]

Parliament opened on November 16, spent a week in such preliminaries as swearing in new members, and then assembled to hear the King's official message from the throne. In the Lords the strong voice of Grenville made itself felt; his contribution to the debate was not lengthy, but he listed aggressions and encroachments of the French Government one after another declaring that all had taken place without remonstrance from the present ministers. He called for 'measures of decision and firmness . . . not by any of the men now in power, but by him to whom this country, to whom Europe, looks up at this awful hour for the preservation of their dearest rights'.[3] Pitt, however, to whom he was obviously referring, was at the time ill, seeking a cure by alternating his port with the salubrious waters of Bath. In the Commons Fox expressed his approval of the general tenor of the King's speech; he declared he saw every reason for continuing the peace and none for becoming warlike.[4] Creevey, the faithful diarist, could write that Fox's speech and conduct were in every respect perfect: 'If he will let them be the models for his future imitation, he will keep in the Doctor and preserve the peace. God continue Fox's prudence and Pitt's gout!'[5] Young Francis Horner, new in Parliament though he already had followed Fox's career for seven years, his first observation of Fox's speaking being no more profound than that Fox 'saws the air with his hands, Pitt with his whole body', now could perceive more of the man and less of the speaker:

The older that man becomes, he seems to acquire a greater dignity of character—the opportunities of retirement seem to have conspired with the growth of years

---

[1] Add. MSS. 47564. *Fox Cor.*, iii, 372. November 18.
[2] *Georgiana*, p. 254. November 1.   [3] *Parliamentary History*, xxxvi, 945.
[4] *Ibid.*, xxxvi, 951–9.   [5] *Creevey Papers*, i, 9. November 25.

in cleansing his fine understanding of . . . intemperance . . . [and] leading him to
. . . comprehensive and philosophical views of political transactions.[1]

It is no inconsiderable achievement for a man to modify his political
image, but the mellow Fox in his forties and fifties had notably
changed from his peak Brooks and Newmarket years.

Fox himself was pleased with his second speech; later that month he
wrote O'Bryen that he had received many compliments.[2] He wrote to
Grey how convinced he was that members of Parliament believed that
peace should continue: 'I have not for many years, certainly not since
the Russian business [1790], found the House so much with me as in
my second and longest speech upon the address, and, as far as I can
judge . . . this part of the country is as much inclined to peace as ever.'[3]
A letter to Holland mentioned that he had been threatened if he spoke
warmly for peace, 'and if those threats were not realised, it was not for
want of inclination in the warriors. *Apologist for France, Agent of the 1st
Consul, no dislike of the power of France,* were dealt about pretty well
both in Newspapers and in the House'; yet Fox nevertheless felt his
audience was sympathetic; so he must have sensed, as any speaker does
when he is sure he is voicing the thoughts of his listeners, a lively
agreement between him and them. In this letter he continued:

To say, as those inclined to flatter me will say, that I have done anything considerable for peace is more than is true; but it is true that, by speaking a pacifick
language more decisively than others dared to do, and by that language being
well received, I have been the means of shewing that the real sentiments of people
are strongly for peace, and it is very important that this should be known.[4]

All of this contrasted sharply with what he had feared might happen,
for he had written to Holland before the debate that he expected to be
abused for uttering pacifist language.[5]

So the lines were being drawn: Grenville at the leading edge of the
war party, Fox at the leading edge of the peacemakers; Pitt yet to be
heard from, Addington weak and ineffectual in office.

Fox's interest was still divided between politics and history; under
the latter heading he was giving thought to the matter of footnotes,
writing to Fitzpatrick that although one might find it impossible to
follow the practice of ancient historians of avoiding notes entirely:
'One ought to put as much into the Text as one can, even observations

[1] *Memoirs and Correspondence of Francis Horner*, 2nd edn (Boston, 1853), i, 219. December
12 [1802].
[2] Add. MSS. 47566. November 28. 'I have had many compliments upon my speech, the
most satisfactory would be that it has had its effect and we shall have Peace.'
[3] Add. MSS. 47565. *Fox Cor.*, iii, 377. Grey MSS. (Durham.) November 29.
[4] Add. MSS. 47574. *Fox Cor.*, iii, 206. December 19.
[5] Add. MSS. 47574. *Fox Cor.*, iii, 203. November 21.

upon other Historians.'[1] In a letter to William Belsham, who had assisted him with his researches, Fox reviewed his plans:

I am very happy my conduct in Parliament has met your approbation, and am going to London to try if possible to keep our Government steady in their wishes for Peace, whether I shall be of any use in this respect I know not; if not, it is a very great sacrifice I make for nothing.—This will among many other things retard my progress in the work to which you allude, and in which I am naturally sufficiently slow, to a degree that with your facility & fluency would much surprise you.[2]

Sir William Fremantle was one of those who was aware of Addington's shaky position: 'The present Administration are endeavouring to strengthen themselves by new arrangements, . . .' he wrote to the Marquess of Buckingham; 'this will be difficult.' He noted, however, for whatever encouragement it might suggest, that at a dinner given by the prince to the 'old opposition', Pitt's name was mentioned, '& Fox pronounced the highest eulogium upon him'.[3]

Debates in the Commons had not been spectacular. In view of the growing menace of France, Parliament had increased the armed forces; in view of the growing debts of the Prince of Wales, Parliament had voted to accommodate them. 'The insipidity of the House of Commons is beyond conception, and I think it is catching,' Fox wrote Grey, 'for the few times I have thought myself obliged to speak, I felt some way as if I was speaking like Addington, and I really believe I was.'[4] To Holland he similarly observed: 'There seems to be a sort of deadness in the House of Commons, worse than even in the worst times of the House of Lords.'[5] No one was superior to Fox in sensing the mood and temper of an audience. The curious state of politics made him wonder what part he should play in it:

'You have in your hands the turn of the scale' is . . . often said to me. First of all it is not so. . . . My plan at present is to have no politicks at all and to take the part upon each question that is most suitable to our general principles and conduct, leaving the political effect, which the debates and divisions may produce, to chance.[6]

Creevey's description, written only days before his next great speech, gives another side:

You would be perfectly astonished at the vigour of body, the energy of mind, the innocent playfulness and happiness of Fox. The contrast between him and his old

---

[1] Add. MSS. 47581. *Fox Cor.*, iii, 391. January 11, 1803.
[2] Fox. MSS. February 3. (Clements.)
[3] ST 164. Stowe collection. March 31. (Huntington.)
[4] Add. MSS. 47565. *Fox Cor.*, iii, 396. Grey MSS. (Durham.) February 28.
[5] Add. MSS. 47575. *Fox Cor.*, iii, 216. February 23.
[6] Fitzwilliam MSS. (Milton), 62/1, 1–3. To Fitzwilliam, April 22. (Northamptonshire Record Office.)

associates is the most marvellous thing I ever saw—they having all the air of shattered debauchees, of passing gaming, drinking, sleepless nights, whereas the old leader of the gang might really pass for the pattern and the effect of domestic good order.[1]

Since the French had steadily encroached upon the provisions of Amiens, the British began to slow their compliance with the treaty and refused to evacuate Malta; when Bonaparte protested, Britain, on May 18, declared war. Then occurred one of the truly brilliant debates in the long confrontation of Pitt and Fox. The discussion opened on May 23, the issue being the renewal of the war; Pitt spoke that day, Fox the next. It was Pitt's first speech in more than a year: more than 200 new members, as Macaulay later pointed out, had never heard him; galleries were so crowded that parliamentary reporters could not gain admission.

Only a brief summary exists, therefore, of Pitt's actual words. Eyewitness accounts relate how he entered the chamber an hour and a half after the speaking had begun. So excited and expectant were members that as soon as Pitt entered, eyes left the speaker and turned to him; amidst cries of 'Mr Pitt! Mr Pitt!' he strode to his seat on the third row behind the ministerial bench, next to one of the pillars. From this position, as Canning remarked to Malmesbury, Pitt could fire over the heads of the ministers, neither praising nor blaming them, but nevertheless supporting the decision to resume the war. When he rose to speak he received a tumultuous cheer, and when he sat down, after about an hour and a half, the applause was tremendous.

The slender account of his speech yields only the main threads of his discourse. Clear evidence existed, he declared, of aggression and hostility on the part of France. The activity of Bonaparte's mission in Egypt was an undeniable act of hostility against Britain; the treatment of Germany was arrogant, the violence offered to Switzerland had excited one universal sentiment of detestation, the continuance of the French army in Holland was another symptom of a deliberate system of ambition. Bonaparte's sending to England a group of 'commercial agents' who clandestinely obtained military information, was a topic on which it was difficult to speak with composure. He urged listeners to recognize that the decision to renew the war was a solemn one, and that it should be waged not merely defensively, to stave off invasion, but offensively; and that finances should be reorganized on the assumption that the war would be long and costly.[2]

In every way it was an impressive speech. 'Detesting the Dog as I do,' wrote Sheridan, 'I cannot withdraw this just tribute to the

---

[1] *Creevey Papers*, i, 13. May 11.   [2] *Parliamentary History*, xxxvi, 1387–98.

Scoundrel's talents.'[1] 'Pitt's speech . . . was admired very much, and very justly. I think it was the best he ever made in that style,' wrote Fox.[2] The House adjourned early—after ten o'clock, according to one report—as if members did not feel in the mood to continue the debate, much less to divide. Fox, who all his life had never hesitated to follow a two-hour speech with a two-hour reply, regardless of time or occasion, elected not to speak that evening; and a motion to adjourn the debate until the next day was quickly agreed to.

Effective as Fox could be in impromptu rebuttal, with several hours' intermission to reflect upon what had been said he could become well fortified indeed. The House was filled to hear the adjourned debate; parliamentary reporters were on hand in the gallery, and put into print undoubtedly the longest and most complete transcript, twenty-six pages, ever prepared of a Fox speech.

Towards the opening of his speech he had a few words to say about various ways not to debate. Many points had been made, he declared, that could not be supported by the evidence in the documents on the table; some points had been stated only in part; others had been omitted, though it would have been only fair to include them; and in some instances speakers had drawn conclusions that did not logically follow from the premises. Fox's colleagues must have feared most of all that he would be offensively pacifistic, but he was content to provide an exposition of what had transpired on both sides, buttressed by a statement of general principles that should govern the conduct of any nation that seeks to substitute, as long as possible, negotiation and mediation for armed conflict.

There was, for example, a disquisition upon the difference between insult and injury. Insult by itself was not a ground for hostility; if there were an insult, the offended nation should demand, and was entitled to receive, explanation. If an injury were actually sustained, the situation was different; even then, however, the injured nation could usually insist upon redress. That evening of May 24, 1803, was not the first time that Fox had expressed this point of view but never had he stated it more clearly. Rather than immediately sever diplomatic relations or launch counter-hostilities, an injured nation should first seek an explanation, making as clear as necessary just how it has been wronged and what kind of satisfaction it feels it must have. Since that speech each decade has increasingly reminded nations of the importance of negotiating first; fighting, when necessary, later.

On both sides there had been much violent abuse—this came under the heading of insults; here Fox quoted Homer: 'Put up your swords,

[1] *Letters of Richard Brinsley Sheridan*, ii, 196. [To Lady Bessborough, May 23.]
[2] Add. MSS. 47575. *Fox Cor.*, iii, 223. To Holland June 6.

and then abuse each other as long as you please.' In a lighter vein he talked about the cargoes of libels that regularly crossed the Channel—a commodity regularly exported, from both countries, in ample quantities—certainly a lesser calamity than war. The insulting demand of the French Government that Britain return French refugees, Fox declared should be ignored; on the other hand, the commercial commissioners, 'in effect no better than spies', should be shipped home at once.

Much more had been made of Malta than Fox thought justified. 'Malta! Malta! plain, bare, naked Malta, unconnected with any other interest! What point of honour can the retention of Malta be to you?' Here Fox had a specific suggestion; ask the Emperor of Russia to mediate this disagreement. 'To obtain [the good offices of the Emperor] for the restoration of peace is, in my opinion, of more real consequence to us, and to all Europe, than our possessing Malta under any circumstances.' Moreover, the principle of mediation might well be extended to Egypt, to Switzerland, to Holland, even to Spain.

Often Fox accompanied his analysis of the logic of a situation with some variety of ridicule or sarcasm; at times his stinging retorts made later conciliation difficult indeed. On this May 24 he made noteworthy comments about the oratory of those who were hustling the country into war, recalling an occasion when Wedderburn, before the Privy Council, called Dr Franklin 'a hoary-headed traitor':

I remember the prodigious effect produced by this splendid invective: so great was it, that when the privy council went away, they were almost ready to throw up their hats for joy, as if they had obtained a triumph. Why, Sir, we paid a pretty dear price for that triumph afterwards! ... There was no want of imagery, no want of figures of rhetoric, no want of the flowers of eloquence,—eloquence seldom equalled, and never surpassed by man, and all exerted to support the war. We know how that war ended, and the damp which was cast upon our ardour at the sight of the bill when it came to be paid.

'So now,' he went on, 'when I hear all these fine and eloquent philippics, I cannot help recollecting what fruits such speeches have generally produced.'[1] A few more minutes, and the three-hour speech was over, ending on the note that before members entered a great contest, they must deliberate at length and completely satisfy themselves that avoiding war was impossible.

The vote was unusually large: 398 to 67. Fox analysed Government support into three parts: Pittites, 58, Grenvillites 36, all the rest ministerial. Even so, Fox far outshone his rival. J. W. Ward, who

[1] *Parliamentary History*, xxxvi, 1437–87. The speech was also printed in *Substance of the speech of the Honourable Charles James Fox, in the house of commons, on Tuesday, May 24, 1803*, etc. (London, 1803).

heard both speeches and who usually was so impressed by Pitt that he declared he would rather listen to Pitt four hours than one, nevertheless wrote:

Fox's speech . . . was . . . a far greater effort of mind. It was much the best I ever heard from him, and stands immediately next to the greatest among those of his antagonist. . . . Don't imagine that from this accidental superiority in one instance, I mean to draw any inference as to the comparative talents of the men. . . . Pitt taking professedly a very narrow, Fox a very wide field, the genius of the one was circumscribed, the other had room to display all his resources.[1]

Fox himself felt pleased with his own speech; he wrote to Lord Holland: 'I dare say you have heard puffs enough of my speech upon the address, so that I need not add my mite, but the truth is that it was my best.'[2] Later he told Grattan that it was the best speech he ever made.[3] Never again did he attain such a height of eloquence—and never again was there such a high level Pitt–Fox debate.

Horner thought Fox's speech unusually distinctive; it was delivered not in his usual high pitch with 'impassioned bursts' throughout, but instead was 'calm, subtle, argumentative pleasantry'. Horner found more wit and humour in it than the text suggests and than Fox customarily used, quoting Mackintosh's observation that 'he never heard so much wit'.[4] Grey was delighted with the speeches of both Pitt and Fox: he called Pitt's 'one of the most magnificent pieces of declamation ever made', and admired Fox's even more extravagantly: describing it as 'the most wonderful display of wisdom and genius that ever was exhibited. It makes everything else shrink into dust.'[5] Ponsonby thought Fox's speech was the finest he had ever heard. While Fox was on his legs, Sheridan received a note from Lady Bessborough, and in his brief, hurried reply, said: 'I have done what I would do for no one breathing but you—Left the House while Fox was speaking to answer your note.' Outside the chamber, scribbling his reply, he could not resist describing the speech in the most glowing phrases: its prudence, management, humour, judiciousness. Sheridan, regretting every instant away from Fox's performance, brought his note to a sudden end: 'I won't write another word. I have lost five minutes. Adieu.'[6]

Mr Speaker, whose diary usually recorded merely the fact of important speeches without comment on them, set down his observation, a true minority report: 'In the debate Mr Fox spoke from ten till one; and in these three hours delivered a speech of more art, eloquence, wit, and mischief than I remember to have heard from him.'[7]

---

[1] Stanhope, iv, 48–50. [2] Add. MSS. 47575. *Fox Cor.*, iii, 223. June 6.
[3] Grattan, v, 200. [4] Horner, i, 229. To J. A. Murray, June 11.
[5] George Macaulay Trevelyan, *Lord Grey of the Reform Bill* (New York, 1920), pp. 130–1.
[6] *Letters of Richard Brinsley Sheridan*, ii, 197–8. [7] Colchester, i, 421.

The papers, however, which for days had discussed the possibilities of impending war both pro and con, though with an undertone of criticism against the Government for its watchful waiting, actively criticized the two debaters and their respective positions. They expressed bitter regrets that their reporters did not get to cover Pitt's speech. It was a 'national calamity', said the *True Briton*, to have missed Pitt's 'eloquent and impressive speech . . . irresistible appeal to the good sense and public spirit of Englishmen'. Most of the comments, nevertheless, favoured Fox, ranging from the *Sun's* observation that Fox had become temperate since long experience had taught him that violent opinion hindered his purpose, to the *Morning Chronicle's*: 'The speech of Mr Fox was undoubtedly one of the best he ever made . . . great impression . . . many members who vote with ministers spoke of it with unmixed approbation.' He did not as some expected advocate the cause of France, but argued the question 'upon principles truly British'. The *Morning Post* thought it one of his most ably argued speeches, 'but we are far from thinking it unanswerable'; especially did the *Post* regret that Fox's speech should go forth to the world while Pitt's was smothered by the exclusion of reporters.

It was left to the *Morning Chronicle*, however, to sound a note that better than any other described a phase of British politics evident then and also during the whole, long period of the Pitt–Fox rivalry. For when other countries look at Britain, it grieved, they must think how wonderfully fertile in talents the nation must be when it can 'lay up in ordinary so many great and able men' (Fox, Pitt, Grey, Windham, Moira, Grenville) at a time of crisis and have a ministry largely made up of men 'neither recommended by birth, connexion, abilities, nor experience'.[1]

Three days later Fox offered a resolution that the Emperor of Russia be asked to serve as mediator. As his plan had Pitt's support and the Government accepted it, the motion was withdrawn. The proposal, asserted the *Morning Chronicle*, was perhaps the most important that could possibly be addressed to a public assembly. The *Morning Post* noted that Pitt was among the first to applaud it: 'We never saw the members of all parties so ardent in their congratulations as on this occasion.' The *Oracle* thought the motion good, though it might only serve to give the enemy time to strengthen itself, but it did cheer the temporary absence of party prejudice. The *Chronicle* further observed that the 'dignified reproof' in Fox's speech would, coming from such a man as Fox, touch Napoleon more than would criticism from someone who lacked Fox's desire, 'which in him is equally a passion and a principle, for the peace and liberty of mankind'.[2] Rumours were circulated

[1] Issues of May 24–June 1.   [2] Issues of May 27–June 1.

that the first consul would accept the offer of mediation, but to chill the rumours came a cold fact: even on the day Fox had spoken, Bonaparte had issued an order arresting British subjects travelling in France. How difficult it is to speak for peace when one combatant prefers war. The two nations therefore continued their aggressive preparation.

29

Fox and Pitt in Opposition
1803-1805

With respect to Mr Fox . . . dismissed from the
Treasury . . . speeches and conduct at the Whig Club . . .
struck out of the Privy Council, he wondered Mr Pitt
should think of presenting such a name.

George the Third

In 1803 Addington's Government was beset by troubles, from west
and east as well as from within its own centre.

The western trouble came from Ireland, where in July rebellion had
broken out again. Robert Emmet, talented young man of Dublin, had
conspired with associates at home and with Irish exiles on the Continent to renew the struggle against British authority. Parliament suspended habeas corpus in Ireland and empowered the Lord Lieutenant
to try before a court martial any lawbreakers who were apprehended.
Emmet was captured, and despite an eloquent defence was executed
along with seventeen others.

The eastern trouble came from France. Napoleon, finances bolstered
by having recently sold the Louisiana country to Mr Jefferson for sixty
million francs, determined to mount a cross-channel invasion against
the English coast. In the spring and summer of 1803 he busied himself
with the plans of the manoeuvre. Boulogne was to be the nerve centre;
along the coast shipyards built flat-bottomed boats, designed as troop
carriers, with a capacity of 50, 80, or 100 men each. Some craft had
mortars in bow and stern; others were designed to carry horses and
field pieces.[1] Years later at St Helena he described how he would have
proclaimed a republic, abolished the House of Lords, freed the country
from a corrupt aristocracy, and established a democracy. Property
would be seized from those who opposed him and distributed to those
who supported him, and thus he would have appeared as the deliverer
of the people.

The English were quick to see the difficulties involved in invading
their island. Invasion craft could not simply be brought unaccompanied
across the Channel but needed powerful naval protection, and Cornwallis at Brest and other admirals elsewhere had been able to blockade

[1] J. M. Thompson, *Napoleon Bonaparte* (New York, 1952). Felix Markham, *Napoleon*
(London, 1963).

large segments of the French fleet. So, despite repeated false alarms and continual speculation about time, place, and strategy, there was little panic. Groups of volunteers were organized who drilled, usually without effective arms; Pitt organized a regiment and as their colonel oversaw exercise and drill. He had much more faith in the volunteers than did Fox. Pitt uniformed them to improve their military posture but Fox declared that the red coats served only to make them better targets. Other preparations also went forward; the coastline was inspected and harbour fortifications strengthened. Formal, detailed studies were made of coastal defences and possible invasion plans. The martello towers still standing on England's southern coast date from this period.

Rumours of invasion filled the papers. Like others, Fox worried about it; he felt a landing was imminent, though he was confident the invading forces could be overcome. He thought he might ask the new Home Secretary, Charles Yorke, whether he could undertake duty in the Westminster neighbourhood, perhaps as a justice of the peace or a sort of colleague to the Lord Mayor. If, however, 'the fools' should 'be afraid of trusting me', he would go to the Prince and 'desire his leave to be by his side on whatever service he is employed'.[1] He wrote Holland: 'Invasion is expected by many immediately, and some go so far as to say the embarkation is to be made tomorrow.'[2] Already Fox was looking ahead to the convening of Parliament when both Ireland and invasion would come up for review. Gradually the danger of invasion passed though it loomed again as a likely possibility the next year; the Irish problem was more persistent.

Under these circumstances the second session of the second Imperial Parliament met at Westminster, November 22, 1803, the forty-fourth year of the reign of George III. The brief address praised the voluntary exertions of the people to defend the kingdom, and reported that the leaders of the late 'traitorous and atrocious conspiracy' in Ireland had been brought to justice. It was approved in both Houses without a vote, although Fox in a short but forceful speech declared that the Irish leaders had disclaimed connection with the French Government. Moreover, their atrocities, which he viewed with horror, were not to be linked with the French situation. Irish hopes were far from satisfied and gentlemen should not suffer themselves to believe that the Irish problem was settled.[3]

[1] Add. MSS. 47581. To Fitzpatrick, September 27, 1803.
[2] Add. MSS. 47575. *Fox Cor.*, iii, 227. October 16.
[3] *Parliamentary Debates*, 1st series, i, 1541–4.

Fox did not speak in the debates that ensued on the Irish question. Saving his argument for the debate of December 9 on the army estimates, he declared that the volunteer system was not adequate to meet the present emergency nor was it a foundation on which to build a strong regular army. He also made reference to the request of the Prince of Wales to be given a military assignment. Later the Prince wrote that a personal friend of Pitt's had declared that he had never heard such a speech as Fox's: 'It not only completely silenced the ministerial phalanx, but left neither friend nor foe a single word to say either respecting me or any other head.'[1]

Trouble from the centre took several forms. There were minor nuisances like the shortage of coins because of hoarding and difficulties in filling out the new income tax blanks; mainly, however, the Government itself needed revision. Among those who worked energetically for a stronger administration was Lord Grenville. Grenville, son of the author of the Stamp Tax, and younger brother of Thomas, Fox's peace negotiator at Paris, had served a term as Speaker of the House, and then, elevated to a barony, served Pitt as Home Secretary and as Foreign Secretary. He had approached Pitt in an effort to enlist his help in removing Addington, but Pitt declined. Pitt's plan was to support Addington in all plain and simple questions; when he differed, he would be content to state his opinions.

Unsuccessful in the negotiation with Pitt, Grenville later, through brother Thomas, approached Fox early in 1804 to form a ministry of the talented men of both parties—the genesis of the administration of All the Talents that was to be formed two years later. Fox had been enjoying literary pursuits ('What can you mean by saying there is little good of the new Poetry in Cowper? what, . . . not *one* of the Sonnets? not the Shipwreck or Outcast? pray read them over again, and repeat your former judgment if you dare')[2] and making progress with his history ('Yesterday and not before died James, Duke of Monmouth &c. It will be well if the Historian has not made as bungling a piece of work with him as the Hangman').[3]

But the proposal from the Grenvilles had to be coped with, so as usual when faced with perplexing decisions he wrote his friends for advice. Fitzpatrick received this urgent summons: 'Pray come as soon as you can. Mrs F. says I should say nothing but *come, come, come,* and she would say it down on her knees. You know she thinks there is no

[1] *HMCR*, Hastings MSS., iii, 228. Prince of Wales to [Francis, second earl of Moira]. December 11.
[2] Add. MSS. 47575. *Fox Cor.*, iii, 236. To Holland, January 18, 1804.
[3] Add. MSS. 47581. *Fox Cor.*, iv, 13. January 1.

adviser but you.'[1] Fox also longed to have Grey at hand, writing to him that he had received a direct communication from a substantial part of the opposition expressing a wish 'to join with us in a systematic opposition, for the purpose of removing the Ministry, and substituting one on the broadest possible basis'. The Grenvilles made clear to Fox that they would have no further connection with Pitt, so the proposed broad-bottomed ministry would give no consideration either to Pitt or to his opinions. Fox wrote further: 'I must consult friends before I come to any determination, and particularly *you*. I own I lean very much to such a junction.'[2] He must have given Grenville's negotiators encouragement, because Lauderdale discovered Fox's leaning towards the Government and objected to it; his reaction in turn came back to Fox, who wrote Grey that 'all I have done' is 'telling them that I have every inclination to act with them, but I think it would be better to agree first in publick and so let the thing come on naturally rather than by any compact'.[3]

Fox was, of course, keenly interested in these negotiations, writing to William Smith, one of his dissenter friends, that he had received a proposition 'of the most frank & handsome nature' from the Grenvilles, to substitute for the present ministry one of the 'broadest basis', with Fox promising his support on such measures as the imperfect defence of the country and on Irish affairs, and even further if circumstances warranted.[4]

Meanwhile the King had fallen seriously ill; for a time his old mental derangement returned and his life was believed in danger. With invasion threatening and the Government unsettled, no time could be worse. Pitt again declined to 'make the turning out this administration the object of his endeavours; that though some of his best friends had united themselves avowedly for that purpose with Fox', he would continue to support the Government.[5] Talk sprang up at once about a regency, which would likely bring in Fox at the head of the Cabinet. Fox could not resist the tendency to meddle; he wrote Dennis O'Bryen that he wanted something in the papers every day about the King's madness, 'in a most decent way, of course'.[6] The King's health improved somewhat though physicians warned that he should not be troubled by distressing problems and so that crisis passed.

Pitt, meanwhile, treated 'as it deserved' an extravagant idea brought to him by Melville, from Addington, that Pitt and Addington become Secretaries of State under a new First Lord of the Treasury, Lord

[1] Add. MSS. 47581. *Fox Cor.*, iv, 19. January 28.
[2] Add. MSS. 47565. *Fox Cor.*, iii, 450–451. Grey MSS. (Durham.) January 29.
[3] Holland House MSS. February 15. (Copy.)   [4] Osborn Collection, 85/15. (Yale.)
[5] Stanhope, iv, 121.   [6] Add. MSS. 47566.

Chatham. Later Grenville and Pitt discussed other arrangements 'on a purely speculative basis'. Pitt suggested that the King would be reluctant to show favour to Fox and certain members of the Opposition. When he added that a new administration would need to propose strong measures to set the country in the proper military and financial posture, Grenville argued that such measures would especially require the united support of all the leading men in Parliament, without exception.

Pitt, according to Grenville, seemed to lean to this notion.[1] But Pitt's correspondence with Melville between March 29 and April 14 is a better index to his own thinking. In considering the possibility of being invited to form a new government Pitt omitted Fox's name from his plans because he was positive that the King would not take kindly to any arrangement with Fox in it. If Pitt were to persist in suggesting to the King 'persons against whom he has long entertained such strong and natural objections,' he could do so only in a manner that would leave the King 'a free option'.[2]

In April Fox and Pitt joined forces in an attack upon the Addington Government, the question being Fox's motion on the state of the nation's defences. Before the debate they thought they might accumulate as many as 200 votes, Fox writing to Grey that he would be happy with 170;[3] actually the minority reached 204 against the Government's 256. The narrow margin of 52 votes alarmed Addington, and at his urging, the King agreed that the Lord Chancellor, Eldon, should consult with Pitt. In the discussions that followed the King made it clear to Pitt, through Lord Eldon, that Catholic emancipation must continue dormant—Pitt was not to propose any alteration in the Test Act. Moreover, Fox was positively not to be admitted to the Cabinet; on this point the King stated his astonishment that Pitt should harbour the thought of bringing such a man to his notice.[4]

Addington's resignation on April 29 brought the problem into sharp focus. The King told Pitt that he might bring the Grenvilles into office but Fox was to be forever excluded. Here was a 'No Fox' that was loud and clear.

This narrative has traced in detail various former attempts to negotiate Fox into office and will not spell out the discussions of 1804.

[1] ST 174. Stowe collection. April 15. (Huntington.)
[2] From *Autograph Correspondence with Lord Melville.* (Clements.)
[3] Add. MSS. 47565. *Fox Cor.*, iv, 49. Grey MSS. (Durham.) April 23.
[4] *HMCR*, Bathurst MSS., 37–8. May 1804. Malmesbury, iv, 299–300. See also Rose's *Diary* for May 5; the king expressed 'an absolute negative' to the admission of Fox, 'saying, that he had been expelled from the Privy Council for his conduct, and that no consideration should prevail with him to accept him now as one of his ministers' (ii, 118). Pitt's draft of a cabinet with Fox as a secretary of state is printed in Stanhope, iv, xi.

Most of the steps taken by various parties were laid down in the contemporary ooze and hardened in the journals and correspondence of witnesses, so that those who wish may inspect the evidence. Let it be said that Pitt earnestly desired Fox in the new Government, in some modest position, but could not counter the King's personal opposition. Nor could Pitt cajole Grenville. Grenville formulated an impressive phrase to heighten and dignify his refusal: he declared he was unwilling to become part of a Government formed 'on a principle of exclusion'. The only way to heal the nation's ills, he wrote, was to bring into the administration the largest possible proportion of the available character and talent—without any exceptions.

The notion of 'principle of exclusion' caught on. It was a good banner to march behind. Fox took the King's dislike calmly and urged Grey, Grenville, and other friends to take positions in the new Government regardless. Grey called his associates together, who agreed, unanimously, not to accept office unless their excluded friends could also have a place. Grenville and his followers reached an identically similar decision. This demonstration of loyalty to Fox was impressive. The new whigs solidly endorsed him, his principles, his potential for leadership.

Old whig Portland, meanwhile, wrote the King an unforgivably mischievous letter, citing a report in *The Times* and adding his own hearsay evidence that at the Whig Club meeting Fox had committed the indiscretion of offering a toast to the radical Sir Francis Burdett. How amazed Fox would have been if he had known that his one-time good friend was tattling to the Monarch. Fox in turn was positive of his own feelings towards Pitt; ever distrustful even of his opponent's best intentions, Fox termed him a mean, low-minded dog and a sad stick. And Pitt was unhappy about Grenville. Even though his own health would suffer, Pitt resolved to teach that proud gentleman politics' grimmest lesson: no man is indispensable. All these major and minor themes reverberated through political circles, and eventually made their separate ways into diaries and letters.[1]

Fortified by Portland's gossip and by his own predilections and prejudices, the King made his point stick; he would see Pitt only if it were agreed that neither Fox nor Grenville were to be mentioned; and if Pitt would not so agree, the King would form an administration 'composed of persons not fond of novelties'.[2] In these circumstances Pitt became first minister and resumed the direction of affairs that he had

---

[1] Holland House MSS. *Fox Cor.*, iii, 455–7, iv, 54–6. Stanhope, iv, 174. *Life of Eldon*, i, 449. *HMCR*, Bathurst MSS., pp. 34 ff.; Colchester, i, 506–7. Rose, ii, 124–5. Fortescue transcripts, May 9 (Clements).
[2] *HMCR*, Bathurst MSS., pp. 37–8. May 1804. Rose, ii, 155–6. Malmesbury, iv, 299 ff.

laid down three years previously. 'Our greatest weakness will be in . . . filling the offices . . . particularly with persons who will be able to assist essentially in debate.'[1] So the King's personal resentment of Fox prevented the formation, at a critical time, of what might have been a powerful and effective coalition Government. Fox in his turn had not been over eager to rush to Pitt. He realized that Pitt would soon need new talent in his administration and would likely approach him and his colleagues again, offering better terms. Fox's tactic meanwhile was to collect as much strength as possible. As he wrote the following year, he and his friends should display every degree of moderation, do anything possible 'to soften the K.'s prejudices', and reject 'those principles of exclusion which we condemn in others'.[2]

Meanwhile Pitt had to take up again the burdens of the struggle with the French. One of his first moves was to devise a solution for the perennial question of inducing the young men of the country to enlist in the armed forces. In general the system in practice had been that a man who was drafted for service in the army reserve could, if he wished not to serve, pay a fine or provide a substitute. Quotas had been assigned to parishes, and any parish not meeting its quota had been required to pay a stiff penalty. To avoid fines and penalties, individuals or parishes had offered high bounties, which had attracted men into the reserve forces who otherwise might enlist in the regular army or navy. The new Chancellor proposed in his Additional Force Bill to remove some of these fines and other obstacles so that men would flow into the nation's first lines of defence instead of its rear echelons. Interest was high in the debates; attendance increased and discussion was lively. The fact that if the Bill failed the ministry might collapse was not lost on Opposition speakers.

The vote of 221 for the second reading of the Bill and 181 against it shows the size of attendance and the narrow margin enjoyed by the new administration. The chief discussion was on the second reading of amendments on June 18, the House not adjourning until half-past four in the morning. In his lifetime Fox had spoken to many full Houses, but never to one with so many members present. The vote was 265 for, 223 against, a majority for the government of 42. That same afternoon, after trifling debate, the Bill was read a third time and passed. Even so, the spirit of opposition was high. Fox wrote to Holland: 'Nothing could have fallen out more to my mind that what has happened: the Party revived and strengthened, Pitt lowered, and, what is of more consequence in my view, the cause of *Royalism* (in the bad sense of the word) lowered too.'[3]

---

[1] Rose, ii, 131. May 10. [2] *Fox Cor.*, iv, 87–9. To O'Bryen, July 7, 1805.
[3] Add. MSS. 47597. *Fox Cor.*, iv, 57. July 24.

By August bad weather and other events turned Napoleon's attention away from invasion to other matters. As the year ended Fox was in better spirits. 'Opposition *seems* now restored,' he wrote to Grey. '. . . Mind, I say *seems*, for if *you* stay away, it will be very far from being really so. . . . Do, for God's sake, make up your mind to one unpleasant effort, and come for the first two months at least of the session.' He concluded: 'I love idleness so much, and so dearly, that I have hardly the heart to say a word against it; but something is due to one's station in life, something to friendship, something to the country.'[1] These moving words reached Grey, who came from Northumberland to be on hand for the debates. The King continued in his determination to keep Fox out of the Government—'His Majesty . . . had taken a positive determination not to admit Mr Fox into his Councils, *even at the hazard of a civil war*'[2]—but Addington joined the Government as President of the Council, operating from the Lords as Viscount Sidmouth.

Neither these activities nor the continual pressure of debts had deterred Fox from undertaking, in June, the construction of a small structure on the grounds at St Anne's. He had had a supply of marble columns on hand, acquired with the grounds or by separate purchase, and when on one occasion a political associate, Lord Newborough, had visited him, the two contrived the notion of utilizing the columns in the construction of 'a little temple'.

Lord Newborough undertook to provide a plan, but Fox himself had various ideas about steps, inscriptions, the portico, and other features. Sculptor Joseph Nollekens visited the construction site on occasion and offered suggestions; after all, Fox had been one of his best clients, since copies of the Fox bust continued in strong demand, and the sculptor could very well take an interest in the debater's building ventures. Over the years the temple has survived numerous changes made at St Anne's by successive owners, and at the time of this writing was in a reasonable state of repair.[3]

The motion against the slave trade came up again in February 1805, and Fox was eager that its supporters should make a good showing:

[1] Add. MSS. 47576. *Fox Cor.*, iv, 71–2. Grey MSS. (Durham.) December 17.
[2] Rose, ii, 156–7.
[3] Letters to Newborough, June 10 [1804] and subsequent dates. Osborn Collection (Yale). I am indebteded for information about the temple and other features of St Anne's to Frank S. Ochs, Hassocks, Sussex, who lived there, 1901–02; to D. W. D. Yates, Chertsey, Surrey; to Dr Frederick Hilton, of Addlestone, Surrey; and to Colin F. Ball, reference librarian, Central Library, Chertsey.

'Pray speak to everybody you can to come down,' he wrote Georgiana from the House of Commons, 'or we shall be lost on the Slave Trade. . . . Pray, pray send any body you see.'[1] The question that day was in the form of an amendment to postpone the Bill for six months; in a thin House it passed 77 to 70. Six months ahead reached to the end of August when Parliament would not be in session. Not until the spring of 1806, three months before his death, did Fox, then ill and weary, have another opportunity to speak for abolition.

'The catholic business' had for many years been one of those subjects near Fox's heart. When in May 1805 the question of relief for Catholics was raised in Parliament, Fox supported it eloquently.

Speeches in favour of religious tolerance are built not only out of facts and instances but also out of masterfully clear thinking upon principles. The present situation, Fox argued, is different from that during the reign of James II, a professed Catholic. Moreover, allowing people to hold lesser positions in the army, the navy and the law, and forbidding them to hold higher positions, puts a restraint 'on the exercise of a man's genius and industry. Take away the hope of higher office and you destroy the greatest incentive to an aspiring mind.' If any particular class of people cannot attain to parliamentary office, you have no real representation, not even virtual representation, no 'sympathy and fellow feeling between the representative and the persons represented. . . . The very substance of representation is, that the members of parliament should not be able to tax their constituents without taxing themselves.' For these and other reasons he urged a settlement of the long-standing Catholic question.[2]

Occasionally a speech receives one of the finest tributes of all: a delayed compliment from somebody who hears it, treasures it in his memory, and years afterwards speaks of it with admiration and wonder. In the gallery during the debates was brilliant young Robert Peel, who spent many days between the time he left Harrow and his matriculation at Christ Church listening to Pitt and Fox and their colleagues. In 1828 Peel found himself Home Secretary, and though he had not been a friend to Catholic emancipation, decided it was preferable to civil strife. In debate on July 3 that year, Mr Secretary Peel paid tribute to Fox's great speech: 'He never heard a speech which made a greater impression on his mind, than that delivered by Mr Fox.'[3] In the debates of

1 Fox MSS. (Clements.) *Two Duchesses*, p. 263.
2 *Parliamentary Debates*, 1st series, iv, 834–54.
3 Quoted in Norman Gash, *Mr Secretary Peel* (London, 1961), pp. 47–8. Peel's comment is in *Parliamentary Debates*, second series, xix, 1611.

1829 that led to the passing of the Catholic Relief Bill, both Peel in the Commons and Grey in the Lords praised the stand that Fox had taken in 1805.

Although Fox had small regard for newspapers as accurate reporters of the parliamentary scene and although he, barring a single exception or two, gave little encouragement to those who wanted to secure better versions of his speeches, he was sensitive to the press as an agency to help shape public opinion.

The question before the Commons on June 20 was a proposed inquiry into public affairs. During this debate, Fox briefly recommended that a new administration be formed embracing 'all that is respectable for rank, talents, character and influence in the country'. No individual should suffer personal ambition 'to stand in the way of the formation of such a ministry'.[1] A few more lines followed in the same vein, then Fox turned to the question proper. Apparently, however, he uttered something further in a subdued tone not heard throughout the chamber: the *Morning Post* attempted to supply the muffled words. Nothing, reported the *Post*, apparently quoting Fox, could justify excluding from his Majesty's councils persons of 'known and extraordinary abilities', but it was now Fox's 'settled and serious resolve' not to accept public office. However—and then came the part that caused much controversy—Fox would be happy (said the *Post*) to support measures 'proposed by those who were now looked upon as his political friends, should they come to act in concert with the present minister'.[2]

Fox, irked to the marrow by this comment, wrote a long letter to O'Bryen, only a part of which has been printed in the collected correspondence. The paragraph, he declared, had not one word of truth; the words were not spoken in a low tone, but 'distinctly and audibly to a House the most silent and attentive that I ever witnessed'. He then set down what he recollected he had said—substantially what appears in the printed debates. He did not want to have his words construed as meaning that he approved a coalition ministry, either of Pitt and Fox, or of Pitt and Fox's friends; moreover, Fox was mortified that his own friends would suspect that he harboured the idea of a juncture. Seeking to meet the newspaper report head-on, he continued:

I have considered this damned paragraph again and again and feel quite sure that much mischief is meant by it. I wish you therefore to get into as many papers as possible [*Chronicle, Press, Herald, Traveller*, and others], the inclosed. . . . I have put into it compliments to myself to make it impossible that it should be suspected to

[1] *Parliamentary Debates*, 1st series, v, 526.   [2] June 22.

come from me. You will of course, after copying it, destroy the original and insert the name of the Paper (which you did not tell me) in which the paragraph originally appeared. Pray attend to this and above all let *me* not be discovered.[1]

The *Post* had insisted that a peculiarity of Fox's public speaking was that he lowered his voice frequently when most speakers would increase their loudness, and although it was inclined to stick to its original story, it printed the following article 'sent to us for insertion' by a 'gentleman of honour and respectability'. Here is Newspaper Correspondent Fox's own version of the incident:

A paragraph appeared in a Morning and Evening Paper of Saturday last, stating that in the Debate of last Thursday Mr Fox expressed himself to the following effect:—'That it was now his serious and settled resolve never to look to nor accept of any public situation; but that he should support to the best of his abilities, the measures of those who were now looked upon as his political friends, should they come to act in concert with the present Minister.' Such are the words imputed to Mr Fox in the paragraph alluded to.

Having stated the imputation, Fox now replied to it:

We are enabled, on the authority of persons who sat close to Mr Fox, and who listened most attentively to that admirable speech, to contradict every word contained in the said paragraph. . . . Mr Fox, undoubtedly, expressed his wish for a comprehensive Administration, and declared that *no personal views of his should stand in the way of so desirable an object*; but he did not drop one expression that could be construed into an approbation on his part of any of his friends (of whatever description) forming a junction with the present Ministry.[2]

The Times and the *Evening Mail* did not print the Fox statement, but editorially stated that Fox did not use the expression attributed to him. The *Star*, same date, also published this article but added, at the end: '. . . Ministry, whom he characterized, with his usual ability, as meriting that contempt in which they are universally held by an indignant public.' The *Chronicle*, same date, published the *Star* version. O'Bryen had done his leg work well.

A letter from Adair to Fox under date of July 7 carried the burden of a conversation between Pitt and the King the previous Sunday, June 30, that Pitt told the King he could not continue longer without the help of Opposition. The King mentioned Fox's speech—presumably that of June 20 with its ambiguous comments on coalition—and Pitt replied: 'It was the most noble one, and that the man who could make it was the fittest to be applied to for advice.' When the King asked 'whether some proposal might be made to the opposition without Mr Fox', Pitt replied 'they ought not to listen to such a proposal, and in my opinion

[1] Add. MSS. 47566. June 23.   [2] June 25.

their acceptance would be of very little use without him'. The King finally admitted that there was great good sense in Pitt's observation; that conditions this year were different from last; nevertheless, Pitt should go on, patching up as best he could. Adair's story was at least secondhand, but suggested that the thirty-year conflict between the Sovereign and Fox might be ended by some kind of truce.[1]

[1] Add. MSS. 47565. *Fox Cor.*, iv, 90–1. Rose, ii, 105–6. July 7.

30

Pitt Dies, Fox Takes Office
1805–1806

The eyes of all sides are fixed on Charles Fox.

Mrs Charlotte Nugent

Our enemies have the merit of being indefatigable.

Charles James Fox

The war went on, Pitt still in office, Fox still on the Opposition bench. The threat of invasion continued, although Fox insisted that the possibility was not so imminent as to make it necessary to curtail the liberties of Englishmen. Although Napoleon, meanwhile, was having troubles of his own, he did not want to abandon the cross-channel attempt. Because of the threat posed by Nelson and British ships of the line, he saw that he had to have his own fleet available to protect the invasion flotilla during its staging and crossing manoeuvres. With two or three days' protection against the British fleet, or even only twenty-four hours, and a favourable wind, he was positive he could 'put an end to the future and to the very existence of Britain'. Hence he sent new instructions to his admirals, but June and July passed with no word whether his instructions had actually reached them or whether they would or could obey. All through August Napoleon impatiently waited —about the time that Fox was writing to Grey that the alarm of invasion was groundless, Napoleon was writing to Talleyrand: 'There is still time—I am master of England.'[1] D-Day would open whenever the French fleet arrived, but it never came.

Meanwhile as Austrian forces crossed the border and marched into Bavaria, Napoleon broke camp at Boulogne and marched with his Army of England into the heartland of the Continent to meet the Austrians. Within a week he fought two critical battles, one on land and one at sea. He won the first when, meeting the Austrian army at Ulm, he surrounded it and compelled the surrender of 30,000 men. The grim news reached London on a Sunday, in the form of a dispatch printed in a Dutch newspaper; Pitt, unable to read Dutch, hunted up Malmesbury, who translated for him, each phrase a shock to the ailing

[1] Thompson, pp. 253–4; Markham, pp. 101–3.

Prime Minister. Napoleon lost the second battle when the French and Spanish fleets, who had outmanoeuvred Nelson with a diversion to the West Indies, had to face the English at Trafalgar. Nelson, signalling that England expects every man to do his duty, won an engagement that crushed the naval power of France and Spain and established Britain as mistress of the seas for more than a century to come.

News of the triumph reached London on a Tuesday, forty-eight hours after the sober message from Ulm. Pitt, getting the word late at night, was so exhilarated by the victory that he could sleep no further. Fox, something less than gracious, wrote his nephew two days later: 'It is a great event, and by it, solid as well as brilliant advantages, far more than compensates for the temporary succour which it will certainly afford to Pitt in his distress.'[1] Fox was still troubled by the disasters on the Continent. It was unequalled madness, he wrote Fitzwilliam, 'to attempt to attack the first military country in the world with an inferiority of numbers, of troops, and still far more of generals.'[2]

Napoleon meanwhile engaged the Austrians and Russians at Austerlitz, winning a brilliant victory that forced Austria and Russia out of the war, ending the coalition. Pitt, in poor health, shattered by the news, left Bath for his recently acquired home in Putney. As he walked down the hall to his bedroom, observing a map of Europe, he is reported to have said: 'Roll up that map; it will not be wanted these ten years.' Fox, usually generous, could not find much sympathy for his stricken opponent. On January 1 he wrote Holland that Opposition should make a strong attack upon the ministry, perhaps even insisting upon a division upon the address or censuring Pitt on the condition of the land forces.[3] On January 2 he wrote further:

As to your News I must know Pitt's Resignation for certain before I believe it, even if he is dying the ruling passion will prevail,
> and in those moments as in all the past
> O! let me keep my Place shall be his last.[4]

In the same letter he had written that if by any chance Pitt were planning to resign, 'for God's sake do all you can to prevent our friends from being eager to come in, until they are sure of being quite and entirely masters'. Everybody concerned must work like drayhorses.

By the time the session opened on January 21, the Opposition had decided not to divide the House; Fox was content to state his position

[1] Add. MSS. 47575. *Fox Cor.*, iv, 121. November 7, 1805.
[2] Fitzwilliam MSS. (Milton) 67/4, 1–3. November 11. (Northamptonshire Record Office.)
[3] Add. MSS. 47575. *Fox Cor.*, iv, 127–9. January 1, 1806.
[4] Add. MSS. 47575. *Fox Cor.*, iv, 130, omits the lines after 'believe it'. January 2.

that the calamities which had befallen British arms on the Continent, because of (here he used favourite words) ill-concerted, ill-supported, and ill-executed plans, should be inquired into. On January 23, twenty-five years to the day after having first entered the House of Commons, Pitt passed away. He had never been a friend of the masses; his death resulted in more newspaper copy than the slender notice taken of his father's exit, but other than an occasional black-bordered sheet, little that was remarkable appeared in print. Next day, on Fox's fifty-seventh birthday, Elizabeth Fox wrote in her journal: 'This is the day of all the year which is to me most dear. It brought into the world him that makes me the happiest of women and God Almighty keep him to me in health.'

On January 27 the motion before the Commons was that the remains of the right honourable William Pitt be interred at the public charge and that a monument be erected to the memory of that 'excellent statesman'. The phrase was not a choice one; sharp memories still lingered in the minds of several as to whether Pitt's policies deserved to be praised, and in the debate that followed almost every other speaker insisted that he did not care to endorse the excellence of Pitt's statesmanship. Fox also felt it his duty to vote against the proposed motion; after opposing Pitt for twenty years, though he paid warm tribute to excellences of character he was not willing to endorse excellences of statecraft; but the division revealed 258 for the motion, 89 against.[1]

Some of Fox's private opinions of Pitt have already been cited. In the debate of that January 27 Fox's long habit of making distinctions persisted at a moment when it would have been more gracious to pass them over. Or the motion itself could have been worded in any of a dozen different ways that would have gained it stronger support. Regardless of Fox's opinion expressed that day, he had stated quite another three days before Pitt's death. Georgiana and her friend Bess had called on Fox; as they entered the house a lady left. Said Mrs Fox:

'That was a mild, gentle little creature who went out, yet she had been rejoicing at . . . Pitt being so ill.'

'Oh, no,' said Fox, 'shocking.'

'It is impossible,' the Duchess and I said, 'to be glad.'

'Quite,' said Fox. 'How can one rejoice in the death of any man? Death is a thing without a remedy. Besides, it is a poor way of getting rid of one's enemy. A fair, good discussion that turns him out is well—but death—no!'

Fox then expressed the view that the news would 'render every debate flat and uninteresting. I hate going to to the House. I think I shall pair off with Pitt.'[2]

---

[1] *Parliamentary Debates*, 1st series, vi, 41–72.
[2] *Dearest Bess*, pp. 133–4.

Eight months later, as this author remarked, Fox paired off with Pitt for all time.

Negotiations for a new government required only a few days. A Cabinet minute of January 24 conveyed the information to the King that the present administration saw no way of carrying on. At the same time a long supplementary letter from the Lord President, the Duke of Portland, after stating his personal attachment to the King, &c, &c, and his grateful remembrances, &c, &c, nevertheless ought to convey to his Majesty's better judgment, &c, &c, the necessity of having recourse to 'some *at least*' of the present Opposition.[1] The King unrelentingly declared that he would not suffer Fox 'to sit in any Cabinet that is to advise him'.[2] Grenville, however, determined to inform the King that nothing can be done except with Fox's fullest concurrence and with the abandonment of all idea of exclusion.[3] When Grenville stated that he must consult with Fox, the King is reported to have replied: 'I thought so and I meant it so.'[4] On January 31 Grenville delivered a paper on which Fox's name appeared as Foreign Secretary; other names included Erskine as Lord Chancellor, Fitzwilliam as Lord President, Spencer as Home Secretary, Grey as First Lord of the Admiralty. Grenville also warned the King that the new Government would expect a few names, 'four or five at the utmost', to be elevated to the peerage. The King adamantly resisted, sending word that he would need to think further about the proposal.[5]

Anxious hours followed as the King's decision was awaited; Fox wrote Fitzwilliam that the Grenville group was not very conciliating, adding: 'I am in daily troubles of every kind. I fear as a Party man I shall make a wretched figure.' His worry about Grenville's support was ill-founded, for before he had finished the letter, Grenville, direct from an audience with the King, called to tell Fox 'the thing is settled', so Fox could write 'on Wednesday some of us shall kiss hands. . . . I

---

[1] Fortescue transcripts (Clements). Sir William Henry Fremantle wrote the Marquis of Buckingham that the King did not seem disinclined to Grenville. 'The great difficulty is Mr Fox to whom he cannot be reconciled.' Stowe MSS. ST 164. [January 24?] (Huntington.)

[2] *HMCR*, Fortescue MSS., vii, 338. Buckingham to Grenville, January 25.

[3] *Ibid.*, vii, 341. January 26. Fifteen years later the Earl of Liverpool wrote to the Earl of Bathurst: 'I was the person in 1806 to advise the late King to waive his exclusion of Mr Fox.' He noted further that when Fox had been excluded the year before, no man could have stood lower 'in reputation, character and credit'; but the day after he had been personally excluded by the monarch, 'his character stood higher in the eyes of the country than it had ever stood at any former period of his political life' (*HMCR*, Bathurst MSS., p. 499).

[4] *Annual Register*, 1806, p. 21.

[5] Fitzwilliam MSS. (Milton), 68A. (Northamptonshire Record Office.) See also Fortescue transcripts (Clements), letter of January 31. *HMCR*, Fortescue MSS., viii, 1.

am hurried to death and must have forgot twenty things'—these last words in possibly the only scrawl to be found throughout the whole of his preserved correspondence.[1] Mrs Fox recorded in her journal that the King had approved the ministry, 'which God Almighty grant may prove a fortunate one for the country and for my angel husband.'[2] Fox wrote Lady Susan his hopes while in office of 'being able to do some great good. . . . What I owe to the publick and to a set of political friends whose attachment to me has been exemplary left me no choice about taking an opportunity which has been so long waited for.'[3]

The complete list of the new Cabinet was quickly made known. Grenville had brought in Lord Robert Spencer as Secretary of State for the Home Department, Windham as Secretary of State for the War and Colonial Departments, and Fitzwilliam, whom Fox had always considered as his warmest friend, as Lord President of the Council. Fox had brought in Moira, a close friend of the Prince, as Master General of the Ordnance; Erskine as Lord Chancellor; Grey, now Howick, as First Lord of the Admiralty; and Henry Petty as Chancellor of the Exchequer. The latter two then and for decades to come were strongly identified with the notions of political and religious reforms that Fox had espoused. Addington, now Sidmouth, was Lord Privy Seal, and brought in Lord Ellenborough, Chief Justice. Sheridan appeared further down the list as Treasurer of the Navy, and the faithful Fitzpatrick as Secretary at War. Pittites, excluded altogether, promptly formed the core of the new opposition.

Two complications immediately arose. Since Grenville already held the post of auditor for life, he did not wish to relinquish it altogether, but obviously could not as auditor review his own treasury accounts. Fox introduced a Bill in the Commons to permit an officer to act in the auditor's office as trustee for Grenville, which passed Parliament in less than a week. The other grew out of the propriety of Ellenborough, the Chief Justice, sitting in the Cabinet. The separation of executive and judicial powers was the central issue in the Commons debate, both sides avoiding any personal attack on Ellenborough and both sides professing to grant the coalition the principle of calling upon all available talent. Legal precedents were cited against the move, but Mr Secretary Fox, always at his best in arguing against lawyers, put in a variety of forms the proposition that the Cabinet council was a body never recognized by law or statute. Castlereagh, Canning, and Perceval spoke in the debate, so the new opposition was out in force. Petty and

---

[1] Fitzwilliam MSS. (Milton), 68/5, 2–3. February 4. Fox added that the difference between the king's list and theirs 'is so little I can not see any at all.' (Northamptonshire Record Office.)
[2] *Mrs Fox's Journal*, entry for [February] 3 [1806].   [3] Holland House MSS. [1806].

especially Sheridan insisted that Fox's point was unanswerable. Sheridan kept both sides of the House laughing, offering the Opposition his sympathy, declaring that every administration, even Mr Fox's, deserved an opposition, but hoped it would not become overcrowded or over numerous. The division was 222 to 64, a comfortable majority of 158.

Meanwhile the electors of Westminster, who had kept Fox in office during his parliamentary secession, returned him without opposition. At that moment England's most experienced and most successful vote-getter, he declared that he was 'a friend to liberty, an enemy to corruption, and a firm and decided supporter of that just weight which the people ought to have in the scale of the constitution'.[1] Once again he was borne in the chair on the shoulders of the multitude. His cherished friend, Georgiana, wanted to see the parade but missed it; 'I arriv'd as ev'rybody was going away. They say, dr soul, he look'd like Bacchus, for the chair was done round with laurels &cc.'[2] Four hundred met at the Crown and Anchor that evening to celebrate with dinner and speeches, Fox toasting the King, and, among others, Erskine, the new Lord Chancellor, and his famous motto, 'Trial by Jury'. As his final toast he offered the one that he and the Westminster electors had so often shared: 'The cause of Liberty all over the world'.

In past years although Grenville had sharply opposed Fox on some issues and had disapproved of his conduct, more and more he became convinced of Fox's better qualities and was pleased to have him in the Government for personal as well as political reasons. One of his first undertakings had been to have Fox restored to the Privy Council. In his turn Fox had been eager that the two should achieve an efficient working relationship. He wrote to Grenville that he wished the coalition to be carried on 'with more than general goodwill and fairness, nay with the most perfect cordiality of friendship', adding that if it were not, 'it shall never be my fault'. Later he suggested an earldom, not that Grenville himself wished it, but that 'such a mark of Royal favour to you would be very useful to us all at this time'. Still later Fox confessed his own uneasy relationship with the King: 'I . . . was so unsuccessful in all my attempts to please him formerly, that I want help at every step.'[3] He evolved an entirely statesmanlike partnership with Grenville. 'Never was anything more perfect than all Lord Grenville's conduct towards Fox,' wrote Lady Elizabeth Foster, who had

[1] R[alph] Fell, *Memoirs of the Public Life of the late Right Honourable Charles James Fox* (London, 1808), ii, 577.
[2] Georgiana, p. 278. [February] 13.
[3] *HMCR*, Fortescue MSS., viii, 46, 49, 63–4. March 1, 5, 23.

seen the two together; 'and as to the question . . . who is first: Is Fox under Lord Grenville or Lord Grenville under Fox? I really believe their great and good minds despise the form. They have united for the publick service and act cordially together.'[1] Fox had by no means won the King's affection, though the King on one occasion declared that it was 'just to acknowledge' that Fox always conducted himself 'frankly and yet respectfully', not treating him like another whig minister 'who, when he came into office, walked up to me in the way I should have expected from Bonaparte after the battle of Austerlitz'.[2]

Messages of praise helped to lubricate the machinery. Dublin wrote that a meeting of about eighty of 'the first class of citizens . . . nobility and gentry' expressed 'the most unlimited confidence in your ministry'. Washington wrote that President Jefferson 'expressed the perfect confidence he had in the wisdom and justice of Mr Fox'. Westminster Hall forwarded the thanks of the meeting to Mr Fox 'for the unparalleled zeal talent and integrity with which in and out of office he has uniformly supported the rights and liberties of the people'.[3] But there were cranks ('For shame rise shake off your chains of idleness . . . if you don't publish this I will write something not to your advantage'). Requests for appointments, promotions, and other favours also poured in. Fox could reflect that certain aspects of the Foreign Secretary's mail had changed little since he turned in the seals of office that bleak night more than twenty years ago.

The Catholic question came up only briefly. Obviously since members of the coalition held contrary views on Catholic relief, and the King's well-known opposition continued unabated, Fox and his friends had reasoned among themselves that although they could not advance the Catholic claims they could in other ways serve the nation. To inquiries from Catholics about his position, he said candidly that an effort in their behalf could not now meet success, and might do harm in the future. He added that if they should after all determine to bring forward their petition, he would support it. They were satisfied by his assurances, and decided to follow his advice.[4]

During April and May Fox scored two brilliant successes.

On April 22, after it was learned that Prussia had taken possession of Hanover, Fox announced to the Commons that the minister to Berlin had been promptly recalled, and the following day the King's message on the subject was debated. Fox opened his statement by appealing for unanimous concurrence, explaining that the Government had been

---

[1] *Two Duchesses*, pp. 285–6. July 2.   [2] *Life of Eldon*, i, 510.
[3] Holland House MSS. March 3, 8, April 5.   [4] *Annual Register*, 1806, p. 25.

reluctant to take this strong step until every attempt at negotiation had 'utterly and completely failed'—a Fox doctrine that on this occasion was greeted with cries of 'Hear, hear!' throughout the House. In the strongest language he denounced Prussian behaviour, nor did he fail to give full attention to the 'pernicious counsels of France'. When he described the transferring of the subjects of Hanover from one country to another, a practice he termed evil and odious, the House again broke out into prodigious cries of 'hear! hear!' on all sides. Never can you have a right of exchanging people, he declared. 'There must be, in every nation, a certain attachment of the people to its form of government, without which no nation can subsist.' Castlereagh seconded, and the question was unanimously agreed to.

On May 30, in committee on the Mutiny Bill, Fox reviewed the military posture of the country. A great navy and the generous use of subsidies to allies were insufficient, as was an army only large enough to defend the island. He insisted he was always an eager and ardent friend of peace, but he sought a peace that would enable the country to retain its continental connections, and not give anything which the point of honour forbade giving up.

If you wish to become a coward and a slave [he concluded], the way is easy: have no opinion, nor maintain any principle of your own, but consult your popularity, and act by the dictates of public clamour; but if you would act wisely and firmly for the public good, you must every day risk your popularity, in the honest discharge of your duty.[1]

Newspaper reaction was highly favourable. Even the violently anti-Fox *Courier* editorialized that it would be impossible to add anything to the admirable statements of Fox and Grenville, and the *Morning Post* declared that Fox had fully redeemed himself from imputations that he would acquiesce in the worst acts and the worst principles of the French Government. It began to appear as if Fox were an Englishman first and a pacifist second, instead of the other way around. *The Times* called his words spirited. Moreover, it used a word not often applied to Fox, patriotic, and expressed its confidence that his sentiments would meet the approbation of all British subjects. Fox could well contemplate the difference between 1800 and 1806 in the reception of his words. At long last he could feel himself speaking with the weight both of parliamentary and public opinion behind him. At long last, having overcome almost every variety of abuse, discouragement, and despair, he had attained a position of commanding influence.

During winter and spring Fox was occasionally ill, and did not take a strenuous part in the daily parliamentary battles. Petty and Windham took the lead in the important debates on the Property Tax Bill and

[1] *Parliamentary Debates*, 1st series, vii, 470–6.

the repeal of the Additional Force Bill. Nor did Fox actively participate in the impeachment of Melville, though he was nominally one of the managers. Rather, his was the heavy artillery, to be brought up as needed.

The days were a mix of the exciting, the grieving, the possible and impossible. Fox helped expose an *assassin declaré* whose avowed target was Napoleon himself, writing to Talleyrand that such a man was at large, and receiving in return a complimentary and appreciative letter.[1] He grieved at the death on March 30 of the Duchess of Devonshire, who had always made her Devonshire and Chatsworth homes a cordial gathering place for their mutual friends, and whose loyalty to him had remained steadfast through a wide assortment of political triumphs and disasters.

With Fox in one House and Grenville in the other, and with Wilberforce's energy and enthusiasm still unlimited, some positive action could be taken toward the abolition of the slave trade. Fox was determined to press forward; his earnestness in this matter, Holland later wrote, kept him attending sessions in the House longer than he wished. Fox had confided that he would like to retire from the Foreign Office in favour of Holland, remaining in the Cabinet without an active post so that he would be at hand to counsel but be free from much of the detail. One evening at his bedside he said to Holland: 'Don't think me selfish, young one. The Slave Trade and Peace are two such glorious things, I can't give them up, even to you. If I can manage *them*, I will then retire.' Grey, now Lord Howick, came with proposals which included a peerage for Fox himself—all designed to protect him from the laborious part of his duties; after a pause he said, 'No, not yet, I think not yet.' Then, later: 'The peerage, to be sure, seems the natural way, but that cannot be. I have an oath in Heaven against it; I will not close my politicks in that foolish way, as so many have done before me.'[2]

The important day came June 10, when Mr Secretary Fox rose in the Commons to propose the resolution that the slave trade is 'contrary to the principles of justice, humanity, and sound policy', and that steps should be taken presumably at the next session to abolish it. His speech was not long. He reviewed the arguments that had been made against the trade over the years by Wilberforce, by the late Mr Burke and by the late Mr Pitt, and reminded his listeners that even those who like Sidmouth and Melville favoured gradual rather than immediate abolition had supported the principle that the trade itself was inhuman and unjust. He recalled that although nearly everyone

[1] FO 27/72. February 18.
[2] *Memoirs of the Whig Party*, i, 249–50. *Fox Cor.*, iv, 469–71.

had favoured abolition in principle, nearly two decades had passed with nothing having been done to implement the principle. Years ago the gradualists, casting about for a date at which they, too, would be willing to see the trade abolished, had fixed 1800; yet now six full years had passed even since that late date. The debate was not lengthy and the vote for abolition was 114 to 15—an anticlimactic finish to a parliamentary struggle that had so long been continued. Debate in the Lords, led by Grenville, was even briefer, the resolutions carrying 41 to 20.[1]

So Fox can be said to have administered the nearly-final blow to the slave trade. The peace, the other of the two glorious things he wished to achieve before he retired, was more elusive. Minutes of Cabinet meetings show that various angles of the negotiations for peace were discussed. On March 2 the Cabinet decided to notify the King of Naples, then in the French sphere of influence and control, that French vessels or troops could not be allowed to seize any part of Sicily. On April 3, the Cabinet held preliminary discussions of the feasibility of laying an embargo on Prussian vessels in British ports as a counter to the occupation of Hanover by the king of Prussia. On April 19 Fox was authorized to write Talleyrand to declare that peace negotiations must be carried on not bilaterally between France and Britain, but conjointly with Russia as well. When the Cabinet decided to make a strong representation to the court of Berlin, protesting the seizure of Hanover, Fox drafted a strong remonstrance, bluntly charging aggrandisement and acquisition. It gave him great pain, he concluded, to be obliged to make such observations 'but his duty to the King and what he owes to his own reputation, which, whatever it may be, stands on the basis of morality and justice, cannot permit him to soften them'.[2] These and other decisions were regularly submitted by Fox to the King, and were promptly, occasionally even cordially, acknowledged.[3]

To undertake the man-sized job of managing the delicate negotiations with France, fate put on the stage the thirty-year-old Francis Charles, Lord Yarmouth, an individual of unreliable character and unstable temperament. Since he had been detained with his family in France after the rupture of the peace of Amiens, Napoleon and Talleyrand chose him to carry a verbal message to Fox on the subject of the

1 *Parliamentary Debates*, 1st series, vii, 580–603; 801–9. See also *The speech of the right hon. Charles James Fox, in the house of commons, June 10th, 1806*, etc. (Newcastle, 1824).
2 Cabinet minute. Holland House MSS. Fortescue transcripts (Clements).
3 Holland House MSS. Fortescue transcripts (Clements).

negotiations. In London, Fox reviewed the status of the deliberations and sent him back, with the approval of the Cabinet, to open further discussion with the French Government.[1] Yarmouth had these advantages as a negotiator: he already had held conversations with the French, and since his family was in Paris, his coming and going would not attract attention in political or diplomatic circles. Fox was convinced, and Yarmouth must have encouraged this conviction, that Talleyrand would negotiate on the principle of *uti possidetis*—that each side would retain the territory it occupied—a critical point as far as Sicily was concerned, since Britain occupied it and Napoleon wanted it for the King of Naples. Fox in fact recalled a striking phrase of Talleyrand's on the matter: 'We will demand nothing from you.'[2]

With Yarmouth in 1806, as with Tom Grenville in 1783, the question arose as to the extent of the powers with which the negotiator was to be clothed. Fox felt it necessary to give Yarmouth only limited authority; he made it clear to the young lord, and Grenville confirmed this fact, that Yarmouth was to proceed entirely on an informal basis, not revealing the fact that he was to have full powers until Talleyrand had confirmed the principle of *uti possidetis*, especially in regard to Sicily. Fox also wanted Yarmouth to bring the subject of the slave trade into the discussion; perhaps France could be led to cooperate in abolishing the trade.[3]

Yarmouth ran into trouble in his first interview with Talleyrand, who insisted that Naples was for France not a militarily sound territory unless Sicily were attached, and who furthermore insisted that Napoleon would not deal with any British envoy who did not have full powers.[4] These facts Yarmouth wrote Fox; Fox in his reply stated that he was 'too much suffering from pain whether from rheumatism or what the Physicians cannot tell' to be able to write at length, but he expressed the thought that to make peace by acceding to worse terms than those first suggested by Talleyrand would be repugnant. In a subsequent, longer letter he repeated his position, bundling the argument into three points, like a debater, so that Yarmouth could have little doubt as to the Government's position. Documents authenticating the full powers were on the way, but Yarmouth should advise Talleyrand that he was not allowed to make use of them or even to produce them formally until the position of Sicily was clarified. Fox also insisted again that Britain would act, in negotiating for peace, only

1 Cabinet minute of June 13. Fortescue transcripts (Clements).
2 *Lady Holland's Journal*, ii, 163. 'Nous ne vous demandons rien.' FO 27/73.
3 *HMCR*, Fortescue MSS., viii, 195, 244. June 22, July 25. Cabinet minute of June 23, Fortescue transcriptions (Clements). FO 27/73, Fox to Grenville, June 26. Holland House, MSS. July 5.
4 FO 27/73. Holland House MSS. July 1.

with her ally, Russia. Through the Russian ambassador in London Fox felt he had been kept sufficiently informed of Russia's desire for peace.

Talleyrand's response was blunt; conditions had changed since the negotiations opened; the point of Sicily would not be yielded. Fox replied that 'the abandonment of Sicily is a point on which it is impossible for his Majesty to concede. . . . The King's troops occupy Sicily for its Defence, but with no right to cede it to France.' Yarmouth relayed Talleyrand's offer that instead of Sicily, Great Britain satisfy herself with Dalmatia, Albania, and Ragusa. Fox replied that each of these was unacceptable—for example: 'Albania is now a province of the Turkish empire, the dismemberment of which . . . both Great Britain and Russia [wish] to prevent.' Fox's hope that the slave trade could be brought into the negotiations was shattered by Talleyrand—'the emperor would discuss that point when the others of greater importance were arranged'.

Meanwhile Talleyrand's negotiations with Russia had progressed further than Yarmouth realized, and suddenly both Fox and Yarmouth received 'mortifying intelligence' of a separate treaty signed between France and Russian emissary Oubril. Yarmouth then revealed his full powers to Talleyrand, a move that caused the British Cabinet keen anguish. 'It is necessary for me to say frankly,' Fox wrote to Yarmouth with restraint, 'that it would have been more satisfactory . . . if your Lordship had waited to know the impression which this new event might create here before you had produced your full powers.'[1] Two days later Yarmouth was notified that Lauderdale had been selected to join him in further negotiations. On August 2 Fox wrote that on any doubtful point Yarmouth was to be guided by Lauderdale's opinion, 'formed as it will be on the fullest knowledge of the sentiments and views of His Majesty's government'.[2] Yarmouth was further rebuked in a letter of August 8, Fox's last official act. For more than four months after the physicians had shaken their heads, he had, to the limit of his strength, kept going.

Yarmouth wrote several letters explaining why he produced his full powers when he did, and what might have happened to weaken the negotiations if he had neglected to step forward with seals and parchment. As the discussions progressed, however, his position became increasingly embarrassing to the British ministry. He drank excessively and was involved in financial manipulations motivated by his inside

---

[1] *Ibid.*, June 26, July 5, July 18, July 26. 'This step of Lord Yarmouth's is very reprehensible' (*Lady Holland's Journal*, ii, 163). 'The . . . transactions of Lord Yarmouth at Paris, are still mysterious to us. . . . I am almost inclined to think that he has given himself out as charged with a more important mission than the fact will confirm.' Sir Robert Adair wrote to Fox from Vienna on July 3 (Fox papers, Clements).
[2] FO 27/73. Holland House MSS. July 28, August 2.

information about the progress of the treaty.[1] Nor did Lauderdale prove to be a masterful negotiator. Talleyrand outmanoeuvred both the Russian and the English representatives, and Napoleon spawned one delay after another.

Fox can be criticized for his opportunistic selection of Yarmouth, although Napoleon and Talleyrand bargained from such a strong hand that they felt little necessity to make concessions either to Russia or to England. Yet long afterwards Pulteney asked Napoleon personally what would have been the best time for the English to have made peace. The reply was, 'when Lord Lauderdale was at Paris, if Mr Fox had lived'.[2] Napoleon ever had a high opinion of Fox. Reminiscing at St Helena, he declared that men like Fox set the moral character of a nation. 'He possessed a noble character, a good heart, liberal, generous, and enlightened views. I considered him an ornament to mankind.' He continued, in mood reflective and pensive : 'The death of Fox was one of the fatalities of my career.' Napoleon, the Russians, the Americans sensed the fairness, the strength, the poise of Mr Secretary Fox.

As early as April, Fox's health had begun to alarm his friends. Now at a critical time in the discussions his health sank rapidly. He could not shake off a bad cold and he suffered from painful aches in his thighs. Office details were no longer allowed to trouble him. Fox would have liked Holland to take the assignment given to Lauderdale, and somehow got the notion that Holland had refused it : 'So you would not leave me, young one, to go to Paris, but liked staying with me better—there's a kind boy.' Holland could never tell his uncle he was not really offered the post.[3]

Even with Lauderdale in Paris, however, the move for peace soon fizzled out. The Russian Government refused to accept the treaty signed by Oubril, and Anglo-French negotiations reached an impasse.

Fox's appointment had brought a breath of fresh air to the Foreign Office so far as the Americans were concerned.

Many months previously, in 1804, James Monroe had arrived in London as the new minister to the Court of St James; he had just successfully negotiated the Louisiana purchase in Paris. Immediately he had sought an interview with Lord Harrowby, Pitt's follower and for a short time his Foreign Secretary, but Harrowby was cold and indif-

[1] See Herbert Butterfield's 1961 Creighton Lecture, *Charles James Fox and Napoleon: The Peace Negotiations of 1806* (London, 1962), for a perceptive analysis of Yarmouth's eccentric behaviour.
[2] The Earl of Kerry, ed., *The First Napoleon* (London, 1925), p. 196.
[3] *Memoirs of the Whig Party*, i, 253. *Fox Cor.*, iv, 473–4.

ferent, 'calculated to wound & to irritate', Monroe wrote American Secretary of State James Madison. 'Not a friendly sentiment toward the U States or their govt. escaped him.'[1]

The topics that Monroe had discussed with Harrowby grew out of boundary disagreements, the effects of the blockade imposed by belligerents upon American ships, and the impressment of American seamen. By a series of edicts and orders in 1804 and 1805 the British had attempted to obstruct commerce between neutrals that transported cargoes to Napoleon. Usually American vessels could evade these orders by interrupting their voyage at an American port and securing fresh clearances; this practice established the principle of the broken voyage. In July of 1805, however, the *Essex* had taken a cargo at Barcelona, landed and cleared customs at Salem, Massachusetts, and headed for Havana. En route, the British seized both ship and cargo, and Admiralty courts, reversing the principle of the broken voyage, sustained the seizure. The action caused an uproar in American mercantile circles.

Fox's wide circle of acquaintances from all the capitals of the world never ceases to astonish. Distinguished Americans recorded in their diaries that they had heard him speak or had met him at social or political occasions. His eloquence and also his kindness and courtesy were widely marked. One of those who had sought him out was Robert R. Livingston, delegate to the Continental Congress, member of Congresses that followed, and in Paris also a prime negotiator of the Louisiana purchase. In London Livingston had had a pleasant visit with Fox and Mrs Fox.

Arriving home after a long overseas stay, Livingston found the capital city boiling because of the *Essex* case. Realizing that Fox might soon come to power and be able to strike a helpful blow, Livingston wrote him about the agitation and dissatisfaction in the United States. Britain now, he warned, was much less in favour than when he left home. The 'very extraordinary adjudication of your courts of admiralty founded upon orders of council justified by no law of nations', nor, he added, 'even by the usage of your own', the 'blocking up our ports by your frigates', and the impressment of seamen all had excited a 'violent spirit of resentment' that were certain to be met by strong, commercial, countermeasures.

Livingston reminded Fox of a promise to call on Monroe; he now again strongly urged that Monroe, well-informed of the new sentiment among Americans, would take pleasure in a frank conversation. From such a conversation Fox could 'derive hints that you so well know how

[1] S. M. Hamilton, ed., *The Writings of James Monroe* (New York, 1900), iv, 196. June 3, 1804.

to improve for the advantage of Britain & the United States'.[1] Livingston could not have known, as he wrote, that the British navy had won its great victory at Trafalgar.

Monroe's interview with Fox, now Foreign Secretary, in February 1806, was conducted in an entirely different atmosphere from that enveloping the conversations with Lord Harrowby. Perhaps Livingston's letter had paved the way, although Fox was invariably well disposed towards Americans. Fox received him 'with great kindness and attention,' Monroe wrote to Madison, 'and in fact put me more at ease in that short time, than I have ever felt with any person in office since I have been in England'. Before the month was out, Monroe had written Fox in detail the causes of irritation between the two Governments: the seizure of American ships and the impressment of American citizens by the Royal Navy.[2] The letter, in short, summarized grievances that led to the War of 1812.

In other interviews with Monroe, Fox showed his cordial attitude toward the American complaints. Monroe sensed, however, that Fox did not, or could not, move rapidly possibly because of disagreement in the British Cabinet. Yet Monroe was able to write on April 18 that Fox had taken steps 'to prohibit the further condemnation of our ships & cargoes'. Monroe thought Fox implied that the prohibition would also apply to the seizure of American ships.[3] The business was a ticklish one. Fox sought to accommodate the Americans, but he had a war with Napoleon on his hands. On May 15 a British order in council established a blockade of the European coast from Brest to the Elbe— in American histories this became known as Fox's blockade. Fox's official note to Monroe explained that neutral ships, carrying neither contraband nor enemy goods, not entering or leaving enemy ports, would not be seized. Furthermore, although the blockade was along the whole coast from Brest to the Elbe, it would be made absolute only along the part from Ostend to the Seine. In this language he permitted a considerable degree of trade with the enemy by way of neutral ports. So at one stroke he removed a measure of the American grievance.[4] Had he lived he might have given a broad interpretation to other areas of conflict. He might have been able to solve the even more aggravating problem of impressment. Holland was member of a commission that framed a treaty, but by the time it got to Washington Fox was dead, and President Jefferson, dissatisfied with some of its provisions, pigeon-holed it. Next year the blockade was resumed.

[1] Monroe Papers, November 14, 1805. (New York Public Library.)
[2] *The Writings of James Monroe*, iv, 411, 417–24. February 12, 25.
[3] *Ibid.*, v, 40 n. To Madison.
[4] A. L. Burt, *The United States, Great Britain, and British North America* (New Haven, 1940), p. 233. *American State Papers: Foreign Relations*, iii, 125.

In this and in other matters the early months of the Ministry of All the Talents were full of promise. Mr Secretary Fox and his colleagues were able to control a good majority in each House. If the King's attitude were not cordial at least it was not menacing. The correspondence of the Foreign Office reflected a statesmanlike candour and fairness but it also revealed strength. Fox was no defeatist; he earnestly desired peace, but only peace with honour.

Long before summer Fox made his last speech in the Commons. It would be pleasant to be able to say that the June 10 speech on the slave trade marked Fox's farewell appearance before a group he had addressed for more than thirty-eight years. Actually half a dozen inconsequential speeches came after that June 10. Such topics as the foreign corps, Chelsea hospital, the West Indies, American trade, faintly echoed the great debates of other years. But Fox felt confident that his administration was building well and would prove to be hardy. Following a favourable division in the Lords on June 17, he wrote to Adair: 'Even the most sanguine of our enemies now think we shall last.'[1]

On June 19 Fox drank tea with Mr Speaker Abbot, talked about Livy's speeches, praised Greek historians, expressed little faith in Adam Smith or other political economists, and contrasted British interest in theology with Greek interest in arts and arms. 'In this desultory talk he was extremely pleasant,' Mr Speaker recorded. In the Commons, Fox, his health obviously failing, spoke briefly on affairs of India. The Speaker thought that day was the last, or very nearly the last time he attended at all.[2] The reports of the debates convey no suggestion that Fox ever addressed the House again. So his parliamentary career ended as it began, with a few short speeches. Ill health was a formidable, final obstacle.

[1] Holland House MSS.   [2] Colchester, ii, 70–1.

31

Death of Fox

1806

The giant race is now extinct.

Francis Horner

In an age when a low fever might suddenly become high, a slight infection massive, a lesser illness mortal, no one could tell whether he would survive an indisposition or be carried away by it. Aches and pains had to be endured with little hope of relief. Physicians were at hand, but fortified mainly with plasters, ointments, leeches, purges, instruments for letting blood. If one recovered, he could be grateful for a constitution strong enough to survive both ailment and healer. If suffering were prolonged he could only pray for the fortitude to endure.

Elizabeth Fox's journal, kept during the spring and summer of 1806, shows her growing alarm about the worsening health of her husband. He never fully recovered from long exposure to bitter cold while attending Nelson's funeral. He worked far too hard. He laboured at parliamentary and official duties when he needed rest and repose. 'Carl dined at the Marquis of Buckinghams came home at nine and was busy writing till near twelve and thank God he seems nice and well and not the worse for the fatigue he has.' This on March 16. 'Carl not quite so well Genl Fitz dined with us a good many people came in the evening which made angel a little cross.' This on April 2. Carl 'did not get to bed until half past three'; his 'cold still bad he breakfasted in bed'; 'he sat up with Ld Yarmouth and Sir F. Vincent writing till three'; 'still worse . . . saw Dr Vaughan'; 'very bad he suffered dreadfully with the pain in his thighs'; 'some days better and some worse but very bad and low the day before yesterday'; 'a badish night owing to the hardness of the poultice'; entries like these through June and July.

As early as the end of June Fox's friends realized his days were numbered. 'I fear that the die is cast respecting Fox,' wrote the Marquis of Buckingham, 'whether his life be protracted a few months or not.'[1] Lady Gower, who saw him June 29, was distressed to see his emaciated face and hands, his sunken bosom, his sallow complexion, his enormous body and legs. 'I cannot tell you the sort of gentle,

[1] *HMCR*, Fortescue MSS., viii, 208. To Grenville, June 29, 1806. 'Fox's state of health is such as gives no hopes of the possibility of his ever resuming his place in the H. of C.' Stowe collection, ST 174, June 29 (Huntington).

suffering, patient expression there was in his countenance,' she added, observing that when Holland told him he looked well, he smiled and said: 'I shall end with being the handsomest Man in England, for everybody who comes in compliments my improv'd looks, and so much improvement must end in beauty.'[1]

Fox was aware of his grave danger and told Holland that he hoped before he died to do 'something for old England that would make her love his memory'. What he had in mind was peace: 'The King they say is very strong for it, and gives Fox his confidence more than could be supposed.'[2] *The Times* hopefully stated that the story of Fox's having fallen asleep at a conference with the chairman of the East India Company was not true. It much preferred to report later that he walked two or three hours in the garden of his home in Stable Yard, St James's, and still later that he held a council of the Cabinet and talked to the Portuguese ambassador. On July 24, however, it noted that the council had met without Fox. By late July the *Morning Chronicle* had learned that Fox missed two council meetings; July 29 it reported that he was in the garden attended by a domestic; July 31 that he planned to resign provisionally unless his health got better fast. Addington, now Lord Sidmouth, called on Fox at Stable Yard: 'His colour is very bad; but his voice was clear. . . . He shook me by the hand at parting, and said he hoped I would come again.' Two days afterwards he wrote that the lack of Fox's assistance 'in counsel and in debate . . . is a calamity of enormous magnitude'.[3] By now Fox's own ailment was a calamity of enormous magnitude, diagnosed as dropsy.

The long hours were spent doing the things Fox most liked. Mrs Fox, Trotter, or Lord Holland's sister read to him, chiefly novels. 'I liked your reading, young one,' Fox told his nephew, 'but I liked it better before I had heard your sister's. That is better than yours I can tell you.' But Holland read to him from Crabbe's *Parish Register*, and conversed briefly with him on the negotiations with Talleyrand and on other political subjects.

Letters arrived regularly from General Fox, on duty in Gibraltar and elsewhere, forwarding all sorts of information that might be valuable to the Foreign Secretary: the advantages of short enlistments, of a re-enlistment pay allowance, of abolishing the 'cat of nine of tails' (which is particularly degrading in the Mediterranean, 'it being the punishment used to the galley slaves').[4] The general did not know of his brother's illness. Letters also poured in suggesting cures and

[1] Castalia Countess Granville, ed. *Lord Granville Leveson Gower, Private Correspondence 1781 to 1821* (London 1916), ii, 205–6.
[2] Beinecke MSS., vault 16. Parry and David Okedon to the Rev. W. L. Bowles, July 21. (Yale.)
[3] Sidmouth, ii, 431–2. July 28, 30.   [4] Holland House MSS. April 27.

remedies; there was talk of fox-glove but physicians thought it too drastic and Fox himself did not wish to take it unless necessary. As fluid accumulated to such an extent that tapping seemed advisable, the physicians asked Holland to counsel Fox to prepare himself mentally for the operation by putting body and mind in a state of complete tranquillity. Fox commented: 'We are neither of us children, and it would be ridiculous to conceal anything,' adding: 'I don't mean to die though, young one; and above all not to give the thing up, as my father did.' He gave directions where to find his will, expressed concern about the situation in which he was leaving Mrs Fox, and then asked Holland to read the eighth book of Virgil. Holland later recalled: 'He made me read the finest verses twice over, spoke of their merits, and compared them with passages in other poets, with all his usual acuteness, taste, memory, and vivacity.'[1]

Sixteen quarts of fluid were drawn. Fox got so much better that he talked about going to St Anne's. Physicians thought this ride, normally of two and a half to three hours, too far for one day, but decided he could go to the Duke of Devonshire's home at Chiswick. Outside the Stable Yard home an inclined plane, covered with green baize, was erected, to help him get into the carriage without exertion; 'a considerable number of people assembled to see him go', and the trip was accomplished without incident.[2] On the 30th he was tapped again and more fluid removed; still, as Mrs Fox wrote, he was able in a day or two to sit in the garden and ride a little in the carriage. 'He kept my hand in his all the time we were out made me kiss him several times and admired the Thames that we saw in the road back from Kew Bridge.' His pleasures were of the tranquil sort: viewing the scenery, looking at paintings, listening to poetry and to instalments from Johnson's *Life of Dryden*.

On Monday, September 8, as he was led about the rooms at Chiswick to look at the pictures, some by Georgiana, late mistress of the house, a 'gush of water burst from the wound' and he became alarmingly weak. 'Most of his intimate friends were at Chiswick,' wrote Lady Elizabeth Foster. 'It was a touching scene to see all those men unable to suppress their grief, and careless to conceal their tears.'[3] On Tuesday, when Fox saw that his wife was not in the room, he asked Doctor Vaughan what he thought of the case and was told that the symptoms were not so good as hoped. Prayers were read by the bedside on Wednesday. 'It was thought all over,' wrote Mrs Fox. On Thursday he seemed better:

[1] *Fox Cor.*, iv, 474–81.   [2] *The Times*, August 28.
[3] *Two Duchesses*, p. 293. To Augustus Foster, September 1806.

'He walked as far as the drawing room with Mr Trotter and talked to him very cheerfully of different books he continued pretty weak all Thursday.' He wanted Holland to inform him exactly what his condition was: 'I told him that we had been much alarmed, but that he was better. I added, however, that he was in a very precarious state.'[1] When Fitzpatrick wrote Fitzwilliam, 'I cannot think there is any hope whatever,' Fitzwilliam hastened to see Fox, who, beyond speech, could only stretch out his hand.[2] Erskine was not at Chiswick to see his old chief but was disturbed: 'I am so agitated with hopes and fears about poor Fox that my stomach is quite out of order and my spirits flat.'[3]

On Friday he was weaker still; 'every moment was expected to be the last,' Mrs Fox wrote. 'I was so low and weak that I could not as I had hitherto done hide my feelings and when he felt that I was almost in hysterics he looked up and said oh fie Liz is this your promise.' They had agreed years before that whoever had to go first, the other should stay by all the time and look cheerful, 'but my God who could do it'. She had sent to St Anne's for one of his favourite chairs—'He sat up longer at a time than he had before done and he looked up at me with a sweet smile and said I like the chair Liz.' That day he learned and bore with fortitude the news that the end was upon him.

Saturday noon, after a quiet morning, he bid Holland good bye, asked his wife to kiss him and said, 'I die happy but pity you.' He mumbled something further but when he saw she did not understand him, he said, 'It don't signify my dearest dearest Liz.' Those, she wrote, were his last words. About three his eyes lost all motion but seemed still fixed on her. At a quarter of six he died. It was September 13.

All this and more she recorded in a journal that she continued to keep for thirty years. With the greatest effort she set down the events of that sad day, ending, as she often did, with prayer: 'Merciful Father let me adore thy great goodness to me oh make me worthy of it and of my dear departed angels affection for me . . . grant great God that it may enable me to make myself more worthy of thee by teaching me humility and kindness to all mankind.'

Lady Elizabeth Foster also noted this final moment. Through the open windows she saw the surgeon and others press their handkerchiefs to their eyes: 'I knew then—I felt it must be so—that he was dead. . . . I left the place and went to the chestnut trees—Mr Allen came to me

---

[1] *Fox Cor.*, iv, 482.
[2] Fitzwilliam MSS. (Milton) 69. September 9. (Northamptonshire Record Office.) *Morning Chronicle*, September 15.
[3] Fitzwilliam MSS. (Milton) 69. September 12. (Northamptonshire Record Office.)

very pale. "Well?" I said. "It is over," he answered. I knew it must be so yet it came like a blow on my heart.'[1]

Not Pitt, not even Nelson commanded so much interest from the press. The *Oracle*, the *Courier*, *The Times*, the *Morning Herald*, the *Sun*, the *Morning Post*, the *Morning Chronicle*, which had long carried daily bulletins from the sick bed, now ran long biographical features in their Monday issues. The provincial press showed equal enterprise in its coverage. In the days that ensued substantial articles appeared in the *York Herald*, the *Kent County Herald*, the *Shrewsbury Chronicle*, the *Liverpool Chronicle*, the *Tyne Mercury*, the *Hull Packet*, and others. Sermons were preached that Sunday and following Sundays. The *Morning Advertiser* attempted to sum up his character in a few words, selecting caps and small caps since lower case would never do: HE WAS A GENUINE WIG OF THE OLD SCHOOL, AND A TRULY HONEST MAN.[2] Magazines published reviews of his career and analyses of his talents. His speeches were quoted and the loyalty of his friends was recalled. When a political enemy published a brief derogatory verse, Lord Byron himself answered with a long panegyrical stanza. Paris dispatches noted the melancholy intelligence of Fox's death, and perceptively commented that he had died before he had demonstrated what he could do for the happiness of his country.

Among the few who did not mourn was George III, now blind. He 'could hardly suppress his indecent exultation' at Fox's death, wrote Holland. His answer to Howick's notification was 'in the coldest possible style, and did not express even sorrow for the event'.[3] Holland, however, may be overstating the case. In the correspondence between the King and Fox is some evidence of cordiality on the part of the Monarch. In July he had expressed concern about Fox's illness. And the day came when he realized that he, like the nation, was left poorer: 'Little did I think that I should ever live to regret Mr Fox's death.'[4] Still, he had never offered to pay Fox's debts, as he did North's, nor offer the services of his own physician, as he did to Chatham. From Downing Street, however, came a sincere tribute: 'I have lost not only a political co-adjutor under whom it was an honour to any man to act, . . . I have lost also a man whose friendship it was a pleasure to cultivate.'[5] The Prince threw himself on the couch and gave way to passionate tears.[6]

[1] *Dearest Bess*, p. 150.   [2] September 15.
[3] *Memoirs of the Whig Party*, ii, 49, 182. The King's note of September 14 simply said: 'The King is sensible of Lord Howick's Attention in communicating to Him the Intelligence of the Death of Mr Fox' (Fortescue transcripts, Clements).
[4] Sidmouth, ii, 435.   [5] *HMCR*, Fortescue MSS., viii, 332. September 14.
[6] *Dearest* Bess, 152.

More than one could recall that the twelvemonth had taken a prodigious toll of England's talent. Cornwallis, Nelson, the Duchess of Devonshire, Pitt, had all passed away. Thurlow died the day before Fox. The Duke of Richmond survived him three months.

With Pitt and Fox gone, the House of Commons had lost its two mightiest voices. Not until Disraeli and Gladstone, half a century into the future, would two parliamentary speakers appear who could repeatedly debate, at a high level, the massive issues confronting the British people. After Disraeli and Gladstone, as yet, no such pair at all. Especially when a nation faces a distressing problem, when its choices seem too irksome and too few, when every scrap of policy needs full public debate, men long for spokesmen on both sides who can provide not only wise but also moving and stirring leadership.

The funeral was delayed until October 10, so that Fox could be buried on the famous anniversary date. The masses of people who had many times cheered him at Westminster Hall meetings, who had applauded and sometimes jeered at the Covent Garden hustings, who had chaired him in triumph through Westminster's streets after elections, now prepared to view the solemn funeral procession. Noblemen and gentlemen who had supported him with equal zeal, and who in addition had paid his debts, had gathered as a committee to organize plans for the funeral. As early as October 8 London papers began to record the names of those in town for the sad event: the Marquis of Tavistock, the Earl of Cholmondeley and his countess, the Earl of Cavendish, scores of others. Some who could not come made their reasons known: 'Lord Anson's severe gout keeps him at home.' Those asked to attend the funeral took the invitation as a great compliment. Already the hustings was erected in front of St Paul's church for the coming election, with much speculation, primarily about Sheridan, as the nominee, but he having refused, Lord Percy was elected and the hustings torn down. The line of procession was announced: Stable Yard to Cleveland Row, Pall Mall, Cockspur Street, Charing Cross, Whitehall, Parliament Street, Palace Yard, the Abbey. The *Morning Chronicle* put a funereal black border around its announcement of the line of march so that no one could miss it. Labourers who worked all through the night covered the streets with gravel—11,530 yards of it, said the itemized bill, at 3*d* per yard. Throughout the day the bells of all the churches in Westminster were tolled.

October 10 was a beautiful autumn day. By nine o'clock men, women and children began to take places along the announced procession route:

at the curbs, in the windows, on the rooftops. For days the papers had carried lengthy notices about the funeral, giving necessary instructions so that the people were well informed about what was to happen, when, and where. The usual warnings against housebreakers and pick-pockets also appeared.

By ten o'clock the whole neighbourhood about St James's 'had the bustle of a birthday'. The Duke of Cumberland had taken the sashes out of his home on Cleveland Row and had put benches in the windows: the rooms were crowded with viewers. The Duke of Marlborough's mansion was completely filled. Pall Mall and other streets were lined with spectators. Hotels at strategic corners were packed.

At eleven o'clock noblemen and gentlemen who were to form the procession began to arrive at the Stable Yard residence. Carriages kept setting down in succession until nearly two o'clock, by which time more than 460 had drawn up. The house being too small to hold the distinguished visitors, they assembled in the garden, where Messrs Marsh and Tatham, funeral directors, arranged the procession. Several of the closer friends entered the residence for a final view of the body, then withdrew to make room for others.

At two o'clock the bells of St James's and St Martin's began to toll. The volunteers then took their places on each side of the streets leading to the Abbey, leaving room in the centre. In slow and stately tread came the Volunteer Cavalry in the lead; six marshalmen in twos, the High Constable of Westminster in ceremonial attire, and so throughout the sorrowing procession with musicians playing solemn music, electors of Westminster, members of the Whig Club, members of the House of Commons. In addition there were trumpets abreast, mutes on horseback, banners carried by gentlemen on foot, banners carried by gentlemen on horseback, physicians and other medical gentlemen. Holland was there as chief mourner (the Prince of Wales, lacking the express permission of his father, thought it wise not to appear in this capacity or any other). Fitzwilliam and Howick were there, most of his old friends were there, the Cabinet and probably every other high official were there. Even without the advantage of the special pomp that characterizes a military funeral or one for a head of state, the procession was stately and moving. The most impressive feature, however, was that the streets were jammed and crowded with people, there not so much to witness a spectacle as to show affection for and pay tribute to their departed spokesman.

What was not detailed in the newspaper stories can be found in the accounts submitted by Marsh and Tatham to the 'noblemen and gentleman directors of Mr Fox's funeral.' A strong elm coffin with very strong outside lead case covered with richly ornamented black velvet was the principal item, but countless yards of velvet, silk gloves, beaver gloves, escutcheons, and ostrich plumes also appeared on the list. Three hundred and forty-three mourning cloaks were for the gentlemen of the Whig Club, electors of Westminster, and others. Various banners were prepared, one 'an emblematic banner painted in oil on each side, representing Brittania weeping under a Cypress, free and resting on the arms of the deceased, £15 15s' (a man to carry ditto, 12s). The large open hearse, covered and richly decorated with black velvet draperies, fringed and tied up with large lines and tassels, the canopy surmounted with a map of very rich ostrich plumes and drawn by six horses with ostrich feathers and velvet coverings, including the expense of building a Hood to erect the Hearse in, and taking it down afterwards, all went in at £485 18s 0d. Included also were sums for six trumpets performing, for the First, Second, and Third regiments of guards bands, for the work of masons in the north transept of the Abbey, for the peace officers on duty. The final bill was nearly £3,000.[1] London papers admitted it was not so brilliant as the final ceremonies for the gallant Nelson (a £14,000 matter), nor even so costly as Pitt's (£6,000), but the Hull *Packet* thought it much more solemn and affecting, much like the funeral of a father attended to his last home by his many children. There was pomp and circumstance, there was costly affectation and pretentious display, but despite the beaver gloves and the ostrich plumes, the black velvet and the caparisoned horses, the gilt silver nails and the escutcheon plates and Britannia weeping under a cypress, there were tears of the common and ordinary, the gentleman and the noble, the writers, the speakers, the statesmen, the officials, those who were and those who sought to be. All knew Fox because they had countless times heard his voice, sometimes in defence of his shortcomings and in explanation of his mistakes, but usually in such keen and clear statement of his hopes for the people and his reasons for those hopes that few could match or master him. Fox belonged to the nation, to the whigs, to Westminster, to London, in about that order; and English men and women were on hand by the thousands to see this Man of the People, with his massive faults and his transcendent virtues, to a final place of rest.

So ended the anniversary of Fox's election to Westminster. 'My angel carried to his last worldly home,' wrote Liz; the ceremony was 'attended by so many proofs from all ranks of people of love and esteem for his memory and deep felt regret for his loss that I cannot but feel gratified that so much goodness was not thrown away upon an ungrateful

[1] Holland House MSS.

world.' She may have wondered, though she did not record her feeling, at the utter lack of public mention of the dead statesman's widow. Names of relatives appeared in print—as being in the procession, as standing around the open grave in Westminster during the final ceremonies—but Mrs Fox's presence can be inferred only from the heading of 'other mourners'. Lady Holland is described as sitting with her three sons, in a gallery hung with black cloth; if the public had any interest in where the widow sat or stood, or how she got to the Abbey, it is not revealed. Yet sermons could be preached on the love and companionship that this gentle woman with the checkered past brought into Fox's life.

The following Saturday she returned to Stable Yard to give up their house—'how agonizing it was to see the room where his dear remains had lived so long'. She received a letter from General Fox, dated on the funeral day; 'he had not heard of our dreadful calamity'. Not for another year did she see him: 'It was God knows a melancholy meeting for us both, he is grown very thin and I think looks very old.' One by one she had to face the people and the places that had entered their lives. St Anne's bitterly renewed her grief; and even Holland House, which she did not revisit until the following May, still had its haunting memories. 'I thought of angel running about the garden and rooms when a child how every place where he was when young is dear to me.' On June 12, 1807, she thought back to an earlier day when they left St Anne's, he for the last time, to have dinner at the Ossory's; he had said, 'I am not well my Liz but it will be a pleasant dinner and if I were to stay at home people would think me worse than I am.'

32

Afterword

Mr Fox has never been answered.

William Pitt

They buried him in Westminster Abbey, inches away from William Pitt.

There was poetry: the maudlin verse of John Taylor ('We come to his tomb, but not to weep, 'Tis freedom's holyday we keep'), the pointed couplet of Sir Walter Scott ('. . . search the land of living men, Where wilt thou find their like again?'), the stately requiem of Lord Byron ('We, we have seen the intellectual race of giants stand, like Titans . . . with a dashing sea Of eloquence between'). There were sermons, obituaries, eulogies, and, after a few weeks, pamphlet tributes and booklet-length lives.

In Fox's career was much that was foolish, much that was trivial, much that was sentimental, much that was wise. So it was also in the years that followed his death.

Fox's eagerness to work with Grenville and even with the King, plus his sense of fairness, his lifetime of political experience, his wide personal acquaintance both in England and on the Continent, and his self-assurance, had proved invaluable assets to the Ministry of All the Talents. Fox's distinctive traits lent strength to the whole. With Fox gone, the ministry proved to be not talented at all. Grenville carried on as best he could, but before Fox had been in his grave a month the Government sought a general election. The reorganized ministry succeeded in passing the law that made the slave trade illegal in 1807. When, however, it proposed to admit Catholics to the higher ranks of the army, the King brought the administration to an end. It had lasted little more than a year.

Fox's will, made in 1805, eventually became public. He divided a five hundred guinea legacy between General Fox's son, Henry, and another young man, identified only as Robert Stephen, 'a youth now living with Lord Viscount Bolingbroke in America'. The reason for this bequest is buried in the past. A similar silence surrounds the identity of Harriet

Willoughby, granted a reversionary interest in a hundred pound annuity.[1] Mrs Fox was named the executrix of the will and received the bulk of the estate. Several were named, including Fitzpatrick, Fitz-william, and Lord John Townshend, to receive presents of books, pictures, or marble. 'There are many others whom I love and value to the greatest degree but these are my oldest connexions.'

He also left behind the manuscript of his history. In 1808 publication was arranged to the satisfaction of his widow, who wrote Holland: 'It is just as my angel would have done and as I wished. All I feel anxious about is to have it well printed, and all his own dear words left.' In another letter she recalled 'the dear angelic looks I used to get while employed in coping [*sic*] it'.[2] The work was cordially received by friends, criticized by others, ignored by professionals. Wilberforce wrote that 'Alps on Alps arise as one proceeds to investigate it.' Francis Jeffrey, great editor of the *Edinburgh Review*, thought it was often unequivocally bad.

Most of Fox's oldest connexions survived him. Although the Bishop of Down had died in 1804, Jimmy Hare had gone to his final obscurity that same year, and the gorgeous Georgiana had died in 1806, others lived on. Fitzpatrick went in 1813; on his tombstone he wanted these words engraved: 'Forty years the friend of Fox.' Lord Robert Spencer, one of his faro bank dealers, died in 1831. Dennis O'Bryen, his public relations adviser, died in 1832. Jack Townshend, his one-time First Lord of the Admiralty, a martyr of 1784, died in 1833. He had considered himself foremost 'the friend and companion of Mr Fox; a distinction which was the pride of his life, and the only one he was desirous might be recorded after his death'. *The Times* for September 26, 1839, noted that Lauderdale died September 10, the same date as Fox, and also that they shared the same birthday, January 24. Fox was ten years the older but Lauderdale lived thirty-three years after Fox had passed away. Lord Holland died at sixty-seven, in 1840. Mrs Fox was even then still alive; *The Times* of July 13, 1841, observed that the widow of the late illustrious statesman had celebrated her ninety-sixth birthday the day before. Her diary establishes her birthday as July 11, and the occasion as her ninety-first, not ninety-sixth. She was in good health, it continued, 'frequently entertaining select parties of her friends at her hospitable table at St Anne's'. Next year she died, three days before her

---

[1] Believed to be a natural daughter of Fox. Farington described her in 1793: 'a little girl of seven or eight years of age, of whom Mrs. Armstead is very fond, though not her daughter' (*Farington Diary*, i, 12, 72). See also Drinkwater, p. 287.
[2] Add. MSS. 47578. January 21, 24.

ninety-second birthday. And Sir Robert Adair, who had basked in the warmth of Fox's friendship during a long lifetime, gained an extra fillip of immortality in the *Dictionary of National Biography*; since he died in 1855, he could be noted as the last leaf on the tree, the final survivor.

In 1809 a group meeting at the Duke of Bedford's decided to raise a fund to erect a monument to Fox in Westminster Abbey. Richard Westmacott, the statuary, 'an artist who has proved himself fully capable of doing justice to such a work', thought a most splendid monument could be raised for £6,000. His proposal was that he should be advanced a third of the sum for purchasing materials, a third of the sum eighteen months later, and the balance upon completion. Among the subscribers were the familiar names: Bedford, Devonshire, Fitzwilliam, Lauderdale, Spencer, Fitzpatrick, Adam. Fixing a minimum contribution of £100, the committee sent a circular to those who might be interested.

During 1809 and 1810 contributions flowed in freely, mostly in the form of promissory notes. Many who sent modest sums expressed the wish that they could have sent more. One who pledged a hundred pounds 'for poor Fox', added, 'I would give a thousand to have him back'. Adam, whose affection for Fox had been demonstrated in similar situations, took charge of this fund, making collections, sending reminders to those whose instalments were overdue, and doing other sorts of paper work. The amount collected was sufficiently large not only to provide a marble monument for Westminster Abbey but also a large bronze statue somewhere else; one site considered was the porch of St Paul's in Convent Garden, overlooking the spot where for twenty-five years Fox had campaigned, but the trustees finally chose Bloomsbury Square, near the British Museum. Fox's statue stands there today, facing a monument of Bedford by the same artist. The statue was erected in 1816 and shows Fox sitting, garbed in a consular robe, right arm extended and left grasping Magna Carta.[1] Not until 1822 was the Westminster Abbey statue erected, the Abbey's records showing that Westmacott and his workmen were to be admitted that year for the purpose of erecting the monument of Mr Fox, but that 'Mr Westmacott must give a list of the Workmen, that no other persons may take advantage of this order, without having business in the Abbey'.[2] The

[1] Fitzwilliam Papers (Sheffield), 115h. Holland House MSS. May 25, 1808; August 2, 1809; February 21, July 18, 1810; May 22, June 11, August 12, 1812; *The Times, Morning Chronicle*, June 20, 1816. *Annual Register*, 1816.
[2] Letter from Lawrence E. Tanner, librarian and keeper. July 29, 1963.

statue is a group of four figures; Fox, in the centre, plus two female figures, as *The Times* described it, 'lamenting over the departed Statesman, and a Negro slave sitting on the steps of the pedestal, with his eyes raised in gratitude to Mr Fox, for the distinguished part he took in the abolition of the disgraceful slave-trade'.[1]

In many ways the memory of Fox persisted. 'Even now, after a lapse of five and twenty years,' Macaulay wrote, 'there are those who cannot talk for a quarter of an hour about Charles Fox without tears.'[2]

He may have been recalling the incident of Sir Robert Adair, who long before had embarrassed Fox and his colleagues so much at the court of Russia; when Adair visited the room in Chiswick in which Fox had died, 'he sat down at the bedside and cried for a quarter of an hour, like a child, a most unexpected and affecting scene'.[3] Some viewed with moist eyes the chair at the Duke of Bedford's where old Mr Fox used to sit, snoring so loud as to disturb the whist players, who would send little Johnnie Russell to wake him by tickling his silk stockings.[4] The Prince wrote Grenville of the deep state of affliction in which he was plunged at the irreparable loss all had sustained.[5] Fitzwilliam also noted that the Prince 'was deeply affected . . . and has never recovered his spirits since'.[6] The Prince's regard persisted for years; as late as 1824 the list of annuities paid out during the reign of King George IV included a sum of £500 to the Honourable Mrs Fox.[7]

Memories of other sorts also lingered. At a breakfast in 1812, Sir George Beaumont said that Charles Fox had greatly contributed to the ease with which women of irregular conduct could be introduced into respectable society by the manner in which he had introduced Mrs Armistead, 'a woman who had been very common, into company after He married Her. His influence in society was such that she visited with him some of the first families'. Taking Fox altogether, politically and otherwise, he had done more harm than any other man of his time—in which opinion artist Joseph Farington, added that he entirely concurred.[8] Thomas De Quincey thought that Fox's screaming voice would remind one of a demon steam-engine on a railway, hissing,

---

1 January 31, 1818.
2 Quoted in John Carswell, *The Old Cause* (London, 1954), p. 298.
3 Add. MSS. 32566, 19. Mitford's Notebooks, viii, 20.
4 Add. MSS. 47601. This story was jotted down by Trevelyan March 3, 1930.
5 *HMCR*, Fortescue MSS., viii, 339. September 18, 1806.
6 *Ibid.*, viii, 356. September 24, 1806.
7 *Letters of George IV*, iii, 499.
8 *Farington Diary*, vii, 126. October 28, 1812.

bubbling, snorting, fuming, and that though he was powerful for instant effect, he was impotent for posterity.[1]

In an important sense De Quincey was right; a speaker so links himself with timely, current issues, like the slave trade, that when these are resolved, the speeches slip back into history's darker corners. Yet Fox was associated also with persistent themes. Sir Philip Francis noted that Fox's principles were appealed to as a standard as late as 1818, 'his name held up, his memory celebrated'.[2] And for decades after 1818, as well. At dinner meetings honouring Fox's birthday or the anniversary of his election for Westminster or other convenient occasions, speakers recalled the great issues with which he was connected. The Whig Club, which during Fox's life had met several times a year, continued its meetings after his death, changed its name in 1811 to 'Fox Club', and still continues to meet.[3] Other groups also celebrated with dinners, toasts, and speeches. From the parade of years, a few examples:

In 1819, at a dinner commemorating Fox's birthday, the chairman asked the assembly: 'Where is the man who can do justice to the character of Mr Fox? (Applause.) He was the friend of the rights of man. . . . He was the friend to peace upon earth. He was the consistent advocate for the abolition of the slave trade. (Applause.)' The Bishop of Norwich, whose convictions were described as those of Mr Fox, was then introduced. The Chairman besought the group to fill a bumper for the toast to Lord Chief Justice Coke, who, so honoured and so fortified, passed easily in his response from high praise of Fox to sharp condemnation of the tory ministry then in power.[4]

In 1822 two hundred attended a meeting at Norfolk, to hear read a letter of Fox's written twenty-one years previously in favour of parliamentary reform. Speakers denounced those who attended Pitt dinners, claiming that following Pitt's principles would lead the country to financial disaster, and parodying the popular Pitt song, 'The Pilot Who Weathered the Storm' by singing a version more to their liking: 'The Pilot Who Gathered the Storm'.[5]

In 1823 five hundred at Edinburgh heard a tribute by the eminent forensic orator and fellow Scot, Sir James Mackintosh. To those who thought Fox was overly zealous, Sir James offered these ringing periods:

[1] David Masson, ed., *The Collected Writings of Thomas De Quincey* (Edinburgh, 1890), xi, 35–6.

[2] Francis, ii, 460.

[3] Letter from Major H. N. Lucas, hon. secretary, Brooks's; Foord, p. 459.

[4] *The Times*, January 30, 1819, quoting the *Norwich Courier*.

[5] *The Times*, January 26, 1822. See also *Morning Post*, same date. Celebrations were also reported at London, Edinburgh, and Glasgow.

Will those who think the principles of Mr Fox were too pertinaciously maintained, assert that we have had too few wars? (cheers) too light burdens? (cheers) too few suspensions of the constitution? (cheers) too many checks to undue power? (cheers) too few violations of personal liberty? (cheers) too many extensions of the liberty of the press? (cheers) too great a control on the prerogative of the Crown? (cheers) too little restraint on the assembling of the people? . . . But it is said, those who hold the opinions of Mr Fox are the advocates of Catholic emancipation and parliamentary reform. We are the advocates of Catholic emancipation and parliamentary reform. (Vehement cheering.)

He then outlined contrary opinions of Mr Pitt, the speaker's pointed contrasts being greeted with cries of 'Hear, hear'.[1]

In 1834, after the enactment of the first Reform Bill, an estimated 100,000 assembled at Glasgow to participate in a monster meeting. At a dinner attended by some 1,500 persons, Fox's name was honoured by a toast. His opposition to the repeal of habeas corpus, the prolonged war with France, and the suppression of liberties at home, were all recalled in elaborate and sentimental language:

In these days [said the speaker] had any man done or said as much as I believe every individual in this room has done or said—aye, or the tenth part of it—he would have been subjected to the tender mercies of packed juries and political judges. (Cheers.) I own my greatest surprise is, that Fox had the courage to persevere so long as he did, . . . had he not . . . felt he sowed good seed, which . . . sooner or later . . . would produce a glorious happiness and freedom in the land. (Loud cheers.)[2]

In Parliament as well as outside, Fox's influence had singular persistence. Three Prime Ministers, Melbourne, Grey, and Russell, in greater or lesser degree helped to perpetuate his principles. From his earliest youth Melbourne had been reared in the Fox tradition. Once he wrote verses to Fox's bust: 'Live, marble, live!'[3] Grey repeatedly asserted that he had learned his political faith from Fox. He uttered a lesser-known tribute in the Lords, on the Libel Bill: 'I had nearly called [Fox] one of the greatest lawyers, but [he] certainly was one of the greatest men this country ever produced.'[4] Russell was a devoted follower of Fox; his eloquent stand in 1828 on the Test and Corporation Acts has already been mentioned.[5] Whitbread, Tierney, Burdett are other names that come to mind. Petty, as Lansdowne, stood high in whig counsels. Those who cherished the memory of Fox had little interest in Fox's mistresses or debts or gambling or the financial manoeuvrings of his father or the coalition

[1] *Edinburgh Star*, January 14. Quoted in *The Times*, January 18.
[2] *Morning Advertiser*, November 1, 1834, quoting the *Glasgow Chronicle*.
[3] W. M. Torrens, *Memoirs of the Right Honourable William, Second Viscount Melbourne*, (London, Macmillan), i, 65.
[4] *Speech of Earl Grey in the House of Lords, May 12, 1817* (London, 1817), p. 48.
[5] See above, p. 262.

with North or his hasty sponsorship of claims of the prince as Regent. What now mattered was that his principles had become a synonym for individual and political liberty.

'Fox was in the class of common men,' wrote William Hazlitt, 'but he was the first in that class.' Hazlitt wrote not only out of literary experience and philosophical contemplation but also as an observer of the political scene; his interest in politics came to the surface in his latter years when he became a parliamentary reporter for the *Morning Chronicle*. Hazlitt at times sharply criticized Fox, observing that Fox lacked certain of Burke's philosophical qualities and even some of Pitt's finer points of debating competence; moreover he realized that one could easily become over-captivated by Fox's personal cordiality and good nature. Setting himself on guard not to exaggerate nor overstate, noting that 'it is difficult to write a character of Fox without running into . . . extravagance', he nevertheless concluded: 'He was a man of a large, capacious, powerful, and highly cultivated intellect. . . . No man's knowledge could be more . . . plain and useful; . . . no man could be more perfectly master of his ideas, could reason upon them more closely. His mind was full, even to overflowing.'[1] Thus Hazlitt; and he knew and heard the best minds of his day. He did not know the young Fox, who had been properly and perceptively ridiculed by Gibbon as he learned, the hard and difficult way, to utter words like 'country, liberty, corruption, &c.', but he did know the image of Fox moulded by later generations, embracing parliamentarians and politicians, literary figures, peers in great houses, and thousands who either could not vote at all or who only barely qualified.

On a Friday, April 12, 1833, Fox's good friend and devoted follower, Thomas Coke, one of those martyrs of 1784, retired. At a dinner in his honour, attended by 500, the distinguished squire of Norfolk could review with pride that he had lived to see trial by jury, Catholic emancipation, the repeal of the Test Acts, and most of all, parliamentary reform. A long lifetime had been necessary to pass these stupendous milestones. Another principal speaker was a son of George the Third, his royal highness the Duke of Sussex, who toasted 'the illustrious patriot and statesman . . . Charles James Fox'. Said the Duke:

We must not forget those champions of former times who boldly advocated the doctrines we now uphold, and who were mercilessly attacked, both in public and private. Happy indeed would it have been if that individual had lived to see the

[1] *The Eloquence of the British Senate* (London, 1808), ii, 466–71.

great work he began, successfully carried through. (Cheers.) . . . We owe a debt
of gratitude to him for having laid the groundwork of those measures.

His simply-worded tribute could hardly have been more moving, nor
less meaningful to that age than to this one. For then, partly from habit,
partly from inspiration, perhaps even partly from prescience, he put a
final toast: 'Civil and religious liberty all over the world.'[1]

It was often said of Charles Fox after one of his compelling speeches,
the debate could not lie better than he had left it. Anybody with half an
eye could have seen him there that evening, his head nodding full
approval, a smile rippling over the fine Atlantic of his countenance.

So much for Mr Fox's principles as they were expressed by those who
had heard his voice and had felt the warmth of his personality.

Now the voice and the person have long gone, and so have the
thousands who heard him in the Commons, Westminster Hall, Palace
Yard, the Shakespeare, Crown and Anchor, London Tavern, the
hustings, the streets. But at this distance of time and place we can inquire into the burden of the Fox message: what he was trying to say to
Westminster electors, to colleagues in party and in Parliament, to
chancelleries on the Continent and in the new world.

Close to his desire was the abolition of the slave trade, one of the
two glorious things he could not give up even to Holland. Here his
position was plain-spoken: the slave trade was morally wrong. He was
not happy with regulating it, supervising it, curtailing it. He did not
want merely to make slaves more comfortable during their overseas
voyage or in their new homes. He did not seek to build a corner of
British prosperity on the trade, nor even to solace himself with the
reflection that a slave ship in time of peace could be a troop ship in time
of war. He did not worry that the Dutch, the French, the Portuguese,
the Americans would flow into the slave market if the British abandoned it. Rather, he insisted that Britain take the lead in abolishing
totally this odious and immoral evil. Wilberforce made more and better
speeches on the subject but Fox supplied the potent combination of
moral earnestness, eloquence, and political power that struck the
mortal blow.

Fox's other glorious issue was peace. He tried to cool the nation's
fire when war was proposed, as he did in 1791 when Pitt waved the
bloody shirt against Russia. He disliked the military effort against
France both at the onset and during the conflict. Again and again he
told the Commons and the people that insult, injury, or other provoca-

---

[1] *A narrative of the proceedings, speeches,* etc. *connected with the dinner to T. W. Coke, Esq.*
(Norwich, 1833), pp. 18–19.

tion should not be allowed to plunge the nation into war until there had been ample opportunity for exploration and discussion. If a nation were insulted, it should ask for and was entitled to receive explanation. If it were injured it should ask for redress. Rather than react violently to an 'indiscriminate provocation thrown out at random', a Government should make clear how it has been wronged, what kind of satisfaction it must have, and even wherein an explanation, if not acceptable, is not acceptable. 'To propose negotiation is not to sue for peace.' Though his opponents branded him with the most obnoxious epithets they could command—American, Dutchman, Spaniard, Frenchman, defeatist, even traitor—he spoke repeatedly for peace. Yet though he despaired that because of war England might be the last country ever to become free, he loved her and her institutions, and, when Foreign Secretary, could and did hold a firm line against her enemies.

The twentieth century, racked by continual warfare both declared and undeclared, can find fresh inspiration in Fox's eloquent plea for exploration, discussion, negotiation.

Fox sought to put an end to penal laws and disqualifications restricting Catholics and dissenters. He argued, and Gladstone powerfully supported the notion less than a century afterward, that no religious test should be required of a public or civil servant. He did not like to judge the religious opinions of men nor persecute them for those opinions. He did not share the fears of Burke and Pitt that if men were allowed to interpret the Bible differently from the mitred fathers of the Church of England, the Church would crumble and totter. Rather, he asserted, both Church and State would emerge the stronger. Fox was accused of playing politics with religious issues in order to gain the franchises of dissenters and Catholics, but any electoral advantage he gained was only a happy byproduct; he was firmly convinced that toleration was not merely a convenient and useful thing but a moral force that in itself was essentially right.

Fox did not live to see peace, nor did he live to see England become a nation free of religious restrictions. Nor did he live to see a solution to still another question, that of parliamentary reform. Fox freely confessed to his intimate friends that he was not so adamant on this issue as on the others. Invariably he seemed out of place when for brief intervals he appeared in the company of those who argued for annual parliaments or other drastic revisions of the constitution. Nor was he ever one of those who sharpened their pens to devise specific formulas for abolishing this or that borough or for extending the franchise. At one time, in fact, he expressed a doubt whether a different mode of election would actually be superior to the present system. In general his position was to adapt the constitution to the change of the times. Let it be propped up where it was sagging and repaired where it was decayed.

Fox simply could not convince himself, as he surveyed the administration's majority of four to one against him, that the people were also four to one against him. Since the sentiment of the people was not proportionately represented in Parliament, let Parliament be modified. The people must have such a share in the government that it can truly embrace their own rights and their own sovereignty. Nor should they placidly await the coming of better days; they should vigorously seize every opportunity offered by public assembly, petition, resolution, and election to make themselves heard. They must be the instrument of their own deliverance.

On another important issue, the rights of juries in trials for libel, Fox scored a prompt success. Here he stood on solid ground, for as one active in the debate of controversial questions, he fully realized that the prevailing libel law would not allow a public-spirited man to discuss such questions in the way they needed to be discussed without exposing himself to prosecution. The debates on his Libel Act cleared away disputed interpretations of the proper function of juries and brought the law into harmony with the growing insistence upon public discussion.

The general body of Fox's ideas about religious and political freedom and about the negotiation of international disputes have a permanent, not a transient, value. Their appeal was not merely to the casual listener of his age but to thoughtful and concerned men of generations that followed.

During Fox's political lifetime the concept of party grew in stature, Fox emerging as one who had a keen appreciation of this instrument of government. Unlike Thomas Jefferson, who declared that if he had to go to heaven with a party he would not go there at all, Fox would much prefer to be out of heaven with a party than in it single.

Fox's notion of party was constructed on an 'aristocratick' base: the existence of an aristocratic element was necessary not only to preserve liberty but to give consequence to the lesser ranks. More than that, Fox regarded party as a collection of men of congenial dispositions and aims; invariably his political companions were close friends that he regarded with affection. Accordingly, the breakup of his party weakened both his personal attachments and his political effectiveness.

Membership in a strong party was, naturally, the only sure way to power. Yet Fox served his party through the locust years of hopelessness and despair. 'The existence and union of our party is useful to the country', he insisted; it must be maintained by exertion and effort. But: 'We must console ourselves with knowing that what we do is right without expecting . . . power . . . or popularity . . . or even fair construction with respect to our intentions.' And even when the times became 'bad, very bad', party might then be most useful, 'and we may be in our proper place'.

Given a party of friendly associates, generously leavened with aristocratic temperament, what could it achieve? It could set an example of 'public virtue and comprehensive understanding'; it could teach men to 'conciliate the good opinion of those with whom they live'; it could keep the country from falling into Mr Hume's 'euthanasia of absolute monarchy'; it could provide its members with a system of beliefs wiser than any person could singly evolve for himself and could thus protect him from poor or hasty judgment. What so much as party contributes to 'the morals and happiness of mankind'? Late in his career he repeated his position, that party was composed of 'men of honour, who entertain similar principles', who conceive that those principles may be more beneficially and successfully pursued by the force of mutual support, harmony, and confidential connection than by any other available means.

When Fox formulated these ideas, he was mainly reviewing ways in which party had been indispensable to him personally. He prized the opportunity of party gatherings to review public issues. Although he read avidly for his own pleasure, he was likely to dig into legal and parliamentary documents only when on the quest of specific facts for debate, and therefore he much preferred to gain information from the counsels of his friends. Throughout his career he summoned his associates to discuss with them parliamentary strategy and tactics: to explore the wordings of motion, to review principal arguments, to determine major outlines of position. Accordingly, he could testify with conviction that one's party fellows served to temper *his* views, test *his* reasoning, verify *his* evidence, appraise *his* policy. This kind of activity is vital if a consensus is to be hammered out that most members will support.

Fox is not associated with the notion of party machinery or party discipline. True enough, he wrote scores of notes to his colleagues urging them to attend important divisions. He was ever an active campaigner, and could walk up and down the streets personally soliciting votes. He took a modest part in the raising of election funds. During his few months in office he was introduced to the problem of patronage. Yet his main contribution was to light the torch, to hold the banner; in other words, to advocate certain ideas, both in and out of Parliament. Many of these became known, not as the Duke of Portland's principles or the Marquis of Rockingham's principles—both of his chiefs were highly inarticulate in front of an audience—but as 'Mr Fox's principles'.

Fox was readily convinced that opposition was an imperative function of party. If he had a bad opinion of ministers, he asserted, he would 'pursue their overthrow by a systematic opposition'. In the political cosmos that he found himself, opposition was natural. But, he insisted, opposition should flow from public principle, from a persuasion that the public welfare is to be served. In the main, especially in his later career, he lived up to this ideal. Good measures are often at first strongly resisted, he argued, but eventually become successful by the perseverance of opposition and the good sense of Parliament. More than any one else in his day, Fox was associated with a systematic, organized, formed opposition. This tiny group of determined, sentimental men kept alive the notion of party. Long after the death of their chief, they kept their standard flying and in the years ahead it served to attract others of like mind.

When all is said and done, historian and biographer must record that Fox achieved the vast part of his accomplishments through his mastery of public speaking.

Many aspects of his competence as a speaker have already been touched on: his methods of preparation, his consummate skill in analysing argument, his natural and convincing delivery, his rapidly flowing language. Fox, however, was more than a skilful persuader, more than an artful performer: he was a fervent advocate of the political necessity of the art of public address itself. No one on either side of the Atlantic, not even excepting Gladstone or Wilson, put speechmaking on a higher pedestal. 'Take away the freedom of speech or of writing,' he once declared, 'and the foundation of all your freedom is gone.' Yet the truest expression of this principle of freedom was not in newspapers, pamphlets, or books, but on a public platform where a lone speaker confronts one and all. 'It is the energy, the boldness of a man's mind, which prompts him to speak, not in private, but in large and popular assemblies, that constitutes . . . the spirit of freedom.' Never suffer the right to speak to be taken away: 'you will then have lost the freedom, the energy, the boldness of the British character.'

Fox had only scorn for those who attempted to modify the freedom of speaking, or curtail it, or bind or encompass it, or police it. 'When the power of speaking is taken away,' he asked, 'what is left but implicit submission?' Surveying the attempt to shackle freedom of utterance, he proclaimed: 'Behold, then, the state of a free-born Englishman!

Before he can discuss any topic which involves his liberty, he must send to a magistrate who is to attend the discussion.' When Englishmen must rejoice or grieve only as it suits the taste or caprice of ministers, 'then I pronounce the constitution of this country to be extinct'. He realized that a man can be punished for abusing his freedom of speech, but he possesses it in the 'first instance'.

Fox displayed a wisdom worthy of the twentieth century when he formulated his belief in the practicality, the social utility, of discussing heated questions in public. Quiet reflection was insufficient; something in the soul and spirit of an Englishman led him to seek to express his views in inns, at the hustings, at mass meetings, in Parliament. Said Fox: 'Public discussion is the best security for public welfare, and for the safety of every good government.' Let those holding unpopular opinions freely express them; the act of expression acted as a vent to release pressure, and thus to prevent an explosion later. 'Do you think that you gain a proselyte where you silence a declaimer?' he demanded. No, he answered his own question; if you offer men no constitutional way of declaring their grievances, you force them 'to more pernicious modes of coming at relief'. Again: 'In proportion as opinions are open, they are innocent and harmless. Opinions become dangerous only when persecution makes it necessary for the people to communicate their ideas under the bond of secrecy.'

Fox therefore anchored his speaking career in the twofold conviction that Englishmen have a constitutional right to express their opinions and that the finest form of expression was the public one. Men naturally approve of the talents they themselves possess, and Fox was in the front rank of a distinguished group of parliamentary speakers. Walter Bagehot once observed that Fox was unable to sit quietly and hear an argument improperly supported or a conclusion illogically deduced. Such utterances brought him bounding to his feet in reply. 'I *must* do so,' Bagehot reported Fox as saying, 'I can't live without discussion.'[1] Aside from relatively inconsequential speeches that fall into this category of forensic nervousness, Fox is primarily to be remembered for his numerous speeches on the issues already enumerated, which, inadequately reported as they are, make up the heart of his public utterance. In addition were half a dozen especially luminous speeches of which only three will be mentioned here: the Westminster Scrutiny speech (Brougham told Macaulay to learn it by heart), the speech on Napoleon's overtures for peace ('But we must pause!') and the speech on War with France ('Ah, that was a damned good speech').

[1] Forrest Morgan, ed., *The Works of Walter Bagehot* (Hartford, 1891), iii, 99. Charles F. Mullett kindly called my attention to this source.

The scores of criticisms that Fox's career induced have already been collected in this volume, and placed somewhat on the back tables. More to the point, scores of tributes have likewise been plucked and harvested and displayed somewhat on the forward tables. Some praise came from neutral observers (Moritz: 'The people yelled "Fox! Fox!" for no other reason than they wanted to hear him speak'), some from close friends (Georgiana: 'His standard is in the hearts of men'), some from critics (Henry Rogers: 'He stated his opponent's arguments so convincingly that friends feared he would be unable to reply'), some from friends-turned-enemies (Burke: 'the greatest Genius that perhaps this Country has produced'). Nineteenth-century historians, impressed by Fox's long struggle against overwhelming odds, saw him the keeper of the light in liberty's tower. Twentieth-century historians find much to admire but also much to blame (reckless . . . rabble-rouser . . . opportunist . . . arrested development). Some of these latter judgments arise from closely reasoned studies made of single issues; one must report on the part of the elephant that he can feel, and Fox is not ennobled by a view that focuses primarily on the coalition, the India Bill, the regency.

Nor is it surprising that this century has sharply criticized Fox for failing to achieve what he could or should have achieved, for failing to do what he could or should have done. The eighteenth century spent many a lively hour in the same pastime. Even Burke, who piously told the electors of Bristol that to quarrel with the imperfections of man was to censure God, ended his days by feasting on Fox's imperfections. Far wiser it is to follow Erskine's observation, that one should judge the great volume of a man's life, the general context of his existence, rather than the frail passages that checker the pages of even the brightest and best-spent career.

Francis Horner, who viewed Fox at middle range, observed that he grew in character and power as years went on. When Pitt and Fox died, Horner wrote: 'The race of giants has become extinct.' His statement was true in that England took a full half-century to rear another. Pitt, who knew at closer range than anyone else the full incisiveness of Fox's argument, who alternately tried to punish him and to invite him into administration, once made a statement here borrowed from its context and regarded as it stands: 'Mr Fox has never been answered.' So it has proved to be: Fox has not been answered on the slave trade, nor on religious freedom, nor on freedom of speech and assembly, nor on political speaking as the expression of man's bold and inquiring spirit. Here is the place to let the debate lie. Here is something for old England and all her children, to make them honour his memory.

Bibliography

ABBREVIATIONS; DOCUMENTATION

Add. MSS.: Additional Manuscripts, British Museum.

FO: Foreign Office Papers, Public Record Office.

Fox Cor.: Lord John Russell, *Memorials and Correspondence of Charles James Fox.*

HMCR: Historical Manuscripts Commission Reports.

PRO: Public Record Office.

Manuscript collections not otherwise identified are housed in the British Museum. Despite the trend to minimize or eliminate footnotes, I have supplied fairly complete documentation, though I have dispensed with references for many lesser details and in instances for materials readily identifiable. As the Fox and Holland House Papers are still undergoing rearrangement, I have omitted folio numbers. Where dates are not given for newspapers, the reader may assume that the citation appears in the issue following the event. With a few trifling exceptions, material within quotation marks follows the spelling, capitalization, and punctuation of the source.

The list below, which is not complete, gives sources consulted.

1. MANUSCRIPT COLLECTIONS

BRITISH MUSEUM: Fox MSS. (Additional Manuscripts, principally Nos. 47561–47581, 47585, 47593–47594, 47601); Holland House MSS. (Additional Manuscript numbers not assigned at time of reading); lesser use of Adair, Egerton, Hardwicke, Rogers, and Poole MSS.

PUBLIC RECORD OFFICE: Selected State, Treasury, and Foreign Office papers.

SHEFFIELD CITY LIBRARY: the Wentworth-Woodhouse Muniments: Burke, Fitzwilliam, Rockingham, Stanhope, Wentworth MSS.

NORTHAMPTONSHIRE RECORD OFFICE: Fitzwilliam MSS. (Milton).

WILLIAM L. CLEMENTS LIBRARY, UNIVERSITY OF MICHIGAN: Canning, Fox, Hartley, Lacaita-Shelburne, Lee, Melville, Pitt, Shelburne, and Wedderburn MSS. Holland House photostats. Adams transcripts. Fortescue transcripts. Letters from William Pitt to Lord Wellesley, 1796–1804.

HENRY E. HUNTINGTON LIBRARY: Hamilton-Greville, Townshend, Stowe MSS.; W. B. Stevens Diary; Sir William Hamilton Autograph Letters.

THE JAMES MARSHALL AND MARIE-LOUISE OSBORN COLLECTION, YALE UNIVERSITY LIBRARY: Fox MSS.

UNIVERSITY OF DURHAM: Fox-Grey MSS.

OTHER COLLECTIONS: Various other British and American individuals and institutions have incidental Fox letters and other manuscript materials. Among them: Bodleian Library, Sir John Murray, Library of Congress, New York Public Library, Princeton University, University of Nottingham, University of Texas, Somerset House.

HISTORICAL MANUSCRIPTS COMMISSION REPORTS: Abergavenny, Bathurst, Carlisle, Charlemont, Donoughmore, Emly, Fortescue, Graham, Hastings, Johnstone, Kenyon, Knox, Lothian, Rutland, Stopford-Sackville, and Sutherland MSS.

Bibliography

2. NEWSPAPERS AND OTHER SERIALS

LONDON NEWSPAPERS: *Adam's Weekly Courant, Daily Advertiser, The Diary, E. Johnson's British Gazette and Sunday Monitor, Evening Mail, The Gazetteer and New Daily Advertiser, General Evening Post, Lloyd's Evening Post, London Chronicle, London Courant, London Gazette, London Evening-Post, London Packet, Morning Chronicle, Morning Herald, Morning Post, Morning Star, Oracle, Parker's General Advertiser, Public Advertiser, St. James's Chronicle, Stuart Star, Sun, The Times, True Briton, Whitehall Evening-Post, World.*

OTHER SERIALS: *Annual Register, Gentleman's Magazine, Monthly Magazine, Notes and Queries, Journals of the House of Commons.*

PROVINCIAL NEWSPAPERS: *Bath Chronicle, Chester Chronicle, Gloucester Journal, Kent County Herald, Middlesex Journal, Westminster Journal.*

AMERICAN NEWSPAPERS: *Aurora General Advertiser, Connecticut Courant, Porcupine Gazette, Virginia Gazette.*

3. COLLECTIONS OF SPEECHES

'A Barrister', ed., *The Speeches of the Right Honourable Charles James Fox in the House of Commons,* 3rd ed., London, Aylott, 1853.

Matthew Brickdale's Notes on the Debates in the House of Commons for the years 1770–1774, vol. v.

Parliamentary History, vols. 16–36, London, Hansard, 1813–1820. Continued as *Parliamentary Debates,* series 1, vols. 1–7, London, Longman, 1812.

Parliamentary Register, various series, 1774–1806, London, Almon (and successors), 1775–1807.

Speeches of the Right Honourable Charles James Fox in the House of Commons, 6 vols., London, Longman, 1815.

Wright, John, ed., *Sir Henry Cavendish's Debates of the House of Commons,* 2 vols., London, Longman, 1841.

4. PAMPHLETS

Account of the proceedings of a meeting of the inhabitants of Westminster in Palace Yard, Nov. 26, 1795, etc., London, Citizen Lee, [1795].

Account of the proceedings of a meeting of the London Corresponding Society, held in a field near Copenhagen House, October 26, 1795, etc., London, Citizen Lee, [1795].

Account of the proceedings of a meeting of the people in a field near Copenhagen House, Thursday, Nov. 12, etc., London, Citizen Lee, 1795.

The beauties of Fox, North, and Burke, selected from their speeches, from the passing of the Quebec Act in the year 1774 down to the present time, etc., London, J. Stockdale, 1784.

Circumstantial details of the long illness and last moments of the Right Hon. Charles James Fox, together with strictures on his public and private life, London, Jordan and Maxwell, 1805.

Facts submitted to the consideration of the friends to civil and religious liberty ... containing the substance of Mr Fox's speech on the repeal of the test laws, London, J. Johnson, [1789]. *History of the political life and public services, as a senator and a statesman, of the Right Honourable Charles James Fox,* etc., London, J. Debrett, 1783.

Jordan's complete collection of all the addresses and speeches of the Hon. C. J. Fox, Sir A. Gardner, and J. H. Tooke, Esq., at the late interesting contest for Westminster, etc., 3rd edn., London, J. S. Jordan, 1796.

A letter from a Manchester manufacturer to the right honourable Charles James Fox, on his political opposition to the commercial treaty with France, Manchester, 1787.

A letter from the Right Honourable Charles James Fox, to the worthy and independent electors of the city and liberty of Westminster, London, J. Debrett, 1793.

A letter from the Rt. Honourable Edmund Burke to the Duke of Portland . . . containing 54 articles of impeachment against the Rt. Hon. C. J. Fox, Philadelphia, Humphreys, 1797.

The life of the right honourable Charles James Fox . . . Albion Press, 1807.

Mr Fox's celebrated speech with the proceedings at the Shakespeare Tavern, on Friday, Oct. 10, 1800, etc., London, J. S. Jordan, [1800].

A narrative of the proceedings, speeches, . . . connected with the dinner to T. W. Coke, Esq., Norwich, J. Dawson, 1833.

Remarks on the members of the house of commons [no place, no publ.], 1780.

A sketch of the character of the late most noble Francis Duke of Bedford, by the Hon. Charles James Fox, etc., London, J. Ridgway, 1802.

The speech (at length) of the Hon. C. J. Fox, against the address to His Majesty, approving of the refusal to enter into a negotiation for peace with the French Republic, London, J. S. Jordan, 1800.

The speeches (at length) of the right honourable C. J. Fox, T. Erskine, &c. &c. &c. at a meeting held at the Shakespeare Tavern, Covent Garden, on Tuesday, October 10, 1797, etc., London, J. S. Jordan, 1797.

The speech of the Hon. Charles James Fox . . . at the Shakespeare Tavern, on . . . 10th October, 1801, etc., London, J. S. Jordan, 1801.

The speech of the honourable Charles James Fox in the House of Commons on Monday, the 3d of February, 1800, on a motion for an address to the throne, approving of the refusal of ministers to treat with the French republic, a new edition, London, J. Debrett, n.d.

The speech of John Horne Tooke, during the Westminster election, 1796: with . . . the speech of the right hon. C. J. Fox, on Saturday June 11, etc., London, [1796].

The speech of the right honourable Charles James Fox at . . . Westminster hall, July 17, 1782, etc., London, J. Debrett, [1782].

The speech of the Right Hon. Charles James Fox containing the declaration of his principles, etc., 3rd edn, London, J. Ridgway, 1793.

The speech of the right honourable Charles James Fox on American Independence, spoken in the house of commons, on Tuesday, July 2, 1782, London, Folingsby, [1782].

Speech of the Right Honourable Charles James Fox, on Mr Whitbread's Motions on the Russian armament, Thursday, March 1, 1792, London, J. Debrett, 1792.

The speech of the Right Hon. Charles James Fox, on the speech delivered to the house of commons, at the opening of parliament, Dec. 13, 1792, etc., 3rd edn, London, J. Ridgway, 1792.

The speech of the Right Hon. Charles James Fox, in the house of commons, on the Irish resolutions, on Thursday, May 12, 1785, etc., London, J. Debrett, 1785.

The speech of the Right Hon. Charles James Fox, in the house of commons, Jan. 4, 1793, on the alien bill, London, J. Ridgway, [1793].

The speech of the Right Hon. Charles James Fox, in the house of commons, Dec. 14, 1792, on that part of the address to the king which implicated our being involved in a war with France, London, J. Ridgway, [1792].

The speech of the Right Hon. C. J. Fox, in the house of commons, on Tuesday, March

2d, 1790, upon his motion for the repeal of the corporation and test acts, London, J. Ridgway, 1790.

Speech of the Right Hon. Charles James Fox, in the house of commons, on Tuesday, March 24, 1795, etc., 2nd edn, London, J. Debrett, 1795.

Speech of the Right Honourable Charles James Fox, in the house of commons, on Friday the 4th of January, 1798, on the assessed-tax bill, etc., London, J. Debrett, 1798.

A state of facts: or a sketch of the character and political conduct of the Right Hon. Charles Fox, London, T. Evans, 1783.

Substance of the speech of the Honourable Charles James Fox, in the house of commons, on Tuesday, May 24, 1803, on the renewal of the war between Great Britain and France, etc., London, J. Debrett, 1803.

The substance of the speech of the Right Honourable Charles James Fox, on Mr Grey's motion in the House of Commons, Friday, May 26, 1797, etc., London, J. Debrett, 1797.

Two speeches of the Right Honourable C. J. Fox the first, on . . . January 31st: the second, on . . . February 11th, 1793, London, J. Ridgway, 1793.

5. CORRESPONDENCE, JOURNALS, MEMOIRS

ALBEMARLE, EARL OF, ed., *Memoirs of the Marquis of Rockingham*, 2 vols., London, Richard Bentley, 1852.

ANSON, SIR WILLIAM R., ed., *Autobiography and Political Correspondence of Augustus Henry, third Duke of Grafton*, London, John Murray, 1898.

ASPINALL, A., ed., *The Correspondence of George, Prince of Wales, 1770–1812*, vol. 1, New York, Oxford University Press, 1963.

ASPINALL, A., ed., *The Later Correspondence of George III*, vols. 1 and 2, Cambridge University Press, 1962–3.

ASPINALL, A. AND E. ANTHONY SMITH, eds., *English Historical Documents, 1783–1832*, vol. xi, London, Eyre & Spottiswoode, 1959.

BALDERSTON, KATHARINE C., *Thraliana: The Diary of Mrs Hester Lynch Thrale*, 2nd edn, 2 vols., Oxford, Clarendon Press, 1951.

BARNES, G. R. AND J. H. OWEN, eds., *The Private Papers of John, Earl of Sandwich*, 4 vols., Navy Records Society, 1932–8.

BARRETT, CHARLOTTE, ed., *Diary and Letters of Madame D'Arblay*, 4 vols., London, Bickers and Son, 1876.

BISHOP OF BATH AND WELLS, *Journal and Correspondence of William, Lord Auckland*, 4 vols., London, Richard Bentley, 1861–2.

BLADON, F. MCKNO, ed., *The Diaries of Colonel the Hon. Robert Fulke Greville*, London, John Lane, 1930.

BOYD, JULIAN P., ed., *The Papers of Thomas Jefferson*, vol. 10, Princeton University Press, 1954.

BRAY, WILLIAM, ed., *Diary and Correspondence of John Evelyn*, London, George Routledge, n.d.

BROWNING, OSCAR, ed., *The Political Memoranda of Francis Fifth Duke of Leeds*, Westminster, Camden Society, 1884.

BUCKINGHAM AND CHANDOS, THE DUKE OF, *Memoirs of the Court and Cabinets of George the Third*, 2 vols., London, Hurst & Blackett, 1855.

BUTLER, CHARLES, *Reminiscences of Charles Butler*, 4th edn, 2 vols., London, John Murray, 1824.

BUTTERFIELD, L. H., ed., Adams, John, *Diary and Autobiography of John Adams*, 4 vols., Cambridge, Belknap Press, 1961.

Bibliography

CHART, D. A., ed., *The Drennan Letters*, Belfast, His Majesty's Stationery Office, 1931.

COLCHESTER, CHARLES, LORD, ed., *The Diary and Correspondence of Charles Abbot, Lord Colchester*, 3 vols., London, John Murray, 1861.

COPELAND, THOMAS W., gen. ed., *The Correspondence of Edmund Burke*, vols. 2–4, Cambridge University Press, 1960–3. Lucy S. Sutherland, ed. vol. 2, 1960; George H. Guttridge, ed. vol. 3, 1961; John A. Woods, ed. vol. 4, 1963.

Correspondence of the late Gilbert Wakefield with the late Right Honourable Charles James Fox, London, T. Cadell, 1813.

THE COUNTESS OF MINTO, ed., *Life and Letters of Sir Gilbert Elliot*, 3 vols., London, Longmans, 1874.

CUNNINGHAM, PETER, ed., *The Letters of Horace Walpole*, vol. 8, London, R. Bentley, 1861.

CURWEN, SAMUEL, *Journal and Letters of the late Samuel Curwen*, New York, C. S. Francis, 1842.

DAVENPORT, BEATRIX C., ed., *A Diary of the French Revolution by Gouverneur Morris, 1789–1793*, 2 vols., Boston, Houghton Mifflin, 1939.

FITZWILLIAM, EARL AND SIR RICHARD BOURKE, eds., *The Works and Correspondence of the Right Honourable Edmund Burke*, new edn, London, Rivington, 1852.

FORTESCUE, SIR JOHN, *The Correspondence of King George the Third*, 6 vols., London, Macmillan, 1927–8.

FRANCIS, BEATA AND ELIZA KEARY, eds., *The Francis Letters*, vol. 2, London, Hutchinson, n.d.

FRASER, SIR WILLIAM, *Disraeli and His Day*, 2nd edn, London, Kegan Paul, 1891.

GIBBON, EDWARD, *The Miscellaneous Works of Edward Gibbon*, London, B. Blake, 1837.

GEORGIANA, DUCHESS OF DEVONSHIRE, *Diary*. In vol. 2, Walter Sichel, *Sheridan*, Boston, Houghton Mifflin, 1909.

GOTTSCHALK, LOUIS, ed., *Letters of Lafayette to Washington, 1777–1799*, New York, privately printed, 1944.

GRANVILLE, CASTALIA COUNTESS, ed. *Lord Granville Leveson Gower, Private Correspondence 1781 to 1821*, 2 vols., London, John Murray, 1916.

GRATTAN, HENRY, *Memoirs of the Life and Times of the Rt. Hon. Henry Grattan*, new edn, London, Henry Colburn, 1849.

GREVILLE, CHARLES CAVENDISH FULKE, ed., *The Greville Diary*, Garden City, Doubleday, 1927.

GRIEG, JAMES, ed., *The Farington Diary*, 2nd edn, 8 vols., London, Hutchinson, [1923–8].

HARCOURT, THE REV. LEVESON VERNON, ed., *The Diaries and Correspondence of the Right Hon. Geo. Rose*, 2 vols., London, 1860.

HARDY, FRANCIS, ed., *Memoirs . . . of James Caulfield, Earl of Charlemont*, 2nd edn, 2 vols., London, T. Cadell, 1812.

HOLLAND, HENRY EDWARD, LORD, *Further Memoirs of the Whig Party, 1807–1821*, London, John Murray, 1905.

HOLLAND, HENRY EDWARD, LORD, *Memoirs of the Whig Party During My Time*, 2 vols., London, Longmans, 1852–4.

HORNER, LEONARD, ed., *Memoirs and Correspondence of Francis Horner*, 2nd edn, 2 vols., Boston, Little, Brown, 1853.

HUTCHINSON, PETER O., ed., *The Diary and Letters of His Excellency Thomas Hutchinson*, 2 vols., London, Sampson Low, 1883–6.

Bibliography

ILCHESTER, COUNTESS OF AND LORD STAVORDALE, *The Life and Letters of Lady Sarah Lennox*, 2 vols., London, John Murray, 1901.

ILCHESTER, THE EARL OF, ed., *Journal of Elizabeth, Lady Holland*, 2 vols., London, Longmans, 1908.

ILCHESTER, THE EARL OF, *Letters to Henry Fox, Lord Holland*, London, privately printed, 1915.

JENNINGS, LOUIS J., ed., *The Croker Papers*, 2 vols., New York, Charles Scribner's Sons, 1884.

LANGDALE, CHARLES, *Memoirs of Mrs Fitzherbert*, London, Richard Bentley, 1856.

LAPRADE, WILLIAM THOMAS, *Parliamentary Papers of John Robinson, 1774–1784*, London, Royal Historical Society, 1922.

LEWIS, W. S., ed., *Horace Walpole's Correspondence*, New Haven, Yale University Press, 1937–61.

LINCOLN, ANTHONY L. J. AND ROBERT LINDLEY MCEWEN, eds., *Lord Eldon's Anecdote Book*, London, Stevens & Sons, 1960.

LLANOVER, LADY AUGUSTA, ed., *The Autobiography and Correspondence of Mary Granville, Mrs Delaney*, second series, 3 vols., London, Richard Bentley, 1862.

MALMESBURY, EARL OF, ed., *Diaries and Correspondence of James Harris, First Earl of Malmesbury*, 4 vols., London, Richard Bentley, 1844.

MALMESBURY, EARL OF, *Letters of the First Earl of Malmesbury*, London, Richard Bentley, 1870.

MAXWELL, SIR HERBERT, ed., *The Creevey Papers*, 2 vols., London, John Murray, 1904.

MCCARTHY, JUSTIN, *Reminiscences*, 2 vols., London, Chatto & Windus, 1899.

Memoirs of the Life of Sir Stephen Fox, Kt, From His First Entrance Upon the Stage of Action, Under the Lord Piercy, till his decease, London, John Sackfield, 1717.

MERIVALE, HERMAN, ed., *Memoirs of Sir Philip Francis*, London, Longmans, 1867.

MOORE, THOMAS, *Letters and Journals of Lord Byron*, 3 vols., London, John Murray, 1833.

MORITZ, CARL PHILIPP, *Travels of Carl Philipp Moritz in England*, London, Humphrey Milford, 1924.

NORTON, J. E., ed., *The Letters of Edward Gibbon*, 3 vols., London, Cassell, 1956.

PELLEW, GEORGE, *The Life and Correspondence of the Right Honourable Henry Addington, First Viscount Sidmouth*, 3 vols., London, John Murray, 1847.

PRICE, CECIL, ed., *The Letters of Richard Brinsley Sheridan*, 3 vols., Oxford, Clarendon Press, 1966.

[ROGERS, SAMUEL], *Recollections of the Table Talk of Samuel Rogers*, New York, D. Appleton, 1856.

ROSCOE, E. S., AND H. CLERGUE, *George Selwyn, His Letters and His Life*, London, T. Fisher Unwin, 1889.

ROSS, CHARLES, ed., *Correspondence of Charles, first Marquis Cornwallis*, 3 vols., London, John Murray, 1859.

RUSSELL, LORD JOHN, *Memoirs, Journal, and Correspondence of Thomas Moore*, vol. 2, London, Longmans, 1853.

RUSSELL, LORD JOHN, ed., *Memorials and Correspondence of Charles James Fox*, 4 vols., London, Richard Bentley, 1853–7.

SMYTH, ALBERT HENRY, ed., *The Writings of Benjamin Franklin*, 8 vols., New York, Macmillan, 1907.

STEUART, A. FRANCIS, ed., *The Last Journals of Horace Walpole*, 2 vols., London, John Lane, 1910.

TAYLOR, TOM, ed., Haydon, Benjamin Robert, *Autobiography and Memoirs of Benjamin Robert Haydon*, 2 vols., London, Peter Davies, 1924.

TAYLOR, WILLIAM STANHOPE AND JOHN HENRY PRINGLE, eds., *Correspondence of William Pitt, Earl of Chatham*, 4 vols., London, John Murray, 1838–40.

TROTTER, JOHN BERNARD, *Memoirs of the Latter Years of the Right Honourable Charles James Fox*, London, Richard Phillips, 1811.

WALPOLE, HORACE, *Memoirs of the Reign of King George the Third*, 4 vols., London, Richard Bentley, 1845.

WHARTON, FRANCIS, *The Revolutionary Diplomatic Correspondence of the United States*, Washington, 1889.

WINDHAM, RT. HON. WILLIAM, *The Windham Papers*, 2 vols., London Herbert Jenkins, 1913.

WRAXALL, SIR NATHANIEL WILLIAM, *The Historical and the Posthumous Memoirs of Sir Nathaniel William Wraxall*, 5 vols., London, Bickers and son, 1884.

WYVILL, CHRISTOPHER, *Political Papers Chiefly Respecting the Attempt of the County of York and other . . . districts . . . to effect a reformation of the Parliament of Great Britain*, 6 vols., York, 1794–1802.

6. SECONDARY SOURCES

ADAMS, W. H. DAVENPORT, *English Party Leaders and English Parties*, 2 vols., London, Tinsley brothers, 1878.

ALDEN, JOHN RICHARD, *The American Revolution, 1775–1783*, New York, Harper, 1954.

ALLEN, JOHN, *Memoirs of Charles James Fox*, Edinburgh, 1820.

Alumni Oxonienses, 1715–1886, 4 vols., London, J. Foster, 1887–8.

ASPINALL, A., *Politics and the Press, c. 1780–1850*, London, Home & Van Thal, 1949.

ASPINALL, A., 'The Reporting and Publishing of the House of Commons' Debates, 1771–1834', in *Essays Presented to Sir Lewis Namier*, London, Macmillan, 1956.

AUSTEN-LEIGH, ed., *The Eton College Register, 1753–1790*, Eton, Spottiswoode, Ballantyne, 1921.

BESSBOROUGH, EARL OF, ed., *Georgiana*, London, John Murray, 1955.

BESSBOROUGH, EARL OF, *Lady Bessborough and Her Family Circle*, in collab. with A. Aspinall, London, John Murray, 1940.

BICKLEY, FRANCIS, *The Cavendish Family*, London, Constable, 1911.

BLACK, EUGENE C., *The Association: British Extraparliamentary Political Organization, 1769–1793*, Cambridge, Harvard University Press, 1963.

BOWRING, SIR JOHN, ed., *Works of Jeremy Bentham*, vol. 10, New York, Russell & Russell, 1962.

BROUGHAM, HENRY PETER, *Historical Sketches of Statesmen Who Flourished in the Times of George III*, 3 vols., London, Charles Knight, 1845.

BUTTERFIELD, HERBERT, *Charles James Fox and Napoleon: The Peace Negotiations of 1806*, London, Athlone Press, 1962.

BUTTERFIELD, HERBERT, 'Charles James Fox and the Whig Opposition in 1792', *Cambridge Historical Journal*, ix (1949), 3.

BUTTERFIELD, HERBERT, *George III, Lord North, and the People*, London, G. Bell, 1949.

CAMPBELL, JOHN C., *Lives of the Lord Chancellors*, vol. 5, London, John Murray, 1846.

CARSWELL, JOHN, *The Old Cause*, London, Cressett, 1954.

CHALONER, W. H., 'Dr Joseph Priestley, John Wilkinson and the French Revolution, 1789–1802', *Transactions of the Royal Historical Society*, 5th Series, viii, London, 1958.

CHENEVIX TRENCH, CHARLES C., *The Royal Malady*, London, Longmans, 1964.

CHRISTIE, IAN R., *The End of North's Ministry, 1780–1782*, London, Macmillan, 1958.

CHRISTIE, IAN R., *Wilkes, Wyvill and Reform*, London, Macmillan, 1962.

CLAYDEN, P. W., *The Early Life of Samuel Rogers*, London, Smith, Elder, 1887.

COLERIDGE, ERNEST HARTLEY, *The Life of Thomas Coutts, Banker*, 2 vols., London, John Lane, 1920.

CONE, CARL B., *Burke and the Nature of Politics*, Lexington, University of Kentucky Press, 1964.

CONNELL, BRIAN, *Portrait of a Whig Peer*, London, Deutsch, 1957.

CREASY, SIR EDWARD S., *Memoirs of Eminent Etonians*, London, Richard Bentley, 1850.

CREASY, SIR EDWARD S., *Some Account of the Foundation of Eton College and of the Past and Present Condition of the School*, London, Longman, 1848.

CURRAN, W. H., *Life of the Rt. Hon. J. P. Curran*, New York, Redfield, 1855.

CURTIS, E. E., *The Organization of the British Army in the American Revolution*, New Haven, Yale University Press, 1926.

DAVIES, GODFREY AND MARION TINLING, 'The Independence of America: Six Unpublished Items on the Treaty in 1782–83', *Huntington Library Quarterly*, xii (1948–49), 2.

DERRY, JOHN W., *The Regency Crisis and the Whigs, 1788–1789*, Cambridge University Press, 1963.

DERRY, JOHN W., *William Pitt*, London, B. T. Batsford, 1962.

DILKS, T. BRUCE, *Charles James Fox and the Borough of Bridgwater*, Bridgwater, 1937.

DRINKWATER, JOHN, *Charles James Fox*, London, Ernest Benn, 1928.

DUGAN, JAMES, *The Great Mutiny*, New York, G. P. Putnam's Sons, 1965.

EHRMAN, JOHN, *British Government and Commerical Relations With Europe, 1783–1793*, Cambridge University Press, 1962.

FAŸ, BERNARD, *Notes on the American Press at the End of the Eighteenth Century*, New York, The Grolier Club, 1927.

FELL, RALPH, *Memoirs of the Public Life of the Late Right Honourable Charles James Fox*, London, J. F. Hughes, 1808.

FITZMAURICE, LORD EDMOND, *The Life of Granville George Leveson Gower*, London, Longmans, 1905.

FITZMAURICE, LORD EDMOND, *Life of William, Earl of Shelburne*, 2nd edn, London, Macmillan, 1912.

FOORD, ARCHIBALD S., *His Majesty's Opposition, 1714–1830*, Oxford, Clarendon Press, 1964.

FORCE, PETER, ed., *American Archives*, vol. 1, Washington, Government Printing Office, 1837.

FOSTER, VERE, ed., *The Two Duchesses*, 2nd edn, London, Blackie and Son, 1898.

GASH, NORMAN, *Mr Secretary Peel*, London, Longmans, 1961.

GEORGE, M. DOROTHY, *English Political Caricature*, 2 vols., Oxford, Clarendon Press, 1959.

HAMILTON, SIDNEY GRAVES, *Hertford College*, London, F. E. Robinson, 1903.

HAMMOND, J. L. LE B., *Charles James Fox: A Political Study*, London, Methuen, 1903.

Bibliography

HARLOW, VINCENT T., *The Founding of the Second British Empire, 1763–1793*, 2 vols., London, Longmans, 1952, 1964.

HAZLITT, WILLIAM, *The Eloquence of the British Senate*, 2 vols., London, 1808.

HENRIQUES, URSULA, *Religious Toleration in England, 1787–1833*, London, Routledge and Paul, 1961.

HILL, GEORGE B., ed., *Boswell's Life of Johnson*, rev. by L. F. Powell, 6 vols., Oxford, Clarendon Press, 1934–50.

HILL, GEORGE B., ed., *Johnsonian Miscellanies*, 2 vols., Oxford, Clarendon Press, 1897.

History of the Westminster Election, etc., London, J. Debrett, 1784.

HOBHOUSE, CHRISTOPHER, *Fox*, London, Constable, 1947.

HOLDSWORTH, SIR WILLIAM, *A History of English Law*, vol. x, Boston, Little, Brown, 1938.

HOWELL, T. J., compiler, *A Complete Collection of State Trials . . . Continued From the Year 1783 to the Present Time*, vols. 23–7, London, Longman, 1817–20.

ILCHESTER, THE EARL OF, *Henry Fox, First Lord Holland*, 2 vols., London, John Murray, 1920.

JAMES, WILLIAM M., *The British Navy in Adversity*, London, Longmans, 1926.

Journals of the Continental Congress, 1774–1789, Washington, Government Printing Office, vols. 22–5, 1922.

JUDD, GERRIT P., *Members of Parliament, 1734–1832*, New Haven, Yale University Press, 1955.

KERR, S. PARNELL, *George Selwyn and the Wits*, London, Methuen, 1909.

KERRY, EARL OF, ed., *The First Napoleon*, London, 1925.

LANDFIELD, JEROME, *The Speeches of Richard Brinsley Sheridan Against Warren Hastings*, unpublished University of Missouri Ph.D. dissertation, 1958.

LASCELLES, EDWARD, *The Life of Charles James Fox*, Oxford University Press, 1936.

[LAURENCE, MR] *History of the political life and public services, as a senator and a statesman, of the Right Honourable Charles James Fox*, etc., London, J. Debrett, 1783.

LEFEBVRE, GEORGES, *The French Revolution from Its Origins to 1793*, London, Routledge, 1962.

LEGG, L. G. WICKHAM, *British Diplomatic Instructions, 1689–1789*, London, Royal Historical Society, 1934.

The Life of the Right Honourable Charles James Fox, etc., Albion Press, 1807.

LYTE, SIR HENRY CHURCHILL MAXWELL, *A History of Eton College, 1440–1910*, 4th edn, London, Macmillan, 1911.

MACAULAY, THOMAS BABINGTON, *Works*, vol. 3, London, Longmans, 1843.

MACKESY, PIERS, *The War for America, 1775–1783*, London, Longmans, 1964.

DE MADARIAGA, ISABEL, *Britain, Russia, and the Armed Neutrality of 1780*, New Haven, Yale University Press, 1962.

MARKHAM, FELIX, *Napoleon*, London, Weidenfeld and Nicolson, 1963.

MARSHALL, DOROTHY, *Eighteenth Century England*, London, Longmans, 1962.

MASSON, DAVID, ed., *The Collected Writings of Thomas De Quincey*, 14 vols., London, A. & C. Black, 1896–1897.

Memoir of the Life of the Right Honourable Charles James Fox, late one of his majesty's principal secretaries of state, etc., London, H. D. Symonds, 1806.

MOORE, THOMAS, *Memoirs of the Life of the Right Honourable Richard Brinsley Sheridan*, 2 vols., London, Longman, 1825.

MORRIS, RICHARD B., *The Peacemakers*, New York, Harper and Row, 1965.

MURRAY, ROBERT H., *Edmund Burke*, Oxford University Press, 1931.

Bibliography

NAMIER, SIR LEWIS, *The Structure of Politics at the Accession of George III*, 2nd edn, London, Macmillan, 1957.

NAMIER, SIR LEWIS AND JOHN BROOKE, *The History of Parliament, 1754–1790,* 3 vols., London, Her Majesty's Stationery Office, 1964.

NICHOLS, JOHN, *Literary Anecdotes of the Eighteenth Century*, vol. 8, London, Nichols, 1814.

PARES, RICHARD, *King George III and the Politicians*, Oxford, Clarendon Press, 1953.

PARES, RICHARD AND A. J. P. TAYLOR, eds., *Essays Presented to Sir Lewis Namier*, London, Macmillan, 1956.

[PARR, SAMUEL], *Characters of the Late Charles James Fox . . . by Philopatris Varicensis*, 2 vols., London, Mawman, 1809.

PRIOR, SIR JAMES, *Life of Edmond Malone*, London, Smith, Elder, 1860.

PRIOR, SIR JAMES, *Memoir of the Life and Character of the Right Honourable Edmund Burke*, 2nd edn, vol. 1, London, Baldwin, Cradock, and Joy, 1826.

RAE, WILLIAM FRASER, *Wilkes, Sheridan, Fox: the Opposition Under George the Third*, London, W. Isbister, 1927.

REID, LOREN, 'Charles Fox and the London Press', *Quarterly Journal of Speech*, xlvii (December, 1961), 4, reprinted in *Parliamentary Affairs*, xv (Summer, 1962), 3.

REID, LOREN, 'Sheridan's Speech on Mrs Fitzherbert', *Quarterly Journal of Speech*, xxxiii (February, 1947).

REID, LOREN, 'Speaking in the Eighteenth Century House of Commons', *Speech Monographs*, xvi (1949).

ROSE, GEORGE, *Observations on the Historical Work of the late Right Hon. Charles James Fox*, London, T. Cadell and W. Davies, 1809.

ROSE, JOHN HOLLAND, *Life of William Pitt*, 2 vols., New York, Harcourt, 1924. Vol. 1, *William Pitt and National Revival*; vol. 2, *William Pitt and the Great War.*

ROSEBERY, LORD, *Tomline's Life of Pitt*, London, 1903.

RUDÉ, GEORGE F. E., 'The Gordon Riots: A Study of the Rioters and their Victims', *Transactions of the Royal Historical Society*, 5th Series, vi, London, 1956.

RUSSELL, LORD JOHN, *The Life and Times of Charles James Fox*, 3 vols., London, Richard Bentley, 1859–66.

SEDGWICK, HENRY DWIGHT, *Madame Récamier*, Indianapolis, Bobbs-Merrill, 1940.

SHEFFIELD, LORD, JOHN, ed., *The Miscellaneous Works of Edward Gibbon, Esq.*, London, B. Blake, 1837.

SICHEL, WALTER, *Sheridan*, 2 vols., London, Constable, 1909.

SOUTHGATE, DONALD, *The Passing of the Whigs, 1832–1886*, London, Macmillan, 1962.

SPARKS, JARED, ed., *The Works of Benjamin Franklin*, 10 vols., Boston, Hilliard, Gray, 1840.

STANHOPE, EARL, *Life of the Right Honourable William Pitt*, 3rd edn, 4 vols., London, John Murray, 1867.

STEPHEN, SIR JAMES FITZJAMES, *A History of the Criminal Law of England*, vol. ii, London, Macmillan, 1883.

STEPHEN, SIR JAMES FITZJAMES, *Miscellanies*, 2nd Series, London, John Murray, 1872.

STIRLING, A. M. W., *Coke of Norfolk and His Friends*, London, John Lane, n.d.

STUART, DOROTHY MARGARET, *Dearest Bess*, London, Methuen, 1955.

SUTHERLAND, LUCY S., *The East India Company in Eighteenth Century Politics*, Oxford, Clarendon Press, 1952.

Bibliography

SUTHERLAND, LUCY S. AND J. BINNEY, 'Henry Fox as Paymaster General of the Forces', *English Historical Review*, lxx, (April, 1955).

THOMAS, PETER D. G., compiler, *Sources for Debates in the House of Commons, 1768–1774*, London, Athlone Press, 1959.

THOMPSON, J. M., *Napoleon Bonaparte*, New York, Oxford University Press, 1952.

TREVELYAN, SIR GEORGE OTTO, *The Early History of Charles James Fox*, New York, Longmans, 1881.

TREVELYAN, SIR GEORGE OTTO, *George the Third and Charles Fox, the Concluding Part of the American Revolution*, London, Longmans, 1912–1914.

TREVELYAN, GEORGE MACAULAY, *Lord Grey of the Reform Bill*, New York, Longmans, 1920.

TWISS, HORACE, *The Public and Private Life of Lord Chancellor Eldon*, 3 vols., London, John Murray, 1844.

VALENTINE, ALAN, *Lord George Germain*, Oxford, Clarendon Press, 1962.

WALPOLE, B. C., *Charles James Fox*, London, n.d.

WATSON, J. STEVEN, *The Reign of George the Third*, Oxford, Clarendon Press, 1960.

WELLS, DAVID F., 'The Keppel-Palliser Dispute, 1778–1779', *School of Arts and Sciences Research Papers*, Georgia State College, Atlanta, number 3, June, 1964.

WERKMEISTER, LUCYLE, *The London Daily Press, 1772–1792*, Lincoln, University of Nebraska, 1963.

WHIBLEY, CHARLES, *William Pitt*, Edinburgh and London, W. Blackwood and Sons, 1906.

WILBERFORCE, ROBERT ISAAC AND SAMUEL WILBERFORCE, *The Life of William Wilberforce*, 5 vols., London, John Murray, 1838.

WILKINS, W. H., *Mrs Fitzherbert and George IV*, New York, Longmans, [1908].

YARBOROUGH, MINNIE CLARE, *John Horne Tooke*, New York, Columbia University Press, 1926.

YONGE, CHARLES DUKE, *The Life and Administration of Robert Banks*, 3 vols., London, 1868.

Index

Abingdon, Lord, quoted, 280–1
Abbot, Charles, 423; notes F's loss of support, 316; 'the debaters . . . rarely take any notes', 344; F's speech a mix of eloquence and mischief, 393
Adair, Sir Robert, 275, 406–7, 419*n*, 435–6
Adam, William, 160, 435; duel with F, 99–102; on Unitarian Church, 282
Adams, John, 152; treaty negotiations, 145, 153, 173, 175*n*; repressive measures during his administration, 306
Addington, Henry (later Viscount Sidmouth), 374, 375, 388, 398; chosen Speaker, 323; Canning's doggerel, 323; resigns, 400; Lord Privy Seal, 412
Addison, Joseph, 24
Additional Force Bill, 402
Alien Bill, 294–6, 320
Allen, Dr John, 24, 24*n*, 25*n*
Americans, treaty negotiations with, 1782, 143–7
Annual Register, 115; regrets secession of men of talent, 149; on Copenhagen House meeting, 315
Anticipation, 112
Aranda, Count de, negotiates treaty, 176
Arden, Pepper, 205
Armed Neutrality, 120, 142; 'armed neutrality', parliamentary faction during regency crisis, 239–40, 245, 247
Armistead, Mrs Elizabeth Bridget, 126, 155–6, 198, 223, 265, 268; letter from F on India Bill, 190; letter from F on Westminster election, 202–3; early days of relationship with F, 221–2; meets Gibbon, 231–2; marries F, 313, 313*n*, 314, 314*n*. *See* Fox, Mrs
Aristotle, *Rhetoric*, 16, 58, 77
Arnold, General, 285
Ashburton, Lord, 157. *See* Dunning, John
Association movement, 103–14
Atkinson, Richard, his role in defeating F's India Bill, 187

Bagehot, Walter, says F could not live without discussion, 445
Barnard, Dr Edward, 12, 16
Barré, Colonel Isaac, 26, 32, 74, 84, 196
Beaufoy, Henry, on repeal of Test and Corporation Acts, 252–3, 255–6
Beaumont, Sir George, quoted, 436
Beauties of Fox, North, and Burke, 195–6
Bedford, Duke of, 285, 305; death, 377–9
Belsham, William, 389
Benares charge, 304
Bessborough, Lady, people shocked by F's delayed announcement of his marriage, 382*n*
Blayney, Benjamin, 16
Bonaparte, Lucien, conversation with F, 384
Bonaparte, Napoleon, 314, 408–9; his overtures for peace, 361–2; greets F, 383–4; discusses Channel Tunnel, 385; assassin's plot detected, 416; praises F, 420

Index

Dunning, John, 23, 65–6, 92, 138; 'influence of Crown has increased',108–11; *See* Ashburton

East India Company, 179, 180–3, 188
Eden, William, 88; quoted, 86; bears Irish demands to Commons, 141–2
Eldon, Lord, 295. *See* Scott, John
Ellenborough, Lord, Chief Justice, 412–13
Elliot, Sir Gilbert, 85–6; observes a 'boggle' on refusing supplies, 197; notes Opposition members missed division, 198; reprobation in which F is held, 293
Ellis, Welbore, 80, 83; quoted, 49, 61
Emmet, Robert, 396
Englishman, The, 95, 98
Erskine, Thomas (later Baron), 114, 284; quoted, 427, 446; supports Libel Bill, 273; defends Paine, 288; Lord Chancellor, 411–12; 'trial by jury', 413
Essay on Woman, 21
Essex case, 421
Evening Mail, 267–8; praises F's Libel Bill, 274–5; indignant at F, 368
Evening Post, notes cub severely rapped, 44; 'F stands high in esteem', 81
Ewart, Joseph, 267

Farington, Joseph, disapproves of F's conduct, 436
Fitzherbert, Mrs Maria, 225–9
Fitzpatrick, Richard, 17, 18, 18*n*, 19, 93, 102, 127, 203, 229, 245, 373, 398, 427, 434; quoted, 118, 118*n*, 173; defends F's resignation, 148; defends coalition, 164, 165; Secretary at War, 166, 412
Fitzwilliam, Earl, 427, 434; quoted, 159; doubts F qualified to head party, 288; dismissed as Lord Lieutenant, 309, 312–13, 326; Lord President, 304, 411–12
Fox Against Fox, 164
Fox, Caroline (F's mother), 9, 11–12; quoted, 37; death, 51
Foster, Lady Elizabeth, 413–14; death of F, 427–8
Fox, Charles James
    biographical details: ancestry, 6–9; birth, 9; childhood, 9–10; at Eton, 11–16; at Wandsworth, 12–13; at Hertford College, Oxford, 16–17; *The Spendthrift*, 17; grand tour, 19; enters House of Commons, 20–4; maiden speech, 24–6; other early speeches, 26–31; at Admiralty, 29–30; dispute with the printers, 32–6; speech on Clandestine Marriages Act, 36–7; resigns Admiralty, 37; Royal Marriage Bill, 37–8; his Marriage Bill, 39; at Treasury, 40; dismissed from Treasury, 44; speaks on American measures, 50–1; share of father's estate, 51; attacks North, 53–5; speaks on North's proposals for conciliation, 54–5; on petition from New York, 58; on Address, 1775, 60; on prohibition of trade with America, 61; inquiry into ill success of British arms, 61; on Declaration of Independence, 62; on proposed secession, 1776, 62; attacks Germain, 63; on Address, 1776, 63–4; suspension of habeas corpus, 1777, 65–6; rift with King deepens, 66; defends Speaker Norton, 66–7; defends Pigot, 67–8; inquiry into state of nation, 1778, 72–83; called Charles Tod, 82; attacks Germain, 86; tentatively approached to join Ministry, 86; speech of November, 1778, 89–90; considers coalition with Ministry, 90–1; denounces Sandwich, 91–6; *The Englishman*, 95, 98; on Irish discontent, 1779, 97–8; talk of coalition, 97–8;

members to prepare speeches, 177; approves F's speech on India Bill, 187; says ministers require a check, 202; applauds F's Westminster victory, 204; impressed by F's competence on legal and theological questions, 256

General Advertiser, 339; scandalous of Ministers not to reply to F, 81–2; involved in Keppel–Palliser dispute, 92; proposes F for prime minister, 138

General Evening-Post, prints samples of F's ridicule, 65; reports interest in F's speech on Test and Corporation Acts, 261; comments on F's French views, 293

George II, 66

George III, 38, 38n, 138, 223, 276, 372; quoted, 55, 69, 93, 95, 109, 121, 132, 284; Address, 1770, 27–8; pleased by increase in majority, 30; incensed at F, 43–4; urges Parliament to stop American disorders, 48; pleased with handsome majority, 52; Address, 1775, 60; 1776, 63; advises North to bring up business while F in Paris, 64; concern with North's affairs, 69; state of the nation inquiry, 1778, 75–6, 79–80; hopes Ministers will speak, 80; says he will never surrender to Opposition, 87; seeks better attendance, 88, 94; ponders coalition, 1779, 98–9; Address, 1779, 99; says F has no principle, 115; opens Fifteenth Parliament, 1780, 119; opens session, 1781, 127–8; delays acceptance of North's resignation, 133; names Shelburne to succeed Rockingham, 147; wishes F kept out of office, 1782, 148; vows support for Shelburne, 168; calls coalition unnatural, 165; declares coalition will not enjoy his confidence, 168; on income for Prince, 171–3; interposition in F's India Bill, 187–90; determined not to submit to F, 194, 196–7; illness, 232, 233–48; opposes repeal of Test and Corporation Acts, 253; disapproves of F's stand on repeal of Test and Corporation Acts, 262; opposes bringing F into Government, 1792, 285–6; his Address on tumults and disturbances, 290; progress of war with France, 300; calls for firmness, 1794, 308; his carriage attacked, 315; pleased by vote, 316, 322; Address, 1796, 323; regrets size of minority, 326; calls F 'open enemy of his country', 327; deplores F's 'art', 331; Address, 1803, 397; illness, 399; determined to keep F out of Government, 400–2, 400n; begins to yield to F's being in Government, 406–7; attitude at F's death, 428–9

Germain, George (later Viscount Sackville), 49, 63, 68, 74, 81, 107, 149, 178; quoted, 60, 122; denounced by F, 119; dropped from Ministry, 131; notes strength of F government, 178

Gibbon, Edward, 52, 83, 109, 123, 231–2; quoted, 24, 148; 'F is commenced patriot', 37; praises F's speech, 53; says Archangel Gabriel would not be heard, 58; 'had never heard a more masterly speech than F's', 63; mixed feelings on Burke–Fox quarrel, 270; F's 'inmost soul deeply tinged with Democracy', 297

Gladstone, William E., 346, 441

Gloucester Journal, notes Pitt's friends voting with F, 210

Glynn, Serjeant John, 30–1

Gordon riots, 113–14

Gower, Earl, 136; President of the Council, 191

Gower, Lady, 424–5

Grafton, Duke of, 23, 146; resigns, 29; opposes coalition, 160

Graham, Mr, auctioneer, candidate for Westminster, 1802, 379–80

Grantham, Thomas, Baron, succeeds Fox as Secretary, 157; praises Pitt's speech, 165

Grasse, Count de, 145

Grattan, Henry, 69, 141, 142; on F's use of language, 338

Grenville, James, 99–100

Index

Index

Mahon, Lord, avers F will not stop supplies, 192
Mahratta war, 181
Malmesbury, 117
Malmesbury, Earl of, 248, 290; notes Burke's complaints about F, 285–6; reports division among whigs, 292; analyses votes on F's speech, 292–3
Malone, Edmund, on Mrs Fitzherbert, 229
'Man of the People', 139
Manchester, Duke of, 71, 176–7
Mansfield, Earl of, Speaker of the Lords in Coalition Government, 166
Mark Twain, quoted, 114
Marsh and Tatham, 430–1
Martin, Samuel, 22
McCarthy, Justin, 113, 339
Melbourne, William Lamb, 1st Viscount, reared in F tradition, 438
Melville impeachment, 416. *See* Dundas, Henry
Middlesex Journal, F spoke 'against liberty', 26
Midhurst, 20
Ministry of All the Talents, 412, 423
Mirabeau, 268
Moira, Earl of, Master General of the Ordnance, 412. *See* Rawdon, Lord
Monroe, James, 420–2
Moritz, Carl Philipp, observes reporters in Commons, 36; describes F as speaker, 139–40, 150
Morley, John, 113
Morning Advertiser, tribute to F, 428
Morning Chronicle, 89, 196, 200, 367; quoted, 178; condemns young cub's conduct, 44; calls F best speaker by far, 65; deplores Ministry's not replying to F, 81; condemns coalition, 167–8; F's able reply, 187; praises F's conduct in quarrel with Burke, 270; criticizes Pitt's speech, praises F's, 311; says Treasury's hired writers have mutinied, 332; calls F's speech one of his best, 394; F's illness, 425
Morning Herald, 187, 196, 198, 200, 212; thinks F's speech resulted in majority on Marriage Act, 125; denounces F's inconsistency, 126; F's pledge to cease gambling, 138; denounces coalition, 167; says F convinced Pitt on Hastings charges, 220–1; notes House calls repeatedly for F, 276
Morning Post, 211; F should teach Americans gaming, 54; thinks North should have F back in Government, 68; F as great as ever Chatham had been, 68; involved in Keppel–Palliser dispute, 92; F's listeners consisted of lowest dregs of mob, 110; deplores coalition, 164; members walk out during F's speech, 167; spectators denounce F, 168; reports public approval of F during regency crisis, 246; praises F's conduct in quarrel with Burke, 270; wonders why Ministry refuses inquiry, 311; hails meeting to petition Parliament, 317; F's language plain and pointed, 332; reports then corrects F's speech, 405–6; says F has redeemed himself by his stand on France, 415
Morning Star, reports F's Newmarket winnings, 256
Morpeth, Lord, praises F, 331
Morris, Gouverneur, describes Burke's and F's speaking, 263
Muir, Thomas, trial for sedition, 300

Namier, Sir Lewis, 20, 38
Napier, Lady Sarah, 345. *See* Lennox, Lady Sarah

Index

Pitt Club, 289, 379
Pitt, Thomas, 185, 186, 196
Pitt, William, 1st Earl of Chatham, 7. *See* Chatham, Earl of
Pitt, William, 17, 123, 137, 269, 270, 276, 277, 278, 300, 316, 317, 325, 352, 353, 406–7, 441; maiden speech, 121; denounces American war, 124–5; Chancellor of Exchequer, 157; begins long contest with F, 158; will not betray Shelburne, 159*n*; approaches F to join Government, 159, 159*n*; opposes Shelburne–North alliance, 160; denounces coalition, 163–4; defends provisional treaty, 165; refuses to form Government after Shelburne's resignation, 165–6; on parliamentary reform, 170; debates definitive treaties, 178; opposes F's India Bill, 189; becomes head of Government, 191; seeks to strengthen Ministry, 192; introduces India Bill, 194; description of Pitt and F in debate, 194–5; Bill thrown out, 196; sentiment grows for union of parties, 196–7; attacked on streets, 199; on Westminster scrutiny, 206–7; replies to F's speech on Westminster scrutiny, 210; defeated on Westminster scrutiny, 212; on parliamentary reform, 214; Irish proposals, 214–18; and Hastings, 220–1, 221*n*; commercial treaty with France, 233–4; and Mrs Fitzherbert, 228; king's illness and regency, 233–48; opposes repeal of Test and Corporation Acts, 252–3, 256, 261–2; on the abolition of the slave trade, 257, 267, 280, 356; Russian question, 265–7, 276–7; praises F, 268; approves Libel Bill, 273; personal characteristics, 282–3; discussions on proposed coalition with Opposition, 285–6, 290; plans for restricting the press, 288–9; defends Alien Bill, 296; his drinking, 298, 357; defends suspension of habeas corpus, 303–4; replies to F's state of the nation speech, 310; defends conduct of war, 316; introduces Treason Bill and Seditious Meetings Bill, 316–17; on Irish grievances, 325–6; faces censure on naval mutinies, 327; dislike of Shelburne, 337; vocabulary praised by F, 338; criticizes F's 'majesty of the people' toast, recommends F be stricken from Privy Council, 354–6; duel with Tierney, 356–7; on Bonaparte's overtures, 362–6; on renewal of war, 390–4; rumours of resignation, 372–4; Addington succeeds him, 374; negotiations with to join Government, 399–402; insists King will not approve F in Government, 400–2; becomes First Minister, 401–2; 'roll up that map', 409; death, 410; 'Mr F has never been answered', 446
Ponsonby, Frederick, praises F, 393
Porson, Richard, 338
Portland, Duke of, 65, 170, 309; at head of coalition Government, 166; seeks income for Prince, 171–3; states position on joining Pitt Government, 192, 196–7; regency crisis, 235, 237, 245; dispute between Burke and F, 266; proposed coalition with Pitt, 285–6, 290; praises F, 294; Secretary of State, 304; describes F's activities as speaker, 318–19; reports F's speech to King, 401
Poynings' law, 141
Price, Dr Richard, 258–9
Price, Uvedale, 19
Priestley, Dr Joseph, 262, 281
Prince of Wales, 294; seeks income for personal establishment, 171–3; Mrs Fitzherbert, 225–9; King's illness and regency, 235–47; mourns F's death, 428, 436
printers, quarrel with, 32–6
Public Advertiser, 131; attacks Speaker, 43; says F would prefer hell with debate than heaven without, 81; deplores Ministry's not replying to F, 81; F's talents would overcome family connections, 106; praises F's arguments against

Index

Walpole, Sir Robert, 7, 131; quoted, 94
Walpole, Thomas, 85
Ward, J. W., praises F's speech, 392–3
Warner, the Reverend Dr, quoted, 116
Warren, Dr Richard, 234–6, 243
Washington, General George, 64, 69, 73, 297, 306
Webster, Sir Godfrey, 325
Wedderburn, Alexander, 28–9, 32, 63, 92, 392; attempted reply to F's state of the nation speech, 78–9, 83. *See* Loughborough, Baron
Wedgwood, Josiah, 216
Westmacott, Richard, 435
Westminster elections, 1780, 3–5, 116–18; 1782, 138–9; 1783, 167–8; 1784, 193–205; 1790, expenses, 264; 1796, 322–3; 1802, 379–81; 1806, 413
Westminster Journal, deplores Ministry not replying to F, 81
Westminster scrutiny, 1780, 118, 208; 1784, 205–13, 222
Whig Club, 289–90, 350, 355, 356, 368, 372–3, 437
Whitbread, Samuel, 284, 438; on Russian policy, 276–7; moves to censure Pitt, 327
Whitehall Evening-Post, 125, 164, 211; satirizes coalition, 166; on Burke–Fox quarrel, 270
Wilberforce, William, 123, 192, 214, 355–6; converses with Pitt about Hastings, 221*n*; praises F's speeches during regency crisis, 247; on abolition of slave trade, 257, 267–8, 279–81; on F as conversationalist, 336; puzzled by F's *History*, 434
Wilkes, John, 16, 21–2, 25, 26–7, 28–9, 35, 203
Willis, Dr Francis, 234–5, 245
Willoughby, Harriet, 433–4, 434*n*
Windham, William, 230, 302, 415; Secretary of State, 412
Woodfall, William, 31, 43
Wordsworth, William, says F loved by poets, 373
World, criticizes F's speech at Hastings trial, 231; on handing the slave trade over to the French, 237; criticizes F's regency stand, 240; reports excitement about regency crisis, 244; notes strong Pitt support, 244; Burke–Fox quarrel excites anxious curiosity, 270; praises F's Libel Bill, 273–4; Pitt's speech superior to F's, 277
Wraxall, Nathaniel William, 101, 132, 162, 217, 336, 343; quoted, 242; describes F in 1781, 120; reports excitement about India Bill, 181; criticizes F's speech on Westminster scrutiny, 211; praises Beaufoy's speech on Test and Corporation Acts, 253
Wray, Sir Cecil, F pays tribute to, 151; opposes receipt stamps, 171; campaigns during Westminster election, 198–205
Wright, John, 25*n*
Wyvill, the Reverend Christopher, 104–5

Yarmouth, Charles Francis, Lord, negotiations with Talleyrand, 417–20
Yorke, Charles, quoted, 119; F mad on subject of peace, 376
Yorke, Philip, quoted, 119
Yorktown, surrender of Cornwallis, 127